Theatre of War

Also by Eric Bentley

Theatre of War

COMMENTS ON 32 OCCASIONS BY

ERIC BENTLEY

The Viking Press / *New York*

First published in 1972 by The Viking Press, Inc.
625 Madison Avenue, New York, N.Y. 10022
Published simultaneously in Canada by
The Macmillan Company of Canada Limited
SBN 670-69807-5
Library of Congress catalog card number: 72-75744
Printed in U.S.A. by Vail-Ballou Press, Inc.

ACKNOWLEDGMENTS

Aldus Books Limited: "Ibsen, Shaw, Brecht: Three Stages" from
Literature of the Western World. Copyright © 1970 by Aldus Books Limited.

Harcourt Brace Jovanovich, Inc.: "Eugene O'Neill" from *Major Writers
of America, Volume II,* edited by Perry Miller, © 1962 by Harcourt Brace
Jovanovich, and reprinted with their permission.

"Bernard Shaw" originally appeared in *The Plays of George Bernard Shaw*
published by The New American Library, Inc., New York, N.Y.

"The Night Is Dark and I Am Far from Home," "Theatre and Therapy:
Preliminary," and "The Unliberated University" originally appeared in
New American Review.

"Treason of the Experts (Thoughts on the Student Discontents)," and
"The Theatre of Interpretations" originally appeared in *The Nation.*

"For the Continuation of Protest" originally appeared in *Playboy*
under the title "Conscience versus Conformity."

"In Bahnhof Friederichstrasse" originally appeared in *Partisan Review.*

"The Naked American" originally appeared in *New Republic.*

For Joe Chaikin

". . . authentic life as the fundamental metaphysical principle
. . . authentic life which unifies and liberates the world . . ."

Preface

"When we are born we cry that we are come/To this great stage of fools."
We instantly recognize that the world is a great stage, and we already knew,
bringing the knowledge no doubt from the realm of the Mothers, that the little
stage of a theatre is the great one in miniature, a model of the world, if not
the universe, around us.

Some of these little stages have been made of ivory, stolen from that famous
Ivory Tower in which the world-weary and the world-shy have taken refuge
from time immemorial; and latterly synthetic ivory—made of money,
actually—has been used, in the name of Entertainment, to serve an essentially
similar purpose; for Neil Simon is not nearer to reality than the lovelorn swains
of yesterday's abstract pastorals. But in our time the towers, whether of ivory or
gold, have been tumbling down, and, even before they did, many of their occu-
pants have left them quite voluntarily. Under threat of proliferating, violent
death, people have been realizing that they are alive, and that life has propelled
them into struggles not of their making. Only within limits do they even get
any choice of which side to fight on. The choice may have been made in advance by the color of skin assigned them, or the size of their parents' income, or
the location of their family's home.

This book records my responses to the great stage as well as the small. The
two are one, and the 1960s, during which nearly all these pieces were written,

was a time when the great stage refused to be ignored, even by those who would have most liked to ignore it. Vietnam clamored for attention, and exacted a commitment. When the whole earth quakes, the tremor cannot but be felt in every cottage, not to pick again on the towers.

Dramatic critics, are they human? When you prick them, do they bleed? Do they respond to anything in life except what actors of the little stage do, under stage lighting, between seven-thirty p.m. and ten? I have assumed that even this, their most narrow and professional response, is not only influenced but conditioned by their responses to events on the great stage. And if you are going to read a critic, it cannot hurt to learn something about him, whether or not you respect his conclusions.

The conclusions may not be the big thing. Surely no one goes to a critic hoping to find a list of right answers to memorize and hand along, spreading rightness around until the world shall be a storehouse of correct opinions? Well, I wonder. Bernard Shaw was one of the finest critical minds of his time, yet what professional readers delighted to do with him was demonstrate that some of his opinions didn't square with some others. That meant, apparently, that he wasn't much of a help.

All that such professional reading bears witness to is the hope that truth can be *provided* by an authority and then *acquired* by memorization of the phrasing. If this hope were a reasonable one, it would also be reasonable to get angry at critics who cannot claim to provide us with truth in this fashion. If, as I believe, this hope is highly *un*reasonable, then Shaw's work could be valued, not as a bundle of transmittable opinions, but as a force that enables the reader to see and feel certain things even if they are not in all ways the same things that Shaw himself saw and felt. It might even be important that a Shaw, revising his work, not eliminate any contradictions so as to win our admiration of his consistency, since there may be less to learn from consistency than from the fact that an intelligent person believed A at one point and, at another, B, which is inconsistent with A. For it is always likely that the truth as seen by an omniscient God would partake of both A and B, even though human reason cannot see how they might be reconciled. Hegel said a thing had vital force only when it contained contradiction.

Men not only contradict themselves at a single moment, they also change their opinions and thus constantly contradict their former selves. Some writers resent this enormously—resent, that is, each self as it becomes *former*—and either let their earlier statements go out of print or keep changing them, presumably with the aim of arriving at *the* truth. Yet the final version of any author's work is but the last one he made before death intervened. Earlier versions are often superior anyway, and no further (if mortal eyes can judge) from *the* truth.

If all this sounds defensive, let me add that this line of argument only makes it all the harder, in the end, for a writer to defend himself. For if it is hard to come to a reader with opinions which are consistent and may be thought correct, it is harder to come to him with qualities which will be accepted in lieu of such opinions, in lieu of consistency, in lieu of *the* truth. Any fool can claim to be right, but it is an unusually rash fool who will claim that, though possibly wrong, he is so *interesting* you will want to go on reading him. For such interest, one wants to assume, would derive from higher qualities of mind and spirit—perspicacity, knowledgeability, wit, compassion, imagination. . . . Yet let any nondogmatist who publishes his writing tremble at his temerity, since implicitly he *is* staking a claim of this kind. Thus, on the great stage of fools, one is an unusually rash fool. One can hope, of course, that this is not the whole truth, since nothing ever is.

E.B.

New York
March 1972

Contents

The Life of

Modern Drama

Bernard Shaw

It was clear from the start that Bernard Shaw was a man of ideas. Later it turned out that he was a fabulous entertainer. But few have granted that the two Shaws were one. The old tendency was to grant that he was a publicist, a critic, an essayist, even a philosopher but to add: "not of course a dramatist." A later tendency was to concede that he was a great showman but to discount his thoughtful side. Neither in the old days, then, nor in the later ones was Shaw considered a dramatist, for even the later generations, so far as I can judge, have thought him only a master of the theatrical occasion, a man with a theatrical line of talk and a theatrical bag of tricks, a highly histrionic jokester—a comedian, certainly, hardly a writer of serious comedy. The fact is that the shock of that long career in the theatre has still not been absorbed. Shaw has not yet been seen in perspective.

In these circumstances it is interesting to go back and look at what happened in the 1890s. In 1891 Bernard Shaw had still not written a play, though he was thirty-five years old. A dozen years later, though he could describe himself as "an unperformed playwright in London," he had written *Widowers' Houses* (1892), *The Philanderer* (1893), *Mrs. Warren's Profession* (1893–1894), *Arms and the Man* (1894), *Candida* (1894–1895), *The Man of Destiny* (1895), *You Never Can Tell* (1895–1896), *The Devil's Disciple* (1896–1897), *Caesar and Cleopatra* (1898), *Captain Brassbound's Conversion*

(1899), *The Admirable Bashville* (1901), and *Man and Superman* (1901–1903).

Let us take for granted that these plays are full of ideas and jokes and ask if they do not also meet the demands of dramatic criticism as such. The drama, everyone agrees, presents character in action. Human actions become "an action" in the drama when they are arranged effectively—when, that is, they are given what we can recognize as a proper and praiseworthy structure. Of character dramatic critics have required many different things. One of them is emotional substance.

Let us ask, then, how Shaw, when he set about playwriting, tackled the problem of structure; and let us ask if he gave his characters' existence the requisite emotional substance.

I

How did Shaw put a play together? To think of questions about Shaw is to think also of the answers he invariably provided to them. In this case, he said, "I avoid plots like the plague. . . . My procedure is to imagine characters and let them rip. . . ." The quotation is from his *Table Talk* but (again: as usual) he said the same thing on many other occasions. One always has to ask not what he means (which may be clear) but what he is getting at. All Shaw's critical prose is polemical, as he freely admitted, and his writing on the theatre is devoted to the destruction of some kinds of drama and their replacement by some others (or one other). Here the enemy is the kind of play which had been dominant throughout the latter half of the nineteenth century—"the well-made play" as perfected by Eugène Scribe. In this dramaturgy the Aristotelian doctrine of the primacy of plot had been driven to an improper extreme. The plot was now not *primus inter pares* but all that mattered. It lost its originally organic relation to character and theme. So it became anathema to the apostles of the New Drama at the century's close. As late as 1946, when Allardyce Nicoll declared that Shaw was himself influenced by the well-made play, the old playwright went into print to deny it.

If the well-made play is defined as having no serious content, if it is defined by the relation (or lack of relation) of its plot to character and theme, then obviously Shaw did not write well-made plays. Yet Professor Nicoll had a point, and a strong one, which was that, for all the disclaimers, Shaw's plays did have plots and, furthermore, that these plots tended to be old acquaintances for those who knew their well-made play. Actually, the playwright had no need to be scandalized, for no dramatist had been more influenced by the well-made play than his own idol of those days, Henrik Ibsen. The Norwegian had begun his theatrical career by directing a large number of these plays; he made an exact imitation of them in his own *Lady Inger of Ostraat;* and he had continued to the end to use many of their characteristic devices. Hence it would have been quite possible for a writer in 1890 to denounce Scribe and Sardou and simultaneously to steal their bag of tricks—from Ibsen. It is doubtful, though, if Bernard Shaw needed to deceive himself in this way. It seems more likely that he took the main situation in *Arms and the Man* from one of Scribe's most successful plays, *Bataille de Dames*.

A situation is not, of course, a plot, and the plot of *Arms and the Man* is not simply lifted from Scribe, even though parts of it may have been. Plagiarism is not the point. The point is that even when Shaw's story diverges from Scribe it remains Scribean. The play *Arms and the Man* is hung, as it were, on the cunningly told tale of a lost coat with a photograph in its pocket. The reader need only go through the text and mark the hints, incidents, accidents, and contretemps of this tale and he will be finding the layout, the play—yes, the plot —of this play. Or at any rate the plot of what could have been a first draft of the play. Shaw, one gathers, did not write such first drafts but, supposing he had, what would be the difference between the first draft and the final one? In the answer to this question lies the secret of Shavian dramaturgy.

A corollary of the view that "plot is all" is this proposition: the cause of any incident is another incident. It is known that Scribe used to chart out a configuration of incidents and then write his play. This is to go far beyond Aristotle. It is to set no store at all by human initiative and assign to events themselves a kind of fatality: they are a network in which mankind is caught. Granted that the conception might in certain hands have its awesomeness, in Scribe's hands it had only triviality, because he manipulated the events till the issue was a pleasant one. It is curious how often that manipulation had to be arbitrary and drastic. Do events, when given their head, rush downward to disaster? To guarantee a happy ending, the well-making playwrights often needed their emergency weapon: sheer accident. Hence the Shavian complaint that well-made plays were badly made after all.

Hence also Bernard Shaw's first drama, which is an adaptation of an adaptation of a well-made play. The subject is one that Scribe and the younger Dumas brought to the nineteenth-century theatre: marrying, or refusing to marry, money. The immediate source is an unfinished play of William Archer's, *Rhinegold*. Archer's source is *La Ceinture dorée* by Emile Augier. When a young man discovers that his young lady's inherited money was acquired by her father in an immoral way, what does he do? William Archer's answer was: he pitches it into the Rhine. One presumes that Archer's action would have been set on a convenient balcony beside that river. Augier's hero is not so privileged. To preserve his honor, he would simply have to forgo the pleasure of marrying the lady, if the author did not provide him and the play with a convenient accident (or money *ex machina*). The whole French economy has to meet with a crisis (war breaks out) so that our heroine's father may be reduced to poverty: it is now honorable for our hero to propose to our heroine. In the well-made play one incident leads to another with a logic that is inescapable—except when the author decides to escape it. Perhaps Shaw's objection was less to the inescapability than to the egregious, last-minute escapes.

His first play, *Widowers' Houses,* may not be great art, but it is a great reversal of custom. Shaw's key decision was to refuse to accept Augier's ending, to refuse to have accident (masquerading as fate or otherwise) intervene. Such a refusal leads a man—leads a born playwright, at least—back and back into the earlier stages of a story and he ends up writing an utterly different play— an utterly different *kind* of play.

Not one but two conceptions of Augier's were being rejected: not just the solution-by-sheer-accident (which condemns a play to meaninglessness) but also the autonomy-of-incidents—something, by the way, which was no part of Augier's conscious philosophy but was imposed on him by the Scribean design. Dramatists are committed to the doctrine of free will. They can say they don't believe in it, but they have to write their plays as if they did. (In this they resemble human beings in general, for your most ardent determinist acts on the assumption that determinism is false.) People in plays have got to be able to make decisions, and these decisions have got to be both real and influential: they have to affect events. I see no reason to object to Aristotle's declaration that plot is the soul of the drama, but Aristotle would have objected to Scribe's attempt to cut the soul off from the body—that is, from character.

What *does* a young man do when he finds that his bride's dowry comes from a tainted source? There are two ways for a writer to arrive at an answer. He can say, "I can think of several answers—on the basis of several different possibilities of 'theatre.' Answer *A* will give you Big Scene *X;* answer *B* will give you Ending *Y;* and so on." Or he can say, "I cannot give you any answer at all until the terms of the proposition are defined, including the term 'tainted.' Above all I need to know who these people are—what bride? what young man?" The first way to arrive at an answer would commonly be thought the playwright's way: the reasoning is "craftsmanlike" and "of the theatre" and would earn a man commendation on Broadway in 1960. The second way is only the human way. That makes it the way of the real dramatist and so of Bernard Shaw.

It could be said that we have this perfectly functioning machine of the well-made play and that a Bernard Shaw is throwing a monkey wrench into it— the monkey wrench of character. That is how it must seem from the Scribean viewpoint. From the viewpoint of dramatic art, however, one would say that this particular engine had been revolving all too fast and uselessly: only when a Shaw slips in the clutch can the gear engage and the vehicle prove itself a vehicle by moving.

"My procedure is to imagine characters and let them rip. . . ." The pertinence of this remark may be now be clearer: if the young man has been "imagined," the dramatist can find the decision he would make as to the young lady's money. But at this point we realize that Shaw's words leave out of account the fact that the situation confronting the young man had been established in advance of the imagining of his character. It had been established by Augier and Archer and by Shaw's own decision to use their work. Hence, Shaw's own interpretation is both helpful and misleading—or, perhaps, is helpful only if those who are helped do a lot of work on their own.

Shaw put *Widowers' Houses* together—how? He took from certain predecessors not only a situation but a story, and not only a story but that clever, orderly, and theatrical arrangement of a story which we call a plot. Then he changed the plot—or, as he would have said, let the characters change it for him. Now had he retained Augier's characters, they could only have caused him to break off the action one scene earlier than Augier did: instead of the happy ending created by a national emergency, we would get the unhappy ending which the emergency reversed.

Characters in a well-made play are "conventional." They behave not according to laws of psychology but according to the expectations of an audience in a theatre. A type of drama in which the plot is given a free hand cannot afford any less passive or more obtrusive *personae*. Conversely, if a playwright abandons the plot-determined play, he will have to be more inventive as to character. To assume the initiative, his characters will have to be capable of it. So Shaw's first contribution to the drama was: more active characters. They were more active, first of all, in the most obvious fashion: they were violent. More important, they made decisions which affected the course of events, and they made them on the basis of their own nature, not of the spectator's. And so these characters were surprising. For a number of years they were too surprising to be acceptable. Like all surprising art, Shaw's dramaturgy was damned as nonart. The critics' formula was: Not A Play.

Augier's hero could not consider being the husband of a woman with a tainted dowry. Shaw creates a hero who has the effrontery to ask the heroine to throw up her dowry for his sake. But the Shavian joke—the Shavian reversal—is already what it would characteristically be in the future: a double one. To this demanding hero he adds an even more demanding heroine: she simply refuses to be poor to preserve her innocence. That is the nub of the first Shaw comedy. Then Shaw works his way out of the apparent deadlock, not by having the heroine weaken (that is, "improve"), but by having the hero renew his strength (that is, "deteriorate"). This the latter does by way of recovering from a shock. The shock comes from without and might be called an accident (like Augier's outbreak of war) except that it belongs to the logic of the situation. It turns out that the source of the hero's own unearned income is the same as that of his girl's father. End of Act Two. In the third and last act, our hero comes around and gets the girl by accepting the nature of capitalism. Socialist propaganda? Precisely: Shaw boasted of it. But he boasted with equal reason that he was writing comedy in the most traditional sense.

"Take what would be done by Scribe, Sardou, Dumas *fils,* or Augier and do the opposite." Is that the Shavian formula? It is certain that Shavian comedy is parodistic in a way, or to an extent, that Plautus, Jonson, and Molière were not. These others, one would judge, took a convention they respected and brought it to the realization of its best possibilities. Shaw took conventions in which he saw no possibilities—except insofar as he would expose their bankruptcy. The injunction "Do the opposite" was not whimsical. Shaw decided to "do the opposite" of Scribe in much the way Marx decided to do the opposite of Hegel—not to stand everything on its head (Hegel, he held, had done this) but to set everything back on its feet again. That was revolutionary thinking, and Shaw's art, for all the polite and charming trappings, was revolutionary art. The usual relations were reversed.

Such reversals as we see in the ending of *Widowers' Houses* are relatively simple. Shaw's weakest plays are those in which he has done little more than turn the ending around: the price you pay for the brilliant ending of *The Devil's Disciple* is that of a rather dull, and decidedly conventional, first act. His best plays are those in which the principle of reversal has pervaded the whole. Such a play is *Arms and the Man.*

The idea of taking two couples and causing them to exchange partners is hardly novel and, as I have said, the little tale of the coat and the portrait is Scribean in pattern, but Shaw can justifiably plead that this is no well-made play because the artifices of the plot are not what ultimately achieve the result. Here is one of the decisive turns in the action:

> BLUNTSCHLI. When you strike that noble attitude and speak in that thrilling voice, I admire you; but I find it impossible to believe a single word you say.
> RAINA. Captain Bluntschli!
> BLUNTSCHLI. Yes?
> RAINA. Do you mean what you said just now? Do you *know* what you said just now?
> BLUNTSCHLI. I do.
> RAINA. I! I!!!—How did you find me out?

With this last query, Raina passes over forever from Sergius's world to Bluntschli's as a result of nothing in the Scribean arrangement of incidents but of words, words, words. It is here that, to many, the Shavian drama seems vulnerable. In drama, actions are supposed to speak louder than words. Writers on the subject invariably know their etymology—"drama" derives from a Greek verb meaning "to do"—and use it as a cudgel. Their error is a vulgar one: action need not be external. It can often be carried by words alone. Shaw used to remark that his plays were all words just as Raphael's paintings were all paint.

There is a degree of legerdemain in that remark, for Scribe too put down his plays in words. What was confusing to readers and spectators half a century ago was that, after indicating unmistakably that he was playing Scribe's game, Shaw proceeded to break the rules. The fact that Bluntschli conquers by words gains its peculiar force from a context in which the opposite was to be expected. To look over *Arms and the Man* with an eye to technique would be to conclude that what we have here is Scribe most subtly interwoven with Shaw. Yet this formulation is inadequate, for who did the interweaving? There was a Scribe in Shaw, and there was a counter-Scribe in Shaw. What makes his works especially dramatic is the interaction of the two.

The passion and preoccupation of Scribe was the idea of climax. To the Big Scene at the end—or, rather, a little before the end—all his arts are dedicated. In Bernard Shaw there was almost as great a predilection for anticlimax. It is the Shavian "effect" par excellence: no other playwright has come near finding so many possibilities in it. The bit I have quoted from Bluntschli and Raina is an apt example. *Arms and the Man* contains a corresponding scene between Sergius and Louka. Where, in a well-made play, Bluntschli and Louka would have to soar to the heights of Raina and Sergius, in the Shaw play Raina and Sergius drop with a bump to the level of Bluntschli and Louka. Such is resolution by anticlimax. It is dramaturgically effective, and it enforces the author's theme. But this is not all of Shaw: it is only the counter-Scribe. The dual anticlimaxes do not round off *Arms and the Man*. What does is not the disenchantment of Raina and Sergius but the discovery that Bluntschli the realist is actually an enchanted soul whom nothing will disenchant. He has destroyed their romanticism and is himself "incurably romantic." This is another point that is made in "mere words"—"mere words stuck on at the end," if you wish—and yet stuck on very well, for they are firmly attached to that little tale of coat and photograph which gives the work its continuity and shape:

> BLUNTSCHLI. —yes: that's the coat I mean. . . . Do you suppose I am the sort of fellow a young girl falls in love with? Why, look at our ages! I'm thirty-four: I don't suppose the young lady is much over seventeen. . . . All that adventure which was life or death to me was only a schoolgirl's game to her. . . . Would a woman who took the affair seriously have sent me this and written on it: Raina, to her Chocolate Cream Soldier, a Souvenir?
>
> PETKOFF. That's what I was looking for. How the deuce did it get there?
>
> BLUNTSCHLI. I have put everything right, I hope, gracious young lady.
> RAINA. I quite agree with your account of yourself. You are a roman-

tic idiot. Next time I hope you will know the difference between a schoolgirl of seventeen and a woman of twenty-three.

In this scene plot and theme reach completion together, and the play of thesis and antithesis ends in synthesis.

The supreme triumph of Shaw's dramaturgical dialectics is to be found in *Man and Superman,* and, for all the blarney in the preface about the medieval *Everyman* and the eighteenth-century *Don Giovanni,* the method is the conversion of old materials into nineteenth-century terms, both thematic and technical. Shaw's claim to be returning to a pristine Don Juan is valid to the extent that the theme had originally been less of psychological than of philosophical, indeed theological, interest. It is also true that Don Juan had run away from his women. However, he had run away from them only after possessing them. In Shaw's play he runs away to prevent *them* from possessing *him.* It is a comic parody of the old motif, embodying Shaw's standard new motif: the courting of the man by the woman. And where the old dramatists and librettists had used the old, "open" type of plot (or nonplot), Shaw substitutes an utterly Scribean "closed" structure.

This very "modern" and "twentieth-century" play is made up of narrative materials familiar to every Victorian theatregoer. We have a hero who spends the entire evening hotly pursued by his foes; a clandestine marriage celebrated in defiance of a hostile father; a lovelorn hero who sacrifices himself so that the girl will go to his rival; a villain whose function is to constitute for a while the barrier to denouement and happy ending. The subplot about the Malone family rests upon two separate uses of the secret skillfully withheld, then skillfully released. Traditional farcical coincidence binds together Straker and Mendoza. The play bears every sign of careful workmanship, all of it School of Scribe, but, as with *Arms and the Man,* as soon as we examine particulars, we find, interwoven with the Scribean elements, those typically Shavian verbal exchanges which constitute further action. Violet's marriage could have been made a secret of in any Scribe play, and Scribe could have been relied on to choose an effective moment for the release of the secret. In Shaw, what creates both the fun and the point of the news release is not the organization of the incidents but their relation to theme:

> TANNER. I know, and the whole world really knows, though it dare not say so, that you were right to follow your instinct; that vitality and bravery are the greatest qualities a woman can have, and motherhood her solemn initiation into womanhood; and that the fact of your not being legally married matters not one scrap either to your own worth or to our real regard for you.
>
> VIOLET (*flushing with indignation*). Oh! You think me a wicked woman like the rest. . . . I won't bear such a horrible insult as to be complimented

by Jack on being one of the wretches of whom he approves. I have kept my marriage a secret for my husband's sake.

An incident which Tanner wishes to use to illustrate his "modern" philosophy thus comes to illustrate a contrasting thesis: that Violet lives by a nonmodern philosophy.

Simple? Yes, but closely linked to a point that is unsimple enough to have generally been missed: Tanner is a windbag. Indeed, the mere fact of the woman courting the man would probably not yield comedy at all, were it not for a further and more dynamic reversal: the woman, who makes no great claims for herself, has all the shrewdness, the real *Lebensweisheit,* while the man who knows everything and can discourse like Bernard Shaw is—a fool. Tanner is, in fact, like Molière's Alceste, the traditional fool of comedy in highly sophisticated intellectual disguise. Ann Whitefield, into whose trap Tanner falls, is the knave—in skirts.

While Don Juan Tenorio is Superman—or is on the road to him—John Tanner, M.I.R.C., is merely Man, and as such belongs to The World As It Is. Of dramaturgical interest is that the kind of plot Shaw evidently considers capable of giving an image of The World As It Is should be the kind that is generally considered (by himself, for instance) artificial, unreal, arbitrary, inane. Shaw the critic championed the new Naturalism, and among French dramatists especially favored Eugène Brieux, who produced dully literal theatrical documentaries. Yet when Shaw wrote an essay entitled "A Dramatic Realist to His Critics," the example of "realism" he gave from his own work was *Arms and the Man*—on the grounds that the characters respond naturally even if the situations aren't natural. We are entitled, then, to insist on his choice of "unnatural" situations. He must intuitively have understood something which, as a critic, he failed to grasp: that plot does not merely reproduce external reality. The violence and intrigue in Shakespeare, which Shaw the critic declared extraneous, provide the objective correlative of Shakespeare's feelings about life, and the "idiocies" of the plot of *Man and Superman* provide an objective correlative for Shaw's sense of modern life. The very fact that Shaw despised Scribe helps to explain the particular use he made of him.

The Don Juan episode in Act Three is neither a well-made play, nor a portion of a well-made play. It stands apart as something appropriately more austere and august. It is not a traditional work of any kind, not even a Platonic dialogue, the relation between Socrates and his interlocutors being quite different. It is not even a debate, for two of the speakers, the Commander and Ann, hardly present arguments at all: they simply represent a point of view. Do even the Devil and Don Juan *discuss* anything? A devil is scarcely a being one can convert to a Cause, and if the Don is busy convincing anyone it is himself. Certainly it is the philosophy of Bernard Shaw that he is given to speak, but is persuasion exercised—even on the audience? Rather, the contributions of the four presences come together as a vision of life and an intimation of superlife.

Man—and superman. The comedy of John Tanner—and the vision of Don Juan Tenorio. Shaw—and counter-Shaw. Thesis and antithesis are, to be sure, of separate interest, and yet, as usual, the great Shavian achievement is to have related one to the other. Tanner seems a wiseman and proves a fool. Don Juan passes for a philanderer but proves an explorer and a missionary of the truth. In our trivial, tawdry, clever, Scribean world, intellect is futile and ever at the mercy of instinct. Take away the episode in hell, and Shaw has written an anti-intellectual comedy. The episode assigns to intellect the highest role. No longer, therefore, is Ann the center and source of things, only a possible mother for superman. Here Don Juan dominates. Here (or rather in heaven) intellect is at home, and the Don is cured of that occupational disease of Shavian heroes —homelessness. He "comes to a good end," only it is not an end, it is an episode, and from these celestial-infernal heights we must descend to earth with the shock of Shavian anticlimax, to earth and to Tanner, from Superman back to Man. One section of the play gets an electric charge from the other.

Of Shaw's "playmaking" one must conclude that he knew how to put together a Scribean plot; that he knew how to subordinate such a plot to his own purposes; and that, in *Man and Superman,* he knew how to take the resultant Shavian comedy and combine it dynamically with a disquisition on (and by) Don Juan.

II

If Shaw's plays are, or begin by being, a parody of the more conventional drama of his time, that parody is by no means confined to the form. We have already seen that the themes, too, tend to get turned around: these compositions not only do the opposite, as it were, but also say the opposite.

What of the emotions? Whatever the ultimate purpose of drama, its immediate impact is a strongly emotional one, and one cannot conceive of a story having an emotional effect upon an audience unless it is an emotional story and has a certain emotional structure. I may be forgiven for stating so rudimentary a principle because the Shavian drama presents us with a paradox: it has flooded a thousand theatres with emotion and yet has often been held to be emotionless.

Of course, this common opinion is absurd, bolstered though it can be with remarks of Shaw's own about being a mere "work machine" and the like. What we confront here is originality. Shaw may not have been an original thinker: he tried, rather, to make a synthesis of what certain others had thought. But he was an original person. What fitted him so well for the role of the enemy of convention was that his natural responses were not those of other people but all his own. His emotional constitution was a peculiar one, and that peculiarity is reflected in his plays.

Sex is, without doubt, the crucial issue. Comedy remains fertility worship, however sublimated, and it is fair enough to ask what Bernard Shaw made of the old sexual rigmarole—courtship and the barriers thereto. It is even fair to use any facts about Shaw himself that are a matter of public record.

On the other hand, one is not honor-bound to side with "modern" opinion against "Victorian" as to what is good and bad. The very "modern" Dr. Kinsey implied that human vitality could be measured in statistics on orgasms. Our subject Bernard Shaw will not pass into any Kinseyite paradise. Though he lived to be ninety-four, he seems to have experienced sexual intercourse only between the ages of twenty-nine and forty-three. "I lived a continent virgin . . . until I was 29. . . . During the fourteen years before my marriage at 43 there was always some lady in the case. . . . As man and wife we found a new relation in which sex had no part. It ended the old gallantries, flirtations, and philanderings for both of us." This quotation is from the letter to Frank Harris, who, as a Kinseyite before Kinsey, wrote:

> Compare his [Shaw's] private life with Shakespeare's. While Mary Fitton was banished from London Shakespeare could write nothing but tragedies. That went on for five years. When the Queen died and Shakespeare's Dark Lady returned, he wrote *Antony and Cleopatra,* his greatest love story. As nothing like that happened in Shaw's life we can only get a text-booky, sexless type of play.

A remarkable blend of ignorance, invention, and arbitrary assumption! For actually Shaw concealed from Harris most of his private life; nothing much is known about Shakespeare's feelings for any woman; and no critic or psychologist of repute has ever argued that a man's writing has to be "text-booky" and "sexless" unless he is carrying on an adulterous romance; a more familiar argument would be that precisely the abstinent man's imagination might well be crammed with sex. But there is no settling the question a priori.

William Archer declared that Shaw's plays reeked with sex. It is a more suggestive declaration than Harris's. It reminds us that Shaw was able to re-create the sexual charm of both men and women to a degree unequaled by any English dramatist except Shakespeare. To be sure, he doesn't need bedroom scenes to do this. Morell has only to talk and we understand "Prossy's complaint." Undershaft has only to talk and we understand why he is a problem to his daughter. To say nothing of the long line of sirens from Candida to Orinthia! Few of the "sexy" ladies of Restoration comedy, by contrast, have any sex appeal at all. One thing Archer is sure to have had in mind is that the women in Shaw pursue a sexual purpose in a way absolutely unknown to Victorian literature. Of all the reversals in Shavian drama this is inevitably the most famous: the reversal in the roles of the sexes. Shaw once committed himself to the view that all superior women are masculine and all superior men are feminine. In his comedies, most often, the woman is active, the man passive. Perhaps by 1960 the theme has been restated *ad nauseam;* to Archer it was startling. As was Shaw's determination to rub the sore places of the sexual morality of his time. *Mrs. Warren's Profession* was for many years too "raw" a play for production in London, and it created a memorable scandal when it was produced in New Haven and New York in 1905. Like most of the major modern dramatists and novelists, Shaw mentioned the unmentionable. He even claimed to have "put the physical act of sexual intercourse on the stage" (in *Overruled*). Archer may well have felt that Shaw could not give the subject of sex a rest: he may not always have been at the center of it, but he was forever touching the fringes.

Here Frank Harris would have interjected, "He was always *avoiding* the center of it." And the interjection is called for. The impression that a man is unemotional in general and sexless in particular does not come from nowhere, nor are the kinds of sex I have been noting what the average spectator is looking for if he demands a "sexy" show. *Overruled* does not really "put the physical act of sexual intercourse on the stage," and, even if it did, it would do so comically, depriving the act of precisely that element which people miss in Shaw, which is not sex in general but the torridity of sexual romance. At that, if this element were simply absent, Shaw might very well have got away with the omission. But it is explicitly rejected. It is not that a Shavian couple cannot end up in bed but, rather, that they are likely to contemplate the idea—and reject it. If the characteristic act of the French drama of the period was the plunge into bed, that of the Shavian drama is the precipitate retreat from the bedroom door.

Harris would be right in reminding us that such was Bernard Shaw's emotional constitution. What other writer has ever created all the normal expectations in a scene between a king and his mistress (*The Apple Cart*) only to reveal later that their relationship is purely platonic? *Captain Brassbound's Conversion* shows the Shavian pattern to perfection. Is there sexual feeling in the play? There is. The process by which Brassbound and Lady Cicely are brought closer and closer is positively titillating. After which, what happens? They are parted. The play has a superb final curtain. "How marvellous!" says Lady Cicely, "how marvellous!" Then with one of those quick changes of tone that mark the Shavian dialogue: "And what an escape!" Is this unemotional? No. But the emotion is not erotic: it is relief at a release from the erotic. Such is the emotional content of this particular Shavian anticlimax.

As far as conscious intention goes, all Shaw's plays might bear the title he gave to three of them—plays for puritans—for that intention is to show romance transcended by a higher-than-erotic purpose. It is a classic intention, an application, really, of the traditional conflict of love and honor, with honor winning hands down, as it did in Corneille and even in one masterpiece of Racine's, *Bérénice*. We are concerned here not with philosophic intention but psychological substance. Where the philosopher insists that Shaw does not cross the threshold of the bedroom, the psychologist asks: Why does he hover at the bedroom door?

We know from the correspondence with Mrs. Pat Campbell that Shaw liked to play with fire. Even the correspondence with Ellen Terry entailed a playfulness not quite devoid of "danger." The boy Shaw had been witness to an odd household arrangement whereby his mother's music teacher contrived to be (it would seem) almost but not quite her lover. A slightly older Shaw has recently been portrayed as the intruder into a friend's marriage like his own Eugene Marchbanks: this is speculation. Let us look at the play *Candida,* which is a fact.

It has a notable Big Scene at the end, which is characterized by an equally notable improbability. A comfortable, sensible, parson's wife doesn't let herself get jockeyed into "choosing" between her husband and an almost total stranger. People—such people at least—don't do such things. A respectable woman's choice was made before the bans were read.

Perhaps Candida is not really respectable? That is the line of interpretation taken by Beatrice Webb, who declared her a prostitute. Will the play, taken as a play, bear this interpretation out? A dramatist's license to have the truth turn out different from the impression given to the audience is very limited, for it is to a large extent by giving impressions that he creates characters. Shaw has given the impression that Candida is *not* a prostitute.

Against this it can be urged that Shaw himself took Beatrice Webb's side and attacked Candida—in remarks he made about her in letters to James Huneker, Richard Burton, and others. True, but was that legitimate? He himself admitted that he had no more right to say what his plays meant than any other critic. One might add that he may have had less, for, when an author intervenes to correct our impressions of his work, he is often intervening to change or misinterpret that work.

Outside the play, Shaw is against Candida. Inside it, he is both for and against her, but he is for her effectually, and against her ineffectually, because the direct impression is favorable, while it is only by throwing logic back into the story when it is over that you can reach an unfavorable judgment. This means, I should think, that, though Shaw's intellect is against Candida, his emotions are for her.

What is it that this play has always projected in the theatre, and can always be counted on to project again? The charm of Candida. This is a reality so immediate and all-pervasive that it is hard for any other element in the play to make headway against it. Leading actresses know this and, hearing their director speak of Candida's essential badness, can afford to smile a Candida-smile, strong in the knowledge that there is nothing a director can do about this badness, once that smile has been displayed on stage as well as off.

I would say that it is a confusing play but that the confusion goes unnoticed because of Candida's charm and may even be the cause of a degree of emotional tension unusual in a Shaw play. Candida is made out of a Shavian ambivalence: he would like to reject this kind of woman, but actually he dotes on her. One quickly senses that he "is" Marchbanks. One also finds he protests (too much) that he is *not* Marchbanks. "I had in mind De Quincey's account of his adolescence in his Confessions," * he wrote, "I certainly never thought of myself as a model." From the pretense of being De Quincey, no doubt, comes a certain unreality in some of the lines. As a character, Marchbanks seems to me not altogether a success because Shaw was hiding. What better image to hide behind than that of the kind of writer he himself was not—a romantic poet? Especially if De Quincey would do the job for him?

It didn't work perfectly except as pure histrionics. (Marchbanks, though a dubiously drawn character, is always an effective stage role, and still seems to correspond to the actors' idea of a poet.) But if no one in the play can reject Candida, there is a noteworthy niche in it for the man whom she will reject. This niche Marchbanks can fill nobly, and has his dramatic moment as he marches into it. His final exit is a magnificent piece of action. Possibly everything before that in this role is just as improvisation. Shaw could not make us believe in the poet's poetry. He does make us believe in his pain and his nobility, for at these points he could identify himself with Eugene completely without having to "think of himself as a model."

Dramatists usually speak of their characters individually, and that could be regarded as strange, because the drama, all through the centuries, has done much less with separate persons than with relationships. The traditional characters are, if you will, simplified to the point of crudity. What is not crude, as treated by the old dramatists, is the interaction of these characters. The dynamics of human relations are fully rendered. If what you do not get is the detailed psychological biography, what you do get is the essence of such relations as parent and child, boy and girl, man and wife.

Now modern playwrights, happily, have not departed from the classic patterns as much as they are supposed to have, and what rings true, emotionally, in *Candida* corresponds to Shaw's ability to find and recreate some of these elemental relationships. An inner obstacle, I tend to think, hampered him somewhat when he tried to "do" the Marchbanks-Candida relationship, but the Morell-Candida relation is both clear and challenging. It is, as Shaw himself said, the relationship of Nora and Torvald Helmer turned around. In Shaw's

* I think this is a slip and that Shaw did not mean *Confessions of an English Opium Eater* but the chapter "Premature Manhood" in *Autobiographic Sketches*.

play the man is the doll. But where Ibsen tells the story of a doll who finally comes to life Shaw tells the story of a seemingly living person who turns out to have been a doll all along. (In other words, the relation of Shaw to Ibsen, instead of being direct, as it might seem, is an inverse one, exactly like the relation of Shaw to other nineteenth-century drama.) Into Morell Shaw can put that part of himself (a child) which finds Candida irresistible, just as into Candida he can put that part of Woman which he finds irresistible—the Mother in her. One would have to be as naïve a psychologist as Frank Harris to consider the mother-and-child relation less emotional than that of lovers.

Or less dramatic. Relationships become dramatic not in the degree of their eroticism but to the extent that they contain conflict. Pure love would not be a dramatic subject at all. Love becomes dramatic when it is *im*pure—when the loving element is submerged in a struggle for power. The axis about which *Candida* revolves is that of strength and weakness, not love and hate, and if one knows Shaw's views on the topic of the "weaker sex" in general the conclusion of *Candida* follows naturally. Instead of the little woman reaching up toward the arms of the strong man, we have the strong woman reaching down to pick up her child. It is remarkable how far Shaw's thought is from the standard "advanced thinking" of his generation with its facile assumptions about equality and comradeship. He is closer to Nietzsche.

Of the ending of *A Doll's House* it has been said: perhaps Nora has walked out in a mere tantrum and will be back in the morning. How much more savage is the ending of *Candida!* Only Strindberg could have written a sequel to it. The cruelty of the heroine, merely implicit in the present play, would have to come to the surface in any continuation of the story. Candida has chosen to let her husband discover his shame. She, as well as he, will have to take the consequences. Let the stage manager hold razors and strait jackets in readiness!

One reason why Shaw got so little credit for his treatment of the emotions is that the emotions he treats are not the ones people expect. The very fact that his favorite device is anticlimax should tell us that what he most insistently feels is "letdown." It may be retorted that, on the contrary, Bernard Shaw was the most buoyant and vivacious of men. That is also true. The axis "strength-weakness" is not more important to Shaw's content than the axis "elation-depression" is to his form. The dialogue ripples gaily along; then comes the sudden letdown. The circus has familiarized us with the pattern. It is the light of heart who take the pratfall. Even as the fool pops up in Shavian comedy in the highly intellectualized shape of a Jack Tanner, so the pratfall is transmuted into an anticlimax that has a climactic force. It has been customary to take these anticlimaxes as expressions of an idea, the idea of disenchantment. It is *the* idea of modern literature, and it is inseparable from an emotion far commoner and far more influential than romantic excitement. There seems to be no name for this emotion, and that too is significant. Let us call it desolation.

You cannot be disenchanted without having been enchanted. One is sometimes tempted to believe that our human desolation might have been avoided if only we had not started out so undesolate. It is not the fact that we don't have things that worries us but that we have lost them—or rather, been deprived of them. Desolation is the feeling of having been driven from paradise.

A friend of Bernard Shaw's said that when he saw *The Wild Duck* the bottom dropped out of the universe. One difference between Ibsen and Shaw is that the former produced this effect on the audience, whereas the latter produced it on the characters in a play. Just as a character in a melodrama loses a fortune, so a character in a Shaw play loses a universe. The experience may be given a playful treatment, as with Raina and Sergius. In the case of Morell, the treatment is only partly playful. It gets more serious as the play *Candida* proceeds. Morell finally loses his image of his wife and of himself. The curtain has to be rung down to save us from the Strindberg play that would have to follow.

What of *Mrs. Warren's Profession?* The starting point was a treatment by Maupassant of the theme of a girl finding out that her mother is a courtesan. In an early version of the tale Maupassant had the girl kill herself. In the later and better-known text (*Yvette*), he saves her life to engineer for himself an ironic-poignant ending: she becomes a kept woman like her mother before her. Curtain! That is the kind of inversion of a suicidal ending which Shaw did *not* go in for. Or not any more. If Shaw had shown a "surrender to the system" (in comical fashion) in the ending to *Widowers' Houses,* he was now intent on showing a rejection of the system. In the first instance, Vivie Warren's revolt represents Shaw's rational rejection of capitalism, but the play culminates in a scene that has no necessary connection with economics, a scene of family crisis, a scene in which a daughter rejects her mother. Which after all is archetypal Shaw. Instead of the emotions of lover and mistress, he renders the emotions of parents and children, and particularly the emotion of the child rejecting the parent. *Major Barbara* is perhaps the grandest example of this archetype. The great last act of *Pygmalion* is the same thing in disguise, for Henry Higgins is the progenitor of the new Eliza, and that is why she must break free of him. Shaw's Joan has a father too—in heaven—and she comes at times almost to the point of breaking with Him. That she does not quite do so is the upshot of a play which, while it shows Joan's isolation from men, ends with a stretching of arms toward the heavenly father. . . . Vivie Warren is already a Saint Joan in that the experience Shaw gives her is that of being desolated. It is the experience he felt most deeply—presumably because it was the experience he had most deeply experienced. In any event, the two long scenes between Vivie and Mrs. Warren are playwriting of a standard England had not reached for a couple of centuries.

The background, however, is blurred. A Scribean climax is arranged to provide *élan* for the announcement that Vivie's romance is incestuous:

CROFTS. . . . Allow me, Mister Frank, to introduce you to your half-sister, the eldest daughter of the Reverend Samuel Gardner. Miss Vivie: your half-brother. Good morning.

FRANK (. . . *raising the rifle*). You'll testify before the coroner that it's an accident, Viv. (*He takes aim at the retreating figure of Crofts. Vivie seizes the muzzle and pulls it round against her breast.*)

VIVIE. Fire now. You may.

Direct climax (as against anticlimax) was not really in Shaw's line, and in failing to parody Scribe here, Shaw has himself tumbled into the ridiculous. Perhaps the following act was bound to be an anticlimax in a way not intended —a mere disappointment. Yet it is hard to believe that the particular disappointments it brings are simply the result of a technical miscalculation. Rather, they involve hesitations about the subject. After so strongly creating the impression of incest, Shaw shuffles the notion off in the next act in a surprisingly ambiguous way. It would be easy enough, from a technical viewpoint, to make clear that no incest had been committed. Why did Shaw leave the situation doubtful? So that Vivie could dismiss the issue as irrelevant? In that case, what is relevant? Why is she giving Frank up? One can think of possible reasons, but what reason is one *supposed* to think of?

Unclarity in the work of so careful a craftsman, a writer, moreover, who has more than once been accused of excessive clarity, surely bears witness to inner uncertainty and conflict. To think of *Mrs. Warren's Profession* in this personal way is to realize what powerful aggressions it embodies. Shaw combined the themes of prostitution and incest in order to make quite a rational point: our mad society draws back in horror from incest, which is certainly not a pressing menace and perhaps not even a bad thing, while it encourages prostitution, which is a virulent social pestilence. But both themes have a resonance far beyond the bounds of intellect. It is as if they proved more than Shaw had bargained for. The incest theme is sounded—all too boldly. Then the young dramatist has no idea what to do with it. He takes it back. Only it is too late. So he half takes it back. After all, what is troubling Vivie does go beyond the rationally established causes. . . . Deep water! And Shaw flounders in it. Which has some interest for the student of the emotions. Even where Shaw's plays are faulty, they are not unemotional. On the contrary, it is because of a certain emotional involvement in the material, not because of incapacity for such involvement, that Shaw was not able to resolve certain problems and truly finish certain plays. *Candida* and *Mrs. Warren's Profession* could be cited in evidence. There is material in both which was not successfully worked through.

Is there similar material in Shaw's collected plays which *was* worked through? Yes, *Pygmalion*. This play might well have proved just as ambiguous as the others, for it might have seemed that Eliza must love Higgins, and therefore that her leaving him is but an overrational afterthought of the author's, like his afterthoughts on Candida. Some people, including, it seems, the author of *My Fair Lady,* think that is just what the Shavian ending is. I, on the other hand, feel—and it is feeling that is in question—that Eliza's rebellion grows organically out of what preceded. She is Higgins' creation. She cannot *be* at all unless she become independent of her creator. If he has "sex appeal," that makes the break more difficult but not less necessary. A girl's father quite normally has sex appeal for her. That is not to justify incest. Here Shaw does cope with incest, and in the shrewdest way—by avoiding it.

The ending of *Pygmalion* is the classic Shavian situation: someone is clamorously refusing to enter the bedroom. The friends of Frank Harris are thereby disgusted. That is their right. But there is a point to be made about Shaw's rendering of emotion. Refusal is emotional. There is more turbulence in conflict between Eliza and Higgins as conceived by Shaw than in romance between them as in *My Fair Lady.*

Man and Superman, on the other hand, might seem to be without emotional substance. The attempt made at a straightforward emotional climax is certainly rather unsuccessful:

> TANNER. I love you. The Life Force enchants me: I have the whole world in my arms when I clasp you. But I am fighting for my freedom, for my honor, for my self, one and undivisible.
>
> ANN. Your happiness will be worth them all.
>
> TANNER. You would sell freedom and honor and self for happiness?
>
> ANN. It would not be happiness for me. Perhaps death.
>
> TANNER. Oh, that clutch holds and hurts. What have you grasped in me? Is there a father's heart as well as a mother's?

If there is capital here, it is the kind that yields no dramatic return, and indeed a criticism of this false climax would lead us to complain of the introduction of the "Life Force" in the first place. There seems no such organic relation between Tanner and Ann as there is between Vivie and her mother, Eliza and Higgins, Candida and Morell. The pair are sometimes compared to Benedick and Beatrice. The comparison is not apt. Shakespeare shows the erotically "dangerous" element in the hostility of his couple. Tanner and Ann draw no sparks from each other. A cynic might say: here there can be no love since there is no hate. There is really no relationship at all except that she insists on having him and he cannot evade her successfully because the author won't let him. In this case, we have either to conclude that Frank Harris's kind of criticism applies or that this is "drama of ideas" and we must not ask it to be otherwise.

Emotional substance? The farce of Tanner and Ann, taken in isolation, has very little; but oddly enough the episode in hell has a good deal, and this spreads itself over the work as a whole. Even here, though, there is a discrepancy between intention and achievement. The final effect of the Don Juan scene is not that we find the positive message inspiring. We find it at best important, at worst gallant, a brave effort to make sense of things that cannot be made sense of. It is all rather like a speech made in wartime saying that our side is bound to win because we are right. Perhaps. But the words that burn with irrefutability are all words expressing not aspiration toward a better future but recognition of a bad present. Don Juan himself is at his best when denouncing people. The speech that steals the show ("And is man any the less destroying himself . . .") is made by the Devil. Which is because it is not only a very reasonable speech but a very emotional one, a speech that springs from that very desolation which Shaw's best people experience.

This note of personal poignancy is not, I think, heard after *Saint Joan* (1923). So much the worse for the later plays. They have considerable merit yet they often lack urgency even when the author makes Urgent Statements in them, and it is interesting that they lack not only dynamic and turbulent personal relationships but also close structure. There had been a connection between the emotional and the dramaturgic construction of the earlier plays; and when one went, so did the other.

I am not proposing here a complete theory of the Shavian drama. Certainly, it should not be implied that that drama is dominated by the emotional conflicts of its author, much less that it ought to be. For that matter, I have had to remark that unresolved conflict sometimes resulted in unresolved art. What I am affirming is that some Shaw plays communicate personal feeling of great intensity and that even some Shaw plays which are less overtly emotional do embody profound feelings, though not of the kind that is usually expected.

(*1960*)

Right You Are

On the face of it, Pirandello's *Right You Are* is the purest instance of "drama of ideas" in the history of the theatre, a veritable exhibition of an idea, the statement of a proposition—namely, that truth is relative and subjective: what seems to me, or you, to be so *is* so. The statement is made in the title *Cosí è (se vi pare)*, explained by a leading character (Laudisi), and embodied in what the author himself designates a parable. Luigi Pirandello seems as single-minded as Aesop, his parable a simple fable, apologue, or exemplum.

If it is rare to find a play so deliberately dedicated to a principle, it is rarer to find one dedicated to a principle that none of us will assent to. What would "assent" mean, anyway? That a certain principle which "seems so" to Pirandello also "seems so" to you or me? What if it did? How can we be sure that it is the same principle as the one he is talking about? Furthermore, if *Right You Are* is true only for Pirandello, why did he write it down? If a man holds the view that views are incommunicable, how can he hope to communicate *that* view? In short, we could not assent to the idea of *Right You Are* even if we would.

Was Pirandello a fool? Had he not taken that elementary lesson in philosophy in which the instructor triumphs over relativism and skepticism by observing that relativism must not become absolute and that the skeptic should be skeptical of skepticism? There is evidence on the point—for example, the following debate:

A — The world is my idea (*rappresentazione*), and the world is purely ideal (*una idealità*). . . . The world—all that is external to the ego —exists only according to the idea one has of it. I do not see what is; what I see, is.

B — Or is not, my dear fellow. Because you may see badly. That existences outside ours should be little more than appearances without reality outside the ego is supposed by the champions of an idealism which the English call solipsism, and you know that it isn't a new notion— English writers following the philosophy of Berkeley have given it fantastic form. And you will know *Through the Looking Glass.* Suppose, my dear fellow, that I, let us say, do not exist outside your ego except as you see me? This means that your consciousness is one-sided, that you are not conscious of me, that you have no *realization* of me within you (to use an expression of Josiah Royce), that your idea does not live for me.

And it must be so. And here, to turn to art, is our true point of difference. For me the world is not solely ideal, that is, it is not confined to the notion I can form of it: outside me the world exists of itself and alongside me; and in my representation or idea of the world I am to propose to *realize* it as much as I can, creating for myself a consciousness in which it exists—in me as in itself, seeing it as it sees itself, feeling it as it feels itself. And so, nothing symbolic and apparent for me, everything will be real and alive!

Since Pirandello * is not A but B we are forced, I think, to admit that he knew what he was doing and are free to ask: if the relativism is a joke, what is serious in the play? In the midst of an earnest discussion in a Westport home,** someone appealed to the maid who was bringing in the tea things, "What did *you* get out of *Right You Are?*" "I guess it just says, keep your nose out of other folks' business," she replied, thus proving all over again how right Molière was to consult his cook. Such is indeed the simple message not only implicit in the action of the play but explicitly stated by Laudisi at the outset as the serious moral conclusion to the frivolous philosophical argument. "Respect what other people see and touch even if it's the opposite of what you see and touch." The reader should go on to ask, as the actor must, not only what Laudisi says but what he does. For more than two acts he tries to discourage people from interfering with the lives of others. In the third act he decides that talk is useless,

* Writing in the weekly journal *Il Marzocco,* March 7, 1897, in reply to Ugo Ojetti (A), *Il Marzocco,* February 28, 1897.
** The present essay was written shortly after I had directed two productions of the play: one at the Brattle Theatre, Cambridge, the other at the Westport Country Playhouse. Quotations from Pirandello plays in this and the two following essays are from my own translations as they appear in my anthologies—*Right You Are* and *Six Characters* in *The Great Playwrights* (1970), *Enrico IV* in *The Genius of the Italian Theatre* (1964).

but his goal is unchanged: he hopes that a *coup de théâtre* may succeed where reason failed—succeed in demonstrating the wickedness and futility of inter-ference.

Pirandello once said he wanted the play to indicate the triumph of the imagi-nation over mere facts, but the imagination he shows us is not a philosophical or literary power of imagining what is not, it is insight into what is, insight by means of sympathy, it is compassion, it is love. While the ostensible principle of his play is an unacceptable metaphysic, the real principle is: love your neigh-bor. To realize how far truth is subjective is to realize that one must respect the subject. Pirandello is defending the person against the dehumanizing influence of society. His special care is for the sanctity of the intimate affections, the right to possess your soul in peace and privacy. These ideas are as old as *Antigone* but have become more relevant than ever with the rise of the police state. And it is not just fanatics who are open to attack. "Many of our best friends" have for years been boosting the public interest and the objective fact above the pri-vate interest and the subjective fact. The inner life of man has been neglected and mocked, without any perceptible public gain.

The seemingly cryptic figure of the veiled lady in *Right You Are* is perhaps the simplest expression of indignation at this neglect in modern literature. She is the inner sanctum, the holy of holies. Her life being love, she has achieved complete self-sacrifice, she has no identity; she exists only in relationship, she is wife to the husband, daughter to the mother; she is what the husband thinks she is, she is what the mother thinks she is, she is what *you* think she is. On the literal plane, all this is absurd, of course, yet hardly more so than the rest of the play. It is all—to quote Pirandello's own perfect characterization—*una gran diavoleria,* a big joke, a piece of deviltry.

Now under what circumstances does a man champion a philosophy he knows to be fallacious? When he wants to enjoy himself and throw ideas about like colored balls. "You're simply being paradoxical," we say to a friend who cham-pions an error with gusto. But the truth is *not* simple. Part of it is that he has been enjoying the comedy of intellect. Another part is that by stating an error he wants to make you more aware of the truth. Laudisi is not quite a devil's ad-vocate. His method is more like the inverse of a *reductio ad absurdum:* he doesn't take plausible premises and prove that they lead to disastrous conse-quences, he takes implausible premises and derives very desirable consequences from them. We have seen how he drives from his "absolute relativism" the prin-ciple of the golden rule. It is also important to see the totality of Laudisi's speeches in the context of other characters' speeches. Laudisi constitutes a sort of frame for the picture or—more correctly perhaps—the spectacles we see the picture through.

Once the "deviltry" of the play is conceded, even its final leap into the realm of symbol seems fully justified. The audience may be cheated of the answer it is waiting for, but it accepts the *image* of the veiled lady unquestioningly. At that point, in performance, there is usually a gasp of astonishment signaling to the actors that the bullet has shot home. And nothing could better illustrate what this play is like than the fact that its climax is an image. If our first discovery is that the idea of the play is not "truth is relative" but "love your neighbor," our second is that *Right You Are* is not, in any narrow sense, a "drama of ideas" at all. To convince himself he had ideas, Pirandello had to redefine the term. "An artist's 'ideas,' " he wrote in his essay on humor, "are not abstract ideas but feelings, sentiments, which become the center of his inner life, take hold of his spirit, shake it, and, by shaking it, create a body of images." *Six Characters in Search of an Author* may have started in Pirandello's mind with an image of Madama Pace's establishment which he took a note of years before. He also tells us that *Right You Are* was born from "the frightening image" in a dream of "a deep courtyard with no exit." * It is with the imagination, not the ratiocinative faculty, that this courtyard is transformed into the home of the Ponzas (the idea of "no exit" being left to Jean-Paul Sartre).

For Pirandello was an artist and, in the fullest professional sense, a playwright. He described one of his plays as "Pinero with a difference," and *Right You Are* is a thriller, almost a who-done-it—with a difference. The audience modestly identifies itself with the foolish busybodies, anxiously asks: Is the girl *her* daughter or *his* second wife?—is led to the one answer and the other in rapid alternation, only to be authoritatively told at the end that the girl is *both* her daughter and his second wife. Luckily, there is another "difference" besides the famous ending—that this thriller contains two other dramas, a tragedy and a comedy.

The tragic action of *Right You Are,* bounded by the arrival and departure of the Ponza-Frola family, derives from an unknown "misfortune"; the exposure of three lives to the public gaze reopens the wound; they decide to leave.

The comic action derives from the conflict between Laudisi and the townspeople (principally, of course, his own family). The three acts correspond to three stages in this conflict. In the first, the "crowd"—in effect a chorus—investigates the lives of the unhappy trio to the point where two of them come forward in turn and make confessions. In the second, the crowd has the "great idea" of confronting Ponza and Frola. Up to this point, Laudisi has practiced dissuasion. But when, in the third act, the police commissioner refuses to write a fictitious explanation that will satisfy everyone's curiosity, Laudisi the peacemaker becomes Laudisi the mischief-maker. He caps the *coups de théâtre* of the first two acts with an even greater one by giving Sirelli the idea of bringing over Signora Ponza. At the end, his point is proved and he is victor.

This comic action is repetitious. Yet, if Acts One and Two of Pirandello's

* See *Almanacco Letterario Bompiani,* 1938.

play present the same drama three times, the very fact that unfriendly critics are not bored but irritated suggests a positive process rather than merely the author's inability to think of something else to say. For one thing, it is repetition and *change*—change in speed and change in magnitude. Farce (and this is farce-comedy) is a mechanism very like many of the weird and whirling vehicles of a fairground. Its favorite trick is acceleration to a climax—which is reached, in Pirandello's play, just before the final meeting of the Ponzas and Signora Frola. In each act, the same drama takes place: the Ponza-Frolas are the actors, the townspeople the audience. But it is a bigger, "louder" drama every time. And the tempo is stepped up. Now, while the repetition that stems from sterility merely bores, positive repetition, especially when accompanied by a crescendo and an accelerando, is dangerously full of life and tends to act directly on the nervous system. In more Dionysian works—say in O'Neill's *Emperor Jones* or Ravel's *Bolero*—this is readily admitted. What we are less ready to see is the manic element in *comic* repetition. Perhaps the final subtlety of *Right You Are* is that the sad and sinister traits that are overt in the Ponza-Frola story lurk also in the farce that frames it: hysteria and madness are not far below the surface. Manic repetition is of the essence of farce, as any page of Molière's prose will testify. John Gay's Macheath is arrested not once but twice, the second arrest being superfluous by the standards of modern dramaturgy, but integral to the pattern of classic farce-comedy. A farce-comedy consists of concentric circles of repetition: around the inner ring of phrases, the outer ring of incidents.

In taking Laudisi to be a comic character, I do not mean that he should be continuously funny but that such a figure is closer to the tradition of clowning than to that of wise uncles, doctor friends, and ministering psychoanalysts. Tell the actor of this part that Laudisi is a *raisonneur,* and you will get spectacles, an avuncular manner, prosy explanatoriness; the philosophy will ride him, not he it. Laudisi is Harlequin in modern dress, a Harlequin who has invaded the realm of philosophy, and who behaves there as he had behaved elsewhere. All his scenes are gags—from the little episode in which he teaches the Sirellis philosophy, through the mirror scene, the butler scene, and the scene with Signora Cini and Signora Nenni on the couch, all the way to his inventing of a ghost story and actual raising up of a ghost. He is what the Italian theatre calls a *brillante,* and should sparkle. He needs the bounding energy, the diabolical rhythm, that we associate with the tradition of the *commedia dell'arte.* The challenge of the part today is that it needs these things much more than what we usually require of our serious actors: subtlety of characterization. The actor of the role of Laudisi does not have the task of helping the audience to understand a complex person with such and such a life history; he serves, rather, the more technical function of a link between the comic chorus and the tragic trio, and also between the action onstage and the audience. He needs a highly developed technique because he has to turn like lightning from one activity to another, from one interlocutor to another, to effect transitions from triviality to seriousness, from tears to laughter, and in the last act to take the play and lift it into the world of fantasy. He needs a personality of strength as well as charm because his presence has to be felt even when he is silent and still.

From the two groups into which the rest of the cast falls, the play demands two distinct ways of acting. One group must play tragedy with a tempestuousness forgotten on our Anglo-American stage and believed to be somewhat foreign to our temperament. The part of Ponza presents the Stanislavski-trained actor with a teasing problem: what to do about the motivation of a character whose motivation is a mystery? I suppose such an actor can invent motives out of whole cloth, but a pre-Stanislavski actor, for whom such questions did not arise, would be in a simpler position: he need not ask why Ponza is nearly fainting, he can just take Pirandello's word for it. Pirandello is pointedly uninterested in the final psychological explanation of Ponza's passion, he is presenting the passion itself. The actor's task is to do likewise—and to do it within the imposed frame of a social type (the white-collar worker). Fernand Ledoux at the Comédie Française has shown that it can be done. Yet, to be sure, the alarming Latin way in which emotion leaps from pianissimo to fortissimo in so few words presents the non-Latin actor with a problem. In all modern drama there is nothing harder to do—or even to decide *how* to do—than the final meeting and exit of the tragic trio.

No less forgotten and just as often considered foreign (usually French) is the style of comedy required from the second group of actors. Here again it is futile to hunt the motive. The actor's attention has to be transferred from individual psychology where nowadays it too often concentrates itself on to the task of cooperation with other actors in a matter of craftsmanship. He must suspend his belief that it is harder and better to act a Chekhov role than that of a Keystone cop. He must not resist Pirandello's method by complaining that the characters are not sufficiently individualized. Who ever said the Keystone cops were not sufficiently individualized? One could praise them for not being *excessively* individualized, though any one of them could always step out of the group and have just as much individuality as he needed.

An author who insists on a character's being six feet one and having an I.Q. of 120 may be said to be creating "closed" characters; an author who leaves the actor large leeway is creating open ones. Traditionally, the theatre deals in open characters. The author's points can be made in a dozen different ways—with actors of different physique using different "line-readings," and so forth. The members of Pirandello's chorus are open characters. Each actor can try his own way of making the main point (Agazzi's self-importance, for example), and it is for the director to decide if the attempt is in place. The nine actors concerned can be asked to make a quick study of their parts and come to rehearsal each with a creation—a Daumier portrait, as it were. In rehearsal it is discovered whether these creations work. If and when they begin to do so, they have to be coordinated. Comic characters most commonly run in pairs. Sirelli is a crony of Agazzi, Signora Cini of Signora Sirelli, Signora Nenni of Signora Cini: ideally all these pairs would become comic couples enjoying as easy and active a relationship as comedian and straight man in vaudeville. A part like that of Signora Sirelli, which barely catches the attention of the reader, in a production by a *maître* like Charles Dullin, becomes a Dickensian gem. The richness of the part stems, technically speaking, from the fact that the actress can play three distinct relationships—to her husband (whom she bickers with), to Laudisi (whom she flirts with), to Cini (whom she patronizes).

No particular style should be imposed on the actors or even spoken of. A true style will come, if at all, as the bloom on a fruit that has ripened by natural growth and good gardening. You can no more tell an actor to perform with style than you can tell him to be funny, and stylization is the last refuge of the theatrical charlatan. Artificial speech and gesture that can be imposed by decree are not worth decreeing. Such "artificial" style as we have admired—say, Gielgud in Wilde—is the product not of a decree but of practice.

The nine chorus members of *Right You Are* will bring with them (one hopes) a technique acquired in farce or vaudeville, but they will not at once be permitted to display their antics because this play needs (as what play does not?) a certain air of naturalness. Only thus can the unnatural and macabre elements have their full effect. The primary aim of the acting must be social satire: we are moving in middle-class circles in a provincial town.

Some caricaturists start with an exact likeness. When they later distort and exaggerate, they take their cue from the truth: only a long nose is made longer, only a small eye smaller, a fat man fatter. This principle applies to the chorus characters in *Right You Are* and to the stage design.

I want my designer to give me an actual room belonging to the right time and place—not necessarily the room in every detail, but enough to suggest its solid, corporeal presence. He must not "stylize" the room with playful fancies of his own. (A common mistake of playful designers is to caricature the pictures on the wall. If the point is, for example, that a picture is sentimental, an actual picture, well chosen, would make the point more forcibly. Openly to make the picture ridiculous is to insult the spectator by instructing him how to respond. And of all instructions, "Now laugh!" is the most risky. The quantity of laughter out front is generally in inverse ratio to that on stage.) The stage designer should limit himself to what is strictly necessary.

"What do the characters *do* onstage?" I was asked by a famous actor who was worried at the absence in the script of all allusion to eating, drinking, and smoking, and the various activities which his naturalistic technique would be helpless without. I do not believe the answer is to insert them; they contribute nothing. "Necessary" means "necessary to the play as Pirandello conceived it," a classic comedy, an elemental tragedy, a slender thriller—anything but a piece of genre painting. What do these people do? They gossip. The furniture of gossip is—the chair. It therefore seemed to me in keeping with Pirandello's almost fanatic lean-mindedness to provide the actors with nothing but chairs. Lester Polakov, our designer, wished to fill the stage with monstrous chairs, their backs five or six feet high, so that the actors would spend the evening threading their way through a forest of furniture. The high backs would mask so much of the stage that the "blocking" problem would be enormous. But someday the idea should be tried.

In both my productions I raised the curtain on an unpeopled stage with a ring of chairs in the center facing inward to suggest that, the day before, perhaps, a circle of gossips had sat there with their heads together. During the first scene Amalia and Dina are rearranging the chairs in a semicircle, and from here on, the chief physical action was the grouping and regrouping of the chairs; for not only is the whole crowd always gossiping, but the Agazzi family is forever receiving visitors, forever setting the stage for the latest drama and preparing an "auditorium" for the onlookers. It seems apt to give Agazzi and his wife a nervous passion for reordering their room. In addition to satirizing the lower-middle-class love of tidiness and symmetry, it is an external, theatrical equivalent of the inner tension and fever.

In Act One the interviews with Ponza and Frola are presented with the chorus forming a semicircle and the object of their scrutiny occupying the only remaining seat, the piano stool, in the middle. In my mind I had the image of an operating room with watching students. In Act Two Pirandello has written a scene with Laudisi on a couch between two ladies. I decided to make the couch the cynosure of all eyes throughout the act by having Agazzi choose it as the projected meeting place for Ponza and Frola. The actual meeting takes place in the open space in front, the chorus standing behind the couch and semicircle of chairs. Here I had in mind a prize ring with a crowd around—or animals in a cage before a crowd of onlookers. The third act is essentially that old standby among theatrical scenes—a trial scene. The drawing room becomes a sort of court of appeals with the Governor as the chief justice. I brought the one large table of the set out of its corner and placed it at right angles to the audience near stage center. When the Governor sat behind it, flanked by Centuri, Agazzi, and Sirelli, a bench of judges was suggested.

The minor details of my scheme were not the same in the two productions I did, nor would they be the same in any future production. The scheme itself is but one possibility among many. I should be interested in trying, sometime, a more naturalistic treatment. Given a cast of trained clowns, I should also be interested in trying a *less* naturalistic treatment: I can imagine a chorus of comedians jumping up and sitting down like jack-in-the-boxes. Directors understandably stress the tragedy more or the comedy more, according to the special abilities of the actors on hand. A French production I saw was delightful light comedy; my own productions seemed to succeed better on the tragic side. The ideal production that one should aim at would be no compromise or halfway house between tragedy and comedy, drama and farce, but a synthesis of the two. I even think I know how the synthesis might be arrived at, and that is by casting English character actors as the chorus and American realistic actors as Ponza and Frola. I would then keep the whole cast on to do *Six Characters* with the same dual distribution.

I have dwelt on the practicalities of staging because no playwright of our time has had a mind more utterly theatrical. In the Appendix to the Columbia University Press edition of the play I discuss the short story which *Right You Are* is based on and find the theatrical version better. An artist of course does not go from one medium to another out of a desire for something better but out of a need for something other. Almost until he wrote *Right You Are* Pirandello said he would not write plays; he feared those misinterpretations at the hands of actors which he later depicted in *Six Characters*. Even after *Right You Are,* he spoke of the plays as a "parenthesis" within the writing of his fiction. If in the latter part of his career he was more a playwright than a story writer it was because the drama—much as he resisted it—corresponded to his vision of life. A poet, whose mind worked in images, he was obsessed, or inspired, by one master-image: that of the theatre. From it he ultimately elaborated his "trilogy of the theatre in the theatre." But already in *Right You Are,* when we see Ponza acting out his drama before his drawing-room audience, we are witnessing "theatre in the theatre."

The notion that "all of the world's a stage and all the men and women merely players" is one of the commonplaces of Western civilization. A charming version of it in Italian runs:

mondo è teatro e l'uomo è marionetta:
se voi guardate bene nella vita
ognun vi rappresenta una scenetta

("world is theatre, and man is marionette:
if you take a good look at life,
everyone in it is playing his little scene")

To say that a man is an actor is normally to condemn him, and the normal procedure of criticism, satire, comedy, is to remove his mask. Pirandello's play *Vestire gli ignudi,* following Ibsen's *Wild Duck,* shows the calamitous consequences of so doing. The collective title of his plays is *Maschere nude (Naked Masks).* People mask the fact that they are masked; Pirandello strips this fact bare and excuses it. The "mask" of his title resembles the *fantasma* (fantasy, ghost) of

Laudisi, the *pupo* (puppet) of Ciampa (who is the Laudisi of *Cap and Bells*), the *pagliacetto* (doll) of Diego Cinci (who is the Laudisi of *Each in His Own Way*). Laudisi's mirror speech makes it clear that error consists not in having a ghost, wearing a mask, but in chasing *il fantasma altrui,* the ghosts of other people, the masks of others, in the belief that these are not ghosts and masks but souls and faces. That there *is* a soul, a center of identity, is not questioned by Diego Cinci at least, for he denounces the false mask of one Prestino on the grounds that it does not correspond with what he "really is and can be."

The word *"maschera"* is also used to define the actors of the *commedia dell'arte* who each played one fixed role. The critic who said Pirandello was not interested in characters but in *maschere* probably meant pretty much what people mean when they damn an author for creating "types," not "individuals": types are assumed to be characters of contemptible cardboard, mere snap judgments on social groups. The roles of the *commedia* are a great deal more. They offer as fair a field to the psychologist as any of the modern typologies, and like the latter they represent a delving below both individual and social distinctions for the very elements of our humanity. Now, several of Pirandello's critics (first among them Massimo Bontempelli, I believe) have noticed the elemental quality in his Ponzas and Frolas and have recorded their impression that the maestro has rendered human nature in its raw and general state prior to individuation. This being so, one is tempted to take the *maschere* in the phrase *"maschere nude"* to mean human archetypes, human beings stripped of the accretions of civilization. If this isn't what Pirandello meant, it is what he ought to have meant. He had every right to claim that he dealt in such archetypes —if only, by the nature of the case, gropingly, by intuition. And the chief function of the theatre in Pirandello's life was that it helped him to do so.

(1952)

Enrico IV

A young man loves a woman and is not loved in return. What is more, he has a rival. In a costumed cavalcade, the rival causes the young man's horse to slip, and the young man falls, faints, and, when he comes to, is the victim of the delusion that he *is* the person whose costume he is wearing: the German Emperor Henry IV. His sister converts a villa into a replica of this Emperor's palace so that the young man can live on as Henry IV undisturbed. After twelve years, however, the delusion wears off. Our man, no longer so young, decides not to let anyone know it and to stay on as Emperor, though sane.

After eight more years, his sister dies. But she had visited him shortly before her death and gained the impression that he might now be curable. She tells her nephew this, and soon after her death he brings a psychiatrist to the villa to see what can be done. The psychiatrist, noticing on the wall portraits of our Emperor and the girl he loved, dating back to the time of the cavalcade, proposes a very precise form of shock treatment. He replaces the canvases by living human beings dressed up like the portraits. They make good likenesses, as one is the woman's own daughter, the other is the "Emperor's" nephew. The Doctor next makes the woman herself dress like the portrait. The idea is that the Emperor will notice that the pictures have come alive, then he will see the older woman, then he will look at himself, and noting in shock the difference between the older couple and the younger will be forced out of his illusion of having remained young, of having remained Henry IV.

The Doctor's plan is of course bound to go wrong, since "Henry IV" has known for eight years that he is not Henry IV. Indeed, everyone else finds this out now from his attendants, to whom he has just released the secret. No sooner has he had an instant to receive the image of the two couples than in rushes everyone to announce the truth and confound confusion. But if the incident cannot have the effect on Henry that the Doctor intended, it does have an effect, and the Doctor's first impression is that it has reactivated the insanity, for Henry seems to accept the younger woman as the elder one, and later on tries to define the whole new situation in terms of this illusion, finally taking the girl in his arms. Her mother's lover—Henry's old rival—protests on the grounds that Henry is sane and able to control himself. "Sane, am I?" says Henry, and kills him on the spot.

That is the story of Luigi Pirandello's *Enrico IV,* and there is a temptation to think of the play as just these incidents with a good many little philosophical essays added. Some of the translations read that way, and Pirandello himself must bear the responsibility for some bad storytelling. The exposition is heavy and overcrowded, as maybe Pirandello realized when he wrote the stage direction that instructs the actors to play it vivaciously. Even the climactic scene of the play is badly articulated, for it is not just that Henry hasn't time to take in what is happening over the portraits—the audience hasn't time either.

Confusion here is presented confusingly, as indeed it is in the whole parallel between the modern young man and the Emperor Henry. One could wish that this Emperor were a man some conceivable audience would know about, so that they could recognize any parallels without effort or, failing this, that the story of the Emperor were so simple that the dramatist could put it across along with his modern plot. The very linking of the two stories certainly makes us assume a point-for-point parallel, but this expectation is disappointed, and bafflement results when, for example, while we see only two women on stage (Matilda, Frida) we are asked to imagine four in the life of the Emperor (Matilda, Agnes, Adelaide, Bertha). Nor—to follow through with the same example—do the modern pair always represent the same two medieval ladies. While one medieval figure (Matilda of Tuscany) is represented by both modern women, one of the modern women (Countess Matilda) represents two medieval women (Matilda of Tuscany, Duchess Adelaide). Some Pirandellians may wish to argue that this is the complexity of deliberate legerdemain and is meant to be bewildering, but others may be permitted to wonder how they can be expected to know this. If one is bewildered as to what is going on, must one not also be bewildered as to the author's intentions?

The question with a work of art that is notably obscure is whether the first puzzling acquaintance one had with it afforded such a premium of pleasure that one wishes to come back for more. In the case of *Enrico IV* there can surely be little doubt. At first encounter, it is hard to get the facts straight—and therefore impossible to get the meaning straight—but there is no doubt of the powerful impression made by the principal images, speeches, and scenes. The general scheme is itself very striking for anyone with the slightest predilection for Gothic fiction, and there are moments of exquisite theatrical poetry—such as the moment in which Henry dictates his life story to Giovanni—which make their mark even before we ask questions about the main drift.

When we do come to these questions, the first question of all is inevitably: what about this German Emperor? Why did it have to be him? I thought I might find some clues when I found mentioned by Benjamin Cremieux the titles of the books Pirandello had consulted on the subject: Voigt's life of Pope Gregory VII and Oncken's *Allgemeine Geschichte*. But I did not find much in these that seemed more to the purpose than an encyclopedia article on the subject unless it was two pictures—of the Abbey of Cluny and the palace at Goslar, respectively. Pirandello worked with the elementary facts of Henry's life as they might be related by any history teacher. Because Henry came to the throne as a mere child, his mother, Agnes, acted as Regent. She came under suspicion of adultery with the Bishop of Augsburg and had to be removed. To this bit of pure history Pirandello adds the fiction that the accusation of adultery was brought by an ecclesiastical friend of the Vatican's: Peter Damiani. Aside from this, all that is filled in of Henry's earlier life is that he had trouble keeping his German barons and ecclesiastics in line. Pirandello, like other people, is mainly interested in what happened when Henry was twenty-six: namely, his arch-enemy, the Pope, brought him literally to his knees and he knelt in the snow hoping that the Pope would give him an audience. His wife, the Empress Bertha, knelt with him, and Bertha's mother, Duchess Adelaide, went with the Abbot of Cluny, another friendly witness, to plead with the Pope and the latter's ally, Countess Matilda of Tuscany.

Here Pirandello adds something of more significance than the involvement of Peter Damiani. "I wanted," he has been quoted as saying, "a situation where a historical personage was in love with a woman who was his enemy." Not finding what he wanted, he created it. Matilda of Tuscany was indeed Henry IV's enemy, but no historian records that he loved her. Pirandello invents this motif, and lets us know it in the play itself by having Landolf remark that Henry secretly loves Matilda even though the historians say nothing about it. It is only through his own Matilda that Pirandello's nameless young protagonist comes to the Emperor Henry IV in the first place. The modern Matilda had already picked her medieval namesake as her role in the masquerade, and that is what gave her young man the idea of being Henry:

I said I'd like to be Countess Matilda of Tuscany. . . . I just heard him saying, "Then I'll be at your feet at Canossa. . . ." I now understood why he wanted to be next to me in the cavalcade as the Emperor . . . because I'd chosen to represent his implacable enemy.

And because he secretly loved her. What the nameless young man finds in history besides a name and the status of an emperor is a relationship of love-hate.

Pirandello's Emperor seems most of the time stuck in his twenty-sixth year (1077), but he has some power to bob about in his private time machine, and is particularly concerned with the years 1076 and 1080. In 1076 at Tribur the German princes had proposed to depose Henry. His famous gesture at Canossa turns out on further scrutiny not to be a sincere and definitive submission before Papal authority but a sly man's effort to head off the prospect of facing his accusers. By 1080 Henry's position had been strengthened to the point where it was not *his* throne that was in danger but the Pope's own. This was an Emperor who, when the Pope was not to his liking, would set up another: the Henry of Pirandello's play prophesies that at Brixen he will declare Pope Gregory deposed. That the historical Emperor outlived by many years both Canossa and Brixen is acknowledged by Pirandello only in the statement that his life contained the material for many tragedies.

It would be a mistake to pursue the historical Henry past the point where Pirandello takes leave of him, or to hunt for more parallels than the play immediately suggests to anyone who knows the historical outline, for beyond this point history will become the play's rival and a victorious rival at that. By putting into the play itself the few historical facts he needs, the author is declaring the other facts off limits. After all, drawing upon some very suggestive incidents and relationships, he has created a plot and characters that are his own and not at all medieval. We perhaps need to brush aside the Gothic trappings altogether for a minute or two if we are to glimpse his characters as they are.

Pirandello is an Ibsenite dramatist. I have suggested elsewhere that for Ibsen man is neurotic and that for Pirandello man is even more deeply neurotic, is indeed never far enough from psychosis to be out of danger of falling into it. Has it been noticed how very far gone are all three of the main characters in *Enrico IV?* Pirandello's full awareness of what he was doing in this respect could be illustrated by the stage directions in which some of the characters—Dr. Genoni for instance—are first introduced. But stage directions stand outside the drama proper, and the dialogue itself is rich enough in evidence. Matilda's character, for instance, is defined in the following passage from Act One:

COUNTESS. . . . I *was* natural in those days. . . .
BARON. You see: she couldn't abide him!
COUNTESS. That's not true! I didn't even dislike him. Just the opposite! But with me, if a man wants to be taken seriously—
BARON. —he gives the clearest proof of his stupidity!

COUNTESS. Don't judge others by yourself, Baron. *He* wasn't stupid.

BARON. But then *I* never asked you to take me seriously.

COUNTESS. Don't I know it! But with him it was no joke. My dear Doctor, a woman has a sad life, a silly life. And some time or other it's her lot to see a man's eyes fixed upon her, steady and intense and full of—shall we say?—the promise of enduring sentiment? (*She bursts into a harsh laugh.*) What could be funnier? If only men could see their looks of enduring sentiment! —I've always laughed at them. More at *that* time than any other. —And let me tell you something: I can still laugh at them, after more than twenty years. —When I laughed like that at *him,* it was partly from fear, though. Perhaps one could have believed a promise in *those* eyes. It would've been dangerous, that's all.

DOCTOR. —Why dangerous?

COUNTESS (*with levity*). Because he wasn't like the others. And because I too am . . . I can't deny it . . . I'm a little . . . intolerant, that's the word. I don't like stuffiness, I don't like people who take life hard. —Anyway, I was too young at that time, you understand? And I was a woman: I couldn't help champing at the bit. —It would have needed courage, and I didn't have any. —So *I* laughed at him too. With remorse. With real self-hatred. . . .

The same conversation gives us all we need to know of the protagonist before he appears. People laughed at him behind his back:

DOCTOR. Ahem, yes, um . . . he was already rather strange . . . exalted, as it were—if I've been following you properly?

BARON. Yes, but after a very curious fashion, Doctor . . . he was damned cold-blooded about it—

COUNTESS. Cold-blooded? What nonsense! This is how it was, Doctor. He was a little strange, it's true: that was because there was so much life in him. It made him—eccentric.

BARON. . . . He was often genuinely exalted. But I could swear, Doctor: he was looking at himself, looking at his own exaltation. And I believe the same is true of every move he made, however spontaneous: he *saw* it. I'll say more: I'm certain it was this that made him suffer. At times he had the funniest fits of rage against himself . . . the lucidity that came from acting all the time . . . being another man . . . shattered, yes, shattered at a single blow, the ties that bound him to his own feelings. And these feelings seemed—well, not exactly a pretense, no, they were sincere—but he felt he must give them an intellectual status, an intellectual form of expression—to make up for his lack of warmth and spontaneity—so he improvised, exaggerated, let himself go, that's about it, to deafen his own ears, to keep his eyes from seeing himself. He seemed fickle, silly, and sometimes . . . yes, ridiculous, let's face it.

Now drama is not made up of character sketches, nor even of characters set side by side: character is rendered by relationships, and relationships are defined in happenings. The happenings in Pirandello are not only collisions (which would be true of much other drama), they are traumatic collisions. His plays hinge on scenes that have the quality of haunting fantasies, like the "primal scene" of psychoanalysis. *Enrico IV* is built upon several traumatic moments. The moment when the protagonist fell from his horse comes first to mind, but of equal weight is the moment, twelve years later, when he woke up to know he was not the Emperor. Then there is the moment, eight years after that, which is the occasion of the action presented on stage, the moment when the other actors in the original drama dare to return to it after two decades: such is Act One. The play moves on to two further traumatic moments: the moment when the planned trauma does not take place, but another one does, as the nameless hero sees the living portraits and the crowd rushes in to say he is sane; and, secondly, the moment in which "Henry" murders Belcredi.

How many readers will notice that the foregoing list omits the most important trauma of them all? I omitted it involuntarily by a kind of "Freudian" forgetting that somehow belongs.

> COUNTESS. . . . A woman has a sad life, a silly life. And some time or other it's her lot to see a man's eyes fixed upon her, steady and intense and full of—shall we say?—the promise of enduring sentiment? . . .

We know she is describing the unnamed one's love for her. He picks up the thread at the very climax of his eloquence in Act Two.

> Woe betide you if, like me, you are swallowed up by a thought that will really drive you mad. You are with another human being, you're at their side, you look into their eyes—how well I remember doing it that day! —and you might as well be a beggar before some door you will never pass through!

In comparison with a murder, or a fall from a horse, the incident is small, but I call it the most important trauma of them all because without it the other traumas either would not have occurred or would have much less significance. At the heart of this Gothic quasi history, this Germanic quasi-philosophical treatise, is a Sicilian melodrama—or opera libretto, if you will—love, jealousy, and revenge. The culmination of such a melodrama is the death of the rival, and the first stage along the violent road to this destination was reached when the rival tripped the hero's horse. Pirandello's plays are variants on such patterns, and Pirandello is giving this particular pattern a new center when he brings the eyes of hero and heroine together, not in the expected exchange of love, but in the unexpected failure to exchange anything. The woman's eyes are a door the man will never pass through. This incident, this situation, undercuts the melodrama because, now, victory over one's rival is fruitless: love is not to be had anyhow. In this way, melodrama becomes drama "of the absurd," becomes "grotesque" in the sense Jan Kott uses the term when he states that in a grotesque work "both alternatives of the choice imposed are absurd, irrelevant, or compromising."

Kott is concerned not with melodrama but with tragedy. "What once was tragedy," he says, "today is grotesque." But this too is a thesis which *Enrico IV* exemplifies. The play has been described as Pirandello's one real tragedy, and in some Italian editions it is subtitled *Una Tragedia*. It is certainly Pirandello's *Hamlet*. Belcredi is its Claudius, Countess Matilda its Gertrude, Frida its Ophelia.* And Hamlet's antic disposition has spread itself over the whole life of the Pirandellian protagonist.

There is *talk* of tragedy in the play. For if the nameless one has chosen to be Henry IV because the latter is the enemy of Matilda of Tuscany, he has chosen him equally because he was the *tragic* emperor, whose life indeed contained "material for many tragedies." (Henry IV is called *il tragico imperatore* in Pirandello's *Rhenish Elegies*.) His aim in life is nothing less than to attain to tragic seriousness, as he makes quite explicit in the speech about the priest who returns to his priestliness from the truancy of a frivolous dream. "Back into his eyes came the same seriousness that you have seen in mine, for Irish priests defend the seriousness of their Catholic faith with the same zeal I felt for the sacred rights of hereditary monarchy."

The protagonist insists on tragedy; the author does not. The protagonist is a character in search of the tragic poet: such is Pirandello's subject, which therefore comes out absurd, grotesque, tragicomic. "Comic" is the conventional opposite of "tragic," even as joking is the usual opposite of seriousness. In Pirandello's play, the protagonist's wish to be serious, to be taken seriously, stems from a feeling that he is *not* serious, that people do not take him seriously. This we are told at the outset, where Matilda speaks of "all the fools who made fun of him," after which Pirandello never lets the theme go. Is Enrico ridiculous, or isn't he? Are people laughing at him or aren't they? Are his actions jokes and jests or aren't they? The words "joke" and "jest" are reiterated obsessively, and always in connection with making a joke or jest of something that should *not* be joked or jested about. Matilda is, in this respect, the agent of the action, since she does, or has done, the laughing. And she has turned from the man she laughed at in fear to the man she laughs at in scorn. *Everything that happens in the whole bizarre series of events is a joke,* bad or good. The idea of the cavalcade

* In my own play *H for Hamlet,* the Henry IV story is replaced by the Hamlet story along the lines here suggested.

was a joke. The tripping of the horse was a practical joke of Belcredi's. The original joke of the masquerade is perpetuated by the re-creation of the Goslar palace in an Umbrian villa. The action we see on stage is meant seriously by its instigators but is turned into a joke by others. The exposition is intended as farce (even if it does not quite work out that way). Genoni is a doctor out of Molière or Ben Jonson. His grand design is closer to *commedia dell'arte* than to the clinic, and Belcredi is there to make us aware of this. A high point in the action is reached when the nameless one reveals to the attendants that he is not mad. The conclusion they draw is that his life in the villa has been a jest. This interpretation produces "Henry's" first great burst of rage. His second, which ends the play, grows out of an act-long quarrel between Belcredi and himself about this matter of joking. "The whole thing was a joke . . . he put on an act so he could have a good laugh behind your back . . . let's have done with this perpetual jesting!" The attendants have told Belcredi the madness was a jest. Belcredi calls the masquerade a joke, and the nameless one counters with: "it wasn't such a joke to me as you think."

The ending of the play, which perhaps seems arbitrary when we detach it from the thematic structure, grows organically enough out of the perpetual tor-turesome question: Is anything more than a jest at stake? The effect of the Doc-tor's shock treatment is to make the nameless one review the whole situation not of course in philosophic calm but in the frenzy induced by the crisis. What he comes back to again and again is the danger of being ridiculous—of his tragedy being reduced to a comedy. Should he, now that he is cured, go out of doors and be a modern man? "To have everyone secretly pointing at me and whispering, Emperor Henry?" When Matilda says, "Who could even conceive of such a thing? An accident is an accident," the nameless one reaches back to the basic fact and premise of the whole fable: "They all said I was mad—even before—all of them!" To this Belcredi retorts, "That was only a joke!" He thinks the retort will make matters better: it makes them much worse since the question of frivolity is even more crucial than that of sanity. The nameless one angrily shows his gray hair. Is that a joke? Then he comes out with the true story of how his horse was tripped. "That must have been a joke too!" Then he defines his own general position as a transcendance of jokes: "not a jest, no, a reality." "And one walks around—a tragic character." Thence to the main situation of the last act, the re-creation of the young Matilda in her daughter Frida. "To me it could hardly be the joke they intended, it could only be this terrible prodigy: a dream come alive." He embraces the living dream. Belcredi cannot believe he is "serious" and protests. Not serious? Not serious? How can the jealous rival prove he is not joking, not play-acting? By using a real sword and producing a real death. In this way the nameless one preserves his image of himself as tragic hero, while Pirandello, by the same stroke, deci-sively detaches his play from tragedy. For, after all, what our hero has just done *is* crazy, *is* ridiculous, and objectively he has tragic dignity just as little as other lunatics who pose as emperors.

In distinguishing between the protagonist's image of himself and Pirandello's image of him, I am declining to take the play as a *pièce à thèse* in which the hero is the author's mouthpiece. It is true he often gives voice to sentiments concerning illusion and reality which we at once spot as Pirandellian commonplaces. Taken as *pièce à thèse, Enrico IV* is very neat indeed. It says that "Henry" was all right till these interlopers came to try and cure him. He was all right both in having recovered from insanity and in having found a solution that is even better than sanity: the conscious acceptance of illusion as a way of life. What the interlopers do bids fair to cancel the solution but "Henry" preserves it and perpetuates it the only way he can. The final murder, thus understood, comes to us simply as a logical conclusion and we respond not with a gasp of horror but with a nod of the head—Q.E.D. Similarly, we have to take the play as wholly abstract: we cannot for a moment take the characters as men and women and ask questions like: What kind of person commits a murder of this kind? What would you make of a murder like this if it happened in your own family circle?

Such an approach overlooks what Pirandello has himself put into this play. Though his "Henry" woos and perhaps wins us with his magnificent speeches about illusion and reality, the action of the play does not confirm Henry's theories (i.e., his hopes). What does he actually conclude when he finds himself sane? That so long as the others do not *know* him to be sane, they will provide him with an unusual privilege: that of living in a dream world for the fun of it with the support of all one's friends. Normally one's friends exact a price: they require that one be really insane. So Henry's opportunity was unique! One's first impulse is to call what he is doing "Living the illusion but being the only one to see through it." But of course the others see through it too. They only don't know that he does. So what we have is a compact based on a misunderstanding created by a benevolent deception. This compact generates a certain amount of good. It would therefore be bad to threaten it. But, on the other hand, it has not produced a little Utopia, not even an ideal state of affairs for a single man. For "Henry's" scheme, in its highest flights, does not work. He would like to insert himself into the eleventh century and simply "be." The pleasure of history, as he expounds it, is to be Henry IV forever. But he is confused as to just how to achieve this. It could mean that he is forever Henry IV at the moment of Canossa, in which case he will always be twenty-six years old. Or it could mean that he is free to move up and down the whole life of Henry IV, enjoying the fact that what happens is already settled and one need not live in uncertainty. The confusion here, clearly enough rendered by Pirandello, is not that of a theory but of a man—a madman.

On whose authority do we have it that the nameless one was ever cured?

Only his own. But will not many a psychotic claim to be well? It is perhaps curious how easily readers of Pirandello accept Henry's own claims. They could say that, in a degree, Henry offers proof that what he says is true: *He* knows he isn't really a German Emperor, and *we* know he isn't really a German Emperor. But is merely the absence of this delusion a proof of sanity? At this point we may well bog down in semantic difficulties. What *is* sanity? It is Pirandello himself, however, who makes us aware of this danger. His punning on the word makes us ask finally if *sanity* is any more *sane* than *insanity*. But without looking for a solution of the semantic problem, can we not go on to say that, sane or insane, the protagonist of *Enrico IV* is presented as a deeply disturbed person? And by "presented" we mean "presented to our eyes and ears"; we are not talking of his mental health eight years earlier. In fact, I have already quoted the passages in which it is heavily underlined that "Henry" had been conspicuously abnormal from the beginning. Is it not perverse, then, to see the murder he commits as a merely symbolic affair? Murder is a serious business, committed in massive rage that has had much time and much reason to accumulate: only thus, generally speaking, can we find it credible. But just such factors are present in the play. The murder (*pace* the semanticists) itself seems crazy. And the rhythm of the action seems to derive from the reactivization of the nameless one's trouble through the incidents we witness. This reactivization is prepared dramatically as early as Act One. What is going on inside "Henry" in that act can scarcely be judged on first reading or seeing: there are too many surprises to take in and one doesn't know what to look for. But then first acts in general are to be appreciated at *second* reading. At such a second reading this first act hardly gives the impression of a sane "Henry," even if we make allowance for deliberate whimsy and playfulness on his part.

Let anyone who thinks the nameless one has constructed a foolproof illusion consider what its major premise is: that time can be stopped. "Henry" *has* stopped time to the extent that he can stay in the eleventh century and never need to jump to the twentieth. Even this, however, he achieved only when he actually thought he was the Emperor: when the twelve years were up he knew exactly which century he was in. As to stopping time in the more vital sense that his own body should stay the same age, the nameless one has no illusions: his gray hairs tell him all. And in exploring Pirandello's handling of the point we learn not only that *he* had no illusions either, but that he handled the matter dialectically and brought it to a conclusion not only different from popular "Pirandellianism" but diametrically opposite to it. His hero tried to go on being the twenty-six-year-old German Emperor, yet not only could not build himself a heaven in fantasy, but longed for the other life, the twentieth-century one, that he was missing. Pirandello audaciously places Henry's confession of this at the end of Act One. Is it contradicted by the fact that when later the doors are opened, and the nameless one could go out in the modern world, he refuses? It is; but the contradiction is that of his character and of a universal human situation. True, he has an alibi: it is too late. But when would it not have been too late? Is this a melodrama in which a healthy Innocent has been deprived of his rights by the Villainous Belcredi? At some moments, *he* can think so; but not at all. And at no moment can *we* think so. This is a story of a life not lived in a world of people incapable of living.

Has the fantasy, then, no positive content at all? It has. Here again the thinking is two-sided and dialectical. "Henry" has found himself a *modus vivendi*, and it is true that the visit of the Doctor and the others destroys this (until he builds up again on another foundation), but the *modus vivendi* was itself imperfect, flawed, full of tragicomic conflict caused by two factors already suggested: the impossibility of the main endeavor (stopping time) and, secondly, the precariousness of the structure of deception and misunderstanding (sooner or later the happy accidents must have an end). It follows that Pirandello's own vision—as distinct from that of some of his Pirandellian spokesmen—is not just of illusion within illusion: there are nonillusions here. Or, stating this differently, illusions are finally only illusions, and one sees through them. It is, on the other hand, no illusion that the nameless one's hair turned gray; or that Belcredi, at the end, is dead as a doornail.

The illusions which many harbor about Pirandello's illusionism come perhaps from assuming that his plays are *about* the philosophy, an assumption it was easy to make when the philosophy was novel and shocking. What is such a play as *Enrico IV* really about? What is at the center of Pirandello's interest, and hence of his play? Necessarily, since he is a major playwright, not a philosopher, what is at the center will not be opinion as such but experience. What he gives us is in fact the *experience* of a man with Pirandellian *opinions,* a man who has applied himself to the Pirandellian task of "constructing himself." That was the meaning of his "play-acting" even in advance of the masquerade. That was the meaning of the masquerade itself and, involuntarily, of the insanity afterward. The point is that "Henry" *always failed.* We even learn in the last act that while he was Emperor (presumably in the "insane period") he noticed his hair turning gray—noticed, that is, that the whole scheme had broken down. In the later phase in which we encounter him on stage he claims to find a solution in *being aware* that one is only an actor in a masquerade, which is preferable, he says, to being such an actor without knowing it. But the play does not show that it really makes much difference whether one is aware of such things or not. Certainly, the four attendants don't "buy" the idea. The one happy human moment of the play, that between "Henry" and Giovanni, is created, significantly enough, by a misunderstanding: Giovanni thinks "Henry" is still mad. And the last act would seem to say that sooner or later any construct is destroyed by life itself.

If the play as a whole embodies a philosophy, that philosophy is pessimistic and materialist, where "Henry" is an optimist and idealist. Just think how this Hamlet-parody differs from *Hamlet* in its last act. Claudius *has* to be killed: heaven itself has said so. And if there is foul play in the killing, Claudius himself is responsible. In *Enrico,* the murder is itself foul play, a vicious and shabby act: a swordsman stabs an unarmed man in the belly. Was Pirandello remembering Eilert Løvborg's failure to shoot himself in the head? At all events, the belly is the least heroic of close-range targets. The thought makes Henry's presumed heroic image of himself all the more fantastic. The note that is struck here is of course the modern one. This is not tragedy, a heroic genre, but post-Dostoevski psychological drama showing the decline and fall of a man through mental sickness to crime.

Are Pirandello's plays more about reality and illusion than they are about love and absence of love? The search for truth is generally conducted by the trivial and bad people in them, while the more serious people seek love. It may be said that the latter often declare love to be unattainable. But what relief there is in seeming to discover the undiscoverability of what one is all the time seeking! Yet love is not inherently impossible to the people Pirandello presents. It has only *become* impossible—and for psychological, not metaphysical, reasons. The whole of *Enrico IV* lies in germ in Belcredi's original description of the nameless one (already quoted) as a man suffering from a strange exaltation and always watching his own exalted state, a sufferer who had fits of rage against himself, an actor who, through acting so much, lost touch with himself, a man who lacked spontaneous warmth, and who, to make up for this, improvised and play-acted to the point of the ridiculous. The same part of Act One lets us see that self-hatred and self-abasement are a sort of family neurosis in which all three main characters are sunk. Here surely we find Pirandello's ultimate reason for lighting on the Canossa story: the Emperor Henry IV has fixed only one thing in the memory of the world, his act of self-abasement before the Pope. All the more interesting, of course, if this Emperor's gesture proves, upon closer examination, to have had low cunning in it. We then realize all the more vividly that there was no humility in the action: it was ignoble through and through.

"In stories like this," says the Gardener in Giraudoux's *Electra,* "the people won't stop killing and biting each other to tell you the one aim of life is to love." Here, too, is the modern note: love can be all inference, while what is exhibited is lovelessness and hate. So with Pirandello, love is absent; present are self-hatred, self-abasement, self-mockery. The "loss of self" here is not mere absence of self, let alone a mere theory that there *is* no self, it is an assault on the self by the self. At the psychological center of this play is psychic masochism, brilliantly suggested at the outset by the nagging, irritable, sarcastic tone in which Belcredi and Matilda address each other. The nameless one's final assault upon himself takes the form of murder. While from the viewpoint of "Pirandellianism" the murder of Belcredi may seem laudable, within the world created by Pirandello in his play it is but the final culmination of this masochism and is to be construed (like most murders, after all) as the ultimate measure taken by the murderer against himself.

If this sounds grandiose, I would suggest that, on the contrary, the present line of thought permits one to speak more "realistically" (i.e. literal-mindedly) about both the play and its protagonist. It is the story of an orphan whose orphanhood has been compounded by insanity and incarceration. We meet him at a time that is especially unfortunate even for a man of many misfortunes. The sister who had been something of a mother to him has just died. This great loss is duplicated on a more trivial scale by the loss of the servant Tony who had played the role of Bishop of Bremen. While he is suffering intensely from the pains of deprivation (just such pains as are responsible for the mental trouble in *Right You Are,* incidentally) the nameless one is arbitrarily confronted with the one woman he has ever loved and the man who stole her from him by the trick which made him a madman. As if these factors would not be enough to produce an explosion, Dr. Genoni then adds his preposterous plot. Genoni's drama did not show the nameless one that he was irretrievably cut off now from Youth as shown in the portraits. It brought to life the portrait of the Loved One and thus seemed to offer the nameless one all he had ever wanted: Matilda when young. At no point is it brought home to us more vividly than here how aware "Henry" has really become of the loss of both Matilda and his youth. Otherwise he would not be so struck by this living image which he knows is not really Matilda. He is not "taken in," but he is overwhelmed with feeling, and, when Belcredi intervenes, the irritability which would be the normal response has reason to be multiplied a hundred-fold in a rage that means murder. Illusions are falling before realities, right and left. And the conclusion is renewed illusion? Not exactly. There will be a pretense of it, that is all: an illusion of illusion. The reality is that the nameless one, already parentless, childless, brotherless before the "play" started, has now lost the Attendants as far as their old roles are concerned, and has reduced himself to an ultimate misery. Not only can he no longer dream of being cut loose from his Emperor, he cannot even live as Emperor either, for the Attendants no longer believe him mad. At the end he is as "cabined, cribbed, confined" as a Beckett character up to the waist in earth or up to the neck in a jar.

(*1966*)

Six Characters in Search of an Author

A man has a wife and a male child. He also has a male secretary. Between the wife and the secretary there arises what the husband considers an understanding of a harmless sort. He wants to help them in some way, but whenever he speaks to them they exchange a significant look that seems to ask how they should receive what he says if they are not to annoy him. But this itself annoys him. He ends up firing the secretary. Then he sends the wife after him. In the wife's view, he fairly throws her into the secretary's arms; and the pair set up house together. The husband, however, does not lose interest in the wife. His continued interest, indeed, though he considers it "pure" (that is: asexual) is a source of embarrassment to the former secretary. When a daughter is born to the lovers the husband is interested in her too—more, perhaps, even, than he had been in the wife. And when she becomes a schoolgirl, he waits for school coming out, then on at least one occasion seeks her out, and gives her a present. The girl does not know who the strange gentleman is. At a certain point the secretary can bear the whole situation no longer, and he takes his family— there are three children by this time—to live somewhere else, out of the stepfather's reach. Subsequently the secretary dies. His family of four is now destitute; they have to sleep all in the same room. And at some point they return to the place where the husband lived. Here the mother gets employment as a kind of seamstress. But her employer's real interest is in employing the daughter, now in her late teens, as a prostitute. The dressmaker's shop is a front for a brothel. One day, the husband, a client of the establishment, presents himself and would have taken the girl in his arms had not the mother suddenly turned up to cry, "But it's my daughter!" After this encounter, the husband takes his wife back into his home, along with his three stepchildren. At the time he is living with his own son, now in his early twenties. This legitimate son is offended by the presence of the three bastards, and wanders from room to room in his father's house, feeling displaced and desolate. The three bastards react to his hostility. The little girl, aged four, drowns herself in the fountain in the garden. The other child, a fourteen-year-old boy, witnesses the drowning, fails to offer any assistance, then shoots himself. The mother, who might have been keeping an eye on the young pair, was, instead, following her twenty-two-year-old son around the house, begging for forgiveness. He rushes out into the garden to escape her, and there comes upon his stepbrother just at the moment the latter watches his sister die and kills himself. After this debacle, the older girl runs away from home. Left behind are father, mother, and son. . . .

I am trying to tell the story of *Sei personaggi in cerca d'autore,* or rather the story of the six characters *in* the play. This is quite hard, and an analysis of the work might well begin with the reasons *why* it is hard. The first reason is pretty much what it would be with an Ibsen play. It is hard to tell the story of, say, *Ghosts* because it comes out in fragments and the fragments have to be painstakingly fitted together. The Ibsenite has, above all, to be able to take a hint; he even has to have the detective's knack of snapping up bits of evidence and holding them in reserve till he can connect them with something else. However, while Ibsen's fragments come together into a complete and coherent picture, like the pieces of a jigsaw puzzle, Pirandello defies a number of the normal expectations and, by the usual criteria, his picture is incomplete. As to *location,* for instance, which in the drama, at least since Aristotle, has always been considered something to have a clear understanding about. In most plays one knows exactly where everything takes place, and in plays where the location is somewhat abstract, there is a convention to make this abstractness acceptable to its audience. In retelling Pirandello's story just now, however, I paused several times, hoping to insert a phrase indicating where someone had gone or returned to. The husband's house could be in Rome, I suppose, but couldn't it just as easily be anywhere else with a climate favorable to fountains? Could I even say, "returned to the city"? Not even that; because the only clues are a school, a house with a fountain in the garden, and a modiste's shop that is also a brothel; things that exist in small towns and villages as well. It is not, of course, that one insists on naturalism, but that one cannot react without a degree of bafflement to not knowing *under what circumstances* the secretary lived with the wife in city, town, or village; how far away he then took her; where the bedroom in which all four slept was to be found; and so on. But the queries as to *place* only lead to similar queries on other topics, and notably *time*. Here at least Pirandello has marked certain boundaries, notably the ages of the four children. Since the legitimate son is twenty-two, and the eldest bastard is eighteen, it follows that the transfer of the wife from husband to lover occurred about twenty years ago. Yet, in the Pirandellian context, how little this arithmetic means! In Ibsen, doing such arithmetic usually proves well worthwhile, but in *Six Characters* it would never be done at all, except by such an undiscourageable investigator as myself, willing to follow any trail. This trail has proved a false one. In the rare instances where exact notation of the passage of time is going to affect our sense of drama, Pirandello does the arithmetic for us. The reiterated statement that the secretary died "two months ago" tells us that the death marks the beginning of the Action that is this play, just as the father's death marks the beginning of the Hamlet action, and the aunt's death the beginning of the action of *Enrico IV*.

Generally, time and space, in the story of the *Six Characters*, are alike rather abstract and are tokens of a pervasive abstractness. *Who is the Father?* The question: What does he do? is no more answered than: Where does he live? To place him, either literally or figuratively, all we can do is remark that his vocabulary marks him as something of an intellectual—a student of Pirandellian philosophy, even—and that his having a secretary and a sizable house (with rooms to wander through and a garden with a fountain in it) marks him as well-to-do. By contrast, wife and secretary are defined as *poor*, the Italian word *"umile"* leaving open whether they were just of humble birth or also humble by nature. Of the elder girl we know that poverty made her a prostitute; and we see that she resents her father. Of the two youngest children we learn little except that their birth was illegitimate. The young man is so withdrawn and silent that we can be told he is a character not fully created because not suited to a play at all: only part of him, as it were, is there. To say the least, then, these are people of no particular background. We can say they are Italians, but our evidence is only that the play is written in Italian. We can say they are bourgeois, yet even for this the evidence is largely negative: in our culture, the bourgeois is the norm, and the speech of this play is normal, except for Madama Pace who, like lower-class New York City today, has a Spanish accent. Incidentally, only Madama Pace has a name. Does that make her the only character portrayed with particularity? Hardly; her name is a symbolic one. It means peace, and is presumably used ironically: she brings not peace but a pair of scissors.

Plays without what are called individual characters, with characters labeled The Father and the like, are no new thing. They were the usual thing in the Expressionist plays of the second decade of the century, the decade during which the ideas for *Six Characters* came to Pirandello.* Is this an Expressionist play, then? One is certainly encouraged to believe so by the stage direction in which the six are introduced. All, says the author, are to wear masks which

> will help to give the impression of figures constructed by art, each one unchangeably fixed in the expression of its own fundamental sentiment, thus: REMORSE in the case of the Father; REVENGE in the case of the Stepdaughter; DISDAIN in the case of the Son; GRIEF in the case of the Mother, who should have wax tears fixed in the rings under her eyes and on her cheeks, as with the sculpted and painted images of the *mater dolorosa* in church.

Here we are being offered abstract qualities as characters, as in those medieval moralities which are the ancestors of Expressionist drama. But the fact is that the stage direction does little to prepare us for what is offered by way of character in the dialogue itself—not abstract qualities or general ideas but emotional conflict of very unusual vividness, vicacity, and fullness. The word "Expressionism" is not the clue we need.

What is? Perhaps the phrase: "dream play." Some of the earliest critics of Pirandello's plays noticed that, in them, "life is a dream." Two features, more than anything else, contributed to this impression: first, the "dreamlike" comings and goings to and from nowhere of Pirandello's people; second, that the author seems haunted, "possessed," by these people. Now the first of these features, appearing by itself, need not signify very much. It is a formal device any author might choose to adopt. It would prove nothing more than that, perhaps, he had read Strindberg. The second feature, however, if further explored, will lead us deep into Pirandello's play, whereupon we shall also learn that, for him, the first feature was not lightly adopted or trivially used.

What is Pirandello possessed *by?* That drama should present the dynamics of relationship, and not separate individual portraits, is in the nature of the genre. But Pirandello is an extremist in this regard. No one has made do with so few

---

* The evidence for this is in two short stories, "La tragedia d'un personaggio" (1911) and "Colloqui coi personaggi" (1915), in a letter to his son Stefano dated 1917, and in a passage (undated) from a projected novel-in-the-making cited in the sixth volume of the collected works (1960). This last-named passage is about Madama Pace's establishment, and suggests the possibility that it was with this image that *Six Characters* began—a tempting point in the light of the interpretation of the play offered above. The letter to Stefano is also cited to this extent in the sixth volume of the collected works:

> . . . But I already have my head full of novelties! So many short stories. . . . And a queer thing, so sad, so very sad: *Six Characters in Search of an Author:* novel-in-the-making. Maybe you understand. Six characters, caught in a terrible drama, who visit me to get themselves put into a novel. And obsession. And I don't want to know about it. I tell them it's no use. What do I care about *them?* What do I care about anything? And they show me all their sores. And I send them packing . . .—and in this way finally the novel-in-the-making turns out to be *made.*

Incidentally, in the projected novel-in-the-making, Madama Pace's shop did have a precise location: Rome.

individual traits and details of background while managing to make the contact between people so electric. This kind of drama, one is tempted to say, is ALL relationship and NO character. Six *Non*-Characters in Search of an Author! Or, translating this from negative to positive: In Search of an Author, these relationships—Man/Wife, Father/Daughter, Mother/Son. There can be little doubt what Pirandello is possessed by: elemental family relationships. Our next questions, then, should be: If he has not offered us a cold typicality but has brought relationships to passionate life, how has he done it? If he has not approached these relationships in the accepted, naturalistic way, how *has* he approached them? And now our queries are turning back on themselves, for Pirandello's method has already been touched on, and is that of dreams, not the dreams of the older literary tradition, either, but the actual fantasies of our actual day and night dreaming. And here it would be well to limit the word "phantasy" to the technical sense given it by Freud when he said, "Phantasies are psychical façades constructed to bar the way to . . . memories" of primal scenes.* (Like Freud's translator, I will spell the word with "ph" when this sense is intended.) This may be only one kind of fantasy among many, but it is amazing how close to the principal images and thoughts of *Six Characters* Freud's definition brings us.

In this play we are never far away from primal scenes, and specifically three of them: incest of father with daughter; the child seeing the parents make love; and sibling murder. Each of these scenes is veiled by at least one layer of phantasy. Even the sibling murder, which comes closest to such a scene, is not actually a murder: the boy refrained from preventing a suicide. In the case of the incest, two layers of phantasy at once present themselves. The girl is not a daughter but a stepdaughter, and the love-making does not quite take place. The most thoroughly hidden of the three primal scenes is that of the son seeing his father in the role of lover; and how strong was Pirandello's wish to hide this scene is shown in the fact that he deleted from later editions this passage from the first:

> Hasn't he [it is the Son, speaking of the Father] acted in such a way as to force me to discover what no son should ever discover? That father and mother are alive and are man and woman, for each other, outside the reality we give them. For as soon as this reality is uncovered, our life is no longer tied to that man and that woman except at a single point—one which will only shame them should we see it.

A single point. One touches one's parents at the moment one is conceived. There, for the one and only time, as the parental genitals touch, are all three of us touching. It is the only togetherness life affords. Such is the painfully vivid

* See letter to Fliess dated May 2, 1897, and the accompanying note. Also *The Interpretation of Dreams*, translated by James Strachey, Basic Books edition, p. 491.

Pirandellian version of this primal scene. It links the Old Testament shame at the sight of parental nakedness with the Pascalian sense of hopeless isolation in an alien universe. The specific veils the scene wears are also of interest. First, this Son has not discovered *anyone* making love. What he has done is notice the erotic quality in a relationship he did not expect to be erotic. It was not that of his father and mother. It was that of his father and his stepsister. But the suspicion is—and it is not the suspicion of the son alone—that the stepsister is taking the mother's place in bed.

A psychoanalyst, Dr. Charles Kligerman, has made an observation that digs deeper into the plot of *Six Characters* than anything, so far as I know, that purely literary critics have said. It is that we have here not an assortment but a *sequence* of phantasies, each more primitive than the last—each belonging to an earlier phase of our lives than the last. "In other words, from adult father/daughter incest there is a retreat to the earlier Oedipal triangle, and then a sudden regression to the primitive sibling rivalry, with wishful phantasy of murder followed by guilty suicide." *

The dramatist cannot be content merely to present phantasies (or fantasies either), he must arrange them in significant progression. It is Dr. Kligerman's thesis, I take it, that the three main phantasies constitute a dramatic beginning, middle, and end. The question is: of what? That they make up the beginning, middle, and end of the six characters' own story is pretty clear. Does that make them the beginning, middle, and end of the whole work? Rather naturally, giving psychology priority over dramatic art, our psychoanalytic interpreter seems to answer this in the affirmative, and backs up his answer with biographical rather than artistic evidence. "The Father, Son and Boy," says Dr. Kligerman, "all represent different levels of conflict within the author." This may well be a true statement on the *sources* of the matter presented. It does not follow that the three characters, once created, are best considered as three aspects of one character. All the characters a playwright "creates" come out of himself, just as his dreams do, and may similarly correspond to parts of himself. The important thing, artistically, is that they then become objectified, and demand to be seen not as aspects of their author but as his creations. If this is true, our protagonist in *Six Characters* has real others (not himself in other forms) to act upon and be acted upon by. This is a man and his son, not a man and himself, though, biologically and symbolically, a man and his son are overlapping categories.

And the end of the family story is not, as I think Dr. Kligerman assumes, the double suicide, but the situation that ensues thereon. It is described thus in the first edition:

> Because, finally, the drama is all in this: when the mother re-enters my
> home, the family she had elsewhere, which was now being, as it were, su-

* "A psychoanalytic study of Pirandello's *Six Characters in Search of an Author*," by Charles Kligerman, *Journal of the American Psychoanalytic Association*, October 1962.

perimposed on the first one, comes to an end, it's alien, it can't grow in this soil. The little girl dies, the little boy comes to a tragic end, the older girl flees. And so, after all the torment, there remain we three—myself, the mother, the son. And when the alien family is gone, we too find ourselves alien, the one to the other. We find ourselves utterly desolated.

The Father is given these words toward the end of Act One.* Later Pirandello must have concluded both that the passage comes at the wrong place and that it is too explicit. He put it off to the very end of the play and did the job without words: the final version states in a stage direction that father, mother, and son are left on stage at the end when the daughter rushes out of their home. They form a tableau with the mother's arms outstretched toward the obdurate son. Which I take to mean that the double suicide is not the final phantasy. Rather, the dramatist insists on returning to the Oedipal image: the family story begins and ends with father, mother, and son. The daughter and two younger children came and went. Their father had gone forever just before we meet them. *The second family is killed off.* We see the effect upon the first family which lives on, bearing the brunt.

So far I have been talking exclusively of the six characters' story, which is complete (as complete as it is going to be) before the show starts: it is all time past. Does nothing happen on stage except a re-enactment of this past? Does nothing happen before our eyes and now, for the first time, in the present? Certainly it does. The six characters enter a theatre and ask the Director to make a play of them. He toys with the idea, finds himself, indeed, devoting the day to trying it out. A negative decision is reached, and that is the end. The first edition actually closes with the line, and it is a very good curtain line: *"E mi hanno fatto perdere una giornata!"*—"And they've made me lose a whole day."

I am describing now, of course, the conceit or *trovata* which gave the play fame, and even notoriety, the idea of an encounter between a company of actors and the roles they might be asked to play. Can it be disposed of lightly? "The plot of the play within a play," Dr. Kligerman says, "contains the essential drama, for the rest is comic badinage . . . and a great deal of discussion. . . ." If valid, this would be a devastating criticism: no dramatic masterpiece would have so much dead wood in it. Conversely, if this is a great play, expressive in all its parts, then both the "badinage" and the "great deal of discussion" will be found to be necessary to its structure. Let us look further into the matter.

Drama is action. "An encounter between a company of actors and the roles they might play": this is a formula for action, but as it stands it is too general. Action has to be more specific than that. Who exactly is doing what to whom?

* I should perhaps say "Section One," as the Italian editions have no act divisions. But many Americans know the play from the translation that names the sections Acts.

We have always to come to this question. Take the first bit of it first: *who is doing?* It needs hardly a moment's reflection on *Six Characters in Search of an Author* to produce an answer that comes from an overpowering impression. *The Father is doing.* If an Action is here being propelled forward by a character, then that propeller is the Father. He is indeed so maniacally insistent that he might seem at times to be lifting the play up bodily. His insistency is a huge motif, and a huge portion of the play. *What* is he doing? He is demanding that his drama be staged. Why? He is persuaded that he will be thereby justified. A hostile interpretation of his character will be rejected, a friendly one endorsed. Does he really believe this? It is hard to say. He is so intent on stressing what should be, it is hard to know if he is confident that it will be. If he gets nowhere, will he settle for less? It looks very much as if the less that he will settle for is the act of pleading itself. He evidently gets a release from just talking, from unburdening himself. He is, among other things, an Ancient Mariner, buttonholing people and inflicting his story on them. And one knows what satisfaction all Ancient Mariners get from this kind of thing, because every one of us is something of an Ancient Mariner. For this mariner, certainly, saying his piece is a matter of life and death. I am reminded of a patient cited in R. D. Laing's book *The Divided Self* as saying that he talked as an act of self-preservation. That is, of course, to imply that his existence was threatened. And the sense of such a threat is felt in all the big talking in Pirandello—that of his Enrico, that of his Ponza and Frola, and that of the Father. The topic, here, is schizophrenia, and Pirandello's plays have become easier to comprehend in the light of studies of schizoid problems written in the past several decades.

It is interesting that in two generations a great dramatist has led the psychologists in providing a classic image of modern man. Ibsen, just before Freud, presented Modern Man as Neurotic. Pirandello, anticipating the study of schizophrenia by a whole school of psychiatrists from Minkowski to Laing, showed how integral to modern life is "the schizophrenic experience." His Henry IV is the schizophrenic as tragic hero.

> . . . the experience and behavior that gets labelled schizophrenic is a special strategy that a person invents in order to live in an unlivable situation.*

In *Così è (se vi pare)*, the Ponza/Frola narrative is an elaboration of such a special strategy, neither more nor less. Such strategies constitute the sanity of the insane, the rationality of the irrational. That is one paradox which Pirandello has in common with recent psychologists. Another is that the sane may not be any more rational. So one can regard the insane as sane, and the sane as insane. In 1967 the thought is no longer new, but new testimony to its truth is printed in each day's newspaper.

* *The Politics of Experience,* by R. D. Laing. New York, 1967.

What is the Father doing? He is talking to live—that is, to avoid getting killed. He is fighting off the arrows of the Indian hordes of the soul. The world's *implosion,* Dr. Laing calls that kind of threat. The Father is also trying to keep from drowning, from inundation. Dr. Laing speaks of *engulfment.* Like a witch doctor, the Father hopes to hold the devils and hobgoblins at arm's length. In short, he is what our grandparents called a lunatic. He is "mad as a hatter." Critics and actors who have resisted this conclusion have never got very far with *Six Characters in Search of an Author.*

Yet the Father's manic behavior on stage is the least of it. In drama, as in life, character is found in concentrated form in men's decisions and actions which entail decisions. What have been this man's decisions? Since he is nothing if not a father and a husband, we must ask what he has done for his son and his wife. When the former was a baby he sent him into the country to be nursed. It would be healthier. This is a rich man who prefers the ways of the poor. But when does he have his son brought back? We are not told, except that it was too late. The boy returned as an alien and an enemy. And the wife? He pushed her into the arms of his secretary. These, too, were good, simple people—also poor—who understood each other. In short, the Father's actions have been such as to destroy his own family by driving them away. Obviously, he is what is usually called schizophrenic, and must isolate himself, even though isolation, in turn, becomes torture. If he can't stand company, equally he cannot stand himself. Desperate measures are taken against the outer world on behalf of the inner world, but to no avail. The inner world feels as insecure as ever, and the Father goes out in search of. . . well, in the first instance, company.

Two is company. That is: company is sex. The Father becomes a client of Madama Pace's, the Pacifying Madam. What, in external terms, goes wrong at her place we know. What does it all signify? Again, it suffices to look closely at the specific data. His wife he considered motherly but asexual. Madama Pace is a mother who sells sex. She is motherhood degraded, and she is sex degraded. As Dr. Kligerman has noticed, she is the "giantess of the nursery," the castrating nanny, and, according to the first version, carries scissors. Perhaps it was defensiveness that made Pirandello omit the scissors from the revised text; surely they are a vivid touch. And the Stepdaughter, whatever else she is, is the Mother when young, the Mother with sex appeal, as in *Enrico IV,* where the Emperor embraces the daughter instead of the mother. What is the substance of the encounter at Madama Pace's? The evil mother offers our man a girl. The girl says: My father just died. The man says: Take your dress off. The good mother rushes in, crying: Stop, that's my daughter! A hideous little instrument of self-torture, this phantasy, though no more so than a thousand others in the chronicles of schizophrenia.

In nothing is the complexity of Pirandello's dramaturgy more evident than in this creation, Madama Pace. She is not one of the six characters. She is conjured up by the spirit of the theatre on the initiative of the Father. What does he mean by this initiative, and what does his author mean? *Six Characters in Search of an Author* can be conceived of as many concentric circles, in which case Madama Pace might well be the innermost circle: play within play within play within play. . . . Now the most helpful insight into plays within plays—or rather dreams within dreams—has been Freud's. He remarked that we dream we are dreaming when we especially wish to disown a particular phantasy as "only a dream." And the phantasies we particularly wish to disown present what troubles us most in a rather blunt form. Madama Pace is not one of the actors, she is not one of the six, she is conjured up by one of the six, or by his "idea of a theatre." Most likely (as psychoanalysts will suggest) she is what troubles Pirandello. Certainly she is what troubles the Father: his mother as "giantess of the nursery," as castrator. Above all, as procuress—provider and degrader of sexual pleasure. The Father is this play's Dr. Faustus, and she is his bad angel.

If she is a go-between, between whom does she go? Between the two families that the six characters consist of. And the story of the six can usefully be seen as a confrontation of these two groups, the legitimate and the illegitimate, pursuing licit and illicit love. Each of the three traumatic situations I have described brings the two groups into desperate conflict: father with his wife's illegitimate daughter, adulterous mother with the legitimate son, illegitimate younger children with the legitimate son. It is appropriate to this play that one finds oneself proposing different ways of looking at it. Each way is likely to have its peculiar advantage. And the schema just provided has the advantage of bringing out the special importance of the Son. He "dominates" two of the bad situations, and is not outside the third one (since he reacts strongly to the "incest"). When we speak of sibling murder, we can cite the Son as the murderer of both younger children.

If the confrontation of the legitimate and the illegitimate families is important to the structure of the play, what of the confrontation we began to look into a few minutes ago, that of the family with the theatrical troupe? Of all the concentric circles, this is perhaps the outermost one. Which in itself might tend to make a psychiatrist regard it as the least important, since the doctor's job is to look for hidden disease and penetrate disguises. Art, however, is not a disease, and in theatre art the disguise is in a clear sense the *ding an sich*. Nor—contrary to what many academic as well as clinical critics assume—does the artist harbor a general prejudice in favor of hidden meanings and against obvious ones. On the contrary, the weight to be given to the most external of the dramas in *Six Characters* must be decided without prejudice against externality. It is wholly a question of what weight, by his own artistic means, did Pirandello give to it.

Well, to begin with, he derived the title of the whole work from it, and considering how unerring his intuition was apt to be in such matters, this "small" item should not be overlooked. Granted that the substance of Action in the work is inner, neurotic, and even schizophrenic experience, what of the ever-present fact that the vehicle of Action is this conceit: characters in search of an author? It is a search with two aspects: the wish for a play to be *written* and the wish for it to be *enacted*. Let us take the second aspect first.

Enactment. If there is anything we are not in doubt about after we have seen this play it is that, for its author, all the world is a stage. *Totus mundus facit histrionem,* as the motto of the Globe Theatre read. But the idea receives a specific application here that is not so obvious. What happens when the actors try to enact the *scene* in Madama Pace's shop? They fail. But the point of the passage is lost when the actors are presented as inept. That kind of failure has too little content. A bad actor is a bad actor, period. What relationship does Pirandello define between the real thing and the re-enactment? Is it not that of a translation that cannot in the nature of things be a faithful one? The best analogy I can find is with the attempt to reconstruct a dream with the aid of notes jotted down upon waking. The notes are very definite, perhaps; but they are fragmentary. There are gaps, and above all the tone of feeling that characterized the whole world of the dream has gone. The Pirandellian re-enactment is incomplete and deeply unsatisfying in just this way.

But enactment is only an offshoot anyway, an offshoot of what is to be enacted: the author's work. IN CERCA D'AUTORE. And *who* is searching for him? Six characters? Not really. There is no evidence that the two children think themselves engaged in such a search. Like children generally, they are dragged along. The older boy definitely objects to the search, practices civil disobedience against it: that is what breaks up the experiment, and precipitates the end of the play. The mother is distressed by the experiment, and gets dragged in against her will. That leaves just two characters who do search for an author —the Father and the Stepdaughter. And only these two had previously pleaded with the author who created them to make them part of a complete work of art:

> . . . trying to persuade him, trying to push him . . . I would appear before him sometimes, sometimes she would go to him, sometimes that poor mother . . . (*The Father*)

> . . . I too went there, sir, to tempt him, many times, in the melancholy of that study of his, at the twilight hour when he would sit stretched out in his armchair, unable to make up his mind to switch the light on, and letting the evening shadows invade the room, knowing that these shadows were alive with us . . . (*The Stepdaughter*)

Even the Stepdaughter has only a conditional interest in finding an author, the condition being that the Father insists on finding him. Then she will meet the challenge. The Father is the challenger: it is his project. And the play *Six Characters in Search of an Author* is his play—not in the sense that other characters are aspects of him but in the sense that he is consistently the prime mover. The story of the six starts from his actions—in marrying, in becoming a father, but even more in driving wife and son out. It starts again from his actions on the death of his rival: meeting the daughter at Madama Pace's, taking the family back into his house. The various family catastrophes stem from him. He is the base of that Oedipal triangle on which the family story rests. Last—and, to a dramatic critic, not least—he takes the initiative in the new and present Action. Our play begins with the arrival of the Father at the theatre, and from then on what we are witnessing is the encounter of the Father with the *Capocomico*. The latter is a Director, not an Author—yet another of the play's special twists—but the question before us is whether he will take on a writer's chores and write, as well as direct, the play into which the six characters would properly fit. As soon as he has decided not to, "our play is done," and Father's day is over.

It is odd that anyone should speak of character conflicts in *Six Characters* without mentioning the one that stands in the foreground and works its way out in the primary Action. I suppose it could only happen because of that prejudice in favor of the secret and murky that I was speaking of. In itself the confrontation Father/Director is an archetypal affair: the confrontation of pathetic suffering humanity with the authorities. And these authorities are portrayed, in almost Shavian fashion, not as hostile and malicious but as open-natured, well-meaning, and far more reasonable than suffering humanity. It is true they are also smug, a little stupid, and very much out of contact—theirs is the life style of bureaucrats and organization men.

Which would just be a picture of normal experience except that Pirandello pushes it, in his usual manner, far beyond the normalities; and Father and Director come to embody two sides of a schizophrenic situation. Through the Father we glimpse the inner world of modern man, through the Director, the outer. Both these worlds are shown as spiritually impoverished. The inner world of the Father contains nothing much besides his two or three phantasies and the pain he feels in failing to justify himself. The Director's outer world is reduced to rituals that preserve the appearances and maintain the occasion, habits, routines, clichés. *All that either the Father or the Director do is repeat themselves,* a factor which is close to the central metaphor of the play: life as theatre. Which aspect of theatre is exhibited in this play? Not performance. Only rehearsal—*répétition*. The stage is bare. The auditorium is empty. The theatre, too, is impoverished and deprived. The bourgeois drama, which had become thrilling through a kind of claustrophobic tension, here dissolves in agoraphobia, its opposite.

What is the Father seeking in the Director? An author who will put him in a play and justify him. In what sense "justify"? First of all, defend him from the Stepdaughter's charge of bestiality by citing .the sexual needs of middle-aged men living apart from their wives, and so on. Is that all? Nothing in *Six Characters* is ever all. If the plot has an outermost circle, the theme hasn't. It reaches out toward infinity, a place where there is either emptiness or God. It should not be too surprising that a great play of dead or agonized fatherhood reverberates with the sense of God the Father, or rather of his absence—the "death of God." A search for an author can easily suggest a search for the Author of our being, and the main metaphor of the play has reminded some people of Calderón's *El Gran Teatro del Mundo*. I only wonder they haven't commented on the opening words of that work: *"Sale el Autor. . . ."* "Enter the Author in a starry mantle with nine rays of light in groups of threes on his hat." This is, of course, God.

It is not necessary to assume that Pirandello had Calderón in mind, or that he thought directly of God at all. God is meaning, God is authority and authorship, God is fatherhood. A poignant sense of the absence of all these burns through every page of *Six Characters in Search of an Author*.

To me, the deepest—or perhaps I mean soundest—interpretation of the search for an author would stress neither God nor literary authorship but fatherhood and I like to think I derive this choice, not from personal predilection, but from the text. The concisest way of stating what the Father demands of the Director in human terms—and Pirandello is always in search of the centrally human—is to say he is asking him to be his father. "Father me." "Rescue me from this maniacal female." "Tell me what is so, reassure me, help me find my place in the story, in the scheme of things, take from me this burden which I cannot bear but which you can." And the Director is very much the daddy of his troupe: that is established at his first entrance. But being the daddy of these lightweight Thespians is one thing, taking on suffering, schizoid humanity is another, particularly in the case of one who calls himself "Father" and should be able to fend for himself. In any event, the Director is another very inadequate Father. Something of a grotesque, he stands in the same relationship to fatherhood as Madama Pace does to motherhood. (Father, Director, Secretary-Lover: three fathers. Mother, Pace, Stepdaughter: three mothers. Another of this play's many symmetries.) But while she castrates, he is castrated: he has the character of the traditional impotent old clown. Our intellectual author transposes this impotence to the literary plane where the Director can prove impotent to make art from the Father's life, life from the Father's art.

In one respect the word "author" is exactly right in suggesting just what a "father" might be expected to provide. When the Father finds the right playwright he will not be content to be given some dialogue in which he can rapidly discomfit his stepdaughter. His ambition goes far beyond that. He is not even saying, "Write a melodrama, and make me the hero." He is saying, "A person is an entity with no clear meaning—an entity close to nonentity—unless there is an author to make him part of (*a part in*) a play."

A severed hand, Aristole has it, is not a hand at all, because it could function as a hand only by belonging to arm and body. A character severed from a play is not even a character. A person severed from his family is not even a person. But what is he? And what can he do about it? We need to watch the words and actions of the Father to find the answer to such questions. Is the Father's quest as hopeless as the effort to graft a hand back onto an arm? Or is success in the quest within the power of an Author—in one sense or another of the word "author"? This is not a play that provides answers. At any rate, it is not a play that provides positive answers. But neither is it a play in which the objects of yearning have been eliminated. Nostalgia pervades it. Nostalgia for what? For some kind of "togetherness." Is this just a regressive fantasy, the longing for the union of embryo and mother? *Child* and mother? There is something here of the modern isolated individual's longing for a social community, but again it is a longing directed backward toward some golden age, not forward toward a new society. By consequence, it is a fantasy not of freedom but of freely accepted bondage.

If only the Father could be part of a play, so he explains in the terms of Pirandello's literary conceit, he would have the permanence of Sancho Panza or Don Abbondio. Interpreting the play, we might translate this back into terms of life, thus: *to have a part in a play* means *to be a member of a family,* and the family is seen as an organism in which each cell lives in and by a happy interdependence. Before such a family could exist, the kind of life we find in Pirandello's play would need to be enormously enriched. It requires a texture far finer than phantasy and fear and guilt can provide. God is love; Father, too, would have to be love. That is the kind of Father this Father is in search of in a play which might just as well be called *A Father in Search of a Father.*

The crowning, and Pirandellian, irony comes when the Director's contribution to the proposed "drama," instead of enriching it, actually impoverishes it further. I am speaking of his work on the *scene* in Act Two. What he starts from is a piece of raw life, or rather a piece of raw erotic phantasy. Give this bit of life or phantasy to a Shakespeare, in the age of Shakespeare, and it becomes *Antony and Cleopatra* with noble enough roles in it for many. All our Director can do is convert it into what in America we would call Broadway drama, in which the already attenuated naturalism of the *scene* has to be further attenuated in the interests of middle-class entertainment.

Shakespeare proves in *Hamlet* that the schizophrenia of an Ophelia can be part of a grand design. Pirandello is interested in showing that in life she would encounter someone like the Director in *Six Characters* or the Doctor in *Enrico IV.* That is to say, she would be on her own. Which is what schizophrenia is. Art is sane. Life is schizoid; and offers only schizoid solutions, as in *Cosí è (si vi pare*). In *Enrico IV,* the schizoid solution is a starting point, then the "sane" people break it to pieces, as it is always the itch of "sane" people to do. One must reckon with this itch in the Director and Actors in *Six Characters.* Yet the play exhibits neither a solution nor a cataclysm—only a constantly re-enacted phantasy, a father journeying endlessly onward like the Flying Dutchman.

Now what the Dutchman was searching for was love. Is the Father's aim all that different?

This is the point at which that "great deal of discussion" which Dr. Kligerman complains of can perhaps be comprehended, for the bulk of it consists of long speeches made by the Father. If, as most critics have assumed, they are really there as exposition of a philosophy, then surely they will be an unwelcome intrusion. What is their content? I'd say that two main points are made, one directed at the Stepdaughter (particularly toward the end of Act One), one directed at the Director (particularly at the beginning of Act Three). The first point is that personality is not unitary but multiple. The second point is that illusion *is* reality. In the context it is not essential that these topics be regarded as interesting in themselves. They are dramatized. Which is to say, they become Action. Just as talking is something the Father has to do to live, so resorting to the particular "talking points" he makes is a matter of urgent necessity for him. If the theory of multiple personality did not exist he would have to invent it. It gets him off the hook on which the incident at Madama Pace's had hung him. He is not necessarily right, however, even though his view coincides with the author's philosophy. From the point of view of drama, I would hold that he is wrong. For the art of drama, as Aristotle explained, takes for granted that actions do define a character. A man *is* what he does at Madama Pace's, and all his talk about really being otherwise is so much . . . well, talk. Whatever Pirandello may have believed, his dramas are drama, and present people as their actions. True, talking is an action—the Father's principal action most of the time—but it is precisely his compulsive talking that inclines us not to accept the endless self-pity and self-justification at face value. The Father *feels* that he is many and not one. But that, as we blithely say, is *"his* problem." He is a very irresponsible man, if sane; and, if not responsible for his actions, then insane. On either assumption, he needs just the philosophy Pirandello gives him. Nothing diffuses responsibility more conveniently than the theory that one is a succession of different people. And if one is insane, one is surely entitled to complain a good deal of that radical disjunction which is one's fate. One may even project it on everyone else.

Freud compares paranoid fantasies to metaphysical systems. It is a comparison that makes some sense in reverse. The Pirandellian metaphysics provides apt fantasies for his mentally disturbed characters.

I gave as the Father's second philosophic idea that illusion is reality. Which is also "what everybody knows about Luigi Pirandello." To say that illusion is reality is, on the face of it, nonsense but can be construed as sense by taking it paradoxically. It is as a paradox that the notion has its primary use to Pirandello. For paradoxes, when expanded, become comedies. The expansion happens, in Pirandello, by doubling and redoubling. Take, in our play, the opposites *life* and *art*. The actors are from *life*. The characters are from *art*. However, nothing begins to "pop" as comedy, as drama, until the author reverses the proposition. The characters are more *real*, are therefore portrayed more as what we regard as people from *life:* they have instincts, impulses, private lives. The actors are less real, and are therefore portrayed as artifacts, as "types," as creatures out of a play. In short, the actors are from art. The characters from life. What one might call the intellectual comedy of *Six Characters in Search of an Author* is built upon this reversibility of the key terms. And what is the truth? Which is "really" life, and which is "really" art? There Pirandello-Laudisi lies in wait for us—laughing. Everything in his little system (or *game,* if we must be up-to-date) works both ways. Nothing is "really" so, because everything is "really" so.

Now a person making use of this system—a person playing this game— can have everything both ways. Which is a very nice way to have everything: it is what we all want, though in proportion as we cease to be childish or sick we learn to do without a good deal of what we all want. The Father, however, *is* childish and sick. The Pirandellian game is after his own heart. In Act Two, he is essentially telling the actors to subordinate their *art* to *life.* All that is wrong with their performance is that it isn't naturalistic, it isn't exactly what happened in Madama Pace's shop. But in his theoretical vein, he usually exalts art *above* life. Similarly, he can use the word "illusion" in a pejorative sense, as when he tells the Director that the actors' lives are more an illusion than the characters' lives, while in the same breath speaking of illusion with respect and a kind of nostalgic awe. All of this is word play, word *game,* inconclusive, and in principle endless—and therefore very depressing. Pirandello can call Laudisi-ism "deviltry" and ask for a comedic tone, but it is black comedy at best: its underside is despair. Pursue any statement the Father may offer as consolation and you will find it lets you down with a bump. For example: art as a solution to the bafflements of impermanence. As a statue you can live forever. The only thing is: you're dead. Petrifaction is no answer, but only corresponds to yet another schizoid wish. And anyone who knows this particular Father will quickly sense that his wish to be a work of art is his wish to escape from flesh and blood—that is, from life. As with other schizophrenics, the great fear of being killed does not prevent him from yearning for death. Indeed it is at this stage of the argument that we realize that the Father's two main points have, for him, the same point: he wants to get out of his own skin. He is "one." But he cites as an alibi that nobody is one, we are each of us a hundred thousand. He is real. But he cites as an alibi that nobody is real. He is trying to nonexist.

His personality can, as it were, be diffused horizontally, losing itself in moments or states of mind, alleged other personalities. Or it can be diffused vertically in vapors of idea. But total nonexistence is too terrifying to flatly accept. One has to try and coax it into acceptability. By paradox. By dialectic. All of which is evasion, though, for a schizophrenic, a necessary evasion.

"If the self is not true to itself, it is in despair," says Kierkegaard. Pirandello depicts a despair so deep that his schizophrenics cannot afford to admit they have selves to be untrue to. The theory of multiple personality is a byproduct of the despair, and, for the Father, a necessary fiction.

The very notion that illusion is reality stems from defeatism. Philosophically, it represents the breakdown of the Hegelian tradition in which there was always a reality to offset appearances. Once the reality starts to be eroded, there will eventually be nothing left but the appearances; and at this point in time philosophers start to advocate *accepting facts at face value*—face value is the only value they have or the world has. Hence, for example, a contemporary of Pirandello's who later became the house philosopher of Mussolini, Giovanni Gentile, wrote in 1916: "The true is what is in the making." *

In this respect, there are only two interpretations of *Six Characters in Search of an Author*. According to one, the play itself endorses Gentile, endorses the Father's philosophic utterances. According to the other, which I subscribe to, the play is larger than the Father, "places" him in a larger setting, makes his pathos unsympathetic. I am not going to argue that the play embodies a positive faith. A critic who recently did this had to rely upon a single sentence that is present only in the first edition.** I am arguing that it is not a philosophical play at all because the philosophy is harnessed to a nonphilosophical chariot. The content is psychopathological from beginning to end.

Perhaps I've said overmuch about psychological motifs. This is an exuberant, excessive, Sicilian work, and from perhaps overmuch suggestiveness may easily come overmuch critical suggestion. Let my last comments be about the form of the work. The first thing a traditional critic—if such a person still exists— would notice about this search for an author is that it respects the unities of time, place, and action. In other words, it conspicuously possesses that compact and classic dramatic structure which the "play in the making" (with its story of the six) conspicuously lacks. The space of time covered is literally the time spent in the theatre plus enough extra hours or minutes to permit the Director to call the session a "whole day"—if we must take *him* literally. Place is given in an equally literal way. And there is something Pirandellian in the fact that such literalness could be a brainstorm. What earned the Maestro the highest compliments for originality was that in this work the boards of the theatre represent—the boards of the theatre. That is to say, they do not represent,

* *The Theory of Mind as Pure Act.* New York, 1922.
** *La giara e altre novelle,* a cura di Giuseppe Lanza. Milano, 1965, page 15.

they are. They are appearances which are the reality: the quintessential Pirandellian principle.

The final point of this handling of place is a dialectical one. The boards of the theatre are to be so definite, so "real" because the "real" streets of the town and country, the gardens, the houses and rooms are to be so shadowy, so "unreal." The interaction of these two elements gives Pirandello a goodly part of his play—and a good deal that is peculiar to his play.

Time also is handled dialectically. Over against this flatly undistorted present on the stage is the story of the six, all of which is already past. The six are trying to pull all this baggage of theirs, as the patient does on the doctor's couch, from the dim, anaesthetic past into the garish, stinging present. The past of the six and the present of the acting troupe are so clearly demarcated that some people see only the one, some only the other, whereas, to realize what Pirandello is up to, we not only have to see both but the constant reaction of one upon the other. There is a further complication. The past and present of the six are *not* clearly demarcated, but, on the contrary, are deliberately mingled, as in dreams. Hence, for example, though the Stepdaughter has already left her parents, here she is back with them, and the younger children, who have died, are alive again. They will die again, and the play will end with the Stepdaughter leaving her parents. . . . But I am afraid that in turning from content to form, I have *been turned back,* by the work itself, from form to content.

One last notation. By an error which was to create a possibly permanent misunderstanding, Six Characters in Search of an Author in its first edition was subtitled: "a play in the making." * But the play in the making is the projected play about the six characters that never gets made. The play that gets made is the play about the encounter of the six characters (seven, finally) with the Director and his acting troupe. This of course includes as much of the unwritten play as is needed. Finally, then, Six Characters became a play fully made. Bernard Shaw said he had never come across so original a play.** It is a su-

* The Italian original reads: *"una commedia da fare."* In the translation most widely read in America, this has been rendered: "a comedy in the making." But in Italian, as in French, a *"commedia"* (comédie) is not necessarily comic, and the word should often be translated as a "play." (That the story of the six should turn out comic is out of the question.) Secondly, if the phrase "in the making" suggests, as I think it does, that there are the makings of a play in this material (which is the opposite of what Pirandello is saying), then it is a mistranslation of *"da fare,"* which means, literally, "to make," and, less literally, "to be made," "yet to be made," "not yet made." Incidentally, "in the making" cited above Giovanni Gentile does not translate *"da fare."* Gentile's original reads: *"Vero è quel che si fa,"* which would be rendered literally: "True is that which is done." ** When Pirandello's preface to Six Characters was published in French translation (Revue de Paris, 15 July 1925), Pirandello added this paragraph (here literally translated) to the text:

If modesty forbids me to accept G. B. Shaw's assertion that Six Characters is the most original and most powerful work of all the theatres ancient and modern in all

preme contribution that says something profound about the theatre and about life seen as theatre and seen by means of theatre. The originality should not blind us to the beauty of the form or to that existential anguish which is the content.

(*1967*)

---

nations, I can't help being aware that their appearance in the history of the Italian theatre marks a date that people won't be able to forget.

When at a later date, this passage was brought to Shaw's attention, he commented:

I have no recollection of the extravagant dictum you quote: but I rank P. as first rate among playwrights and have never come across a play so *original* as Six Chracters [*sic*].

—*The Shavian*, February 1964.

Eugene O'Neill

(For Perry Miller)

[James] O'Neill assumed the role of the Christus in an adaptation of the Oberammergau Passion Play. In later years he always seemed most proud of having played this part, claiming to have been the "only actor on the English-speaking stage who has impersonated our Saviour." As late as 1918, James O'Neill still felt very strongly about the desirability of putting on this play. He declared that "it would be a relief after all the filth we get. . . . People have seen so much lewdness on the stage that they have become nauseated by it."

—From *The Curse of the Misbegotten*
by Croswell Bowen

Jamie jeered. "The curtain of eternity has been there a long time and I don't think that you're the one to tear it down. . . ." "The answer is that there is nothing behind the curtain when you do tear it down," Gene said. . . . "Life is a farce played by a baboon who feels in his invertebrate bones a vision that, being an ape, he cannot understand. He scratches his fleas absently, with melancholy eyes, and then hangs upside down on the nearest branch and plays with his testicles."

"My trouble is that there is nobody who wants to play with *mine!*" Jamie said. . . .

—James O'Neill, Jr., and Eugene O'Neill,
as reported in *Part of a Long Story*
by Agnes Boulton

ACT II. SCENE 3. *Platform of the Château d'If. Steps cut in the rock. Door of secret dungeons. Enter two gaolers carrying a sack enveloping a form.*

FIRST GAOLER. Are you ready?
SECOND GAOLER. Ready! (*They swing the sack into the sea.*)
FIRST GAOLER. An ugly night on the sea.
SECOND GAOLER. Aye, under, too. (*Exeunt. The moon breaks out, lighting up a projecting rock. Edmond Dantès rises from the sea. He is dripping, a knife in his hand, some shreds of sack adhering to it.*)
EDMUND (*on rock*). Saved! Mine, the treasures of Monte Cristo! The world is mine!

—James O'Neill's version of *Monte Cristo*

I'm going on the theory that the United States, instead of being the most successful country in the world, is the greatest failure. . . . We are the greatest example of, For what shall it profit a man if he shall gain the whole world and lose his own soul?

—Eugene O'Neill, speaking to the press, 1946

I

The son of a famous romantic actor, his infancy and youth were spent in the atmosphere of the theatre while his father, James O'Neill, toured the country in *Monte Cristo* and Shakespearean repertoire. After a year at Princeton and a brief career as a reporter in New London, Connecticut, O'Neill went to sea on a Norwegian barque and at the end of two years earned his Able Seaman's certificate. In 1914, following a year in Professor [George Pierce] Baker's famous English 47 class at Harvard, he devoted himself exclusively to playwriting. Since then no fewer than thirty plays have come from his pen, and the whole world has sought to do him honor. Awarded the gold medal for drama by the National Institute of Arts and Letters and the degree of Litt.D. by Yale University, three times winner of the Pulitzer Prize for drama, he achieved his highest accolade when he was given the Nobel Prize for Literature in 1936. Eugene O'Neill's plays have been translated into almost all languages and have been performed in every civilized country of the world. His plays, next to Shakespeare's, are read by more people than are the works of any other dramatist, living or dead.

The foregoing is from an anonymous Note on the Author in *Nine Plays by Eugene O'Neill* (Modern Library). The tone is a little euphoric and one wonders where the statistics come from that would prove O'Neill is read by more people than Bernard Shaw. My reasons for quoting the excerpt are, first, that it does give an outline of the facts up to 1941 (when it was written) and, second, that it gives them in a distinctly typical way—typical of the O'Neill literature, typical of that American middle-brow culture which has been O'Neill's principal audience, typical of the world we live in and its Hollywoodian way of thinking about writers. The long and short of it is that O'Neill was a worldly success—in contrast, say, to E. E. Cummings, of whom Mr. Gilbert Highet has written: ". . . he has never made a really solid impact on his world. Up to this time, for instance, he has not been awarded the Pulitzer Prize. . . ."

The tone of a Note on the Author might be unimportant, only in this case the writer's assumptions are symptomatic enough to be significant. Not only, in his account, is the Harvard class a famous one. Harvard is famous too. Likewise the playwright's father. And the university at which he spent an undergraduate year. And when the playwright wrote plays, up rose "the whole world" and cried Hooray! "in almost all languages. . . ."

All of which provides an excellent cue for the question: *What really happened?* By way of answer I shall rehearse a few well-established facts.

The author's father, James O'Neill, was indeed famous: he was a star actor. Eugene O'Neill was born into the theatre and, as it happened, literally on Broadway, New York City. But Broadway is not much of a home to anyone and was not at all a home to Eugene O'Neill. "My first seven years," he has written, "were spent mainly in the larger towns all over the U.S. . . . I knew only actors and the stage. My mother nursed me in the wings and in dressing rooms."

It hardly even makes sense to say he was "sent away to boarding school"— away from where? (He went to school in Riverdale and Stamford.) The only approximation to a home that his parents ever acquired was a summer place in New London, Connecticut, which, therefore, was to play a role in their son's life.

The year at Princeton (1906–1907) was a flop—otherwise it would have been four years at Princeton. O'Neill liked to make it out even more of a flop than it was, for he sometimes lent his authority to the myth that he had been expelled for throwing a bottle through President Woodrow Wilson's window. It turned out that the only person he had abused was the stationmaster. To top things off, he didn't take his exams.

At this point, the anonymous Note is seriously misleading. "After a year at Princeton and a brief career as a reporter in New London, Connecticut, O'Neill went to sea on a Norwegian barque . . ." The word "barque" is very choice; the rest is fudge. The period under review is 1909–1912. There were three voyages (to Honduras, South America, and England, respectively), not one, and each time O'Neill returned to his father—either to the New London summer place or a theatre somewhere. He also got married, stayed with his wife long enough to get her pregnant, attempted suicide, and was divorced.

Nineteen-twelve was the most important adult year in O'Neill's whole formation. This was the year in which he not only worked as a reporter but also began to have his own work published. It was the year of his first divorce. It was the year of his romance with the girl whom he calls Muriel in *Ah, Wilderness!* And it was the year when he went to the hospital with tuberculosis.

I have no intention of putting down the facts of a whole lifetime—that has been done by others—but am setting the intellectual stage for interpretation. It is the early years, for any man, that are formative. No need, at this date, to stress the importance of childhood, but there is a critical age of which much less has been said: the first years of manhood. This is a particularly trying time for the children of the famous—enviable as Fame seems to anonymous annotators and the anonymous millions. Or, rather, just because Fame is so enviable, it is embarrassing, to say the least, if your own father has got it. The problem of rivaling and replacing the father—or at least establishing one's own place on his level—is compounded. The only complete solution is for the son to be a Goethe or a Mozart, and then it's Father who has his problems.

That solution was not open to Eugene O'Neill. He did say that his father would someday be known only as the father of Eugene O'Neill, and the prophecy has proved correct, but it was a disingenuous prophecy. For acting—or acting before the days of movies—is automatically forgotten, while even a second-rate writer can "live" for a generation or two, and actually O'Neill's rank among dramatists has turned out to be about what his father's was among actors: high but not quite among the highest.

O'Neill was unable to defeat his father and then love him. He remained forever in the original state of ambivalence with which he first rebelled.

And the mother? As a girl she had been taken to see James O'Neill play Sidney Carton in Cleveland and had fallen in love with him, though she was by no means of the theatre herself, and had indeed thought of becoming a nun. Life proved less romantic than *A Tale of Two Cities,* and, as the world has learned from *A Long Day's Journey into Night,* Ella O'Neill took to drugs.

As the world knows from the same source, there was an elder brother, James, Jr. He was an alcoholic. He also kept company with prostitutes and made sure that his younger brother went along with him from time to time.

In the work of Eugene O'Neill the ideas of "nun" and of "mother" often go together. He was very much an Irishman, and the Virgin Mother composed an image he could not do without. He liked to use the phrase, "God the Mother." Otherwise, in the works of O'Neill, femininity is found largely in whores. The vices of James, Jr.—drink and whoring—are the standard recourse of any O'Neill character who has received a setback.

O'Neill married three times. From what has been published on the subject, it would seem clear that he looked less for a wife than for a mother—looked, indeed, for the image of the young Ella Quinlan, whom he had never known —and that he thought sometimes, in his second and third marriages, that he had found her. It would seem, too, that he was greatly loved by his wives but experienced the utmost difficulty in accepting love. It may well be that he portrayed this aspect of himself in Hickey, the salesman who kills his wife because she keeps forgiving him.

And his playwriting? The art of an artist is often outrageously left out of account by his biographers, as if it were not as much a part of his life as his relations with men. Thoroughly wise to this error, a psychoanalyst has shown that the writing of drama came as the solution, or partial solution, to O'Neill's main problem in living. Dr. Philip Weissman * points out that O'Neill's mode of living in the critical years 1909–1912 constituted the "acting out" of the cruel ambivalence in his relation to his father. He would flee, and then return, time and again. But in 1912 that stopped: he had started writing. He wrote the story of his ambivalence again and again and again; devoted his life to doing so; was able to live only by doing so.

That isn't all Dr. Weissman says, but even this much helps us to understand the peculiarity of O'Neill's endeavor. He is no Broadway playwright writing to entertain, to make money, or to be one of the boys. Nor is he a man of letters with an interest in the whole give-and-take of literary, political, or scientific discussion. He lives, as it were, in a trance, writing and rewriting the story of the two Jameses, Ella, and Eugene. Or parts of the story. Or the story at a remove.

Whatever the isolation of writers from the average middle-class citizen, they at least belong to families, and as children were not so isolated after all. Yet in having the kind of family background most Americans think they want— namely a Famous one—O'Neill had a hideous and painful upbringing. Some think talent thrives on that sort of thing. More probably, he was born strong and made his way through innate strength. The handicaps were enormous, and his writing is marked by them. What important American writer has known so little of America—any part of the country or any class of its people? It is so taken for granted these days that the artist is isolated, is "alienated," that it is hard to realize that some artists are much more isolated than others. O'Neill was the outsider of outsiders. He did not "belong" in the beginning, and he did

* "Conscious and Unconscious Autobiographical Dramas of Eugene O'Neill," *Journal of the American Psychoanalytic Association,* July 1957.

not try to belong later on. As a youth, he hankered after the *Lumpenproletariat* in waterfront dives or in Greenwich Village. When he made money, he used it to take himself away not only from the dives but from everyone. He chose the life of the luxury villa. Children embarrassed him, especially his own children, to whom, as to at least two of his three wives, he was extremely cruel. One son committed suicide, the other became a drug addict. Only his daughter made a go of things—on her own. Ever since he was in the sanatorium in 1913 he characterized himself as an invalid, and while occupied with his largest work —during World War II—he fell victim to Parkinson's disease. During the thirties he had separated himself even from his audience by not releasing plays for publication or production. His last years were a living death: he was separated even from his work. His hands shook too much to allow him to write; and he could not compose orally.

If there is much success worship in America, there is also a widespread belief that successful people are unhappy. Like unsuccessful people, they are. What distinguishes them from other folk is that they must suffer the effects of success. In other words, Eugene O'Neill had to try to cope, eventually, not only with his father's success but with his own.

For he did have success, and not merely in the newspaper sense of the word. He had success in solving the particular problem to which he had addressed himself: rivaling and replacing his father. How better, in any case, can a man outdo an actor than by becoming a playwright? The actor is the playwright's mouthpiece and victim. At least he can be; and O'Neill, Jr., made sure that he would be. His father's theatre—the Victorian theatre of Booth and Irving— was an actor's theatre. The modern theatre would be a playwright's theatre, and Eugene O'Neill was one of the principal playwrights who made it so.

The texts of the plays bear a relation to James O'Neill, Sr., not merely in frequently portraying men who are like him but in doing so in a style he could never have accepted. O'Neill, Sr., was, as the *New York Times*'s obituary put it in 1920, "the last of the old school . . . a lover of all that is true and good in dramatic art, always holding up with authority the best traditions of the American stage." Early that year he had sat in a box at the première of his son's first Pulitzer Prize–winning play, *Beyond the Horizon*. Afterward he said to his son, "People come to the theatre to forget their troubles, not to be reminded of them. What are you trying to do—send them home to commit suicide?" Which certainly was to hit a bull's eye; for to send one particular person home to commit suicide was, in a symbolic sense, precisely the intention.

The public discussion of O'Neill has by this time gone beyond the above-mentioned anonymous Note and embraced the fact—announced so openly in *Long Day's Journey*—that he was his father's enemy. The anonymous annotator's success story has been undermined, and another school of interpretation has taken over the public mind: the school that finds fame interesting *as an or-*

deal. At this point, books and articles on O'Neill come to resemble books and articles on, say, famous actresses who tell it to Gerold Frank. In journalism, one stereotype follows hard on the heels of the next.

The newer school of thought will be willing enough to concede that the young O'Neill reacted against the elder O'Neill's type of theatre. "James O'Neill," we read in Croswell Bowen's *The Curse of the Misbegotten* (1959),

> was seeing the passing of his kind of American theatre with its old-fashioned, flamboyant acting. Melodrama, pathos, blood and thunder, hearts and flowers were already a little passé. They were yielding to the neo-realism —to the interpretation of contemporary experience—that constitutes the serious aspect of Broadway today, and which his son was inaugurating.

And again: "Before O'Neill, the American theatre had been cheap, sentimental, and tawdry. It was 'afraid of its own emotions,' as Eugene said. . . . It would not be too great an exaggeration to say that the emergence of an important American theatre is due . . ." et cetera.

Now it is true enough that Eugene O'Neill expressed contempt for *Monte Cristo*. As far as that goes, he even described his father, on one occasion, as the worst actor in America. The two statements may be equally personal and uncritical. Even if they are not, what does the younger O'Neill claim to be rejecting in the older theatre? Only, it would seem, what was feeble about it—hearts and flowers, no doubt, but not "melodrama, pathos, blood and thunder" by any means. What does the same commentator say of one of O'Neill's early plays? *"The Web* is remarkable in that it includes many of O'Neill's characteristic elements: violent death, cruelty, and a good deal of theatrical action." Exactly— these are the characteristics of melodrama.

Ambivalence is ambivalence. If Eugene O'Neill hated his father and his father's great role of Edmond Dantès, he also loved them. The proposition that he rejected Victorian melodrama will be useless to criticism unless it is accompanied by its opposite: O'Neill undertook to free melodrama from what was cheap and tawdry and ineffective, and to write a melodrama that would be truly melodramatic—a *Monte Cristo* raised to the *n*th power. If the rebellious son wishes to destroy the father, in his ambivalence he wishes nothing so much as to validate him and, if necessary, to rehabilitate him.

Eugene O'Neill is generally at his best when he sticks to melodrama, but Mr. Bowen's words about a "serious" and "important" aspect call our attention to a problem. Even good melodrama does not have the reputation it might have. That much is clear even from Mr. Bowen's own tone. And what the son does to, with, and for the father must win recognition—must have a good reputation, must gain prestige. Hence the paradox that though the younger O'Neill succeeded in melodrama he was not thereby satisfied. He had to be serious too. And he had to be acknowledged as such by pundits, professors, and institutions who award prizes even more august than Pulitzers—such as the Swedish Academy.

We have seen that he succeeded in his adventure into seriousness. The Swedish Academy and "the whole world" seriously approved. It remains a question, though, whether the seriousness was *artistically* successful, whether it even had any spontaneity, or any underlying purpose other than its author's private and neurotic one.

II

The writing career of Eugene O'Neill falls into three parts:

I. 1912–1924

The most notable premières were:

1920: *Beyond the Horizon*
      The Emperor Jones
1921: *Anna Christie*
1922: *The Hairy Ape*
1924: *Desire Under the Elms*

II. 1925–1934

The most notable premières were:

1926: *The Great God Brown*
1928: *Strange Interlude*
      Lazarus Laughed (Pasadena, California)
1931: *Mourning Becomes Electra*

III. 1934–1953

There were no O'Neill premières between 1934 and 1946. The last three named below were posthumous.

1946: *The Iceman Cometh*
1956: *Long Day's Journey into Night*
1957: *A Moon for the Misbegotten* (Columbus, Ohio)
1958: *A Touch of the Poet*

Eugene O'Neill's earliest efforts are somewhat ludicrous, not least because the form of the one-act simply would not carry the kind of weight he tried to put on it. Soon he was wise enough to reduce the load, and the result was a kind of one-act not quite like anything else that had yet been produced in the genre. The little plays of the sea, later gathered together under the title *The Moon of the Caribbees* (1919), are sketches of maritime life organized largely by a certain sense of romance, of "poetry." Brevity was an admirable discipline, preventing O'Neill from launching upon the *longueurs* that ruined many of his later works. Though people nowadays think of O'Neill as the author of very long plays, he was in fact one of the many modern playwrights who have difficulty filling up more than one act. A lot of his best work is in the one-act form, and some of his seemingly full-length works are but one-acts slightly extended—I don't necessarily mean padded. *The Emperor Jones* is one of O'Neill's more satisfactory creations. Essentially, it is a long one-act, and the culmination of all his work in the one-act form between 1912 and 1920.*

Anna Christie is a play which proceeded splendidly for one full act but then went to pieces in the effort to become a full-length play. The tragedy of "old davil, sea" and its victory over Chris Christopherson was spoiled by the comedy of Anna and her Irish boy friends. Two one-acts do not make an integrated full-length play, and O'Neill confessed his own dissatisfaction with the result. Nonetheless, *Anna Christie* remains a landmark. Such richly colloquial dialogue had not been heard in the American theatre before. Here the genteel tradition —of Clyde Fitch and the rest—ended, and the rhythm of modern life—in a sense Whitman himself would have recognized—was heard on the New York stage.

O'Neill's dialogue has often been adversely criticized, and not without reason: it is often prosy and ponderous; his ear was not a fastidious one; nor was his knowledge of real dialects—as against stage dialects—particularly sure. Even so he was responsible, more than any other one man, for a change in the tone of stage dialogue in general, and people "talk O'Neill" on the American stage to this day. Such an author as Tennessee Williams may introduce local variations from New Orleans or St. Louis but the basic pattern is still, I think the O'Neillian blend of vernacular with a kind of artifice that wavers between rhetoric and lyricism.

The best commentator on O'Neill's work as a whole, Edwin A. Engel, has shown that evolution is the idea behind both *The Emperor Jones* and *The Hairy Ape* and that, while in the latter we see a man vainly trying to evolve, in the former we see him looking back at the stage he has evolved from. I would add that the Darwinian philosophy is less important than the psychological implication, which is the same in both cases: namely, regression. To be sure, Yank does not regress. It is O'Neill who regresses; and we with him. People who talk lightly of O'Neill the Able Seaman forget that his visits to stokeholes and waterfront dives were the slumming of an ex-Princeton undergraduate and son of a Broadway celebrity. That *this* man chooses to identify himself with Yank and Brutus Jones is what is significant—a maladjusted young Bohemian who, in real life, goes slumming.

To go to sea can be itself the ultimate regression—to go to sea as O'Neill went to sea, not for any practical reason but in evident quest of certain purely

* My topic is dramaturgy. On O'Neill's attitude to Blacks, in this play and *All God's Chillun Got Wings*, there would be more to say. Paul Robeson did star in both.

psychic satisfactions, and particularly, one would think, in quest of the mother he had never (sufficiently) had.

That it is not always desirable for an artist to become too conscious of what he is doing can be amply illustrated from the career of O'Neill's son-in-law, Charles Chaplin. When people explained to Charlie what was going on in his early films he unloaded their explanations into his later films, which, consequently are weighed down with explanations. Though the artist, qua artist, does not explain himself, in our day, explanatoriness has become the besetting sin of the cultural climber: Charlie Chaplin thought by explanations—symbolism, message, philosophy—to come up in the world.

Up to a point, O'Neill's background was similar and his ambition identical. The parents in both cases belonged to the popular theatre. The sons in both cases wanted all this and culture too. Here "culture" means recognition from people who write about such things. Here "people who write about such things" means the critics of those newspapers and magazines who lay down the law. Even if these men were giants of disinterested thought it would not be wise for a Chaplin or an O'Neill to have them constantly in mind. Since by and large what they have is not brains but vested interests, to pay much heed to them can only be a mistake.

The Hairy Ape has many of the merits of *The Emperor Jones* and the first act of *Anna Christie* but also marks the appearance on the scene of Eugene O'Neill the Intellectual. You only need to read it once through to gather that an explanation is expected of you. You only need to read it a second time to discover that the explanation has been supplied by the author in his dialogue. You only need to read it a third time to realize that this is precisely what is wrong with the dialogue. Perhaps for a brilliant reader three readings would not be needed, but for most, surely, the phonetic spelling will conceal for a while the far less uncouth mentality of the author. One cannot help thinking that the uncouth accents are only a device to cover intellectuality. Yank would not have talked about "belonging." The conception comes from the intelligentsia who have talked of nothing else for the past hundred years.

Desire Under the Elms is a better play because it springs more directly from O'Neill's needs and preoccupations. So central is this play that Dr. Weissman has been able to take it as a sort of first draft of *Long Day's Journey into Night*. In other words, it deals with O'Neill's relations with father and mother.

Directly incestuous relationships are avoided, in fiction as in other fantasy, by making the mother-figure only a stepmother. The device is at least as old as Euripides, and is familiar to many of us from Schiller's *Don Carlos*. A modern touch is added by O'Neill, who brings the story nearer to overt incest by stressing that Eben Cabot has a "fixation" on his dead mother—as well as an affair with his live stepmother. That Eben loves both his mothers and hates his father is perhaps not so remarkable in modern writing as that the stepmother murders their child to prove she loves Eben. In the context, there is some logic in this act, because Eben has been told she bore the child only in order to get an inheritance. The murder does disprove the allegation. The question that arises is whether, even so, it is credible. Infanticide is a crime that has often been committed. Nonetheless, few women will kill their child just to prove a point. What is beyond debate is that O'Neill's fantasy gave birth to a woman who commits an atrocity that is not only inhuman but also quite rare because it is quite unfeminine. O'Neill's plays are full of items like this, which are of interest chiefly in relation to their author's life and make-up. Psychoanalysts to the contrary notwithstanding, this is a limitation.

Though it has a flaw near its center, *Desire Under the Elms* remains a superior play because most of the time O'Neill stays well within his emotional range, within the kind of world that is truly *his* world. The landscape is neither pretty nor varied. The father is an Old Testament tyrant recreated with something of the appropriate majesty. If in many later plays O'Neill tends toward the overabstract, here the father is not derived from a bare idea. He seems to grow from the soil. The soil is given a reality, not, to be sure, through true local color, or sensitivity to the life around him, but by a curiously vivid sense of the bovine which O'Neill found, surely, in some marshy tract, not of New England, but of his soul. It is a nauseating play, but nausea is at least a thing of the senses, and one must grant that O'Neill at his best could communicate strong emotions, particularly negative ones. I am not even convinced that the negative emotions he most readily commanded are those he has been praised for commanding, such as terror. Are they not, rather, the mean and masochistic feelings? One may admire *Desire Under the Elms,* but one can hardly relish it.

III

O'Neill's more ardent admirers have been admirers above all of his second phase (1925–1934). The rest of us feel compelled to regret that this phase ever happened, vain as it always is to scold artists or tell them, even beforehand, that they mustn't do what their hearts are set on doing.

I have stressed that playwriting was for O'Neill something much different from what it is for your Broadway entertainer. It may be well to elaborate at this stage a point of Dr. Weissman's. O'Neill was so disturbed in the period 1909–1912 that he kept alternately fleeing from and returning to his father. That activity constitutes neurotic "acting out" and nearly went as far as suicide. Then it subsided considerably. Why? Presumably because O'Neill, in 1912, took up writing. At first he wrote precisely about the voyages and the returns, a theme, which, for that matter, he would revert to later. The career of O'Neill should interest those who see a connection between art and neurosis, and it would indicate that art is not so much a symptom as an attempt at cure. O'Neill was never cured—which of us is?—and he deserted wives—one in 1909, it is true, but one also in the middle twenties—as he had deserted parents. Yet it is quite tenable that only his writing kept O'Neill going at all. And why did it? Not, obviously, because it was art, but because it seemed a weapon in a personal battle. Everything we know about O'Neill suggests that he never emerged from the Oedipus conflict but remained in the immature and adolescent relation to both father and mother.

What O'Neill did was to take Victorian melodrama and add. When what he added was chiefly his own personal vehemence—as attached to his own complexes—the result could be impressive and even unpretentious. When he added more than this, the result was to many even more impressive—and very pretentious indeed. The *New York Times* was impressed. Which is to say that middle-brow culture was impressed, as well it might be, for what had O'Neill added to melodrama but the stock of ideas and attitudes which constitute middle-brow culture? O'Neill may have flunked out of Princeton but, down the years, he had been reading, reading, reading, and was now a rather formidable autodidact. He had a theory of theatre which I for one am so far from taking issue with that, on the contrary, I would applaud nearly all of it.

What was this theory? We have seen that O'Neill wanted to reintroduce the powerful emotions fearlessly. That perhaps was the main wish, and one that could not harm him unless he had it too much in his *head*. He also saw through the cult of character—the schoolteacher's idea that playwrights must portray "individuals, not types"—and realized that even better than "individuals" are archetypes. He also realized that no kind of character—even an archetypal one—is enough, that the playwright should try to get at "the Force Beyond," at the part of the world that is *not* contained in the characters themselves, and at the problem which Goethe himself thought transcended all problems, that of belief.

In short, Eugene O'Neill saw through not only the tawdry everyday commercial theatre of his father's time but also through the drab or homey naturalistic theatre of his own time and ours. Like most autodidacts, he had a nose, too, for the kind of reading that would mean most to him, and this nose led him unerringly to the philosopher who, of all philosophers, has entered most deeply into the spirit of tragedy, and who also happens to be the philosopher who laid the foundations of modern psychological understanding: Friedrich Nietzsche. One result of all this thinking of O'Neill's, and all this reading, was that he was able to reinvent Expressionism on his own. For I believe we can take him at his word when he tells us he knew very little of the German Expressionists. There is ironic justice in the fact that one of the German Expressionists considered *Lazarus Laughed* the best of all Expressionist plays.

Unfortunately, all this proves no more than that Eugene O'Neill came to some good conclusions. No number of good conclusions will make a good play. And he also came to some bad conclusions. More precisely, he came to adopt an outlook which could affect actual playwriting—for the worse. There is no word for this outlook that I know of. I will call it psychologism. It proceeds by substituting notions about people's minds for actual observation of people's minds and contact with them.

Now an artist can often get by with very few formulations, provided he enjoys very lively contact with people. He need not *know* what people are like but he certainly need *sense* what they are like, and he certainly must be able to communicate that sense. O'Neill came to maturity in the era of psychologism. Freud was then—as now, I suppose—chiefly a fad. One had to know his name. One had to bandy Freudian phraseology, actual or supposed. O'Neill had some canniness, it is true, and tried to avoid being a faddist. He denied having read much Freud. But in that atmosphere nonreading was insufficient protection. Freud was "in the air." Worse: Jung was in the air. Then too, O'Neill said he *had* read Jung.

More important than the leading psychologists were the hundreds of nonleaders whose books and articles flooded the market. One of O'Neill's closest associates, Kenneth MacGowan, was coauthor, with Dr. G. V. Hamilton, of a psychiatric treatise, *What Is Wrong with Marriage?* The heading for a chapter entitled "Oedipus Rex" reads: "Evidence that supports Freud's dictum of the part the mother-image plays in a man's choice of his wife . . . The happiest group of men have wives on the mother-pattern. Yet the fear of inbreeding makes men marry away from the mother." The next chapter is headed by the words: ". . . fear of incest, added to the fear of inbreeding, makes the women even less fortunate than the men in their marriage choices." This chapter is entitled "The Tragedy of Electra."

When Malcolm Cowley visited O'Neill in 1923, the latter

> picked up a green textbook-type volume from the table and explained that it was William Stekel's treatise on sexual aberrations, *The Disguises of Love,* recently translated from the German. He said there were enough case histories in the book to furnish plots to all the playwrights who ever lived. He turned to a case history of a mother who seduced her only son and drove him insane.

The poet Meredith wrote: "passions spin the plot." It was left to O'Neill to imagine that case histories spin the plot. There could be no more clear-cut example of the kind of half-baked thinking that mars his work. *Strange Interlude* stands condemned right there: it is a gigantic appendix to Dr. Hamilton's *A Research in Marriage.* "My husband is unable to give me a healthy child. What shall I do?" In the spirit of the lady columnist running her readers' private lives, O'Neill writes out not, to be sure, what we *should* do but what Dr. Hamilton or Dr. Stekel says we *have* done.

I do not find *Strange Interlude* boring. Though not low-brow, it is soap opera, and soap opera doesn't have to be boring, it only has to be foolish. Soap opera larded—or should one say lathered?—with would-be serious and up-to-date ideas is doubly foolish. The solemn farce got its deserved comeuppance when Groucho Marx—was it in *Animal Crackers?*—did an imitation of its manner.

Groucho used the comedian's privilege of attacking the weakest spot, which was the device of asides placed at the service of psychologism. The things that people think and don't say were written into the dialogue as long and numerous asides, delivered while everyone on stage stood petrified. The petrifaction would have been bearable had the monologues been bearable, but the principle behind the latter was simple-minded. It was that when a man is saying to a woman, "I love you!" he is murmuring to himself, "No I don't, I hate you, you bitch!" Of which the reverse form, even commoner in O'Neill, is: "I hate you, you bitch!" followed by: "Oh, what a cad I am, I don't hate her at all, I love her!" If, as one might certainly maintain, ambivalence is the main theme of O'Neill's writing, as of his life, this is no adequate way to present it.

What about the mask? It is the very prototype of theatrical artifices, and it was O'Neill's idea that it could be used to express ambivalence. For example, a mask may express innocence, while the face is haunted with guilt; a mask may exude confidence, while the face exudes timidity. This is one of a very few ideas by which *The Great God Brown* stands or falls. It proved more interesting in discussion than effective in the theatre. So did the idea of having two actors play opposing sides of the same man in *Days Without End* (première 1934).

More of course was involved than technical devices. The plays of O'Neill's middle period were a very bold attempt to realize on the stage the vision of theatre of O'Neill's generation. This was particularly the vision of three of his close associates, George Cram Cook, Robert Edmond Jones, and Kenneth MacGowan. Jones was the most gifted American stage designer of his day. He and MacGowan had toured the European theatres shortly after World War I and had returned to write and rhapsodize about "the theatre of tomorrow." Like all such dreams, this one had a good deal to do with yesterday. It had specifically to do with Wagner and Nietzsche, Adolphe Appia and Gordon Craig. The vision was of a release from realism, a release upward, as it were, toward the sublime and downward toward the instinctual. Cook's particular enthusiasm was Greece. It is Cook whom O'Neill is echoing when he speaks, in a letter, of the Greek dream being the noblest of them all. The word "dream" recurs a good deal, and the reference is less to Freud than to Apollo, whom Nietzsche regarded as a symbol of the dream world in contrast to Dionysus, who stood for drunkenness. The word "Dionysus" recurs even oftener. Bred a Catholic, and educated in popular Hellenism by Cook and others, O'Neill liked to see life as a conflict between the ascetic and the pagan spirit. Hence the name of the hero of *The Great God Brown,* Dion Anthony—Dionysus the drunken God and Anthony the ascetic saint. Closely related to Dionysus is "the great god Pan," with whom O'Neill contrasts the American businessman of the Babbitt era—the great god Brown.

One can only say of these antitheses what I have already said about O'Neill's whole theory of drama. In themselves they are splendid and full of possibilities. Very similar antitheses underlie tragic art of the greatest epochs. It was a contemporary of Shakespeare's who wrote:

> O wearisome condition of humanity!
> Born under one law, to another bound,
> Vainly begot and yet forbidden vanity,
> Created sick, commanded to be sound.
> What meaneth nature by these diverse laws,
> Passion and reason, self-division's cause?

And it was certainly permissible for O'Neill to champion passion against reason—instead of reason against passion as the Elizabethans had done. This he was inclined to do in the middle twenties when he took a Nietzschean position. Once, in the early thirties, he seemed, rather, to champion Anthony against Dionysus in a play that ends in reconciliation with the Catholic Church, *Days Without End.* But this was a momentary point of rest, not a final conclusion.

The question was never of the permissibility of the ideas themselves but of O'Neill's ability to handle them—or, more exactly, of their suitability to the kind of work which he could do in art. In *Hamlet* the conflict between passion and reason is deeply sunk in an Action as well as in characters inwardly felt. Neither passion nor reason have to be mentioned by name, and, when they are, we do not have an embarrassing feeling of "There goes the main theme again." This embarrassing feeling is just what we do have in *Strange Interlude* when we hear:

> a lot to account for, Herr Freud! . . . punishment to fit his crimes, be forced to listen eternally during breakfast while innumerable plain ones tell him dreams about snakes . . . pah, what an easy cure-all! . . . sex the philosopher's stone . . . "O Oedipus, O my king! The world is adopting you!" . . .

and:

> she has strange devious intuitions that tap the hidden currents of life . . . dark intermingling currents that become the one stream of desire . . .

and:

> Perhaps he realizes subconsciously that I am his father, his rival in your love; but I'm not his father ostensibly, there are no taboos, so he can come right out and hate me . . .

and:

> Yes, perhaps unconsciously Preston is a compensating substitute.

and:

> I was only a body to you . . . I was never more to you than a substitute for your dead lover!

and:

> I can remember that day seeing her kiss him . . . it did something to me I never got over.

These passages prompt the question: In what way should literature be psychological? It is good that great writers should be psychologically deep, and that Freud should say so, but is it good that an artist should read Freud and reproduce him? Is it good that characters should sum themselves up, should spend their time diagnosing themselves—and everyone else? That, by consequence, human character should come to the audience in the form of summation and diagnosis? On the contrary, it is a disaster. The drama should provide an image of experience and character such as might be analyzed later. To begin with analysis is to put the cart before the horse—with the same result: immobility.

What is true of psychological ideas is true of all ideas in drama. The playwright Hebbel put it with witty overstatement: "In drama, no character should ever utter a thought: from the thought in a play come the speeches of *all* the characters." Now, if this principle applies to the relatively modest ideas of *Strange Interlude,* how much more is it called for when we confront *The Great God Brown* and *Lazarus Laughed*! So little are the ideas of these plays sunk in the action and the characters that neither action nor characters have any effective existence except to illustrate the ideas. And if there are obscurities, as in *The Great God Brown* there certainly are, they are cleared up not by more work on action or character but by a letter to the newspapers explaining the philosophy and the symbolism.

Lazarus Laughed is probably the most ambitious American play ever written by a gifted playwright. It cries out to be compared with the work which presumably prompted its writing, Nietzsche's *Thus Spake Zarathustra.* ("This book," writes O'Neill's second wife, Agnes Boulton, "had more influence on Gene than any other single book he ever read. It was a sort of Bible to him, and he kept it by his bedside. . . .") Both works would ring out an old era, and

ring in a new. Both authors would denounce the old era with the terrifying finality of a Jeremiah and, in hailing the new, reach the highest peaks of ecstasy.
Nietzsche, however, was a master of ideas, and was not attempting drama. In
Lazarus the ideas are too few and too grandiose ever to become active and interesting, while not enough is done by way of dialogue, action, and character to
give us a real play. And if O'Neill had not had much success in depicting self-
division, it was a false way out that he found in *Lazarus* when he picked a hero
who was not divided.

O'Neill's Lazarus has little to do with the Biblical character and a great deal
to do with the Greek god whom Nietzsche had already opposed to Christ:
Dionysus. Following Nietzsche, O'Neill takes Christianity to be life-denial, the
religion of Dionysus to be life-worship. One worships life and denies death. In
that perhaps rather peculiar sense, one believes in immortality. "The fear of
death," O'Neill wrote,

> is the root of all evil, the cause of all man's blundering unhappiness. Lazarus
> knows there is no death, there is only change. He is reborn without that
> fear. Therefore he is the first and only man who is able to laugh affirma-
> tively. His laughter is a triumphant Yes to life. . . . And life itself is the
> self-affirmative joyous laughter of God.

Whatever we make of this as philosophy, we can hardly make much of it as
theatre or psychology. Theatrically, O'Neill asks laughter to do more than laughter *can* do. For an actor to be laughing so often and so loudly when he isn't
even amused is to court confusion, even assuming he can keep it up. Laughter
is not a pretty noise or a majestic one, a fact that is related to the psychic side.
Laughter is not a suitable symbol of, or outlet for, affirmation because there is so
much about it that is inherently and unmistakably negative. Laughter sounds
aggressive for the good reason that it *is* aggressive. It is impossible to hear roars
of laughter in which one is not personally involved without wishing to shut
them up.

O'Neill was not always kind to his audience. *The Iceman Cometh* opens with
a lot of men asleep on stage. In the theatre, sleep is contagious, and some audiences have at once dozed off. Did O'Neill hate not only his family but his public? Lazarus's laughter would prove very annoying. Was that O'Neill's unconscious intention? If so, it is a pity that no conscious intention interfered. It is
hard to resist the conclusion that O'Neill sometimes liked to flout his own theatre sense because he identified it with his father. If the laughter of Lazarus
stems from thought, it is an instance of the way in which a playwright should
not be a thinker.

Though not more ambitious, *Mourning Becomes Electra* is a much longer
play than *Lazarus Laughed* and is ambitious enough to invite the comparison
with Aeschylus. Some of the most respected critics of the time, such as George

Jean Nathan and Joseph Wood Krutch, thought it could sustain the comparison. For a time it was possible for many intelligent people to think of this play as at least one of the supreme American masterpieces like, say, *Moby Dick* or *The Scarlet Letter*. Today there is no need to take issue with an opinion which is gone with the wind: it can serve only to educate us in the ways of the world. And there is an interesting human and historical problem: what was it about *Mourning Becomes Electra* that at first made a big impression and later did not?

The idea behind the play is that of an equivalent in terms of Freudian, or perhaps Jungian, psychology to the *Oresteia* of Aeschylus: an equivalent and, following the reasoning of the man in street, an improvement. As Croswell Bowen puts it, *"Electra* is based on sound modern concepts of psychological and biological cause and effect, not upon the inspiration of the Furies." It is certainly based on concepts. That may be the main trouble. Whether these concepts are so much sounder than Aeschylus is also open to debate. They are certainly more depressing. The *Oresteia* celebrates the establishment of community: it shows the rule of law take the place of the vendetta. *Mourning Becomes Electra* shows the vendetta going on and on and on. In place of the liberating, creative, and inspiring ideas of Aeschylus come ideas that at best are sobering.

The key terms reverse their meanings. Where Aeschylus describes a curse that can be lifted in the name of a justice that is real and that can be assured by a human nature not wholly lacking in wisdom, for O'Neill living is itself a curse, death is a release, and justice is not the opposite of revenge but the same thing.

The psychology of *Mourning Becomes Electra* runs as thin as the philosophy. One thing leads to another in all too naïve and mechanical a way. It is as if a couple of psychoanalytic concepts, taken in ridiculously simple form, were held sufficient to demonstrate what tragic life is like. Daughters, for example, hate their mothers and love their fathers. This must have seemed a thrillingly novel idea in 1931, or how could anyone have thought O'Neill's presentation of it anything but monotonous? To do without the Furies is nothing but a loss if all you put in their place is the rhetoric of psychologism.

Orin grows to resemble his father, and Lavinia her mother. Such a development comes under the heading, in psychiatry, of "psychotic identification," and it seems that O'Neill has been "confirmed" by recent medical writers. Dr. Weissman congratulates him on his insight, but is it so remarkable? Isn't this particular "insight" in the logic of the whole argument? Isn't it also very much in the spirit of melodrama? And finally, do such "insights," however correct, constitute dramatic art?

Insofar as any big play can be summed up in a sentence, cannot *Mourning Becomes Electra* be summed up in this one: Eugene O'Neill feels that people wish to kill each other? O'Neill seems to have been imbued with hatred as Saint Francis, say, or Gandhi was imbued with love, but how creative is mere hatred, even in art? Certainly, it is permissible for O'Neill to keep inventing people who kill each other or want to, but isn't it equally permissible for us to wonder that they don't have any other interests?

The question sounds like a jibe, and those who leap to O'Neill's defense might ask if one could not wonder the same about the frantic characters of Strindberg and Dostoevski. I doubt it. The world of Dostoevski's people, and even of Strindberg's, is a far larger one than that of O'Neill's. The Captain in Strindberg's *The Father* is a scientist and his intellectuality is made quite real to us. The Captain's fury attains to full dramatic force just because we have been made to feel his love of knowledge. Does not every author who presents the negative side have to make us feel the positive side even if he never shows it? Is an artist ever really a monomaniac? Must he not always be able to *imagine* an alternative even if he does not propose one? Dostoevski often did propose one. Not all his characters are possessed, unless one were to say that some are possessed by Christian love. O'Neill sometimes presents an alternative—but inadequately. The few characters not propelled downward by the death wish are mere dummies. Peter and Hazel, in *Mourning Becomes Electra*, are examples.

For all his reading, O'Neill remained horrifyingly barbaric. Culture existed for him, it would seem, only as those books he lifted ideas from and in no degree as culture—the cultivation of the spirit and the tradition among men of such cultivation. In this respect, *Mourning Becomes Electra* stands at the opposite pole not only from the Greeks but from such characteristic attempts to revive Greek tragedy in modern times as Goethe's *Iphigenia in Tauris*. There, the poet's search was expressly for whatever in the myth might tend to the schooling of man and the taming of the beast in him—whatever might tend to the enhancement of life in possible sweetness and grace. Reading or seeing Goethe's play, we enter his mind and find it a spacious and truly edifying dwelling place. The paradox of *Mourning Becomes Electra* is that O'Neill took up a great testament of humane culture in order to spit in the face of humanity.

How is it no one said so? People bring such charges against authors much less guilty of them. Obviously, if O'Neill's points got across at all they did not carry a sting—which is to say they did not carry conviction. For when all is said against O'Neill's ideas, it must yet be admitted that such ideas might have gone to the making of very powerful drama. They did so when Wagner used them. (For is not the "tragic philosophy" of *Mourning Becomes Electra* much less that of Nietzsche than of Nietzsche's archenemy, the author of *Tristan and Isolde* and *The Nibelung's Ring?*) If initially one tends to reject this *Electra* because of the view of life it presents, one rejects it even more emphatically because it does not get this view across the footlights.

We are now perhaps in a position to answer the question as to what people were impressed by back in 1931: not by the nihilistic view of life, which did not come home to men's business and bosoms, but merely by the rhetoric of psychologism. One might not know exactly what the main intent was but certainly much of the talk in scene after scene was close enough to the talk at the cocktail party before the show. Now even dead ideas can seem to come alive in a play when they happen to be alive in the current conversation of the public, and surely such ideas—though they may not be the main themes of the plays —come up in all the plays of O'Neill's middle period. They return to their graves as soon as they are no longer part of the current chatter, "the new small talk."

IV

By 1930, the success story was written: Eugene O'Neill was far more prominent in the American theatre than his father had ever been and a Nobel Prize winner, Sinclair Lewis, was telling the Swedish Academy that:

> had you chosen Mr. O'Neill who has done nothing much in American drama save to transform it utterly in ten or twelve years from a false world of neat and competent trickery to a world of splendor and fear and greatness, you would have been reminded that he has done something far worse than scoffing—he has seen life as not to be neatly arranged in the study of a scholar but as a terrifying, magnificent, and often quite horrible thing akin to the tornado, the earthquake, and the devastating fire.

How to survive such praise? After the success of *Mourning Becomes Electra,* what O'Neill attempted was to re-enter his past. In *Ah Wilderness!* (première 1933) he based a play upon that same New London summer of 1912 which later would yield *Long Day's Journey into Night.* After reading both plays, one comes to doubt that O'Neill meant even the latter to be pure autobiography. In any case, it is almost incredible that both plays present the same O'Neill in the same year. In neither play does he see himself as the actual twenty-three-year-old who was already a father and was in the process of being divorced. In *Ah Wilderness!* he sees himself as an adolescent and a virgin, dreams of belonging to a regular American home in a regular American town, and so relives the kind of childhood he had never lived in the first place. In *Days Without End* he dreams himself back into the Church of his fathers. Incidentally, the priest he consulted on theological matters got no impression that O'Neill wanted more than to dream. The two plays belong to a moment of wistful pause, and perhaps of hesitation, before O'Neill embarked upon the most grandiose of his grandiose schemes: a cycle of plays in which he would write the spiritual history of his country. Six of these plays were undoubtedly completed, and five others planned. But in 1953 O'Neill sat down with his wife in the Hotel Shelton in

Boston and tore up all the finished plays. "We tore them up bit by bit, together," says Mrs. O'Neill, "I helped him because his hands—he had this terrific tremor, he could tear just a few pages at a time. It was awful. It was like tearing up children."

Why Mrs. O'Neill cooperated in the tearing up of O'Neill's children shall remain, for the present at least, her business. A writer's life, on the other hand, belongs to the world, and the world has already speculated on Eugene O'Neill's reasons. All he said was: "I don't want anyone else finishing up a play of mine." But the plays, says Mrs. O'Neill, *were* finished—except for cutting. It is impossible not to connect this terrible act—which any fellow writer feels in the pit of his stomach—with O'Neill's many other destructive acts. He had killed himself as son, as father, and several times as husband—why not also as writer?

Everything that happened since the plays of the early thirties remains somewhat mysterious despite the labors of the biographers. O'Neill had lived the life of a wealthy man ever since he *became* a wealthy man in the early twenties. If he changed now, it was mainly to let it be known that he was going off— presumably forever—to work on the giant project. He seems to have worked on it regularly until 1939, and to have resumed it with less assiduity several years later. Shortly before the end of World War II O'Neill had a stroke. Afterward a tremor of the hands which he had had for some time was much more marked, and he could not write. Echoing Mrs. O'Neill, I have already said that since he could not compose orally his writing days were over. This is an incomplete statement. Many men would have gradually learned to compose orally. Mrs. O'Neill says, "He died when he could no longer work—spiritually died and was dragging the poor diseased body along for a few more years until it too died." This does not explain why his will to work was insufficient to overcome his aversion to dictation. One must assume that this will was already dead or dying. Following such a clue, one might then move backward into the mysterious years when the Cycle was being written. Did the plays of the Cycle, when finished, disappoint O'Neill? One, *A Touch of the Poet,* has survived and is certainly not among, say, his dozen best plays. Did the Cycle, in O'Neill's opinion, deserve to be destroyed? He seems never to have expressed the opinion that it was, as it was meant to be, the crown of his writing career. Could it be that most of the writing he did in California did not represent his further development as a playwright but a progressive withdrawal from the theatre, a long day's journey into night? This is not a conclusion drawn by Dr. Weissman but he provides evidence for it.

If O'Neill's "love affair with the world" was over, he sometimes longed for his old mistress, and we find him dropping the Cycle in 1939 and writing two of his best plays: *The Iceman Cometh* and *Long Day's Journey into Night*— as well as *A Moon for the Misbegotten,* which is by no means one of his worst. To think of O'Neill's "final period" will always be to think of *The Iceman* and *Journey*.

Both are explorations of the year 1912. Neither is merely a memoir. *Long Day's Journey* does seem wholly a memoir the first time one reads it; at least it did when the facts of O'Neill's background were not yet public knowledge. One read the play with amazement at what the O'Neills went through. Dr. Weissman soon pointed out that O'Neill had omitted facts of the utmost relevance, such as that Edmund is not represented as a father and divorcé. Dr. Weissman conjectures that these facts had been "repressed," and thinks that Barrett Clark also did a little "repressing" in his biography. This conjecture I find uncalled for. Clark said what he was allowed to say, and tried to give the impression he was supposed to give. O'Neill never stated that *Long Day's Journey* was pure history, and he was a good enough playwright to know that history and drama must ever be distinct. O'Neill "played" with the facts of 1912 in no less than four dramas—*Hughie* is the only one not already mentioned here—and always in a different style, always with a different angle on the facts. In *Long Day's Journey* the camera is still at an angle to the subject, though admittedly a less oblique one.

If O'Neill was nihilistic in his views, and Bohemian in some of his conduct, he was not disorderly in his work. Indeed his work spelled order for him, just as it spelled somewhat better mental health. *The Iceman Cometh* and *Long Day's Journey,* prompted to some extent by the outbreak of World War II, were islands of order in the sea of a personal and more than personal chaos.

Long Day's Journey is a kind of classical quartet. Here O'Neill eschews the luxury of numerous minor characters, crowds, and a bustle of stage activity. He has a few people and they talk. This has given the public an impression of shapelessness. Bowen says, "The play is essentially plotless . . . the deliberate formlessness of it all is enervating. Still, it is a dramatic achievement of the first order. . . ." A biographer—in this case at least—is not a critic, or one might ask him how a piece of enervating formlessness can be a dramatic achievement of the first order. *Long Day's Journey* is a dramatic achievement which at first glance *seems* formless. Later, one discovers the form. The play has the outward calm and formality—not formlessness!—of French classical tragedies. Like them, and like *The Iceman,* it observes the unities. The form reveals itself in the interrelationship of people. The principal relationship here (dramaturgically speaking at least) is that between Edmund and his mother. The classical dramatist has to pull together on one day events which in actuality happened over a longer period. O'Neill found his action and his drama in the —presumably fictitious—coincidence of Mary's final relapse into drug addiction with the discovery of Edmund's tuberculosis. But a situation is only a premise of drama, not its realization. Before we have drama, the situation must move, and the dramatist must have discovered what makes it move. In *Long*

Day's Journey Edmund has come to the point where he needs his mother very much. He is moving toward her. And only a short while ago he would have had a chance. But she has now relapsed, with an obvious finality, into drug addiction. She too is moving. She is moving away from Edmund, away from everyone. She is moving to the point—reached during the play as its culmination—where no one can reach her any more. That Mary moves away just when Edmund moves toward her is—in terms of dynamics—what makes possible the play and enables O'Neill to rescue it from "formlessness."

Admittedly, this is to speak only of two of the four main characters. Before the play is over we have got inside each of the four. As people, James, Sr., and James, Jr., may be just as salient: in the dramatic structure, as I see it, they are subordinated to Mary and Edmund because the action turns on the question: What is happening to the latter pair?

Sincerity has done far more for O'Neill in this drama than ambition could ever do for him in the "big" plays of the second period. In the handling of ambivalence, for example. Had it ever really been necessary to invent devices to show the phenomenon? The method O'Neill used in the later play was to work through to his feelings, and then let them speak. It is the hard kind of sincerity, and he must surely have been gratified to see how—under this dispensation—a character can turn from expressing his hate to expressing love without any kind of device at all. It "just happens."

The process called "working through" implies deliberately living through an experience a second time, to the end of understanding and liberation. If Aristotle's word catharsis implies a sort of thorough cleaning out of the emotional system, then it exaggerates what normally happens to us at the theatre, even when there's a tragedy on. Perhaps it is not spectators but authors who experience catharsis. Mrs. O'Neill has given the following account of the composition of *Long Day's Journey:*

> He came in and talked to me all night. . . . He explained to me then that he had to write this play. He had to write it because it was a thing that haunted him. . . . I think he felt freer when he got it out of his system. It was his way of making peace with his family and himself.

Catharsis, if I understand what Aristotle meant, is a matter of physical and mental health, but I cannot hold wholly mistaken the now discredited view that he may also have had moral considerations in mind. Whether or not Aristotle had them in mind, moral considerations do at once come up. Catharsis means purgation, and purgation is purgatorial. After it, if one is lucky, one is ready for heaven. It is the road on which a man learns to forgive.

The deeply human thing about this often inhuman artist, Eugene O'Neill, is his concern to be forgiven—and to be capable of forgiving. The absence of catharsis is a notable, and ugly, feature of the "big" plays. As Engel has put it, instead of catharsis, O'Neill proposes narcosis or necrosis. Not that even *Long Day's Journey* ends with anyone on stage actually forgiving anyone. Their journey is truly into night, not into love, but the dignity of the ending lies in what is *not* said. There throbs in the final speech that sense of an alternative, that sense of having lived and of having deserved to live, which I deplored the absence of in the "big" plays:

I had a talk with Mother Elizabeth [says Mary Tyrone]. . . . I told her I wanted to be a nun. I explained how sure I was of my vocation, that I had prayed to the Blessed Virgin to make me sure and to find me worthy. I told Mother I had had a true vision when I was praying in the shrine of Our Lady of Lourdes on the little island in the lake. I said I knew as surely as I knew I was kneeling there that the Blessed Virgin had smiled and blessed me with her consent. But Mother Elizabeth told me I must be more sure than that, that I must prove it wasn't my imagination. She said, if I was so sure, then I wouldn't mind putting myself to a test by going home after I graduated and living as other girls lived, going out to parties and dances and enjoying myself, and then if after a year or two I still felt sure, I could come back to see her and we would talk it over again. I never dreamed Holy Mother would give me such advice! I was really shocked. I said of course I would do anything she suggested but I knew it was simply a waste of time. After I left her, I felt all mixed up, so I went to the shrine and prayed to the Blessed Virgin and found peace again because I knew she heard my prayer and would always love me and see no harm ever came to me as I never lost my faith in her. That was in the winter of senior year. Then in the spring something happened to me. Yes, I remember. I fell in love with James Tyrone and was so happy for a time.

V

The Iceman Cometh was almost as much of a new departure for O'Neill as *Long Day's Journey,* and it is equally the end of a long day's journey for the author. It marks the end of his voyagings after new forms and a "theatre of tomorrow." Here, finally, O'Neill settles for the theatre of yesterday. The form of *The Iceman* is conservative and contains nothing that would have surprised his father. The Jones-MacGowan rejection of realism is itself rejected. We are back with the kind of theatre of low life which Gorky envisaged for his *Lower Depths.* Gorky's naturalism was not, however, the dramaturgic model. There is nothing episodic about *The Iceman.* The structure is unified and, though large, almost symmetrical. It is possible that O'Neill was compulsive in this, and allowed himself too little freedom. Note the stage manager's pedantry with which he lays down in a lengthy stage direction just where everyone is to sit!

This is how I summarized the main action of the play in my book *In Search of Theatre:*

> There is Hickey, and there is Parritt. Both are pouring out their false confessions and professions, and holding back their essential secret. Yet, inexorably, though against their conscious will, both are seeking punishment. Their two stories are brought together through Larry Slade whose destiny, in contrast to his intention, is to extract the secret of both protagonists. Hickey's secret explodes, and Larry at last gives Parritt what he wants: a death sentence. The upshot of the whole action is that Larry is brought from a posturing and oratorical pessimism to a real despair. . . . Larry is . . . the centre of the play, and the audience can watch the two stories being played out before him.

The summary is accurate enough, but what strikes me after a ten-year interval is that it betokens more interest in the intellectual than in the emotional dynamics of the play. I continued:

> The main ideas are two: . . . that people may as well keep their illusions; second, that one should not hate and punish but love and forgive. . . . In a way the truth-illusion theme is a red herring, and . . . the author's real interest is in the love-hate theme. . . . O'Neill is unclear . . . it is his play, and not life, that is unintelligible.

I now think that the play becomes more intelligible if we follow up this hint: "the author's real interest is in the love-hate theme." Hickey really hated his wife, as Parritt really hated his mother. These are the repressed truths which it is the function of the action to bring to the light of day. In Hickey's case:

> I remember I heard myself speaking to her, as if it was something I'd always wanted to say: "Well, you know what you can do with your pipe dream now, you damned bitch!"

The implication could hardly be clearer, yet what follows can be confusing. "Good God," Hickey cries, "I couldn't have said that! If I did, I'd gone insane! Why, I loved Evelyn. . . ." The idea appeals to Harry Hope. It gives him an "out." It gives all the men an "out." It enables them to discount all that has happened and return to their pipe dreams. Hickey is taken aback at this turn of events. After all, had he not embarked on his long, long narrative with exactly the opposite purpose in mind: finally to persuade them to abandon their dreams? He starts to object: "I see what you're driving at, but I can't let you get away with—" Then he thinks twice about it and, after a pause, gives in: "I *was* insane." He has decided to let them keep their dreams after all. Why? It is not a simple question. Ten years ago I would probably have answered: because he now sees the need which weak people have of illusions, for I thought of the play as a footnote to Ibsen's *The Wild Duck*. Today, I would find the clue in O'Neill's own stage direction: "Harry Hope's expression turns to resentful callousness again." It is to check this "resentful callousness" that Hickey agrees to be considered insane. Ten years ago, I wrote: Hickey "is a maniac," and there is a case for applying such a word to men who murder their wives under the illusion that they love them. Nonetheless, the dramatic point is different. Hickey regards himself as sane, but is willing to be regarded as insane by the others, so that Harry Hope will stop being "resentfully callous" to him. We are back with the love-hate theme.

And there is a whole dimension of *The Iceman Cometh* about which I find nothing in my earlier account of the play: the drama of love and hate, merely recounted in the speeches of Hickey and Parritt, is re-enacted in the drama of this very recounting. One recounts *to* someone. This play presents what Theodore Reik calls the "compulsion to confess." The intent of Hickey's confession —whose weight and position make it the climax—as of his previous shorter declarations, is to bring "peace." The source of this peace is his supposed love for Evelyn. But where previously, before the men tried unsuccessfully to drop their dreams, Hickey's speech-making did elicit love—made this well-liked salesman even better liked—now they are all angry at him. They hate him. And Hickey, like many O'Neill characters, if not all, is a man completely at the mercy of other people's love and hate. As Evelyn's love drove him to hate and kill her, so the men's hate drives him to declare himself insane—and rush toward the electric chair.

Aristotle said that the chorus should be regarded as a character in the play. The men in Jimmy the Priest's are the chorus of this play, and a way of looking at the action perhaps just as valid as the one I have quoted from myself would be to take it as arising from the reciprocal relationship of Hickey and the chorus. Nowhere more than in the scene where the men rise up and try to make a new life do we feel the power of O'Neill's playwriting. We see, as various critics have noticed with approval, a pipe dream take shape before us. But is that just an incidental bit of virtuosity? Is not the chorus equally important—and dramatic—in the final scene?

An analogy can be drawn between *The Iceman Cometh* and *Lazarus Laughed*. If they are very different, it may well be because the pattern has been exactly, and perhaps deliberately, reversed. *Lazarus* was O'Neill's attempt to affirm life and love, and put down death and hate. Most of his life, as in *The Iceman Cometh*, death and hate dominated his thoughts and seemed to him to dominate the world: it is no bridegroom that cometh with love,* it is an iceman—bringing death. As for love, it is only lust—as is implied by pop-

---

* "Behold, the bridegroom cometh" (Matt. 25:6). In the Biblical context, the bridegroom himself symbolizes death, and the moral drawn is *memento mori:* "Watch therefore, for ye know neither the day nor the hour wherein the Son of man cometh."

ular sayings concerning housewives and their affairs with icemen. Now if we have in mind these two contrasting attitudes to life and death, we can take Lazarus and Hickey as corresponding figures. Both are salesmen to a clientele. Lazarus is selling love and everlasting life; Hickey is selling hate and everlasting death, but where Lazarus is candid, Hickey claims to be selling—precisely what Lazarus is selling! The earlier play is direct; the later, ironical. This is one factor, I believe, that makes *The Iceman* the superior play, and it would seem that O'Neill's natural bent was toward what is called "realism," for what seems awkward and "arty" about the chorus in *Lazarus* falls into place in the everyday setting of *The Iceman*.

That the average spectator at *The Iceman* is not forced to think of a "chorus" at all but can just think of men shows something good about the play. At the same time, those who wish to explore O'Neill's mind cannot but be interested in the Nietzschean intention behind the "realistic" disguise. The Dionysian element is still large—even if it appears under the form of alcoholism or a birthday party or the euphoria of a drummer's "pitch" with its background of Midwestern revivalism. The chorus remains an integral part of the drama and has its own curve of action. As in *Lazarus Laughed,* the crowd is excited and inflamed by a Savior, only later to be disenchanted. They end in *Lazarus* shouting, "Hail to Death!" They end in *The Iceman,* first in complaints, and then in the noisy relief of a return to pipe dreams.

In this way, *The Iceman Cometh* is seen to have its own peculiar emotional dynamics, and the ending effects a negative catharsis: the expenditure of emotion leads not to a new beginning but to the admission of exhaustion. There is something audacious and almost Quixotic about the application of so much histrionic ingenuity to such negative ends. "Life's a tragedy, hurrah!" the young O'Neill used to say in humorous acknowledgment of a contradiction that vitiated all his thought. It is futile enough to profess pessimism in any art—but above all, perhaps, in the drama. For a play cannot but be playful.

If in *Long Day's Journey* O'Neill transcends his usual vision, *The Iceman Cometh* is the quintessence of O'Neillism. I have already tried to show how the word "justice" loses its meaning in O'Neill's world. Of necessity, the word "punishment" must also lose. If by justice, O'Neill means only revenge, by punishment he means only inflicted suffering—as when a boxer "takes a lot of punishment." Hence, in *The Iceman,* though there is a Dostoevskian sound to the word when we hear that Parritt seeks punishment, he actually is seeking only suffering and a conclusion. He is a masochist. He wants Larry to hurt him, and he has lost the wish to live, or will have as soon as he is hurt. He wishes his own death—the only alternative in O'Neill's bleak world to wishing other people's death. Life equals murder and suicide.

This conception deprives O'Neill of what would normally be the dramatic content of his material. Our story would normally be dramatic so long as we think of our men—Hickey and Parritt—as seeking punishment as we understand punishment, and, after all, one of them is heading for what we take as the very embodiment of punishment under its usual definition: the electric chair. But if life is not a blessing, death is not a punishment: in which case *The Iceman* has a happy ending!

We suffer some confusion of the feelings as to the direction, happy or unhappy, in which the main characters are traveling, but, in a very clever play, O'Neill does something very clever about this: Hickey's punishment is over before the cops arrive; Parritt's punishment is over before he kills himself. By that token, their punishment takes place before our eyes during our whole evening at the theatre. Parritt is punished by Larry Slade, not at the end—which is a release—but all through. Hickey is punished by all the men—again, not at the end but all through, except for one moment of vertigo when it seems they may be transformed.

This is where the pipe dreams of the three main characters come in. The illusions are what stand between them and the punishment they seek. In what he thinks about illusions, O'Neill is systematic. Best is not to lose one's illusions and die as soon as possible. Second best is not to lose one's illusions and die later—like most of the men in *The Iceman*. Third best is to lose one's illusions and die as soon as one does so—like Hickey and Parritt. The worst fate of all is to lose your illusions and live on. This fate is reserved for Larry Slade —whom, on this interpretation as on others, we find to be the central figure in the composition. Now the spectator figure in literature is nearly always a portrait of the author. I imagine that Larry Slade represents a piece of self-criticism on O'Neill's part, that O'Neill puts into Larry his own tendency toward an empty and oratorical pessimism (an inversion of the official optimism of American society), and, since it is not in the cards that either Larry or O'Neill should turn optimist, the most that can be achieved is that the pessimism should turn from spurious to genuine. Larry learns sincerity, which was what O'Neill was learning in the final phase of his career.

Larry learns sincerity, which is something; not love, which would be everything. However, O'Neill does try to cope with love in *The Iceman Cometh*, and the topic is a suitable one with which to close this consideration of the play and of O'Neill's whole "life in art." Taking my cue from O'Neill's own words and those of his biographers, I have spoken of ambivalence as a central fact, perhaps *the* central fact, both of the life and the work. If the word "ambivalence" implies an exact balancing of opposing attitudes, the formulation, finally, seems inexact. The relevant attitudes, in O'Neill's case, are love and hate, but we do not find them balanced: we find the former swamped by the latter.

This is not surprising in itself. The negative emotions are more prominent than the positive ones throughout the whole of literature. What is important, and disappointing, about O'Neill is that, while he does deal with love, it is always a very inadequate kind of love that he deals with, while the hate he feels would be adequate for blowing up the universe. I do not speak just quantitatively. It is the quality of the love that is insufficient—I mean of course for the purposes which O'Neill himself proposes. If we consider, for example, the relationship of Hickey and his wife Evelyn, we learn that she loves him, and we are given to understand that her love is simply wonderful because she keeps forgiving him. But to reread Hickey's long account is to realize that O'Neill, as his habit was, has equated true love with maternal warmth while leaving sex to prostitutes. Yet he does not use this fact to characterize Hickey with, because it is not a fact he can *see* as an artist. It is a fact that he is involved in as a man. The perfect marriage which Evelyn offered was the union of mother and child. What the play "ought" to have been about is Hickey's unresolved Oedipus complex, but it could not be about this because O'Neill's Oedipus complex was unresolved.

Which helps to explain, I think, why Freudian critics, upon reading O'Neill, prick up their ears and reach for their pencils. He needs them to finish a job that he could not finish himself. Ibsen said, "to be a poet is chiefly to see," and I am assuming here that in literature the writer's complexes are not wallowed in, they are seen. And one can see only from a distance. The fantasies which derive from a writer's troubles must not merely exist; they must be transcended. They resemble the ordeal by fire and water: you have to pass through, yes; but you also have to emerge on the other side. Perhaps this is a matter of character, perhaps of talent, perhaps of both; or perhaps our terminology is inadequate and neither "talent" nor "character" tells the whole story. But anyone who uses psychoanalytic ideas at all must start out with at least a tentative answer to this question: Why cannot any literate person with an Oedipus complex write an *Oedipus Rex*?

The Iceman Cometh is a typical O'Neill work in that, while it has high merit, it does not achieve the transcendence I am speaking of, but substitutes the standard O'Neill pessimism—or rather a more sincere brand of it, as I have also tried to show. It is arguable, as I have indicated, that O'Neill did achieve transcendence in *Long Day's Journey into Night* and perhaps in some of the plays of his youth. An author's talent is often most abundantly at work in his least "serious" efforts, and it may well be that such an item as *The Emperor Jones* will withstand time better than the big plays, just as *Charley's Aunt* withstands time better than *The Second Mrs. Tanqueray*. The reed withstands the hurricane better than the oak.

(*1960*)

Bertolt Brecht

Do not write that you admire me!
—B.B.

Brecht, 1960. A writer, as Aristotle might say, is either fashionable or unfashionable. Neither condition is desirable. To be fashionable is to be celebrated for the wrong reasons, and to be unfashionable is not to be celebrated at all.

In the past ten years Bertolt Brecht has passed from the depths of unrecognition to the heights of a chic celebrity. Such a change is not without interest to the gossip columnist or even the social historian. To the serious reader—and to the serious theatregoer if he exists—it is a bore, and in the history of the drama it is just a bad thing. Brecht has died, and what we have chosen to inherit is a cult, an *ism.*

Is it so long since the same thing happened to Ibsen? For half a century a foggy phenomenon called Ibsenism, and many plays distinguished only for their Ibsenism, have stood in the way of Henrik Ibsen. Only after many years was any favorable change discernible, and by 1960 it was possible for Raymond Williams to write, "Ibsenism is dead, and Ibsen is very much alive."

Alas, poor Brecht! He stands where Ibsen stood in 1910: he is dead, and Brechtism is very much alive. But history need not repeat itself. War can be waged on Brechtism in the name of Brecht. More shrewdly: the cult of Brecht might be exploited to arouse a deeper interest in the work of Brecht. The coming of the cult has this to be said for it, that the old air of secrecy has gone. Brecht's works are at least there to be read. There is even such a thing as Brecht scholarship. And a real discussion of Brecht could and did begin when such critics as Martin Esslin and Ernest Borneman broke through the taboos by which the priests of the cult hoped to keep their idol holy, if unreal.

The errors that have been promoted by the cultists and the dilettantes will be exposed gradually as genuine criticism proceeds, but one error needs pointing out in advance as it is shared by the enemies of the cultists, particularly by those critics whom the cult has most infuriated. This is the notion that there are two Brechts, who correspond to the period before his conversion to Marxism (1928) and the period after. The early Brecht is a good thing, the later a bad, just as to many Communists and fellow travelers, the early Brecht is a bad thing, the later a good.

It would be strange indeed if a poet could cut his creative life so neatly in half. I believe that one can get the impression that Brecht did so only if one is blinded by political prejudice. If Brecht had a divided nature, it was—as the word "nature" implies—divided all his life long. Such a division is discernible in every major play. Otherwise, the lifework of Brecht has a most impressive unity: what is found in the late plays is found in the early ones, and vice versa. This is not to say that there is no development, nor is it to deny that Brecht *attempted* something like the total change which the doctrinaires on both sides attribute to him. One might say he providentially failed in this attempt. More probably, he surely if dimly knew what he was doing. Behind the attempt to change was the knowledge that one cannot change that much that fast, and a wily, conniving refusal to go to all lengths in attempting the impossible. This is speculation about the fact of unity in Brecht's work. About the fact there can be little doubt.

Necessary to the appreciation of this fact is the discovery or rediscovery of the early plays, particularly *Baal* and *In the Swamp*.

In the Swamp (Jungle of Cities)

Emotional dynamics. Brecht's later plays were so unconventionally constructed that the dramatic critics, being the men they are, were bound to think them badly constructed. *In the Swamp* is well constructed and, for all the absence of act divisions, is constructed in a fairly conventional way. Brecht's originality shows less in the overarching main structure than in the details of his rendering of the emotions and their dynamics.

The word "dynamics" may at first seem inapplicable because the subject is passivity, but human passivity has its own negative dynamics, as has a donkey that refuses to budge, a possum that pretends to be dead, or a poodle that begs to be whipped. It would be arbitrary to assume that there is less drama in cessation than in initiation, in refusal than acceptance, in surrender than resistance —nor is the passive man consistently passive. He is passive so much that occasionally he has to be the opposite. He overcompensates for inaction by action that is rash, sudden, and extreme. No lack of dynamics here! Combining the negative dynamics of refusal with the insane lunges of passivity interrupted, the young Brecht makes a drama out of apparently undramatic materials. Very modern materials: critics have not been slow to see the connection between the Brecht of 1920 and the plays of Beckett in the fifties. If only Beckett had a quarter of Brecht's constructive power! It seems to me that the later author, for all his true theatricality, cannot find the emotional dynamics to animate a full-length play. . . .

Speaking of the aggressions of the passive type of person, the works of Brecht embody aggressions of colossal proportions, and make a special appeal to persons who harbor such aggressions of their own. I have known many Brechtians intimately: one and all, they are persons positively possessed by aggression. This is something to think about when you read some of the current French and British Brechtians, who can give their writing a coolness of tone that accords with the theories of the Meister. Those theories came into being to create such a rational coolness of tone and conceal the heat and irrationality of the aggressive impulse.

The menagerie of Bertolt Brecht. Between the art of Bertolt Brecht and the discussion of that art a great gulf has been fixed. Maybe it was Brecht who fixed it by becoming a Marxist and letting us know about his art, even his early art, only in Marxist terms. If you read about Mackie the Knife in Brecht's Notes, you would expect anything but the Mackie the Knife of Brecht's own play. The Notes are all about capitalism and the world about us. The play shows . . . well, what? If this type of figure must be characterized in one word, that word will have to be "grotesque." Yes, a grotesque figure may *represent* capitalism and the world around us, but here we are changing the subject back to the author's intentions. What has he *done?* He has created a group of grotesques. This type of creation in no way results from Marxism: it antedates Brecht's reading of Marx. What one should rather observe is the way in which Brecht, when he joins the left, brings his menagerie with him. All he has to do is rename his jackals Capitalists.

By this time (1960), there are many people who approve of Brecht on the grounds that he was a Communist, but is that why they are attracted to his work? Rather, he is approved for one reason and enjoyed for another. Some of the enjoyment may indeed be rather improper, almost illicit. An unbeatable combination!

Amerika. The menagerie is all complete in *In the Swamp.* In Garga and Shlink we already hear the sentiments and accents of Peachum. Worm and Baboon are our first Brechtian henchmen. The nickelodeon plays "Ave Maria," a Salvation Army officer shoots himself after uttering the last words of Frederick the Great, and a lynch gang goes into action at the bidding of the police! It is the Amerika that was discovered not by C.C. but by B.B. It is the Amerika of *Mahagonny* and *The Seven Deadly Sins*.

Homosexuality. The modern subject par excellence? Yet still an unusual subject for a play when Brecht wrote *In the Swamp*, and it seems that people can read this play and miss it. They miss a lot. If homosexuality is not talked about, it is as fully implicit as in Genet's *Deathwatch*.

There is candor and candor. If homosexuality is now a standard subject of sentimental commercial literature, that literature can be trusted to impose its own limitations on the subject as it did on previous "daring" subjects. For example, Broadway plays on the theme only permit us to *discover* that the hero is homosexual just as older plays let us discover that the unmarried heroine was pregnant.

Homosexuality can appear in commercial culture only by way of pathetic romance. A homosexual disposition is accepted as arbitrarily *there*. Society is "arraigned" for its failure to see this. Here, as it were, is a group of people who prefer strawberries to raspberries, and society has made the eating of strawberries illegal: pathos! Brecht, on the other hand, while he doesn't tag characters with clinical labels, reaches what clinicians will recognize as the big facts.

One reason the treatment of homosexuality seems not very explicit in *In the Swamp* is that the author clearly puts sex in its place, the place for the kind of sex he has in mind being entitled Masochism. As in Genet, a gay eros is subordinated to the struggle for power; in which struggle Brecht's characters tend to wish to lose.

Nihilism: a query. Discussions of Brecht's philosophy—of this period *or later*—would gain from an understanding of his emotions and attitudes. His philosophy as of this period is always described as Nihilism, but is Nihilism a philosophy? Is it not rather an emotional attitude in a philosophically minded person? The philosophy is pessimistic, yet pessimism becomes nihilist only when espoused with resentment and rage. Nihilists are destroyers, though to study particular nihilists is often to find that they were very passive men. Are they men who become active only in destruction? And when they are converted to Causes which make high moral claims, can their Nihilism be discarded as a mere opinion?

A Man's a Man

A new Brecht. The protagonists of the earlier plays—Baal, Kragler, and Garga—were mouthpieces for Brecht's own yearnings and agonies. We are still not as far as he liked to think from the agonized-ecstatic dramas of the Expressionists. With *A Man's a Man* emerges the Brecht the world knows. The transition is rather an abrupt one, and I wonder that more has not been made of it. Formally speaking, it could be taken as a switch from tragedy to comedy. Brecht's final attitude would be vehemently antitragic. The newfangled notion of epic theatre can be construed as a synonym for traditional Comedy.

Influences. None, luckily, are as marked as those of Rimbaud and Büchner on *Baal* and *In the Swamp,* yet surely Chaplin runs these pretty close. It would be hard to prove this, of course, though Brecht's admiration of Chaplin is a matter of record, and the latter's influence is obvious enough in such later plays as *Puntila* and *Schweyk in World War II.* As far as *A Man's a Man* is concerned, one needn't stress Chaplin individually: I would judge the influence to be that of American silent-movie comedy in general. It was this influence (among others) that enabled Brecht to write, as he already wished to, much more impersonally. He was able to dispel the Expressionistic penumbra, and draw his own creatures on white paper, as it were, in hard black lines. Georg Grosz may have been as valuable to him as Chaplin.

Later revisions. He succeeded so well that later he was able to believe that *A Man's a Man* was Marxist before the fact: all it needed was a few extra touches, and it would be the model anticapitalist and antiwar play. The extra touches involved the omission of the superb final scenes (Ten, Eleven), and hence the blurring of the crucial Bloody Five—Galy Gay relationship. It was perhaps the puritanism of his friends in the Communist Party that made Brecht omit the castration episode (as it certainly made him tone down or omit the racier jokes). Brecht's famous revisions were often doctrinaire and seldom improvements.

Structure. The first published version of *A Man's a Man* has a very clear structure. The accident to Jip provides only the point of departure. At the center of the action is Uriah. It is Uriah who decides that, since men are all interchangeable, Jip can be replaced: it is just a matter of picking out Galy Gay, making sure that Jesse and Polly go along, and then keeping at it. While Uriah conducts his experiment on Galy Gay, Bloody Five conducts one on himself. What's in a name?—the phrase would make a good title for the play. Bloody Five changes into a civilian at the bidding of Widow Begbick. His humiliations in the role persuade him to change back again and cling to the name Bloody Five at any cost. "It is not important that I eat; it is important that I am Bloody Five." Well, Bloody Five is successful by his own standard, but Galy Gay is even more successful by drawing the opposite conclusion: one shouldn't make a "fuss about a name" and "it is very important that I eat." Final Curtain.

Pirandello. Within this clear structure, there are some less clear, but no less fascinating, things, such as the one piece of spoken verse in the play (Scene Nine, Sixth Number), in which Brecht goes far beyond a sociological statement and enters the depths of personal confusion. Indeed, the whole of the Fourth and Sixth Numbers bears witness to a very intimate kind of distress concerning lack of identity, and the vehicle that Brecht finds to carry the sense is singularly Pirandellian:

> URIAH. Fire!
> (GALY GAY *falls in a faint.*)
> POLLY. Stop! He fell all by himself!
> URIAH. Shoot! So he'll hear he's dead!
> (*They shoot.*)

Is A Man's a Man *topical?* In some ways, not. As of 1960, our Galy Gays wouldn't be so easily persuaded that war is pleasant. In some ways, too, this play was old-fashioned even in 1925. The imperialism envisaged seems to be that of the nineties ("We're soldiers of the Queen, my lads"), of jingoism, and the days when swords still had glamour, and Orientals seemed to some a lesser breed without the Law.

The play belongs to the era of Georg Kaiser's critique of the Machine Age —man dwarfed by his machinery and caught in it—whereas in 1960 John Kenneth Galbraith tells us that the machine is on the decline and that in the Affluent Society persons will be important. This last argument, however, is not really damaging to *A Man's a Man,* for *in what way* are our new managers and executives important? As organization men—as interchangeable ciphers. In their world, Bertolt Brecht's message is still pertinent: a man is most definitely a man.

Martin Esslin has remarked that the play is a prophecy of brainwashing. A good point, but the fable of brainwashing is combined, at least in the first published version, with one that contradicts it: a fable of a sorcerer's apprentice or Frankenstein's monster. Uriah's brainwashing of Galy Gay can hardly be deemed successful if then Galy Gay eats Uriah's rations! Perhaps the right conclusion is that Brecht's fable happily transcends the topical applications that will crop up from time to time. Of the latter, here is one from the *Nation,* June 11, 1960:

> Rockefeller, the most intellectual advocate of strong Civil Defense, detailed his argument in the April, 1960, issue of *Foreign Affairs.* . . . Rockefeller's words harmonize with the ponderous theorizing of other *Foreign Affairs* contributors who talk in terms of number and percentages instead of horror and anguish, as if war were a chess game. . . . When we concentrate on numbers, survival, and victory, as Rockefeller does, and drive from our minds visions of writhing bodies and screaming flesh, then war becomes thinkable. . . .

Cruelty. It would be hasty to imagine that, in finding his own genre, Brecht could change his emotional system. The emotional patterns of *In the Swamp* are found in the later plays in this or that disguise.

The Brechtian world revolves about an axis which has sadism and masochism as its north and south poles. In one play after another, Brecht saw the humaneness in human nature swamped out by inhumanity, by the cruelty of what he at first thought of as the universe and later as capitalist society. The standard ending of Brecht plays is the total victory of this cruelty. If, near the end of *Days of the Commune,* he indicates in a song that the workers may do better later on, the fact remains that he chose as his subject a classic defeat. *In Brecht's world, badness is active, while goodness is usually passive.* That antithesis is well rendered in *A Man's a Man* in Uriah and Galy Gay. It will be the making of the split good-and-bad ladies of *The Seven Deadly Sins* and *The Good Woman of Setzuan,* and, as Ernest Borneman has added, the passivity is not simply good, it has its perverse aspect. Galy Gay relishes his humiliations.

At the end of *King Lear* Kent sees the world as a rack on which human beings are stretched. That's Brechtian. People talk of the lack of emotion in his plays. Perhaps they mean in his theory of his plays, or perhaps they mean the lack of pleasant emotions. Being tortured is a violent emotional experience, and Brecht's characters, from the earliest plays on, live (it is his own metaphor, taken from Rimbaud) in an inferno. Shlink is lynched, Bloody Five castrates himself, Galy Gay is brainwashed. . . . What of the later plays written (we are told) in the spirit of rationalistic positivism and permitting the audience to keep cool? Self-castration occurs again in *The Private Tutor. The Good Woman* is the story of the rending asunder, all but literally, of a young woman. In *Courage* we watch a mother lose all three children by the deliberate brutality of men. In *Galileo* (as not in actual history) everything hinges on the threat of physical torture. Though torture cannot very well (*pace* Shakespeare) be shown on stage, Brecht devised scenes which suggest great physical violence without showing it and push mental torment to the limits of the bearable.

Are we to take plays like *A Man's a Man* and *Mahagonny* as forecasts of the Nazi regime or even as comment on the already active Nazi movement? If so, we shall have to characterize as "Nazis" certain characters in the very earliest Brecht plays. Hitler (as Brecht saw things) was not born yesterday.

The scene in which Mother Courage is asked to identify the corpse of her son is thought by some to derive straight from such incidents in recent history —one of which is shown directly by Brecht in "The Zinc Box" (*The Private Life of the Master Race*). But is not the essence of the matter already present in that scene in *A Man's a Man* where the corpse of Galy Gay is supposed to be in a crate and the actual (or former) Galy Gay makes a tormented speech about it?

Brecht the stage director was always insisting that the perpetrators of cruelty not be presented demonstratively. Instead of gesticulating and declaiming, they were to be businesslike, *sachlich*. The actors usually found the reason for this in "the Brecht style," "the Alienation-effect and all that," but what Brecht chiefly wanted was just to make the cruelty real instead of stagy. And he had in mind a different sort of cruelty from that which the average actor would tend to think of—the cruelty of men who live by cruelty and by little else, men who can order tortures as matter-of-factly as an actor orders a cocktail. Here Brecht pierces through into the pathological—the pathology of a Himmler or an Eichmann.

Whatever else is said of cruelty in Brecht's plays, the nature and quantity of it defeat any attempt on the spectator's part to remain detached in the manner recommended in Brecht's theoretical writings. Brecht's theatre is a theatre of *more than usually violent* emotion. It is a theatre for sadists, masochists, sado-masochists, and all others with any slight tendency in these directions—certainly, then, a theatre for everybody.

Saint Joan of the Stockyards

Here Bernard Shaw's Joan enters the menagerie of Bertolt Brecht, Chicago being its location in no less than three Brecht plays—*In the Swamp* and *Arturo Ui* are the others.

Parody. Parody is more important to modern than to any previous school of comedy. Already in Shaw parody had become very serious, a way of calling attention to dangerous fallacies.

It has been said that good parody parodies good authors and does not decrease one's respect for them. The authors parodied in this play are Shakespeare, Goethe, and Schiller, and certainly they are not the target. One could begin to explain what the target is by mentioning that many supporters of Hitler could and did quote all three of these authors a great deal.

To Shaw, Bertolt Brecht's attitude was ambivalent. Already, in a tribute he paid the older author in 1926, Brecht had said in passing that the most treasured possessions of Shaw characters were opinions. What Brecht thought of the right to your own opinions had already been indicated in certain speeches of Shlink and Uriah. Hence he is at pains to ensure that *his* Joan is entangled in circumstances, not besieged by epigrams.

Whether Brecht had understood Shaw is another matter. It is by circumstances—those of the capitalist system, as interpreted by a Marx or a Brecht—that Shaw's Major Barbara is trapped, nor are the opinions of Brecht's Joan Dark held to be immaterial. It is to an opinion (atheism) that she is finally won over, and Brecht tips the audience the wink that, had she lived any longer, she would have accepted that last word in opinions: communism.

Now as to Brecht's use of works by Goethe and Schiller, Shakespeare and Shaw in this play, the first two had better be ignored by readers of an English translation, for even the reader who spots the allusions to *Faust II* and *The Maid of Orleans* is still in the dark. The "light" is the reverent acceptance by the German philistine public of their classics, a reverence that precludes any positive critical interpretation. To the English-speaking audience, the Shakespearean blank verse should, on the other hand, have something to say. For we know the emptiness of our Anglo-Saxon acceptance of Shakespeare, and we can see how serious Brecht's verse has to be to express the utter falsity of the mode of life depicted. In the Brechtian parody, this falsity is quite the reverse of self-proclaimed. The speeches of Mauler and Cridle and the rest are a good deal more dignified, intelligent, plausible than most speeches in the Congressional Record.

Shavianism. As for Shaw, as I said, ambivalence reigns. He is parodied and he is plagiarized. The borrowings are less from *Saint Joan* than from *Major Barbara*. The essence of Brecht's tale, like Shaw's, is that a girl of superior caliber joins the Salvation Army but is later disenchanted by discovering that the Army is involved in "the contradictions of the capitalist system." (Shaw and Brecht were the only good "Marxist playwrights"—partly, no doubt, because they regarded the dialectic as dramatic and not just as philosophically valid.) More interesting still is the adoption by both playwrights, in their maturer vein, of fine young women with shining eyes and a limited or nonexistent interest in men as the bearers of the banner of the ideal.

Communism. On the Communist question this play is discreet but clear. The Communists are mentioned by name just once, a mention that is at once a genuflection.

Yet the Communist critic Ernst Schumacher observes that Brecht's treatment of the masses is "abstract"—for him a very dirty word. The Communist critic Kurella observed that such bourgeois converts to leftism as Brecht were obsessed with the conversion of bourgeois to leftism. It was a Communist critic who shows no knowledge of Brecht's work, Christopher Caudwell, who wrote the classic denunciation of such converts in the last chapter of his *Illusion and Reality* (1937). Though today many on the left are shocked to hear Brecht accused of "unconscious dishonesty," that formula was applied by Caudwell to the whole class that Brecht belonged to: bourgeois writers with Communist leanings.

Official, or semiofficial, Party writers never had much of a liking for Brecht's attempts to deal with working-class life. It is true that he got it all out of books, out of brief slumming expeditions, out of his imagination. *The Menagerie would do very well as Capitalists, but how to render the Proletariat?* Generally, we get those incarnations of sterling simplicity that many believe in and few have met with—I paraphrase one of the few great proletarian artists,

D. H. Lawrence. The mother in Brecht's adaptation of Gorky's novel is an example. Another tack is that of agitprop: treat the workers as a group and present them on stage as a singing or verse-speaking choir. *Saint Joan of the Stockyards* belongs to Brecht's agitprop phase.

Galileo

History. The historical understanding played no part in the writing of *Galileo,* nor did Brecht pay his respects to historical accuracy except in the broad outline and in certain details. True, not a great deal is known, but quite enough is known for us to be sure that the historical Galileo was nothing like this; nor were his problems of this type; nor did his opponents resemble those whom Brecht invents for him.

Galileo is not a Marxist play either. What Marxist historian would accept the unhistorical major premise: namely, that if an Italian scientist had refused to renounce Copernicus in 1633 "an age of reason would have begun," and hence our age of unreason would have been avoided? What Marxist historian could accept the notion that a Catholic scientist of the seventeenth century, whose best friends were priests, who placed both his daughters in a convent as young girls, was halfway a Marxist, resented convents and churchgoing, doubted the existence of God, and regarded his tenets in physics as socially revolutionary?

But it is one of the open secrets of dramatic criticism that historical plays are unhistorical. They depend for their life on relevance to the playwright's own time—and, if he is lucky, all future times—not at all on their historicity.

It might, of course, be asked, why a playwright would choose historical material at all, and pretend to be limited by it? There are reasons. For one, he relies on the public's ignorance of the secrets, closed or open, of dramatic criticism. Audiences assume that most of what they see in a history play did happen, and it may be that most of the "history" in the popular mind comes from such sources. By popular, I don't mean proletarian. I met a Hollywood director at the première of *Galileo* and asked him what he thought of it. "As a play? I don't know," he answered, "but it is always thrilling to hear the truth, to see what actually happened!" Well, the joke was not on Brecht, and this incident helps to explain why historical plays are still written.

The character of Brecht's Galileo. It is a play—not fact but fiction—and one of the criteria by which playwrights are judged is their ability to create characters who can, as it were, "take up their bed and walk," who can assume the frightening autonomy of the six who once stood in the path of Pirandello. This play lives, to a large extent, by the character of the protagonist, a character which Brecht cut out of whole cloth—that is to say, created out of his own resources. What makes this Galileo a fascinating figure is that his goodness and badness, strength and weakness, have the same source: a big appetite and a

Wildean disposition to give way to it. His appetite for knowledge is of a piece with his appetite for food, and so the same quality can appear, in different circumstances, as magnificent or as mean. I don't see how the theory of epic theatre could do justice to the ambiguity here. It calls for a theory of tragedy. The problem is not social and conditioned but personal and inherent.

Whatever the theorist makes of it, that particular ambiguity is very satisfyingly presented. It is perhaps the play's chief exhibit. There is another ambiguity, equally fascinating, if not equally well defined. In this work, the self-denunciatory impulse in Brecht, not to speak again of masochism, has a field day. His Galileo denounces himself twice, and the two denunciations are designed to be the twin pillars upon which the whole edifice rests. The first of them, the historic abjuration of Copernicanism, was, we may be sure, what suggested the play in the beginning. The second was Brecht's invention.

One can hardly hear either for the crackle of dialectics. The first is immediately condemned by Andrea (Cursed be the land that lacks a hero) and defended in a very Brechtian proverb by Galileo (Cursed be the land that *needs* a hero). Then Galileo changes his mind, and in the last scene (as performed), the argument is reversed. Andrea takes the line that the abjuration had been justified because "science has only one law: contribution," Galileo having by now contributed the Discorsi. Thereupon Galileo whips himself up into a self-lacerating fury: "Men like me should not be tolerated in the ranks of science!" He who had made the great False Confession, which according to Brecht destroyed him in the eyes of the good and just, now makes the great True Confession, *which is his destruction in his own eyes and before the eyes of the only person in the story with whom he has an emotional relationship.*

It is theatre on the grandest scale, and I call the conception fascinating because it is an attempt to bring together the most widely divided sections of Brecht's own divided nature: on the one hand the hedonist and "coward," on the other the "hero"—and masochist. It is hardly necessary to say that "no masochism was intended." Any element of masochism destroys, of course, the Marxist intention of this finale, but, once again, *Brecht is not Marxism,* Brecht is Brecht—and Galileo is *his,* not Marx's, prophet.

Here the conscious and the unconscious motives are so directly in conflict that complete clarity cannot result. What we get is an impression of improbability. We recognize that the final self-denunciation is all very moral, but we are not convinced that the old reprobate would actually make it. Such a person naturally believes, "Cursed be the land that needs a hero." What changed his mind? There would be a drama in such a change, and one wouldn't like to miss it. When Brecht simply *announces* the change, Galileo seems only his master's voice—a very different thing from being, as he was till then, his master's embodiment.

The matter is even less clear than I make out. It is almost possible to believe that Galileo is only scolding himself (for which we give him credit) and in general is the same man as before. In giving his manuscript to Andrea, he pretends he is, as usual, giving way to weakness, succumbing to temptation. The incident, particularly in the 1938–1939 version, is very endearing. In this respect, the man is true to character to the end, and one has to admit his character has its points. It is possible, in the main to stay pro-Galileo. A familiar Brechtian feature! Moral disapproval goes one way, but human sympathy goes the same way. On stage the apparatus of Alienation is called into action *as a fire brigade.* The whole effort of the Berlin Ensemble production is to counteract the natural flow of sympathy to Galileo. These actors know this particular job well. They have performed it for *Puntila;* as I write, they are performing it for a *Threepenny Opera* in which Mackie is not to be allowed any charm; and they try in vain to perform it for *Mother Courage.*

Galileo as a portrait of the artist. The term "portrait of the artist"—for novelists and dramatists at least—is a relative one. A character may be three-quarters self-portrait and one-quarter a portrait of someone else or sheer invention. The proportion of self-portrayal may indeed be anything from zero to a hundred per cent. There is sense in speaking of a portrait of the artist only when the relation to the artist is very marked and of special significance. In the present case, it is.

As already noted, there is a lot of Brecht in Baal, Kragler, and Garga. Then Brecht did not sit to himself for a long time. Which presumably means that he split himself up into *all* his characters. He often put the idealistic part of himself inside one of the young ladies with the shining eyes. He was likely to let the nonidealistic part of himself into the rogue of any play.

Why Galileo Galilei? W. H. Auden says the poet cannot portray the poet, and points to Shaw's Marchbanks as an awful example. But the poet can portray the poet by pretending he is something else, such as an architect (Solness) or a philosopher (Jack Tanner)—or a scientist (Galileo). Marxism considers itself scientific, which is one reason why it appealed to Brecht. Then there is the matter of History again. Whether or not the playwright is scrupulous about the historical record, a historical play carries the Idea of Fact.

Getting rid of one's personality, Brecht had written at the time he gave himself to social causes, was an amusing business. If only the subjective did not exist! If only one *were* history! And science! And by the time one *is* history and science—in this play, *Galileo*—it is interesting that one still has the same human constitution as before. One is a genius, one would like to be committed to a cause, but one is a rogue.

Rogues and knaves. Rogues are different from knaves—at least in plays. Uriah is a knave. He is the Enemy, the Cruel World, Capitalism, et cetera. So, I think, is Peachum. They are nothing if not active, while your rogue, though applying himself busily to this or that, is fundamentally passive. Widow Begbick is a rogue and in a late version of the script sings a song celebrating her passivity. She calls it not resisting the current of the river. Macheath is more rogue than knave, and it is passivity, in the form of "sexual submissiveness," that defeats him, as the story indicates and two long songs emphasize. Brecht in fact created a long line of rogues of whom Mother Courage and Puntila are only the most conspicuous. They differ from the knaves in being likable, even charming. Whatever disapproval we might feel is canceled by the fact that their roguery is unsuccessful and was predestined to be so. Or it is successful in a very small and unimportant area. Brecht will make sure we understand that our hatred, if given primarily to them, is misdirected.

Or will he? The problem is complicated by the extent to which the rogue is always Brecht himself. His enjoyment of himself was qualified by an unusually large quota of self-hatred. The former would show itself in first drafts; the latter would be given full play in later revisions, not to mention notes and other outside comments. (The early versions of *Puntila* and *Galileo* are especially revealing.)

Heroism, martyrdom, masochism. It has been pointed out that the passive sufferers of Brechtian drama are offset by the heroic resisters. It has also been pointed out that what the heroes do is as passive as what the sufferers do: they obey, consent, submit. Galileo, then, is given his choice of two kinds of passivity: submit to fear or submit to torture. The passive characters of the early plays (Galy Gay, Shlink) had submitted to torture—masochistically. Galileo submits to fear and later denounces himself—most masochistically, as we have seen—before Andrea. Had he submitted to torture, that would have certified him a hero and therefore no masochist. Such would be Brecht's alibi. But he didn't use it. And it is not a valid alibi because writer and character are distinct in this: that the portrayal of nonmasochistic heroism can itself be a masochistic act.

In any event, it is not really heroism, but martyrdom, that is at stake, and it is well known that only a thin line divides masochistic submission from true martyrdom. If Galileo were tortured, you would get not a tragedy but, from Brecht's viewpoint, a happy ending, with Galileo a martyr of science. Here, however, we use the term "martyr" in a debased way. In Brecht's view, Galileo should have been willing to die because the news of his refusal to recant could have been exploited by the right side. This is the kind of thing we have in mind in modern politics when we say, Let's not ruin such and such a man or we'll provide our opponents with a martyr. Anything further from the original idea of martyrdom could hardly be imagined.

Gluttony: a deadly sin. The most famous line Brecht wrote is: *"Erst kommt das Fressen, dann kommt die Moral"*—Eating comes first, morality second. It is one of his passive and charming rogues speaking (or rather, singing): Macheath. The sentiment is one that the passive and charming Brecht would endorse, but that the active and activist Brecht would denounce. He denounces it in *Puntila* where a tale is told, in tones of awe, of a young man named Athi whose heroic deed it was to starve rather than eat food that came from his capitalist foe. In this context—again it is the context of Brecht's own mind and work that matters—Galileo's love of food takes on more meaning. I rather think Laughton got the part because Brecht had seen the ravenous eating he did in the *Henry VIII* film. (In *Galileo,* Laughton tore a chicken apart in exactly the same way.) Galy Gay's superiority to Bloody Five in *A Man's a Man* consists in his knowing that "it is very important that I eat," and his transformation in the final scene is shown mainly in his wolfing the rations of the three others. *In the Swamp* culminates in a conclusion written in a similar form of words, though containing no reference to food. "It is not important," says this particular passive protagonist (Garga), "to be the stronger one, but to be the living one." He is providing the reason for all that gluttony—as well as the provocation for Athi's hunger strike. Such, by the way, are the kinds of details through which the unity of Brecht's work is discovered.

It will be recalled that Brecht's word both for commercial entertainment and for the sensuous, thought-inhibiting, action-inhibiting high art of our era was: culinary.

The Good Woman of Setzuan

Anna-Anna. Already in *The Seven Deadly Sins,* Brecht had made of his usual antithesis—kind vs. cruel, humane vs. inhumane, natural vs. unnatural, idealistic vs. realistic—a division within the same person. The world being bad, the good person requires a bad half if he is to survive. In this proposition, there is no contradiction between Brecht's natural constitution and Marxism, provided the negative side be identified with capitalism. Even the key role of the economic motive was something Brecht had worked out on his own: in *A Man's a Man,* written before the conversion to Marxism, we find Uriah able to hold on to Galy Gay only by the lure of a "deal."

Drama schematic and abstract. Brecht did not like the word "abstract." He made a personal motto of the phrase "truth is concrete," and in this most of the literary world, on both the sides of the Iron Curtain, agrees with him. What are they all agreeing to? The word "concrete" is an abstraction, and all art is abstracted from life, with considerable subtraction and distortion along the way —just think of the Brecht menagerie!

But I would not try to empty the antithesis concrete/abstract of all meaning. It makes sense to say *The Three Sisters* presents life more concretely than does the *Oresteia,* and it is a fact that writers today emulate this concreteness rather than that abstractness. Even so, most nonmodern drama was more abstract, and modern drama continually reverts to relative abstractness. After Ibsen (concrete), Expressionism (abstract).

Brecht believed that he reinstated the concrete. But did he? On the contrary, beginning with *A Man's a Man,* he created a dramaturgy as schematic and abstract as any workable dramaturgy well could be. With its numbering, its blackboard demonstrations, its many unashamedly two-dimensional characters, it is surely the abstractest thing in drama since the Spanish *autos* of the seventeenth century. Nor am I speaking merely of the *Lehrstücke.* Beginning with *A Man's a Man,* and not least in *The Good Woman of Setzuan,* Brecht's drama is all schematic and abstract, more so perhaps than is acceptable to the theatre public of most countries today.

A Man's a Man has the form of a scientific demonstration. One draft actually ends with the words *Quod erat demonstrandum. The Good Woman* is similar. As in the earlier play, the first sequence of action presents a premise or hypothesis. Then comes the action, which is divided into clearly demarcated sections, each proving its own point. As Shen Te puts it at the end, she had only tried:

1. to help her neighbor,
2. to love her lover, and
3. to keep her little son from want.

These are the three main sections and "actions" of the play. When Shen Te has failed in all three respects, even with increased help each time from her alter ego Shui Ta, she makes her appeal to the gods. There is nothing they can do. Q.E.D.

It sounds dismal! And what could have been a worse fate for the theatre than the theories and "schemes" of Brecht without his talent, which so often works not hand in hand with the theories and "schemes" but at daggers drawn with them? This much must be granted to those who abhor the schematic and the abstract: the schematic and the abstract never amount to theatre, drama, literature, art, *by themselves.* Yet, if what is added is not the "concrete" characterization and milieu that we are used to, what is it? In other words:

What is epic theatre, actually? In the first instance, a misnomer, and this Brecht, in effect, has admitted. The word "epic" suggests too many things or the wrong things. In England and America there is the added trouble that our schools don't make much use of the old triple division of literature: epic, lyric, dramatic. There is a lot to be said for *not* using it, as the dramatic is not a separate genre running parallel to the others without touching them. The dramatic has traditionally embraced epic and lyric elements.

But "epic" does make a good antithesis to "lyric." In *Illusion and Reality* Caudwell makes them so different it would be hard to conceive of the same person excelling at both, harder still to find him combining the two in one work.

Caudwell's theory, oversimplified, is that the lyric writer writes himself while the epic writer writes the world. Even my oversimplification helps in explaining Brecht, who was originally a "lyric" poet, but who, when he discovered the world, tried to do without the self altogether and create a wholly "epic" drama.

Brecht never really succeeded in writing a novel—i.e., never became a fully epic writer. He remained the Poet as Playwright, and if we speak not of intentions but attainments, we should call his theatre a "lyric theatre." The name would certainly bring out his qualities, rather than his defects.

There are defects—or perhaps "deficiencies" would be the word—in the area where the novelist or epic writer excels, namely, in the full presentation of individual character. Brecht would show at his worst in a comparison with Ibsen, but Ibsen—the "modern" Ibsen, that is—would show at his worst in a comparison with Brecht, for he tried to cut out the lyric element by the roots.

"Lyric theatre" would also prove a misleading term. There would be confusion with opera or with decorative drama written in verse like, say, Christopher Fry's plays. Caudwell's formula guides us to a deeper interpretation of the lyric: the writer's relation to all of life is always at stake in it. The "lyricism" of *The Good Woman of Setzuan* is not isolated in the songs or bits of spoken verse. Rather, these are emanations of the spirit in which the whole play is composed. The prose, too, is poetry—not decorative and external but structural and integral.

Epic theatre is lyric theatre. The twentieth century has seen a series of attempts to reinstate poetry in the theatre. Brecht made the most successful of these attempts. How? If it was not because he was a better poet—and one can scarcely maintain that he was a better poet than Yeats or Eliot—why was it? Cocteau's phrase "poetry of the theatre" as distinct from "poetry *in* the theatre" helps us toward the answer. As early as 1920 Eliot had completely debunked the kind of drama that is poetic chiefly in consisting of mellifluous or even exquisite lines. Nonetheless, his own interest continued to be in the poetic line and the way it was written: the free verse of *The Cocktail Party* is offered as an alternative to the blank verse and stanzas of the Victorians. Now, though Brecht too had his alternative forms of dialogue to offer, they are but a part of a Grand Design to replace the Victorian drama in all departments. And it is the design as a whole that provides the answer to the question: What kind of lyric theatre? The poetry *of* the theatre is not a poetry of dialogue alone but of stage design, of lighting, of acting, and directing, nor is it enough that these be "imaginative"— to use Robert Edmond Jones's word for his vision of a poetry of the theatre—they must also be called to order—subordinated to the statement which is being made. For this theatre is no firework display. It is not there to show off the theatre arts, together or individually, but to show off the world around us and the world within us—to make a *statement* about those worlds. Hence, while Jones's designs often look better in a book than on the stage, photographs of the Brechtian stage, thrilling as they are, fall short of doing justice to the phenomenon itself. There is this difference too. Jones was adding his own vision to that of an author: two inevitably somewhat disparate contributions were made toward what would be at best a happy combination. In the Brecht theatre, though others made contributions, he himself laid the foundation in every department: he was really the stage designer, the composer, and the director. The production as a whole, not just the words, was the poem. It was in essence, and often in detail too, *his* poem.

Collaboration. It has not escaped attention that, following the title page of a Brecht play, there is a page headed: *Mitarbeiter*—Collaborators. It has escaped attention only that these names are in small type and do not appear on the title page of the book or, presumably, on the publisher's royalty statements.

All the collaborators, and many who have witnessed the work of collaboration, have testified to Brecht's penchant for collaborating. We learn that at one period he didn't like to write alone and sitting down but only pacing the floor and talking with several "collaborators." We hear of his willingness to snap up a phrase or notion applied by an onlooker.

Yet Brecht had no talent at all for collaboration if the word carries any connotation of equality, of give and take. His talent was for domination and exploitation, though the ethics of the procedure were in this sense satisfactory, that his collaborators were always people who wanted and needed to be dominated and exploited. That this should be true of friends and mistresses who never wrote anything notable of their own goes without saying. It is true also of the Big Names, including the biggest name of all—that of Kurt Weill. Weill has no more enthusiastic and enthralled a listener than myself: the success of his music for *Mahagonny* and the other Brecht works is not in question. But how was that success achieved? Brecht sometimes intimated that he himself contributed some or all of the tunes of *The Threepenny Opera*. For years I considered this a boast. Later I came to believe it. For I saw the way Brecht worked with composers, and I listened to the music Weill wrote before and after his collaboration with Brecht. Weill took on the artistic personality of any writer he happened to work with. He had no artistic personality of his own. For a theatrical composer this is conceivably an advantage. I am not arguing that point. I would only mention in passing that what goes for Weill goes for Hanns Eisler. The music of both is parasitic. When parasitic upon Brecht, it is nearly always superb. Parasitic upon second-raters, it is second-rate. And when they attempt music that is not parasitic at all, music that is bolstered by no writer, music that is not imitative of any composer, or even music that is not in some sense serious or flippant, a parody of other music, they court disaster. What kind of stage designs has Caspar Neher made for other playwrights? Often, very good ones, but in what way? Either in his

Brecht style or in some established mode that would not mark off his work from that of any other eminent modernist. The "originality" of Neher is concentrated in the work he did for Brecht. Since that work was inspired *by* Brecht, it is clear that the word "originality" is in need of redefinition.

Brecht dominated not only the collaborators who were present in the flesh but also the dead or absent writers whose works he adapted. *The Threepenny Opera* is not a "steal" but a new work and just as "original" as John Gay's *Beggar's Opera*. In no case can the success or the character of a Brecht work be attributed to the writer or writers whom he drew upon. Though you might, for example, believe that Brecht "ruined" Lenz's play *The Private Tutor,* by that very token you can hardly attribute the proven effectiveness of the new play to Lenz.

Hence, what is interesting is not the legal issue of plagiarism—a hare started by Alfred Kerr long ago—but a critical problem: how was it that Brecht arrived at his results in this particular way? Perhaps the burden of proof is on those who regard the opposite procedure as normal, since it is only in recent times that "life" and not literature has come to be regarded as the usual source for a dramatist's plots and characters. The most "original" playwright of all, Shakespeare, is also the one who keeps scholars busiest studying his literary sources. Molière notoriously said he took his material wherever he found it—and the place he meant was literature or the theatre, not "life." Why did Brecht return to the earlier method? The question can hardly be answered *en passant,* but one thing is clear: that in exploring the whole range of dramatic art, Brecht rediscovered the many-sided significance of collaboration.

The heart of the matter is, perhaps, that the individual artist contributes less to his art than is commonly supposed. A large contribution is always made by collaborators, visible and invisible. Drama, being narrative in a concentrated form, relies even more on the collaboration of others than does fiction. The dramatist draws, for example, on more "conventions" as a welcome short-cut —conventions being unwritten agreements with the audience. Similarly, he is inclined to use not the raw material of life but material that has already been "worked" by another artist. It takes all sorts of collaboration to make dramatic art, the final collaborative act being that which unites performer and spectator.

The book from which most modern comments on this last subject are— directly or indirectly—taken is *The Crowd* by Gustave LeBon. There is a fatal equivocation in it. LeBon fails to distinguish between the crowd in the concrete (say, a thousand people of any kind in a theatre) and the crowd in the abstract (the masses, etc.). Slurring over this simple difference, he enjoys himself reaching unwarranted conclusions.

In English we would call the first phenomenon the audience and the second the public; and it occurs to me that English is unusual in having these two words. In French the audience is called *le public,* in German, *das Publikum.* Language seems to put English-speaking persons in immediate possession of a useful distinction.

We have heard much too much of the contribution the audience makes to a show. The audience laughs or cries, is attentive or fidgety, creates an atmosphere, sets up a current of psychic electricity between itself and the players. . . . All of which is to speak of the problems that arise at the end of the whole process of writing and rehearsing. No essential problem can be solved at that late point, as has a hundred times been shown in the history of American "out-of-town tryouts," without, of course, anyone's learning the lesson.

The audience's collaboration is one thing, the public's is another. There comes to mind Synge's historic statement that all art is a collaboration between the artist and his people. Synge correctly observed that something had gone terribly wrong in modern times. In my terms: the problem of the modern theatre is the problem not of the audience only but of the public as well.

One sign of this is that the audience problem can often be solved, while the problem of the public remains where it was. The problem of the audience has been that it has lacked homogeneity, common purpose, warmth. You can get these things by picking an audience of people united in a common faith. I would say T. S. Eliot solved the audience problem when he put on *Murder in the Cathedral* in the cathedral at Canterbury. Here is a theatrical "experiment" that succeeded. But that audience did not help Mr. Eliot to write his play. The public was not only not collaborating; it was absent, indifferent, even hostile.

Bertolt Brecht's radical reconsideration of theatre and drama includes a reconsideration of both audience and public. The trade unions and other large groups who would buy out the house once a week in the Germany of the twenties obviously represented a new audience and might also suggest the idea of a new public that corresponds to a new working-class culture. Seen in this connection, Brecht's communism will not appear as unplausible as it does to many of his readers in America today. Such readers would do well to remember that an artist will accept almost anything if it seems to offer a future for his art.* Brecht accepted communism as Pascal advised accepting supernatural religion: as a bet according to which you have everything to gain and very little to lose. Concerned for the integrity of the theatre art, Brecht looked to proletarianism as the only way in which the artist could regain the kind of collaboration which Synge in 1900 thought was barely available any more.

Now, in his estimates of power and political success, Brecht showed shrewdness. At a time when the Soviet Union was considered weak, and the huge social-democratic movement in Western Europe tended to be anti-Communist, Brecht put his money on Moscow. There is little need, in 1960, to explain what

---

* "Only by crawling on his belly can an unpopular and troublesome man get a job that leaves him enough free time." Thus spake (Brecht's) Galileo.

a sound investment that was—if political success is the criterion. What if we apply other criteria—especially the very simple one of an audience and a public for Brecht?

As far as the public goes, one normally considers it as collaborating with the artist while he is planning and writing. Brecht, however, believed that he belonged with the public of the future. Only socialism could give his works a home. He once told me in so many words that if world socialism did not come about he did not expect his works to have any future at all.

The Soviet Union gave Brecht the Stalin Peace Prize. East Germany gave him a place to live and a large subsidy for a theatre. Does this amount to a public? Did Brecht's plays find their proper habitat? Did epic theatre establish itself as the theatre of the Communist countries?

There was a small production of *Threepenny Opera* in Russia some thirty years ago! Despite the visit of the Berlin Ensemble in 1957, the Russians are still (1960) not doing Brecht plays. Nor are most of the East German theatres. The failure to find a public is total. On the other hand, Brecht has found an enthusiastic audience. But it consists of just the sort of people he ostensibly didn't want—chiefly the liberal intelligentsia of "decadent" Paris and London.

As for what Brecht really wanted, we find the same ambivalence in this field as in others. When in America, he was brave about being ignored on Broadway. "Why expect them to pay for their own liquidation?" he once said to me. But he fretted about it too, and made a few stabs at crass commercial success. His attitude to the Western *avant-garde* theatre was similar. The "so-called *avant-garde*" was not important, but, under certain conditions, it would take up his plays. What conditions? I once asked him. "Well," he replied, "if I were a Frenchman—or if I became the rage in Paris." And to be the rage in Paris —"intellectual," "advanced," almost "revolutionary" Paris—is, as far as worldly success goes, the highest achievement of Brecht to date.

Even aside from politics, it is questionable whether Brecht could have had what he wanted. There comes to mind George Lukacs's statement that, in the great ages, the drama flowed "naturally" from the existing theatre, while, from Goethe on, the poet-dramatist rejects the theatre, writes plays which are "too good for it," and then calls for the creation of the kind of theatre which will be good enough for the plays. Brecht saw the weakness of the post-Goethe position—without being able to escape it. If there is any theatre you cannot see a man's plays naturally flowing from it is a theatre that doesn't yet exist! If there is any public that is not a collaborator it is a public that isn't yet there! We all applaud the work of the Berlin Ensemble, but that institution is not the product of a new proletarian society. Its audience is the bourgeois *avant-garde*. Its leaders—Erich Engel and Helene Weigel—are noble relics of the culture of the despised Weimar Republic. As for Bertolt Brecht, the point is not so much that he didn't succeed in getting any plays written about the doings in

East Germany as that, if he had, they would inescapably have been the product of the mind and sensibility that made *In the Swamp*. Has it escaped notice that the East German critics have been happier with Thomas Mann, who made no bones about being bourgeois, than with this uncomfortable Bavarian rogue?

Has The Good Woman of Setzuan *dated?* This query is not as easy as it sounds, because all plays "date" in many respects, even though some go on being played and read forever. In this case, the question is: Does the play belong irretrievably to the Depression Era? It does presuppose general unemployment on the one hand, and, on the other, slave-driver capitalists, like those of the factory system in the classic era of capitalism as described by Marx and Engels. An audience which does not presuppose these things will not cry, "How true!" as often as the author would like. Today's audience knows, for example, that the composer who in the thirties predicted the swift demise of American capitalism in *The Cradle Will Rock* today receives Henry Ford's money to write about American injustice in the Sacco-Vanzetti case.

But such changes in background are negative factors. They only explain why a play will not receive an artificial "lift" from the audience. To the extent that *The Good Woman* is a good play and not absolutely confined in relevance to the Depression, it can command an audience. I see no reason to limit the interpretation of Brecht's plays to what is known to be his own understanding of them. As Shaw would put it, he was only the author. He was neither the audience nor the arbiter. During the Stalin era *The Good Woman* presented a good picture of current tendencies in Soviet society, with Shui Ta as the necessary "realistic" correction of the earlier idealism, and Yang Sun as eventually a high Party functionary, rising by the path of Stakhanovism. More permanently, the two sides of Shen Te, as they arise from the divided nature of Brecht, express such a division for all of us, and the tendency thereto which exists *in* all of us.

Mother Courage

Beyond place and time. It would be rash to expect this play to be any more historical than *Galileo* is. The vein of cynicism in which Mother Courage sings and speaks of war is the tone of the twentieth century, more particularly of Bertolt Brecht, and not that of seventeenth-century peasant women. Like Brecht's Galileo, she has all the negative side of Marxism under her belt, lacking only the positive belief in social progress.

Indications of place mean no more than indications of time. You can tell that from the way Brecht would change both. "The Song of the Great Souls" in *Mother Courage* (Sweden, Germany, etc., the seventeenth century) is taken bodily from *The Threepenny Opera* (England, nineteenth-twentieth centuries). "The Song of the Fishwife and the Soldier" seems, from its setting in *Mother*

Courage, to tell a German tale. The omission of the one word "Volga" conceals the fact that an earlier rendering had set it in Russia. An action can be transported thousands of miles by the changing of a single word! In short, there is no concrete locality in Brecht's drama. Place, like time, is abstract.

This feature represents an inheritance from Expressionism. Brecht's work is continuous with that of the Expressionists to the extent that he tried to construct an abstract model of his subject. *Mahagonny* and *The Threepenny Opera* provide not a socialist-realist report on capitalism but, as it were, the Platonic idea of it.

But Brecht sank his roots much deeper in human history than the Expressionists did—and in the history of the abstract in drama. Obsessed with religion, a subject he could not keep away from for more than a few pages at a time, he often thought in terms of traditional religious abstractions. He wrote a *Seven Deadly Sins* and talked of writing a *Dance of Death.* His first and best book of poems had the form of a manual of piety. Converted to communism, his mind ran not forward to some Artwork of the Future but back to the cantata and the oratorio. His "invention," the *Lehrstück,* is a sort of Catholic morality play revised by a Marxist reader of Luther's Bible.

The deadly sins and the Christian virtues. We have seen that *The Good Woman* is a schematic and abstract study of the three parts of Shen Te's goodness, love of her neighbor, love of her man, and love of her offspring. *Mother Courage* is equally schematic, and is also tripartite. The action divides into three sections at the end of each of which a child is killed. Each child represents one of the virtues. Eilif is called The Brave Son. Swiss Cheese is called The Honest Son. Kattrin is characterized by Kindness in the little charade of the black cross. In that charade the whole action is seen in advance. In "The Song of the Great Souls," near the end, it is summed up retrospectively and abstractly—that is, in terms of the virtues themselves. Caesar, too, was brave and got killed. Socrates was honest and got killed. Saint Martin was kind and died of the cold. As it was demonstrated in *The Seven Deadly Sins* that natural and healthy impulses become as sins which society will not tolerate, so it is demonstrated in *Mother Courage* that the cardinal virtues are not for this world. In other words, *Mother Courage* is quite close, in what it says, to *The Good Woman.* For that matter, it is close to *The Threepenny Opera,* where also "The Song of the Great Souls" —under the name of "The Song of Solomon"—can be taken as a summary of the play as a whole. Brecht is one of those artists—Ibsen and Conrad are others—who do not really change their subject from one work to the next but, all their life long, worry the same point.

Such an artist soon becomes a bore unless that point is of great moment and unless he can present it in various aspects. How can the principle of variety be applied to the notion of the virtues? One way is by irony. Eilif's bravery turns out in the end to be only what is wrongly called bravery: like Galy Gay, he is transformed into a foolhardy bandit. Another way to variety is by parallelism and contrast in character and narrative. Not only is one brother offset by a second, the daughter is offset by another kind of daughter (of joy). Yvette's career yields the one success story in the play. This has its own irony. Yvette's success is doubly ambiguous: it is accompanied by physical and moral deterioration, and it is exhibited with (the author's) disapproval. Kattrin, by contrast, is a failure at the start and becomes more of a failure all the time, but just as Brecht had drawn an analogy between Swiss Cheese and Christ, so he makes of Kattrin his own type of hero—the activist—and confers upon her a kind of glory.

The positive hero. At this point, the virtue which Kattrin represents comes within range of the virtue of the "positive hero" of Soviet literature. But that was not the kind of abstractness to which Brecht was naturally drawn. He is careful not to make Kattrin an idealist. It is not for an idea that she dies but, on the contrary, because, on the subject of children, she is not rational: she is a *Kindernarr,* crazy for little ones. If Brecht moves toward the abstract in this characterization, the abstraction is not Philanthropy but Mother Love, an instinct which is celebrated in a whole series of his plays. Another touch that belongs very much to this poet, rather than to a school of thought, is that Kattrin cannot speak. In the world depicted, Virtue has no voice, or at least, if she has, even the poet cannot find it. And yet there is rebellion. "The stones begin to speak," says the scene heading. And Mother Courage had called Kattrin "a stone in Dalarna." (Symbolism with a vengeance! Though "symbolism," in Brecht circles, was as nasty a word as "abstraction," like "abstraction; it will prove a necessary word to the true critic of Brecht.)

Brecht chose to be the voice of the voiceless. Such was the positive side of his impulse toward radicalism, a side sometimes obscured by his readiness to excuse Stalinist brutality.

> Und die Einen sind im Dunkeln
> Und die Anderen sind im Licht.
> Und man siehet die im Lichte
> Die im Dunkeln sieht man nicht.*

Precisely to *bring* light into this darkness was the mission of Bertolt Brecht, who had all the makings of a popular, though not of a proletarian, poet.

The "drum" scene is possibly the most powerful scene, emotionally, in twentieth-century drama. Any actress playing Courage might be hard put to it to hold her own, and, if one Sovietized the play, Kattrin would be the protagonist. To put her mother center stage was to invite the complaint that the play was not truly Marxist but pacifistic, defeatist, and bourgeois. But Brecht did put her mother center stage, and did not entitle his play *Dumb Kattrin.*

* "And these are in the dark, and those are in the light, and you can see the ones in the light: those in the dark you can't see." From the film of *The Threepenny Opera.*

That Brecht should have proved the leading Communist writer of the Stalin era is perhaps the most striking of all the Brechtian contradictions. The "positive hero" is one of the few ideas which Stalin and Zhdanov contributed to literary discussion, and Brecht stood for nothing if not the opposite. His protagonists from Baal through Azdak are nothing if not *negative* heroes. Brecht got angry when actresses made Courage noble and even, supreme error! courageous. For this writer's first weapon—and here again he stands in direct contrast to Stalin's writers—is irony. Nicknamed Courage by a fluke, as she readily explains, the lady represents, in the first instance, the diametric opposite of courage, namely, cowardice, and the diametric opposite of active virtue, namely, passivity. That she keeps herself busy—works her hands to the bone, in fact—is an added irony. Such are the "ridiculous superhuman efforts" which Brecht's Galileo attributes to the peasantry in general: they are passive in the class struggle, which is to say, in history. As in her previous incarnation as Widow Begbick, Mother Courage is content to flow with the tide—even though her own song (of the fishwife) tells where the tide inexorably leads, namely, to death.

Critics of *Mother Courage* could hardly fail to observe that people in it die, but they don't seem to have noticed that dying is implicit in the play from the first scene on—a scene which begins with the song, "Let your men drink before they die!" and ends with the prophecy of the death of all three children. The vision of death and the prospect of death is what is most vivid about the play. The spirit it is shot through with is, in fact, that of the death-wishing Brecht of the early plays: Mother Courage is a new spokesman for the old disenchantment. If Brecht put some of himself into Kattrin and she sums up Brecht the activist and lover of mankind, he put even more into his passive and negative heroine, Mother Courage the coward.

The final touch—which I think only one critic (Esslin) has spotted is that, in the last instance, Mother Courage does have courage, not the kind that Brecht officially favored, not the kind he could have admitted, perhaps, to be there at all, but surely the kind he must have covertly respected since he makes it command respect in the play. This is, to borrow a phrase from Brecht's friend Paul Tillich,* "the courage to be"—in this case, the courage to exist in the face of a world that so powerfully recommends nonexistence.

Critics who confront *Mother Courage* may need to speak not only of abstraction and symbolism but also of the tragic. But this we have already found to be true of *Galileo*. We shall find it true of *The Caucasian Chalk Circle* as well.

Why the Thirty Years' War? Because in German history it is the *locus classicus* of death—the death not of individuals but of cities and populations.

---

* I do not know how much of a friend, but it happens that the only time I have seen Dr. Tillich was in Brecht's New York apartment on East Fifty-sixth Street. (Until I saw him in Cambridge in 1960.)

Brecht had seen World War I, and could foresee World War II. Even if the play did not find a permanent place in the repertoire, it would always remain a great document of our age of world wars, as Grimmelshausen's *Simplicissimus* is a great document of the seventeenth century.

To some extent Grimmelshausen was the inspirer of *Mother Courage*. His work certainly brought to Brecht a sense of death, decay, and disaster, corresponding rather closely to his own, yet insofar as the sources—or provocations—of the play are literary, there is an author who has an even better claim to be considered the main source. If the Thirty Years' War had been lived through by Grimmelshausen, it had been seen in perspective by a much better-known German writer who also happens to be Germany's most widely admired dramatist, Friedrich Schiller.

The left-wing intelligentsia of the twenties had it in for Schiller. Erwin Piscator deglamorized *The Robbers* by making it a picture of the class struggle à la Marx. Brecht was strongly anti-Schiller. There were times when he seemed to see himself as *The* Anti-Schiller, a sort of German equivalent of The Anti-Christ. If Schiller gave the heroic view of the war—classical in its dignity, romantic in its presentation of women—Brecht would give the antiheroic, anticlassical, antiromantic worm's-eye view. *Mother Courage* stands to *Wallenstein* as *Saint Joan of the Stockyards* to *The Maid of Orleans*. This is a two-sided statement, for, as I said above, Brecht did not merely parody the classics. His procedure in his *Saint Joan* contrasts with that of modernizers in general who take an old theme and vulgarize it. No work of Brecht's is so resolutely stately. He was trying to find an equivalent for Schiller's sublimity. As for *Mother Courage,* it might well have been suggested by the first part of the *Wallenstein* trilogy.

The Caucasian Chalk Circle

Charm and naïveté. How is this play built? The incident of the chalk circle takes up only one scene. What is the rest of the play there for? So that we can get to know the Judge? But he doesn't appear till the second half. What is the first half of the play there for? It would be hard, I think, to find a satisfying reason in the doctrinaire terms in which Brecht and his colleagues discussed plays. Why couldn't a reason be found along traditional artistic lines? Not all the play is didactic. Was not Brecht capable of relaxing a little, telling a touching story, and filling it out with a poem and a song?

He was. Not the least of the many disservices of his theorizing to his cause was to obscure the presence in his work of the primary attributes of good theatre. Take such a thing as *charm*. The word has been pre-empted, latterly, by advertisers of clothing and cosmetics. That isn't the word's fault. Only the most egregious art-snob or the blindest art-theorist can overlook the role of charm in art. In the theatre, which directs itself to the eyes and ears, it is primary. Goethe himself speaks of going to the theatre to gaze at beautiful bodies. What beauty is to the body, charm is to the word, to the person. How vacuous to discuss the "thought patterns" in *As You Like It* and not allow for the charm of Rosalind's personality! How portentous to deal with Shaw as Marxist, Wagnerite, vegetarian, antivivisectionist, and pass over the fact that his characters woo us and win us—not with their philosophy but with their charm! Another of the open secrets of Brecht was that while he attacked other forms of charm he had his own. Being a dramatist, he passed it on to his characters, particularly to those with whom he was strongly identified—Galy Gay, Macheath, Galileo, Mother Courage, Azdak.

Something similar needs to be said of *naïveté*. The word has been used more and more in our century because more and more people have come to regard themselves as *not* naïve—as subtle fellows. It is now the usual word with which to strike down an argument you cannot answer, an opponent whose weak spot you cannot find. It is pleasant, therefore, to find Brecht, in his last years, saying a good word for naïveté. He regarded it as a sort of ultimate goal for any stylist.

In question here, then, is not the kind of simplicity an artist starts out with at the age of nineteen; for that matter, his style may well be at its most "complex" at that age. In question is the simplicity that is achieved when much complexity has been worked through and worn down. To the truly naïve reader, such not-really-naïve art is "deceptively" simple. The late lyrics of Brecht are a case in point. They are positively cryptic. The sense is between the lines. It is doubtful if Brecht is really simpler than poets who parade their "difficulty."

Of the charm of *The Caucasian Chalk Circle* there is no doubt. As to whether the presentation is naïve, that is a matter of definition. In any case, naïveté of style would be no guarantee of unambiguousness of import. Like many another wily Bavarian peasant, Bertolt Brecht could be devious in very simple words. And in case the word "devious" gives offense, I hasten to add that what we call deviousness in behavior becomes, in literature of genius, richness of texture and fullness of significance.

Chinese boxes. The Berlin critic Friedrich Luft has said that while the younger Brecht wished to use theatre to alter the world, the later Brecht took a step back when he said the theatre should only show the world to be alterable. I'm not so sure that even the earlier Brecht theatre had such direct designs on the world as had the theatre of Erwin Piscator or Clifford Odets, but I agree that some sort of withdrawal took place later. I would place it in the late thirties. And the true explanation is the simple one: that Brecht was forced by Hitler into a withdrawal from political life in his own country. Living among foreigners who did not know him or his language, he could not be the kind of writer he had recently decided to become: the Party activist. He was forced into that very withdrawal which most artists crave and which the activist seeks to avoid. Those of us who knew Brecht in exile can testify to the extent of the withdrawal. It is to Hitler, then, that we owe the big plays of these years, plays which were much more deeply meditated, drawn from sources deeper inside as well as more remote in time, than those of the preceding years.

I mean chiefly *Galileo, Mother Courage,* and *The Caucasian Chalk Circle,* the last of which marks an end point. I have read most of what Brecht is known to have written afterward, and I find him taking no new steps—only retracing old ones. In the sense here suggested, *The Caucasian Chalk Circle* is his last play. It is certainly the play of deepest withdrawal. The form, puzzling at first, can be seen as Chinese boxes, one inside the other, Azdak's story being a box within the Grusha story, the innermost box (to my mind) being the narrative of Azdak's two big songs.

The first of the songs is a description from the time of Azdak's grandfather of the miserable state of the people and the appalling conduct of the ruling classes. The second of the songs describes a popular revolution. It is based on an ancient document which Brecht had already quoted in his essay on five ways of telling the truth. The further back we go in time the closer we come to what Brecht regards as present and future. The flashback is used, as it were, in order to flash forward. The urgent and the ultimate are presented in a dream within a dream, a memory within a memory. All of which is stressed precisely when the socialist moral is stated at the end: Azdak "disappeared and was never seen again," and his time became a legend of a "brief golden age."

The Prologue. And we are not surprised when we read that West German theatres put the play on as a "charming fantasy," or that the dialecticians of the East rise up in wrath to explain the Prologue. The Prologue is set not in older times but at a date later than the year when Brecht started work on the play. If the rest of the play, without the Prologue, might be taken to be "unreal," the Prologue is set in what for a Communist of that era was the most real of all real places, Soviet Russia. It might also be assumed that, once the Prologue is played, you can't forget it, and so everything that happens all evening is seen in direct relation to it.

Now it seems to me quite likely that this was what Brecht intended, and certainly the Prologue was not added after Brecht got to East Berlin—it was present in the first manuscript I saw of the play (1946). The question is whether we can take the will for the deed. If the little Prologue cannot function as some of Brecht's friends would wish it to, it is not for lack of good intentions but for lack of weight.

Brecht and tragedy. The last time I saw Bertolt Brecht (June 1956) we spoke of Ernst Busch's performance as Azdak, and Brecht said the actor had missed the "whole tragic side of the role." I think the comment has the highest interest for Brecht criticism because Brecht usually talked *against* tragedy, and those who have found "a tragic side" in his work have assumed that he was unconscious of it. What *is* tragic about Azdak? On the surface, the part is all racy and ironic comedy, but, aside from anything he says, Azdak performs an action near the beginning of his part of the play which casts a good deal of light on the whole: *having let the Grand Duke escape, he denounces himself to the authorities for so doing.* It is a very bizarre incident, in itself hard to believe, and, as acted by Busch, flatly incredible. What is its moral and psychological content? First, self-denunciation, as often in Brecht and Stalinist culture generally, is seen as good. Azdak is doing what Galileo abysmally failed to do: taking his punishment. Second, the "goodness" is canceled by the fact that the authorities surrendered to are bad. The tragedy of Azdak, as found in this incident, is that his effort at heroism is reduced to absurdity by the circumstances. *"Doch die Verhältnisse, sie sind nicht so,"* to quote Mr. Peachum—"That isn't how things are." *The tragedy of Azdak is that his life is a comedy.*

The incident has a third aspect. It carries a note of personal poignancy to the degree—the very considerable degree—that Azdak represents his author. There is nothing tragic, of course, in Brecht's willingness to denounce himself. What is tragic is his suspicion that the authorities he might denounce himself to were no better than those he had rebelled against. If *The Caucasian Chalk Circle* is implicitly dedicated to Stalin, also implicit is the question: What if Stalin should prove a grand duke—or a mad czar? One can hardly forget that *Galileo* and *The Caucasian Chalk Circle* followed in the wake of the self-denunciations of Radek and Bukharin.

I am not concerned here with evidence that has been coming to light that, in the fifties, Brecht was more than worried about Stalinism in East Germany. My point is rather that this more-than-worry—this haunting suspicion—antedates "East Germany." Disenchantment was indeed burnt deep into Brecht's personality, and it would be naïve to think that it affected only his thoughts about capitalism. Stalin's pact with Hitler in 1939 was a baffling blow, and Brecht (as he once told me) had not been able to say, with Nexö and others, "Well, Hitler is a socialist too." He was full of doubt, dread, and guilt, as some of his poems testify—and as some of his conversation testified. And what makes most credible Wolfgang Harich's claim in 1956 that Brecht belonged to the anti-Ulbricht, anti-Stalin "rebellion" is that Brecht had for a long time kept ajar that door to non-Stalinist thoughts which better Communists kept tightly shut. I have heard him defend Ignazio Silone in company that was horrified, and in June 1956 the book I saw open on his desk in East Berlin was the American edition of Koestler's *The Invisible Writing.* . . . The dark lining to Azdak's comic coat of many colors is the tragedy of the disenchanted revolutionary.

Azdak, oddly enough, has much in common with Galileo—Brecht's Galileo. Not only are they both of them rogues in the sense defined above, they both embody the same contradictions: for instance, of talking, particularly about sex, like men about town, but behaving more like hermits. They are essentially solitary. Azdak comes out of solitude and returns to it. Galileo is progressively detached from the world and his friends. Both characters reflect the isolation of Brecht.

I recall exchanging letters with Brecht about certain rather elementary and even banal problems of communism and literature. I was brought up sharp by his remarking that *I was the only person with whom he discussed such things.* Now I was not a member of what was regarded as his circle of intimates. As a non-Communist, I was, in a sense, not even *persona grata.* I suddenly realized that Bertolt Brecht, surrounded by disciples and "comrades," lived, intellectually at least, in a state of total isolation. Behind that Iron Curtain, it is not only the Pasternaks who have lived alone, nor, perhaps, was it only behind the Iron Curtain that Brecht lived lonely amid the crowd. Things were no doubt quite similar in California, where *The Caucasian Chalk Circle* was written.

Why labor a commonplace? However antitragic a poet's philosophy, if he is truly a poet, the tragedy of his life will find some echoes in his work. To the question: Was this what Brecht meant when he spoke of the tragic side of Azdak, one must answer, in the first place, Obviously not, but, in the second place, Yes.

"Theater ist einfältig, wenn es nicht vielfältig ist." This punning dictum of Brecht's can be freely translated: Theatre is simple-minded unless it is open-minded, or: The dramatic poet has a one-track mind unless his mind runs on several tracks. One sometimes has to quarrel with Brecht's "contradictions," but *to quarrel with* can be *to pay homage to.* In any event, there are authors who *must* be quarreled with—not because (or not only because) they are wrong and you are right, but because this is the only way they can be encountered. Was anyone ever able to read Nietzsche without fighting him? There are philosophers whose views you just memorize: Nietzsche makes you fight. He is "wrong"—but he is hard to answer! He is "wrong"—but unlike those who are right he is hard to ignore or forget! What is a philosopher for, finally? And even if you decide that a philosopher is there to provide you with correct opinions, is that what an artist is for? There is another view, namely, that the artist is there to experience and express the contradictions, whether or not he can resolve them. If this view is valid, a critic is not captious when he points out what those contradictions are, nor is he accusing the artist of stupidity or deceitfulness if he remarks that some contradictions were less conscious than others. The criticism that is unworthy of Brecht (here I return to my starting point) is the criticism that ignores or denies the contradictions. Precisely *this* criticism is either disingenuous or simple-minded and makes Brecht so.

If there is a tendency now, in Paris or East Berlin, to put Brecht on a pedestal, one should recall that the older German poets are already on such pedestals, and that Bertolt Brecht spent quite a lot of energy trying to pull them down.

(1960)

Baal

The fame of Brecht's later plays has been bad for the reputation of his earlier ones, and in combating this phenomenon one is combating some powerful preconceptions. It is assumed, for example, that a major writer steadily improves. Early works are automatically placed in such categories as "juvenilia" and "apprenticeship." Also, the earlier work is judged by criteria suggested by the later. Brecht himself judged his early work by criteria suggested by the later. Which compounded the problem, and created the cliché. The cliché reads as follows: The later Brecht was a great man who had found himself in finding a great philosophy. The early Brecht was a confused and misguided young fellow who would never have come to any good—had he not found the great philosophy and, through it, his greater self. In other words, the early work represents the sin from which Marxism redeemed him. The early Brecht is the unregenerate Saul; the late Brecht, the Sainted Paul. Now this cliché is the more important because it is taken over—with a little rewording—by many non-Marxists. It can be taken over without misgivings by anyone who is prepared to assume that to go from despair and pessimism to some sort of "positive" philosophy is necessarily to become a finer artist.

To protest at this cliché should not be to reverse it. An artist is not confronted with the alternative: progress or regress. More normal is simply development—with ups and downs. And that, in my view, is what the career of Brecht has to show. This much, however, must be said on behalf of his early work: that had he died immediately after writing it, he would, in time, have been classed with other such youths of amazing poetic genius as Büchner and Rimbaud.

In time. His work, like theirs, could not be assimilated by the contemporary public. It was too original. In any case, the broader public takes up "unpopular" work only on the basis of some misunderstanding. Brecht himself was to become popular through misunderstanding when the German bourgeoisie would take *The Threepenny Opera* to its big clammy bosom in the belief that the philosophy of the piece was summed up in: *Erst kommt das Fressen, dann kommt die Moral.* If an author cannot be understood, it is important, for his bankbook at least, that he be misunderstood, but *Baal*—Brecht's first play except for high-school juvenilia—did not get across in either way. It was intelligible, in the 1920s, only to persons who themselves had unusual insight into our life and times. In a prologue which Hofmannsthal wrote for the Viennese première in 1926, the older poet put his finger on the very pulse of the play: ". . . all the ominous events of Europe," says one of his spokesmen, "which we have witnessed these last twelve years are nothing but a long drawn-out way of laying the weary concept of the European individual in the grave. . . ." Oscar Homolka, who played Baal, receives this speech from Hofmannsthal: "We are anonymous forces. Psychological possibilities. Individuality is one of the fantastic embellishments which we have stripped from us. You'll see how I'm going to play Baal."

We are taught in school about "the end of heroism" in the drama of the eighteenth and nineteenth centuries. The hero of tragedy was replaced by the individual of the nineteenth-century novel and play. Ibsen's work is par excellence the drama of that individual. Yet even here, where the dramatis personae are most individual, individuality is seen as threatened. Failing to be a hero, Master Builder Solness manages to be an individual—but only just, for the threat of complete disintegration is ever-present. In the dream plays of Strindberg the individual is dissolving in mist and mysticism. Here, instead of personalities, there are memories, bits of experience, cross references, images, names, momentary encounters. In Pirandello's plays of around 1920 the nonexistence of the individual is proclaimed, but to sustain the form of a play Pirandello reverts to the traditional types, a little dressed up in Ibsenish "biography." Hence there is an element of contradiction between the *theory* that there is no such thing as continuity in character and the presentation, in practice, of people who *are* continuous and of a piece. Yet Pirandello does more than state the idea of discontinuity: he also projects the state of soul of those who believe in this idea, those who feel discontinuous with themselves, the disoriented, the metaphysically as well as neurotically lost: men of the twentieth century.

Baal is neither a Strindbergian dream play, nor a Pirandellian "play in the ιaking." What was in part a theory for the older men is here wholly a practice, state of being, a fact of life. Few of us did see how Homolka played Baal, yet ιe script itself suggests vividly enough the truth of his remarks. Baal is a stripped" character—is man stripped of character. There is a paradox about ιhe Victorian Man of Character, the Independent Individual of the age of individualism, which is that he was formed by that age and belonged utterly to that society. The rejection of the individual that comes with the twentieth century, and especially after World War I, is a rejection of the society around him, and even of society as such. Baal is the asocial man.

It would be natural enough to call him amoral, and his actions stamp him as what Freud called polymorphous perverse: sensuality is acceptable to him in itself, and he does not limit himself to the "outlets" which society approves. However, if this were the beginning and end of Baal, the play that bears his name would simply be a tract favoring the noble savage, a return to an innocent paganism. Nothing could be further from the text before us. The image of an innocent paganism is present in it, but is by no means the image of the play as a whole. Baal beholds the innocence, the amorality, of Nature all around us, but from a distance and with longing and envy. The *sky* would be an ideal mistress indeed, but how far off it is, how unreachable! Between us and primal innocence stands the world, which includes that very society of men which one would reject.

"Screw the world!" Those three syllables sum up a whole school of modern art and thought. Lautréamont had given the idea "sodomitic" form even earlier:

Oh that the universe were an immense celestial anus! I would plunge my penis past its bloody sphincter, rending apart, with my impetuous motion, the very bones of the pelvis.

The prologue to *Baal* reads:

> And that girl the world who gives herself and giggles
> If you only let her crush you with her thighs
> Shared with Baal, who loved it, orgiastic wriggles.
> But he did not die. He looked her in the eyes.

No innocent enjoyment of beautiful Nature here! If Lautréamont is sadistic, Brecht is cooly defiant. He looks "that girl" in the eyes. How much lies behind such a look! How much pain and despair, how much living!

Though all drama tends to be about guilt, one might expect that a drama without individuals, without respect for society—a drama without ego or super-ego, one might be tempted to put it—would be an exception, would be "beyond guilt." One has read here and there that to give up the individual is to give up the whole notion of responsibility, but it is not so unless one is uttering a tautology: to give up the individual is to give up *individual* responsibility.

Responsibility and guilt remain, and only seem the more unwieldy, the more oppressive, for not being neatly tied to this person and that action.

Brecht does make Baal seem cut off from the meaning of his own actions: from his killing of Ekart and his virtual killing of Johanna Reiher. Only with difficulty, looking back on the play, can one say to oneself: *It is a play about a murderer.* And yet by any humane standard murder is only one among Baal's several offenses and amid his consistent offensiveness. The immediate reason for this difficulty is to be found in Brecht's special perspective. He lends Baal a quality of innocence, but it is an innocence on the other side of guilt. Our minds, which are used to thinking here of a duality (guilt-innocence), have to stretch themselves a little to think in terms of three instead of two: innocence (1), guilt, and innocence (2). This innocence (2) is the subject of much of Brecht's writing in this period. It could even be said that around 1919–1921 his favorite subject was the innocence that can accrue to extremely vicious, even extremely criminal, people. It is as if one were to speak of regained innocence in an old whore.

Dostoevski, it could be added, does speak of such innocence. It is even inherent in Christianity, and was written out once and for all in the New Testament story of Mary Magdalene, but Brecht's second innocence has no such authority behind it. It has no one's blessing except his own. It carries no fringe benefits in this world or the next. It is not a state of beatitude that endures or that presages endurance. It is no more than a poet's feeling, an inspired hunch, a momentary dream, "just a thought"; hence its peculiar pathos. If it holds out a hope, it is a hope neither of utopia here nor heaven there, it says merely that a life could—at moments—be conceived of that is not quite so bad:

> *träumt er gelegentlich von einer kleinen Wiese*
> *mit blauem Himmel drüber und sonst nichts.*

> (He dreams at times about a little meadow
> A patch of blue in the sky and nothing more.)

There *is* a dream of celestial bliss in Brecht's early work, but it has the character of an ephemeral image, something that crosses the line of spiritual vision and is gone, a small loveliness sandwiched in between huge horrors. (Thus too, in a not so early work, the fragile lyric "Die Liebenden" is inserted in the story of *Mahagonny* between copulations that are paid for.) Insofar as Dostoevski managed to believe in a real heaven, he could see it as transcending and swallowing up all that is unheavenly, even as eternity swallows up time. In Brecht it is hell—hell on earth—that is eternal, heaven that is swallowed up. The pathos of unbelief is pervasive in Brecht's lifework. It is his personal pathos, but cogent and significant because it is also the characteristic pathos of the whole epoch.

For in the modern era, from Kierkegaard to Graham Greene, even the believers are not sure they really believe, they are sure only that they should. They are able only—like Brecht when later he came to "believe" in communism—to "commit" themselves to a belief—i.e., take the consequences of joining the ranks of the faithful even though their faith is not really felt. Hence, *Baal* is solid and firm where the Brecht plays that affirm communism are, in that affirmation, rather shaky and hollow. *Baal* conveys the actual *Weltgefühl* of Bertolt Brecht throughout his career. A play like *The Mother* articulates the *Weltanschauung* which he agreed to commit himself to in the hope that a better *Welt* might come out of it after which the original *Weltgefühl* would change by itself. Even if this plan had all worked out, it would not make *The Mother* a better work of art than *Baal;* just the contrary. If all Brecht's later plays had been on the pattern of *The Mother,* his later works would simply have proved inferior to the earlier.

Brecht's "heaven" is momentary, and does not redeem. The guilt remains, and the guilt is all the greater for not being only a guilt for specific offenses. When the individual disappears, what is left is the race. And the race is seen by Brecht as burdened with a primal curse—that which caused the Greeks to repeat that "not to be born is the best for man," and the Christians to formulate a doctrine of "original sin." If at moments we think that Brecht takes Baal's crimes too lightly—murder, after all, is murder—we quickly realize that in saying, "Baal is no worse than the rest of us," he is not taking a high view of Baal but a low view of the rest of us. He is saying we are ourselves no better than murderers. We may even be worse than Baal, in that we may have missed the romance with the sky, and the dream of the little meadow. We may be Baal minus the poetry.

And—what is partly the same thing—minus the pleasure. For though Baal's pleasures are finally poisoned by guilt and ended by aggression, they were not impure at the source. On the contrary, the search for pleasure is the one truly affirmative element in the play, and the reason why the poetry of the play retains a directly and even ingenuously romantic aura. Baal really was seeking

Immer das Land wo es besser zu leben ist.

(Ever the country where there's a better life.)

More than thirty years later, Brecht was to take a look back at this play and speak of the love of pleasure, the search for happiness, as its subject. The comment is to be taken the more seriously in that *Baal* is, in all other respects, so unacceptable to the later Brecht; but the human longing for happiness "which cannot be killed" (as he put it) was a theme he was ready to pursue at all times. He reports that he tried to pick up the thread of *Baal* twenty years afterward in an opera-libretto about a Chinese god of happiness. (True, he had come by then to believe that Russia was "the country where there's a better life" and that "happiness is—Communism." With the early Brecht, it is as if he was striving to break through to a hedonism as radical as that of Herbert Marcuse or Norman O. Brown. That guilt and anxiety blocked this path may, in one respect, however, have been fortunate: he was a dramatist—conflict was his raw material.)

In the fact that Baal is respected by Brecht as pleasure-seeker (though some readers may come to the play with an unfortunate puritanic prejudice) lies part of the reason that he is not pure villain. Walter Sokel has written of him eloquently as a parody of those Expressionistic heroes whose life was a sacred mission, but since Brecht considered the Expressionist missions spurious, he makes Baal's mission genuine. Baal is an ambiguous, ambivalent figure: part monster but partly, too, the martyr of a poetic hedonism. And the positive element is more prominent than the negative because it is Baal's special contribution— his monstrousness he has in common with a monstrous world. (Later, the peculiar acidity of *The Threepenny Opera* would come from the implied proposition: "We on stage may be little crooks; but many of you out front are big ones.")

Yet if in the figure of Baal the more sympathetic element prevails over the less, in the play of *Baal* the poetry of life is overwhelmed by the prose, the beauty by the horror. If, as I tend to believe, a good play amounts finally to a particular vision of life seen as a whole, then this play is a vision of life as an inferno, and the occasional faint gleam of beauty only makes the ugliness look more intensely black. Baal will let no one persuade him he has lost all chance of pleasure. But self is something he lost so long ago its discovery is never in the cards. One might better put it that he never had a self. Whereas in Ibsen the self is threatened, and in Pirandello it is *said* not to exist, in Brecht both the Ibsenite self and the Pirandellian discussion are so far in the past they are totally forgotten. There remains the horror: Lowell's "horror of the lost self." And this horror belongs even more to the play than to the protagonist.

"We possess nothing in the world—a mere chance can strip us of everything—except the power to say *I*." So said Simone Weil. What then can a poet say for whom there is no *I* to affirm? "Nada y pues nada y nada y pues nada. Our nada, who art in nada, nada be thy name. . . ." From Hemingway, in this famous passage published in 1933, to Samuel Beckett in the 1950s with his "nothing is more real than nothing," contemporary poets and poet-novelists and poet-dramatists have found themselves confronted and surrounded by nothingness. Brecht found himself in this situation in 1918 at the frighteningly youthful age of nineteen or twenty. *"Das Schönste ist das Nichts."* ("The most beautiful thing is nothing.") Googoo says this in the thirteenth scene of *Baal*. Brecht says it in every scene of *Baal*. Man, here, is alienated from the others and from himself, to the degree that both others and self may be said to nonexist, to be nothing. This idea—better: this sentiment, this lacerating conviction—gives a new poignancy to the old "ashes to ashes, dust to dust." If death is, on the one hand, an ironic ending to pleasure and beauty, it is, on the other, a direct, unironic continuation of the universal nothingness, the omnipresent death-in-life.

Baal is about nothingness. By that token it is also about death. Brecht might well have taken yet another idea from the playwright who most influenced him, Büchner, and called his play *Baal's Death*. The mythic Baal was a fertility god, a god of life. This mythological (i.e., unpsychological) drama presents the archetypal battle of life and death, Eros and Thanatos. Traditionally, such a story would follow the pattern of rebirth: death followed by resurrection. Brecht who was always to parody the traditional patterns is doing so already in his first play where death is followed by . . . death.

Some readers have found the play formless. What it finally achieves in the way of organic form must perhaps remain a matter of opinion but analysis will demonstrate at least that there is some very deliberate patterning here. *Baal* is the play in which the protagonist dies three times—in three ways that are poetically diversified. First, he dies as "Teddy," and speaks his own funeral oration (as Galy Gay is to do in *A Man's a Man*.) Second, he relates his own death in the poem, "Death in the Forest." Third, there is his actual death scene, with which the play ends. The identity of the three deaths is clearly established by the identical forest setting and the identical cruel attitude of the dying one's fellow men. ("The coldness of the forests will be with me to my dying day," Brecht said in a famous poem; and he could have said the same of the coldness of those who are in attendance at the dying day—one thinks forward to the death of Swiss Cheese and, for that matter, the death of Brecht's Jesus in his "Song of the Hours.") Perhaps the whole play was planned as a kind of air and variations on the theme of dying. The drowning of Johanna is less an action than a leitmotif.

A final word on the Baal myth and Brecht's attitude to it. A writer from Augsburg, Brecht's native town describes the poet's room at the time that he wrote *Baal:*

> . . . over the bed [was] a lifesize picture of his idol Baal, that Semitic-Phoenician deity of insatiability which Christianity had declared the principle of evil. . . . Caspar Neher had drawn it in the then current style of Masereel after Brecht's model, a male vamp named K. from Pfersee near Augsburg.

And this is probably to place the emphasis correctly: what would interest Brecht is that Baal was the enemy of the Christian-Judaic, puritanic, ascetic tradition. Perhaps he knew, too, that in the Canaanite *Poem of Baal* this god had an enemy, Môt, "the god," as Theodore Gaster says, "of all that lacks life and vitality." The very name Môt means death. Standing for fertility, Baal was also the god of rainfall, and the association of fertility with rain is something Brecht would remember when he created his comic fertility god—the Bloody Five of *A Man's a Man*.

Gaster's book *Thespis* reports many things which it is tempting to connect with Brecht's play, such as that the god Baal copulated with a calf, and that "Baal's enveloping robe is . . . identified with the sky," and that, at his death, Baal "fell into the earth." In relation to the recurrent image of a corpse floating down a river, it is startling to read in Gaster that the motif is common in the folklore of Brecht's part of the world:

> In many of the seasonal mummeries representing the rout of the Dragon, or the expulsion of Death, Blight, or Winter, he is *flung into the water*. Thus, at Nuremberg, the traditional song specified that "we bear Death into the water." . . . At Tabor, Bohemia, it was said that "Death floats down the stream" . . . and at Bielsk, Podlachia, the effigy was drowned in a marsh or pond. . . . In Chrudim, Bohemia, Death was flung into the water on "Black Sunday" [one of Brecht's early poems refers to Black Saturday]. . . . In Silesia, children used to throw the effigy of Death into the river . . . while at Leipzig this was done by the local prostitutes and bastards. . . .

There is enough here to guarantee that Brecht's *Baal* will sooner or later be interpreted wholly in terms of myth and ritual. Such interpretations will be unbalanced—but surely less unbalanced than those that try to make sense of *Baal* on the lines of what was conventional drama in 1918.

Historians have shown that, in *Baal*, Brecht was mocking the Expressionists. Specifically, he sought to debunk Hanns Johst's image of the poet as ecstatic visionary amid the wicked materialism of the surrounding world. In effect, though, the young Brecht had taken on a much larger antagonist than any Expressionist playwright. He had made a *tabula rasa* of the modern drama as a whole and on that bare surface had erected a primitive and already sturdy structure of his own. For better or for worse, a new era in dramatic art dates from this play.

(1963)

Edward II

If Brecht's early works have been neglected and underrated, *Edward II* must surely be the most neglected and underrated of them all. I was told by several persons that they assumed the play would not turn up at all in an English-language edition of Brecht's works, "since it is a translation from the English, and who wants to have Marlowe translated back from the German?" My reply is that the same point was made, earlier, about *The Threepenny Opera,* with as little justification. Brecht was uninterested in translation and probably incapable of it. Anything he touched became inalienably his own.* It is true that he was prepared to lift many lines from other authors, not to mention incidents, but even lines and incidents reproduced by Brecht without change are always utterly changed by their new context. The work of other authors was infinitely suggestive for Brecht, but *what* it suggested was entirely his own affair, and would have surprised those other authors very much indeed.

Even when people are told that Brecht's treatment of Marlowe's *Edward II* is "free," what they expect is Marlowe cut and edited, as by an expert stage director or scholarly popularizer who aims at providing the "essence of Marlowe." Possibly Brecht uses almost as much of Marlowe's plot as that kind of adapter, and quotes almost as many of the lines, yet his aim—to realize which he has to write in many lines of his own, and invent new incidents—is diametrically

* See also page 109.

opposite. Telling a tale that is only outwardly, and not at all points even outwardly, the same, he tells it about quite different people to the end of embodying quite a different theme and communicating quite a different vision of life. The remarkable thing is how much of the original can be absorbed in what is essentially a brand-new play. An aspect of Brecht's genius for which he has not yet been given full credit is his gift of assimilation. How many fruits he sucked dry! This is not to say it was a matter of indifference what fruit came his way. To speak less metaphorically, the material must be transformable, but must also, in its as yet untransformed state, have something substantial to offer. And Brecht had an uncanny way of finding what offered him most, whether it was a particular Japanese Noh or a play by Marlowe that few Germans had even heard of. Which, no doubt, is yet another aspect of his genius.

What was it that Marlowe's play did offer him? Many things, a number of which will emerge as we proceed. What first comes to mind is the subject—a Brechtian one—of a homosexual relationship seen as a fatal infatuation, seen, moreover, as masochistic in relation to the male principal and as sadistic in relation to women. Secondly, the form. Speaking on general lines, one would have to say that the form of an Elizabethan chronicle play offered Brecht that distance from immediate experience which later he would bring under the heading of *Verfremdung* or Alienation. England in the Middle Ages is, in other words, another of his exotic-grotesque pseudo milieus. Thinking specifically of Marlowe's *Edward II,* one would want to add that it has a remarkably expressive pattern of action which can be taken over and perhaps in some respects improved upon. According to this pattern, the hero becomes a more sympathetic person as his fortunes grow worse, while his chief antagonist becomes more and more repellent as he has more and more success.

If that—plus a lot of usable incidents and lines—is what Marlowe had to offer Brecht, in what did the Brechtian transformation consist? Anyone interested in the technique of playmaking—the carpentry of it—might learn much from watching the young Brecht reduce the number of characters from about forty to about twenty and simplifying the incidents to match this reduction. In one who was only just starting out as a playwright, the technical achievement alone was one to mark him as a dramatic genius, but probably little of this simplifying was done for its own sake. Brecht had no objection to a bewildering complexity, as his other plays of this period show. The point—as with his more famous transformations of later years—was to turn things completely around, to write a counterplay, to *re*write Marlowe, to correct him, to stand him on his feet.

A reader of Marlowe who starts to read the Brecht is surprised and perhaps disappointed very early on by Brecht's omission of the most famous purple patch in the play, Gaveston's speech about the fun which he and Edward will have together:

I must have wanton poets, pleasant wits,
Musicians, that with touching of a string
May draw the pliant king which way I please:
Music and poetry is his delight,
Therefore I'll have Italian masks by night,
Sweet speeches, comedies, and pleasing shows,
And in the day, when he shall walk abroad,
Like sylvan nymphs my pages shall be clad;
My men, like satyrs grazing on the lawns,
Shall with their goat-feet dance an antic hay;
Sometime a lovely boy, in Dian's shape,
With hair that gilds the water as it glides,
Crownets of pearl about his naked arms,
And in his sportful hands an olive tree,
To hide those parts which men delight to see,
Shall bathe him in a spring . . .

If the topic is homosexuality, would not such a passage seem relevant? Reading on, one finds that it is not relevant—is not *possible*—to the experience Brecht depicts, the world he creates. A whole dimension of the poet Marlowe is not usable, and it may well be the dimension which most of his English-language readers find the most attractive: Renaissance sensuousness finding expression in luxurious words and sinuous rhythms.

Brecht's refusal of the Marlovian line is not motivated by modesty. The Brechtian "counterplay" is always a sort of serious parody, converting the sublime to the grotesque. In Marlowe the steady roll of the blank verse has an effect comparable in solemnity to the rhymed Alexandrines of French classical tragedy. The Brecht version intersperses iambic pentameter with shorter lines —and sometimes with longer ones—that break the pattern and shatter, as it were, the icon. As with the form, so with the content. The homosexuality in Marlowe is at once aesthetic and ambiguous. Sometimes seeming conscious, physical, and even animal, it seems at other times but the Elizabethan cult of poeticized friendship. When the Elder Mortimer says Edward will get over it soon, we aren't compelled to disbelieve him. As for Brecht, some readers have had the impression that he wanted to be "shockingly frank" and sensational in the modern manner. That is not the point. It is not even true. Whereas Marlowe's Gaveston is seen not just as bedfellow but even more as royal "favorite," and a marriage we need not regard as phony is being arranged for him with a princess, Brecht's Gaveston is a sexual partner first and last. The word "whore" is bound to recur, as it does, if, as we do, we keep hearing what his enemies think of him.

A reader who looked at the end of the play first, even though there is no sex in it, would receive the same jolt from Brecht's changes as the reader who looks at the opening scenes. When Marlowe's Edward has to give up not only Gaveston but this world, what he is left with is the Christian religion— that is, the hope of a next world. His friend Baldock provides the cue:

> Make for a new life, man; throw up thy eyes,
> And heart and hand to heaven's immortal throne. . . .

And so the lyric afflatus prompted in the beginning by sex is sustained in the end by religious sentiment:

> Yet stay a while, forbear thy bloody hand,
> And let me see the stroke before it comes
> That even then when I shall lose my life
> My mind may be more steadfast on my God. . . .

And:

> I am too weak and feeble to resist.
> Assist me, sweet God, and receive my soul.

Now, though Brecht's Edward also ends up as a metaphysician, the metaphysics is a travesty of Christianity (close in its wording to an acknowledged parody Brecht wrote on the subject, the "Great Thanksgiving Hymn"):

> Therefore
> Who is dark, let him stay dark,
> Who is unclean, let him stay unclean.
> Praise deficiency, praise cruelty, praise
> The darkness.

And we find, in this ending, an instance of the same words coming to mean the opposite when used by Brecht. I refer to Mortimer's summing up, his speech about the wheel of fortune. In Marlowe's play this Elizabethan commonplace concerning the fate of "magistrates" is not felt to be contradicted by an affirmative treatment of young Edward's accession to the throne: by a turn of fortune's wheel Mortimer gets his deserts, but the accession of Edward III is an improvement and a purification. Brecht on the other hand, through Mortimer, turns the argument against the new King, as much as to say, "Your turn will come." Here, the wheel of fortune is an image of a philosophy that hovers over the whole play: history goes meaninglessly round and round.

Luckily, it is not the only philosophy in the play, or it would reduce all the characters to mere pawns on a historical chessboard. No one could see or read Brecht's *Edward II* and feel that this is what they are. Brecht's Edward is far less passive than Marlowe's. This is indeed Brecht's most decisive divergence from his source, and it is in looking further into it that we begin to discover what Brecht put into the play to make up for the Marlovian elements which he so drastically cut. Whether he came out with a play which is better or worse than Marlowe's is, I think, a question not to be asked: their plays are, finally, so different as to be incommensurable. But I do think that, like many another great play, Marlowe's has shortcomings and that Brecht sometimes found solutions where his predecessor had found none. This much by way of explanation, if what follows gives the impression that I do consider Brecht's a better play.

Marlowe's eloquence has rightly been praised, yet there is something about his eloquent *Edward II* that is dramatically unsatisfying. "Edward sings too many arias," one tends to say: yet the fact that he does so serves to conceal a dramatic weakness, which derives from Edward's passivity. Thinking about the shortcomings of Marlowe's play, one recalls W. B. Yeats's rejection of passive suffering as a dramatic subject. Whether or not it should be rejected out of hand, passive suffering certainly presents problems which are seldom solved. Looking at this particular narrative, one finds two nodal points in it: the point where Edward gives Gaveston up, and the point where he gives the crown up. Both are actions which are not actions. "That's Edward," Marlowe might have said. It is a proposition which is reversed by Brecht, whose Edward refuses to give up either Gaveston or the crown. He loses them anyway, of course; so, from a cynical point of view, there's no difference between the two Edwards. There is all the difference in the world from a tragic point of view—and is not *Edward II* the one play of Brecht's which can be called a tragedy in any accepted sense?

However this may be, we are confronted here with opposite characters in opposite stories. One play is about a weak man who, under pressure, gives up his friend first and his crown later, and interests us only in his very human weakness and by virtue of the faint halo that is cast around it by all the grace and poeticizing. The other is a play about an infatuated man, made palatable to us in the beginning by no poetry or charm, but earning our admiration, gradually and with difficulty, by a surprising loyalty both to his friend and to his idea of himself as king. Marlowe's play, for all its magnificent rhetoric, is a little monotonous because Edward for so long stays the same, repeating himself not only in words but in action (or rather in inaction). Though the young Brecht is often spoken of as mainly a lyric poet, nothing marks him more unmistakably as a dramatic genius than the way in which he was able to make Edward change not just at the end but throughout the play. We see a different Edward in the middle of the play already when we find him toughened by a soldier's life in the open. That is of course only the outward form and result of a toughness which, Brecht makes us realize, must always have been there. It is not out of a clear sky that Edward, when facing his worst and final sufferings, proves then most strong and most serene:

> . . . such water hardens my limbs which are now
> Like cedar wood.
> The stench of excrement gives me boundless greatness!
> And the good sound of drums keeps me awake,
> Though weak, so death won't find me fainting but
> Waking.

Now, if one had to illustrate Marlowe's gift of character creation from *Edward II*, one could not say very much about any character save Edward himself. If Brecht eliminated about twenty of Marlowe's figures, he did so in order to develop more fully the four leading personae, who, after Edward, are Gaveston, the Queen, and Mortimer. I have already tried to suggest what he made of Gaveston. To that broad suggestion should be added that Gaveston is here given further touches of reality that belong to the situation of a young man who has not so much worked hard to get a Great Personage's attention as he has had this attention forced upon him:

> I . . . do not know
> What it was about me of too much or little
> That made this Edward, now the King,
> Unable to leave me alone
> For my own mother found nothing in me
> Any different from the extremely
> Usual, no goitre, no white skin. . . .

Because Edward is really infatuated, Gaveston does not have to be a seducer or even a schemer, and the pattern is more human, more typical, and, finally, more dramatic this way. The downfall of Gaveston has the more poignancy because it is so much more than he "asked for."

If Gaveston, in the Brecht, is less the standard wastrel, the Queen is far less shadowy. It is remarkable how skillfully the young Brecht was able to mark the stages in this character's development. Whereas in Marlowe the Queen's liaison is suddenly there, and mentioned, in the Brecht we see it happen step by step, and feel the inexorable logic of it. The drama in the material is found by underlining her reluctance on the one hand and Edward's aggressive misogyny on the other. (The dynamics of sexuality—hence its drama—are always better seen in the sadistic and masochistic components than in the romance.) Again, there is great technical accomplishment in the modern play; but, again, that is subordinate to a larger human matter: in this case, the Queen's gradual loss of all sense of herself and, therewith, of reality generally. Nowhere is Brecht's audacity more marked or, to my mind, more triumphant than in the scene entitled "The emptiness of the world makes the Queen laugh." No topic, of course, has been more often dilated upon by modern writers than this "emptiness in the world." Credit is due to Brecht not for taking the subject up but for showing in a succession of dramatic encounters how the Queen *discovers* the void.

In Marlowe, Edward has but one partner and foil: Gaveston. In Brecht, he has three: Gaveston, the Queen, and Mortimer. The contrast is a strong one between the infatuated, stubborn king and the lost, embarrassed, not stupid, fundamentally rather innocent boy friend. The contrast is strong, too, between Edward and his queen. Though this Edward has been able to become a father, everything else we know of him seems homoerotic. Gaveston is not the whole story. Even in his isolation, later, Edward is the man's man, finding strength on horseback and in the tent, an aging Hippolytus. And even the asexuality of his final phase is part of the complex. The Queen, on the other hand, is "all woman." She will be loyal to her man as long as she is allowed to be, but when this loyalty is mocked and, as it were, forbidden, she will drift to another man. There is a convincing morbidity in this drift as Brecht shows it, since it is a drift to her former man's principal enemy and opposite.

Principal enemy and opposite: that is why Mortimer is the principal partner among Edward's three. And therein lies another achievement of Brecht's. Marlowe's play suffers because his Edward has no adequate partner once Gaveston drops out in the middle. In Brecht's play Gaveston is less important from the start than Mortimer, and so is the more expendable: if all four characters are mostly Brecht's own inventions, Mortimer is ninety-nine per cent so. Marlowe's young Mortimer is a barbaric young man who is capable of having at Gaveston with his sword to cap an argument. We feel he takes over the Queen only because that's what barbarians do. It is Brecht's idea that Mortimer was a scholar, and has to be won from his books before he enters the political arena at all. More original still, his meditations have already led him to Solomon's conclusion: all is vanity. What for the Queen is a destination was for him a point of departure. The absolute "nullity of human things and deeds": what a premise for political action! The conception permits Brecht to create, in the first instance, an effectively tragicomic scoundrel and, in the second, to define the perfect antithesis to Edward: Edward is the man of feeling, Mortimer of reason. But so long as the contrast remains so general it has little human interest or dramatic force. These it derives from an "action" that gives it concrete expression and by further "interpretation" of what reason and feeling, in this context, signify. Mortimer remarks that Edward "Antaeus-like . . . draws strength from the soil." Antaeus was the son of the Earth Mother, and Edward himself says:

> Dull-eyed, you Mortimers do arithmetic, and
> Burrow in books like worms.
> But in books there is nothing about Edward who
> Reads nothing, does not do arithmetic,
> Knows nothing and has intimate ties with Nature.
> He's nourished by quite different food.

One thinks of poems, novels, or plays in which Nature and Reason confront each other and are both benign. Nature can, for example, imply a utopia of noble savages; Reason can be the law of a God who is all-wise and all-good. In the world of the young Brecht, such benignities have all been replaced by horrors of disenchantment. Some bizarre but solid paradoxes result. The "Nature" of Edward is precisely what for the world at large passes for *un*natural:

> Oh, Spencer, since words are rough
> And only part us heart from heart
> And understanding is not granted to us
> Amid the deafness nothing remains except
> Bodily contact between men.

The "Reason" of Mortimer is hardly that of the optimistic Rationalist. At best it is that of some of the French existentialists who see the whole universe as hostile and Reason as the element that, if you're lucky, reduces the hostility to temporarily manageable proportions. The final paradox is a certain fundamental agreement between Edward and Mortimer. Both see the world as impossible but suggest the hope that it may at times become "possible" if we appeal to what is most human in us. What they disagree about is the character of our humanity, Mortimer finding it in reason, Edward in feeling, which—in Brecht's context —makes of the former a Machiavellian or even fascistic politician, and of the latter . . . a homosexual. Obviously, from the point of view of almost any modern theatre public, this whole story is "beyond good and evil."

A minor character in Marlowe's play compares Gaveston to Helen of Troy:

> Monster of men,
> That, like the Greekish strumpet, train'd to arms
> And bloody wars so many valiant knights . . .

Brecht, who at any point can take what one Marlowe character says and give it to some other character, not only gives this comparison to Mortimer, but also makes of it the longest and perhaps most important speech of the play: a sort of centerpiece for the whole drama. From it we learn that such a relationship as that of Helen and Paris or Gaveston and Edward is the source of human trouble, but not because society considers it immoral. It makes no difference to Mortimer "whether Helen was a whore/Or had a score of healthy grandchildren." It is simply that "the ear of reason had . . . been stopped up." In other words, Mortimer offers himself and his own philosophy as the nearest the world can come to any solution. His opposite, Edward, represents the worst that the world can know; infatuation, surrender to pure feeling.

At bottom, Mortimer's philosophy is less paradoxical than contradictory, for if we believe him when he tells us the world is nothing, we are hardly disposed to take him up on it when he offers to save that world from passion. The poet is able to indicate by the tone of Mortimer's speeches that they can scarcely be accepted at face value:

> Because a few hats are off and on the ground
> Before a son of a bitch, the English people
> Push their Island over the precipice.

Well, any tears Mortimer sheds over this prospect are crocodile tears, since disaster is for him normal and natural and inevitable, and, in the play, we know this without even going through the logical reasoning, since Mortimer, though not the usual villain, is still the villain.

Edward, though not the usual hero, is still a hero. This story is, if you like, yet another of those modern defenses of the sensitive homosexual destroyed by a cruelly hostile world, and can be confidently recommended to the broad public such stories apparently command. If at bottom Mortimer's philosophy is contradictory, if his rationalism is finally irrational and his reason unreasonable, Edward's antirational view, the world being what it is, is rational.

> Amid the deafness nothing remains but
> Bodily contact between men.

If the Trojan War was as mad and meaningless as, say, World War I, then isn't it possible that what Paris and Helen did in bed was the only part of the whole transaction that had any human value or even much human substance? Whatever you and I, in the context of our own lives, make of this question, isn't it cogent for Edward, in the context of Brecht's play, to answer the comparable question in the positive: the relationship between Edward and Gaveston—not seen "poetically" as by Marlowe but in all its physicality—provided something to hold on to, which is more than could be said for anything else that transpires in the play, with a single exception I shall revert to in a moment.

Brecht's brilliant complicated dialectic is seen in the endings to which Mortimer and Edward come, which are "the same" but also "the opposite." Both men end quietly, accept their end philosophically. There is something stoical, and hence traditionally tragic, about both endings. Mortimer's is the more ostentatiously so (he has two big speeches, the bull speech, and the wheel-of-fortune speech), and the ostentation "gives the show away"—that is, gives away that he *is* putting on a show. He enacts the very parody of a hero's death. That he is really *un*heroic is clear in that he closes with a taunt toward the young king. Edward's heroism is genuine, and his power to endure is that other "something to hold on to" which I just mentioned.

Heroic courage is the tragic virtue, and Edward has it. Mortimer's courage, if we take it to exist at all, is unheroic because it needs to be propped by hatred and cynicism: it is easier to die if you are spitting hatred against others all the while and if you truly find all living worthless anyway. (Hence the abundant unheroic courage of modern militarists.) Not the least interesting feature of Brecht's Mortimer is that he has known this all along:

> . . . frightened like one burned to death
> I wrap myself in the skin of another man:
> This butcher's son.

Here, quite early in the action, Mortimer thinks of the skin of Gaveston as a cloak in which he can hide. Our strong man is weak. Our courageous man is unheroic.

I have indicated that what makes a hero out of Edward in Brecht's play is that, unlike Marlowe's protagonist, he *can* say no. His two refusals, spaced out in the way they are, do much to give the play its grand and cogent structure. Edward can say no because he possesses the primordial, Promethean tragic virtue of sheer endurance. The effect and meaning of this are much heightened by Brecht, because he gives Edward much more to endure. Less ethereally poetic, the Brecht play is far more brutal than the Marlowe. If some of the more external barbarities (like bringing on Mortimer's head) are discarded, far more real torture is inflicted. At times the story itself is changed to this end. It is Brecht's doing that Edward had the chance to save Gaveston and missed it, giving Mortimer his chance to turn his knife in the psychological wound:

> had you
> Not drowned their words out with your drums,
> Had not, that is, too little confidence
> And too much passion, too swift anger
> Troubled your eye, your favorite Gaveston
> Would be still alive.

As for the sequence where Edward is asked to abdicate, Brecht not only changes the action to a refusal to abdicate, but also makes it essentially a contest between Edward and Mortimer. (In Marlowe's abdication scene, Mortimer is not even present.) This contest has the character of a cat-and-mouse game. While the cruder tortures of the Gurneys are mostly kept off stage, the pressure inflicted by Mortimer upon Edward's spirit—Mortimer's attempt to brainwash him—is all presented and is of the very essence of this play.

If the tale of Edward's imprisonment and death is mostly taken from Marlowe, who had mostly taken it from Holinshed, Brecht's changes are still considerable, and underline both Edward's final victory and the horror of the conditions which failed to defeat him.

> This dungeon where they keep me is the sink
> Wherein the filth of all the castle falls . . .
> And there in mire and puddle have I stood . . .

That is Marlowe. Holinshed had spoken of "a chamber over a foul filthy dungeon full of dead carrion," but Brecht paints a picture which is not only more revolting than Marlowe and Holinshed but belongs to a different pattern and intention. Where his Edward stands is nothing more nor less than the cloaca, and we see him there actually steeped in excrement and presumably continuing to be shat and pissed on before our eyes. So ends Edward the playboy. The Baalian quester for pleasures, for anal pleasures, ends in the sewer. It would be a mistake to consider the young Brecht merely fascinated by filth, though he may *also* have been fascinated by it. There is dramatic appropriateness and irony in Edward's final condition. For one thing it is very close to the primal condition, the situation of the human being born *inter faeces et urinas,* and it is not just that Edward finds himself there, but that there he achieves strength, and even serenity.

In its own Schopenhauerian way, Brecht's *Edward II* is a heroic tragedy, and as such is unique in the lifework of Brecht, for while he would often portray courageous action and the self-sacrifice it entails—as with his Kattrin, the son in *The Mother,* the revolutionaries in *Days of the Commune*—the context of the later heroism is imposed by the author's optimistic progressivism, which negates tragedy as traditionally accepted. Edward's heroism belongs to the category of the traditionally tragic in that is is not utilitarian but serves only (only!) to demonstrate that man is not a worm.

Of course, for Brecht personally, there is a continuing thread from this early hero of his to the truly "positive heroes" found here and there in his later works. It is to be found in that ability to say no which for Brecht had such very urgent importance. For this there are clear historical reasons, notably the inability of his own people, the Germans, to say no to the Mortimers of the Nazi Party. "Will none of you say NO?" cries the chorus before the last scene of Brecht's chronicle of life under the Nazis, while the scene itself ends on the decision to issue an anti-Nazi pamphlet consisting of the one word "no." Conversely (the word is needed often in expounding the works of this great dramatic dialectician) the person who cannot say no is a constantly recurring figure of the Brecht *œuvre.* He is depicted most flat-footedly in the poem "On Giving This World One's Endorsement," which depicts and denounces the average fellow traveler of Nazism. He receives his classical definition in Galy Gay of *A Man's a Man,* and he gets subtle, two-sided, definitely dialectical, and possibly ambiguous treatment in Herr Keuner, Mother Courage, Schweyk, Galileo, and Azdak.

Perhaps *Edward II* should make us rethink the whole topic of Brecht's development. Generally, all the early plays are lumped together as negative in spirit, and in them the men who can't say no are spotted and reported on by the critics. Actually, for all the despair that floats free in these plays, they frequently bear witness to a kind of human strength. In the introduction to his translation of *Drums in the Night,* Frank Jones makes us aware that Kragler is one of Brecht's strong men. If we had not noticed it, it is because we take his abandonment of the revolution as irreclaimably "negative." No doubt the later Brecht wanted the Kraglers of this world to be disapproved of, but the Brecht who wrote *Drums in the Night* presented Kragler's achieving of independence as positive.

It is interesting that in Brecht's plays the men of sheer action are generally bad, whereas good actions tend to come, if at all, from people who have hitherto been markedly passive. Whereas the men of action in *Mother Courage* keep busy slaughtering people, good actions get performed after long preparation by persons who were so gentle they seemed till then quite inactive, such as Swiss Cheese and Kattrin. If the passive people of the early plays never become doers-of-good, the principal ones do shake themselves out of their passivity: Kragler, for example, at the end of *Drums,* and Garga at the end of *In the Swamp.* Baal is characterized, on the one hand, by an extreme passivity, yet, on the other, is a sort of nonspiritual Don Quixote in quest of happiness. Perhaps only *A Man's a Man* is a study of complete inability to say no, and even there the joke, in the original version, is that once Galy Gay is reconstructed he becomes a Leader: he has moved from the camp of the amiably passive to that of the brutally active. At any rate, when the young Bertolt Brecht chose Marlowe's *Edward II* as the basis for a play, one could only have supposed that he chose it as one of the classic studies of passivity and weakness, and one could only have expected he was himself interested in presenting to the world a man who couldn't say no. That he presented a man who *could* say no, and this long before he heard any talk about "positive heroes" or even studied Marxism, should give his critics pause.

Close to all the other early plays, *Edward II* is especially close to *In the Swamp* and *A Man's a Man.* All three dramatize a contrast between two men, depict a struggle between two men, and in similar terms. It is a question of the actual or virtual rape of one by the other, and it is a question of the masochistic pleasure which the raped one takes in the rape. "It was the best time," as Garga succinctly puts it, after being seduced and taken over by Shlink. In *A Man's a Man* Galy Gay is "raped" by the British army in the form of a machine-gun unit, but the character-contrast is with Bloody Five upon whose quest to identify him *as* Galy Gay, not Jeraiah Jip, the story is built; and by a very suggestive quirk Bloody Five speaks at one point of the possibility of raping Galy Gay. However, the contrast is almost wholly in terms of the active/passive elements, rather than hetero/homo.

In Marlowe's *Edward II* one could believe that the King was seduced by Gaveston. What we notice first about Brecht's rendering is that the responsibility rests more with the King, who is infatuated, while Gaveston preserves a degree of detachment. But the Brechtian "rape" is no more directly sexual in this play than in *A Man's a Man*. It is again a military rape. The rapist is neither the King nor Gaveston but Mortimer, and Brecht reworks the plot to give the King's part in this relationship a decisive and unmistakable masochism. Where in Marlowe Mortimer simply escapes, in Brecht he is released by the King for no clear reason. The reason is *made* clear by the subsequent action and, more specifically, by the King when questioned about it later:

> I spared Mortimer for the wicked pleasure
> It gave me to do just that.

Sparing Mortimer gave pleasure, in the first instance, for its sheer arbitrariness: the King did it for "the hell of it," "for kicks." But what hell, and what was it that kicked? Surely the part of Edward which wanted his enemy to win, the part of Edward which wanted to lose. To the sad logic of the old tragic tale from Holinshed and the old tragic drama of Marlowe, Brecht adds a further kind of doom: a psycho-logic. It entails transferring the homosexuality to Mortimer, for not only is Mortimer drawn very dynamically into a close relation with Edward, he desires Edward's wife, a fact which, in this context, must be taken as homosexual girl-sharing. Here *Edward II* is close to *Baal*.

Brecht's tragedy has a puritanic aspect. His hero has been a heterosexual before the play opens; becomes a homosexual later; and, later still, withdraws, through friendship, and, even more, through friendship betrayed, into heroic solitude. At the end he is almost a saint. The role of Mortimer has a precisely contrary movement. He begins in bookish isolation and then plunges headlong into Edward's world. When he takes over the Queen he is, as it were, experiencing Edward's hetero- and homosexual phases at the same time, and this fact is presented in what may strike the reader as an Elizabethan rather than a Brechtian vein, namely, as morally heinous. Yet, if such puritanism seems a far cry from the pansexuality propagated by the character Baal, the play of *Baal* also bears witness to much sexual nausea, to much hatred of sex and therefore much fear of sex, and what is perhaps the finest lyric in the play proposes a romantic, asexual purity as an alternative:

> He dreams at times about a little meadow
> A patch of blue in the sky and nothing more.

While a first impression of Brecht's *Edward II* may make us say how much "more sex" there is in it than in Marlowe's play, the point of the sex is not sex itself. A vulgarized Freudianism, which finds sex hidden at the bottom of everything, would be the worst of all critical philosophies to bring to a play in which the surface itself is all sex and at the bottom is . . . what? My metaphor itself smacks too much of popular Freudianism. Literary subject matter cannot always be neatly split into manifest and latent. In *Edward II* it is less a question of sex concealing something else than of being part of a larger whole, part of a human fate which is a sexual fate but not exclusively so. Hence, while Edward's relation with Gaveston is more blatantly sexual than it had been for Marlowe, that does not prevent the poet Brecht from finding in it an image of a fate that is not just sexual:

> Against the hour when the corpse is found
> Prepare a worthy grave. And yet
> Don't hunt for him!
> He's like the man who walks into the woods
> And the bushes grow up thickly behind him and
> The plants shoot up again and
> The thicket's got him.

One cannot ask that a theatre audience that sees *Edward II* should have read Brecht's "Ballad of Friendship," his "Ballad of Cortez' Men," and his "Fort Donald Railroad Gang," in order to feel more at home with such a treatment of the theme. Perhaps indeed the passage just quoted is more powerful if it comes as an astonishment. Of a sudden we then see Gaveston as part of that vast organism, Nature, to which Edward acknowledged so close a relation. A self-devouring organism: Gaveston was part of it and is swallowed up by it. Specifically by a *thicket*. The word is the same as in the title of *Im Dickicht der Städte* (*In the Thicket of the Cities*). And for all the jungle beasts, tigers, wolves, or wild bulls, that haunt *Edward II,* a *Dickicht* is, incidentally, not a jungle: only density of vegetation is implied, not the presence of wild animals. Edward pictures a Gaveston not torn to pieces by beasts but stifled by the under- and overgrowth. And it is soon as if he had never been: what flourish are the grasses, the plants, and the trees. The image is cosmic rather than clinical.

Even Edward's final triumph over sex should not be taken as the farthest reach of the poet's imagination in this play. This heroism is more than a new-found chastity. The chastity is itself but an aspect of something else: independence. Edward had not been able to do without Gaveston. He had not been able to do without the Queen even when he insulted and rejected her: a contradiction she spotted and taunted him with. He could not do without his last loyal retainers until the chief one proved *dis*loyal and betrayed him. (The Baldock episode is another brilliant innovation of Brecht's.) It is only when he *is* without all these people he "could not do without" that Edward finds he not only can do without them, but also that he is now a man, he is now himself, for the first time. It's like a hypochondriac cripple who does not discover he can stand upright and walk without assistance until his crutches have been brutally torn from him.

It has been remarked—it could hardly not be—that *Brecht's plays present victimization,* and many have got the impression that his early plays show and represent a mere wallowing in it, but this is to see what one might call the primary movement of the action and not the countermovement that ensues and for the sake of which the play was written. *Each of these plays is actually a cry of: Don't fence me in!* Baal may be cruelly left to perish, but he has lived, and under the open sky: he didn't let them fence him in. Kragler wouldn't be fenced in even by an ideology which the author of *Drums in the Night* would —much later—accept. (That is, of course, not all he wouldn't be fenced in by.) *In the Swamp* ends as Garga breaks loose from Chicago itself, the cage in which the whole action had been enclosed. The paradox of Edward's final posture is that he is physically fenced in but spiritually liberated. There is nothing more they can do to him, and this in two senses: that he cannot suffer worse humiliations and that his fearlessness is an iron barrier which they cannot cross: he has fenced *them* in. In each case, Brecht shows a man giving way to pressure, and hence exhibiting human weakness; but in each case there comes the countermovement: the worm turns, the weak man shows strength, and the ending is in some sense a victory. Even Galy Gay, in the original conception, not the Marxized version, is getting his own back at the end. "He'll have our heads yet," say those who once had called him "a man who can't say no." These endings are not pious, renewing our faith in human goodness, while the sun comes up at the back, and soft music plays. That kind of ending stands rebuked by the young Brecht. But so does a kind of ending he was more likely to have had in mind: the ending of the typical naturalistic play in which life is simply too much for pathetic little homo sapiens and someone jumps in a lake at the bottom of the garden or shoots himself in the next room.

(1965)

Galileo

Brecht was all wrong about the seventeenth century in general and about Galileo Galilei in particular. His main assumption is that the new cosmology gave man only a peripheral importance, where the old cosmology had given him a central one. In actual fact, this argument is not found in the works or conversation of Galileo, or of his friends, or of his enemies, or of anyone in his time. Discussing the point in his *Great Chain of Being,* the historian Arthur O. Lovejoy observes that the center was not held to be the place of honor anyway: prestige was out beyond the periphery, where God lived.

So much for the universe. As for the new scientific attitude, for Brecht it apparently is summed up in the pebble which his Galileo likes to drop from one hand to the other to remind himself that pebbles do not fly but fall. In short, the scientist notices, in a down-to-earth way, what actually goes on: he accepts the evidence of his senses. In this he is contrasted with the theologian, who uses imagination and reasoning. Which is all very well except that the little parable of the pebble does not characterize the stage to which physical science was brought by Galileo. It does cover his initial use of the telescope. That was a matter of looking through lenses and believing his own eyes. However, no startling conclusions could be reached, and above all nothing could be proved, without doing a great deal more. What happened to physics in the seventeent¹ century is that it became mathematical. This meant that it became not mc concrete but just the opposite. After all, the evidence of one's senses is that the sun goes round the earth. That the earth should go round the sun is directly counter to that evidence. The average man today accepts the latter idea on pure faith. So far as he knows, it could be wholly untrue. For the demonstration lies in the realm of the abstract and the abstruse.

Brecht is no nearer to the kind of truth that interests a biographer than he is to the kind that interests a historian of science. A good deal is known about the historical Galileo Galilei. For example, he had a mistress who bore him three children. The most human document of his biography is his correspondence with one of the daughters. The love between these two may well have been the greatest love of his life, as it certainly was of hers. But Brecht is interested in none of this, nor can it be retorted that the details of Galileo's professional life preoccupied him. Much is known of the trial of Galileo, and the material has the highest human and dramatic quality, on which various biographers have capitalized. But Brecht passes by the trial "scenes" too. Even the character of his Galileo seems only in part to have been suggested by the personality of the great scientist. The historical Galileo was a proud, even a vain, man. This makes him the villain of Arthur Koestler's book *The Sleepwalkers,* and, to be sure, it contributes to the villainous element in Brecht's Galileo, though Brecht is less concerned than Koestler to nag him, and more concerned to show that there are social reasons why excessive self-reliance fails to get results. Yet Galileo's self-reliance *would* have got results—as Brecht tells the story—but for a quality which has to be invented for him: cowardice. The axis of Brecht's story is passivity-activity, cowardice-courage, slyness-boldness. To make his story into a play, Brecht exploited whatever ready-made material came to hand, but must himself take full responsibility for the final product.

Would Brecht have admitted this, or would he have claimed that he was writing history? If I may be permitted to draw on my memory of Brecht's conversation on the point, I'd say he had a variable attitude. Sometimes he talked as if he had indeed taken everything from the historical record; other times (and this is true in the printed notes too) he would admit to changes but maintain that they didn't distort history; at other times still, he would talk as if he had an entirely free hand (as when in 1945–1956 he changed Galileo's big speech in his last scene).

Whatever Brecht thought he was doing, what good playwrights always do was perceived by Aristotle and confirmed by Lessing. When Aristotle observed that tragedy was more philosophical than history, he was noting that drama has a different logic from that of fact. History can be (or appear to be) chaotic and meaningless; drama cannot. Truth may be stranger than fiction; by the same token, it is not as orderly. Or as Pirandello saw the matter: the truth doesn't have to be plausible but fiction does. The facts of Jeanne d'Arc's life, as the historical record supplies them, did not seem to Bernard Shaw to have either plausibility or interest, for the historical Jeanne was the victim of the machinations of a vulgar politician (the historical Cauchon). The story becomes plausible and interesting by the replacement of this Cauchon with an invented one who can oppose Jeanne on principle. Now the antagonists of Brecht's Galileo would be inconceivable had Shaw not created Warwick, Cauchon, and the Inquisitor, and, equally, Brecht's Barberini and Inquisitor could not get into his play except by replacing the Barberini and the Inquisitor of history. The historical Barberini seems to have made himself a personal enemy of Galileo, and the Inquisitor (Firenzuola) seems to have intrigued most mercilessly against him, but Brecht follows Shaw in having his protagonist's foes proceed solely from the logic of their situation. In this way the central situations of both *Saint Joan* and *Galileo* take on form and meaning. It is a paradox. The historical truth, rejected for its implausibility, has the air of an artifact, whereas the artifact, the play, has an air of truth. The villains of history seemed too melodramatic to both authors. The truth offended their sense of truth, and out of the less dramatic they made the more dramatic.

If what playwrights are after is fiction, why do they purport to offer us history plays at all? People who ask this question generally have in mind the whole expanse of human history and see it all as available to the playwright, yet a glance at history plays that have had success of any sort will reveal that they are not about the great figures of history taken indiscriminately but only about those few, like Julius Caesar, Joan of Arc, and Napoleon, whose names have become bywords. Another paradox: only when a figure has become *legendary* is he or she a fit subject for a *history* play.

Are such figures as Shakespeare's *Henry IV* or Strindberg's *Eric XIV* exceptions? Not really. Within Britain, at least, the kings were legends: certainly Henry V was, as a great deal of ballad lore attests, and *Henry IV* is a preparation for *Henry V*. Something similar is true of Strindberg's histories: Swedish history was suitable for plays insofar as it was the folklore of nationalism. Because the historical dramatist is concerned with the bits of history that have stuck in people's imagination, he may well find himself handling bits of pseudo history that are the very *product* of people's imagination. Is it likely that William Tell actually shot an apple off his son's head? What is certain is that Schiller would never have written a play about him had that story not existed.

Again, why do playwrights purport to put history on stage? Is it because the events of a history at least *seem* more real, since many spectators will assume that such a play *is* all true? After all, very much of our "knowledge" of the past is based on fiction. Has not Churchill himself claimed to learn English history from Shakespeare? Was Shakespeare's distortion of the Anglo-French quarrel just Providence's way of preparing Churchill for the Battle of Britain? So should we be prepared to see a modern, Marxist playwright distorting history in order to prepare young Communists for some future Battle of Russia? The proposition is not as remote as it may sound from Bertolt Brecht's *Galileo*. The question is whether the factual distortions have to be accepted at face value. It seems to me that even for spectators who know that a history play is bad history, such a play might still seem to have some sort of special relevancy, a more urgent truth.

Writing on Schiller's *Don Carlos,* George Lukacs has suggested that, while playwrights and novelists depart from the *facts* of history, they still present the larger *forces* of history. But the forces of what period in history, that of the ostensible action, or that of the playwright? To me it seems that the claim of the chronicle play to be close to history is valid only if it is contemporary history that is in question. *Don Carlos* belongs to the eighteenth century, not the sixteenth; Shakespeare's histories belong to the sixteenth century, not the fifteenth. Now obviously there is a departure from the contemporary facts. It is not even possible to be close to these facts, since nothing factually contemporary is there at all. What is it that the historical dramatist finds in the earlier period? In Brecht's terminology, it is an alienation of the subject. The familiar subject is placed in a strange setting, so that one can sit back and look and be amazed. What kind of strangeness? It is a matter of what strangeness will throw the subject into highest relief, and of what strangeness a particular writer's gift can re-create. But the strangeness is, anyhow, *only* a setting, and within the setting there must be a situation, a grouping of events, an Action, which provide a little model of what the playwright believes is going on in the present. Dramatists may spend decades looking for such settings and such Actions, or hoping to stumble on them.

Sometimes a sudden irruption of the past into the present will call the dramatist's attention to the new relevance of some old event. The canonization of Jeanne d'Arc in 1920 was such an irruption. It prompted the writing of a play which seemed to be about the age which burned Joan yet which was actually about the age that canonized her though it would burn her if she returned. Like *Saint Joan* and all other good history plays, *Galileo* is about the playwright's own time.

Like many of Brecht's works, it exists in a number of different drafts, but it is unusual among them in taking two broadly different forms. There are two *Galileo* plays here, both of which exist in their entirety, the version of 1938, and the version of 1947. Partial analogies to the changes exist in other Brecht plays. For Brecht, it was no unique thing that he should create a winning rogue and then later decide he must make the audience dislike him. The revisions of both *Mother Courage* and *Puntila* show this. But in Galileo the change was more radical.

Brecht became interested in the historical Galileo at a time when he was preoccupied with friends and comrades who remained in Germany and somehow managed to continue to work. Prominent in his thoughts was the underground political worker plotting to subvert the Hitler regime. He himself was not a "worker," he was a poet, but a poet in love with the idea of science, a poet who believed that his own philosophy was scientific. It is easy to understand how Galileo came to mind! And to think of Galileo is to think of a single anecdote (incidentally not found before 1757):

> The moment he [Galileo] was set at liberty, he looked up to the sky and down to the ground, and, stamping with his foot, in a contemplative mood, said, *Eppur si muove;* that is, still it moves, meaning the earth.*

His study was the universe, and its laws are what they are, irrespective of ecclesiastical pronouncement. "Still it moves!" And Galileo can now write a new, epoch-making work, and smuggle it out of the country with these words:

> Take care when you travel through Germany with the truth under your coat!

This sentence puts in a nutshell the most striking analogy between the first version of Brecht's *Galileo* and the present, the present being the 1930s, in which, indeed, truth in Germany had to be hidden under coats. It was the time when Wilhelm Reich had copies of his writings on the orgasm bound and inscribed to look like prayer books and in that form mailed from abroad to Germany. It was the time when Brecht himself wrote the essay "Five Difficulties in Writing the Truth." The fifth of these difficulties, and the one which Brecht gave most attention to, was the need of "cunning in disseminating the truth." Although Galileo is not included in the essay's list of heroes who showed such cunning, the whole passage is quite close to the thought and frame of mind reflected in the first version of the Galileo play. Even the special perspective which caused Brecht's friend Walter Benjamin to say its hero was not Galileo but the people is found in sentences like: "Propaganda for thinking, in whatever field, is useful to the cause of the oppressed." The early version of *Galileo* is nothing if not propaganda for thinking.

The later version of *Galileo* is also about the playwright's own time, but this was now, not the thirties, but the middle forties. Brecht has himself recorded what the motive force of the new *Galileo* was:

> The atomic age made its debut at Hiroshima in the middle of our work. Overnight the biography of the founder of the new system of physics read differently.

To a historian it would seem bizarre to suggest that he should reverse a judgment he had made on something in the seventeenth century on account of

* For further details, see *Discoveries and Opinions of Galileo,* translated by Stillman Drake (Garden City: Doubleday Anchor, 1957), p. 292.

something which had just happened in the twentieth. To a dramatist, however, the question would mainly be whether a subject which had suggested itself because it resembled something in the twentieth century would still be usable when asked to resemble something quite different in the twentieth century.

In the thirties, as I have been saying, what presumably commended the subject of Galileo to Brecht was the analogy between the seventeenth-century scientist's underground activities and those of twentieth-century left-wingers in Hitler Germany. But that is not all that Brecht, even in the early version, made of the *exemplum*. The abjuration was defined as an act of cowardice, and the act of cowardice was then deplored for a precise reason, namely, that more than certain notions about astronomy were at stake. At stake was the liberty to advance these and any other notions.

> ANDREA. . . . many on all sides followed you with their eyes and ears, believing that you stood, not only for a particular view of the movement of the stars, but even more for the liberty of teaching—in all fields. Not then for any particular thoughts, but for the right to think at all.

> GALILEO. . . . a member of the scientific community cannot logically just point to his possible merits as a researcher if he has neglected to honor his profession as such and to defend it against coercion of every kind. But this is a business of some scope. For science demands that facts not be subordinated to opinions but that opinions be subordinated to facts. It is not in a position to limit these propositions and apply them to "some opinions" and "such and such" facts. To be certain that these propositions can always and without limitation be acted on, science must do battle to ensure that they are respected in all fields.

After Hiroshima, Brecht deleted these speeches, in order to substitute another idea. The point was no longer to demand from the authorities liberty to teach all things but to demand from the scientists themselves a sense of social responsibility, a sense of identification with the destiny, not of other scientists only, but of people at large. The point was now to dissent from those who see scientific advance as "an end in itself," thus playing into the hands of those who happen to be in power, and to advance the alternate, utilitarian conception of science:

> GALILEO. . . . I take it that the intent of science is to ease human existence. If you give way to coercion, science can be crippled, and your new machines may simply suggest new drudgeries. Should you, then, in time, discover all there is to be discovered, your progress must become a progress away from the bulk of humanity. The gulf might even grow so wide that the sound of your cheering at some new achievement would be echoed by a universal howl of horror.

In this respect, *Galileo* I is a "liberal" defense of freedom against tyranny, while *Galileo* II is a Marxist defense of a social conception of science against the "liberal" view that truth is an end in itself.

If this philosophic change is large enough, it is accompanied by an even larger change in the dramatic action. In *Galileo* I, a balance is struck between two opposing motifs. On the one hand, Galileo is admired for his slyness and cunning, while on the other being condemned for his cowardice. The admiration is never entirely swallowed up in the disapproval. On the contrary, we give Galileo a good mark for conceding his own weakness. Then, too, Brecht brings about a partial rehabilitation of his hero in two distinct ways: first, by stressing the admirable cunning of the underground worker who can write a new masterpiece under these conditions and arrange to smuggle it out to freer lands; second, by defining his hero's lapse as a limited one, thus:

> ANDREA. . . . it is as if a very high tower which had been thought indestructible should fall to the ground. The noise of its collapse was far louder than the din of the builders and the machines had been during the whole period of its construction. And the pillar of dust which the collapse occasioned rose higher than the tower had ever done. But possibly it turns out, when the dust clears, that, while twelve top floors have fallen, thirty floors below are still standing. Is that what you mean? There is this to be said for it: the things that are wrong in this science of ours are out in the open. . . . The difficulty may be the greater; but the necessity has also become greater.

Indeed there is something good about the new book's having a disgraced author. It must now make its way on its own, and not by authority; which will be a gain for science and the scientific community. And dramatically it means a lot that *Galileo* I ends with the emphasis on the renewal of friendship between Galileo and Andrea. The old scientist is after all able to hand his work on, as to a son.

Revising the play after Hiroshima, Brecht decided to condemn Galileo far more strongly, and in fact not only to render an unqualified verdict of guilty, but also to picture a shipwrecked, a totally corrupted human being. The sense of the earlier text is: "I should not have let my fear of death make me overlook the fact that I had something more to defend than a theory in pure astronomy." The sense of the later text is: "To be a coward in those circumstances entailed something worse than cowardice itself, namely, treachery." In the early text, Brecht alludes to the Church's belief that Galileo risked damnation for squandering the gift of intellect. In the later text, it is clear that Galileo sees himself as already in hell for having *actually* squandered (betrayed) the gift of intellect, so what we see in the penultimate scene of the later text is a portrait of a "collaborator," a renegade. And Brecht's Notes stress that Galileo should register a malign, misanthropic contempt for Federzoni, as well as shouting in sheer self-hatred to Andrea:

> Welcome to the gutter, dear colleague in science and brother in treason: I sold out, you are a buyer. . . . Blessed be our bargaining, whitewashing, deathfearing community!

Which version is better? There can be no doubt that many improvements were made throughout the play by which the later version benefited, but as far as this penultimate scene is concerned, it is not clear that, in making it more ambitious, Brecht also improved it. To show the foulness of Galileo's crime he has to try to plumb deeper depths. The question is whether this befouled, denatured Galileo can be believed to be the same man we have seen up to then. The impression is, rather, of someone Brecht arbitrarily declares bad at this stage in order to make a point. Which would be of a piece with Communist Party treatment of the betrayal theme generally. One moment a Tito is a Jesus, and the next a Judas. There is, perhaps, an intrusion of unfelt C. P. clichés about traitors and renegades in the later *Galileo*. One cannot find, within the boundaries of the play itself, a full justification for the virulence of the final condemnation.

If the crime of Galileo, in the earlier text, being less cataclysmic in its results and less anguished in its style, at first seems less dramatic, it is actually rendered *more* dramatic by the tragicomic relationship in which it stands to Galileo's Schweykian cunning. Personally I find the ambiguity of the earlier ending more human and more richly dramatic as well as more Brechtian and more consistent with the rest of the play.

Sidelights are provided by performances of the play, and their background. It seems to me that even Ernst Busch, the Galileo of the Berlin Ensemble production, could not make real the image of a corrupted Galileo. Busch was very much the Old Communist. He never seemed the sinner in hell but, rather, the Party member who had strayed and was now practicing self-criticism. Charles Laughton would seem a likelier casting. Brecht said Laughton felt guilty for having stayed in Hollywood during World War II instead of returning to fight for Britain, and this sense of guilt, he said, was what would come in useful in *Galileo*. Laughton did indeed have subtly personal ways of making guilt seem real that would have delighted Stanislvaski himself. When he made his entrance after the abjuration, he seemed, as Brecht said, a little boy who had wet his pants, but, in the last scene, when Brecht wanted the audience to reject Galileo in horror, Laughton made sure they accepted him in pity—while loving him at the same time for the way he outwitted the Inquisition. In other words, the actor put something of *Galileo* I back into *Galileo* II. Perhaps it is hard not to. The *action* (Galileo smuggling his new book out) is apt, in a theatre, to speak louder than mere *words* of denunciation, but then again the way in which Laughton "stood out" from his part was not exactly what the Brechtian theory bargains for. It was through an actorish narcissism that he kept aloof; and that limited his power to communicate the content of the play. It also made the sinister and self-defeating pride of the scientist dwindle into a movie-star's showy and nervous vanity. Laughton had a unique equipment for this role. It is unlikely that anyone again will combine as he did every appearance of intellectual brilliance with every appearance of physical self-indulgence, yet actorish vanity allowed him to let the brilliance slide over into drawing-room-comedy smartness. Narcissism prevented him from even trying to enter those somewhat Dostoevskian depths into which Brecht invites the actor of the final scene, version two.

Brecht added a detail in the later text which could help a great deal to define that "tragedy of pride" which is certainly a part of this drama. Galileo is offered the chance to escape the Inquisition if he will accept the patronage of the industrialist Vanni, yet he is not an astute enough politician to see the wisdom of such acceptance, and prefers to believe not only in the authorities themselves but in his own ability to go it alone. Laughton, by seeming not to take in what Vanni was saying, threw this little scene away. The effect was not of arrogant overconfidence, merely of lack of rapport or maybe, again, trivial vanity.

It was also through Charles Laughton that the notion was first spread around that *Galileo* not only touches on the atom bomb but is essentially concerned with it. Here is Brecht himself in this vein:

> Galileo's crime can be regarded as the original sin of modern physical science. . . . The atom bomb, both as a technical and as a social phenomenon, is the classical end product of his contribution to science and his failure to society.

But such a meaning does not emerge from the story as told either by historians or by Brecht. Had those who wished to stop Galileo and scientific advance had their way, there would be no atom bomb today. Contrariwise, if we accept the Brechtian premise that Galileo could have changed history by making an opposite decision, then he would have changed history by joining hands with Vanni the industrialist, and the atom bomb might have been invented a little earlier —say, by Wernher von Braun.

In East Berlin today Heinar Kipphardt's play about J. Robert Oppenheimer begins in the setting left on stage from Brecht's *Galileo,* and the newer play "shows what society exacts from its individuals, what it needs from them," as Brecht said his *Galileo* did. However, one is struck by the extreme difference between the two main dramatic situations—that in which it is Reaction that suppresses discovery, and that in which it was inhumane to push *for* science and the *making* of a discovery.

One American production of Brecht's *Galileo,* at my suggestion, posted up the following words for the audience to read after the abjuration scene:

I was not in a policy-making position at Los Alamos. I would have done anything that I was asked to do.

—J. Robert Oppenheimer

I now think there is too much sensationalism in this idea, for Galileo has not offered to do "anything" he might be "asked to do" at all, and dramatically it makes a big difference that he is not being asked to do something but being asked not to do something. He is being asked not to pursue his researches. Then he goes and pursues them anyway, muttering, *"Eppur si muove."*

The story to which the Oppenheimer dossier leads, when interpreted by a Marxist, is told, not in Brecht's *Galileo,* but in Haakon Chevalier's novel *The Man Who Would Be God.* Here the faith the protagonist stands for is obviously Marxism. He betrays it and his best friend (who is also his best Comrade) in order to become the man who can make Reaction a present of the atom bomb. The ending resembles *Galileo* II to the extent that both protagonists are shown as burnt-out ruins of their former selves; but Chevalier's man does not practice self-criticism.

Chevalier makes it clear he thinks the Action of his story describes a curve like that of Greek tragedy; and this curve may suggest, too, the Action of Brecht's play. The rhythm of both novel and play, we might at first think, is: from battle to defeat, loyalty to betrayal, commitment to alienation. But of course Galileo's writing of religious tracts for a cardinal in no way resembles Oppenheimer's devising of a monstrous weapon. For one thing, while it is quite credible that devising a monstrous weapon would give a man delusions of satanic grandeur, thus corrupting him, Galileo's obligation to turn out a little conformist journalism is merely a boring chore.

It is true that *Galileo* II touches on, or almost touches on, many of the problems which were created or augmented by the atomic bomb. Still, even *Galileo* II is not based on Oppenheimer folklore but on Galileo folklore; and a preoccupation with the similarities, by blinding critics to the enormous differences, disables judgment and is, in my view, a disservice to Brecht the dramatist. It prevents the Action as a whole from being perceived. If we begin by assuming that the play is about the atomic scientists, we shall end by complaining that Brecht doesn't get to the point till very near the end.

If *Galileo* is not "all about the atom bomb" is it a tragedy of pride? One might begin to answer this question with the observation that no tragedy of pride would end in its hero's lacking, not only pride, but even self-respect. At the end, supremely, the true hero reveals his true heroism, and if lack of self-respect has been in question, as in Conrad's *Lord Jim,* then what he will do with his self-respect at the end is precisely to regain it. *Galileo* (I or II) is more of a tragedy of *lack* of pride; but that, to be sure, is no tragedy at all. Brecht himself, speaking of his play in terms of a commitment abandoned and betrayed, indicates that he has nothing against writers like Copernicus who never made a commitment. Copernicus simply left his book for men to make what they would of it after his death. Galileo embarked on a campaign to change the world, then quit. Brecht shows the trend of his own thinking about the play by the use of words like "opportunism," "collaboration," "betrayal." To these one must add the equally Brechtian term: "capitulation." To begin full of fighting spirit, to end capitulating ignominiously: this is the rhythm of life as Brecht so often depicted it and so deeply felt it. In *Mother Courage* the "great" capitulation—Courage's own—is over before the first curtain rises. We find it only in certain speeches and a retrospective song. In *Galileo,* on the other hand, it is the hinge of the whole Action. The play is a tragicomedy of heroic combat followed by unheroic capitulation, and the ending of the later version is of the harrowing sort common in tragicomedy when it achieves greatness: no noble contrition, no belated rebellion even, but savage, misanthropic self-hatred. This Galileo is the victim of his own curse upon Mucius:

> He who does not know the truth is merely an idiot. But he who knows it and calls it a lie is a criminal.

Received "into the ranks of the faithful" he is exiled from the ranks of mankind, *and that by his own decree.*

That the horror of *Galileo* II, Scene Thirteen, did not fully emerge in the 1947 production Brecht was inclined to blame on Laughton. It was one of the few passages, he says, which the actor had difficulties with. He did not seem to grasp the playwright's plea that a condemnation of the opportunist must be inherent in the condemnation of those who accept the fruits of the opportunism. Not using the squint-eyed, worried grin he had worn in the abjuration scene, Laughton here robbed the opening of the big speech on science of its supercil-iousness:

> It did not entirely emerge [says Brecht] that you are on the lowest rung of the ladder of teaching when you deride the ignorant and that it is a hateful light which a man emits just to have his own light shine. . . .

Laughton failed to make his audiences feel that "that man sits in a hell worse than Dante's where the gift of intellect has been gambled away."

But could not Laughton be partly excused for not playing what Brecht calls the low point of the action on the grounds that this low point is hardly reached in the writing? When we ask this we are asking a question not only about the dialogue of the penultimate scene but also about the scene that sets it up: the abjuration scene. This scene represents an extreme instance of Brechtian method. Brecht well knew that the obvious way to write the scene is to confront Galileo with his enemies. Some playwrights would make you sit there three hours for the sole pleasure of seeing this happen at the end.* Brecht's reason for doing otherwise is clear: the people he wishes to confront Galileo with are—his friends. In the theatre, Scene Twelve is a truly marvelous scene, with its off-stage action, its two groups waiting on stage (the friends and the daughter), its climactic, anticlimactic entrance of Galileo Galilei, the collapse of Andrea, and the laconic, meaning-packed summing up of Galileo's retort to him: "Unhappy is the land that *needs* heroes!" This line has a partly new meaning in *Galileo* II, being now far more ironical, yet it contains a direct, unironic truth still, expressing, as Brecht says, the scientist's wish to deprive Nature of her privilege of making life tragic and heroism necessary. Yet the scene is perhaps a shade *too* oblique. One senses the presence of an intention which is not entirely achieved: to avoid the hackneyed, overprepared climax of conventional drama in the big, long trial scene by bringing down the hero with a flick of the wrist. The abjuration is there before one is ready for it. Our man collapses without a fight. Something is gained. There is a special interest in collapse being so prompt, so sudden, so actionless, after all the overconfidence that had gone before. The Brechtian avoidance of psychology does pay off here in shock, but I wonder if it doesn't force the playwright to omit something we need, at once for continuity of narrative and later for our understanding of Galileo's descent into hatred of himself and contempt for others?

To condemn Galileo for his abjuration, one must believe, first, that he had a real alternative and, second, that this alternative was worth all the trouble. Thirdly, his enemies must be as convincing in their way as he is in his, or the whole conflict lacks magnitude. Now, to take the last point first, the enemy figures in *Galileo,* though done with adroitness, are markedly less impressive than those they are roughly modeled on—the enemies in *Saint Joan.* As to Galileo's alternative, the trouble is not that we may feel asked to believe that the *historical* Galileo had such an alternative, the trouble is that, unless we can see all history and society in these terms of progressives and reactionaries, we shall not respond as Brecht would like us to. Faced with this kind of objection, Brecht used to say that *all* plays require agreement with the author's philosophy. But do they? Don't they require, rather, only a suspension of disbelief, a temporary willingness to see things through the playwright's spectacles? And is that

* Not a mere speculation. The only Galileo play I have read that precedes Brecht's is by the nineteenth-century French dramatist François Ponsard. Ponsard's final curtain line is: *"Et pourtant elle tourne!"* I doubt very much that Brecht had read Ponsard, but, if he had, one would be able to say he took the older work and stood it on its head (or feet) in his usual fashion. Ponsard gives us a wholly noble Galileo and is at pains to free the scientist from the *possible* charge of cowardice. He confronts Galileo with a tragic choice between Science and Family: as a noble hero, he must of course choose the latter. The Family is represented by his daughter; and so concern for his daughter's welfare becomes the high cause for which he suffers. How tempting to conclude that Brecht did read Ponsard and decided on the spot to have his Galileo ride roughshod over his daughter's happiness!

the issue here? Could not the terms of this conflict be objected to on the grounds of the very philosphy Brecht did accept, Marxism? It seems to me that a Marxist should object that the dialectic of history and society is here excessively attenuated, and that the result is a melodramatic black and white. The fact that this story cannot be thought of as actually taking place in the seventeenth century does become a dramatic defect *by being called attention to*. In this it resembles the story of Mother Courage, who is condemned for what she did, though what she ought to have done instead (namely, help to destroy the system) was not in the seventeenth-century cards. There is something absurd in condemning her, and there is something absurd in asking Galileo Galilei to strike a blow for the philosophy of Bertolt Brecht. If Cardinal and Inquisitor are abstract and simplistic, so is the play's rendering of the alternative to them, as shown in the character of Federzoni, the idealized worker. *Federzoni is made of wood,* and so, even more obviously, are various smaller characters, introduced to make points, like Mucius the Renegade and Vanni the Business Man. Before Galileo is arrested, Brecht offers him through Vanni the alternative of working for the rising bourgeoisie. The point is made, but only by being mentioned, as it might be mentioned in an essay. It does not register as drama, because Vanni exercises no pull on Galileo; and this is because he is a mere mouthpiece.

These weaknesses would be cruelly displayed by any director who labored under the misapprehension that this was a Shaw play. *Galileo* can suffer by being compared to *Saint Joan* in that Shaw puts much more thought into drama and finds much more drama in thought. *Saint Joan,* on the other hand, might suffer a little by comparison with *Galileo* if what one was after was not thinking but poetry—whether the poetry of the word or the poetry of stagecraft.

"The hero is the people." Walter Benjamin's hyperbole applies, not to the prosaically imposed "vulgar" Marxism of the Federzoni figure, but to the impact of Galileo's life upon the commonalty, a topic to which two whole scenes are devoted (Nine and Fourteen). The people are the hero in that the final interest is not in Galileo himself but in what he did, and what he failed to do, *for* the people. And here an objection on historical grounds—to the effect that the seventeenth-century populace did not react in this way, or that Galileo wrote in Italian instead of Latin, not to reach the people, who couldn't read, but to reach the middle class—cannot be upheld, because the poet has created a vision that transcends literal reportage. Scene Nine usually goes over better with an audience than any other scene in the play. Cynics may say that is because it is a creation of the director and composer. The design remains Brecht's own. The little scene gives us an image that resembles the image of Azdak in *The Caucasian Chalk Circle*. In each case, the common folk, in their long night of slavery, are given a brief glimpse of a possible dawn, and Brecht is able to convey this, not discursively, but in direct, poetic-dramatic vision.

And, of course, it is a matter, not just of a scene, but of the whole play. As we work our way back from the last scene, through the scene of abjuration, to the long preparation for the abjuration scene, we can discern the curve of the whole Action. One might find the key to this Action in the phrase "The New Age." It is a favorite Brechtian topic, and Brecht explains in the notes to this very play of *Galileo* that the phrase "The New Age" brought to his mind the Workers' Movement as of the beginning of the twentieth century:

> . . . no other line from a song so powerfully inspired the workers as the line, "Now a new age is dawning": old and young marched to it. . . .

This is the theme that is sounded in the very first scene of *Galileo,* and again I wish to make a somewhat more than parenthetic allusion to Charles Laughton, since here Laughton the adapter conspired with Laughton the actor to evade an important issue. The actor found the speech about the New Age far too long, so the adapter cut most of it out, and had the remainder rebuked by an Andrea who says, "You're off again, Mr. Galilei." But it was Mr. Brecht who was off again, and a really long speech is needed here, a veritable paean to the idea of a New Age, or we cannot grasp the importance of the conception or the sentiment in the main design. The paean is a poem, though in prose. It creates a sense of that Enchantment, which will later, as the very climax of the Action, turn to Disenchantment (ambiguously in one version, unequivocally in the other). In *The Caucasian Chalk Circle,* we learn how much too early the carpet weavers tried to establish a people's regime, and for how short a time Azdak's people's regime can eke out its fluky existence. In *Galileo* the point is that the coming of such a regime is actually postponed by the protagonist's principal act. And though we cannot take this as history (of the seventeenth century) we can certainly make sense of it as politics (of the twentieth century).

It has become customary to cut the last scene (Fourteen), but this is because directors insist on believing that Galileo is the hero. If the people are the hero, the last scene is a needed conclusion and a needed correction of Scene Nine. The people will not emerge into the dawn in the sudden ecstasy of Carnival. The journey out of night is long and slow, all the slower because of Galileo's abjuration and all analogous capitulations. At the end, the play abuts upon the Marxist realization that the people must learn not to rely on the Great Men of the bourgeoisie for their salvation: they will have to save themselves. But discreetly enough, this is not spelled out. Brecht speaks here through image and action. The smuggling out of the new book has a somewhat different meaning in *Galileo* II. It is less of a triumph for Galileo, but it does take up the theme of *eppur si muove* and partially redeem it from the cynicism which, especially in this version, it must carry. The earth continues to revolve, and even the bad man can continue to contribute good science. Or, on a more literal plane: though a social setback is recorded, science marches ahead—in which contrast, that between a rotten society and a flourishing science, we again glimpse the twentieth century.

A further comment is perhaps needed on the protagonist of Brecht's play. What does this Galileo—not the Galileo of the historians—finally amount to? The topic can be approached through the following passage from Isaac Deutscher's life of Trotsky:

> He [Brecht] had been in some sympathy with Trotskyism and was shaken by the purges; but he could not bring himself to break with Stalinism. He surrendered to it with a load of doubt on his mind, as the capitulators in Russia had done; and he expressed artistically his and their predicament in *Galileo Galilei*. It was through the prism of the Bolshevik experience that he saw Galileo going down on his knees before the Inquisition and doing this from an "historic necessity," because of the people's political and spiritual immaturity. The Galileo of his drama is Zinoviev or Bukharin or Rakovsky dressed up in historical costume. He is haunted by the "fruitless" martyrdom of Giordano Bruno; that terrible example causes him to surrender to the Inquisition, just as Trotsky's fate caused so many Communists to surrender to Stalin. And Brecht's famous duologue: "Happy is the country that produces such a hero" and "Unhappy is the people that needs such a hero" epitomizes clearly enough the problem of Trotsky and Stalinist Russia rather than Galileo's quandary in Renaissance Italy. (Brecht wrote the original version of *Galileo Galilei* in 1937–8, at the height of the Great Purges.)

Unless Mr. Deutscher has his hands on some version of *Galileo* not known by anyone else to exist he can't read straight. *Galileo* II *cannot* be taken the way he proposes, since the capitulation, there, is denounced as loudly as he could wish. If we assume, as perhaps we must, it is *Galileo* I he is talking about, then how could he take the Church (Stalinism) as something Galileo "could not bring himself to break with," in view of the fact that this Galileo cheats and outwits the Church triumphantly? Or maybe Mr. Deutscher never got to the penultimate scene? Brecht's Galileo is not haunted by the martyrdom of Bruno, either, and if Bruno is Trotsky, then Trotsky hardly comes within the purview of the play at all. Does Mr. Deutscher take "Happy is the country that produces such a hero" to be about Trotsky? If so, inaccuracy has again tripped him up, as the line actually reads: "Unhappy is the land that has no heroes!" and the reference is to Galileo's failure to be heroic.

But Mr. Deutscher's incursion into dramatic criticism raises the question whether he claims to describe Brecht's conscious thoughts or things that crept in in the author's despite? If the former, then the Deutscher thesis is highly implausible. Brecht may have been troubled by inner doubts, but on the whole he must be said to have given his approval to the Moscow trials, much in the spirit of his close friend Feuchtwanger, whose ardently Stalinist book *Moscow 1937* is mentioned by Mr. Deutscher. Besides, the abjuration in *Galileo* 1 is in part a means to an end, which is to go on writing subversive things. Though reprehensible, it is also a neat trick, and no occasion for Slavic breast-beating. That Brecht, in that period, would knowingly have depicted Stalin simply as the enemy is improbable in the extreme.

Yet it may well be true that not only the Nazi but the Bolshevik experience found their way into the play, especially into its later version, which Mr. Deutscher doesn't seem to have read. The Bolshevik idea of self-criticism, going to all possible lengths of self-denunciation and a demand for punishment, undoubtedly exerted considerable sway over Brecht. In 1944–1945, he is using it in *The Caucasian Chalk Circle,* in a passage so "Russian" that Western audiences have trouble following the argument. If we are now guessing at unconscious motives, instead of just noting the provable ones, we might by all means guess that the self-denunciation of the new version of *Galileo,* written in 1945 or so, was put there to correct and place in proper perspective the famous self-denunciation before the Inquisition around which the story is built. The abjuration is a spurious piece of self-denunciation. It cries out, Brecht might well have felt, for a real one, and the real one, by all means, suggests the world of Zinoviev, Bukharin, and Rakovsky. However, if this interpretation is valid, Brecht's unconscious made, surely, the same identification as his conscious mind, namely with Stalin, not with his enemies, who are felt to be guilty as charged.

But wasn't the Nazi experience far more important to the play than the Bolshevik one? The real complaint against Galileo is that he did not rise up like Georgi Dimitrov at the Reichstag trial in Leipzig and denounce his judges. The real complaint is against German physicists who announced that there was such a thing as Aryan physics as distinct from Jewish physics. The real complaint is against the conspiracy of silence in which most German scholars and writers took part in those years. Brecht's poetry of the thirties reverts again and again to this subject.

> *Aber man wird nicht sagen: Die Zeiten waren finster*
> *Sondern: Warum haben ihre Dichter geschwiegen?*

(But men won't say: The times were dark, but: Why were their poets silent?)

And Brecht's personal relation to this subject? He was by no means silent, but he knew how to take care of himself. He did not volunteer in Spain. He did not go to Moscow to risk his neck at the headquarters of Revolution. And undoubtedly such guilt as was felt (if any was) by Charles Laughton at not taking part in the Battle of Britain was felt by Brecht a thousand times over at not taking more than a literary part in any of the battles of his lifetime. This guilt, one can readily believe, is concentrated in the protagonist in whose footsteps some people think Brecht trod when before the Un-American Activities Committee he cried, "No, no, no, no, no, never," at the question, "Have you ever made application to join the Communist Party?"

"The sick inmost being of a poet," Jean Paul has it, "betrays itself nowhere more than in his hero, whom he never fails to stain with the secret weaknesses of his own nature." Brecht felt in himself a natural affinity with the shirker and the quitter. In that respect, the late play *Galileo* looks all the way back to the earliest plays, and especially to *Drums in the Night*. A whole row of Brecht protagonists belongs to this species in one way or another (Baal, Galy Gay, Macheath, Mother Courage, Schweyk, Azdak . . .* and what gives these figures dramatic tension is that their natural passivity has either to be redeemed by the addition of some other quality (as with Schweyk's intuitive shrewdness and humanity) or worked up into something much worse that can be roundly denounced. This working up took Brecht a little time, as we know from the revisions of *Mother Courage* and *Puntila*. It was a quarter of a century before Brecht made it clear that Kragler, of *Drums in the Night,* was to be utterly rejected, and the wholehearted rejection of Galileo's "crime" took Brecht nearly ten years to make—ten years and two atom bombs. Brecht, one might put it, was a moralist on second thought, and, however moralist-critics may judge him as a man, they can hardly deny that this "contradiction" in him was dramatically dynamic and productive.

Galileo is a self-portrait in respect of incarnating the main contradiction of Brecht's own personality. That can hardly fail to have interest for students of his work, but it can hardly be the main point of *Galileo* if we judge *Galileo* to be a good play, since good plays are not, in the first or last instance, personal outpourings. A writer writes himself, but a playwright has written a play only when he has written more than, or other than, himself. Even should his material

---

* To this list, except that he is not the protagonist of a play, belongs Herr Keuner. And interestingly enough, Brecht introduced into *Galileo* I a complete "Keuner story," thus:

> Into the home of the Cretan philosopher Keunos, who was beloved among the Cretans for his love of liberty, came one day, during the time of tyranny, a certain agent, who presented a pass that had been issued by those who ruled the city. It said that any home he set foot in belonged to him; likewise, any food he demanded; likewise, any man should serve him that he set eyes on. The agent sat down, demanded food, washed, lay down, and asked, with his face toward the wall, before he fell asleep: will you serve me? Keunos covered him with a blanket, drove the flies away, watched over his sleep, and obeyed him for seven years just as on this day. But whatever he did for him, he certainly kept from doing one thing, and that was to utter a single word. When the seven years were up, and the agent had grown fat from much eating, sleeping, and commanding, the agent died. Keunos then wrapped him in the beat-up old blanket, dragged him out of the house, washed the bed, whitewashed the walls, took a deep breath, and answered: No.

The speech is given to Galileo in Scene Eight, and Brecht is able thereby to differentiate Galileo from Andrea, in preparation for later scenes. "The pupils laugh. Only Andrea shakes his head. ANDREA: I don't like the story, Mr. Galilei."

stem from himself, the test is whether he can get it outside himself and make it not-himself. He has to let himself be strewn about like dragon's teeth so that other men may spring up, armed. In *Galileo*, a contradiction that had once merely been Brecht's own, merely a character trait, is translated into action, into an Action, and this action, reciprocally, attaches itself to someone who is neither Bertolt Brecht nor the Galileo Galilei of history. Though he bear the latter's name, he is a *creation* of the former, and surely a very notable one. It is not just that Brecht's Galileo is contradictory. Such a contradiction would count for comparatively little if the *man* who is contradictory were not both deeply, complexly human and—great. Nor is greatness, in plays, taken on trust or proved by citation of the evidence. Rather, it must be there as a visible halo, and felt as an actual charisma. As the man speaks, moves, or merely stands there, his greatness must, for his audience in the theatre, be beyond cavil. In this play, Brecht proves himself to be, with Shaw, one of the very few modern playwrights who can compel belief in the greatness of their great ones.

It would be a pity if we were so busy arguing the *Problematik* of science and authority that we overlooked an achievement of this sort. After all, playwrights should be allowed their limitations in the stratosphere of science and philosophy, since their main job is down on earth, giving life to characters. The role which, however, misleadingly, goes by the name of Galileo Galilei is not only notable in itself, and functions well in the Action, as I have tried to show, it also solves a very real problem posed by Brecht's subject. Our world is no longer in the center of the universe, *ergo* man has lost his central importance in the scheme of things. If this proposition is not of the seventeenth century, it is very much of the twentieth, and it had always been important to Bertolt Brecht. He places it at the heart of Garga's nihilism in *In the Swamp* (*Jungle of Cities*), and of Uriah Shelley's in one of the versions of *A Man's a Man*. Man is absolutely nothing, is Uriah's premise and conclusion. And yet Galileo Galilei, who (allegedly) made this discovery, is something? Is this in fact the ultimate contradiction about him? He is assigned his share in worthlessness and nihilism (if nothingness is divisible), particularly in the later text, but the main point is in the contrast between this discovery of nothingness and the something-ness, the greatness, of the discoverer. God, as Brecht's Galileo puts it, will be found, from now on, "in ourselves or nowhere." Man will be great, not by the role assigned to him by Another, nor yet by his position in space, but by his own inherent qualities. If *Galileo* II verges on being merely a repudiation of its protagonist, then, as I have already intimated, it carries Brecht's vision of things less completely than *Galileo* I. But even in *Galileo* I the "crime" must be taken very seriously, because it is an abdication of what he alone among the characters has to offer (human greatness) and if human greatness were wiped from the record, then the "discovery" that "man is nothing" would be the truth.

Or are the sterling but more modest merits of Andrea and Federzoni sufficient to justify existence? In the terms imposed by the play, it is not clear that they are. That these two men disapprove of the abjuration tells us nothing to the purpose. They were never put to such a test, nor could they be since, not possessing greatness, they could never have had as much to lose as Galileo had. "The people are the hero." I have conceded that there is much truth in Benjamin's dictum, but the thought in the play is dialectical, many-sided, ironic, and the individual greatness of the protagonist is essential to the scheme. In the final crisis he is an antihero, and that is bad (or, in the first version, partly bad). What I am stressing, as a final point, is that he is also a hero: the hero as great man; human greatness being what offsets the Copernican blow to human narcissism.

> It was . . . a time which called for giants and produced giants—giants in power of thought, passion, and character, in universality and learning. The men who founded the modern rule of the bourgeoisie had anything but bourgeois limitations. On the contrary the adventurous character of the time inspired them to a greater or less degree. . . . But what is especially characteristic of them is that they almost all pursue their lives and activities in the midst of the contemporary movements, in the practical struggle; they take sides and join in the fight. . . . Hence the fullness and force of character that makes them complete men.

I don't know if this passage from Engels' *Dialectics of Nature* suggested the theme of Galileo Galilei to Brecht. It *is* cited in the Berlin Ensemble program of his play. Reading it, one reflects that, of course, Galileo, according to Brecht, was one who at a crucial moment was disloyal to his "side" in "the fight." That can hardly be unimportant. The character will stand, as Brecht intended, as an exemplar of a certain kind of weakness. But will it not stand, even more impressively, as the exemplar of human greatness, a proof that greatness is possible to humankind? For that matter, would the weakness be even interesting if it were not that of a great (which is to say: in many ways, a strong) man?

(1966)

Mother Courage

The role of Mother Courage is hard to play and is always being miscast. Why? "Because middle-aged actresses are such ladies and lack earthiness." But who has succeeded in the role? Outstandingly, Helene Weigel. Is she very earthy, is she notably proletarian? On the contrary—there is nothing proletarian about her except her opinions. Then what is it those other ladies lack that Helene Weigel has? Among other things, I would suggest an appreciation of the role, an understanding of what is in it, and above all the ability to portray contradictions. For whenever anyone says, "Mother Courage is essentially X," it is equally reasonable for someone to retort: "Mother Courage is essentially the opposite of X."

Mother Courage is essentially courageous. That is well known, isn't it? Tennessee Williams has written of the final moment of Brecht's play as one of the inspiring moments in all theatre—inspiring because of the woman's indomitability. On she marches with her wagon after all that has happened, a symbol of the way humanity itself goes on its way after all that has happened, *if* it can find the courage. And after all we don't have to wait for the final scene to learn that we have to deal with a woman of considerable toughness and resilience. This is not the first time she has shown that she can pick up the pieces and continue. One might even find courage in the very first scene where we learn that she has not been content to cower in some corner of Bamberg but has boldly come to meet the war. A trouble shooter, we might say on first meeting the lady, but the reverse of a coward.

Yet it is impossible to continue on this tack for long without requiring an: *On the other hand.* Beginning with the reason why she is nicknamed "Courage" in the first place.

> They call me Mother Courage because I was afraid I'd be ruined, so I drove through the bombardment of Riga like a madwoman with fifty loaves of bread in my cart. They were going moldy, what else could I do?

Did those who gave her the name intend a joke against an obvious coward? Or did they think she was driven by heroic valor when in fact she was impelled by sheer necessity? Either way her act is utterly devoid of the moral quality imputed. Whether in cowardice or in down-to-earth realism, her stance is Falstaffian. What is courage? A word.

Somewhere hovering over this play is the image of a pre-eminently courageous mother who courageously tries to hold on to her young. More than one actress, offering herself for the role, has seen this image and nothing else. Yet valor is conspicuously absent at those times when Mother Courage (however unwittingly) seals the fate of her children. At moments when, in heroic melodrama, the protagonist would be riding to the rescue, come hell or high water, Mother Courage is in the back room concluding a little deal. For her, it is emphatically not "a time for greatness." *She is essentially cowardly.*

A basic contradiction, then, which the actress in the role must play both sides of, or the play will become the flat and simple thing which not a few journalistic commentators have declared it to be. An actress may be said to be beginning to play Mother Courage when she is putting both courage and cowardice into the role with equal conviction and equal effect. She is still only beginning to play it, though; for, as she proceeds with her interpretation, she will find that, in this play, courage and cowardice are not inherent and invariable qualities but by-products.

Of what? We can hunt for the answer by looking further into particular sequences of action. It is not really from cowardice that Mother Courage is in the back room concluding a little deal when her children are claimed by the war. It is from preoccupation with "business." Although *Mother Courage* is spoken of as a war play, it is actually a business play, in the sense that the incidents in it, one and all, are business transactions—from the deal with the belt in Scene One, through the deal with the capon in Scene Two, the deal with the wagon in Scene Three, the deals with bullets and shirts in Scene Five, through to the economical funeral arrangements of the final scene. And since these transactions (except for the last) are what Courage supports her children by, they are "necessary." Those who condemn her have to face the question: What alternative had she? Of what use would it have been to save the life of Swiss Cheese if she lacked the wherewithal to *keep* him alive? The severe judge will answer that she could take a chance on this, provided she does save his life. But this is exactly Mother Courage's own position. She is fully prepared to take the chance if she has to. It is in determining whether she has to that her boy's life slips through her fingers: life or death is a matter of timing.

To say that Swiss Cheese is a victim of circumstances, not of Courage's character, will not, however, be of much use to the actress interpreting this character. If cowardice is *less* important here than at first appears, what is *more* important? Surely it is a failure in understanding, rather than in virtue. Let me elaborate.

Though only one of Brecht's completed plays is about anyone that a university would recognize as a philosopher, several of his plays present what one might call philosophers in disguise, such as Schweyk, the philosopher of a pub in Prague, and Azdak, the philosopher of a Georgian village. To my mind, *Mother Courage is above all a philosopher,* defining the philosopher along Socratic lines as a person who likes to talk all the time and explain everything to everybody. (A simple trait in itself, one would think, yet there have been actresses and directors who wish to have all Courage's speeches shortened into mere remarks. Your philosopher never makes remarks; he always speechifies; hence such abridgment enforces a radical misinterpretation of character.) I do not mean at all that Courage is an idle or armchair philosopher whose teachings make no contact with life. On the contrary, her ideas are nothing if not a scheme of life by which, she hopes, her family is to do pretty well in a world which is doing pretty badly.

Here one sees the danger of thinking of Mother Courage as the average person. Rather, she resembles the thoughtfully ambitious modern mother of the lower-middle or better-paid working class who wants her children to win scholarships and end up in the Labour Cabinet.* (Minister of Education: Kattrin. Chancellor of the Exchequer: Swiss Cheese. Minister of War: Eilif.) Has it escaped attention that if one of her children turns out a cutthroat, this is blamed on circumstances ("Otherwise, I'd have starved, smarty"), while *the other two are outright heroes?* Anyone who considers this an average family takes a far higher view of the average than is implicit in the works of Bertolt Brecht.

What is the philosophy of this philosopher? Reduced to a single proposition, it is that if you concede defeat on the larger issue, you can achieve some nice victories in smaller ways. The larger issue is whether the world can be changed. It can't. But brandy is still drunk, and can be sold. One can survive, and one can help one's children to survive by teaching each to make appropriate use of the qualities God gave him. The proposition I have just mentioned will apply to this upbringing. A child endowed with a particular talent or virtue should

* This "comment" was written on the "occasion" of the play's production in London.

not pursue it to its logical end: defeat on such projects should be conceded at the outset. The child should cunningly exploit his characteristic talent for its incidental uses along the way. In this fashion the unselfishness of a Swiss Cheese or a Kattrin can be harnessed to selfishness. The result, if the philosophy works, is that while the world may shoot itself to blazes, the little Courage family, one and all, will live out its days in moderate wealth and moderate happiness. The scheme is not utopian. Just the opposite: the hope is to make optimism rational by reducing human demands to size.

The main reason it doesn't work is that the little world which Mother Courage's wisdom tries to regulate is dependent upon the big world which she has given up as a bad job. Small business is part of the big war which is part of the big business of ownership of *all* the means of production and distribution. No more than the small businessman can live in a separate economic system from the big can the small philosopher live in a separate philosophic system from the big. *Mother Courage,* one can conclude, exposes the perennial illusions of the *petit bourgeois* scheme of things. This has of course often been done before in modern literature. But usually only the idealism has been exposed. Mother Courage, on the other hand, could claim to be a cynic. She has the theatre audience laughing most of the time on the score of this cynicism—by which *she* deflates illusions. Cynicism is nothing, after all, if not "realistic." What a cynical remark lays bare *has* to be the truth. Brecht makes the truth of his play the more poignant through the fact that the cynicism in it ultimately favors illusion. Mother Courage had gone to all lengths to trim her sails to the wind but even then the ship wouldn't move. So there is irony within irony (as, in Brecht's work, there usually is). Courage's cynicism can cut down the windy moralizing of the Chaplain easily enough, but only to be itself cut down by a world that cannot be comprehended even by this drastically skeptical kind of thinking.

What alternative did Mother Courage have? The only alternatives shown in the play are, on the one hand, the total brutalization of men like the Swedish Commander (and, for that matter, her own son Eilif) and, on the other hand, the martyrdom achieved by Swiss Cheese and Kattrin. Presumably, to the degree that the playwright criticizes her, he is pushing her toward the second alternative. Yet, not only would such a destiny be completely out of character, within the terms of the play itself it is not shown to be really preferable. Rather, the fruitlessness of both deaths is underlined. Why add a third?

Given her character, Mother Courage had no alternative to what she thought—or, for that matter, to the various "bad" things she did. In this case, can she be condemned? Logically, obviously not; but was Brecht logical? The printed editions of the play indicate that he made changes in his script to render Mother Courage less sympathetic. In other words, after having made her thoroughly sympathetic in his first version, Brecht later wanted her less so. One can see the sense of the changes in polemical terms: he did not wish to seem to condone behavior which is to be deplored. But to make this point, is it necessary to make Mother Courage a less good person? Personally I would think not, and I should like to see *Courage* played sometime in the Urtext of 1940 and without the later "improvements." But one should not minimize the complexity of the problem. Like many other playwrights, Brecht wanted to show a kind of inevitability combined with a degree of free will, and if it doesn't matter whether Courage is less good or more, because she is trapped by circumstances, then the play is fatalistic. I tend to think it *is* fatalistic as far as the movement of history is concerned, and that the element of hope in it springs only from Brecht's rendering of human character. Brecht himself is not satisfied with this and made changes in the hope of suggesting that things might have been different had Mother Courage acted otherwise. (What would she have done? Established socialism in seventeenth-century Germany? One must not ask.)

Brecht has stressed, in his Notes, that Mother Courage never sees the light, never realizes what has happened, is incapable of learning. As usual, Brecht's opinions, as stated in outside comments, are more doctrinaire than those to be found embodied in the plays. It may be true that Mother Courage never sees that "small business" is a hopeless case, though to prove even this Brecht had to manufacture the evidence by inserting, later, the line at the end: "I must get back into business." She does see through her own philosophy of education. The "Song of Solomon" in Scene Nine concedes that the program announced in Scene One has failed. The manipulation of the virtues has not worked: "a man is better off without." The song is perhaps more symbolic, as well as more schematic, than most Brechtians wish Brecht to be, for there is a verse about each of her children under the form of famous men (Eilif is Caesar, Swiss Cheese is Socrates, Kattrin is Saint Martin), but more important is that this is the "Song of Solomon" (from *The Threepenny Opera*) and that Solomon is Courage herself:

> King Solomon was very wise
> So what's his history?
> He came to view this world with scorn
> Yes, he came to regret he ever had been born
> Declaring: all is vanity.
> King Solomon was very wise
> But long before the day was out
> The consequence was clear, alas:
> It was his wisdom brought him to this pass.
> A man is better off without.

I have heard the question asked whether this conclusion was not already reached in the "Song of the Great Capitulation" in Scene Four. Both songs are songs of defeat (Brecht's great subject) but of two different defeats. The second is defeat total and final: Courage has staked everything on wisdom, and wisdom has ruined her and her family. The first is the setback of "capitulation," that is of disenchantment. When Yvette was only seventeen she was in love, and love was heaven. Soon afterward she had learned to "fraternize behind the trees"; she had capitulated. It is perhaps hard to imagine Courage as a younger and different person from the woman we meet in the play, but in the "Song of the Great Capitulation" we are definitely invited to imagine her as a young woman who thought she could storm the heavens, whose faith seemed able to move mountains.

Scene Four is one of several in this play which one can regard as the whole play in miniature. For Brecht is not finished when he has set forth the character of Mother Courage as one who has passed from youthful idealism to cynical realism. For many a playwright, that would no doubt be that, but Courage's exchange with the angry young soldier leads to other things. We discover that Mother Courage is not a happy Machiavellian, boasting of her realism as an achievement. We find that she is deeply ashamed. And in finding this, we discover in Courage the mother of those two roaring idealists (not to say again: martyrs) Swiss Cheese and Kattrin. "Kiss my arse," says the soldier, and why? His bad language had not hitherto been directed at her. But she has been kind to him only to be cruel. If she has not broken his spirit, she has done something equally galling: she has made clear to him how easily his spirit can be broken. When you convert a man to the philosophy of You Can't Win, you can hardly expect to earn his gratitude at the same time.

In the way Courage puts matters to the soldier we see how close she came to being a truly wise woman. We also discover in this scene that, despite the confident tone of her cynical lingo, Courage is not really sure of herself and her little philosophy. She teaches the soldier that it is futile to protest, but she apparently does not know this herself until she reminds herself of it, for she has come here precisely to protest. Here we learn to recognize in Courage not only contradiction but conflict. She knows what she has thought. She is not sure what to think.

And this is communicated by Brecht in a very bold—or, if you prefer, just poetic—manner. For while Courage does not give herself to despair until the end (and not even then for those who can take at face value her: "I must get back into business"), she had correctly foreseen the end from the beginning: the despair she gives herself to had been there from the moment of capitulation. At times it would strike her between the eyes: she is very responsive and, for example, has worked out the Marxist interpretation of religion for herself. Scene Two contains a song she had taught Eilif as a boy: it accurately predicts the manner of his death. In Scene One she predicts doom for the whole family in her elaborate pantomime of fortunetelling. It could be said that everything is there from the start, for the first thing Mother Courage does is to try and sell things by announcing an early death for her prospective customers. The famous "Song of Mother Courage" is the most extraordinary parody of the kind of song any real *vivandière* might try to attract customers with. Mother Courage's Come and buy! is nothing other than: Come and die! In that respect, her fortunetelling is on the level, and her wisdom is valid.

Scene Four, I have been saying, is one of several in this play which one can regard as the whole play in miniature. The main purpose of the play, for Brecht, was, I think, to generate anger over what it shows. Yet Brecht realizes how pointless angry plays have been—and angry speeches outside the drama. It is said that Clifford Odets's *Waiting for Lefty* made millionaires angry for as long as it took them to get from their seats to where their chauffeurs tactfully waited for them at the end of the block. Such is the anger of the social drama in general.

There is the anger of a sudden fit, which boils up and over and is gone. And there is the anger which informs the work of long years of change. *Why* can't the world be changed? For Mother Courage, it is not from any inherent unchangeability in the world. It is because our wish to change it is not strong enough. Nor is this weakness innate. It is simply that our objection to the present world isn't as strong as it once was. What is outrageous does not outrage us as it once did. Today, it only arouses the "short rage" of Brecht's soldier—and of Courage herself—not the long one that is required. Because we—they—have capitulated.

Capitulation is not just an idea but a feeling, an agony in fact, and is located not just in the scene of the Great Capitulation but in the whole play of *Mother Courage*. Everything that happens is related to it, above all the things that are furthest away from it, namely, the deaths of Swiss Cheese and Kattrin. And if these children are what their mother made them, then their refusal to capitulate stems from her, is her own youth, her own original nature.

The ultimate achievement of an actress playing this role would be that she made us sense to what an extent Courage's children are truly hers.

(*1965*)

The Caucasian Chalk Circle

In the prologue to *The Caucasian Chalk Circle,* the people of two collective farms in Georgia debate their respective titles to the ownership of a piece of land. Up to now it has belonged to one farm, but now the other claims to be able to make better use of it. Who should own *anything?* Should possession be nine-tenths of the law? Or should law and possession be open to review? That is the question Brecht raises. In the first draft of the play, the date of this bit of action was the 1930s. Later, Brecht shifted it to 1945 for two reasons: so that the land can be approached as a new problem, in that the farmers on it had all been ordered east at the approach of Hitler's armies; and so that the farmers newly claiming it can have partially earned it by having fought as partisans against the invader.

The Prologue is a bit of a shock for American audiences. Here are all these Communists—Russians at that—calling each other Comrades, and so on. That is why, until recently, the Prologue was always omitted from American productions. In 1965, however, it was included in the Minnesota Theatre Company's production without untoward incidents or, so far as I know, outraged comment. With the years the Prologue had not changed, but the world had. America had. The existence of the U.S.S.R. is now generally conceded in the U.S.A. That Communists do use the title "Comrades" is taken in stride. There is even understanding for the fact that the playwright Bertolt Brecht sympathized with communism in those days, even more consistently than Jean-Paul Sartre and Peter Weiss do today.

However, disapproval of the Prologue is not caused merely by the labels. A deeper malaise is caused by the *mode* of the dispute over the land. Land has always been fought over, often with guns. The expectation that some individual should pull a gun, or threaten to, is part of our stock response to the situation, but in the prologue, this expectation receives a calculated disappointment. The conflict is, or has been, real, but a new way of resolving it has been found, a new attitude to antagonists has been found. Not to mention the new solution: the land goes to the "interlopers," the impostors, because they offer convincing evidence that they will be able to make better use of it. Both the conclusion and the road by which it is reached imply a complete reversal of the values by which our civilization has been living.

And Soviet civilization? Were we to visit Georgia, should we actually witness such decisions being made, and being arrived at in Brecht's way? It is certainly open to doubt, even in 1966, while, in 1945, nothing could have been more misleading than Brecht's Prologue, if it was intended to give an accurate picture of Stalin's Russia. We hear that Soviet citizens have themselves complained that, quite apart from the political point, they find nothing recognizably Russian in this German scene.

Is it thereby invalidated? "The home of the Soviet people shall also be the home of Reason!" That is certainly a key line in the Prologue, but the verb is "shall be," not "is." That Brecht aligned himself with socialism, and saw the Soviet Union as the chief champion of socialism, is clear, yet is only to say that he saw Russia as on the right path, not by any means as having arrived at the goal. Let the worried reader of the Prologue to *The Caucasian Chalk Circle* also read Brecht's poem "Are the People Infallible?" * in which the poet speaks in this vein of the death in 1939 of the Soviet playwright Tretyakov: "My teacher who was great and kind has been shot, sentenced to death by a People's Court as a spy. Suppose he is innocent? The sons of the people have found him guilty. On the supposition that he is innocent, what will he be thinking as he goes to his death?" In any case, to prove Brecht wrong about Russia would not necessarily be to prove him wrong about socialism.

A socialist play, is this a play for Socialists only? That, ultimately, is for non-Socialists to decide. From Brecht's viewpoint, a lot of people are potential Socialists who might—at this time, in this place—be very surprised to hear it. In principle it is a play for all who are not identified with those it shows to be the common enemy, and in actuality it may turn out to be a play even for some of those who *are* identified with the enemy, since they may not recognize the identification, preferring a life-illusion. French aristocrats applauded *Figaro*.

* Full text in *Tulane Drama Review*, Summer 1966, and *Nation*, April 18, 1966.

The Threepenny Opera must have been enjoyed by many who, very shortly afterward, voted for Hitler.

The Prologue shows a country (forget it is Russia, if that offends you) where Reason has made inroads upon Unreason. Unreason, in *The Caucasian Chalk Circle,* takes the form of private property, and the laws that guarantee it. "Property is theft," and, by paradox, a private person who steals another private person's property, infringing the law, only re-enacts the original rape of the earth, and confirms the law—of private property. The characters in *Chalk Circle* who most firmly believe in private property are most actively engaged in fighting over private property—whether to cling to it or to grab it.

Where is private property's most sensitive spot? One learns the answer whenever a businessman announces that his son will be taking over the business or whenever a spokesman for all things holy comes to his favorite theme of mother and child.

> . . . of all ties, the ties of blood are strongest. Mother and child, is there a more intimate relationship? Can one tear a child from its mother? High Court of Justice, she has conceived it in the holy ecstasies of love, she has carried it in her womb, she has fed it with her blood, she has borne it with pain . . .

This is the voice of one of the spokesmen for all things holy in *The Caucasian Chalk Circle,* and so, when the possession of a child has been in dispute, whether at the court of Solomon in Israel, or before a Chinese magistrate in the year 1000 A.D., the question asked has been only: Which womb did it come out of? Which loins begat it? The ultimate *locus* of private property is in the private parts.

Plato had other plans. He knew that a given parent may in fact be the worst person to bring up his or her child. Our concern, he assumes, should be to produce the best human beings, the best society, not to sacrifice these ends to an, after all, arbitrary notion of "natural" right. The point about an umbilical cord is that it has to be cut. Children should be assigned to those best qualified to bring them up. . . . Plato's Republic *is* "the home of Reason."

The Georgia of *The Caucasian Chalk Circle* is not. After a Prologue which provides a hint of what it would mean to begin to create a home for Reason on this earth, the play transports us to a world which, for all its exotic externals, is nothing other than the world we live in, *our* world, the world of Unreason, of Disorder, of Injustice. Those who are upset by the idealizations of the Prologue, by its "utopianism," need not fret. The play itself provides an image of life in its customary mode, soiled, stinking, cruel, and outrageous.

Even in a jungle, lovely flowers will spring up here and there, such being the fecundity of nature, and however badly our pastors and masters run our society, however much they pull to pieces that which they claim to be keeping intact, nature remains fecund, human beings are born with human traits, sometimes human strength outweighs human weakness, and human grace shows itself amid human ugliness. "In the bloodiest times," as our play has it, "there are kind people." Their kindness is arbitrary. No sociologist could deduce it from the historical process. Just the contrary. It represents the brute refusal of nature to be submerged in history and therefore, arguably (and this *is* Brecht's argument), the possibility that the creature should, at some future point, subdue history.

For the present, though—a present that has spread itself out through the whole course of historical time—the sociologists win, and man is not the master but the slave of society. History is the history of power struggles conducted (behind the moralistic rhetoric familiar to us all from the mass media) with minimum scrupulousness and maximum violence. To give way to the promptings of nature, to natural sympathy, to the natural love of the Good, is to be a Sucker. America invented that expressive word, and America's most articulate comedian, W. C. Fields, called one of his films *Never Give a Sucker an Even Break*. Which is the credo of Western civilization as depicted in the works of Bertolt Brecht.

In *The Caucasian Chalk Circle* a sucker gets an even break. That seems contradictory, and in the contradiction—or contradictiousness—lies the whole interest of the story. Or rather of its second part. In the first part, we see the inevitable working itself out. The sucker—the good girl who gives way to her goodness—is not given any breaks at all. She is punished for her non-sin, her anti-sin. She loses everything, both the child she has saved and adopted, and the soldier-fiancé whom she has loyally loved and waited for. She is abandoned, isolated, stripped, torn apart, like other people in Brecht's plays and our world who persist in the practice of active goodness.

> The Ironshirts took the child, the beloved child.
> The unhappy girl followed them to the city, the dreaded city.
> She who had borne him demanded the child.
> She who had raised him faced trial.

So ends Part One: a complete Brecht play in itself. In Part Two Brecht was determined to put the question: Suppose the inevitable did not continue to work itself out? Now how could he do this? By having a Socialist revolution destroy private property and establish the rule of Reason? That is what he would have done, had he been as narrow and doctrinaire as some readers of his Prologue assume. But what is in the Prologue is not in the play itself. For the second half of his play Brecht invented a new version of the Chalk Circle legend, which is also a new version of another idea from literary tradition, the idea that the powers that be can sometimes be temporarily overthrown and a brief Golden Age ensue.

Who will decide the case?
To whom will the child be assigned?
Who will the judge be? A good judge? A bad?
The city was in flames.
In the judge's seat sat—Azdak.

Inevitably, necessarily, a judge in the society depicted in *The Caucasian Chalk Circle* must assign a child to its actual mother. In that proposition, the law of private property seems to receive the sanction of Mother Nature herself— that is to say, the owners of private property are able to appeal to nature without conscious irony. Such an event, however, would give Brecht at best a brief epilogue to Part One. What gives him a second part to his play, and one which enables him in the end to pick up the loose ends left by the Prologue, is that the judge is Azdak, and that Azdak is a mock king, an Abbot of Unreason, a Lord of Misrule, who introduces "a brief Golden Age, almost an age of justice."

> The reign of Zeus [says F. M. Cornford in *The Origin of Attic Comedy*] stood in the Greek mind for the existing moral and social order; its overthrow, which is the theme of so many of the comedies, might be taken to symbolise . . . the breaking up of all ordinary restraints, or again . . . the restoration of the Golden Age of Justice and Lovingkindness, that Age of Kronos which lingered in the imagination of poets, like the after-glow of a sun that had set below the horizon of the Age of Iron. The seasonal festivals of a Saturnalian character celebrated the return, for a brief interregnum, of a primitive innocence that knew not shame, and a liberty that at any other time would have been licentious. Social ranks were inverted, the slave exercising authority over the master. At Rome each household became a miniature republic, the slaves being invested with the dignities of office. A mock king was chosen to bear rule during the festival, like the mediaeval Abbot of Unreason or Lord of Misrule.

In this case, how is the play any different from the Prologue, except in the temporariness of Azdak's project? Its temporariness is of a piece with its precariousness, its freakishness, its skittishness, its semiaccidental character. Only with a touch of irony can one say that Azdak establishes a Golden Age or even that he is a good judge. The age remains far from golden, and his judging is often outrageous enough. But his *extra*ordinary outrages call our attention to the ordinary outrages of ordinary times—to the fact that outrage *is* ordinary, is the usual thing, and that we are shocked, not by injustice per se, but only by injustice that favors the poor and the weak. Azdak did not rebuild a society, nor even start a movement that had such an end in view. He only provided Georgia with something to think about and us with a legend, a memory, an image.

So much for the ideological *schema*. The play would be too rigidly schematic if Brecht had just brought together the Good Girl with the Appropriate Judge, using both characters simply as mouthpieces for a position. There is more to both of them than that. Azdak is one of the most complex figures in modern drama.

Discussing the role of the Ironical Man in ancient comedy, F. M. Cornford remarks that "the special kind of irony" he practices is

feigned stupidity. The word Ironist itself in the fifth century appears to mean "cunning" or (more exactly) "sly." Especially it meant the man who masks his batteries of deceit behind a show of ordinary good nature or indulges a secret pride and conceit of wisdom, while he affects ignorance and self-depreciation, but lets you see all the while that he could enlighten you if he chose, and so makes a mock of you. It was for putting on these airs that Socrates was accused of "irony" by his enemies.

This passage sets forth what I take to be the preliminary design of Azdak's character, but then Brecht complicates the design. Azdak is not simply an embodiment of an ironical viewpoint, he is a person with a particular history, who needs irony for a particular reason—and not all the time. It is through the chinks in the ironical armor that we descry the man. *Azdak is not being ironical when he tells us he wanted to denounce himself for letting the Grand Duke escape.* He supposed, it seems, that, while the Grand Duke and his Governors were busy fighting the Princes, the carpet weavers had brought off a popular revolution, and, as a revolutionary, he wished to denounce himself for a counter-revolutionary act.

What kind of revolutionary was he? A very modern kind: a disenchanted one. Those who like to compare Azdak the Judge to Robin Hood should not fail to compare Azdak the Politician to Arthur Koestler. Before the present revolt of the carpet weavers, decades earlier, there had been another popular uprising. Azdak maintains, or pretends, that this was in his grandfather's time, forty years ago, and not in Georgia, but in Persia. His two songs—which lie at the very heart of our play—tell both of the conditions that produced the uprising and of the uprising itself.* The pretense is that revolution represents disorder, and the suppression of revolutions, order; and that Azdak is appealing to the Generals to restore order. This last item is not a hollow pretense or a single irony, for Azdak has not championed revolt. He has withdrawn into his shell. His job as a "village scrivener" is the outward token of the fact. In a note, Brecht advises the actor of the role not to imagine that Azdak's rags directly indicate his character. He wears them, Brecht says, as a Shakespearean wears the

---

* Azdak's "Song of Chaos" is adapted from a translation of an ancient Egyptian lament, brought to notice in 1903, but dating back to about 2500 B.C. The document describes a state of social disintegration and revolt, appeals to the King and other authorities to take

motley of a fool. Azdak is not lacking in wisdom. Only it is the bitter wisdom of the disillusioned intellectual, and, in Brecht's view, a partly false wisdom prompted not alone by objective facts but quite as much by the "wise" man's own limitations.

Azdak has the characteristic limitation of the Brechtian rogue: cowardice. Or at any rate: courage insufficient to the occasion. He is Brecht's Herr Keuner saying no to tyranny only after the tyrant is safely dead. At least, this is how Azdak is, if left to himself. Yet, like other human beings, he is not a fixed quantity but influenceable by the flow of things, and especially by the people he meets. A passive sort of fellow, he acts less than he *re*acts. Our play describes his reaction to a new and unforeseen situation, and especially, in the end, to a single person: Grusha. Which gives the last section of the play its organic movement.

Azdak needs drawing out, and what Brecht does is expose him to a series of persons and situations that do draw him out. (That he also brings with him into the Golden Age his unregenerate self creates the comic contradictions. It is hard, through all the little trial scenes, to tell where selfishness leaves off and generosity begins: this is a source of amusement, and also enables Brecht to question accepted assumptions on the relation of social and antisocial impulses.) The Test of the Chalk Circle with which the action culminates does not follow automatically from the philosophy of Azdak but is a product of a dramatic development. At the outset he is in no mood to be so good or so wise. He has just been mercilessly beaten, but then he reacts in his especially sensitive way to all that ensues, and above all to the big speech in which Grusha denounces him:

> AZDAK. Fined twenty piasters!
> GRUSHA. Even if it was thirty, I'd tell you what I think of your justice, you drunken onion! How dare you talk to me like the cracked Isaiah on the

---

action. Brecht reverses the point of view, as his custom is, but since he does so ironically, he is able to stay close to such words of the original as the following:

Nay, but the highborn are full of lamentations, and the poor are full of joy. Every town saith: 'Let us drive out the powerful from our midst.'

Nay, but the son of the highborn man is no longer to be recognized. The child of his lady is become [no more than] the son of his handmaid.

Nay, but the boxes of ebony are broken up. Precious sesnem [*sic*] wood is out in pieces for beds.

Nay, but the public offices are opened and their lists [of serfs] are taken away. Serfs become lords of serfs.

Behold, ladies lie on cushions [in lieu of beds] and magistrates in the storehouse. He that could not sleep upon walls now possesseth a bed.

Behold, he that never build for himself a boat now possesseth ships. He that possessed the same looketh at them, but they are no longer his.

(Translated from the Egyptian by A. M. Blackman, and published in *The Literature of the Ancient Egyptians* by Adolf Erman. London, 1927.)

church window? As if you were somebody. You weren't born to this. You weren't born to rap your own mother on the knuckles if she swipes a little bowl of salt someplace. Aren't you ashamed when you see how I tremble before you? You've made yourself their servant so they won't get their houses stolen out from under them—houses they themselves stole! Since when did a house belong to its bedbugs? But you're their watchdog, or how would they get our men into their wars? Bribe taker! I don't respect you. No more than a thief or a bandit with a knife. Do what you like. You can all do what you like, a hundred against one, but do you know who should be chosen for a profession like yours? Extortioners! Men who rape children! Let it be their punishment to sit in judgment on their fellow men! Which is worse than to hang from the gallows.

AZDAK. Now it is thirty.

She could hardly know how she got under his skin. Her denunciation, quite guileless and spontaneous, happens to be couched in just the terms that come home to him. For she is representing him as a traitor to his class. Who does he think he is, who is now setting himself up as a Lord over his own people? Well, in his own view, Azdak *was* something of a traitor to his class, but he has been busy for a year or two trying to make it up to them, and now Grusha is providing him with the happiest of all occasions to prove this. His decision to give her the child grows out of his sense of guilt and out of his delight in opportunities to make good.

One could say, too, that his earlier confrontation with Granny Grusinia prepares the way for the later one with Grusha. Here, too, he has to be drawn out, partly by threats, but even more by finding again his original identification with the cause of the people. Between them, Granny Grusinia and Grusha are the Marxian, Brechtian version of the "eternal feminine" whom our blundering, uncourageous Faust needs, if he is to move "onwards and upwards." Hence, although the Chalk Circle incident occupies only a minute or two at the end of a long play, it is rightly used for the title of the whole.

The incident not only clarifies the meaning of Azdak, it also brings together the various thematic threads of the play. In the first instance, there is the stated conclusion:

Take note what men of old concluded:
That what there is shall go to those who are good for it, thus:
Children to the motherly, that they prosper,
Carts to good drivers, that they be driven well,
The valley to the waterers, that it yield fruit.

But this was never in doubt. Any spectator who has spent the evening hoping for a surprise at the end courted disappointment. He should have been warned by the Prologue. In an early draft Brecht planned to let the decision on the collective farms wait till the Chalk Circle story has been told. That, however, is politically ludicrous, if it means, as it would have to, that Soviet planners depend on folksingers in the way that some other leaders depend upon astrologers. And an infringement of a main principle of Brechtian drama would have occurred. In this type of play there should be no doubt as to what is going to happen, only as to how and why.

The valley is assigned to the waterers already in the Prologue, and already in the first scenes that follow we see that Michael has a bad mother but has been befriended by a better one. What remains to be said? On what grounds can we be asked to stay another couple of hours in the theatre? One sufficient reason would be: to see Grusha *become* the mother. This is not Plato's Republic, and Grusha is no trained educator in a Platonic crèche. In the first phase of the action her purpose is only to rescue the child, not keep it: she is going to leave it on a peasant's doorstep and return home. We see the child becoming hers by stages, so that when Azdak reaches his verdict in the final scene, he is not having a brainstorm ("Grusha would be a splendid mother for this child") but recognizing an accomplished fact ("She *is* the mother of this child"). Another paradox: in this play that says possession is not nine-tenths of the law we learn that (in another sense) possession is ten-tenths of the law.

It should not escape notice that, in the end, the child becomes Simon Shashava's too:

> GRUSHA. You like him?
> SIMON. With my respects, I like him.
> GRUSHA. Now I can tell you: I took him because on that Easter Sunday I got engaged to you. So he's a child of love.

Michael had been a child of the lovelessness of his actual mother and the lifelessness of his actual father, but now it turns out that he will have a father who has been spared death in war and is very much alive, and a mother who did not love him at his conception, nor yet at his delivery, but who loves him *now*. The term "lovechild" is applied to bastards, and Michael, who was legitimate in the legal sense, however illegitimate humanly and morally, will now become a bastard in a sense which the story . . . legitimizes.

> Your father is a bandit
> A harlot the mother who bore you
> Yet honorable men
> Shall kneel down before you.
>
> Food to the baby horses
> The tiger's son will take.
> The mothers will get milk
> From the son of the snake.

Brecht's play broadens out into myth, and we hear many echoes—from the Bible, from Pirandello—but it is more relevant to see the phenomenon the other way around: not that Brecht lets his story spread outward toward other stories, but that he uses other stories, and mythical patterns, and pulls them in, brings them, as we say, "down to earth," in concrete, modern meanings. Most important, in this regard, is Brecht's use of what a recent scholar has called festive comedy. *The Caucasian Chalk Circle* is not an *inquiry* into the dispute over ownership presented in the Prologue but a *celebration* of the assignment of the land to "those who are good for it."

A main preoccupation of this oldest form of comedy in Western tradition was with Impostors. The point of comedy was, and has remained, to expose the imposture. *The Caucasian Chalk Circle* does this, for what could be a more gross imposture than the claims to either rulership or parenthood of the Abashwili couple? But Brecht does not leave the ancient patterns alone. Even as he turns around the old tale of the Chalk Circle, so also he plays his ironic, dialectical game with the patterns. *For Azdak and Grusha are impostors too.* That is what makes them brother and sister under the skin. In the impostor-mother, the impostor-judge recognizes his own.

> As if it was stolen goods she picked it up.
> As if she was a thief she sneaked away.

Thus the Singer, describing how Grusha got the baby. He is too generous. Legally, she *is* a thief; the child *is* stolen goods; and Azdak has "stolen" the judgeship, though, characteristically, not on his own initiative: he is, if you will, a receiver of stolen goods. The special pleasure for Azdak in his Chalk Circle verdict is that, at the moment when he will return his own "stolen" goods to their "rightful" owners, he is able to give Grusha and Simon "their" child in (what they can hope is) perpetuity.

I have called the irony a game, for art is a game, but this is not to say that Brecht's playfulness is capricious. In the inversion lies the meaning, and it is simply our good fortune that there is fun in such things, that, potentially at least, there is fun in *all* human contradictions and oppositions. The old patterns have, indeed, no meaning for Brecht *until* they are inverted. For instance, this important pattern: the return to the Age of Gold. We, the modern audience, Russian or American, *return* to the Age of Gold when we see Azdak inverting our rules and laws. Azdak *returns* to an Age of Gold when he nostalgically recalls the popular revolt of a former generation. On the other hand, the Age of Azdak is not, literally, an Age of Gold at all. It is an age of war and internecine strife in which just a little justice can, by a fluke, be done. Nor is the traditional image of a Golden Age anything like a revolutionary's happy memories of days on the barricades: just the reverse. Finally, Brecht repudiates our hankering after past Ages of Gold altogether. That revolutions, for Azdak, are identified with the past is precisely what is wrong with him. In *The Caucasian Chalk Circle* we move back in order to move forward. The era of Azdak has the transitory character of the Saturnalia and so is properly identified with it. After the interregnum is over, the mock king goes back into anonymity, like Azdak. But the Prologue suggests a *regnum* that is not accidental and shortlived but deliberate and perhaps not *inter*. And then there is the ultimate inversion: that the Golden Age should be envisaged not in the past but in the future, and not in fairyland or heaven, but in Georgia.

The Russian Georgia. But ours is included, at least in the sense that the play is about our twentieth century world, and in a specific way. As Brecht saw things, this century came in on a wave of democratic hope. A new age was dawning, or seemed to be. So universally was this felt that the most powerful of counterrevolutionary movements, the Hitler movement, had to represent itself as Socialist and announce, in its turn, the dawn of a new age. It could bring in no dawn of its own, of course, but in Germany it certainly prevented the arrival of the dawn that had seemed imminent.

This grouping of forces is what we have in *The Caucasian Chalk Circle*. A true dawn is promised by the rebellious carpet weavers. It never arrives, because the Ironshirts are paid to cut the weavers to pieces. At this point, when a triumphant Fat Prince enters, very much in the likeness of Marshal Goering, Azdak points at him with the comment: There's your new age all right! The thought of the new age, the longing for a new age, hovers over *The Caucasian Chalk Circle* from beginning to end, and any good production should seem haunted by it.

The Prologue will say different things to different people as to what has already been achieved and where, but to all it conveys Brecht's belief that the new age is possible. What his audience is to be haunted by is not a memory, a fantasy, or a dream, but a possibility.

(1966)

Ibsen, Shaw, Brecht

For David Daiches

I

Matthew Arnold expected from poets in general a "criticism of life," and many today would not only agree but add that this criticism should be a social one. Some will even argue that it *must* be a social one, since literature, in their view, is by nature social. Society, that is, can be regarded as providing both the source and substance of literature. It can also be maintained that to a communicate a thought to another person—even more, to a group of other persons—is to socialize it.

As for the drama, it has often been regarded as, in several senses, yet more social than other kinds of literature. Sense one: the theatre appeals most strongly and helpfully *to* society.

> The theatre is the most potent and direct means of strengthening human reason and enlightening the whole nation.
>
> —Mercier, Du Théâtre, 1773

Sense two: the theatre has an especially close connection with the social conditions of the moment.

No portion of literature is connected by closer or more numerous ties with the present condition of society than the drama.

—Tocqueville, *Democracy in America,* Part Two, 1840

Sense three: drama is pre-eminently the genre in which what is currently the characteristic type of relation of man to man is represented.

Thus investigation as to which type of man is suited to dramatic art coincides with the investigation of the problem of man's relation to other men.

—George Lukacs, *The Sociology of Modern Drama,* 1909

Finally, modern drama, drama since Ibsen, has frequently been regarded as still more social than earlier drama, as peculiarly concerned with social problems: a thesis which can best be documented in the lives of the three dramatists to be discussed here.

Though Henrik Ibsen would seem to us today to have been concerned with modern social problems from the very beginning, he did not seem so in his early works to the leading Scandinavian critic of the time, George Brandes, who criticized *Brand* (1865) as reactionary and read the playwright (as well as the rest of the world) this lesson:

What keeps a literature alive in our day is that it submits problems for debate. Thus, for example, George Sand debates the problem of the relations between the sexes, Byron and Feuerbach religion, John Stuart Mill and Proudhon property, Turgenev, Spielhagen and Emile Augier social conditions. . . .

—Inaugural Lecture, 1871

To which Ibsen replied: ". . . your work is a great, shattering, and emancipating outbreak of genius," and, "what cannot withstand the ideas of the times must succumb." Undoubtedly Brandes' writings which, as Ibsen said, disturbed his sleep also led him toward his great "modern period." Some fifteen years after Brandes' Inaugural Lecture, Henrik Ibsen's plays disturbed the sleep of George Bernard Shaw and led him to modernism and to the theatre. In 1886 he took the part of Krogstad in a reading of *A Doll's House* (1879) staged by Karl Marx's daughter, Eleanor. In 1890 he gave a Fabian lecture about that play. In the next year appeared the first book on Ibsen in English: Shaw's *Quintessence of Ibsenism.* One year more and Shaw's first play, *Widowers' Houses* was ready. "It deals," Shaw said in a preface, "with a burning social question, and is deliberately intended to induce people to vote on the Progressive side at the next County Council election in London." It will be noted that Shaw is pushing the idea of problem literature further than Brandes had. Not debate now, but political pressure, if on a modest municipal scale. The scale would be enlarged later. In May 1895 a magazine called the *Humanitarian* asked a number of public men to answer the question: "Should social problems be freely dealt with in the drama?" Shaw answered:

> We are . . . witnessing a steady intensification in the hold of social questions on the larger poetic imagination. . . . If people are rotting and starving in all directions, and nobody else has the heart or brains to make a disturbance about it, the great writers must. In short, what is forcing our poets to follow Shelley in becoming political and social agitators, and to turn the theatre into a platform for propaganda and an arena for discussion, is that whilst social questions are being thrown up for solution almost daily by the fierce rapidity with which industrial processes change and supersede one another . . . the political machinery by which alone our institutions can be kept abreast of these changes is so oldfashioned . . . that social questions never get solved until the pressure becomes so desperate that even governments recognize the necessity for moving. And to bring the pressure to this point, the poets must lend a hand. . . .

If Shaw pushed the idea of problem drama further than Ibsen, Bertolt Brecht pushed it further than Shaw. The changes correspond, of course, to stages of history—and disillusionment. In 1871 there still seemed time for debate. In the 1890s it still seemed worthwhile to put pressure on governments, local and national. All Brecht's playwriting came after the definitive collapse of nineteenth-century civilization in World War I. By that token, it also came after a crucial attempt to build a new civilization by means other than parliamentary debate and propagandist pressure, namely, by Revolution. The question that arose now was whether the theatre could be of any use at all. Could the modern world even be portrayed in it? Brecht answered that it could, if it was portrayed as alterable. For him, to portray it as alterable was to help to alter it, beginning with an alteration of the means of portrayal, an alteration of the theatre itself:

> . . . half a century's experiments . . . had won the theatre brand-new fields of subject matter and types of problem, and made it a factor of marked social importance. At the same time they had brought the theatre to a point where any further development of the intellectual, social (political) experience must wreck the artistic experience.
>
> —"On Experimental Theatre," 1939

> . . . *The Mother* is a piece of anti-metaphysical, materialistic, non-Aristotelian drama. This makes nothing like such a free use as the Aristotelian theatre does of the passive empathy of the spectator; it also relates differently to certain psychological effects, such as catharsis. Just as it refrains from handing its hero over to the world as if it were his inescapable fate, so it would not dream of handing over the spectator to an inspiring theatrical

experience. Anxious to teach the spectator a quite different practical attitude, directed towards changing the world, it must begin by making him adopt in the theatre a quite different attitude from what he is used to.

—Notes to *The Mother*, 1933

By means of a new kind of theatre, Brecht would work on audiences in a new way and, by changing them, would help to change the world.

So far, so good. The quotations just made from our three authors are unequivocal, and suggest accurately enough three clear phases of recent history. What they hardly begin to suggest is the actual tenor of the three writers' creative work. I have only been citing, really, the official stance of each man: the quotations are from theoretical works, not from plays. If one wanted to document from actual theatre what has here been cited as principle, it would be easier to document the Brandes–Ibsen position from plays by Alexandre Dumas *fils;* the Shaw position from plays by Eugène Brieux; and the Brecht position, perhaps from Erwin Piscator's production experiments, perhaps from Brecht plays which most critics would regard as his weakest efforts. Here, for example, are the first and last speeches of Brieux's *Damaged Goods* (*Les Avariés*), cited in the translation for which Shaw wrote a preface:

1. [Before the play begins, the manager appears upon the stage and says:] Ladies and Gentlemen, I beg leave to inform you, on behalf of the author and of the management, that the object of this play is a study of the disease of syphilis in its bearing on marriage.

2. DOCTOR. This poor girl is typical. The whole problem is summed up in her: she is at once the product and the cause. We set the ball rolling, others keep it up, and it runs back to bruise our own shins. I have nothing more to say. (*He shakes hands with Loches as he conducts him to the door, and adds in a lighter tone*) But if you give a thought or two to what you have just seen when you are sitting in the Chamber [of Deputies], we shall not have wasted our time.

These passages correspond exactly to the young Shaw's idea that drama should put pressure on the people's parliamentary representatives. The significant thing is that no such passages occur in any play by Shaw. Even if they did, we could be sure they would have an entirely different tone.

Even where the theoretical remarks of our three authors are consistent with their respective practice, they really give no idea what that practice is. Were the plays to disappear, the prefatory remarks to survive, posterity would receive a wholly misleading impression of what the plays had been like. Which ought not to amaze us. An author's official positions are one thing; his creative achievements are another. It is minor authors, moreover, who make movements and are content to exemplify their principles. Major authors may start movements or join them; they don't become submerged in them. To read Zola's proclamations, you might gather that novel-writing was a science, and that once you've mastered the latest teaching on heredity and environment you can put a novel together. Perhaps. But it wouldn't be a Zola novel, which is a remarkably "unscientific" work, compounded of Gothic imagination, great human warmth, and even a macabre sense of humor. . . .

I am not going to argue that Ibsen, Shaw, and Brecht are *not* social dramatists, only that the definition of the word "social" may need enlargement if it is to fit them, and that, in any case, each must be regarded not as a member of a school or an example of a trend but as an individual genius, making his own peculiar and wondrous explorations. Though all three have had imitators, the results do not show that any of the qualities for which we value them are imitable. Their criticisms of social phenomena may not be unique in the form in which we can abstract them from the work, yet they are unique in the emphasis and color given to them in the setting of the work. Which is why it is to that setting that we must pursue them.

II

"The object of this play is a study of the disease of syphilis in its bearing on marriage." Nine out of ten students, questioned about this sentence would guess that it referred to Ibsen's *Ghosts* (1881). Captain Alving had syphilis, and as a result his son Oswald is becoming an idiot in front of our eyes. Brieux would use this story as a pretext for urging us to have all possible measures taken to combat venereal disease. We get no hint whatsoever as to whether Ibsen would urge anything of this kind. What is *his* interest in the story? Oswald's collapse is the central happening. What does Ibsen do with it?

The question can be answered only in terms of the whole play, a fact which is in itself significant and, as it turns out, a tribute to Ibsen's genius. Oswald is an Orestes for whom the Furies (Erinyes) do not turn into Wellwishers (Eumenides) in accord with a poet's desire to affirm life and, by implication, the phase of life which his culture is passing through. He is irreclaimably doomed by "ghosts." Ibsen generally knew what he was doing, and never more so than in his choice of title for this play. Not *The House of Alving,* not *Mrs. Alving,* not *Oswald,* though any of these titles would have been in the classical tradition.* Rather, he chooses a title in the tradition of *The Eumenides* and *The Bacchae.* In ancient literature these are unusual titles because they stress extra-human forces, normally left in the background. Such forces come into the foreground at certain crises of history: Aeschylus celebrated the creation of the dem-

* If it be objected that the traditional titles of Greek tragedies were not—or were not in all cases—given them by their authors, I reply that it is sufficient for my present argument that they *are* traditional titles.

ocratic city state, Euripides pronounces a doom upon the whole Hellenic experiment. Ibsen is a Euripidean playwright dramatizing the crisis of middle-class culture in his own day and somewhat beyond. Accordingly, his "ghosts" are neither furies nor bacchantes. What they are is very precisely, if complexly, worked out. They are ghosts, to begin with, in the most ordinary sense, that of superstition. Overheard in the next room by Mrs. Alving, Oswald and Regina sound like the ghosts (*revenants,* returned spirits, spooks) of Captain Alving and Regina's mother. *Sound like:* the word "ghosts" is in the first instance a simile. In the second, it is a metaphor for Captain Alving's legacy of disease: this is how syphilis enters into Ibsen's scheme of things. But it is not where he leaves his presentation of ghosts. They are more than superstition and more than physiology. They are cultural and social: they are a matter of the characters' beliefs and attitudes, their decisive and therefore dramatic beliefs and attitudes.

When Mrs. Alving hears the ghosts in the next room she is brought that much nearer telling Oswald what she at that point believes to be the whole truth about his father. The simile drives her to explain the metaphor, and that would be where a conventional nineteenth-century play would have ended. Ibsen's last and greatest act is still to come. In the process of telling this truth, Mrs. Alving finds that it is *not* the whole truth. Under the traumatic influence of those events or discoveries which are Ibsen's plot, she finds herself telling a different story and realizing a different truth: that not only Alving but she herself was responsible for the debacle. She was a victim of the third kind of ghost, the ideological ghost. When she had tried, as a young wife, to flee from her husband to Parson Manders, who loved her, Manders had turned her away from the door, and she had consented to be turned away and to return to Alving. Not all the reading she then did in modern literature could erase the facts of her non-modern actions. In her fantasy life she wants liberation from bourgeois culture. In actuality she cannot defy the marriage laws; cannot contemplate the incestuous union of her son with his half-sister; cannot practice mercy killing.

Corresponding to this double twist whereby Mrs. Alving's narrative turns from husband-denunciation to self-discovery, there is doubleness, too, in the main narrative line. Oswald's collapse, I have said, is the central happening. One could even say it is the *only* thing that happens on this stage, and that once it *has* happened the play is over, the play of the superstition simile and the physiological metaphor. But this is to overlook the happenings within the breast of Mrs. Alving, for *Ghosts,* finally, is the story of Oswald *as witnessed by his mother.* The final effect is the effect upon her. She is the on-stage audience. Such had been her fate from the beginning. What she now does, or fails to do, with her son she had previously done, or failed to do, with her husband: she reduces herself to the position of helpless, agonized onlooker. Oswald's paralysis, physical, unaccompanied by suffering and exceptional is as nothing to hers as she stands there holding the lethal pills and not using them: with a life still to live, in unbearable agony, and typical of a whole class of people, a whole phase of history. At this point we see how different from furies or bacchantes, and how much more modern, Ibsenian ghosts are. Pale as they are by comparison, they are far more negative because they have no possibility of transformation into Eumenides. They are inertia, where what is needed is movement. They are regression, where what is called for is progress. They are imprisonment and death where what is "desired" is liberation and life. I put the word "desired" in quotation marks because the authenticity of the desire is in question. In the situation depicted, hope is mere cultured fantasy and modish liberalism. Wherever the seeds of life are shown to be still faintly alive, as in Oswald's hankering after joy *and after his half-sister,* they are precipitately, hysterically exterminated by Ibsen's enlightened abortionists.

It is tempting to call Ibsen the most ironical dramatist since Sophocles, for, with him, nothing that glitters is gold. Now such irony would not be interesting if it were a merely technical fact, if it had the impact only of trick or mannerism, but only if (a) it imposes itself as the author's authentic mode of vision and (b) if it succeeds in redefining the author's subject for us, the public. To establish that it is indeed Ibsen's mode of vision one can only refer the skeptical back to his work. On the redefinition of subject, one might cite yet again the notion of ghosts. People who have noticed that Ibsen's ghosts are not furies have perhaps failed to notice that they are not a curse rooted in real crimes, as in Greek drama and the mythology on which it is based, or on original sin, as in much Christian literature down to, say, T. S. Eliot's *Family Reunion,* based as it is on the Orestes legend. In *Ghosts* there is a clear reference to the Old Testament idea of the sins of the fathers being visited upon the children. Yet it would be disingenuous to cite this idea without noting that Ibsen inverts it. The idea that emerges from *Ghosts* is that what Alving did was not sin after all, it was the unfortunate result of his legitimate joy in life. Can we conclude that Mrs. Alving was the sinner? Not that either. What was wrong was that she *believed* Alving sinned. What was wrong was what gave her this belief: her education, her culture, her background, her epoch, and her class—in a word, her society.

Here we have the deeper sense in which Ibsenite drama may truly be called social. Not to harp too long on one string, it can equally well be illustrated from *Hedda Gabler* (1890). One need only cite the ending. Hedda shoots herself to avoid being in Judge Brack's power. But Brack himself had indicated that she had other alternatives. The whole passage is worth quoting. Brack knows that Løvborg shot himself with Hedda's pistol:

BRACK. . . . The police have it.
HEDDA. What will the police do with it?

BRACK. Search till they find the owner.

HEDDA. Do you think they will succeed?

BRACK. . . . No, Hedda Gabler, not so long as I keep silent.

HEDDA. . . . And if you do not keep silent, what then?

BRACK. . . . One could always declare the pistol was stolen.

HEDDA (*firmly*). It would be better to die.

BRACK (*smiling*). One says such things; one doesn't do them.

HEDDA. . . . And if the pistol were not stolen and the police find the owner, what then?

BRACK. Well, Hedda, then, think of the scandal.

HEDDA. The scandal?

BRACK. The scandal yes, which you are terrified of. You'd naturally have to appear in court, both you and Mademoiselle Diana. She would have to explain how the thing happened, whether it was accident or murder. Did he threaten to shoot her, and did the pistol go off then, or did she grab the pistol, shoot him, afterwards putting it back into his pocket. She might have done that, for she is a hefty woman, this—Mademoiselle Diana.

HEDDA. What have I to do with all this repulsive business?

BRACK. Nothing. But you will have to answer the question: why did you give Ejlert Løvborg the pistol? And what conclusion will people draw from the fact that you did give it to him?

HEDDA. That is true. I didn't think of that.

BRACK. Well, fortunately, there is no danger as long as I keep silent.

HEDDA. . . . That means you have me in your power. . . .

BRACK. . . . Dearest Hedda . . .

HEDDA. . . . No longer free—not free . . . No, I won't endure that thought, never!

BRACK. . . . People manage to get used to the inevitable.

Why couldn't Hedda, as Brack suggests, tell the police the pistol had been stolen? In her own mind, the answer is that she could not tell such a lie. Why not, considering that she is quite a fluent liar? Because this lie would hurt her image of herself as aristocrat. It would be petty. She'd commit hara-kiri to avoid it. Nonsense, says Brack, such suicides have been abolished by bourgeois respectability. In any event, Brack is toying with Hedda. He himself would no doubt publicly deny that the pistol was stolen. He moves on to his principal threat. Unless he keeps his peace, there will be a scandal. What is a scandal? It is not wrongdoing itself: Løvborg is not being accused of iniquity and if Mademoiselle Diana shot him it was in self-defense. It is not sin or wrongdoing that Hedda finds repellent but talk about it, being talked about, having her "name dragged through the mud." Which is all the more ironic in that *she* really is a sinner in this whole affair. True, she will be accused of a wrong: placing a pistol in the hands of an unbalanced man. To most people, however, the man would remain the responsible party. Hedda will just be a dubious character who was implicated, will just be—an object of scandal. She will have a bad reputation.

Reputation is the social value par excellence: the value that is totally social. It is the equivalent of credit in financial matters: if people think you have it, you have it, for it is what people think. If, therefore, "people"—a given social system—are given a positive valuation by the dramatist, reputation will also be seen positively. It will be seen as Honor and, despite its basis in opinion, be regarded as the rock on which civilization rests. So it is in the classic drama of Spain. Now Hedda, as a character, has some vestige of this feeling for genuine honor. This is one component of her statement that rather than lie she would kill herself, and it is a component of her actual suicide. It is seen in a corrupted, sick form in her fantasies of a heroic death for Løvborg, and it is because *he* didn't "do it beautifully" that *she* has to do it beautifully. What prevents her suicide from being truly beautiful? The fact that it is only a transcendence in one aspect, while being mainly an evasion of responsibility, an enactment of defeat, an expression of a simple death wish. Vaguely Hedda had wished death from the outset, and accordingly was shown toying with her pistols in Scene One. Now she finds the energy to use them in what had all along been the "logical" way. Prodded by fear, and not of God but of scandal; not of wrong but of talk about wrong and about her.

"One says such things, one doesn't do them." "People manage to get used to the inevitable." "People don't do such things." So Judge Brack in the last couple of minutes of the play. The idea had been stated earlier by Hedda herself: when Mrs. Elvsted spoke of the shadow of a woman standing between herself and Løvborg. (We sense that it is Hedda herself.)

> HEDDA. Has he told you anything about her?
> MRS. ELVSTED. He spoke of her once—vaguely.
> HEDDA. What did he say?
> MRS. ELVSTED. He said that when they parted she threatened to shoot him.
> HEDDA (*with cold composure*). What nonsense! No one does that sort of thing here.

"Here"—that is, in bourgeois society, Brack's society. Brack's calculations are exactly as dependable as the social order itself. In this society a woman will take an uncongenial lover, and even let a man have a blackmailer's power over her, rather than create a scandal. Brack did not misunderstand the social system, except in assuming that it had completely assimilated everyone. He is fooled by a vestige of aristocracy, however decadent, in Hedda. Adultery would have been all right. As for dishonor, had she been Hedda Tesman through and through, even in this there would have been no problem. But she was Hedda Gabler, the general's daughter.

If the play had been written not by Ibsen but by Judge Brack or even by an enemy of Brack's who belonged to Brack's milieu—that is, by someone who lived wholly within the bourgeois scheme of things—then it would have been social drama on a familiar pattern, and would have ended with Hedda as Brack's mistress and victim. The "social drama" of Ibsen gains another dimension from his own ending and all that goes with it. Since the values of his society are not the values of the play, but only the rejected values *in* the play, the vision of the whole is a much broader one. In other words, Ibsen presupposes alternatives to his society.

One need not be surprised that he has generally been regarded as a pessimist. His spirit, like the spirit of tragic artists in the past, is shot through with a sense of *curse* and *doom*—a curse upon the life he sees around him, the doom of his fellow men and the form of noncommunity they have wrought. That the Judge Bracks in his audience find him totally negative is entirely correct from where they sit, and not entirely incorrect from where anyone else sits, since Ibsen put down on paper what he saw, not what he would have liked to see. Nonetheless, what he would have liked to see is present as something more than a fantasy of the impossible. The "ghosts" that in fact doom Mrs. Alving, the fear of scandal that in fact dooms Hedda Gabler, are not divine or diabolical, nor do they partake of any necessity other than the historical. Which is to say they are necessary only for a time. "They have their day and cease to be." They are *un*necessary.

Napoleon said: Politics is fate. The view that permeates the modern epoch after Napoleon is that *history* is fate, and though history has been seen in various ways there is one characteristically modern way: history as evolution. Which is to imply a possible, if not an inevitable, progression. That Ibsen was captivated by this vision is spelled out in his letters and speeches, and was dramatized in an early play, *Emperor and Galilean* (1873), which as an older man he still made a point of endorsing (after-dinner speech in Stockholm, 1887). Now, since drama deals with collisions, it may be natural that what preoccupied the playwrights, when they were inspired by the modern historical outlook, was a single factor: the collision of two epochs. Friedrich Hebbel stressed this in the 1840s. Ibsen's comment on Brandes' Inaugural Lecture of 1871, already cited, contains these formulations:

No more dangerous book could fall into the hands of a pregnant writer. It is one of those works which place a yawning gap between yesterday and today. . . . What will be the outcome of this mortal combat between two epochs I do not know, but anything rather than the existing state of affairs, say I.

Emperor and Galilean presents the clash of the Pagan and Christian epochs. Christianity wins out but is not seen by the young (or old) Ibsen as the solution. As a guideline for such positive solutions as may be worked for there hovers the vision of a Third Kingdom. So in the modern plays of Ibsen, there is a break with the past, but it is not a liberation from the past: for that we must wait long after the fall of the final curtain. Even certain "final curtains" which at first seem optimistic prove not to be so under further examination. *Little Eyolf* (1894) is a clear instance, *When we Dead Awaken* (1899) a more debatable instance. Ibsen had no optimism about optimists: he depicts them as weaklings (Rosmer is the classic case) who fall headlong into pessimism, and "optimism" is hardly the best word to describe the positive conviction that underlies the critical thought and negative emotion of Ibsen himself. One can only say he withstands the luxury of pessimism; shows the evils depicted to be unnecessary; and therefore entitles us to retain an irreducible minimum of hope—not of heaven, and not for oneself alone, but for human society, for civilization.

III

Ibsen made tragedy modern by infusing it with his sense that society is fate. In comedy, society has always been fate; and Ibsen can also be seen as fusing the tragic and comic traditions in his own essentially tragicomic vision. But the "society" of older comedy had been as immutable as the fate of older tragedy. Shaw and Brecht followed Ibsen in presenting an evolving, historical fate, of which the theatrical form might best be suggested by some words of Chekhov's: "You live badly, my friends. It is shameful to live like that." For people don't have to live like that. It need not be necessary for people to live like that.

But how shall it come about that they *won't* live like that? Bernard Shaw's simplest (but by no means only) answer is that he will talk them out of it. "I write plays with the deliberate object of converting the nation to my opinion . . ." (Preface to *Blanco Posnet*). And Shaw was also inclined to see Ibsen as engaged in that kind of effort. "Every one of them [Ibsen's plays] is a deliberate act of war on society as at present constituted. . . . [Ibsen undertook] a task of no less magnitude than changing the mind of Europe with a view to changing its morals" (*ibid.*). Brecht once said that for Shaw a man's most precious possession was his opinions, and part of Shaw remained ever hopeful of robbing people of their most precious possession, offering them his own by way of reparations. Behind Shaw's remarks in this vein is the Victorian liberal tradition which sees culture as the final locus of free trade. Presupposed are open ears and sympathetic souls. Not presupposed are conflicts of interest along class lines or "false consciousness" as a mode of intelligently deceiving oneself. Shaw himself learned to be highly critical of this liberalism, yet it played a part in putting together his own conception of a drama in which all characters genuinely can claim to have something to offer. "They are all right from their several points of view; and their points of view are, for the dramatic moment, mine also. This may puzzle the people who believe there is such a thing as an absolutely right point of view . . . nobody who agrees with them can possibly be a dramatist . . ." (Epistle Dedicatory to *Man and Superman*). One need not be scornful of Shaw's wish to "convert the nation." During the first half of the twentieth century the English nation was converted to many socialistic notions, and Bernard Shaw could take a great deal of credit for this. But another idea of drama is implicit in this description of the several points of view which all embody part of the truth. Also there is hyperbole as well as humor in the idea that the whole nation was Shaw's audience. In fact, his plays were addressed to the educated bourgeoisie of all nations and were about that class, whether his characters wore the tailcoat or the toga, the pinstripe trousers or the doublet and hose. Shaw came to manhood in the century of the second great wave of *philosophes* and, with the others, he helped the educated middle class to criticize itself. Ibsen had touched their guilt feelings. Shaw touched their funny bone. Which is to say that Ibsen showed their complicity in crime, while Shaw showed incongruities, inconsistencies, absurdities, both in the crimes and the complicity. What comedy may lack in depth, it can make up in scope. The subject matter of Ibsen's tragic plays is limited and forever the same. In his comedies, on the other hand, Shaw would "cover the field": war and peace, the capitalist system, education, biology, religion, metaphysics, penal law, the Irish Question, the family, the various professions (medical, martial, clerical) . . . anything and everything.

More precisely speaking, it is in the prefaces and attendant pamphlets, articles, and treatises that the field was covered *in extenso*. The plays did what plays more characteristically do: brought certain crucial conflicts into sharp focus. Indeed one might well say that it was in prefaces and the like that Shaw did his best to convert a nation while in the plays he provided comic relief. But it was comic relief of a highly ironical kind for, in it, the subjects of the prefaces are seen, not in a simpler form, but in a form which is even more complex, being more human and concrete. The difference between preface and play has sometimes been viewed as one between the propagandist and the artist, the latter, in turn, being considered "universally human." Shaw's critics are free to choose their terms, and even to invoke shibboleths. To some of us, however, it seems mistaken to think of the plays as any less social in their commentary than the prefaces. Surely comedy was always the principal vehicle of sociological thought until academic men had the unhappy idea that the comic sense was not necessary in the field and founded the science of sociology. In any event, Shaw's comedies bring social principles to the final test, asking what they mean in the lives of human beings. Some critics will perhaps see a claim to the "universally human," a claim to be asocial, parasocial, metasocial, in Shaw's own statement that his plays present a conflict of free vitality with various abstract principles and impersonal institutions, but just as the principles and institutions are specific ones, and Shaw's satirical thrusts are directed at them, so the free vitality is seldom merely the Life Force in the abstract but is to be found in the actual life generated in a character by Shaw the comic artist.

A recurring type in Shaw's comedies is what, with apologies to Nietzsche, we may call the superman: a human being who is not divided against himself but is all of a piece and lives directly and happily from the primal vital spring. Caesar, Undershaft, and Joan are examples. There are no such people in the comedies of Aristophanes or Plautus, Machiavelli or Jonson, Shakespeare or Molière. Superior people stem from the epic and tragic tradition: and so, if Ibsen can be said to have given tragedy a comic twist, Shaw can be said to have given comedy a tragic one. Yet even tragic heroes are traditionally supposed to have a flaw, whereas the Shavian superman is flawless, an Achilles invulnerable even in the heel. Perhaps only one great tragic writer had regularly risked such protagonists: Corneille. And the result was that his tragedies verged upon comic effects that were not intended.

Invulnerable in himself, as a dramatic creation the Shavian superman has not proven invulnerable to dramatic criticism. There are obvious dangers to the comic art in the presence, at its center, of a man who knows all the answers like Undershaft, especially since it is not just verbal answers he knows but practical ones. For drama is *praxis*. The plot of *Saint Joan* is not helped by the fact our heroine couldn't do wrong if she tried. That she at one point pleads guilty in the trial is only a momentary hesitation that makes her final position the more heroic. Similarly, the Shavian Caesar's vanity is only the charming, humanizing foible of a great man, not a flaw undermining his greatness.

Has criticism been as ready to see why Shaw went in for this sort of hero as it has to note the reasons why he shouldn't have? Such a "why" might not be specially significant if explored in biographical, psychological terms, citing factors in Shaw's life that impelled him to seek flawless heroes, but it surely has much interest in relation to modern social drama. It relates to what Ernst Bloch has called *das Prinzip Hoffnung*—the principle of hope as the very foundation of the modern radical outlook, as of the religions and mythologies in the eras of their full vitality. As the religions and mythologies had a golden age in the past which one could hope for the return of or a heaven in the sky which was eternally there, so modern radical philosophy has a future in which this earth is a home for men.

When society is fate, a historical fate, the dialectic of drama, I have suggested, will be found in an interplay between epochs. One sees this first, as Ibsen did, as an interplay between past and present: the theatre exhibits a present into which the past ("ghosts") erupt, but, as Ibsen also knew, this is a simplification. There is a third factor, the future, and if art has a normative function—"it is always a writer's duty to make the world better" (Samuel Johnson)—the future is suffused by a definite sentiment, the sentiment of hope. Indeed, in the modern situation, one must perhaps say that, if art is to have something positive about it, the most likely locus of the positive will be the future, golden ages in the past having become as inconceivable as heavens in the skies. The past, so far from being golden, hangs like lead about the necks of modern characters. The past is the dead weight of failure pressing upon the present and tending to kill the future. Such is the modern view of the past, personal and neurotic, social and historical. Thus, unless the modern artist is to acquiesce in a blank future, a future murdered by the past, he has to postulate and imagine a positive future. Which is to say that he has to discover the grounds for hope both within his own breast and in the world about him and, having discovered just what his hopes are, he has to work with them, go to work *on* them.

This Ibsen the thinker certainly believed. Ibsen the artist felt on firmer ground with the past and present, hence the fact that most of his plays provide a far more desolate image of life than his proclaimed philosophy. Shaw and Brecht, if they lived in a time of yet greater public catastrophes, by that very token felt themselves closer also to whatever positive solutions were going to be found. They clearly resolved, at whatever cost to their art as art, to inject a far larger positive element into it than Ibsen had usually done. For them, even more than for him, art was not for its own sake but the sake of the future. Like Ibsen's, their art would help exorcise the ghosts of the past—"let the dead bury their dead"—and help terminate the life-in-death of the present. Less ambiguously than Ibsen's, their art would help "us dead" to "awaken."

Which in itself would have been sufficient reason for them to discontinue Ibsen's investigations of neurotic weakness. If they can be meaningfully referred back to him at all, it would be to his one or two attempts at a simply positive hero, and notably Dr. Stockmann in *An Enemy of the People* (1883). Such a superman was to find a place in both Shavian and Brechtian drama, though in different guises, corresponding to different nationalities and generations. Shaw's most characteristic and impressive superman is Undershaft, a radical critic of normal bourgeois procedures and shibboleths, yet himself a hero of bourgeois civilization—and a scintillating bourgeois intellectual to boot. If we look in the plays of Brecht for characters who are solid and all of a piece, who always are right and always do what is right, we shall find them only in the guise of the rebel as revolutionary: examples are Pavel in *The Mother* (1932) and several of the Communards in *Days of the Commune* (1949).

There are not many such supermen in Brecht or even in Shaw. Both playwrights remained Ibsenites to the extent that they dealt primarily, if not with neurotic weakness, with divided characters. Pavel is a revolutionary from the outset, but the protagonist is his mother, who is not a revolutionary till near the end: meanwhile the play has shown her inner divisions. Particularly the Brecht characters who have universally been found most human and interesting —Mother Courage, Galileo, Azdak—are divided people, brave and cowardly, passive and active, good and bad. Even in Shaw, the superman didn't always have to be protagonist. He could fill a character role such as that of General Burgoyne in *The Devil's Disciple* (1897) or Sergeant Meek in *Too True to be Good* (1932).

Shaw generally placed his supermen over against men who were human-all-too-human, average products of a given epoch and class. In these encounters he was able to give the age-old contrast of ironist and impostor a thoroughly actual and relevant treatment, and his own divided nature preserved him from super-manic dramaturgy on a Cornelian scale. The ironist did not defeat the impostor too easily. Some plays (*Heartbreak House* [1919], for instance) are principally about impostors and contain no outright supermen. In some, such as *John Bull's Other Island* (1904), the emphasis is strongly on a single impostor (Broadbent). Again, a favorite Shavian device and achievement is the ironist-superman who ironically turns out not to be a superman after all but human-all-too-human. Such are Bluntschli (*Arms and the Man*) and Tanner (*Man and Superman*). Nor is it true that a Shavian character who embodies free vitality must have su-perhuman capabilities. He may be an impotent priest like Father Keegan (*John Bull's Other Island*) or a senile crackpot like Captain Shotover (*Heartbreak House*).

He may be a she. Shaw was a feminist, not only after the more political and abstract fashion, but in his human and artistic instincts. He tended to identify both himself and free vitality with the Eternal Feminine and to identify the enemy with the society-ridden male. Hence, if we are looking for the positive element, for bridges to the future, for foundations of a socialist humanism, his women are just as important as his supermen. And this can be true in the least political of his comedies. *Pygmalion* (1913), for instance, is the tale of the incubation and liberation of a woman. With Tanner and the rest, Henry Higgins is a superman *manqué*, a clever ironist who proves to be an impostor, a Pygmalion who is only a Frankenstein.

A woman is the key to a Shaw play which has been widely misunderstood, *The Doctor's Dilemma* (1906), a play which will also permit us to illustrate another feature of Shaw the social dramatist: that he delights to drive his critique beyond what is its ostensible main point to another point which is its dialectical opposite. Sometimes the very topic is not the ostensible one but another and contrary one. So with the "dilemma" in the choice between saving the life of an immoral genius or that of a moral mediocrity: it is thoroughly immoral. Only God can rightly assume such powers of life and death. A mere man can only plunge into folly or worse. The mere man in Shaw's play chooses to believe that his hand is pushed toward sacrificing the immoral genius by a solicitude for the latter's wife, who can thus be kept ignorant of her genius's immorality and so preserve her romantic image of him. However, we, the audience know that it is not solicitude that is forcing our man's hand but desire: he wants to marry the widow. The "dilemma" is a false one, and its falsity is brought home to him in dramatic action. When he runs into the now widowed lady, he finds she has already remarried. He is amazed because it had never occurred to him that she might have found him resistible. "Other people" were a somewhat unreal category to him, pieces on a chessboard. His error over the widow sprang from the same complex as his error in setting up a false dilemma.

Would it be fair to conclude that the social drama of the medical profession became a "universally human" or at least wholly psychological drama? No. In drama any subject has to be humanized, has to be steeped in the juices of humanity, but surely "social" and "human" are not opposites? The topic here is private enterprise in medicine. The author's view is that medicine should be socialized. He is discreet enough not to state this view in the play. His play will show—in the flesh—private medicine as it exists. At one pole there are the more obvious impostors, the outright fools, who are lined up at the outset. The doctor-dramatist James Bridie has complained that they are *too* foolish (in *Shaw at 90,* edited S. Winsten, London, 1946), but then Shaw exhibits the less foolish kind of impostor in our hero, the man of the dilemma, Sir Colenso Ridgeon, a superman who, like Tanner, like Higgins, is not a superman at all.

If Sir Colenso is less of a superman than he supposes, Jennifer Dubedat, the widow, is more fully human than she had appeared. She did not really need an inspiring, mendacious image to live by after all, nor could she consent to be a marionette on Ridgeon's string. In counting on his idea of the inevitable female reaction, Ridgeon left out of account the woman, the human being. So the parable remains political. Medicine should be socialized to free us from the caprices and fantasies of the Ridgeons—all the more so if they can disguise their self-centered wishful thinking as objectivity and generosity. Next proposition: there exists a counterforce to Ridgeonism, namely, free vitality, sometimes and not at all accidentally embodied in women. Paradox: precisely where Ridgeon looked for compliance as the feminine contribution, he met with resistance and with his comeuppance.

The social drama, as practiced by nongeniuses like Brieux, ran into fatal clichés. That Bernard Shaw just did not notice the limitations of a Brieux is an index to his missionary zeal and to the strength of his commitment to a social criterion in drama. "Incomparably the greatest writer France has produced since Molière" (Preface to *Three Plays by Brieux,* 1909), Brieux was the kind of playwright that the propagandist-in-a-hurry within the breast of Shaw could not help envying, yet some deep intuition as to where his own calling lay kept the envy from growing into emulation. Let those who once considered that, as against Shaw, Brieux really came to grips with social problems take note that today Brieux cannot be seen as coming to grips with anything, whereas the playful Shaw must be seen to have come to grips, in play as well as preface, with the main problems of the era.

"We are coming fast," Shaw wrote in one of his theatre reviews (1896), "to a melodramatic formula in which the villain shall be a bad employer and the hero a Socialist." In his first and third plays, completed in the early nineties, he had provided a socialist critique of capitalism without recourse to this formula. In the first, *Widowers' Houses,* it was as if he set out to make the bad employer his hero while making the rebel against capitalism his villain. Yet that, though it "sounds like Shaw," is not it, either. The capitalist Sartorius is a scoundrel who knows he is a scoundrel, whereas his adversary Trench is an exploiter who thinks he is outside the whole process of exploitation. Comedy has always been less inclined to scowl at iniquity than to laugh at a lack of self-knowledge, and so it is in this comedy of nineteenth-century capitalism, as in all the rest of its author's lifework.

Shaw's third play, *Mrs. Warren's Profession* (1894), is founded on an inno-cent girl's discovery that her mother is a procuress and ex-whore. That would make mother a villainess and daughter a heroine if melodrama were true to life, but actually—and comedy has as its yardstick the actuality of society, of life as people live it—innocence is not of itself heroic, nor is membership in an antisocial profession—and all professions, according to Shaw, are conspiracies against the public—an act of personal iniquity. If Mrs. Warren has a sin, it consists only in a belief which she shares with most of mankind: that you can't buck the system. If you can't lick 'em, join 'em; and she has joined 'em. In the end her daughter, for her part, really *is* a heroine to the extent that she is trying to buck the system. She has taken that first step which in the 1960s would be called "dropping out." But she has also ceased to regard her mother as a villain-ess or herself as more wronged than others who are living on tainted money. What money is not tainted? Under capitalism you can either, as worker, have your earnings stolen or, as capitalist, do the stealing and live on the pro-ceeds.

These two early plays are socialist not only in implying that socialism would be the remedy but also in their rendering of the *comédie humaine* generally. Just as the ultimate source of trouble in *Ghosts* and *Hedda Gabler* is both social and unnecessary, so the ultimate source of trouble in *Widowers' Houses* and *Mrs. Warren's Profession* is social and unnecessary. When the Mrs. Alvings are truly liberated, when the Heddas don't give a damn about scandal, life will be differ-ent. When there are no landlords to exploit slumdwellers, when there are no white slavers to buy and sell sex, life can be better. Meanwhile, it is ridiculous to condemn the individual landlord, pimp, or whore. Ridiculous. Deserving of ridicule. A proper object of laughter. A proper subject for comedy. Needed, then, for the comic play on these themes: the plausible capitalist, the worshiper of the god of Things As They Are, and, over against him, the idealistic rebel against capitalism who does not even know that the stocks and shares he lives off are investments in the same shabby business as the landlord he denounces. Needed: a procuress and ex-whore who is a very honest, agreeable, intelligent woman utterly devoted to a daughter who, well brought up as she is, will undergo a trauma when she finds out what money she has been well brought up on. . . .

The two plays present capitalism in miniature, and in this could be regarded as models for Brecht's *Threepenny Opera* (1928) and *The Rise and Fall of the City of Mahagonny* (1930). The perspective of all four comedies is suggested in some lines of Simon O. Lesser (*Fiction and the Unconscious* [1957]):

> The attitude of most comedies is that of an urbane and tolerant friend, amused rather than censorious about that blond he saw us out with the night before. . . . Other comedies are caustic and the reverse of indulgent, but they suggest a scale of values against which the shortcomings and misdeeds of the characters seem trivial . . . granted that the little people [this kind of comedy] sets before us are far from admirable, they, and by inference we ourselves are no worse than anyone else.

Bernard Shaw called the two types here adumbrated *Plays: Pleasant and Unpleasant,* a phrase he used as the title for all his early plays (1892–1898). The "unpleasant" play, as exemplified by *Widowers' Houses* and *Mrs. Warren's Profession,* was certainly a precision tool in social criticism for which their author has scarcely yet received due credit, a dialectical tool. You can smile all evening at the amusing crimes of Sartorius and Mrs. Warren, but when, on your way home, you realize that the whole social order is run this way, you will smile on the wrong side of your face.

Shaw, for his part, seems to have found the "unpleasant" mode constricting. Like Swift, he "served human liberty," and the schematic early plays afforded his enterprise far too little elbowroom. They had, for example, no room for his supermen and, if they had room for rebellious women like Blanche Sartorius and Vivie Warren, they kept the rebellion within too narrow bounds. Even the impostors were miniatures compared with those to follow. Shaw once spoke of the need a dramatist has to let his characters rip. That is what he was not able to do in the earliest plays; the mold in which the plays were cast seemed to forbid it. There is far more freedom later. There is the growing freedom of the playwright as he learns his craft and gives his genius its head; also, characters are placed in situations in which *they* have freedom in its ultimate form: real freedom of choice on crucial issues. Both kinds of freedom had been lacking in *Widowers' Houses.* Not only had the journeyman playwright acquired no kind of ease or daring in handling the structure. Inside the box of his plot, and in the box (with one side missing) of the Victorian stage-scene, he presented a version of humanity boxed in by the capitalist system. It was clear, cutting, even devastating writing, but no wind of freedom blew from that stage to that audience. One thing needed was that characters should not just be worked upon by circumstances; they should work on the circumstances. History, by all means, can determine their mode of existence; but they in turn must work upon history.

Saint Joan (1923), for example, could not have been written by the playwright of the early nineties. He wouldn't have known how to let her rip. In this play we breathe the air of human freedom, and again this is both an artistic, technical matter and a matter of the outlook defined by the art and technique. The closed, boxlike form of the nineteenth-century well-made play was progressively abandoned by Shaw. As a chronicle, Saint Joan is rather compact, but that it is a chronicle at all means open windows, fresh air, amplitude.

IV

Half a dozen years after the première of Saint Joan, Bertolt Brecht wrote Happy End, which a couple of years later had grown into Saint Joan of the Stockyards. It can serve here as a cue for continued analysis of Saint Joan itself and for an exploration of the difference between Shaw and Brecht. The relation between the two dramatists was never closer than here, since Saint Joan of the Stockyards owes much not only to Saint Joan but to Major Barbara.

As usual with Brecht, one can begin with surprise at how much he saw fit to borrow. "A Salvation Army officer forsaken by God" could be considered the central image of Major Barbara, and Brecht appropriated it. That the officer is a girl, with all that femininity connotes of delicacy in feeling and ardor in aspiration, is not lost on Brecht, either, and the general reason for the loss of God is the same in both authors: the dependence of the otherworldly institution upon a capitalistic world. However, though both authors rely upon a Marxist analysis of the Salvation Army, they approach the subject from opposite ends. Shaw shows that the teetotalism of the Army, being promoted by brewers' money, is compromised at the start: the "idealism" of an Army officer has to be either ignorant or corrupt. Realizing this, Major Barbara feels emptied out, devastated, abandoned by her God. She will remain in this state of mind and heart until a niche is found for her within the existing social order. The finding of such a niche is the psychospiritual solution to what has already been shown as a psychospiritual problem. Brecht, on the other hand, is little concerned with the usefulness of capitalism to the Salvation Army. He is concerned with the usefulness of the Salvation Army to capitalism. If his Joan, too, suffers a psychospiritual crisis—and she does, though the phrase itself begins to let us down in a Brechtian context—it is from the sensation not of being deserted but of being cheated. God has not gone: he was never there. Joan discovers not a void of unbelief but an active atheism which offers an alternative to deity in the idea of Man On His Own—man's fate is man himself. It is at this point that one can imagine the playwright Brecht asking whether, if one Shaw play wouldn't do his job for him, another might serve the purpose. Though *Saint Joan of the Stockyards* is mostly a *Major Barbara*, ultimately it is indeed a *Saint Joan:* for Barbara turns into Joan when Brecht's protagonist moves from false to true consciousness and from passivity disguised as action to action which is positive and revolutionary.

Brecht probably noted what most of Shaw's critics have missed: that Shaw himself goes part of the way toward making Joan a revolutionary leader whose final support comes from the people. She is his only nonbourgeois superman, for even his Caesar is bourgeois in spirit, as is his superking Magnus, and this fact yields much more broadly conceived political drama than Shaw was wont to attempt. In the great scene (Five) which is the turning point of the story, Joan stands forth as the patron saint of all future National Liberation Fronts:

> Common folks understand . . . they follow me half naked into the moat and up the ladder and over the wall. . . . You locked the gates to keep me in; and it was the townsfolk and the common people that followed me, and forced the gate. . . . I will go out now to the common people, and let the love in their eyes comfort me for the hate in yours. You will all be glad to see me burnt; but if I go through the fire, I shall go through it to their hearts for ever and ever.

Though, unlike Shaw's Major Barbara, Brecht's Joan Dark has, in the Communist Party, an alternative to both the Salvation Army and big business, unlike Shaw's Joan she is not permitted a true martyrdom but only a fake one. Her death is a "setup," and so she remains in death what she had been in life: a victim. The politics of *Saint Joan* and *Saint Joan of the Stockyards* are thus revealed, in their respective endings, to be diametrically opposite. Shaw calls for a democracy of supermen that shall be worthy of his democratic superwoman. Brecht appeals for solidarity among those people (the working class, the victims) by whom the myths of sainthood will be shattered along with the social order which the myths serve to flatter and conceal.

In nothing, perhaps, is the difference between Shaw and Brecht more marked than in their presentation of the capitalist villain. Both authors are at the top of their form: Undershaft is one of Shaw's most telling characters, and Pierpont Mauler is one of Brecht's. Underlying both creations is the Marxist principle that the individual capitalist is not to be equated with the system. To Shaw, this means that while the system may be rationally flimsy and morally outrageous, the individual capitalist may be rational, plausible, intelligent, and charming. To Brecht, it means that, while the system may be omnipotent and devoid of conscience, the individual capitalist may well have a sense of guilt but, sensing also his own powerlessness, will hold on to his position, anyway, seeing no alternative:

> Just think, if I—
> who have much against it [the system], and sleep badly—
> were to desert it, I would be like a fly
> ceasing to hold back a landslide.
> —*Saint Joan of the Stockyards* (Scene Eight)

Therefore, though Mauler doesn't feel sorry for mankind, because "mankind is evil," he is distinctly sorry for himself as the presumably nonevil exception. He pities himself as he pities slaughtered cattle: both are true victims. The alleged victims—of the working class—are just those who, being bad, met with a bad fate.

One could elaborate indefinitely the different *schemata* behind Undershaft and Mauler. The result is two characters who stand at opposite poles of comedy. Undershaft is a maker of comedy—of amusing speeches and of dramas that will have a chilling comedic effect to begin with and a happy ending later. He is an entertainer, entertaining his workers in a model factory, and entertaining Shaw's spectators whenever he comes on stage. Even in his family's home, he is the Father as Entertainer. If Undershaft represents comedy as the highest possible degree of *charm,* Mauler is so close to the opposite pole of *the nauseating* that some will want to deny him the epithet "comic" altogether. What also may strike some people as uncomic is that he is so emotional; whereas Undershaft is nothing if not cool, keeping his head "when all about him," etc. Mauler loses his head—is a headless hen throughout, twitching with desperation. He suffers vociferously, the aggrieved victim of a social system in crisis. And what a system! Brecht reported that when he first studied capitalist economics, his reaction was not: How unjust! but: It will never work! To the extent that it worked, it kept its helpers and servers at fever pitch watching the fluctuations of the market. Thus it is that the Pierpont Maulers experience the extreme tensions of the roulette player.

If we think such painful tensions out of place in comedy, we are forgetting the sufferings of, say, Jonson's Morose or Molière's Harpagon, but comedy, to use Brecht's word, "alienates" the emotions so that we feel no sympathy. And in alienating the emotions so that we feel no sympathy, comedy is the exactly correct vehicle of this author's intention and philosophy. We are to recoil from Mauler and his colleagues in horror and disgust, and we do so because they are made ridiculous, which is only to say that they are seen through the eyes of comedy. To those who would assume that comedy might somehow make such figures pleasant and therefore acceptable, there would be several answers. One is: no, this is "unpleasant" comedy. A second is: no, the danger would lie in the more direct portrayal of gangsters as villains, whereby their villainy, conveying emotional intensity, gains a fascination by no means reduced in being called "evil" fascination, etc. One could see a Hollywood movie of that era, such as *Scarface,* and draw the conclusion: "Scarface's life was good while it lasted. How can one be upset by a premature death in a society that offers such empty living? Better to live dangerously. Gangsterism has glamour." Conclusions of this sort can be blocked by such "alienation" of the action as we see in Brecht's gangster play, *The Resistible Rise of Arturo Ui* (1941)—or in *Saint Joan of the Stockyards.*

In Andrew Undershaft and Pierpont Mauler we find our socialist playwrights equally determined to remove a mote from the public's eye. But not the same mote. For Shaw, the target is the person who will exonerate the system by characterizing the businessman as bad. For Brecht, the target is the person who, will exonerate the system by characterizing the businessman as "human." Shaw is portraying a businessman who is human and who, better than that, better than the mass of proletarians as well as bourgeois, is *super*human. Brecht is portraying one whom the folklore of capitalism will see as a superman (man of distinction, VIP, member of the power elite) but who is actually subhuman, a worm. The difference, here, between Shaw and Brecht reflects the passage of time between the writing of *Major Barbara* and the writing of *Saint Joan of the Stockyards,* yet not so much the steady ticking of the clock as the gigantic Happening of World War I, a dual happening in that it consisted of (a) the destruction of one world and (b) the boldest attempt since the French Revolution to bring a new world into existence. Though an orphan and rebel, Undershaft still very much belongs to the Victorian salons he despises. There still *exists* a world of salons in which his brilliant repartee is not really unwelcome. Mauler, on the other hand, is truly homeless, has nowhere nice to go, is trapped between the stock exchange and the stockyards. Whatever Undershaft's objections to the upper-class London of his wife and son, he actually enhances its claims on our respect by adding to the formal elegance of its furniture, dress, and accent his own elegance of word and thought. He is its crowning adornment, so that, from the vantage point of the 1960s, though we may cry: *obsolete!* we cannot restrain a sigh of longing for the snows of yesteryear. Whereas Mauler's world has no more aesthetic appeal than the slums where his class enemies live. Like the slums, it is ugly, nasty, stifling, and macabre, a kind of Inferno.

Saint Joan of the Stockyards is not just a play that happens to be different in kind from *Major Barbara* because time has passed, nor even because in that time a war and a revolution both occurred. It also reflects deliberate conclusions on the subject of social theatre which Brecht reached during the 1920s. That was the decade in which he put together his theory of an epic theatre— "epic" in the sense of "narrative," as against lyric and dramatic. Richard Wagner had perfected a lyric theatre, and in this had been echoed even by poets who could do without music, from Yeats to Maeterlinck. Ibsen had perfected the modern "dramatic" theatre, "dramatic" in the classic, Sophoclean-Racinian tradition with its unity of time, place, and action, "modern" in its psychological, indeed psychoanalytical emphasis. Brecht's scheme of things began with the rejection of Wagnerism and Ibsenism. As for Shavianism, he would not so much reject it as develop it—if to an extent that would have made it unrecognizable to Bernard Shaw.

The essence of Shavianism in dramaturgy was the assumption that the modern world could best be placed on stage in the form of serious parody, a double form of parody as it turned out, for Shaw consistently parodied both the behavior of men and the patterns of dramatic art. In his mind, the two were so closely related as to be at essential points identical.

> The truth is that dramatic invention is the first effort of man to become intellectually conscious. No frontier can be marked between drama and history or religion, or between acting and conduct.
> —*Plays, Pleasant and Unpleasant,*
> 1898, Preface to the Pleasant Plays

Shaw proposed to stand all the nineteenth century's idealisms on their feet. Hence his subjection of melodrama, in theatre or in life, to the test of reality. For such purposes, already in the nineties, he was demanding a nonillusionistic stage.

> For him [William Archer] there is illusion in the theatre: for me there is none. . . . To me the play is only the means, the end being the expression of feeling by the arts of the actor, the poet, the musician. Anything that makes this expression more vivid, whether it be versification, or an orchestra, or a deliberately artificial delivery of the lines, is so much to the good for me, even though it may destroy all the verisimilitude of the scene.
> —*Saturday Review,* April 13, 1895

Now what I have just called the essence of Shavianism was never challenged by Brecht. On the contrary, his plays, like Shaw's, are to a very large extent parodies both of conventional plays and of conventional behavior. In the passage just quoted, Brecht would no doubt have been dissatisfied with the phrase "expression of feeling" while at the same time enthusiastically accepting Shaw's invitation to a nonillusionistic theatre in which "versification, or an orchestra, or a deliberately artificial delivery" would not be out of place.

Perhaps the most damaging thing ever said about Shavian theatre was Egon Friedell's remark to the effect that Shaw's message was like a pill which he had covered with the sugar of entertainment, and the nice thing was that you could suck off the sugar and put the pill back on the plate. Seeing how much truth there was to this, Bertolt Brecht resolved to write "Shavian" comedies which could not be disposed of in this way. Such are the theory and practice known as epic theatre. Brecht once said his efforts could all be summed up as an attempt to restate in theatrical terms the famous thesis of Marx: "The philosophers have only interpreted the world in various ways: the point would be to change it." Shaw had of course wanted exactly the same thing but, as the young Brecht would see the situation, had been too nice to his audience, and got shrugged off for his pains. The early theoretical work of Brecht is taken up with a condemnation of "culinary" theatre—theatre in which you just enjoy eating, as in a restaurant. It seemed almost as if the guests in the modern theatre-restaurant swallowed all their food without chewing it. Perhaps the answer was to serve them crunchy solids instead of smooth fluids? Certainly one must not, as Wagner had done, melt down the whole meal into a single smooth liquid but, rather, delight to break it up into dishes of various and contrasting consistencies.

Brecht was aware of a cultural situation which was being discussed in his time and has been discussed since, particularly by writers of German background from Herbert Marcuse to Hannah Arendt. Modern bourgeois civilization—to use the food metaphor in another way—*devours* everything, good or bad. It not only pours forth musical rubbish in the elevator or supermarket in the form of Muzak. It is also capable of serving up the "Ode to Joy" from the Ninth Symphony in a radio or television commercial and at the same time claiming to be spreading "culture" around. Against this kind of exploitation the music of Beethoven is as helpless as Mrs. Warren before the white slaver or the Chinese coolie before the colonialist. Being dead, Beethoven can do little about it, but what of the living artist?

Brecht's answer was that he can make his art less fluid and saccharine with certain crunchy and pungent ingredients as alienation devices. The German for "alien" is *"fremd."* Marx had seen the worker under capitalism as *entfremdet,* alienated. Brecht proposed actually to *make alien (verfremden)* the familiar elements of the theatre experience. A paradox, yes, since alienation is the problem and the antagonist, and communism will mark the end of alienation. But communism is a good way off, even in Socialist countries. Meanwhile, *the artist can resist being consumed,* can help prevent the whole inherited culture from being poured between the Leviathan's jaws and gobbled up. Brecht's theatre is an attempt at a different mode of communication. The result would inevitably be that some would not receive any message at all; but those who did receive one would know they had. It would not be lost in the fine print. It would stand out. It would command attention, and perhaps incite to action.

It was with such ends in view that so many of the treasured devices of traditional theatre were dropped. The lighting was to be plain white and diffused over the whole stage. In this way the cult of *Stimmung* (mood) would be countered. To the same end, illusionistic scenery must go, for the paradox of scenery that "looked like the real thing" was that it induced dream states in the audience. What was needed instead of a hypnotic trance was alertness. Actors would have to change their ways. Instead of attempting an hallucination of unrealities suddenly present ("I am Dracula") they must exhibit realities that can be recognized as such and have thus belonged to our past ("This was a man"). For the Stanislavski actor who spoke in the first person and the present tense and absorbed all stage directions into a living illusion of the actual thing, Brecht proposed an "epic" actor who seemed to be using the third person and the past tense; as for the stage directions, at least as an exercise, they could be read aloud. . . .

This is not the place to itemize every feature of Brechtian theatre, either in its early or epic phase or in the final phase when Brecht was beginning to substitute the term "dialectial theatre." Too much theory would be misleading, at least if accompanied by too few looks at the practice. One must even take care, as I suggested above, not to assume that Brecht's theories correspond exactly and in all ways to his practices. Even if they did, practice is no more deducible from theory than the beauty of an Italian landscape is deducible from the map. Just as the Ibsenite drama could never be deduced from existing notions of social theatre, and Shavian comedy could never be deduced from free-floating notions like "discussion plays" and "propaganda," nor yet from Shaw's own Prefaces, so Brecht's achievement as a playwright, even as a social playwright, could not be deduced from theoretical writings, even his own. On the contrary, it is possible to make bad mistakes about the plays by too readily assuming they must be what the theories describe, no more, and no less.

Whenever active artistry is at work, many concrete elements come into being which escape the net of general ideas. You may read in Ibsen's workbooks that "marriage for external reasons . . . brings a nemesis upon the offspring," and this idea is obviously in *Ghosts:* yet it neither makes *Ghosts* a good play nor gives it its particular tone, style, character—its mode of being. This latter stems—if indeed the source may be isolated in a single phrase—from Ibsen's *ironical use* of the idea and of all his other materials. So with Shaw. Many of the ideas of, say, *The Intelligent Woman's Guide to Socialism* (1928) are also to be found in the plays, sometimes in similar phrasing, but they neither constitute the merit of the plays nor give them their life as theatre, as art. *A dramatic context ironizes;* and to say "dramatic irony" is often a little like saying "dramatic drama." A Shavian dramatic context sometimes ironizes to the point of conflict with the presumably intended idea. Thus it is not clear that, in the final act of *Major Barbara,* Shaw solved all his problems. One may feel that Undershaft is so strong a character that an intended balance is upset and a desired synthesis is missed.

One would like to turn the attention of critics exercised by Bernard Shaw's opinions to something far more pervasive in his work than any particular opinion, and far more likely to endear some people to him, while putting other people off, namely, his habit of teasing. His opinions come from here, there, and everywhere, but his teasing tone is, somehow, his very self: it is present throughout both his plays and his other writings. Shall we ask what his various avowals signify, and not ask what this central fact about him signifies? That would be like getting seduced, and not asking who seduced us.

Teasing is a complex phenomenon, but it is easy to see at least two ingredients: humorous acceptance of failure (to persuade) and a degree of aggression toward the unpersuaded. On the few occasions when Shaw did not tease he expressed complete exasperation. Teasing could be regarded as indicating either a disguised acceptance of defeat or a good-natured refusal to accept it, and it is not surprising that, as to Shaw's humor generally, some have seen it as just another weapon of an optimistic fighter, while others have found in it a tacit admission both of defeat and defeatism. But those are not the only possible alternatives. It is also possible for a man to be thinking: *"Even if* we fail, *even if* we are mistaken . . ."

When Tolstoy expressed disapproval of Shaw's humorous approach to religion, Shaw replied: "Suppose the world were only one of God's jokes, would you work any the less to make it a good joke instead of a bad one?" That a man allows for failure is not to say he thinks it has to be; and both Shaw's teasing and his humor in general serve to communicate neither optimism nor pessimism but, rather, *to ironize whatever topic comes up,* thus making the thought dialectical, and the form dramatic. The pessimist can surely find in much of the teasing an admission of difficulty—of possible impossibility, as it were. The optimist can congratulate the teaser on his admirable poise, the confident way in which he gets on top of his subject. But the shrewd psychologist will want to stress that, by teasing, Shaw insures that he is always in an active relation to his audience: whenever he is not pushing he is pulling. And to be sure, what those who reject Shavian theatre reject it for is commonly what those who relish it relish it for. Here is an author who "never lets you alone." You are either stimulated and delighted or provoked and put out.

Such is the concrete Shaw, as against the man whose views were thus and so. Of Brecht it has been said that, though his views were Communist, his concrete existence contradicted those views. Even if this formulation is correct, it need not be taken as so damaging either to Brecht or to communism as has been assumed. Some tension between existence and idea is surely inevitable. What Christian is simply an embodiment of Christianity? If such a person existed, he would not, in any case, turn out to be a Christian *artist.* Always more concrete than theory, art must always give a different account of the world, unless by sheer lack of merit (as with Brieux) it fails to be art. To the political artist, art presents a particular opportunity, which is not, as is commonly thought, simply to restate his political views and thus extend the political battle to another front, but, instead, to *test abstract principles in concrete situations,* to show what politics means in the lives of people. Contradictions enter the picture automatically, for, since the concretely human is the writer's special field, when he brings it into play it brings with it the contradictoriness of its people. Bertolt Brecht was a contradictory man, so is the present writer, and so are you, dear reader. Why not, also, Brecht's Galileo?

> *Das heisst: ich bin kein ausgeklügelt Buch*
> *Ich bin ein Mensch mit seinem Widerspruch.*

(And so: I am no wire-drawn book. I am a human being with his contradiction.)

It should therefore come as no surprise that the socialist humanism of Brecht is more adequately rendered in a many-sided and problematic work like *The Caucasian Chalk Circle* (1945) than in the more explicit presentations, closer to Marx and Lenin, such as *The Mother* or *Days of the Commune.* Again the author's sense of humor—and specifically his ironizing of everything—is our best clue. When, as in the two plays just mentioned, Brecht writes of class comrades he abandons this irony—understandably, to be sure, as it was likely to turn against them. Yet it was evidently hard to find anything to take its place: a friendly attitude, however commendable morally and politically, has no particular aesthetic merit, no energy as art. Another author might perhaps have found another solution. Brecht the artist, like Shaw the artist, cannot be severed from his sense of humor. By his lyric gift, eked out by Hanns Eisler's musical genius, Brecht was able to raise both *The Mother* and the *Commune* well above the average level of political plays. It is just that to see what he can do—and, at that, writing on socialism itself—you have to turn to works that have been steeped in his irony.

Ernst Bloch * has written that, in the work of all the great poets and philosophers, there is a window that opens upon utopia. One might add that sometimes (as for example in Shaw's *Back to Methuselah, 1921*) it is open too wide. What is engaging about *The Caucasian Chalk Circle* is the irony in the utopianism, particularly in the wake of a prologue that presents the Soviet Union as much closer to utopia than it actually was. In this play Brecht used the idea of the Lord of Misrule who for a brief interregnum turns the existing society and its values upside down. Which, if the existing society is an antihuman one, would mean substituting a genuine humanism. To be human for a day: that is the formula. But there is a catch in it. What we are likely to get is a flat, unbelievable virtuousness. Brecht does not give us this, arguing, as it were, that if the whole society was monstrous then even the misrule would be grotesque: in

* In the following three paragraphs I plagiarize myself somewhat. The source is the previous chapter, *The Caucasian Chalk Circle.*

its origin a fluke, it is by nature a freak. The fact that by definition it will have no future affects its character: it is only a truancy, not a liberation. All of which would have remained so much theorizing except that Brecht was able to write the poetry and the comedy, the narrative and the character, by which the word became flesh—by which, signally, the Lord of Misrule became *ein Mensch mit seinem Widerspruch:* Azdak—the disenchanted philosopher as quasi-revolutionary activist.

Does the irony undercut the author's activism? As with Shaw, there will be those who think that it does, and with this much justification: that as they read or see the play, they find themselves responding more fully to the despair than to the hope. And it is always likely, *a priori,* that despair will outweigh hope in a work of art, since despair is a pervasive established fact that tends to pervade the past and the present, whereas hope tends to be just a project, located, as it is, in that frail, as yet merely imagined spot, the future. But it seems to me that Brecht has linked despair and hope in lively dialectical interplay; and that while there are many moments when despair predominates, hope remains at the end. Which is all that hope need do. It need not bring in the kingdom. It need only survive.

The question is whether the good society is felt, nostalgically, to be in the past (that is, to be over) or whether it is felt, hopefully, to be in the future, that is, in the making, felt to be a possibility and "up to us," something we can work on, a matter of *praxis.* The old notion of the Age of Gold has little meaning in *The Caucasian Chalk Circle* until it is inverted. We, the audience, return to the Age of Gold when we see Azdak inverting our rules and laws. In thought Azdak returns to an Age of Gold when he nostalgically recalls the popular revolt of a former generation. On the other hand, the age of Azdak is no Age of Gold but an age of war and oppression in which by a fluke a little justice can be done. That, for Azdak himself, revolutions are identified with the past is what is wrong with him. The era of Azdak itself has the transitory character of the Saturnalia in which, after the brief interregnum is over, a mock king goes back into anonymity. But the important Prologue suggests a *regnum* that is not *inter.* The ultimate ironic inversion among the many in the play is that a Golden Age should be envisaged not in Arcadia but in Georgia. In this way, what is planted in the minds of at least a sympathetic audience is not a memory, a fantasy, or a dream but a possibility. That this should be open to doubt, and that certain audiences can respond differently, is a tribute to the dialectical complexity of the piece, the subtlety of its method.

"What is a modern problem play but a clinical lecture on society?" Bernard Shaw asked in 1901. If the works of Ibsen, Shaw, and Brecht may fairly be described as modern problem plays, then our answer must be that they are *much* besides being clinical lectures on society. They are tragedies, or comedies, or tragicomedies of so special a kind that only close analysis can bring out their pecularity, let alone their merit. They are dramatic art, and they are dramatic art in motion: we see the "problem play" developing from one Ibsen play to another, from one Shaw play to another, from one Brecht play to another. There is also a development from one *author* to another. And since people are individuals and unique, geniuses—if an Irishism may be permitted—are even more individual and unique. The problem play, ultimately, was whatever Ibsen or Shaw or Brecht made of it. Yet there is reason to say that it remained the problem play. If it has been my aim in this "comment" to suggest that far more art and artifice went into this form of play than has hitherto been assumed, it has equally been my aim to demonstrate that the social drama was indeed social, from *Ghosts* and *Hedda Gabler* to *Widowers' Houses* and *Mrs. Warren's Profession*, and from *Major Barbara* and *Saint Joan* to *Saint Joan of the Stockyards* and *The Caucasian Chalk Circle*.

(*1969*)

The Drama of Modern Life

In Bahnhof Friedrichstrasse

Summer 1965. If the Berlin Wall didn't exist it would have to be invented. What could symbolize better how we are placed on earth side by side but insist on living divided from each other, however irrationally? But then, and this too is symbolic, the Wall has cracks in it. Through one crack the S-Bahn (elevated railroad) runs from West Berlin to the Friedrichstrasse Bahnhof. When you get off the train, nothing tells you, if you are a foreigner, what to do. If you look up you see a couple of guards with rifles or submachine guns slung across their backs, perched on a kind of balustrade up near the roof. If you look down, there are stairs indicating that West German visitors should go down them. When for lack of other suggestions you too follow them, you come to a ticket booth, and there ask where foreigners should go. You are aware that your question goes not only to the person you speak to but several others, including policemen, People's Policemen. You are sent around corners to a point you later come to regard as the world's real center. At some former date in history it was doubtless just a right-angle bend in a corridor of an old-fashioned railroad station. Fitted up with new railings, and armed guards, while its lights and furnishings have been left in a primitive state, it is pure nightmare, and the right angle is part of a diabolical plan. Waiting rooms had something of this poorly lit, dirty desolation in the old railroad stations, and this is a railroad station, and you are waiting. Only not for a train. You are waiting to be adjudged harmless.

Well, you are harmless, aren't you? But is that good? Or should you, rather, be the very person they wish to apprehend—one who is plotting mischief, arranging to build tunnels through the Wall, or to bring people through the checkpoints on other people's passports? What would Antigone be doing? What would Karl Marx be thinking?

The world of Ulbricht. Walter Ulbricht and myself actually touched, at the Kammerspiele the other night, when he put in an unannounced appearance at *La belle Hélène*. The Offenbach opera had been adapted by Peter Hacks, whose play *Worries about Power* was withdrawn in a hurry not long ago for its political unorthodoxy. Or rather just for showing that East Germany has its economic and human problems. Everybody keeps staring at Ulbricht to see how he responds to Helen. At the appropriate times, he smiles, he claps. He is much smaller than his photographs suggest, only comes up to my chin when we pass in the aisle. His violence is no more apparent from his person than Goldwater's or Lyndon Johnson's. How hard history is to believe! No wonder people met Stalin and concluded he had *not* committed any atrocities: he too was very small. Was even Eichmann banal, as Hannah Arendt says? That is hardly the word for Goering and Goebbels, anyhow.

And what of our century's greatest hero and supreme symbol, the man with the Charlie Chaplin mustache? I have been able to see him on film several times since returning to Germany. Reunion with an old friend? He copied Chaplin, and then, in *The Great Dictator,* Chaplin copied him. Twin symbols of our century? And Chaplin a Communist sympathizer. But Chaplin's skit on Hitler is only mimicry, not portraiture. He renders inimitably the non-German's impression of the Führer's voice and the German language. He projects actually the Cockney conviction that everyone on the Continent is temperamental to the point of lunacy. Above all, he gives far too favorable an impression of Hitler's technique. In comparison, the historical Adolf, in film clips selected for public perusal by his own propaganda ministry, is positively gauche. One can well understand that German aristocrats with nothing against the Final Solution would have been shocked to the soul by his awkwardness. Hitler was a hick from the Austrian backwoods. The radio flattered him. For if he took lessons in gesture and body movement he never got out of the beginner's class. In the newsreel clips, you see him fumble and hesitate with his hands. His voice must have had a fascination for many—*si monumentum requiris circumspice*—but what he did was chiefly to misuse it, tormenting himself into paroxysms of would-be eloquence. The ultimate in Naturalism: when oratory is not achieved at all, what we have *must* be sincerity. The contrast with the empty stateliness of German public speaking generally is remarkable: and there indeed one glimpses the source of the gentleman's success. He embodied suppressed resentment against the old Establishment, and his very incapacity found an echo in every Spiessbürger's breast: here "our own" inarticulateness was mirrored—and was turned into its opposite, partly by growls, groans, and shrieks, but even more by action. Yours not to reason why, yours but to do and kill.

In the Friedrichstrasse Bahnhof one always ends up thinking about Hitler. Deadest of Germans, he is also the most alive. "*NS-Vergangenheit*." This is the phrase applied to all Germans with a shady past: one speaks of their "national socialist past." Of course, most Germans over forty-five have something of an *NS-Vergangenheit,* and this is very noticeably true at the professional level, since professional people occupy positions of leadership or at least prestige. Communists, like Jews, are exceptions. The Volksgemeinschaft did not include them, and so they feel themselves entitled to claim that their State, the DDR, has been purified from Nazism, while they mercilessly expose Nazism in the Federal Republic. In this, however, they participate in the general German hypocrisy, since they too—perforce—have used many ex-Nazis, especially lawyers, in important positions. And the very man who hands out the most virulent Party propaganda on East German TV, Karl Eduard von Schnitzler, was an enthusiastic supporter of Hitler's war effort up to the moment when he was captured by the British in 1945.

By chance I met the person who interviewed Von Schnitzler at that time on behalf of the BBC, which was looking for Germans who would be willing to take part in anti-Nazi broadcasts. "Don't you hate the British?" he asked Von Schnitzler. "I did," the latter answered, "I did till a few days ago. My heart was full of hatred for them. When I saw our planes and how many there were of them, my heart was full of hate for England." "But now it isn't?" "No, last Wednesday, I saw the British planes, and how many there were of *them.* England, too, is a great power, I said to myself. And the hate for England died in my heart." The hate must have died also for the chief enemy, Soviet Russia, since a few years later, Von Schnitzler switched from West to East German radio and television.

Today he presides over a couple of weekly TV programs—both remarkable in their way. On one he shows clips from West German television. (I don't know what the East/West division has done to copyright—probably destroyed it entirely. They rob each other's TV programs quite freely, it seems.) The idea is to see the Westerners condemned out of their own mouths. Some of them, of course, stand condemned out of their own mouths without any assistance from Herr Von S. Some of them—Heinrich Lübke, for instance— need only be seen and heard. When I hear President Lübke's flabby, flaccid enunciation I am ready to believe anything of him. Actually, the "assistance" Von S. renders has the reverse of the intended effect. The intention is so evidently malicious, the absence of any interest in the truth as such so very obvious, one's sympathy inevitably goes to the victim. Besides which, Von S.'s logical specialty is the *non sequitur.* He is forever drawing consequences that aren't there, forcing a meaning on a speaker that is obviously contrary to the intention. There is so much misleading talk of the diabolical efficiency of the to-talitarian systems! We owe our lives to their inefficiency and silliness. If they were not as inefficient and silly as ourselves they would have won the last war.

Take the Wall. Take this very corner of the Bahnhof Friedrichstrasse where I am sitting. A few weeks ago a young British friend of mine was here. He had come to Berlin to put on a show and had all his wages in his pocket—they amounted to a couple of hundred dollars. He knew no German, didn't fully un-derstand what he was told about papers, thought it all didn't matter much any-way, and failed to mention on these papers how much money he was carrying. That was on the way East. Returning at eleven p.m., after seeing a play at the Berlin Ensemble, he gave a confusing account of what he now had. Then, to show how honest he was, and how there was nothing at stake, he produced *all* his cash for the customs officials to see. Result: he was immediately taken into custody for fraud. They held him till five the next morning. Kafkaesque scenes were enacted. An interpreter was called in whose chief interest was fishing for compliments from my friend on his good English. He was absurdly friendly. But the watches of the night were jogging by, and Bahnhof Friedrichstrasse is a very grim place, especially when you are under guard and confined in what is vir-tually a solitary cell.

My friend got his money back, but only some months later, and after all kinds of wires had been pulled by all kinds of VIPs and Organizations. He got his money back: that's my point. The whole operation was inefficiently con-ducted and in any case futile. Had my friend really been breaking the rules he would have been in no trouble at all. He would have hidden the money they didn't want him to have somewhere on his person. For, normally speaking, no one is ever searched. Which of course makes nonsense of the view that the Wall is there to stop traffic in money.

Why don't they search people, by the way? Are they just staggered at the thought of how many man-hours it would take up? Are they reluctant to add to the already considerable irritation people feel at procedures at the Wall? Is their fear of black-marketeering in money not really all that great?

I don't know the answers to these questions, and that too is my point. The natural response to this "world of the Wall" is not the blustering indignation of the politicians and the reporters of the popular press but rather bewilderment. The American press—*Time,* especially—seems lacking in real reporters, preferring philosophers—bad philosophers. What is said emanates from a theory, not from observation. A recent instance was *Time*'s reporting of the East German decision to make Western visitors to East Berlin buy some East money at *their* rates. *Time* represented this money as a fee, as if one were not allowed to spend it. And they repeated their usual description of the customs officials and police as "surly." These men can indeed be surly and worse, but just as often they are jovial and all smiles. For this is not Whittaker Chambers, it is Kafka. When they smile, *you* are surly, as often as not. You ask yourself what in hell they are so cheerful about.

Yes, it's one's own moods one must watch, as they are affected, not only by the moods of others, but by the bureaucratic process itself. One evening I got so furious, here at the Wall, I turned round and went home without ever getting through. I had been on my way to the theatre, which was about five minutes away—but on the other side. I had handed in my passport, it had disappeared into the Rooms Beyond, and I was left watching a queue that seemed totally stationary. What was infuriating about the guards was that they were doing nothing—and not surlily à la *Time,* but imperturbably. I thought I'd get a rise out of one by demanding my passport back and announcing I was returning home. He remained imperturbable and gave me the passport. No impropriety that I could report to *Time's* Berlin office! I drove back home in redoubled rage.

And this incident had a sequel with another significant twist—or do I mean significantly lacking in significance? As long as my rage lasted I was resolved never to go through the Wall again. I canceled a speaking engagement I had had in East Berlin. Yet rage subsides, and gives place to sullen resentment. I wanted to see that show, and turned up again at show time, sulking vigorously to an audience of fellow visitors only. For the customs men and police, though they are always the same individuals, and one gets to know their faces well, have obviously been instructed *not* to get on familiar terms with visitors, and each time one is greeted as a total stranger by someone who is less and less a total stranger, which also helps the resentment grow. But this time, of all times, the young man handling my papers decided to know me. Reading my name out from my passport, he asked, "Mr. Bentley? Did you give an interview to the press that was quoted on the radio?" Oh my God, I thought, my little tantrum set them to checking up on me, now doubtless they have rooted out some unpleasant remarks I've made about something in East German theatre, and I'm about to be banished from their territory forever. "What interview was that?" I asked nervously. "A few months back," said the young man, "you said East Berlin also had good theatre. *Was* it you?" So, I was getting a *good mark.* They wanted me to feel appreciated. This was as near as they could come, maybe, to apologizing to me for the other evening? Or was there no connection? Was it entirely by chance that the young man had become communicative? The smile he gave me when returning the passport and letting me through was not of the routine kind but genuinely interested and friendly. Or was it?

The Friedrichstrasse Bahnhof feels like a jail. You have the sensation that you may never again see the light of day. Then suddenly—when the process of filling out forms and being looked at is over—you are out and on the street. What have you emerged into? Just a street? Nothing in East Berlin, at any rate for the visitor, is *just* anything. It is that thing in a setting of uncertainty and ghostly unreality. A lack of gay faces, *Time* will have it. That's the formula they've found. One sympathizes with their plight, given that their readers demand the absolute truth in a very few words of very bad English and in a form that disturbs no conventional preconceptions. A lack of gay faces? Sometimes it is, rather, a lack of faces altogether—I mean where one expects faces to be, as, above all, in the streets of a big city. The neighborhood of the Volksbühne is very eerie in this way. The Volksbühne is a big new centrally placed theatre in the imposing, forbidding style of Soviet Classical public buildings. This having been a bombed-out area, every building in sight is brand-new, spick and span. But why are there no people around? One would think it was five in the morning. In East Berlin five in the afternoon very often seems to be five in the morning.

Is West Berlin any less freakish, though? What can one make of half a city, surrounded by barbed wire and wall, in the midst of an enemy zone? (The proposition is as preposterous as it is unprecedented. And the problems are solved preposterously.) Well, obviously one can make propaganda, and on the grandest scale. Khrushchev could bluster about invasion, and Bobby Kennedy could bluster about using the atomic bomb. Ideals soar higher than spaceships whenever the word "Berlin" comes up in Moscow or Washington. It is a useful word, but expensive, of course. It is expensive to stand guard over Ulbricht— or over Brandt. But there is profit as well as loss. West Berlin is a city to invest in, East Germany is a fine place to rob. And then there are the games that East and West play with each other! Sometimes Moscow and Washington tire of them, but Pankow and Bonn, never. Every issue, however real, becomes a game, played with Teutonic earnestness and *furor*. Both sides are always right. And wrong. Pick your issue according to your allegiance and zest for battle. The final joke is that for all their pleas of independence, or even of dependence on Russia or America, they are dependent on—each other. Behind the pretense of not even being on speaking terms, West and East Berlin officials have to be meeting all the time. The very feces of West Berlin are taken care of by East Berlin—boy, do they need each other!

If the elaborate patterns of life in the East bloc suggest meaninglessness, the no less elaborate pattern of East-West relations suggests fakery. To this latter pattern, of course, one comes better prepared. That every moral gesture or utterance should be a phony is something one has been brought up to, whatever one's origin. Berlin provides only new examples. On arriving in West Berlin, I was informed that the elevated railway, being East property, was being boycotted by the West, and I should not invest my twenty pfennigs in it, but as an observer, I felt I had a prior obligation to observe. Upon observing, I found the El full (or half full) of other Westerners, albeit mostly of such as didn't have too many pfennigs to invest in the politicians' high ideals. Checking back with the secretarial lady who had given me the warning, I found that her own ideals really weren't all that high—her objection to the El was precisely that dirty and ill-clad people were to be seen on it. Let them eat cake—and travel on the (more expensive) subway! The same lady expressed surprise that I was willing to visit Wedding. I was visiting something as respectable as an art gallery there, but it is a working-class section.

What a wonderful essay could be written if there were a Swift around on the way both sides *make* free with the *word* "free." The East, as is known, has real freedom, instead of formal freedom. But that's nothing. The West has plain old genuine Freedom, of which the capital F reaches God. And far from having a subtle, wire-drawn, Jesuitical definition, this freedom has one unambiguous meaning: that you're not in the East bloc. Spain and Portugal are free, Taiwan and South Vietnam are free. So do not run away with the idea that the Free in Free University (of Berlin) means that no charge is made for tuition. On the contrary. It means that the faculty may be Nazis but that they certainly aren't Communists. Hence, there is no great parad·x, at the Free University, of that formal freedom which the Marxists make fun of. Free speech, for example, does not exist there. The Rektor recently stopped Erich Kuby from speaking there. (Kuby is a liberal journalist, whose work has recently appeared in *Der Spiegel*. His crime was having made a joke about the word "free" in the phrase "Free University.") In welcoming Saragat to the special freedom of this particular borough, the same Rektor reverently invoked the name of the one important Italian philosopher who supported Mussolini (Gentile).

The biggest recent scandal at this Free institution occurred in my own field of theatre and drama. When the Free University was set up in 1949, with all the trumpets of Freedom blaring, the man they chose to represent this field was a man the German public of that time knew pretty well, by the name of Hans Knudsen. They knew him because he had been the drama critic (or noncritic, after Goebbels abolished criticism) of the *Völkischer Beobachter*. At the Nazi University of Berlin, Knudsen stood by while his old master Max Herrmann was deprived of all his resources in preparation for his death (in 1942) in Theresienstadt. Knudsen didn't just stand by. He promoted the "philosophy" of anti-Semitism in the field of Theaterwissenschaft. What happened last winter was that documents proving this were published in a Berlin newspaper—photostats and all. It also came out that Knudsen got his title of Professor under the Nazis only by the personal intervention of Alfred Rosenberg. Even a dean who wrote "Heil Hitler!" before his signature didn't want to accept him. That was in the years 1943–1944. Five years later he was taken on without any known demur by the Free University. And the Free University would never to this day have taken any stand against Knudsen had it not been shamed into it by the liberal press.

The liberal press. There is one. That is one of the best things about West

Germany, and one which, of course, has no parallel, *can* have no parallel, in the East. The East limits itself to exploiting all the dirt about the West which the liberal press of the West prints. The Knudsen affair was duly gone over in *Theater der Zeit,* the East Berlin theatre magazine. The paper that "broke" the story had been the *Spandauer Volksblatt,* the paper of dissident but non-Communist West Berlin youth. Sprightly as it is, the *Volksblatt* has very limited news coverage. There is not a first-rate *news*paper in all of Berlin. For that you have to go to Hamburg (*Die Welt*) or Frankfurt (*Frankfurter Allgemeine*). The most important political journalist in Germany today—more important even than Walter Lippmann in America—is Rudolf Augstein, the editor of *Der Spiegel.* The world heard something of Augstein's arrest at the instance of Franz Josef Strauss a year or two ago. The incident symbolizes the confrontation of liberal journalism with Old Germany. Fat, foxy, philistine, and ferocious, Strauss is a figure straight out of the Georg Grosz cartoons of forty years ago; Augstein is a Georg Grosz of words instead of drawings. You need to follow the *Spiegel* issue by issue to appreciate the insistency of his guerrilla war against the Germany not only of Hitler but of Adenauer, and not only of Adenauer but of Erhard, and not only of Erhard but of Ulbricht.

One should not see the old Nazis and the neo-Nazis as the chief danger. That is a trap. Only in New York has *The Deputy* been picketed by men with swastika armbands. In Germany those who a generation ago would have worn swastikas are now happy enough with the Hammer and Sickle or the Stars and Stripes. The voice of the Monster may in future have a sound quite unlike Adolf Hitler's screeching falsetto. It will more likely sound like Caspar Milquetoast or Walt Rostow. The old brown and black shirts have been bleached white, and in their white shirts the new men fly to the United States for honorary degrees.

Günter Grass is maintaining that the answer to Erhard is Brandt. I have seen this mentioned in the American press. But how many Americans know of Pastor Martin Niemoeller's declaration, "Tasks of Politics in 1965," in which he recommends the spoiling of as many ballots as possible in this year's elections as a protest against the mere pretense of democracy which in his belief is the federal system? True, even in Germany an attitude like Grass's gets more public attention than one like Niemoeller's. *Public* attention. Western Germany is to a large extent a publicity operation, staged, as it were, by the Chamber of Commerce. When in New York, Erhard told of having sat in the ruins of the Nuremberg Stadium back in 1945 with his "good friend Henry Luce" and telling the good Henry there was one way in which Germany could be rebuilt and that was by free enterprise. Today Krupp is the richest man in Europe, and the social democrats are as eager as ever to prove themselves no different from nonsocial democrats.

Günter Grass is clutching at a straw, but who wouldn't, when there is nothing else to clutch at? Or is there? Peter Weiss thinks there is. He has clutched at the Russian bear itself and must now find out if (as an artist at any rate) he can survive a bear hug. The encounter has been a curious one to watch, and one did literally watch it, as it, or significant moments of it, was shown on East German TV. On the little screen one saw Weiss telling the East Germans that *their* understanding of his Marat-Sade play was the right one. In other words, Marat is the hero, and Sade the villain. Funnily enough, this was not what Weiss had told the presumably Communist director of the West Berlin production, Konrad Swinarski. Meanwhile some months passed, and those months seem to have marked the conversion of Weiss, if not to Communism then to fellow-traveling. He now says one must choose between East and West and he has chosen the East.

Can anyone over thirty-five confront the politics of Grass on the one hand or of Weiss on the other with other than a despondent feeling of *déjà-vu?* Why should a solution be found in the Social Democrats of 1965 any more than it was in their predecessors of 1914 or 1933? And why should the East Bloc be embraced at the very time it has shown itself not to be a bloc at all? And just following the time when we learned that the outrages of which the Soviet regime had been accused during the Stalin years actually were committed?

Official communism and official anticommunism are both bankrupt, yet my friends tell me that pronouncing "a plague on both your houses" is too negative. Too negative for what? Am I to minimize the shortcomings (i.e., crimes and outrages) of one of the two sides, just to enable myself to become a hypocritical champion of the other? Isn't that too positive by half? Surely the main objection to Stalinism yesterday, as to "Johnsonism" today, is that, in the name of an uncertain moral result, it asks us to accept, deny, and conceal the certain immoral means? A "purely negative" attitude might well be preferable to any choice between such positive alternatives. But is it necessary to be purely negative? That would be to assume the Wall is solid and perpetual. Actually there are cracks in it. Bahnhof Friedrichstrasse, as I was saying, is one of the cracks.

About five minutes walk from the Bahnhof, on the East side, lives Wolf Biermann. Now there's a Communist, if you like, though hardly the Parisian fellow-traveler type, cleverly justifying every twist and turn of official policy, or deftly shifting the subject to "how about the Negroes in the South?" Strictly speaking, Biermann is an ex-Communist, but then too he says he wouldn't "choose freedom" and go West if the Wall were opened to him and the streets of welcoming West Berlin were covered with gold.

Biermann is a poet and singer. "He has had the best publicity East Germany could give any man," said the friend who guided me to his apartment. "What's that?" I asked. "Walter Ulbricht," was the reply, "publicly read Biermann out of the Party, and if that wouldn't bring a poet to the attention of the public I don't know what would." Wolf Biermann sang for me. He writes both the words and the music. There was an "American" song—Woody Guthrie—Pete Seeger style, a little mixed up—about the civil-rights worker William L. Moore who was murdered in the South. That's routine, of course, for any radical songster. Far from routine is Biermann's song about the Communist who escaped from Buchenwald in 1939, got to Moscow, and there was shot by Stalin on information supplied by the Nazis. Far from routine is the song about the East German citizen who was beaten up by the police for dancing free style. "You wait there," says Biermann in another poem, "seriously certain that I'll go swimming into the net of Self-Criticism for you; but I am a pike: you'd have to tear me limb from limb, chop me up, put me through the meat grinder, if you want me on bread!" Well, maybe they do want Biermann on bread, the meat grinders are certainly on hand, but the political point is clear: today the opposition comes from within. The opponents of the Communist governments are not necessarily friends of Lyndon Johnson and J. Edgar Hoover, or even of Leo Cherne and Sidney Hook; they are other Communists, with a non-Stalinist view of communism. Isn't there a lesson there for our people too? For the dissident young in the Western countries are not young Whittaker Chamberses wanting to work for the "Gay Pay Oo." The issue is not treason, or even desertion. And anyway, going over to the other side, whichever the other side is, has less and less drama because it has less and less significance, whether the "defector" is Peter Weiss or Uwe Johnson. *It is staying that counts now,* but staying not as a hired man of a regime but as a thorn in the flesh of a regime. So one does not cross the Wall to make headlines, one stays on one's own side of it—to make trouble.

And so the Wall is accepted? By no means. It is the fighting of the Cold War that favors this Wall—and Walls to come, as, maybe, between North and South Vietnam. But more and more what the writers and other artists are feeling is that they should put themselves at a distance from the regimes and their wars and address themselves to just people—which, as a minimum, means "to each other." Wolf Biermann and I were able to speak "to each other," without my seeming to be a Communist, and without his intimating that he wished to "choose Freedom," and I was considerably more at home that I could be sitting down with my ex-Dean McGeorge Bundy or with the trustees of Columbia University which has given doctorates to McNamara, Lodge, and Erhard.

Martin Buber comes to mind:

> That people can no longer carry on authentic dialogue with one another is not only the most acute symptom of the pathology of our time, it is also that which most urgently makes a demand of us. I believe, despite all, that the peoples in this hour can enter into dialogue. . . . To the task of initiating this conversation those are inevitably called who carry on today within

each people the battle against the anti-human. Those who build the great unknown front across mankind shall make it known by speaking unreservedly with one another, not overlooking what divides them but determined to bear this division in common.

Such a front does exist today. One would have to be deaf and blind not to find it in Prague or Warsaw—or, to go by reports, in Moscow, Hanoi, and maybe even Peking. It is one of the big reasons why the unrest in the United States should not be explained away or otherwise made light of. American youth has more to lose than its beards and dirty jeans, and more to defend. Even Vietnam is not all that is at stake, though it would be enough. Even World War III is not all that is at stake, though, if it happened, it would engulf all else. At stake is the honor of mankind, an irreducible human something without which mankind would not deserve to survive and without which one would not even want it to survive.

Does one want it to survive? *Really?* This will be the crucial question in the years ahead. I look around the corridor in Bahnhof Friedrichstrasse. There are the officious little guards with their high black boots and their military breeches. And here are we, their victims, waiting, waiting in the dirty gray-brown corridor. To this corridor all the aeons of evolution have led. And if I suddenly run to the door, the rifle of that fellow over there will slip from his shoulder, and he will shoot me down. Just outside is the new Glass House, through which one returns to the West. Glass, so no one can hide. The House of Tears, the East Berliners call it. Does one wish to survive? I should understand the Easterner who said no, and as a Westerner I should also fine it hard to say yes, if what the world offered was what the Western regimes are currently offering—if, that is, the world were nothing more than the world's regimes, the world's two sets of regimes. But it isn't. And I can't agree that the outlook is blacker than ever before. That the outlook is extremely black is nothing new. New, so far as I can judge, is only a certain positive aspect to the whole situation. Youth movements, peace movements, etc., etc., are bursting out everywhere, there is more and more widespread unrest, and less and less inclination to accept either the world as it is or the measures proposed by the regimes to change it. It always was, and it remains, unlikely that the good will triumph, but can it not be said for the present state of affairs that at least it provides some of us with a vocation?

(*1965*)

Thoughts on the Student Discontents

Last spring, the president of Columbia University said that teachers should think twice before giving students advice in areas where they have no special expertise. How many times should university presidents think before giving teachers advice in areas where they have no more expertise than their faculty? And what is all this about "expertise" anyway? When is expertise ever required of people except when they are already judged to be wrongheaded? Are professors who support highly patriotic wars asked to have expertise in warfare or even in patriotism? Are they not, so far as their presidents are concerned, merely praised for their high sense of duty? Similarly, students who protest against a war are asked to have expertise, while those who support it are allowed to be ignoramuses. Undoubtedly their ignorance is a big help. Similarly, too, McGeorge Bundy and his friends try to disqualify criticism on the plea that their critics don't have access to essential information: if we all had access to the data Mr. Bundy has access to, we would all reach his conclusions. Since we don't, we must trust him.

We are hearing a lot about trust these days, and the man we are above all to trust is Lyndon Johnson. Which is too bad, as he is not an unusually trustworthy person. I voted for him at the last election because I considered that he had virtues not shared by his opponent. An unusual degree of trustworthiness was not, however, one of these. People used to ask about Richard Nixon: Would you buy a used car from this man? Well, which of us wouldn't prefer buying a used car from Barry Goldwater to buying one from Lyndon Johnson? The very quality for which Johnson is most admired—political dexterity—carries with it the defect of trickiness. He strikes me also as a man lacking in all conviction. That seems to be the source of his strength: he is without prejudice. He could at one time talk and act like a segregationist, but he *really* didn't mean it: he doesn't *really* mean anything. He is like a lawyer: totally willing to take his client's side, and give his all to it, with every outward sign of sincerity and felt fervor. When his client is the public, this makes him a very democratic figure, and when his client is only part of the public, he will show great skill in (a) wooing other parts; and (b) pretending that he has already wooed and won all parts. However, from time to time, the unforeseen happens, and someone actually speaks *against* Johnson or even acts against him. It doesn't seem right, but it happens. And right now in the United States that is the one fly in the political ointment. Everything is under control. All would be well. We would have the best of both worlds—all the comfortable advantage of peace and welfare added to the heroic afflatus of a just war—if it were not for this impudent indocility, this active mistrust. Even the Bible, though warning us not to put our trust in princes, says nothing against Presidents.

Trust the President. Trust Mr. Bundy. Both Mr. Bundys. Also Mr. Rusk. And until recently there was the supremely trustworthy Adlai Stevenson. Yet Adlai Stevenson was caught lying in the United Nations when he denied that the United States had anything to do with the Bay of Pigs invasion. We have all lied in our time, but maybe not in such a big way. Besides we don't all ask everyone to take us on trust. Then again, some lies make for practical problems. Let me again cite the Bay of Pigs. In connection with that adventure a government spokesman defended lying. It might be a patriotic duty, he said. Maybe so, but we would like to know when our leaders are *not* lying, so we can talk over the truth—the actual facts—with them. When Mr. Bundy implies that if we knew the inside story about Vietnam, we would approve of each stand our government has taken, including no doubt stands that contradict one another, is he patriotically lying? Is Johnson's explanation of what he did in the Dominican Republic a tissue of lies?

Consider one admitted lie. Debating on TV with John F. Kennedy on October 22, 1960, the Vice President of the United States let the people know that, so far as his government was concerned, United States support for an anti-Castro invasion was out of the question. Kennedy's plea for such support he called "the most shockingly reckless proposal ever made in our history by a Presidential candidate during a campaign." Nearly four years later the *New York Times* announced: "Mr. Nixon subsequently explained in his book *Six Crises* that he believed Mr. Kennedy had been endangering the security of the invasion plan . . . and therefore felt obliged to attack a plan he privately supported." It follows from this that when the intelligent citizen hears one of his trustworthy pastors and masters attacking a plan, any plan, he should ask himself whether maybe the said pastor and master isn't privately supporting that plan. Perhaps these trustworthy folk could actually be trusted if one made a habit of reversing all their statements? Could one trust them to support a thing privately *if* they are publicly attacking it? I wouldn't count on it. What we *can* probably count on is that at the moment when we are confronted with any crisis, we shall not be placed in possession of the facts that govern the outcome.

Mistrust is a better guide than trust to what actually seems to have been going on in all the great crises of the past few years. That one no longer trusted Stevenson in 1960 was lucky, and those who trusted Kennedy at that time must surely have got a shock from Arthur Schlesinger's account of the Bay of Pigs in 1965. In 1960 the team was being loyal to the captain. The Bay of Pigs was all set to be mentioned in some future "1776 and All That" as "a Good Thing," and Kennedy had approved the invasion on the ground of High Ideals. One gathers, however, from the Schlesinger memoir that what really interested Kennedy was . . . public relations. He wanted to be known as Strong, and the formula was Strength through Guns. Hence, anyone who died in that unfortunate encounter died to keep Kennedy's reputation up. Which brings military campaigning into the area of political campaigning; and one again had the impression that the two were quite close in the summer of 1964 when, in his turn, Johnson wanted to seem Strong. The question at the time was whether Goldwater could make Johnson seem an Appeaser. Just at that moment, the American Navy was attacked by the Vietnamese. At least that was what we were told, and considering where the Navy was, it didn't seem too improbable. Johnson's ideals soared sky-high (i.e., the order was given to drop bombs), and whatever Vietnamese got killed can today rejoice in heaven or elsewhere that Johnson was elected.

Since being elected, Johnson's main point about the Vietnamese has been that he keeps asking them all to negotiate but they won't. Another provable if patriotic lie is involved. Hanoi is now known, even in the United States, to have also offered to negotiate. Arthur Miller brought this up recently, and a Johnsonian magazine that reported the matter tried to refute Miller with the observation that the terms offered by Hanoi were unacceptable. So: "refusal to negotiate" means "refusal to agree to our terms." Besides which there might be something to say of the tactic of *bombing* an antagonist, ostensibly as a way of forcing him to negotiate, but actually as a way of forcing your terms on him. Only to a public-relations man is that any different from plain old war. But we are ruled by public-relations men. Which is another reason why, much as we may admire the flexibility of the gentlemen, we cannot reasonably be asked to give them our trust.

A corollary of Grayson Kirk's remarks would seem to be that professors who *are* experts do have the right to hand out advice. One question would be: Expert in what? History? Geography? Political theory, and communism in particular? Southeast Asia, and Vietnam in particular? Then again, aren't experts purchasable? Can't anyone have the experts he can afford? And can't anyone hire experts to defend any position he likes to take? Above all, will not the entrenched positions, in the nature of things, be well defended? Won't Soviet experts *on* capitalism be experts *against* capitalism? And isn't just the converse true of American experts on this subject? Even if I am wrong here, do the experts ever agree on anything? And, if they don't, which ones should we be guided by? Are there experts on choosing-among-experts and, if so, do *these* experts agree?

A moment's thought about such difficulties can only cause us to wonder why there is so much talk of expertise all of a sudden. Isn't the main commitment of democracy, for better or for worse, to the nonexpert—i.e., people at large? For America, the country with the strongest populist tradition in the world, it is certainly strange doctrine that we should all be dissuaded from independent thinking and individualistic action. Even willful rebelliousness is sanctified here by tradition, the country being founded on a Revolution which reasonable conservative gentlemen (Edmund Burke, for example) showed to be quite unnecessary. It is bizarre indeed that today the rebels and protesters should be placed on the defensive, and even stigmatized as un-American. Isn't the boot on the other foot?

On Vietnam, as on other things, the experts do disagree, and the predictable experts *are* predictable—Communist experts defend the Communist position, and vice versa. So there is nothing for the rest of us to do but either be totally passive or come to grips with the situation as best we may. It can only be called curious that persons who are nothing but passive should get a good mark for patriotism and political virtue generally, while those who take a stand contrary to the Establishment are found at best inexpert and at worst immoral. We can all respect a young man whose convictions impel him to risk his life in the army, but surely no reverence is due to someone whose sole achievement is that he got drafted?

The argument behind the patriotic line of college presidents and other Establishment figures is this. America is not a Communist country, and therefore we need not believe Communist experts. It is an anti-Communist country, and therefore we should follow the advice of the anti-Communist experts. Now one can respect this logic to the extent of admitting that there are only two sides in a war and thus, if one took a side other than Johnson's side in the Vietnam war, one would be fighting against the Army of the United States and alongside many Communists. But then, unless one *is* a Communist, *one is not advocating fighting for Hanoi but a cessation of fighting by all parties.* President Johnson has been urging recently that the Vietnam demonstrations are against the national interest. Of course they are against the national interest if his policy is *in* the national interest, but that is the question. Antiwar talk is *always* against the interest of a government at war: does that mean that antiwar talk is to be permitted only when there is no war to be anti? That such talk brings comfort to "the enemy" may well be true. In a given case, the enemy may deserve comfort and, even in other cases, such talk has to be heard, surely, before it can be assessed. And it may have to be heard even after that, given a belief in something that many anti-Communists do profess belief in—freedom of discussion.

Still, it will be urged, simply not volunteering in North Vietnam's army is not enough to detach one from the Communists. All the Party would demand of a United States citizen would be antiwar propaganda, and this all who oppose the Vietnam action are providing. Aren't Communists strange bedfellows, especially for the young, antiwar liberals of our college communities? The answer to this is: Certainly, but to eschew strange bedfellows would be to eschew politics itself—which is, of course, what many of the old want many of the young to do. Since political conflicts, like wars, tend to have only two sides, a willingness to make alliances with the lesser foe against the greater is of the essence of politics. Naturally, there is often a question which *is* the lesser foe. Some people would be happier if Roosevelt had joined with Hitler against Stalin. That he did the opposite, however, gives our present-day pacifists an august precedent for their strange sleeping around. It is a matter of Beggars Can't Be Choosers. Against an imminent and total threat you accept any help available, and leave the question of your indebtedness to be answered later, if it can be: otherwise there may be no "you" to answer it.

I am not one of those who are blithe and unskeptical about "working with the Communists." "Whoever sleeps in their camp wakes up one morning to find himself robbed"—this is a quotation from myself, and a statement I do not repudiate: it was based on considerable personal experience. Many of the Communists I knew are still there, and many of the practices I deplored are still current. At the same time, it would be ridiculous to assume that communism has not changed in the past ten years. Yet this is, in general, what *is* assumed in Washington and in American Embassies round the world, and it is not just a matter of communism maybe not being as bad as they think, but of its being a good deal different from what they think, and indeed of its not being just one thing any more, as they assume it to be. We have grown used to laughing at the Communist use of the word "capitalism," because for us the one word cannot sum up the multifarious ways of business, but our own men now use the word "communism" in just such a manner. If communism were indeed One and Indivisible, Russia and China would have combined to keep America out of Vietnam—or would have joined America in destroying civilization. Johnson, Rusk, and Company would not have been able to show us what great moralists they are but for a division in the Communist ranks which Washington has not yet learned to understand!

I have just spent a year behind the Iron Curtain as a "lackey of capitalism" (i.e., paid by the Ford Foundation), and, meeting American officials here and there, charming fellows most of them, have gained the impression that they have no idea what a Communist, today, is like, nor yet what it is like to be a citizen of a Communist country. Some have not studied communism in any form. Others have studied it as if in preparation to be secret agents; others as if the only aim were to get an A in anticommunism. Now I would be the first to recognize that one might learn theology from an atheist, but I also think a theology student should at some point get to know what theologians are like.

One of the assumptions of the American official class is that living under communism is a fate worse than death. A corollary dogma is that everyone else thinks so too, except for a hard core of Communists and fellow travelers. Now whatever truth these two dogmas had in Stalin's day, they have both become provably false. It is not that everyone you meet behind the Iron Curtain likes his government, but the spirit of the Hungarian Revolt of 1956 is no longer widespread, partly because it is now known that no help is forthcoming from the West, partly because life in Hungary—and many other places—is now a good deal pleasanter. Also, though it is a shock for the few Americans who bother to find out, many Easterners think that, while the East is bad, the West is worse. Vietnam is cited as a vivid example. "What the Russians did in Budapest was outrageous; what the Americans are doing in Vietnam is *more* outrageous, first, because Vietnam is not on their frontiers and, second, because this is an endlessly continued and calculated outrage, not just a single mad lunge." This is not a quotation from one Easterner but from a thousand. Since anti-Communist zeal is seen as driving Americans into actions characteristic of Stalinism at its height, and since at just this time Russia and other Eastern countries have been de-Stalinizing themselves to a certain extent, many Easterners have come in recent years to think worse of America and better of their own regimes.

That the Communist movement exploits the word "peace" is very true. So do all political movements in all countries, now that open praise of war is no longer successful claptrap. But the Communist-led section of the peace movement is actually on the level to this extent, that the interests of communism can in general be better served by peace than war. Perhaps war only serves its interests when, as in Vietnam, a capitalist power takes the offensive, and so drives *patriots* into the arms of the Communist Party. For while the official class in America can think of the struggle as being between communism and a Free World, the Communists are on to the fact that the living political force in Asia (as in Africa) is neither communism nor belief in a "Free World" but nationalism. It would probably be impossible for the Orient to see any war America might wage against a small country there as other than a war of white imperialism against native nationalism. As to Vietnam, they can make a strong case that is not in the least undermined by Johnson's insistence that he has no territorial ambitions in the East, because everyone there is well-aware of the invisible imperialism of investments, which can be defended by soldiers flown to any territory whatever in a matter of hours.

To live under a Communist government is not necessarily a fate worse than death. It is not even worse than living under a Saigon government with a hundred and forty thousand American soldiers as its palace guard. (Premier Ky has been quoted in the British press as saying that Hitler is the only modern leader he admires.) On the contrary, it would be very hard indeed for any ordinary Oriental—and perhaps for any ordinary human being—to prefer the life in Saigon (1950–1955–1960–1965–?) to the life in Hanoi. I saw something of both in the TV programs of the German networks, West and East. Nothing from either network to recommend Saigon rather than Hanoi. Much (in the East presentations, naturally) to recommend Hanoi rather than Saigon. But of course I am not speaking only of visible amenities. The *New York Times* ran a story about the way in which poor South Vietnamese families can improve their lot, namely, by making their daughters into American camp followers. Hanoi seems to have more attractive plans for the poor. And, inevitably, going over this ground, one returns to the famous remark of Eisenhower's explaining how fortunate it was the Vietnamese were never granted free elections: eighty per cent of the population "would have voted for the Communist Ho Chi Minh."

At this point, the Establishment will ask if, then, I am proposing to *appease* the Communists? And some will add that people like me (or is it people like them?) appeased Hitler in the thirties. How about Walter Lippmann, for instance? Wasn't he some kind of an "appeaser" in the thirties? And, if he was, doesn't that explain his advocacy of "appeasement" now? And entitle us to disregard him? This was strongly implied in a recent article in the *New York Times Magazine,* "A Professor Votes *for* Mr. Johnson" by John P. Roche, and surely Mr. Roche does not stand alone. The Cold Warriors, self-styled and otherwise, all bank very heavily indeed on an historical analogy which they seldom expose to full view, that between the present and the thirties, and specifically between the present-day Communist powers and the Nazi-Fascist powers of a generation ago. To me it seems that these people are so determined to play Churchill that they would feel badly let down if the Soviets refused their assigned role as Hitler Germany. Yet wouldn't it make sense—from the Communist viewpoint—for the Soviets to do just that? Well, in that case some people are determined to play Churchill against an *imaginary* Hitler Germany.

The slur on Mr. Lippmann, and on those of us who read his comments on Vietnam with sympathy, falls to the ground if this pet analogy of the Cold

Warriors is not a good one. I think it is a mistake to wish an analogy upon an as yet unwritten page of history, to try, as it were, to force the future to resemble the past in order to prove a point, but in this case can one not go further and declare this particular analogy inept? The dynamics of Germany 1925–1945 and those of Russia 1945–1965 are not at all similar. The ideology and background of the two regimes are not at all similar, and the leadership is not at all similar. Nor is the relationship of the rest of the world *to* these two phenomena at all similar, for, to go no further, Hitler was congenial to many in the West precisely as a bulwark against Bolshevism. Professor Roche makes his comparison specific by equating Poland 1939 to Vietnam 1965. Unhappy similitude, if true, and one that makes me tremble at the thought of 1966! But how little true similarity exists! Among a dozen factors missing from the Vietnam situation is anti-Semitism. Many thought war against Hitler justified by the single aim of liberating the Jews. For all the anti-Semitism that has been unearthed in Russia, I know very few Jews who feel threatened by the Soviet Union as they had to by the Third Reich.

I think Professor Roche's other arguments can be answered too, but he is an expert, and had better be answered by experts: I confidently hand him over to those he has shrugged off with quips. What I have a vivid sense of, after reading this piece, is his style. A quotation will bring it to mind:

> Even our bombing pattern in the North has followed a careful etiquette of "controlled response": we have observed what Herman Kahn would call the "city threshold" and only went after a few of the S.A.M. missile launchers when they began to broaden their protective mission beyond Hanoi–Haiphong. We are, in short, fighting a carefully limited war in the effort to attain a perfectly reasonable objective. . . .

It must be pleasant to feel that such a thing as bombing can be neatly combined with perfect reasonableness, but some of us find this coolly babbling prose unconvincing, if not corrupt, and I think I for one shall start praying at night, God save me from Professor Roche's careful etiquette! Someone lives in a dream world, he or I; for I am one of those who cannot think of the American action in Vietnam otherwise than in terms of outrage.

It is true that history is one outrage after another, and that the Communists have perpetrated some gigantic outrages in their time, but is America to be excused her atrocities on the grounds that others commit them too? Is she even to lead the way in outrage now because others have led the way at some other date? Or, if it is a matter of evening up the score, wasn't a tremendous step toward that made at Hiroshima? And are not further steps taken almost monthly in the Deep South? . . . I miss in Professor Roche's exegesis the note of concern. If he does not understand my indignation, I do not understand his nonchalance.

I am not an absolute pacifist. That the problems of international relations will get solved by the peace movement as we know it seems to me even more unlikely than that they will get solved through the "normal channels" of governmental negotiation, and on Vietnam I support that eminent nonpacifist Charles de Gaulle in advocating, first, a cease fire and then a neutralization of South Vietnam. Is even de Gaulle considered a fellow traveler these days? Or an appeaser at least? He *is* considered an "impossible" fellow, but isn't this because he has let down the team, and made it much harder for them to represent a more reasonable position on Vietnam as appeasement and fellow-traveling? Let de Gaulle's motives be what they may, it is certainly true that he represents millions of people in the world today who, while firmly rejecting communism, reject American interventionism just as firmly. And there is this too to be said. De Gaulle, whatever else he may have done, has not changed. The traits of character that may be complained of in him today were there twenty-five years ago. And the independence of spirit which enabled him to do what he then did is operative again now. Does anyone really believe that Harold Wilson is more enthusiastic about the American role in Vietnam than de Gaulle? He is only much more easily overawed by superior power.

This is another discussion. Here I am concerned with the peace movement, which is united only in its opposition to American policy in Vietnam, and not in affirmation of any one remedy. Even from a nonpacifist viewpoint, the present peace movement may serve a good purpose. It takes all sorts to make—or remake—a world. It may even be that it is best for the intellectual to represent something other than the viewpoint that is, or even is going to be, dominant, and that one should ask how much he modifies the existing state of things, rather than what he would do if he were in power.

It seems likely that what most menaces the world today is neither communism nor imperialism as such, but the possession of so much power by so few men, be they "Communists" in Moscow or "imperialists" in Washington, especially since the official view of each side is that it has a monopoly of civic virtue. In this situation, the critical act, the intellectual's act, can have historic importance—whether it be Yevtushenko criticizing Soviet anti-Semitism or Robert Lowell refusing an invitation from Lyndon Johnson. In such ways is the claim to a monopoly of virtue challenged. Which in turn means the regime concerned will be that much less ready to *act* in the name of virtue. Such protests are against "the national interest" not only in encouraging the enemy abroad but also—which the Authorities are naturally not so apt to mention—in discouraging the trigger-happy friends of power at home. For the world's danger is what the *Dr. Strangelove* movie said it was. Not literally, of course. It was quite beside the point for the experts to refute Terry Southern *et al.* by solemn proof that the Bomb cannot be exploited by a single "kook" in the war department. The point was, rather, that our whole world is, in all too real a sense, crazy; anything is possible; and the worst really can happen.

In this situation the classic function of the intellectual—to be the voice of reason amid the clamor of the world's irrationality—attains a peculiar urgency. The intellectuals can hope, must hope, to discourage the generals and the politicians from blowing the world up in one of their fits of patriotic (or proletarian) virtue. *Discouragement* is of the essence, and it was good to note that Lowell *had* discouraged even the ebullient Texan who is our commander in chief. There is evidence that even the Soviet leaders cannot brush off their critical poets like so many flies. They aren't flies anyway, they are mosquitoes, and they sting. Behold, then, both these sets of crusaders, full of martial ardor and the spirit of '76 (or '17), and then look at the leaders of the intelligentsia not only refusing to cooperate, but treating the claims of the Ideal (or Real) as a phony—as a balloon to be pricked. The crusaders get discouraged. "Revolutionary defeatism" is Lenin's phrase, I believe, but we can now use it against some of his successors, as well as against czars and commissars nearer home.

Intellectuals of the world unite! In a degree, they have already done just that. Living behind the Iron Curtain, I was surprised to what an extent the intelligentsia there has the same gripes—and hopes—as ourselves. And they have to fight off the same facile accusation of disloyalty with the same entirely sincere answer: no, they don't wish to "defect" to the "other side," they wish to remake their side or, if that is not immediately practical, to restrain it from practicing what it preaches, to prevent it from having the courage of its professed convictions, to *dis-courage* it. To me, the universal presence of such *dis*couragement is profoundly *en*couraging. We seem to be approaching a point where the political leadership of the world, both worlds, may be disowned by the intellectual leadership.

Discouragement, deflation—this is the negative side. There is much negative work to do, and the talents of an intelligentsia, from a Terry Southern to a Dwight Macdonald, may be specially apt for this work, but the intention, naturally, is positive, and there is a corresponding body of positive labor before us. It is the work of active and contagious love. Here the pioneers have been Martin Luther King and Pope John XXIII. Whether or not one can envisage the world acting on the lines laid down in his encyclical *Pacem in Terris,* one can surely believe that the spirit the encyclical embodies might influence the world. If one cannot believe this, one's view of politics is *wholly* cynical. I for one had as soon merely give politics up as a hopeless mess. Not to give politics up in this way is to bear witness to a degree of faith in human possibility. But this faith intellectuals have to possess, if only to justify their own existence as the carriers of—intellect. This witness is precisely their duty.

So when I am asked if I think our students are entitled to protest, I must not limit my answer to a patronizing yes, but must go on to congratulate the younger generation on boldly bearing witness at a time when so many of their elders were pussyfooting around discussing *whether* witness should be borne. This is not to say all forms of protest are proper or even shrewd. Some are obviously idiotic; some feeble; some morally ambiguous; some morally wrong. The same could be said of the forms of nonprotest. But the discontent itself is more than justified, it is necessary. For aside from its political effects, it is helping, in an age of phony virtue and real murder, to keep alive both the body and the spirit.

(1965)

For the Continuation of Protest

There is a danger of loss of momentum. Indignation has a natural rhythm, it boils up and over and is gone. Protest movements cannot keep going indefinitely. It is sometimes amazing how quickly the life can go out of them, merely by a sudden switch of attention to something else. And one protest movement's gain is another's loss. The civil-rights movement has already lost momentum, because public interest switched to Vietnam. Will the indignation over Vietnam subside? There are many who hope so, and many who are willing to provide helpful distractions, new targets, real or illusory, for public concern. In a recent discussion Arthur Schlesinger, Jr.,* represented the Vietnam demonstrations as a nuisance. They hamper Senators like McGovern and Fulbright in doing what they are trying to do. Mr. Schlesinger wanted demonstrations limited to the civil-rights movement. Perhaps his comments matter little to us dissidents because, after all, Mr. Schlesinger is in general agreement with the policies of the Administration. But I've heard it said recently, even by those who are not, that the demonstrations and petitions are becoming dull and useless, a sort of bad habit, monotonous. Useless, of course, they have been, so long as the war continues. But finding them tiresome is to apply wrong criteria. They are not entertainments anyway, they are not subject to aesthetic standards. They are political

* When this "comment" appeared in *Playboy,* all criticism of Arthur Schlesinger was omitted on the insistence of the editors.

measures, and politics *is* tiresome, and worse than tiresome. I find in these arguments only a warning to us all not to be too easily discouraged. Was it to be expected that a war would stop because we have signed petitions, written articles, attended marches and meetings? Of course not. But that is no reason for assuming that such activities have no effect. The effect is cumulative, and the accumulation has to be gigantic: more and more signatures, articles, speeches, marches, meetings, until the protest is irresistible. On the possibility Mr. Schlesinger mentioned that such activities actually hamper real efforts at peace, what is the evidence for that? Only a certain *feeling* registered by Senator McGovern: he is embarrassed by all those poor relations misbehaving themselves at the gates, when inside his own domain he is asking for all the right things in a way believed to be more effective and certainly far more genteel. Even Senator Fulbright in recent days has felt compelled to speak somewhat disapprovingly of the protest movement in the form it takes in universities. Or rather he feels he can approve of it only as an alternative to panty raids. Surprising to what an extent public men these days have sex on their minds: Mr. Schlesinger, in the same discussion, said that the motive of the demonstrations was only to provide orgasms. But how is this any truer of the protest movements he disapproves of than of those he approves of? Surely people demonstrate for civil rights also to get their orgasms? People have been known to run for the Senate with such motives, even if only to discover later that they were impotent. And why does a man try to become President? Take Lyndon Johnson. He is a great admirer of the self-sacrifices of others. He shows no inclination to sacrifice his own life in Vietnam. He has always shown, on the contrary, that he knows how to take care of number one. . . . I am not *introducing* this kind of *argumentum ad hominem,* you understand, I'm only suggesting that it is a boomerang. All movements, on both sides of all social conflicts, contain people with motives that can be found fault with. Is that an argument against a particular side in a particular conflict? No.

Is it true that the present peace movement hampers the cause of peace? There is little reason to assume so. On the contrary, it would seem to me that, though Senators Fulbright and McGovern may be irritated by the pacifists, they are also influenced by them, spurred on by them. Senator Fulbright says that this country is succumbing to the arrogance of power. Now he cannot claim to find such an attitude in the peace movement. As he looks around, must he not be forced to say to himself: "Though a lot of people are succumbing to the arrogance of power, I do discern a few, besides myself and Senator McGovern, who are not succumbing to the arrogance of power, who indeed seem determined not to let this nation succumb to the arrogance of power." If in Washington there are doves as well as hawks, is it not fair to ask where the doves find any encouragement? Do they not draw their sustenance from the discontent which we say is "in the air"? Diffused discontent is indeed one of the salient features of the world we live in. McGeorge Bundy may choose to state that very *few* people disagree with him about Vietnam and may imply that these few are all in places like Harvard, which Mr. Bundy at this point doesn't overvalue. But if these people are so few, why does so cautious a public-relations man give them so much publicity? Why does he get them mentioned—mentioned yet again —in the *New York Times?* Why did President Johnson keep on mentioning Robert Lowell after a certain incident last summer (1965) in the social life at the White House? There are very few Robert Lowells. There are very few poets, and of them very few are invited to the White House. My point is, then, not that the importance of Robert Lowell was asserted by Robert Lowell but that it was taken for granted by Lyndon Baines Johnson. And by importance I mean political importance. I mean that—with all due credit to Mr. Lowell for the personal strength he showed—such protests don't get made when only one man feels that way, when only a few men feel that way. To take a more distressing example. Two young Americans have burned themselves to death on account of Mr. Johnson's war. Two is a very small number indeed. But those two young men were not lunatics. There can be disagreement on the moral and psychological content of their action, but all must agree that such deeds will only happen in a certain climate of opinion and feeling, under a particular historical pressure. The very fact that young Americans have not acted this way before should awaken curiosity even in those who feel no sympathy. . . . I am vastly understating the case in an effort to meet opponents halfway. I actually believe that the self-immolation of those boys bears witness to a perfectly enormous spiritual malaise, to a collective guilt comparable only to that of the Germans.

Of course the peace movement is too small. If it were not, there wouldn't be a war. We have to make it bigger. If we didn't intend to make it very much bigger, big enough to be successful, we might as well plead guilty to Mr. Schlesinger's criticisms and frankly abandon ourselves to orgasm hunting. At the same time, people like McGeorge Bundy have stressed the smallness of the protest for reasons of their own. It isn't as small as all that. Nor can we let it be assumed that everyone who hasn't yet stood up to be counted on our side can definitely and irrevocably be counted on Johnson's side. There are plenty of people who will not stand up and call themselves atheists who yet have no measurable belief in God. Around a small, aware protest movement of thousands, there may well exist a half-aware, half-protesting, certainly uneasy bloc of millions.

But it is important that people on our side concede one thing very clearheadedly. The labor movement in America is lost to radicalism, is lost to conscience itself. I don't say this is irrevocably so, and I don't speak of all workers taken individually. I speak of the movement as at present organized, as at present led. It has been bought off. It has been appeased by higher wages and government sanctioning of the right to strike for higher wages still.

Religion is no longer the opium of the people, but the popular diet is still opium. Today it is television that is the opium of the people, and not just television, but rather the whole Kitsch culture of which television is only the most ubiquitous part. I would like to add my voice to that of Professor Havemann of East Berlin, who made the point that the menace of capitalism must now be seen in new terms. We must see it, he urged, not in terms of poverty, or not *just* in terms of poverty, but in terms of the Kitsch culture with which it enchants and bewitches its still captive millions.

Our President would probably like to believe that, by means of TV, he can give the millions a positive enthusiasm for his war. This is a possibility, certainly, if by "enthusiasm" one understands the kind of self-righteous rage that results from having your relatives killed by those you can choose to believe are malignant enemies of all that is good. In other words, enthusiasm might possibly be generated, but only by getting GIs killed in far greater numbers than heretofore.

What our Kitsch culture has contributed up to now has not been enthusiasm but insensibility. Television is an anaesthetic for the national conscience. On the little screen, you can let anything roll by and just grunt. The Nazis must regret very deeply that they didn't have this instrument on hand in their day. I fancy they needn't then have kept the gas chambers a secret. The little screen would have made them acceptable. What's that we see there? Burning Jews? The things they think of! But, look, the commercial says the gas ovens help maintain free enterprise; anyhow, if you don't like that program, turn the knob.

Lyndon Johnson is the President, let's not forget, not only of America but of Kitsch culture, and the aim of his wars is to confer Kitsch culture upon other nations, maybe all other nations. Sometimes it looks as if the only people who have noticed this, or noticed it with any deep disapproval, are André Malraux and General de Gaulle.

But only sometimes. More often one is made aware that this is what the world calls the American Way of Life and that the world doesn't want it, thank you very much. At this point, our opponents will interject: well, how about the Communist Way of Life? Does the world want that? And can we wish it upon the world?

Let my rejoinder, since it has to be very brief, take this form: Why must we want the whole world dominated either by what is called the West (namely America) or by what is called the East (namely Russia and China)? And if it is gradually becoming dominated by one or the other, or partly by one, partly by the other, why do we have to aid and abet the process? Within both the Eastern and Western blocs there are movements for greater independence. Had Ho Chi Minh not been full of the spirit of such independence, he would already have called in far more help from Russia or China. To this spirit in Ho the United States owes the (very limited) success it has had in the war. But there is a similar spirit of independence in some parts of the West. I have already mentioned France. It is a big mistake to ascribe the French attitude to the willfulness of one man. Rather, one should note that in the recent elections all the larger groupings were equally anti-American. France is no more willing to be part of an American empire than Vietnam is willing to be part of a Russian or Chinese empire. Nationalism is still real, and the love of independence is still real, more so than any of the great powers feel in a position to acknowledge. Yet they fail to acknowledge it at their peril.

Well, here we all are at our read-ins, our protest meetings, our various gatherings of the class that is notoriously dissident in the United States today: a class that consists of students, teachers, scholars, writers, artists, dentists, doctors, lawyers. People call it the professional middle class, but it actually cuts across most of the class barriers and includes the greatly richer and the greatly poorer. We are being told to make little of ourselves. We are few and should get fewer. We are impractical and should remove ourselves even further from practice. We have our heads in the clouds and should take our torsos and limbs up there to join them.

That we should get this advice is quite in order. It would be stranger if we didn't. But let us not use our self-doubt, which can be one of our virtues, as a weapon that strikes down our other virtues. The practical people, the realists, have created the present situation in Vietnam. We couldn't have done any worse than that.

But there is a far more important point. Just because there has been a demoralization of the labor movement, and it is at present not possible to call on the labor movement for anything, a responsibility has devolved upon us. The very fact that we are sensitive to these issues gives us the obligation to act on them. Recognizing that modern civilization is, among other things, a device for the killing of consciences, we have the obligation to do what the conscience we still claim to have dictates.

And this, as I see it, is the issue in Vietnam: conscience vs. lack of conscience. Johnson and Rusk and their associates also claim to be acting in good conscience and for what their consciences dictate. But, as McNamara has put it, their opponents have assailed their credibility. That is correct. That is just what we do. We claim to be able to demonstrate that these men cannot be believed by a rational creature. Even when they are telling the truth, they cannot be believed, for reasons explained by Aesop in his fable of Wolf Wolf.

Have you and I never told lies? Is politics conceivable without lying? We have. It cannot. But at the same time, politics also requires a certain minimum of truth-telling or the WolfWolf situation appears. The saying that there is honor among thieves has the same significance: a degree of honor is *necessary* to thieves if they are to steal efficiently. Now these minimum demands on truth and honor have not been met by the United States Government in its handling of Vietnam (or Cuba, or Santo Domingo, or no doubt various other places). And this has become a thorny practical problem, since it accounts for the present alleged intransigence of North Vietnam. The Vietnamese suspect trickery in every proposal, because prudence tells them they *must* suspect trickery in every proposal. Our right-wing politicians run around asking if Communists can be trusted to keep to any treaty, anyway. They are too busy to notice that Communist politicians can give chapter and verse for believing that Americans can't be trusted to hold to any statement, in a treaty or otherwise.

Now the thing held against intellectuals by politicians, held against so-called liberals by so-called realists, is that the former are only interested in truth, rather than in getting things done. No doubt there are times when that is a limitation. But today unconcern about truth and the deliberate flouting of truth have become the problem. This is an age in which, when a Harvard intellectual goes to Washington, he learns to lie for the Cause. Now, if all intellectuals went to Washington to lie for the Cause, who would be left to interest himself in the truth? Today, the intellectual has a mission again because he has been left alone with the truth, left alone guarding the truth. I have said the struggle is between conscience and lack of conscience. Is that an oversimplification? Perhaps. But, in any case, the danger that confronts us in discussing Vietnam is not oversimplification but the opposite: overcomplication. When American policy there is defended on anything other than the level of Johnson's empty rhetoric, it is defended in supersubtle political terms. Experts are then cited, experts political and military. Many other countries are brought into the discussion. Skeptics are given to understand they don't know enough about Southeast Asia. A tough attitude is taken to all ideal values, and even to the matter of killing and wounding, because what we are talking about is the complications.

To the tough political and military arguments there are tough political and military answers, which have been offered by Senator Fulbright, by Walter Lippmann, and others. Yet these tough answers are not the real answer; they only constitute corroborative evidence. The protest movement is a spontaneous assertion of the conscience, based on the belief that the matter, at bottom, is complicated only if you choose to complicate it. *For* the Johnson policy in Vietnam there is an *argument,* just as there was an argument for dropping the atom bomb, for saturation bombing of Dresden, yes, even for removal of the Jews from Germany, and an *argument*—buttressed with statistics and with pleas for understanding of history and geography—is *all* there is for any of these policies. To assume that these arguments *have* to be answered is to fall into a trap. One may be glad they *are* answered, by Walter Lippmann or anyone else. But we are not against these people because of the argument. We are against them because we are outraged by them. We cannot support them; we cannot willingly acquiesce in them; we are compelled to oppose them. This is how it is with Auschwitz. This is how it is with Hiroshima. This is how it is with the bombing of Vietnam. Such things are *inexcusable*.

It is true that, unless we are absolute pacifists, we countenance killing anyway. But that does not prevent us from limiting rather strictly the occasions on which we countenance it. In the discussion I have referred to, Arthur Schlesinger said that, as to the use of arms, we had all sanctioned it against Hitler, why all the hullabaloo about Vietnam? He said he couldn't recall that people like us had had qualms of conscience back in the thirties and forties. He couldn't *recall* that we had; but we had. Even those who went out as volunteers to use arms for Spain had a great tussle with themselves before they did so. I belong to that generation and was not able to believe in the legitimacy of military action till 1942. Besides which, the kind of boys who went to Spain, if they returned today, would not volunteer for America. They would probably prefer the National Liberation Front. The Vietnamese are a people fighting for their existence; and Ho Chi Minh is fighting much more to keep out foreign interlopers, even those on his own side, than any of the governments in Saigon, which are all puppets of the United States.

Expediency can be allowed to go just so far. Surely there must be things one would not do in the interests, real or supposed, of any cause. Some killing might be regarded as legitimate if one is convinced it is in the interest of a truly worthy cause. Is the killing in Vietnam in the interests of Vietnam? Is it in the interests of the United States? Is it in the interests of some other states (I reject the phrase "the Free World")? Some think it is. But evidently it is not clearly established that it is, since many think it isn't. A Buddhist leader recently said that his country was oppressed by two forces, the Communists and the Americans. Europe—not to mention Asia—is full of people who cannot see any merit in the American policy. The number of Americans whose consciences are troubled is larger than McGeorge Bundy might care to admit. The people can be wrong, but the point remains that there is no consensus, the issue remains at best doubtful, and the question arises whether it is right to go on killing as if we were certain when we are at best doubtful, when the possibility exists that it is all a ghastly mistake, and the mild-mannered men of Johnson's cabinet may go down in history as no better than gangsters.

The overwhelming reasons needed to justify military action with today's military means are simply not on hand. And again I am understating my own view of the case to try and meet the opposition halfway. The actual truth, in my judgment, is that American methods in Vietnam are so outrageous that, like the methods of the Nazis, the conscience rejects them out of hand and without going into details. The Vietnamese people cannot be sacrificed in this way, even if one could believe they were being sacrificed in a good cause. The triumph of such a cause is uncertain anyway, while, meanwhile, America is committing certain murder on a gigantic scale and threatening to commit it on an even wider scale if she doesn't get her own way.

There is an old religious objection to that sort of thing which, to me, is still valid. It was to the effect that you are not allowed to help God that much. It argues a lack of faith in your God to think that your cause will perish if you don't insure its success by methods entailing so serious an infringement of God's laws. God doesn't need anyone's help so much that they have to commit outrages to insure His victory. In common-sense terms, if that's what our ideals require for their realization, let's not bother having them realized.

In the last analysis, since everything is possible in this huge, many-sided, and finally baffling universe, we who protest have to admit that our opponent may be right, and therefore that we may somewhere along the line have slipped. Suppose that there is something that may fairly be called the Free World, and suppose it really is important to defend it with arms against something that may fairly be called communism, and suppose that this defense, to be effective, has to be offensive.

I can suppose it. I can entertain the notion in my mind for moments, even minutes. But when I look around and see who represents this standpoint and what they do about it, I have no interest in helping. If people want to die in such a cause, they can. The fact should not concern us any more than that they also kill for it.

Who can look around the world of the mid-twentieth century and get the impression that its true meaning has been correctly grasped by Dean Rusk, Lyndon Johnson, and McGeorge Bundy, and not by Pope John XXIII, Martin Luther King, and Martin Buber?

The twentieth century is Auschwitz, and Hiroshima, and Vietnam. This our realists have done for us and will be delighted to do again in the name of the unusually high ideals which realists normally boast. But there is something else in the air. It is the third and most neglected of the three ideals of the French Revolution—fraternity. The "ecumenical spirit" would be the theological term. It is the thing not to have missed about our time, I feel, or one may well have missed everything. I am one of those who cannot believe that good is likely to result from all these experiments in crime and outrage that are supposed to preserve us from tyranny, etc., etc. If we have to bet on a course of action (and I suppose we do, and I suppose this is actually what commitment means), then I am betting against all that and would wish to put my small weight behind the contrary kind of attempt, the attempt to make fraternity—some degree of fraternity—real on this planet.

(1966)

How D'You Feel About Vietnam?

And now today here I come again, marching again at the
same old job—same old, brand-new job—marching again
with all free men. I am the ring of steel around Democracy; the ramparts that you sing about; I am the Citizen Soldier; the Nation in arms. I am the eyes of the cannon, the
marching refrain, the brain of the tank, the nerves of the
plane, the heart of the shell. I am the Liberty Bell; the salt of
our youth. I am the fighting man of every outpost from
Alaska to Hawaii to Korea and beyond; from Panama to
Puerto Rico to Greenland, and beyond. Whatever the need
—for the spirit of Liberty, for the future we're making—
I, the American soldier, am the ultimate weapon.
                    —*Army Information Digest,* September 1963

Mr. [Hubert H.] Humphrey said the war in Vietnam was
being waged to keep alive the hope of freedom in Southeast
Asia. The United States, he said, has a duty to keep "strong
men" from gaining power through aggression. "A new world
has come into being," he said, ". . . it is a world that renders
obsolete the old dogmas of world domination by the use of
force. . . . In Vietnam, now, the struggle is essentially a
struggle not between two doctrines . . . but, rather, a strug-

gle between those old values and these new values." Mr.
Humphrey brought the Legislature almost to a frenzy of applause by reciting portions of the pledge of allegiance to the
flag in a resounding voice.
—*New York Times,* April 25, 1967

"If we know where Charlie is, we can zap him easy," said a
Marine captain. . . . A certain casualness about killing is a
mark of military professionalism, for killing after all is a soldier's business . . . the professionalism of the magnificent
American Army in Vietnam seems to this reporter to mark
the end of the long era of American innocence, and the final
half-unaware acceptance by the United States of the agonizing
responsibilities of a great world power.
—Stewart Alsop, *Saturday Evening Post,*
January 14, 1967

There is a certain sloppiness about the current use of the expression "I feel
that . . ." in lieu of "I think that . . . ," yet abuses of language have their reasons, and the reason for this one is that feelings do underlie opinions. Though
truth itself is objective—a thing is true or untrue irrespective of what you or
I feel—assent is subjective, and only happens in affective situations that are
favorable. We have, as we say, to be receptive, and being receptive is a matter
of the mood of the moment, and, beyond that, of one's whole life history up to
the moment, the set of one's personality, the established flow of one's sympa-
thies and antipathies.

Aristotle has it that learning is a pleasure. The recognitions which constitute
learning are savored as they are imbibed, like other food and drink. I wonder if
the unusually gifted or receptive child is not really the one with the greatest capacity for enjoyment. In his autobiography Bertrand Russell mentions that his
discovery of Euclid as a child gave him an ecstatic pleasure such as men expect
to find in romantic love. Intellectuals who are mediocre, like Dr. Timothy
Leary, will want romantic love instead of Euclid and then will find the natural
supply of it so deficient that they resort to artificial aids. A man is what he
loves, says Meister Eckhart. Russell for a while *was* mathematics, as Dr. Leary *is*
drugs and verbal diarrhea.

Elementary arithmetic provides little spurts of pleasure, as the infant mind
receives the sensation of mastery: if it doesn't, then arithmetic is not learned.
Now, if feeling plays an integral part in learning at such an elementary level,
instead of being eliminated at the more advanced level it plays a progressively
greater part all the time, and the advanced student in any field is the supreme
hedonist; which is the basis for Bernard Shaw's remark to the effect that Isaac
Newton must have got a lot more fun out of life than Casanova. The Casanova
complex arises from acute lack of pleasure. When we suffer from lack of plea-

sure (yes, "we": it is something we all do) we go straight to sex in an effort to correct the situation. The current cults of sex stem from a failure of mind which is also a failure of feeling.

I am mentioning these things because we have so often been advised to look at the objective facts about Vietnam that we may well have omitted to look at the subjective facts about Vietnam. More correctly: among the objective facts are the subjective factors. People who look at the objective facts about Vietnam end up taking a stand about them. Now, however much they are backed up with reason and truth, stands are emotional. However much can be said for any cause by way of fact and by way of argument, it is still a question why we were so interested in the first place and why in the end we decided to invest so much emotion, so much of ourselves, in that cause. I come here to the subject of Commitment. To be committed is not to favor the idea of Commitment, it is to *make* commitments and stand by them. The test of the authenticity of a particular commitment is whether you would stake your life on it. To commit one's whole being takes courage, a moral quality that requires very substantial emotional backing. It is a matter of "feeling convinced." This feeling has to accumulate, has to attain a certain volume. It also has to have a certain density, so that it will stick, so that it will not blow away. To have the wish to be committed without having what it takes to be committed would be worse than not even having the wish, for in this case one is likely, when the moment comes, to let the cause down. No opinions have any value unless the state of one's feelings is what the situation requires.

What is the present state of our feelings? I have been asking around, and since my personal contacts are limited in number, I have reached out for further contacts through the printed word. Having subscribed to the *New York Times,* I pick up its Sunday *Magazine* and come across a great deal of evidence and a still greater deal of assertions. The *Magazine* has printed at least two pieces in the past year dealing with the state of mind and heart of that section of the community to which I belong—university people who are protesting against the war in Vietnam. One was by Russell Kirk and said that we are imprudent and should stick to the campus, where we should practice contemplation—I suppose, imprudently. The other was by Lewis Feuer and said that we are snobbish, self-destructive, compulsive, vain, unbalanced, nutty, and—last, not least—antidemocratic. It would be a fair conclusion from both articles that we are so inflamed with wrong notions that we are a danger to the community and should be locked up. Mr. Kirk would accept the American university itself as the penitentiary, while Mr. Feuer's worry is precisely that that is where we are: so he has left us, and is now content to defend this revolutionary Republic from the home of the United Empire Loyalists.

What is it about the state of *our* feelings that sets up such a crisis of feeling in Mr. Feuer? He presents us with a double image: of students carried away by what he calls generational revolt and of a faculty—our part of the faculty—carried away by such an arrogance of power as makes Lyndon Johnson seem as gentle as Jesus. If I am not amazed to find Mr. Feuer telling me I envy my pastors and masters, I am surprised to discover how long I have allegedly been doing it:

> Alienated Intellectuals . . . suffer from the ailment which has afflicted intellectuals since the time of Plato on: the sense that they have ideas but no power, the frustration arising from the feeling that though they regard themselves as an elite fit to rule, they have not always been recognized as such by society. It is an alienation stemming basically from an obstructed will to rule.

This is hardly history but as bad poetry it has a certain lurid power. We are seen as a class that has harbored its resentments for two and a half thousand years and is now cutting loose a bit. About time, I'd say; and I hope we get somewhere. But, to stay with the argument—or should I say the image?—Mr. Feuer is here representing our resentment as having no grounds worth mentioning other than our own nasty natures. "It is alienation stemming basically from an obstructed will to rule." I myself don't feel a will to rule but, even if I did, I couldn't consider this "obstructed will to rule" basic. Basic would be the thing that obstructed it—not myself but a system which obstructs *my* will to rule without obstructing Lyndon Johnson's will to rule.

As for Mr. Kirk, he thinks that only an exclamation mark can do justice to the notion that Staughton Lynd might take part in government, and yet he has no exclamation marks for those who do "take part in government" and who are slaughtering the Vietnamese people. But then this is a culture, isn't it, in which there would always be exclamation marks for Bluebeard, who on half a dozen nights killed his half dozen wives, but seldom for a President who sends out half a million men to burn, shoot, and bomb every night for a year? Mr. Kirk writes:

> In the politician, prudence is the chief virtue; but the ideologue, sheltered by academic tenure and campus immunities, demands we work instanter a radical reformation of man and society; and he knows not prudence. Fancy Dr. Staughton Lynd, or a professor of the Birchite persuasion, as Secretary of State!

Again, bad poetry instead of history. Prudence has always been a rarity among politicians; and men with a talent for ruling have all too often been the most imprudent of mortals. Not caution but *hubris* is the main tradition of the political leader as we have known him over the course of three war-ridden millennia, and, not to be too remote about this, what about the prudence of Harry S. Truman who ordered the dropping not only of one but of two atom bombs? What about the prudence of Robert Kennedy threatening the use of the atom bomb at the Berlin crisis of 1961? What about the prudence of John Kennedy and Lyndon Johnson in steadily increasing the number of Americans in Vietnam? What about the prudence of General Eisenhower who says the Vietnamese war must be won even if it takes atomic bombs to win it? How much more imprudent than all these has Staughton Lynd actually been? Well, he flew to Hanoi; and it is imprudent to fly by Chinese Airlines.

What do Mr. Feuer and Mr. Kirk feel? Mr. Feuer feels upstaged, and sadly reports that our part of the faculty is "charismatic." Students like us. Evidently they like him less; alas, poor Feuer. What Mr. Kirk feels is: uncomfortable, now that politics isn't left to the prudent, as in the days of Napoleon or Alexander the Great. In his prudent, surrealistic dreams we remind Mr. Kirk of the John Birch Society. (Revilo spelled backwards is Lynd.) Well, if the feelings of Mr. Feuer and Mr. Kirk prove, finally, rather insignificant, significant is: their lack of feeling. They can be as abusive as they like about *us*. Who cares? But where is their response to the world we did not make?

This is a point in my argument where the *obj*ective factors need mentioning, for our feelings are justified, if at all, as a response to them. The official view of the war in this country is this: There are two Vietnamese nations, and the northern one has invaded the southern one. This, like other invasions, was completely wrong in itself, and is doubly a menace because the invader is Communist. We are innocent and beneficent, and automatically go to the defense of all the invaded against all invaders. We do this with redoubled conviction, energy, and strength when the invader is Red. For we believe that communism has already reached the permissible limit, and we also are quite sure that we are the proper, if not the sole, judges of what is permissible. Wherever "world communism" reaches out one inch farther, we will push it back by whatever means is needed to do so, and however many people, Communist or otherwise, get killed in the process.

Such is the official view, and we of the opposition believe it to be a tissue of extremely dangerous falsehoods. This fact in itself explains the present state of our feelings to a considerable extent. What explains it fully is that we cannot really confront our opponent because he has surrounded himself with a barrage of lies. This we feel assured of because of the number of times we have caught him at it. Good faith is gone. We cannot engage in debate lest next week we are to be told that what Mr. Nixon or Mr. Schlesinger said this week was merely what he had had to say in the interests of national security and *of course* wasn't true. We live in fear of the lies that will be exposed tomorrow, of the illusions that are deceiving us today.

This situation gives our feelings that additional touch of vertigo which makes our opponents represent us as crazy. They have a point, as did the sage who said that, in this world, not to lose your head would be to have no head to lose.

But what about *them?* As between insanities, must we not prefer our own? If one had lived in the neighborhood of Auschwitz, one might very well have had morbid and inaccurate fantasies about what was going on inside, but how about the people who said nothing bad was going on inside at all? (Analogies can be misleading, but this one is not.)

However, let's not be defensive about the dissident responses—the angry feelings—that are to be observed in America today. It is only reasonable to expect some of them to be just as indefensible as the responses and nonresponses of the Establishment. And they are. Lenin himself spoke of one kind of communism as an infantile disorder; and at least one section of every social movement—by tradition, perhaps—always dedicates itself to sheer infantilism. Today this wing of the protest movement calls itself the Underground, and, in its subterranean posture, feels it is being radical when it is only being self-indulgent.

Allen Ginsberg went to Washington to present the case for drugs before a Congressional committee. On the same day, and presented on the same TV newscasts that evening, was an officer of the United States Army who confessed to the same committee that he had been killing people in Vietnam because he was under the influence of drugs. Now we all know that Allen Ginsberg has in mind the use of drugs in different circumstances and with different ends in view. Nonetheless, if he had had the political skill of an intelligent sixteen-year-old, he would have dropped his pert little plea for psychedelics, and addressed his national TV audience on the subject of Vietnam and the United States Army. Time spent arguing for Allen Ginsberg's right to take drugs would be more humanely, more intelligently spent today trying to save Vietnamese lives from American soldiers, all too many of whom *already have* their marijauana and even their LSD.

How bright was it to prepare a poster reading HO CHI MINH IS A VIRGIN for the April 15 (1967) march? Can the boy who painted those words on a sheet make real to himself, with or without the help of drugs, that, as he paints, Vietnamese families are being maimed and killed? We are accomplices in that crime in any case, but we become accomplices much more directly by giving aid and comfort to the enemy, the enemy in this instance being American press photographers.

It has been said that, in this country, Suburbia and Bohemia are adjacent. The Bohemians are only the rebels against the Suburbs, and ambivalent rebels at best, leading a rebellion not much more creative than the notorious fun and games of suburban life itself. East Village is Scarsdale on its night out. Such is the fantasy life of the upper middle class, and it is a crassly commercial thing. The money paid for the funny clothes seen in the East Village finds its way out to Westchester millionaires holding stock in the garment industry. The Underground is financed from Barney Rosset's mansion, well above ground in East Hampton.

If the hippies didn't exist, they would be invented by men who live in Mamaroneck and work on Madison Avenue. They do exist, but are the sons of bishops and college presidents. One must not, of course, make them victims of the genetic fallacy: their origin would not matter if they had really pulled clear of it. But not only do they still live on the bishops' money, they haven't even given up God. Their allegiance is with society as it is, and the most conservative American is not Barry Goldwater but Andy Warhol. Mr. Warhol told the press that New York City is perfect as it stands; and one realizes that, for his purposes, it is. If one's purpose is not to taste the delights of Babylon but to free Israel *from* Babylon, why, then, one might make Barry Goldwater a present of Andy Warhol, however surprising each might find the mores of the other.

The pleasure-lovers will obviously be the first to leave the peace movement if being in it ceases to be a pleasure—if, that is to say, the war takes a heavier toll and large sections of the public come to feel (feelings, again!) a far greater bitterness against those of us who "prolong the war by giving aid and comfort to the enemy." Fair-weather friends are even less welcome than usual in territory where the weather is seldom fair.

There is a yet deeper objection to the Underground—to the extent that it professes any interest in helping to end a war. Its gaiety is the desperate kind, and at this point in time—spring 1967—the peace movement can only say of despair: "That's all we need."

For indeed the whole movement is threatened by despair just because, for all, and not just for the hippies, the protests have been enjoyable (refreshing, amusing, inspiring) but have been a failure. "Nothing to be done," as the clowns in *Waiting for Godot* put it, a phrase to be translated into American by: "Leave it to Lyndon." Before the mind's eye flashes the image of the Gadarene swine rushing down a steep place into the sea.

The present state of our feelings? "I feel I should be in jail," a friend of mine told me the other day. I see his point, (as I saw the point of Norman Morrison, who burned himself to death) and sense the depth of his concern. Even if certain such actions had not some higher and, as it were, sacramental value, there is something to be said, even politically, for more drastic acts of civil disobedience by those who are capable of them.

Individually, each of us must do what he must do, and probably jail will come, before long, to more of us than actually seek it. At the same time, I must record the impression—sticking to the theme of our feelings—that it is out of mere *exasperation* that many of my friends and colleagues are spending their time devising more and more drastic gestures. Having failed to win the many, the few are offering to do ANYTHING that might attract attention, and so to make immediate and very heavy sacrifices, even the supreme one.

Now I have conceded in advance that commitment is commitment to the death. This surely gives me all the more right to ask whether, today, exasperation is not driving us to make the big sacrifices when they are not called for and might not prove worthwhile. (Like the sacrifices of GIs in Vietnam—irony indeed.) My friend's guilt feelings are propelling him toward jail, but I happen to think that this particular man is more of a threat to Lyndon Johnson when he is at large. For our sake, as well as his own, I don't want him in jail. I don't want him to proceed right now from our mild parading protests to the ultimate protest of incarceration or death. I want him to take the tamer but shrewder step from protest to politics.

My statement on the hippies—namely that they are the middle class in fancy dress—wouldn't have to stop with the reflection that they aren't a big help on a peace march. It could go on to the further conclusion that we need to win for the peace movement a sizable part of middle-class America, hippies included. The East Village is not to be given up for lost because, for that matter, Scarsdale itself is not to be given up for lost. Bombs fall on hippies and squares alike.

One can assume that millions of Americans support the war. One can assume this for many reasons, not least because wars always get a lot of support, but perhaps mainly because, well, I'd be for the war myself if the only information I'd had about it was the information which most of our countrymen have had about it, the information presented on TV and in most newspapers and magazines, for in that case, I would quite sincerely believe in the official view as stated above.

On the other hand, this war commands *less* support than other wars have. In one class of the community—the professional class—it is not even unusual to be against it. A large section of this war's most immediate targets—students, aged seventeen to twenty-five—are dead against it. Nor, I think, can it be said that during the years 1964–1965–1966–1967, the opposition has shrunk, or that the feeling of malaise has been reduced. In many contexts, we have to regret that guilt feelings spread like a stain, but in this context we may live to be glad they did. Right now they *are* spreading, under the impact, in the first instance, of terrible news from the battle front but also from a dozen lesser sources, such as the opinion of average citizens in other countries, not to mention the influence of outstanding individuals from U Thant to Martin Luther King. (One should not omit from this list individuals whose dissent is timid, at any rate not if they wear a triple crown.)

All this being so, it is premature to assume that "public opinion" cannot be influenced. However, it is influenced *adversely* by too close an identification of the peace movement with radicalism. Some of us are, in one sense or another, radicals, but what we should be proposing today, in my view, is the formation of a broad front with nonradicals for the performance of a single task: the stopping of a war. Those who find themselves compromised by such a collaboration need not be discouraged. They can all return to quarreling as usual the moment peace is signed.

I know the arguments against this, and I don't suggest that one should put all one's eggs in any particular nonradical basket, certainly not Robert Kennedy's, and not even William Fulbright's. The latter said on April 27, 1967: "In the final analysis, I will support our country right or wrong," and thus served notice ·hat he will withdraw his opposition any time the heat is on. This is a very weak position, since the whole tendency of American foreign policy is to provoke the Socialist Bloc into some giant act of war which will shock everyone from the hippies in San Francisco to the doves in Washington into acceptance of war. And so a person in my position must feel that, in the long run, he can't trust Fulbright. Still, in the short run, he can collaborate with him, and Mr. Fulbright can collaborate with people he considers a little nutty, like us. To refuse to do this, and call, as some of our speakers are doing, for a "break with the reactionary part of the peace movement" is to resign oneself to failure, and therefore is no less self-indulgent than psychedelic antics.

There is only one job right now—to end a war—for none of the other jobs can get done till this one has got done. The criterion for each action is whether it contributes or not. That is why to say hippie or square, reactionary or radical, may not—at a given juncture—be pertinent, and why things describable by any of these labels may all be useful.

Feeling is running high in the country, and it runs even higher among the peacemakers than among the warmakers because *for* this war there is only an argument, whereas *against* it there is a sense of moral outrage. We are therefore so little apologetic for our "emotionalism" that we can at best only pity those who are *not* outraged; and if our feelings present a problem it is not that they blind us to truth but that, at times, they run away with us. At these times some of us (not just the hippies) are self-indulgent and happy-drugged, while others of us (not just the jailbirds) achieve an almost catatonic despair. Either way this is to leave the world to Bobby Kennedy or such another to set right, and he is not going to make it. Our sense of cussedness, our sense of humor, if nothing else, bids us espouse what the objective situation might not seem to sanction: hope. Hope is mandatory. And we feel hopeful.

Finally: we are We. The first person plural, banned from the grammar of politics by Stalin and McCarthy, is back again. "Our" particular first person plural. It, too, represents a feeling—the feeling of fraternity.

(1967)

The Night Is Dark and
I Am Far from Home

For Conor Cruise O'Brien

The word "alienation" has been used in a variety of ways. What I have in mind is the feeling that many of us have of not belonging to the American Way of Life. The American Way of Life is written with initial capitals or within quotes—that is to say, we dissociate ourselves from it even as we mention it. It has *alienated* us, made us *enemy aliens*. All our actions are *Un-American Activities* and have to be looked into by committees and punished by literal or figurative jail sentences, deportation, exile, death. We are the disaffiliated, the disenfranchised. We are public enemies, foreigners, refugees, displaced persons, outlaws . . .

The opposite of being alien is being native, indigenous, fulfilled, in harmony with one's surroundings, at home. The environment makes one welcome, and one gratefully repays it with respect, praise, loyalty. Such is patriotism in a healthy situation. It is not an opinion, it is a formed attitude to a fact, the fact of belonging.

If the opposite of being alien is to belong, belonging may be active or passive. The passive belonger acquiesces in, approves, applauds, what the active belonger does. The active belonger plants the flag on the conquered territory; the passive belonger salutes it and him. In modern times, the lower middle class as a whole has delighted in the passive role. And modern society has therefore aimed at giving the working class a lower-middle-class mentality.

Active belonging means belonging to what nowadays is called the power elite, the Establishment. Such belonging doesn't necessarily *look* active. It is the privilege of the rich to be passive personally while *operating* actively through their wealth. Because it dominates, they can exercise domination. But without lifting a finger. Listless aristocrats are no longer the persons the society most respects. Society prefers people who not only do dominate but look and sound as if they do, like Hitler. This is a doubly active form of belonging. It is in this perspective that we should see the modern preference of the social climber to the born gentleman. The latter is still something; the climber is more. From the log cabin to the White House. From the Austrian village to mastery of the world. That is the strongest modern image, the archetype of archetypes.

What is really shocking about Norman Podhoretz's book *Making It* is that the author, if we take him seriously, believes this archetype to be irresistible and is telling us that those who might claim to find it resistible are hypocrites. In the light of this "insight," the alienated are only those who failed to "make it," and all their plaints are cries of "sour grapes."

There is another aspect to the Podhoretz case: the Jewish aspect. Until Podhoretz, so to speak, young Jews had all had the option of either trying to "make it" or of renting a cold-water flat and belonging to the intelligentsia. Podhoretz claims to be making the revelation that the stairs of the cold-water flat lead ultimately to Westchester. The Jewish intelligentsia is the WASP Establishment's loyal opposition. The Jewish Mafia can even be Dean Rusk's bodyguard. Chosen some time ago by Jehovah, the Chosen Race has now "made it" with Lyndon Johnson. The model from now on won't be Maimonides or Spinoza, Heine, Marx, or Freud. It will be Arthur Goldberg.

What is the strategy of *Making It?* On the face of things, it is to force an admission from the reader—*"vous! hypocrite lecteur, mon semblable, mon frère"*—that he himself is no better but either enjoys making it or envies those who do. The name for the philosophy behind this is cynicism. Cynicism, however, is always either ironical or uncertain of itself, and Norman Podhoretz either meant just the opposite of what he pretended to say or he is *not sure* whether he meant what he pretended to mean. If he is not sure, his uncertainty could contain the mute appeal: "Show me I don't really mean it," as when a man says; "I'm in despair. Isn't this weak of me?" in the hope of making someone retort; "Oh no, you're not, you're very brave."

I tend to think that Norman Podhoretz is trying to convince us he has overcome alienation. On the face of it, the evidence is overwhelming. He gets phone calls from the White House and so forth. But alienation and integration are not synonyms for failure and success, or for opposition and conformism. The words represent a state of being which the outer circumstances may conceal.

Sometimes one wonders if our present society is one which even the people it rewards most extravagantly can be at home with. James V. Forrestal committed suicide at precisely the time when the scope of the present military-industrial complex defined itself. There is a sense in which Dorothy Day is at home in this world and Lyndon Johnson is a frantically maladjusted intruder. But these are paradoxes which, when unraveled, only confuse one's original understanding of what the words mean. It is by a professional alienation from society as it is —its conditions and its ideology—that a saintly person can sometimes find a real home in holiness. In such instances—Buddha and Saint Francis are others—the rejection of society is quite overt. The fine clothes are stripped off and the saint moves from the city, which society made, to the fields, which society didn't make. The comrades sought after by such figures—Jesus is another example—are society's rejects. The New Testament is very clear about this. "Give all you have to the poor and follow me," says Jesus to the rich young ruler. This is not the establishment of a new society. This is the rejection of all society. Those whom society has *not* rejected must themselves do the rejecting, says Jesus. To those who reject the kingdoms of this world he offers his kingdom, which is not of this world. To those who leave home he offers a home from home.

What Jesus offered the poor in spirit has an analogue in what, at a much later date, the romantic poets offered the impoverished imagination. William Wordsworth is a Saint Francis of poetry, finding in a oneness with the countryside and country folk the communion which society proper denied him. The Lake District, in those days before tourists, superhighways, buses, and planes, could be a home.

It was the habit of many radicals a generation ago to scoff at these religious and poetical conquests of alienation. A wiser radicalism will not feel any need to do so, will, in fact, need *not* to do so, because saints and poets were not running away from the home that is what radicalism has in view but (a) were finding it where it could be found and (b) were at the same time defining it for any who might later find it elsewhere. They are not to be seen as enemies of the future. That they befriended a certain aspect of the past—peasant culture or whatever—only makes them enemies, like ourselves, of the present.

When Marx said religion was the opium of the people, it was; but this religion had nothing in common with that of a Saint Francis. Literature and the arts also function mainly as drugs, but that is because most art is bad art, as most religion is bad religion. Even good art and good religion can be badly used.

I am saying that alienation is overcome by a Saint Francis or a Wordsworth. The limitation of this conquest is obvious: it is only a personal one, a solution for *them* and perhaps a small circle of intimates. The new home provided by religion or poetry is a "home from home." The original nonhome—the city, the civilization, the communal entity, polis or nation or whatnot—is unaffected. Today we are not content to think that a saint or a poet can construct a little home-from-home for himself. We like to think that our civilization itself can become a home, not just for an Establishment but for a people, and not just for one people but for all.

Since nothing like this has ever been achieved in all history, it is a vision of remarkable audacity. We need look no further afield than the streets of the city where these words were written—New York—for the evidence that civilization is still the direct opposite of a home for men. The other evening, seeing a film on TV, my son heard one of the characters say people could learn to live by giving instead of grabbing. His comment was that this must be an old film, since today people wouldn't have that much faith in goodness. My son is eight years old. His environment—protected, comfortable, middle-class—has already demonstrated to his satisfaction that the United States is not a home for man. If and when I let him see the daily exploits of American military power on the seven-o'clock news, he will find out just how right he was.

We cry peace when there is no peace. We cry brotherhood and drop atomic bombs. Is it, then, an error, a giant absurdity, that in a time of unprecedented violence we envision an unprecedented fraternity? If the violence has the last word, it *will* have been an error and an absurdity, though there may be no one left to see the joke. However, those of us who are rash enough to make the affirmation are not at all disposed to minimize the threat to it. That the possibilities have been polarized seems to us in the nature of the case. This may be hard for the imagination to grasp but that's the imagination's problem. As in the Garden of Eden—after the fall—possibilities for good are also, and equally, possibilities for evil. If the goodness we envision is on the grand scale, so the disaster, if it comes, will be colossal.

Yes, to think of this subject is to think of both Eden and Armageddon, Creation and Doomsday. And of course the two sets of forces—those of birth and those of death—are not separate. They encounter each other all the time. There is a relationship between them, the relationship between violence and transformation. What *is* this relationship? From the Marxist tradition we have received images such as violence is the midwife of social change. That is not misleading. Conventional liberals are shocked by it, particularly if anyone proceeds to act as if it were valid, yet American history affords examples both in its Revolution and its Civil War. Let me cite a more recent fragment of evidence. I paid a call on a local Congressman. He seemed to be against the war in Vietnam, and I wanted to know if he would do something about it in Congress. Instead he lectured me on the restraints placed upon action by the two-party system. Very little could ever be done, he stressed: one must simply learn not to expect much. Then he added: except in a time of social chaos. Then he added: and of course we may be headed for just such a time.

I was tempted to say at once, *"Well, I can only hope so."* It was the one chance he offered me. Revolt. Black power. Rioting. If we would prove to him that things had gone so far, he would go down to Washington and say, "In *these* circumstances, yes, I can ask for withdrawal from Vietnam." In this manner the program of Rap Brown and Stokely Carmichael is conjured up and, in a sense, even justified by the hedging, "square" white middle class. . . .

Violence is the midwife of social change. Not the only midwife of social change; but the choice lies first and foremost with those who resist change. The Bastille fell in 1789 largely without violence. That was because there were no guns to defend it. The French monarchy did *not* fall without violence. That is because it was defended with guns.

The wars that stand between us and the goal—making a home for man —are not to be seen as roadblocks only: they may prove to be the road to the goal. The logic of Che Guevara and Régis Debray is not farfetched. "Since the battle is the road to the goal, make sure you win it." Dean Rusk and Lyndon Johnson should have no quarrel with that logic since they propose to do likewise—fighting, of course, on the other side. Yet the fact that *they* killed Che, and that he didn't kill *them,* forces us to reconsider the entire logic. Guns do not win all struggles, and this is lucky for us, since, in many struggles, our enemies have all the guns.

Certain it is that the struggles—both those with guns and the others— will decide whether the goal modern humanity has set itself will ever be reached. These struggles will decide if our alienation will be overcome, if the planet can be a home for man and not just for the imagination of individual saints and poets. War will have to be abolished. The nation state will have to be abolished. Capitalism will have to be abolished. The road is long in struggle and suffering. It may not be long in years. Many now living might live on to see the Day if they live out their three score and ten, but how many of them will?

We can expect to live out the days that remain to us in alienation. That is why we are justified in looking the phenomenon in the face. We can hardly glory in it, but we can come to terms with it. What are its dangers and possibilities?

The dangers stem from misjudged self-congratulation, from forgetting that alienation is a misfortune. To make a parade of being alienated is like making a parade of a wooden leg. It also confuses alienation with mere opposition and presupposes that all members of the Establishment are not alienated, whereas in fact the Establishment draws constantly on alienated intellectuals of a certain type and plays their alienation for all it is worth. (Many alienated intellectuals, myself for instance, were invited to John F. Kennedy's Inaugural.)

The thought of self-congratulation among the alienated brings to mind the hippies. I don't want to join in the current joking against the hippies. They are a more admirable group of Americans than will be found in the country clubs or in the conventions this summer of the Republican and Democratic parties. The trouble is that they are *children* of the country club and of the Republican and Democratic parties. My complaint against them is not that they are too alienated but that they are not alienated enough. It is only when rebellion is incomplete that it runs to so much external display. A real rebel, like A. J. Muste or Dave Dellinger, is willing to wear the uniform of the bourgeoisie, like any labor leader.

One should not limit this kind of criticism to hippies. The wish to look like a rebel is commoner than the wish to be one. This supposedly individualistic country has always, as Stendhal and Tocqueville noted long ago, lived under the tyranny of public opinion. As much as Germans, Americans like, above all else, to run with the pack. If they leave the Established pack, they run with the Alienated pack. Their uniform clothes—in either case—mean too much to them, like their uniform hair styles, modes of speech, and so on. One danger of alienation is that it brings the dangers of nonalienation with it. Many people don't tackle the problem of alienation at all but think merely in terms of staying in or dropping out. At a recent peace meeting which I attended in Town Hall, one speaker got a round of applause immediately after he said he was a college dropout—before he explained why he dropped out or what he did with his freedom from education. That applause indicates a prejudice in favor of something entirely negative and without content.

To the hippies, as I've said, it is not easy to be fair. Lecture audiences, I find, begin to titter as soon as hippies are mentioned. Also, they are not a compact group. The views of the various persons called hippie are neither identical nor unchanging. Sometimes there are changes toward an attitude I can recognize as more satisfactory—in which case hippieism may have been a necessary stage along life's way, but among many who are called hippies there is a dangerous degree of passivity. This shows itself in their profession of the religious virtue of humility, as well as in their code of Live and Let Live. These high principles can be the mask of mere noninterventionism and indifference.

In relation to the war, it has been always to be asked how many of those who are against it today will drop their opposition when the heat is on, when American casualties are really heavy, when the government feels it has to have National Unity, sky-high morale, etc. Some hippies like to say there would be no wars if everyone was a hippie, a remark which shows too easy a disregard for intelligence. And indeed another common fault of hippies is that they are anti-intellectual or even unintelligent in principle. There would be no wars if everyone was a Quaker; or even if everyone was a sheep; so what? Everyone isn't; war is; and war has so strong a personality—has so much, as we say, "going for it"—that it will drag us all along in its iron chariot unless our opposition is *much tougher than this*. Today religion is not always opium for the people.

Religiously inspired individuals stand at the head of the peace movement. But religion can too easily be the opium of the hippies; just as opium—and other drugs—can be their religion.

This last comment is not a passing quip. The drug-addicted subculture makes up one large constituency of the Alienated. Without pursuing the experiments oneself, one can grant what is claimed for drugs by the experimenters—that they do something which, by vague metaphor at least, can be called expansion of consciousness. This fact has suggestive value. It suggests what pleasures may be awaiting us on the other side of alienation. But drug experience is not the only experience that does this. Bernard Shaw wrote of plain, undrugged sexual intercourse, "I liked sexual intercourse because of its amazing power of producing a celestial flood of emotion and exultation of existence which, however momentary, gave me a sample of what one day may be the normal state of being for mankind in intellectual ecstasy."

One day. When this earth is a home for man. Meanwhile it is the fate of such experiences to be occasional, momentary, unpredicted, casual, or accidental. I would not be taken as expressing merely Puritanic disapproval of drug culture or the other sexual explorations of today—though Puritanism has its point —but rather, while admitting that such pleasures might one day proceed naturally from the life the community is leading, as warning anyone who needs it that their social function now is almost inevitably going to prove escapist.

Art was defined in the nineteenth century as "the quickest way out of Manchester," and drugs in the twentieth are the quickest way out of Manhattan. To wish to get out of Manhattan is natural enough, but if we are addressing ourselves to the question of a home for man, our task is to remake the places where men are, not to leave them.

"To get out of Manhattan." Gauguin's Tahiti no longer beckons, and the Virgin Islands are full of the Manhattan rich. There is no escape except into fantasy. That is the solid material base of drug subculture, and that is also what is wrong with it.

The wrongness is evident in more ways than one. What starts out as the exploration of an alienated *avant-garde* can easily end up identical with the masturbation fantasies of the business executive and his staff. Andy Warhol's movies are an instance. The *avant-garde* here makes itself the source of supply for the stag movies in Scarsdale and Greenwich, and what was a flight *from* the Establishment becomes a headlong rush back *into* the Establishment—and provides a flight—or should I say a trip?—for the Establishment. I have already cited Andy Warhol's statement that New York City under Lindsay was perfect. Which is to say that Warhol denies the very existence of alienation: to him New York is already a home for man. Such is the decadence of one section of our intelligentsia. I offer it as a sample of the refuse that any revolution would have to sweep into the garbage can.

Just as the *im*perfections of New York City have to be seen with a cold, clear eye, so alienation—if it is to have possibilities—must be seen as the unhappy state that it is. And even when possibilities open up, we need to be constantly aware of the hazards. The Alienated have their hysterias. Their detachment lends itself all too easily to every sort of irresponsibility, and to sudden changes of direction especially capitulations and betrayals. Cut loose from their moorings, the Alienated have the freedom, excessive, dangerous, and pointless, of a boat adrift; which is no freedom at all since such a vessel's course is determined by the winds and waves. It is very important that Alienated man not mistake himself for Liberated man. (Classical instance: Ibsen's Gregers Werle.)

On the other hand, if Alienated man does not see himself as moving *toward* liberation, his alienation has dangers but no positive possibilities. Are there such possibilities, and if so what are they?

We should undoubtedly not be discussing alienation, here in New York in 1968, had it not been discussed by the young Karl Marx in his *Economic-Philosophic Manuscript 5*, written in 1844, published in 1932, and it is Marx and Engels who present a clear case for regarding the negative phenomenon of alienation as fraught with positive possibilities. Indeed, in their exposition, it is from the very negativity that the possibilities arise. I quote from Engels' *Housing Question:*

> In order to create the modern revolutionary class of the proletariat it was absolutely necessary to cut the umbilical cord which still bound the worker of the past to the land. The handweaver who had his little house, garden, and field, along with his loom, was a quiet, contented man "in godliness and respectability" despite all misery and despite all political pressure; he doffed his cap to the rich, to the priests, and to the officials of the state; and inwardly was altogether a slave. It is precisely modern large-scale industry which has turned the worker, formerly chained to the land, into a completely propertyless proletarian, liberated from all traditional fetters and free as a bird; it is precisely this economic revolution which has created the sole conditions under which the exploitation of the working class in its final form, the capitalist modes of production, can be overthrown.

I am reading from the translation published in Moscow, and it contains an error which shows that even the Moscow translator was confused by Engels' dialectic. The worker is *not* free as a bird, *at home* with nature. He is free, at best, as a Robin Hood *exiled* in nature, and this is what Engels said. The mistranslated word is *"vogelfrei,"* which looks as if it means "free as a bird," but actually can mean proscribed, banned, banished, outlawed. Such a passage provides the basic reason why Marxism placed its hope of revolution in the proletariat. The reason was not a liberal and sentimental admiration for the moral character of workers, though Engels at times, like subsequent Marxists, does show such admiration.

The reason lay, not in the workers' characters, but in their historical situation. Being stripped bare by the bourgeoisie, they did not even wear the *spiritual* clothing of that class and its civilization. They were without prejudice, and so could see the world as it was. They were without property, and so had no inducement to be defensive. Passivity offered only continued and increasing oppression. "You have nothing to lose but your chains and a world to win:" the *Communist Manifesto* states the objective side definitively. There is a subjective side. Whether or not the world was won, revolt gave a positive meaning to existences become wholly negative, made men out of things, offered a foretaste of community and home to the dispossessed, homeless, slumdweller.

Now George Meany's well-heeled following does not resemble the forlorn proletariat described in Engels' *Condition of the Working Class in 1844* or the first volume of Marx's *Capital*. Instead, it supports colonialism and war.* From being the great hope for revolution, through its character as a disaffiliated group, the working class in America has effected a merger with the lower middle class and become what principally makes for cohesion within the established social system. This more than any other single factor is what has enabled the ruling group in the United States to follow its interests as it saw them with a minimum of interference. It did not need to suppress the traditional freedom of dissent. There *was* no dissent of the kind that gave trouble, though of course it's always nice to have around the kind of dissenting chatter that makes no difference.

In the light of these facts, it is interesting to look back on the history of American radicalism in our time. In the thirties there was much militancy. It was the era of the Depression and the New Deal, but World War II brought national unity, which meant that the left was lost, like a drop in a bucket. An attempt was made to revive it in 1947–1948, but there were at least two strongly countervailing factors: first, the compromising of the Socialist movement all over the world by Joseph Stalin, which could no longer be passed over as it had been in the thirties; second, the launching of a counteroffensive in the United States by the House Un-American Activities Committee and other such bodies, including a subcommittee headed by the other Joseph, Joseph McCarthy. When the left was not disenchanted and discouraged by one Joseph, it was intimidated and discouraged by the other. Even in the sixties one often stumbled on further evidence of the vast power of both Josephs, in large and small things. I know many who will not join in any of the current antiwar activity even though they agree with it. They have been so hurt by McCarthyism they can never again "do anything of that kind." McCarthyism works; and if you are twenty years old now, you should ask yourself whether you can withstand all future attempts to cripple the radical in you.

* By about fifty-six per cent to forty-four per cent, however, not six hundred to one, as Mr. Meany would have us believe. *New York Times,* February 18, 1968.

Had the trend of the late forties and early fifties continued, by 1960 the American people would have been handed over, bound hand and foot, to what is variously called the military-industrial complex, the power elite, the Establishment. This Grand Design was in the cards, and very influential people worked hard to achieve it. Hard and subtly, for it could all have been done without recourse to the un-American style of Adolf Hitler. There would have been no little black mustaches. No straight-arm salutes. No swastikas. Possibly no anti-Semitism. It could probably all have been done within the proprieties. Without an extension of censorship. With the press free in the sense in which it is free now. And all around, the *dolce vita* of the affluent society: on the money you make off wars in the Pacific you can take your cruises in the Mediterranean. Such is the American dream, new style, and the dream is to impose it on everyone else under the name *Pax Americana.* Between United States power and the realization of this dream abroad stands the military might of her official enemies among the Great Powers and the determination of the guerrillas and the NLFs. But what stands between United States power and the realization of that dream here in the United States? Neither of the political parties, not even the dissident groups within them. No leaders of organized labor. The possibilities narrow themselves down to two groups: Negroes and a section of the largely white professional classes, and, of course, these are the people that come closest to Marx and Engels' description of the Alienated, even though they aren't all proletarian or even poor.

It is possible that United States power can be contained by China and the Soviet Union, especially if other countries follow the lead of France in withholding support. It is possible that the United States can be defeated by the guerrillas in Vietnam and in all countries the United States Army intrudes upon. Another possibility is that it cannot. If there is still a group of "Great Powers," America is really the single Superpower, and if the others cannot unite, they may simply be unable to hold America off.

If this should prove to be the case, then the hope of the world rests with the dissidents in America itself, and only Americans will be able to save the world from America. If this *may* be so, it becomes our job to provide for the possibility that it *is* so. From which much else follows. Leaving America would not seem a good idea until it becomes clear that the dissidents here are totally blocked. Which is not so now. Even United States power has not abrogated laws of human dialectics. Things still work both ways. That freedom of speech which may be conceded by the ruling group as a luxury-they-can-afford can also be exploited by a nonruling group to the point where it is something different. It is up to the latter to *make use* of such freedoms *against* the powers that concede them.

How was it that the Grand Design of the McCarthy era went wrong? Why wasn't every section of the nation "included in"? Here blacks are a topic to themselves. I will only remark in passing that the Grand Design would have encompassed them too, had *all* Negro leaders praised Freedom House and LBJ, had all the rank and file shown nothing but an interest in joining the white middle class. It is in this perspective that Black Power shows a plus, not a minus, sign.

But because I am a white writer, artist, scholar, teacher, talking chiefly to other white writers, artists, scholars, teachers, it behooves me to speak more especially of *our* part in things. This would be a point, too, at which to speak of the hippies in a more friendly fashion. Insofar as they are well-heeled boys and girls who, at some cost to themselves, and with difficulty, reject the Westchester way of life, the Greenwich, Connecticut, way of life, all honor to them. What they are doing at least proves that the Great American Way doesn't work. The affluent society would like to abolish conflict. Success and money provide gracious living in the suburbs and exurbs, and there's your brave new world. What else is the aim of it all? What else is being defended against greedy yellow Communists? What other happiness has life to offer? This is the thesis anyway; the antithesis has been told to get lost.

Only, true to the logic of human nature and human history, it refuses. The sons and daughters of suburban high living rebel. Quit. Drop out. They *feel alien;* and they move to *alien* ground. This moving does no good, but without it—without what is implied in it—no good could be done.

Something happened around 1960 for which the world may someday be grateful. It was a reversal of a main trend. I have represented it as happening according to dialectical law: trends develop their own contradictions, and friends give birth, as it were, to their enemies. Whether it's really as inevitable as that I don't know. We may just have been lucky. Credit should perhaps be given to human will as well as to historical forces. Whatever the explanation, a revolt happened, and this revolt differed from other revolts—including the Negro revolt—which are revolts against acknowledged failures, because it was a revolt not only against failure *but also against what America considered its successes.* It was a revolt against the American Way of Life. The parents had said, "We have labored three generations to give you this, darling." And the younger generation replied, "You know where you can shove it."

For our class, this revolt comes before any concern with civil rights, poverty, or war. Of course, the concern is *connected* with the revolt. Just what the connection is might be expressed this way: "After feeling the worthlessness of your affluent culture to the marrow of our bones, we are compelled to look into it all a little further, to ask how it happened. Well then: we ask *at whose expense?* and we discover the poor. We look at the poor and we see they are not the same *color* as we are. Looking at all those who are not the same color as we are, our eyes make the journey from Mississippi to *Vietnam.* And then finally we have it. The primal shame and the ultimate one. The bombs that kill the Vietnamese today were manufactured yesterday and sold to the government for money. On that money our parents live in nice places. The garden party at Greenwich is as elegant as anyone could wish. Truman Capote is there with Princess Lee Radziwill. The fine flower of our society. The peak of Western Civilization. But look at these people more closely. They are dripping with blood." However high the wages, however gracious the living, this is a civilization that lives by oppression at home and aggression abroad. It is when young people see this nightmare—a nightmare they do not invent but discover—that they become deeply alienated.

The most optimistic conclusion that could be drawn from the facts as I have presented them would be that what Marx hoped from the proletariat could be delivered by an alliance between the Negroes and the white professional classes, and this is a dream we do see gleaming in the eyes of some radicals these days. Since protest is having no effect, the argument runs, let us follow the lead of Che Guevara, Régis Debray, and Stokely Carmichael, and be guerrillas. I note that what is used in defense of this position is, above all, *contempt for peaceful methods*. A remark made at the recent Havana Congress is worth citing. "When they hear the word 'revolver,'" said one militant about the less militant, "they reach for their culture." A very rough joke. Rough because it is drawn from Nazi sources, and what the Nazis meant by it is not reversed by the new formulation. That is one point. There is a more important one. In the United States the biggest and best guns belong to the cops, the National Guard, and the Army. As far as Black Power goes, I have suggested what must be conceded in its favor. One need not be so starry-eyed that one does not see its limitations. Not the least horrible aspect of a horrible general situation is that United States power drives so many into acts and attitudes of futile desperation. I attended a gathering lately when a speaker got a quick round of applause by stating that if we couldn't change America at least we could destroy it. One appreciates the excruciating sense of impotence out of which such a declaration comes. It remains simple-minded and infantile because the point is never reached at which "we" can conclude that America cannot be changed. *I* may fail to change it but *you* younger people may yet succeed—provided, that is, that *I* don't destroy it. And, even if it could be proved that America is unchangeable, what really would be the interest in the building of funeral pyres? If America is really unchangeable, it will destroy itself without assistance from the likes of us.

The other day I met a girl who very much agreed with the proposition: "If you can't change it destroy it." Finding her so much more radical than I myself, I whipped out of my pocket a couple of documents for her to sign. One would have committed her to tax refusal; the other to aiding and abetting draft resisters. Before deciding that America should be totally destroyed, would she change America this little bit? To my dismay she declined. It was the universal bonfire that appealed to her, not positive change. I conclude that we have a lunatic fringe on the left and that it fully matches the one on the right for lunacy.

Was this girl excessively alienated? I don't think so. Consider. Our Establishment believes above all in violence while infuriating us with hypocritical speeches *against* violence. We say to Ho Chi Minh, "Stop your violence and come reason with us." Then we add, "And if you don't we'll smash your face in." In this situation it is inevitable that some of our radicals should wish to match the Establishment's violence with their own. *In doing so, though, they want "in."* They want to be invited to the Garden Party, and are promising that their hands too will drip with blood.

Why not address ourselves to the fact which prompts all the futile gestures: it is that America is *not* on the verge of that total overturn which we would like to see and which we feel to be necessary. Therefore it is futile to say: a few more fires this summer, a few more guns, and a revolution will occur, and our alienation will be overcome. As far as politics are concerned, we must concentrate on immediate goals, above all on the stopping of the war. As far as the longer term is concerned, what is needed is the *preparation of ourselves* for the future we should like to see. We have by all means to endure alienation, but it is not a merely passive endurance. We fight it because we have a vision of a promised land, an eventual home. In this suffering and in this fight we need what some people will call an ideology, some a religion, and others yet again a cultural program. The aggressions of the United States in this time would be wrong in any case, but they are doubly wrong because the culture which the United States has to offer the other nations is a bad one: bad religion, bad philosophy, bad art. America is smashing up old cultures, and preventing new ones from being born, both at the same time, and is replacing what it destroys with the corrupt rhetoric of public relations and the cultural junk of its mass media. What Newark and Detroit are today, cities conquered by the United States— if they remain standing—can hope to become tomorrow.

Let them assimilate, in our own population, those who are assimilable, but let those who are too alienated for that have the courage of their alienation and accept the responsibilities. This means holding on to good ideology, good religion, good poetry—holding on, in short, to the *imagination* in its purity, its nakedness—and not only holding on but making new ideology, new religion, new poetry.

I was saying that the artist, like the saint, could achieve only in personal fantasy what we hoped would eventually be achieved in social actuality. This statement needs now to be enlarged. What begins as personal fantasy may become social reality. It is then that the poet is seen to be, in Shelley's phrase, an unacknowledged legislator. The word "prophet," in this connection, is misleading. It only suggests that the poet, like Nostradamus or readers of tea leaves, has his own strange ways of guessing what others will do. What I am asserting is that he contributes, and can contribute, at a very early stage. This is the stage not of a guessing game, nor of systematic planning, but of the formation of images. In saying this I am thinking not only of Shelley but also of William Blake.

The alienation of our class will not be overcome by individual action alone, but certain individual actions lay the groundwork for general change. To imagine is an individual action par excellence. Nothing can happen in society that has not first been imagined by individuals. This dictum, alas, applies just as well to bad as to good social creations. Auschwitz existed in the fantasy of anti-Semites long before it was actuality. The fantasy of American planes and ships running wild in the skies and seas of the whole world was to be found in "Superman" and other comic strips long before America's U2 was brought down over Russia and her spy ship was seized off Korea. If only such money and energy could be given to positive causes!

The Communist parties a generation ago were parading something called socialist realism. It was corrupted by Stalinism and deservedly came in for much ridicule. Nonetheless the original rationale had been right. The premise was that literature had bogged down in mere description of conditions, and that something more positive was needed. Now if you look at, say, fiction in America today it is still in that naturalistic tradition. What floats the fictional successes of the Grove Press is still what floated fictional successes half a century ago: *shocking frankness,* etc.—that is, mentioning a little more than was mentioned the last time of what goes on in bedrooms in the dirtier parts of town. This literature once had great value; it is now used up. In drama the situation is similar. I see *A Day in the Death of Joe Egg,* and I say: not *another* play telling us that everyday life is trivial, empty, sordid and contemptible? Even our negative literature will be different, like *Candy* perhaps, or *Catch-22,* grotesque, fantastic, "far-out." An alienated class, if it is not merely to drown in Alienation, needs a literature that does not merely reflect Alienation.

It needs literature and art that begins to prefigure the next phase: the Integration by which Alienation can be ended and transcended. In this, literature and art join with religion, not the decadent kind that is the opium of the people, but the active and fresh religion as it has been seen in our time in Pope John XXIII, in Martin Buber, and in A. J. Muste. For if I am speaking now of faith, hope, and love (and I am), I am speaking of them as facts of life, big with earthly possibilities.

(*1968*)

The Unliberated University

I would grant at the outset that the university is often taken far too seriously. The literature of all education is for burning. Bertrand Russell was shrewd when he said that the most encouraging thing about a man's education was the ease with which, given the right circumstances, it would simply drop off. If only educators would, as simply, drop dead! For most education, judged by any exacting criterion, is shabby stuff. All that is generally attempted, under any social system, is to produce the right cogs for those particular wheels. We have the gall to talk of "brainwashing" as if it were the invention of the heathen Chinese when what Western education has usually been is a brainwashing of our entire juvenile population, the fitting of billions of square pegs into the round holes of our precious Culture.

Somewhere in mid-adolescence this process is considered more or less completed, but thousands of the billions are kept on for a further working over at the university. I am referring to what Commencement Day speakers call education for leadership. The University has an ROTC and is itself a training corps for the officers of the whole social system. Again the aim is that the supply should meet the demand: the person should find his place and do in it what is expected of him and what is anyway all he is trained to do. Training implies certain achievements, though not necessarily any values. The theory of education has always been strong on values—that's what it's there for: as ideological applesauce—but the essence of education, where it has been more than training, is that it provided the equipment whereby each student could exist in that station and function to which his parent's income level had brought him. The ideology could even be fairly tame, except of course in time of "national emergency."

If one learns that Columbia University has ties with the Institute of Defense Analyses, or even the CIA, how can one go through the motions of amazement and sudden outrage? What do you expect it to have ties with? Who owns Columbia? This question was indeed asked—eventually. It should have been asked uneventually. The answer should have been known all along. Who owns Columbia, and how did they come to own it, and to what end do they own it? The fun thing about these "provocative" questions is that the answers are not really secrets and were not secrets even before the great revolt of spring 1968.

If any social system will have the universities it feels it needs, is it not clear that the physics department will be tied in with the government? Lyndon Johnson could hardly have manufactured his hydrogen bombs home on the range. And if he needed the physicists, whom did he not need? No physics, these days, without math, without chemistry, without . . . And even Johnson did not live by bombs alone, he also needed "political scientists," the university term for men who explain why the bombs must be dropped by *us* and, equally, must *not* be dropped by *them*. . . . To presuppose a university not entangled in this sort of net is to presuppose that the nation-state does not exist, which is to presuppose that modern history has not taken place.

Then what was all the shouting about? Had Columbia suddenly formed some closer tie with the social system than before? On the contrary. Grayson Kirk had just announced he was for stopping the war in Vietnam! And as for the gym, which earned itself the name of Gym Crow because it was to have a separate door for you-know-who, a few years earlier it would have had *no* door for them: facilities for "the Community" (Morningside term for niggers) were added to the gym project as a concession to newfangled notions, and Grayson Kirk continued to be bewildered as to why some people seemed to think one door was worse than none. . . .

No wonder that so many at Columbia thought the uprising irrational. Like all uprisings, it was. Which is the basis for the conservative case against them. To "rise up" is to dismiss the appeal to reason as insufficient. And with the basic "irrationality" of all such activity went particular irrationalities, both large and small. Which again is not surprising, since so few of the rebels knew anything about education. One of the more comic aspects of the whole rebellion was the effort to set up a program of liberated classes. You can easily "liberate" some subjects: you just replace whatever was said before with "the Marxist interpretation." The only trouble being that there is no Marxist interpretation of most subjects: capitalist math equals Communist math. This makes math a boring enterprise for the rebel.

Yet, though all uprisings have many irrational sources, and work themselves out in many irrational ways, some uprisings are defensible on rational grounds; and all have a kind of logic. Though it seems a little unfair that Columbia got attacked in 1968 for continuing to serve its usual purpose, the logic here is that it was the usual purpose that came under attack. But, great heavens! as all the old dodos have been saying, is this not to attack the whole social system? It is. The matter is there in a nutshell; the dodos got the message.

But maybe they overdid it when they announced from their various national pulpits that nothing more than sheer willful, sadistic, pointless aggression was involved. J. Edgar Hoover defined the aim of the rebellions as "to smash first our educational structure, then our economic system, and finally our government itself" (*New York Times,* September 1, 1968). Which would certainly be a revolutionary theory of revolution, since hitherto the custom has been to shake the government and then have the educational structure fall into your revolutionary lap. In politics, the extremes meet, especially in absurdity, and it is true that lunatic individuals were to be found around Columbia last spring whose social fantasies resembled Hoover's. I am not sure, though, that most of them were "students for a democratic society." If one bumped into someone who was muttering, "Set fire to the place! Columbia's gotta go!" (and one did), it was usually some older "member of the Community," though not necessarily a black one. There were also dubious younger people, never recognizable as Columbia students, inciting to arson and general rapine. Some doubtless were police provocateurs. Columbia was where the action was last spring; the gang was all there.

The statement that "the students just wished to destroy the University" is a loose one, raising the questions: Which students wished this, Is it true they wished this and nothing else, and, Did they consistently wish it and not just in moments of outrage? Clearly no survey could find a way of registering all the possible variations, and in any case statements on the subject were never based on any attempt at comprehensive knowledge. They were based at best on impressions and at worst on ideology, generally the latter. It is important to remember that a class or group that is threatened with ruin can hardly help seeing the prospect of such ruin as the end of the world, of "all civilized values," etc., etc. Should one even resent this? *"Cet animal est très méchant/ Quand on l'attaque, il se défend."* ["This animal is very naughty: when you attack it, it defends itself."] Respect the rights of the brontosaurus.

Attempting to base myself not on ideology but on personal impressions, I would say that among the Columbia radicals—a few notable eccentrics apart —there was at worst a willingness to exploit Columbia in the interests of a larger cause. And clearly the concern of the "outside agitators" was of this sort. Tom Hayden has no noticeable interest in education, let alone in Columbia. I do think his aims are positive, but he assumes (as do I) that much demolition is needed before there can be rebuilding, and I suppose that Columbia figures in his scheme of things (though not in mine) more in the demolition phase than in the other. Even this must be left vague, as he is not much concerned with Columbia one way or the other. He hit us and ran, writing up his defense of hit-and-run tactics in—where else?—*Ramparts*. I suppose he was within his rights, though I feel I'm also within mine in regretting that he didn't confer his favors on City College instead: it, too, borders on Harlem. He made it harder for radicals at Columbia to "bore from within" and presented the Columbia authorities with their best argument, viz., that their enemy was not concerned with the welfare of the place. (He was quoted by Grayson Kirk himself. Admittedly, the thought of Kirk curled up before a log fire with a copy of *Ramparts* is captivating.)

With the thesis that the aim was "the destruction of Columbia" went the thesis that there was a "hard core" of destroyers who were the real cause of the whole fracas. Some equate this hard core with SDS as a whole, some with SDS leadership, some with an element in SDS which, in their view, is the element that always comes out on top. Here again we run into the impossibility of verification. SDS can be called a hard core (if you like the metaphor) in that its Columbia membership before the busts was only about seventy, but there was always much more variety and disagreement even among these seventy than their Establishment critics ever bothered to discover. A minor sensation was created at one point by an announcement that the busts were simply the execution of a plan made by national SDS months before. But the only relevant content this statement has is that such plans had been bandied about for years. Anyone who witnessed the Columbia incidents witnessed the great uncertainty of SDS leadership at many crucial points and the improvised and sometimes ludicrously accidental results. Beyond this, there is a failure in such journalistic theories of action to distinguish between initiation and control, between, if you like, the sorcerer and his apprentice. The rebellion started with a small SDS rally. It culminated in a strike of several thousand students. Were the several thousand the humble servants of SDS? If at all, only in very limited respects. The strike was preceded by the occupation of buildings by about seven hundred students. The Establishment theorists believed that these people were all under Mark Rudd's thumb. This was just believing what one wished to believe. (It seems that Columbia informed the cops that there were only a couple of hundred students in the buildings: the figure was a product of the "hard core" theory.) In actual fact, the seven hundred not only had such differences with each other as seven hundred people will, but also developed new differences in their new situation. Each occupied building had its own character. Rivalries and even enmities arose. . . . All in all, what is most relevant about the theory of the hard core, as well as about the theory of total destruction, is that both spell paranoia. Even the "outside agitator" is none other than our old friend the "foreign Communist" in slight disguise. Most important of all, according to the paranoid scheme, the larger number of subversives who cannot be included in the "core" are classified as fellow travelers—that is, as (this word too is classic) "dupes." Now it seems to me that anyone who knew a goodly number of our five thousand striking students knew also that they were *not* dupes. Of the many hypocritical evasions that came out of Low Library, perhaps the most hypocritical of all was Grayson Kirk's statement that the five thousand were merely squeamish about police violence. Not that that isn't a good thing to be squeamish about. But the evidence on the spot (the place where Kirk never was, except in another sense) was that a lot of people who had wished to rebel for a long time at last found the right occasion, the full justification. You only had to listen, in those extraordinary weeks, to students pouring their hearts out to realize that this was so. And one must make it a chief ground for complaint against Kirk and the others that they always wanted to talk about the seventy and not the seven hundred, let alone the five thousand. The background of many of the Columbia administrators is in some form of social science. Yet, I would suggest, real social science would address itself primarily to the five thousand—would not refuse to acknowledge that they rose up in rebellion last spring but would ask *why* they did. Would indeed ask *them* why they did. But there, of course, we move outside the world of Grayson Kirk.

To be fair, Grayson Kirk's adjutant, David Truman, was reported as mentioning the real background of the revolt. I am not referring to his attack on Dr. Benjamin Spock's alleged encouragement of permissive parenthood, which was just one of the many comic *gaffes*. I am referring to a *cri de coeur* by Truman to the effect that none of these awful things would have happened at Columbia but for that nuisance of a war in Vietnam. This was not a matter of political dissent, of "disagreeing with the foreign policy of the Johnson-Humphrey Administration." I have mentioned that there was no special reason for challenging Columbia University in spring 1968—unless, which is a gigantic proviso, you wished to challenge the whole way of life of which it is part. That is just what the Columbia students did wish to challenge. Now "Vietnam" is not the whole way of life. Not literally. But nonliterally?

Any regime, I suppose, lasts as long as it can hide its contradictions from its citizens. (In America, I heard William Buckley say on TV, class war is something we simply don't have.) What happened in the lives of student citizens in the 1960s was the unmasking of a very great contradiction. It came to their attention in this form. The university said to them, (1) "Don't meddle in politics. Your job here is to study," but then added, (2) "When you graduate, your deferment will end, *and off to Vietnam with you.*"

The simplest way this contradiction can work out in practice is in the proposition: be a bookworm till the call comes, then be a killer. Since this is nakedly psychotic, a certain regard for sanity, or at least for the proprieties, suggests evasions. The simplest evasion I know of was advanced at a Columbia faculty meeting when a colleague said he had it from a high official in Washington that the government would be glad to fight this war with high-school dropouts: if college students would just be docile, they would also be let alone even after graduation. But this formula belongs to the time when the Johnson-Humphrey Administration thought it was winning the war.

Between 1941 and 1945 students did go more or less happily straight from book to gun, but then that war was *just,* in the opinion of almost all of them. Just and unavoidable. Though, like all wars, the Vietnam war was represented as just by those who waged it, they were disbelieved on an unprecedented scale. Even the dumbest undergraduate, the least prepared to make any moral judgments whatever, would hear the news wherever he went on his vacation abroad. "You Americans are waging an outrageous, unjust war." He would hear it not only from young Communists but from old anti-Communists. He would hear it if he had an audience with de Gaulle; he would hear it, in muffled tones, if he had an audience with the Pope. The Great Contradiction came to be recognized more and more widely as not only crassly stupid but also gravely immoral.

The next step was to recognize the magnitude of the outrage. At first you assumed the unjust war was but another of the myriad atrocious incidents of history in general and imperialism in particular—like, say, the repeated Russian use of tanks in East Europe. But Vietnam was not over in a week. It dragged on. Hypocritically not called a war at all, it was, one slowly had to realize, a major war. Even official figures proved that, as did certain comparisons. The point was rather soon reached when the United States had poured more bombs on North Vietnam than Hitler had poured on all his enemies put together.

No less significant than the size of the crime was the way in which the people at large were kept from seeing it and hence from sensing the depth of the immorality. This brainwashing of the people can be illustrated even from those denunciations of the war that received general publicity, for they were denunciations of marginal offenses. The Kennedy brothers stressed corruption in Saigon; Johnson could therefore answer that there was corruption everywhere. Robert Kennedy, regarded as a bold man, was really only speaking of America's having gone *too far*—presumably in the right direction. Fulbright's thesis of the "arrogance of power" is inadequate in a similar way, for this kind of arrogance is only the defect of the virtue of solicitude; so Fulbright got what was coming to him when he was accused of isolationism or *lack* of solicitude. . . . Alas, the actual function of these plaintive protests was: to help Johnson cover up.

Maybe he didn't even need the help, for what is called the American Way of Life is a cover-up job from beginning to end and represents the victory of public relations over truth. The American Establishment is better prepared for a career of crime than any other Establishment in history just because it *looks* so uncriminal. *Of course* America did not invent fascistic methods and imperialistic policies. On the contrary, America denounced them. It promoted antifascist and anti-imperialist ideology. Above all it created a Way of Life—the affluent society—whose every appearance contradicted all assumptions about fascism and imperialism. Instead of Nuremberg rallies, black shirts, screaming speeches: TV discussion panels, business suits, Rotarian manners. . . . This is a topic to itself but it has relevance to "Vietnam" in that it helps to explain how so many, even of those who felt that all was not as it should be, utterly failed to sense the breadth and depth and crudity of the offense. Which has its prototype in the American failure to realize what America did, earlier, to the American Indian. A minimum of declarations that Indians don't deserve to live. In an era when most oratory was humanitarian blather, they were just killed off. So today. No anti-Vietnamese ideology. Good Vietnamese are on our side. We are trying to stop bad Vietnamese from being "violent." Which is just part of our general effort to stem the tide of Russian and Chinese "violence." . . . From all which it follows that the real villain is not some idiot rightist who may hate all Orientals on principle. The real villain is the smooth, mealy-mouthed, liberal ideologue who can support such a war for his own reasons and in his own way. Hubert H. Humphrey is the man not only of the year but of the decade and, if we don't look out, of the epoch, and on the list of those who supported him for the Democratic nomination, summer 1968, was the most "modern" of Columbia's administrators, then regarded as Grayson Kirk's successor: David Truman.

What "Vietnam" has meant to the young generation is a radical disjunction between word and deed, profession and fact, education and life, culture and history. It all seems summed up in that miserable creature of the Frankfurt trials who during World War II (a) worked on a thesis in praise of the humanism of Goethe and (b) as an officer at Auschwitz helped to massacre the Jews.

At first blush this would not seem to "apply to America," some of whose best friends are Jews, and whose Hubert Humphreys are such affable fellows. There are differences; I have just tried to define some of them; but they are mostly in the area of what the PR world calls personal style. And even Auschwitz went in for some degree of idealistic pretense. Over the gate stood the inscription: WORK MAKES YOU FREE—which is easily translated into American as Rehabilitation (or in Vietnam: Pacification) Center. In any case I am not denying that it remains scandalous in most of America to speak of a Humphrey and a Himmler in the same breath. On the contrary, I am crediting the current ideology with this and many similar achievements. My point is that, under pressure from Vietnam, many of the young have escaped the ideological cage. Which, to be sure, is exactly what makes them "anti-American" and creates between them and their elders the famous Generation Gap.

The Vietnam war released young Americans from their belief in the household gods, their loyalty to the household priests, high and low. The young could no longer be appealed to, since all appeals were assumed to be in bad faith. That's how it is with "law and order." That's how it is with the Establishment's complaints about "resort to violence." Law and order is *their* law and order, arbitrary and illegitimate. As to violence, *they* are the chief users of it—Martin Luther King had said that very bluntly just before he earned the Establishment's admiration by becoming a corpse. "Rap Brown shouldn't resort to violence. Ho Chi Minh shouldn't resort to violence. You and I shouldn't resort to violence. Violence should be resorted to by Lyndon B. Johnson and Hubert H. Humphrey." What a laugh.

Even the Negro question belongs under the head "Vietnam," first because the war is "a racist war," second because, to an indecent extent, it is being fought by American blacks, and third because the problem of violence can be confronted only if we think of Saigon and Detroit together. No American can discuss violence in good faith without bringing in both the war and the Negro question. No American can discuss *student violence* in good faith without bringing in both the war and the Negro question. The main point was made in Charlie Chaplin's film *Monsieur Verdoux:* "I, Bluebeard, have killed my half dozen wives, and thus brought down upon my head the indignant wrath of your society. You kill millions of wives in your unjust wars, and your society says: please do it again whenever you feel like it." Anyone who gets Chaplin's point is bound to feel that, however wrong student violence may be, it is a drop in the bucket compared to the violence of Hubert Humphrey—and of "professors for Hubert Humphrey."

Next, the question of legality and legitimate methods. The friends of authority reiterate *ad nauseam* that in a democratic society "like ours" you are limited to peaceful reform. Rebellion is great in Commie countries; but not here. Laws must be obeyed so long as they exist, and changed, if at all, by persuading a majority to vote for such a change. Nothing is said about how damned convenient such doctrine is to those who preach it, though this is what catches the attention of young people and makes them mad. Well, their anger is improper, period. A little discussion might be allowed as to whether the electoral system is a fair one: but even this discussion terminates with the declaration that "we" are improving it. . . . Again, it is "Vietnam" that dramatizes the fraudulence. Suppose I work at stopping the war through "legitimate" channels. It means I use my freedom of speech to talk around a few Democrats or Republicans. Fine. We have seen that a little headway can be made on a project like that. The snag is that, meanwhile, the war continues; we are responsible for murder after murder. I can send the Vietnamese a telegram stating: HOPE BY 1969 TO HAVE A MAJORITY CONVINCED IT IS WRONG TO CONTINUE KILLING YOU. But just think what they would have the right to say to me by way of answer! Slow, "legitimate" methods are not legitimate at all, if in what is called "the meanwhile"—a stretch of time as real as any other—illegitimate and irremediable crimes are allowed to be repeated. If we see, here, how "freedom of speech" becomes the tool of gangsterism, we can recognize, too, that teaching children in school simply to favor freedom of speech, irrespective of context, is . . . well, highly opportune from a highly immoral viewpoint. For again the old liberal ideology functions as a front for everything the old liberals were against.

What does this have to do with the Negro question? Race relations is the one area in which a lot of Americans now allow that so-called illegitimate methods can be legitimate. These Americans are reconciled to the proposition that you can recommend peaceful and legal methods till you are blue in the face but that certain demands in this area are going to be met regardless. If the Negro cannot get his equality by approved methods he will seize it by disapproved ones. All the talk against violence will cut no ice; *and this is known and accepted in advance.*

It does not follow that what is conceded to the Negro community, which has been wronged so deeply and so long, will be conceded to any group that may claim such a concession; but, on the other hand, if the Negro's point is granted in principle—and it is—there is no way of limiting it to Negroes only. Conservatives in our time are naturally worried that nowadays *everyone* is claiming the right to illegal and violent opposition. Not everyone is entitled to it. But some people are entitled to it; that seems agreed. Must one have black skin to belong to their number? I state the question as it presents itself to white students today. Contrariwise, one can ask the university authorities why they spend their energy talking up law and order instead of trying not to let situations develop in which legitimate changes can be secured—in time—only by "illegitimate" methods? The importance of the clause "in time" I have illustrated from the Vietnam war. It is too late to use legal methods to stop that war when it has run its course. . . .

It is important to see that this is how the question of illegality and violence generally arises in the modern, and especially in the American, context. It is important to see the sense in which right and center critics are correct when they identify lawbreaking and violence with the left. It is important above all to recognize that if the left were unwilling to risk such lawlessness it would not only lose many particular battles, it would become empty ideology, false consciousness, mere blah. Conversely, the insistence of right and center that the left should content itself with discussion and verbal persuasion is precisely an insistence that free speech be fruitless speech. To revert yet again to the Great Example of Vietnam, it is not merely that the war continues as we while away the time in free discussion but that *it is the purpose of free speech in our society to let the war continue.* Talking is a *way* of letting it continue; just as illegal resistance is a direct challenge and threat to its continuation.

So there has to be forthright criticism of free speech as it currently functions in the United States, even though, when we offer it, we shall be denounced as totalitarian, and students who offer it will be compared with the Nazi students of 1933. It will be our job to expose the speciousness of these rejoinders. More important is that we do more than speak. If we don't, we ourselves run the risk of resembling the Auschwitz guard who is writing on Goethe's humanism. In other words, our humanism, today, needs to be linked to a humanistic politics —to humanistic change, to humanistic action. The thought is, of course, a commonplace of the left. Herbert Marcuse has given it particular emphasis, pointing out that the left could have no real successes unless the humanistic philosophy of an intelligentsia were linked with the felt need of a larger class for liberation. That's the politics of it. What I would call attention to, here, is the mental hygiene of it. Humanism can be *healthy* only when linked to the appropriate social action.

Whereas, what actually happens to the traditional humanistic values in our universities? In the first instance, they function as pure hypocrisy, which anyone who wishes to may penetrate. It is not all that hard to see that Mr. X is really getting his honorary degree because he is rich and not for all the humanistic reasons given in the eulogy, but the very fact that this is so obvious and crass tends to obscure the larger fact that humanistic values, even when *not* hypocritical, are still fraudulent. The fraud may consist in a claim to relevance when there is no relevance. Teachers in the humanities often assume that there is value in the mere handing along of ideas about value. An educated person, by this criterion, is one that has heard the news—knows that Plato said thus and so, and that Aristotle disagreed with him, and so on. This scheme of things would only create a utopia of quiz kids. At best what we get is a cult of culture—and we are back again with our Auschwitz guard who, of course, believes that knowing what Goethe said makes him a cultivated, a superior person. Humanistic values within the usual framework must either operate as "false consciousness" in a directly vicious way or wander off into sheer irrelevance—the void of academic escapism. And escapism offers no real escape. The professor who may himself hate all modern politics and take refuge, say, in medieval studies will be used by the masters of modern politics to illustrate their claim that they promote humanism, diversity, freedom, and what have you.

Try to conserve humanistic values merely as ideas to which people give assent and you end up with nothing but oratory. Such oratory either serves no function at all and is quickly forgotten, or it serves the function of concealing unwelcome facts and maintaining false consciousness. Aggression masks itself in a rhetoric of liberation, imperialism in a rhetoric of internationalism (anti-isolationism). No wonder that the Establishment today stresses the right to dissent! Radical ideas are there to be agreed or disagreed with: talked about and talked through, talked out of existence. It is important to keep them out of the realm of action not only because one is against them but also because one knows they are vitiated by being reduced to a purely verbal existence. A living humanism would not permit its adherents to be officers in Auschwitz—or in Saigon. Nor could it persist as a doctrine merely expounded and verbally affirmed. It exists as praxis or not at all, and those who would keep it alive, or bring it back to life, must at all costs create such a praxis, if it does not already exist.

It was the thesis of Marx and Engels that such a praxis did already exist in the struggle of the proletariat for liberation from the bourgeoisie. The theory of a socialist humanism could be kept from hypocrisy and ossification by the theorist's identification with the struggle. A hundred years of history forces a reconsideration of the Marxian diagnosis. But does it force a reconsideration of the underlying point, namely, that humanism must be rooted, not in theory alone, but in the felt needs of humanity and in the great social movements which arise to meet those needs? I think not. No humanism would have any vitality, any health, in the United States of our period, which did not ally itself, to begin with, with the vital needs of blacks. No humanism would have any vitality, any health, in the world of our period which did not ally itself with the vital needs of oppressed peoples everywhere. The enemies are racism, colonialism, and war itself. All are masked by a rhetoric of antiracism, anticolonialism, and antiwar, but the rhetoric is destroyed as soon as one points the finger at racist practice, colonialist practice, and the practice of war. A denunciation of Russian aggression in Prague by Lyndon Johnson is canceled out by the bombs he simultaneously drops on Vietnam. On the intellectual front, a living humanism spends its energy pointing such things out, and thereby destroying the intellectual front of the enemy. But it is in close and constant liaison with the nonintellectual front, nonviolent or violent, legal or illegal, pleasant, in short, or unpleasant.

In the United States of the sixties this meant liaison with the civil-rights movement first and then later with the peace movement. Now, at the close of the decade, we are learning how closely interrelated the two are. One must work in both areas at once. As to strategy, a turning point was reached in 1967–1968 which is summed up in the formula: from protest to resistance. On that, in radical circles at least, there was general agreement. Less easy to agree on were the specific targets.

How about Columbia University? Was it the right target to pick at this point? One qualification it did have: it was a sitting duck. Grayson Kirk was perfect casting for Louis XVI; and so on. But here we are in the realm of comedy or at best journalism. If the aim was more serious than the making of easy headlines, was Columbia still a good target?

The query is academic in more senses than one. Even if national SDS considered that it had picked Columbia, essentially Columbia was chosen by none but itself. The word "chosen" is a euphemism. What happened was that the place exploded and couldn't help itself. Granted that SDS applied the match, our main interest must be in the size of the powder keg.

Why Columbia? What I have said above about the younger generation and Vietnam applies to the whole country. But only Columbia revolted. It follows that Vietnam was not the only reason. The special and peculiar reason lay in Columbia's relation to Harlem. It is to be noted that among the original points of protest those that were not about student discipline were only two: the University's affiliation with the Institute of Defense Analyses and the construction of a gym in Morningside Park—Vietnam *and Harlem*. And in the somewhat accidental, or at least improvised, sequence of events that led to occupation of buildings and then to a strike of several thousand students, black students played a role even more crucial than most of the printed accounts have recognized. For reasons of his own, Grayson Kirk stressed that the blacks behaved better than the whites. He hadn't actually believed so at the time, since the blacks were thought to have guns and flew the NLF flag from Hamilton Hall balcony. According to what the blacks themselves have said (in *Partisan Review*), the whites withdrew in consternation from Hamilton Hall, seeing how much further the blacks were prepared to go. Only as challenged by the blacks did the whites occupy buildings at all.

Granted that a revolt in 1968 was inevitable; granted, too, that it was legitimate, even fortunate; should the University be permanently under attack until it "mends its ways"?

First of all, it cannot, in the revolutionary sense, mend its ways under its present ownership, and no basic change of ownership will take place unless there is a revolution. Is a revolution imminent? If it is, Columbia might as well wait till there's a revolutionary government. If it is not, plans should be made for the interim. These would have to be plans for relatively minor reforms. Silly, in this case, to complain that the reforms *are* minor! Silly, too, to play at insurrection all the time.

Besides, as Marcuse has stressed, the university is not the best target anyway, because it is not one of the worst segments of the community. On the contrary, it is one of the best (or least bad, if you prefer). It certainly is a principal source of student radicalism. And not merely by contact of student with student. It is important to see how much the generation gap has been exaggerated and how much too much the faculty have been spoken of as a single bloc. If figures like Kirk have existed as rejected fathers on the other side of a generation gap, figures like Marcuse himself have been accepted father figures. If students have rejected "the faculty" and the Establishment generally, they have done so under the influence of another part of the faculty—the influence of men like Herbert Marcuse, Noam Chomsky, William Appleman Williams, Christopher Lasch, and, at Columbia, C. Wright Mills.

It is true that the university "co-opts" these men to the extent that it buys the right to boast of its tolerance of them and at the same time buys their tolerance of it. A bargain for the university, but, I feel, a bargain for us radicals too. Though our views are and should be regarded as subversive by the authorities, we are tolerated. The motives for tolerating us are not altruistic, but not only have we to value being tolerated, our unwritten contract—the bargain or deal to which we owe our appointments—obliges us to tolerate those on campus whom *we* regard as subversive, who are likely to include just about everybody in authority. The bargain is also a gamble. Their calculation is that they can afford us, that they can absorb and survive us. Our calculation is that in the end we shall absorb and survive them. Somebody has to prove wrong; but meanwhile both parties can wear a smile; and even if they wear a scowl, or occasionally curse and swear, the unwritten compact is still there; and is still being honored.

The university is not only not my enemy. Even in politics, it, or a large part of it, can sometimes be my friend. For example, there is a big fight on now to decide whether the universities will hold on to a degree of independence from government or whether they will come more and more under government control, the scientists (as I have put it) inventing the atom bombs, the political scientists inventing the lies that will be told about them. Particularly insidious are what Noam Chomsky calls the New Mandarins: those of my colleagues who take jobs in or near the White House in order to see that the American atrocities are efficiently executed and enthusiastically received. Opposition to this tendency comes not only from radicals but from defenders of the liberal tradition of independent thought. An alliance between the two groups on this issue is not only opportune but wise. It will have far more success than either group could have on its own. It is therefore good that the radicals are around to make such an alliance and do not allow themselves to be driven out on the grounds that they are enemies.

A section of the university radical movement has exaggerated certain tendencies out of all recognition. One Columbia student represented the Law School as existing solely for the support of "the corporate structure" when at the very moment he spoke he himself was being supported in the courts by a graduate of the school, free of charge. There are lawyers and lawyers, just as there are professors and professors. Similarly, it is a mistake to represent the liberal-conservative tradition as wholly spurious or effete. When Fulbright asks scholars to stick by their high vocation and not join Walt Rostow in the White House, he is indulging in neither deception nor empty oratory. He is in touch with exactly the same historical forces as we would claim to be, and is joining with us on the concrete position taken. Our radicalism presumably makes some sense to him in this area; and his liberalism deserves some better welcome from us than merely to be dismissed as old-fashioned twaddle.

I suggested conceding at the outset that a university will inevitably represent the governing class both in direct propaganda and in all manner of indirect indoctrination and conditioning-for-the-world-as-it-is. On the other hand, one must avoid the megalomania of considering one's own activities and views as the only countervailing force, even when multiplied by the similar activities and views of those who completely agree. Such megalomania leads only to an impotent self-righteousness. It's first political result is the refusal to make those alliances without which there is no success. "Strange bedfellows," cries the megalomaniac at the first sign of any such alliance, as if, in politics, bedfellows were ever not strange.

People who were not on Morningside Heights last spring may wonder why I go over this familiar ground. Being on Morningside Heights forced me to do just that. The existence of a certain authoritarian strain among the young radicals reminded us older ones of Stalinism. Clearly, there were quite a few on the Heights who would at least have taken Lenin's side against Rosa Luxemburg. But there were many of us, too, who saw the force of Rosa's arguments all the more vividly in this small red spring of 1968. Rosa believed that institutions wither without diversity and conflict. It was something to remember in the face of an assumption that all Columbia needed was indoctrination along one consistent line. Even if the topic were only the education of young radicals (and it isn't), the question arises: Should a young radical never encounter a reactionary viewpoint? One should study one's enemies. But that's not all I mean. I'm thinking, rather, of the service rendered any of us when we hear a contrary viewpoint brilliantly formulated. Only then are we really forced to come to grips with it. For that reason, even a university that defined itself as radical would need brilliant reactionaries on its faculty. More yet: the actual content of a subject may be better communicated within a "reactionary" frame than otherwise. Here a classical example was provided by Marx and Engels when they observed how much more was to be learned about modern society from the Catholic monarchist Balzac than from progressive novelists. It is a lesson some of our radicals still haven't learned, and some are so far from having learned it that they would rather, as Chomsky put it, that Karl Marx had burned down the British Museum than worked there on *Das Kapital.*

Would the ideal education for young radicals be nothing more than at indoctrination in radicalism? Of course not. Yet that at best is all we shall get if we begin by breaking up even the positive features of the present system. To avoid this one must begin by agreeing that such features exist and by identifying them—a not impossible task. Whether you like it or not, there is time for the task, since, unless I am much mistaken, no general revolution is imminent in these United States, and we shall have to live with the existing system, willy-nilly, for quite a while.

In case anybody under twenty-five still wants advice from a man over fifty (and actually I know that many do) here is mine: "Be more opportunistic, at least in this respect: grab the education that you can get and that you or your parents are paying for. Understand that this education will have the limitations which, given the history of Western civilization up to this point, it must have. But seek out the exceptions and the freaks. Seek out sheer merit whatever the circumambient ideology. Seek out fine men of learning, fine critics of life: they exist. Explode in revolt when you have to, but not when you don't have to. If you feel you must be a full-time reformer or revolutionary as of now, then go out—out from the university—and be one. The university is for students who don't yet feel quite ready for this mission or any other. It is for people who feel the university will help *make* them ready. If you conclude that it can help make you ready, then enroll. After that, by all means exploit the university for your own purposes, but in the way in which it can successfully be exploited and your interests duly served. Concede that the unliberated university can still be of use; discover exactly what use it can be to you; then use it."

(1968)

The Greatest Show on Earth

Readers of my **Thirty Years of Treason** *might well ask why so many of the wit-*
nesses before the Un-American Activities Committee, as there cited, are perform-
ing artists. I would not duck the imputation of professional bias, but only add
that the Committee showed this bias too. Its first substantional target in the
thirties was the Federal Theatre, and throughout its great decade
(1946–1956) it reverted again and again to the performers, whether movie
stars, Broadway actors, or folk singers. If we remark that one of the Committee's
star witnesses and stanch supporters became Governor of California, we should
not forget that, until this happened, Ronald Reagan was known to the public
exclusively as a movie star. Things changed in the sixties, but in what way?
Radical politics became street theatre. For that decade the testimony included in
my book is that of agitators pure and simple. They were the star performers of
their time.

There have always been other theatres besides the professional playhouse and
the political arena, notably the law court, the church, and the schoolroom. Wit-
nesses from each of these are presented in my book. They bring their theatres
with them, and we hear the characteristic intelligence, style, and tone of each set-
ting. Then again, the particular environment imposed by the Committee asserts
its own theatrical character. The transaction was known as investigation. The
scene is the Old House Office Building in Washington—or Room 1105 in

the United States Court House, Foley Square, New York—or some other high rectangular chamber in some other government building somewhere, designed in the grand Greek post-office manner. In the early years, before TV, many HUAC hearings were heard on the radio. Later, some were seen on TV. So these dramas were present to a national audience until the day when Speaker Sam Rayburn forbade all this nonsense. Since the hearings continued to be nationally reported in the papers, the occasion was not, even later, contained within the room where it took place. As in a play, the actors of this "real-life drama" did not really talk to each other at all. They talked for an audience, and could confidently assume that this audience was not limited to guests physically present. Since there was a stenographer at work, and this worthy handed over his records to the Government Printing Office, the Committee did not even limit its audience to the living. If it played to the gallery, in the gallery was sitting none other than Clio, Muse of History.

I

If there were a God, and we could know it for sure; if this God badly needed us to know it, needed also homage from us and much support; if, moreover, godly people were by definition free people and their freedom took concrete form in a socioeconomic system called Free Enterprise; if, conversely and consequently, the two cardinal errors for human beings were NOT to believe in God and Free Enterprise, BUT to believe in No God, or even any other definition of God, and in socialism, or even any other definition of freedom; then it was reasonable of the Congress to create the House Committee on Un-American Activities in 1938, and the thirty-odd years of that Committee's work may be seen as a contribution to the good, the beautiful, and the true.

To those who think this is to place too much emphasis on religion, HUAC being by no means a religious body, I must reply that by all means there is something false and grotesquely exaggerated in the emphasis, but that the falsity and exaggeration are the Committee's own. God and Free Enterprise undoubtedly are the twin pillars of the edifice they defend. That this edifice may be a castle in the air is only to add that we are dealing here with pure opinion, indeed with ideology, the falsest of false consciousness. Such notions may have small weight in the realms of truth or logic but may nonetheless— or all the more—be deftly woven into the fabric of history. As theory, anti-Semitism was tenuous, abstract, even absurd, but the ovens of Auschwitz were of solid iron and the charred remains were of real bone. The ideologues in such cases are shrewd enough not to argue with the professors of philosophy. Their criterion is whether a given notion strikes an answering chord in classes of men whose support they and/or their masters need. Once it does, professors of philosophy will not be lacking in the ranks of those who affirm that it's a mysterious universe we live in, rationalism has lots wrong with it, and everyone knows two times two is five.

Whether or not Free Enterprise is of any use to God, He has always been of much to it. To base Free Enterprise on Him is to found it on a rock—upon the unchangeably true, upon the conveniently undebatable. And, by paradox if not magic, it is also conveniently to dissolve Free Enterprise in a mist of vagueness and undefinability. We have here the great example in modern history of having it both ways, which in logic is bad but in traditional politics—the art of manipulating human beings—is the principal end in view. You hear it said, these days, of almost everything that if it didn't exist it would have to be invented, but the great Voltairean formula was devised to describe the human need of one idea only: God. There is irony in the formula, but Voltaire was no atheist. What hurts in his irony is the strong suggestion that precisely those whose affirmation of God is prompted by their interests are irreligious: they are using God, and the God they are using is just a social force, a psychosocial factor in their political constituency: it is the members of HUAC who are the atheists, the materialists. No wonder they protest (too much) against atheism and materialism! Conscious atheism in others is their arch enemy, first, because it challenges their own right to use the word "God," a right they most sorely need, and second, because they are themselves atheists, if unconscious ones, and fear having this fact exposed by atheists who are out in the open. Among the various ironies, perhaps the supreme one is that, for these people, real believers in God—believers in a real God—are the ultimate atheists, for in pointing to a Being who exists outside this world, they discount the God of the Chamber of Commerce and the FBI, the God who is a concrete social fact. Not much preferable are those whose definition of God, though human, has a different social orientation, Paul Tillich, for instance, who saw "Faith" as a synonym for "ultimate concern." The lower middle class's concern for conformity and status is hardly ultimate. If its God is the one God, Tillich's is no God. "That guy Tillich was a socialist from way back."

Socialists are atheists in that they propose to take charge. Under capitalism, God is in charge. The basic idea of the capitalist economy, of the whole capitalist civilization and era, was *laissez faire,* which Bernard Shaw translated: "letting things slide." That's because Shaw was an "atheist." *Laissez faire* would not be letting things slide if old Nobodaddy (the "socialist" Blake's word for God) were everyone's Daddy and were up there arranging for the survival of the fittest through open competition, a preponderance of booms over slumps, freedom of soul through freedom of trade, and so on. To a purely rational mind this may seem a somewhat ridiculous role for God to play, but to a practical apologist for capitalism it could only seem exactly what rescued his system from absurdity by elevating luck into law, chance into destiny. Though capitalism has also had its professional economists to sell *laissez faire* to the academic establishment in the jargon of social science, that was a minor matter besides satisfying the popular need for a mythology.

> The rich man in his castle
> The poor man at his gate
> God made them high and lowly
> And ordered their estate

In this form, the mythology goes back long before the nineteenth century: you mustn't meddle with the class structure, because it has divine sanction. The classical economics of the nineteenth century added: you mustn't meddle because, under God, the system runs itself better than men could ever run it, rich men get richer, an occasional poor man gets rich, and if the poor chiefly remain poor, or even get poorer, such is life under God.

And America was the classical country of the classical economics. Whereas Europeans in trouble always now tended to see capitalism in its death throes, and socialism just round the corner, Americans saw capitalism as everlasting like its God, and socialism as a totally uncalled-for idea, cranky, perverse, alien, in a word—*un-American*. One of those oversophisticated West European countries like France or Germany might have a socialist government for a while, but presumably that could be taken care of.

It was against this background that the news of October broke in 1917. Ten days shook the world. It was a young American that said so, and all America realized, with a shock, that capitalism could be overthrown in a big, sprawling, underdeveloped, "new" kind of a country—a country unlike France and Germany but like say, China . . . and America. The Chinese surprise would not come till 1949, but meanwhile radicals with their bombs had to be pounced on in the United States. What would later be called McCarthyism might well be dated from the national hysteria that attended the Red scare of 1919–1920 when Attorney General A. Mitchell Palmer played the role that was later played by Joseph R. McCarthy. And 1919 was also the year when the United States Government first investigated "efforts being made to propagate in this country the principles of any party exercising . . . authority in Russia." In 1930 came the Hamilton Fish Committee in the House of Representatives. Speaking of a resolution to investigate "all entities, groups, or individuals who are alleged to advise, teach, or advocate the overthrow by force or violence of the Government of the United States," Fish commented, "It is not the purpose of this resolution to interfere with any group except the Communists in the United States, and we propose to deport all alien Communists." In the middle thirties Representative Samuel Dickstein would fain have deflected investigative ardor toward the Nazis, but in 1938 HUAC was formed, Dickstein was not on the Committee, and its Chairman, Martin Dies of Texas, would make sure that any interests the Committee might have outside of communism would be diversionary as to purpose and ephemeral as to duration.

The years 1929–1931 brought an even greater shock than 1917 to a middle class that had once thought itself secure. Capitalism didn't seem everlasting even in America now. The economy had broken down. *Laissez faire* had indeed meant letting things slide—into an abyss. After 1929 even ideas on how to save the capitalist system would tend to be proposals to have the government interfere. Blasphemy and presumption! Such ideas were doubly threatening: if they worked, then classical economics had to be dropped by its own champions; if they didn't work, men would think of dropping the whole capitalist system if by that time it hadn't dropped itself.

Popular ideology generally takes the form of melodrama, and the melodrama that had come out of the Red October of 1917 might be expressed in the dictum: "Life is a battle against Soviet Russia." How many people subscribed to this notion in the twenties would be hard to say. They were just a fringe of the middle class, perhaps, the most insecure section of that class, the most vulnerable to paranoia. Certainly the image was there, and was a vivid one, something to masturbate to. Alien Russia and rabid Red made a good combination; and the adjective "un-American" said it all. In the twenties, there was already this much behind the fantasy: Russia was indeed an alien and forbidding place, it did adhere to communism, which was an alien and forbidding doctrine, it did send agents to the United States, and American Communists did fraternize with their Russian comrades and were apt to return from trips to Moscow with a headful of plans for the furtherance of the cause.

In the thirties the fantasy received a new charge of reality. Not only were Americans far more receptive, the Soviet Union was far more active. Communism does have to be world-wide if there is going to be lasting communism at all—Stalin and Trotsky didn't really differ as to that—and the fact that one country has already had its revolution does make it a world headquarters and by that token a threat to the (prerevolutionary) world. It is understandable, then, that if a Soviet spy like Whittaker Chambers could believe he was making a sizable contribution to the overthrow of capitalism in the United States, persons of equally lurid imagination in the other camp would believe such contributions were being made. It is equally understandable that many would agree with Chambers that this is how socialism most characteristically does spread. James Bond was not yet invented but he would be born out of the fantasies of precisely that generation. In Chambers we see the impact of art (mythology, group fantasy) on life; and we see the same thing in Chambers' enemies, who of course, as Chambers was the first to admit, were also his friends: moving straight over from his pals in the Party to men like Luce, Nixon, and William Buckley, he never knew—never wished to know—what most of us think of as normal America, normal humanity, a ghastly irony in the life of one whose first ideological affair was with the proletariat.

It was interesting to be in America in 1939. Some groups of Americans, I recall, especially in upper-middle-class circles, were predominantly Anglophile, and spoke of little but the need of aid to Britain, possibly adding something about the threat to France. But there were others whose attention was overwhelmingly on the Soviet Union, and their attitudes tell us a lot about *them*. The Soviet Union was supposed to have betrayed them. BUT the Soviet Union had never owed them anything—on the contrary. The Soviet Union was supposed to have done the unthinkable in making a nonagression pact with Germany. BUT wasn't it equally unthinkable that anti-Communist America would ever join with the Soviet Union in a war? Yet it did so for the whole period 1941–1945. The 1939 crisis is important also in relation to the Communists themselves. No sympathizer with the CPUSA, I don't feel hurt that the Party lost members at any point, but the "moral crisis" of 1939 reveals itself as a phony in a very clear-cut fashion. The accusation against the Party was betrayal of its professed principles. Now its professed principles are Marxist. Did those who left the Party proceed to maintain Marxism in its purity against the non-Marxism of the CPUSA? By no means. Most of them, so far as I have been able to ascertain, became regular fellows, and certainly quite a lot just switched sides in the greatest show on earth, the number-one melodrama of the twentieth century, the battle of Free Men against the Soviet Union.

One Communist sympathizer who did not make the phony switch in 1939 was J. Robert Oppenheimer, and yet, such is the irony of history, he turned out to be the greatest melodramatic protagonist of them all. If we are to believe the friend who is up to now the only source of information, Oppenheimer continued to sympathize with the Party and the Soviet Union during 1940, and it would have been strange indeed if he had switched in 1941, for in June of that year Russia became the ally of Britain in war against Hitler. In 1942, however, Oppenheimer was chosen to head the Manhattan Project and work on the atom bomb for America. It didn't take him more than a year, if that, to be converted to belief in The Great Melodrama: in 1943 he was so eager to give information to the secret police about his former comrades that one of the security officers thought he was currying favor. Later, when this period of Oppenheimer's life was reviewed by the Atomic Energy Commission, his one supporter among the three "judges" had this to say in his defense: "He hated Russia." But some people are hard to please, and the other two judges didn't feel Oppenheimer could be trusted to hate Russia uninterruptedly.

Hate Russia! Research on the bomb was started because it was feared Hitler might also come up with one. Then it was used, not indeed against Russia, but against Japan at the moment when Russia was ready to aid the Allies in the East and share the victory with them. The view of Russian historians is naturally that the two hundred thousand who died at Hiroshima did so that they might be saved from the Red Army. Better dead than Red. Whether that is whole truth, it is obviously true in some degree. It can be confirmed by all manner of evidence. To cite a small example, the American commander in the Pacific, Douglas MacArthur, was visited in 1945 by Churchill's top commander, Alanbrooke, who reported of MacArthur, "He considered the Russians a greater menace than the Nazis had ever been." That remark forces us to look back and note the consistency of Western statesmen from the time (1919) when Churchill had supported the White generals against the Red Army, through neutrality in Spain in the thirties, through a World War II in which the real betrayals were their own, to that grand design for Southeast Asia which started to go into action in 1950 and is still dragging catastrophically on in Vietnam as these words are written.

If the idea that life is a battle with Soviet Russia was fantastic in the twenties, and still fairly absurd in the thirties, the possibility of actual war between the Russian and American governments in the forties made it seem realism itself. One had many friends in 1945 who expected America and Russia to go for each other's throats the moment they were through with Germany, and we have learned since that the Nazis had entertained not unreasonable hopes of this several years earlier: they sensed the force of The Great Melodrama. If what happened was only the Cold War, that also represents the triumph of the melodrama, all the more so as the two giant powers are fighting wars with the small countries as proxies. Moscow fights Washington in Prague; Washington fights Moscow in Saigon.

The triumph of The Great Melodrama was also the triumph of the HUAC. The forties and fifties were the days of the Committee's dubious glory. After all, its only real scoop, ever, was the Hiss case (1948). This one time the HUAC grabbed the headlines and kept them and in the course of ruining Hiss made two historic reputations, that of Whittaker Chambers and that of Richard Milhous Nixon. Whatever the gaps in Hiss's evidence, he would easily have been saved had Chambers chosen any other point in time for his "revelations." Hiss was a victim not of justice but of the clock: 1949 was a devastating year for the United States. Russia was found to have an atom bomb, and China went socialist. How far hysteria went in the West may be gauged from the fact that the possibility of just up and atom-bombing Moscow was raised there by . . . Bertrand Russell! Heads had to roll, and Hiss's did. New men must present themselves, and Nixon did. Someone must help the heads to roll and the new men to make their bow, and Chambers did. On the assumption that Hiss was guilty, not only as charged but guilty of espionage, the Committee could be said to be doing just what it had always wanted to do. It had come into its own.

Which was fun while it lasted. But it didn't last long because other committees wanted to get into the limelight, and Senator McCarthy's subcommittee succeeded. Meanwhile The Great Melodrama had reached a climax in the court-

room of Judge Irving Kaufman, who accused two alleged Communists of causing the Korean war and, in effect, got a jury to agree with him. The speech he
made on April 5, 1951, when sentencing the Rosenbergs gives as pithy a description of The Great Melodrama as can be found anywhere, as well as exem-
plifying that melodrama in murderous action:

> They [the Rosenbergs] made a choice of devoting themselves to the Rus-
> sian ideology of denial of God . . . and aggression against free men
> everywhere. . . . I believe your [the Rosenbergs'] conduct . . . has already
> caused the Communist aggression in Korea with the resultant casualties ex-
> ceeding 50,000, and who knows but that millions more of innocent people
> may pay the price of your treason? Indeed by your betrayal you undoubtedly
> have altered the course of history to the disadvantage of our country. . . . I
> . . . assume that the basic Marxist goal of world revolution and the destruc-
> tion of capitalism was well known to the defendants. . . . I must pass such
> sentence upon the principals in this diabolical conspiracy to destroy a God-
> fearing nation which will demonstrate with finality that this nation's secu-
> rity will remain inviolate.

I. F. Stone was one of very few Americans who maintained that the Korean
war was not started by "Communist aggression" at all but by the machinations
of an imperialistic United States, intent on controlling Southeast Asia; but there
again it was a question of timing. Americans in large numbers did not become
receptive to that kind of argument for another dozen years. Even in 1964 William Fulbright and Eugene McCarthy were unreceptive when Wayne Morse
and Ernest Gruening applied the argument to Vietnam. Much blood had to
flow, much cruelty and much idiocy had to be brought to their attention before
even they came around, reminding one of the question in Shaw's *Saint Joan:*
"Must a Christ die in every generation for the benefit of those with no imagination?"

II

Since, so far, I have been writing about the anti-Communist Establishment, it
would be possible for a visitor from Mars, following my account, to assume that
the Communists and their sympathizers were entirely admirable and innocent
victims of "McCarthyism," that they, accused of conspiracy, were themselves the
target of a conspiracy they in no way invited. At this point, one must speak specifically of the Communist Party—not of communism, much less of radicalism generally. In the time of Stalin, the CPUSA made two decisive commitments which have nothing necessarily to do with communism: one was to
Soviet Union, the other to a tactic of secrecy. The two commitments were all
too intricately intertwined, as secrecy was a Russian tradition, and had indeed

—in the times of the czars—been a harsh necessity.

The commitment to Russia had two distinct features: it was a commitment to a foreign power and it was a promise of unquestioning obedience. Now, either of these features might have been tolerable—without the other. Talking orders from a boss who is on the premises is not unusual, nor so objectionable if you have chosen the boss and can quit at will and without reprisals. That Russia would always have had advice to offer would also have been harmless enough. What made trouble was that, whenever Moscow spoke, everyone else had to jump to attention. Not till the 1960s did the national CPs learn to talk back, if then. It is true that Moscow's modes of interference were often exaggerated by their enemies. Fewer people received direct orders from Moscow than our "radical right" imagined. The thing was: they didn't need to. Stalin only had to sneeze, and they all caught cold. Discipline, which is a thing our own left today could use some of, which indeed is morally legitimate and politically necessary, became, as military discipline so often has, a mere pretext for outright domination of one man by another, and reduction of the dominated to a subhuman status. Since domination is bad for the dominant too, making them conceited, arbitrary, and cruel, we had here a trend exactly opposite to that which communism—the philosophy of Marx and Engels—had laid down.

If the combination of unquestioning obedience with allegiance to a foreign power was damaging, the combination of both with a tactic of secrecy was fatal. A Communist was not now to be defined as a member of a political party as that term is understood in the United States. He was a "secret agent of a foreign power," and since we were at war with that power—not in fact, perhaps, but in the kind of fantasy that becomes fact—he was "guilty of treason." Spy and traitor—this is "Communist" defined after the heart's desire of militant anti-Communists. And the CPUSA handed them its confirmation of the formula on a silver platter. This is why the Hiss case was the biggest event in the history of HUAC up to that time, and it may explain, too, why Hiss was so tight-lipped about communism and has remained so.

It is time now, I believe, to cease regarding the case as a personal duel between Hiss and Chambers. Politically, it was the Committee's attempt to nail down its thesis about Communists. It held that it succeeded; most of conservative America readily agreed; what is perhaps more interesting, a large part of liberal America was seduced into agreement. And in the long sweep of history, the personal victor was not Whittaker Chambers, who shriveled up and died, but Representative Richard M. Nixon of California, who was quoted by the Associated Press as saying:

The hearing [on Hiss] is by far the most important the Committee on Un-American Activities has conducted because of the nature of the evidence and the importance of the people involved. It will prove to the American

people once and for all that where you have a Communist you have an espionage agent.

Now the proof that Hiss was a spy was never conclusive. Chambers, as Hiss's
lawyers would eventually argue, may have committed forgery by typewriter in
order to frame Hiss. Suppose Hiss had got up one day and said, "Look, I was
never an agent. What I was is known as *a Communist:* I was a Marxist, I believed in socialism through revolution." He would have been falling into a semantic trap. A Communist is *by definition* an agent. (True, this definition became definitive precisely through the Hiss trial, but it was widely current
earlier.) And if Hiss was indeed a Communist, this must have been why he
never said so. This and the whole code and tradition of secrecy in which the
CPUSA had enveloped itself. So (again on the assumption that he was a Communist) he gambled and fought the whole battle on the question whether he
had been an agent. If he had won, no one would have found out if he had done
anything—even read the *Communist Manifesto.* If, on the other hand, he was
found to be an agent, then obviously he was a Communist too, and would be
used to prove the Nixonian axiom: "where you have a Communist you have an
espionage agent."

In fact, of course, Hiss's being an agent, if he was, would NOT prove that he
was a Communist, since there could be other reasons for undertaking agentry,
and often are. Conversely, those who know the milieu will confirm that not only
were many Communists not agents, but many wouldn't have been able even to
conceive of being agents. Again, what was unfortunate to the point of the cata-
strophic was the over-all Stalinist commitment to secrecy and to Russia: it constantly created situations which went part way to espionage even when they
didn't go the whole way, and it involved people who really could never have
lived with themselves as spies, or even as nonpatriots, in actions that smacked
of snooping and/or of divided allegiance.

I am not overlooking the arguments by which the CP could be defended. If
you are a Socialist, and socialism is achieved in one country, that country may
reasonably enough come to mean a great deal to you, and indeed there are
many Americans whose warmth of feeling toward a foreign power—Eire, Israel are examples—goes pretty far at times, as do their machinations on behalf of such powers. It can also be argued that what is in the interests of the
one socialist country must be in the interests of America too—the socialist
America we are working for—so that there is no possible conflict of loyalties.
Certainly, the pro-Soviet leftists of the thirties did not see themselves as anti-
American. For many of them, the then current CP slogan, "Communism is twentieth-century Americanism," was on the level. Any Russian aid in a revolution
would have been regarded as analagous to French aid in 1776. The Russians

would help to overthrow General Motors as the French helped to overthrow George III.

Few, of course, had projected any such thing. Had they done so, they would have run upon problems. In the American Revolution, there was small possibility of the French taking over George Washington, who in the first place professed no allegiance, public or secret, to them. Soviet Russia was simply too big a friend and did business in the wrong way—by overmuch secrecy and by outright domination. That she did so was part of a larger fact: that something had gone dreadfully wrong with socialism in Russia, possibly through mistakes of Lenin (and Leninism) in the early days, certainly through the dictatorship of Stalin in the thirties. I state the case baldly. The CPUSA denied every word of it, and still does. This is hardly the place to have it out with them, but whatever conclusions one has reached bear directly on one's judgment of "allegiance to a foreign power" in general. The degree of allegiance an Irish American feels to Eire may be very considerable, but Eire can't do much about it and Eire isn't much of a threat to anything.

I had the peculiar experience not long ago of reading in the same week *Soviet Communism, a New Civilization?* (1935) by Sidney and Beatrice Webb, and *Journey into the Whirlwind* (1967) by Eugenia Semyonova Ginzburg. Both present a picture of Russia in the thirties. The Webbs saw a beautiful new civilization there, leading the way for the rest of the world. Their only serious complaint is that discussion of fundamental principles wasn't encouraged. Eugenia Ginzburg could have got along very nicely without discussion of fundamental principles. She was a Communist in Russia and asked nothing but to be allowed to live on and work as such. She was forbidden to. And she was forbidden to on no rational grounds but on unhappily familiar irrational ones. She was confronted with human cruelty organized on the largest scale—by that very Soviet government which the Webbs admired so much. I'm afraid the Webbs wouldn't have believed such things possible even under capitalism. Under socialism they were impossible by definition. Yet Eugenia Ginzburg can be disregarded only if (a) she is a liar or (b) her case isn't typical. I defy anyone to read the book and believe it is mendacious, and, alas, no one can look further into the record and not find it to be typical.

The revolution had been betrayed. Trotsky was right. And therefore this was a strange time indeed to decide that communism was twentieth-century Americanism. It was a strange time for a popular front in which communism would commonly be equated with the most idealistic forms of liberalism. At this point the tactic of secrecy reveals another dimension. *The very nature of Soviet Communism was being kept a secret from its liberal friends.* In some ways, the CP was secretive even vis-à-vis its own members: this, too, Miss Ginzburg's history illustrates. But there was no incentive in Russia to pretend to be a Jeffersonian democrat. In America there was. And in the era in which the Party to which they owed absolute obedience practiced terror that went far beyond expedient callousness into orgies of meaningless sadism, American Communists wore the sheep's clothing of idealistic liberals. If, contrariwise, a truly idealistic liberal could be suspected of communism, the error was to be attributed not alone to the paranoia of the right but equally to the hypocrisy of the left.

And hypocritical leftists were not above exploiting the situation quite grossly. In the matter of invoking the Fifth Amendment, for example. While Joe McCarthy, on his side—or, for that matter, Sidney Hook—taught a credulous public to believe that anyone who invoked this amendment was a Communist, Communists edged non-Communists toward invoking it just in order to prove McCarthy and Hook wrong and, more broadly, to blur the lines between communism and noncommunism in their own interest. An incident I myself recall from the fifties is of such a non-Communist being actually blackmailed into invoking the Fifth Amendment by his Communist "friends," the threat being that if he didn't do it, they would report his attendance at such-and-such "Communist-front" meetings. The same horrible irony obtains in this last clause. It was the right which decided which organizations were "fronts." An unscrupulous, over-Machiavellian left could get certain results by accepting a definition it knew to be false. After which any discussion as to which organizations "really" were fronts could not but be Pirandellian. If they were fronts at all, they became so, in some cases at least, by being called so by the right and by being accepted as such by the one section of the left which was given to such shenanigans. That section was the Communist Party.

Absurd of course is all the rightist rhetoric about communism, means, and ends. This rhetoric reiterates that the peculiar evil in communism is the belief that the end justifies bad means. The absurdity here rests in the disregard of the fact that politics in general is committed to acceptance of bad means, otherwise politicians would never support war, let along the system of secrecy and deceit (espionage and diplomacy) that goes with it. If communism was worse, it was not a matter of principle but of degree. Yet even that was not the main point, which was that of communism more was expected. Communism was supposed to be a new game, and all the Stalinists were proposing was to beat the veterans of the old game. Stalin had *more logical* concentration camps than Hitler, or so it could be claimed for a time and up to a point: in the end they were so far beyond all logic that the act of comparison becomes surrealistic, ludicrous —and inhuman. Let us suppose for the purposes of argument—or for the purpose of breaking off that particular argument—that the amount of cruelty in the Hitler and Stalin regimes was exactly equal. The Russian disaster would be many times worse than the German because it is more than a disaster, it is also a tragedy, the greatest historical tragedy of the past hundred years, because, beyond all the physical suffering, it represented the desolating disappointment of the great hope of our era: the hope of socialist humanism, the hope, to put it modestly, of a society which, through socialism, shall be less oppressed, less insecure, less miserable.

Just how close any part of the CPUSA was to the giant misdeeds of the Soviet government in the late thirties I do not know, but there is plenty on the record to document that, while a degree of Machiavellianism is common to all politics, the Communists delighted in maximizing that degree and have the worst record of perhaps any radical organization that ever existed for intrigue, unscrupulousness, and inhumanity. If this is even approximately true, then we cannot think of an attack upon them—however inhuman and unscrupulous *it* may be—as comparable, say, to Hitler's assault upon ordinary citizens of Jewish origin.

One of the best studies I have read in the field is *Witch Hunt* by Carey McWilliams. After twenty years, most of McWilliams' arguments stand up very well, and some are more pertinent than ever, as for example:

> Even a majority enjoys no real immunity from the modern forms of psychological warfare which governments use to coerce consent. Nowadays large majorities can be manipulated by carefully timed headlines, revelations, and a thoroughly unscrupulous exploitation of the silence and secrecy surrounding many phases of government.

Under American law, nothing save a "clear and present" physical danger could justify coming down hard on any group of citizens of any persuasion, including communism. McWilliams' book might be regarded as a scholarly elaboration upon such views of freedom of speech as have been reiterated over the years by Justice William O. Douglas and Justice Hugo Black. He identifies a real sickness, a veritable fever, within American society, demonstrates its ravages, and suggests, for cure, adherence to the principles laid down in the Constitution and the Bill of Rights.

But it is characteristic of the liberal writing of the time (1950) that so little is said of communism. The whole problem is seen as that of the witch-hunters themselves. On one point, however, McWilliams shows more curiosity than did the liberalism of the day: secrecy. Generally this was passed over almost as if the CPUSA was as open in its dealings as any other group. McWilliams acknowledges that it was not, and even advances a justification for secrecy, and a dignified precedent: the Abolitionists also withheld their plans from the public. But I'm afraid the CPUSA can only suffer further from any comparison with the Abolitionists. Of course, all parties involved in revolutionary, warlike, and maybe just political action will use a degree of secrecy. There is secrecy in withholding a press release till the right moment. Again, the difference from Communist practice is not one of principle but of degree; yet moral differences are often differences of degree; such differences can be enormous.

The Abolitionists had a deserved reputation for integrity. The opposite is true of the Communist parties of the Stalin era.

Descending from the high plateau of politics to simple personal prudence, one might defend American Communists who were secretive to avoid losing their jobs. Surely secrecy of that sort is often fully justified. If only the secrecy of the CP had stopped there! But not only was it a Machiavellian scheme of life with widely spread nets, it was a veritable mystique, respected and adhered to beyond all rational plan. It was a way of life. And therein more than a revolution was betrayed. Marxism was betrayed. The whole tradition of radicalism was betrayed. I cite the *Communist Manifesto:*

> The Communists disdain to conceal their views and aims. They openly declare that their ends can be attained by the forcible overthrow of all existing social conditions. Let the ruling classes tremble at a Communist revolution.

That such an "open declaration" is likely to be dangerous is obvious. That the declarer may lose his job stands to reason. Though he might forgivably do a little trembling, the emphasis of Marx and Engels is all on the trembling the other side would do.

Quite a contrast to HUAC's Hollywood hearings of 1947. The Ten went to jail and in various degrees suffered further privations later. But what were they fighting for? Materially speaking, for the maintenance of their—in some cases—absurdly high level of income. Ideologically speaking, neither for Marxism nor for Stalinism, but for the classical liberalism of Hugo Black and William Douglas, as embodied in the First Amendment. Why? What sense did that make? That wasn't the kind of people they were, obviously, whether or not they were all card-carrying members of the CPUSA. But, alas, they did *not* disdain to conceal their views. They lacked candor, and if that, humanly speaking, is quite a common lack, it is an impossible lack for real radicals. For, to radicalism, candor is no adornment, it is of the essence. It is love of candor that makes men radical thinkers: a distaste for pretense, an awareness of the prevalence of false consciousness, and a yearning for realities, an appetite for true consciousness. While in action Stalinist Communism ran to terror on a big scale, in thought it went just as far astray by creating its own "false consciousness." Abandoning that strenuous and joyful quest for reality which is the spiritual life of radicalism, it addressed itself instead to the traditional task of wrapping realities in empty forms of words. So, in the HUAC hearings, the rhetoric of John Howard Lawson merely counterbalances that of the Committee. Bullshit equals bullshit.

III

It is with this in mind that Richard Rovere wrote, "The investigators and the investigated have seemed richly to deserve each other." The witticism is sharp, but what exactly is implied? If a torturer and the man he is torturing are equally terrible fellows, should one extend an equal lack of sympathy to both? Rovere does praise Walter Goodman, the principal historian of HUAC, precisely for "the evenhandedness of his contempt for the Stalinist Left and the Yahoo Right." * But aside from the question whether contempt is a sufficient response, there is a failure to distinguish here between the mere disaster of Yahoo rightism, and the tragedy of communism in the Stalin era. A Yahoo is a Yahoo, but the left was not by nature Stalinist: the Stalinization of non-Stalinoid human beings was a tragic process—how could anyone who has been on the inside, the real side, of any of this contrive to be merely contemptuous? If your brother goes wrong, you aren't contemptuous, you are devastated; and the Stalinists were our brothers, while the Yahoos were not. I speak for radicals.

Rovere and Goodman could reply that they are not radicals, and this is very true. The question remains whether their contempt for hangman and hanged alike yields any insight, let alone constitutes a tenable position. All that comes through to me is a certain delight in feeling superior to both sides: a message less about the sides than about the observer. The stance is narcissistic, and it fails to do justice not only to the investigated *but also to the investigators.*

No radical critic can bring to the investigators the kind of understanding that comes from sympathy, but a combatant does not fall, either, into the error of underestimating the enemy. Contempt entails doing just that, for in the fire of contempt, a knave shrivels into a fool, a monster into a shrimp. With this in mind, I would criticize what, over the years, I have found to be the prevailing view of HUAC among those who consider themselves agin it. It is that the HUAC hearings are an irrelevant side show beside the circus tent of American politics. As a theatre man, I may be permitted to remind anyone who needs it that actual side shows were intended to lure customers into the tent: they were never irrelevant. Metaphor aside, I think it can be demonstrated that—amid so many stupid things said—HUAC itself was usually the reverse of stupid and, so far from being irrelevant or remote, was always close to the center of the political struggle. These men had their ears closer to the ground than any of your bland, clever, literate liberals.

We shall never know *how* close unless some band of revolutionaries manages to corner the FBI files, for undoubtedly the historian's key to The Whole Truth in this field lies in the connection between HUAC and the FBI. There is general agreement that it is close, which indeed can be proved from the public record, but just what it means in specific detail could only be shown from FBI files themselves. In the matter of informing, for example. The public got the impression that informers just ran to Washington and talked to HUAC while America eavesdropped. In fact, HUAC carefully dramatized the act of informing

* Foreword to *The Committee* by Walter Goodman.

for purposes of waging political warfare: to intimidate some, to encourage others, and so on. It was theatre or, if you like, ritual: a rite of purification that would also put the fear of God (HUAC's man in heaven) into the as yet unpurified. The public confessions were as nothing to the private confessions that preceded them. One could spill all the beans to J. Edgar Hoover or one of his merry men; then HUAC would serve selected beans to the great American public via the great American press. HUAC also had its own investigators to whom beans could be privately spilled. Before we would know The Whole Truth we would need to have the records of their sessions too, as well as of "executive sessions" of the Committee, which also seem to have specialized in intimate, if not necessarily true, confessions. If the American people is not the freest ever, it may be the best supervised and most listened in on. Everything from Eleanor Roosevelt's hotel-room conversation to Martin Luther King's extramarital relations is there on tape for nationwide broadcast at the appointed time. For Big Brother isn't of 1984, he has been watching us for some decades now. Some think his name is Hoover. In which case his Little Brother's name is HUAC.

Linked in the first instance to the FBI, HUAC is linked in the second to the courts. Congressman John Rankin described it as "the grand jury of America," and in 1946 it became the only House committee ever to have the right to subpoena witnesses. The game was then to place them in a position where the House itself would cite them for contempt of Congress. At best they would then go to jail, at worst spend some uncomfortable, expensive years keeping out of jail: such was the alternative to purification. The Committee won either way.

That HUAC has usually been extremely smart is best shown in its choice of targets and therewith of headlines. One could work backward from 1970 and demonstrate this year by year. This year they are doing the Panthers. Last year they did SDS. In 1968 they were investigating the Chicago "conspiracy" even before Nixon got to the White House. In 1966 it had been "Bills to make punishable assistance to enemies of U.S. in time of undeclared war"—i.e., the left wing of the peace movement. They had got to women's liberation as early as 1962 (Women Strike for Peace). They were on to the Oppenheimer Case as early as 1947, though for the public it didn't become a case at all till seven years later. "Alger Hiss the Spy" was a HUAC discovery or invention, as you will. They had a large share in making history of the Great Informers: first and always foremost Whittaker Chambers, but, scarcely less creative and aggressive, Elizabeth Bentley, Louis Budenz, Harvey Matusow. They shot two Eislers with one stone—a third Eisler, who got in touch with Hoover in 1946. In 1939 they wrecked the Federal Theatre, that first effort at socialist humanism in American institutions. In short, they have always been on the ball, and we needn't ask Our Father to forgive them, for they do know what they do.

The HUAC's most notorious target of all was Hollywood, and to be sure they chose it because, in Arthur Miller's phrase, they were "cheap publicity hounds."

Yet if we impute this motive alone we fall into the trap of overstressing the HUAC's frivolity and thereby underestimating its seriousness. In our America, publicity is no marginal phenomenon, and its ballyhoo, though unreal in one sense, is, in mere common sense, reality itself. At best we may hope to make it unreal later on. For now, the advertising is the most real part of television—TV exists for it, not it for TV, time is money, and TV has Father Time in a wallet on its back. The image is more important than the man, whether the name be Narcissus or Nixon, and the unreal is our quintessential reality, our *Ding an sich*. The marriage of HUAC and Hollywood was made in heaven, which in turn is situated between Fifth and Park. Today, if the HUAC were still in its prime, it would no doubt be wooing the TV networks, but in 1947 Hollywood was still the principal dream factory—always excepting Washington itself.

The two sets of dreamers—power wielders too, since their dreams had power, black-and-white power, not to mention Technicolor—were meant for each other and had to get together. Paranoia being what it is, and The Great Melodrama being what it is, they had to get together against the Enemy, especially the Enemy Within, the "Trojan Horse in America," the Russian agent in the White House or Disneyland. A big show? Well, naturally: the greatest show on earth, enacted by professionals of both entertainment businesses, West and East, Hollywood and Washington. It was the only time in history that the earth seemed likely to be taken over by its greatest show.

IV

How should those of us who are "unfriendly" to such a committee behave when subpoenaed by it? I have been saying that, traditionally and essentially, radicals disdain to conceal their views. The simplest thing for them to do, then, would be to go to Washington and answer all questions about these views. But this would be to recognize the Committee's authority or at least existence. Should they do that? Albert Einstein thought not and, in 1953, formulated what I. F. Stone, who supported it, called the Einstein Pledge. Einstein saw the Committee's work as a kind of Inquisition that threatened the integrity of all intellectual workers. They should therefore be conscientious objectors against it, breaking the law of the land in the name of a Higher Law, like Saint Thomas More—and be prepared to suffer for this as he did.

But just as conscientious objection to military service may be applied in various degrees and at various stages along the line—one can serve in the Red Cross or one can refuse even to go to the induction center—so it has been possible to fight the Committee without taking the Einstein Pledge. Most unfriendly witnesses have responded to their subpoenas and have then confronted HUAC with some tactic calculated to help their own cause. The most famous tack has been invocation of the Fifth Amendment to the Constitution—which offers the privilege of not testifying if you judge that your testimony might prove self-incriminating. Some witnesses cited several amendments, and many invoked just the First, which guarantees freedom of speech and association.

In themselves all these choices were legitimate, even if, as Telford Taylor has shown in his book *Grand Inquest,* there was widespread misunderstanding of what the Fifth Amendment was all about. (It was never intended as a way of protecting associates; rather, and specifically, as a means of *self*-protection, whether one was innocent or guilty. When Lillian Hellman, in 1952, tried to use the Fifth to shield others while exposing herself she was performing legal gymnastics—unwittingly, of course; and in retrospect it would seem that both the ethics and the politics of her strategy were exemplary.) If there was a question, it was not really of the tactics themselves but of good faith. Was refusal to speak the honest and courageous gesture it purported to be or a disingenuous way of hiding something both from the Committee and from the world?

As I have stressed, it is the Communist Party, of all radical groups, that has made a specialty of a politics of bad faith. To match it one has to look to its arch-enemies in the Establishment, such as Richard Nixon, a man fascinated by Communist skulduggery. And it was the Communist Party that gave Joe McCarthy the pretext for his otherwise preposterous concept, "Fifth-Amendment Communists," and, for that matter, which gave Sidney Hook the pretext for his more sophisticated presentations of McCarthy's notion. The CPUSA, rendering suspect everything they touched, forfeited what is nowadays called "credibility," which perhaps wouldn't have mattered very much except that they thereby damaged the "credibility" of every other radical group in America. What one has to complain of, then, is less that some people's silence was in bad faith than that the good faith of what was no doubt the large majority of unfriendly witnesses before HUAC was brought into question by the bad faith of the others. Which was a double misfortune: a misfortune in ethics, since a real wrong was done by some human beings to others, and a misfortune in political warfare and "public relations" since irreparable damage was done to reputations, both of causes and of individuals.

What a pity that such a topic comes to us almost exclusively in the crude blacks and whites of journalism! For, that way, it is not just nuances of gray that are lost but the whole spectrum of colors. What I have said of the CPUSA is far from true of many members and sympathizers of that organization, for the Party was monolithic chiefly in the fertile fantasy of its enemies: it had human beings both in and around it, many of them very fine people indeed. When its most famous sympathizer, Paul Robeson, took the position before HUAC that everyone in fact knew where he stood, it was true. He may have respected certain formal taboos of CP tradition—like avoiding the mention of communism and its Party when addressing a non-Communist audience—yet it would be ludicrous to suggest that Paul Robeson ever kept the public from knowing who he was and what he believed. When he refused, on principle, to answer the sixty-four-dollar question before HUAC, he had already answered it before California's "little HUAC," the Tenney Committee. But by the time he came before HUAC, he had decided to say, in effect, "I'll tell the public but I won't tell you." He was far from alone in this decision. A party may have betrayed a Revolution, but that does not make a traitor of each of its individual supporters—a traitor either to Revolution or to their country—for no man is an institution incarnate, and despite reports to the contrary, very many Stalinists continued to be men.

Much as one may favor open declarations of faith, it would be unfair, without knowing each from the inside, to censure those individuals who did not make such declarations. Their secret was not always that they held membership in the CPUSA. There were often private reasons for silence: one person was protecting another or believing he was. Besides which, there was much sincerity, if not always as much clearheadedness, in the individual's commitment to silence. Even today many on the left will not go along with such a condemnation of the CP as I have offered here. And yesterday—well, yesterday *Journey into the Whirlwind* had not been written and, although evidence of the nature of Stalinism had been published, it was much easier, then, to overlook it. The Webbs were a scholarly couple, yet their only comment on the murder of Trotsky (in the 1942 revision of their book) was that he fell at the hands of one of his own followers! At the time this was a common version of what happened. The full truth had not yet been written. But one notes also a refusal to be suspicious that is highly inappropriate to the subject.

It would in any case be a mistake both tactical and moral to go after individuals in a kind of reverse McCarthyism. Let the dead bury their dead. In the 1960s a new generation came to life. As far as HUAC is concerned, it began with Women Strike for Peace. The HUAC wanted to know if they were a Communist front. One questioned such people, didn't one, and they hedged on their answers? If they said they accepted Communists into membership of their organizations they would add that that was only because they were so broadminded. So one pressed on and asked, Are you so broad-minded you accept Nazis? Then they said, Oh no, that was quite different and, bingo, one had them in the trap: they were, too, a front for Communism. Only Dagmar Wilson didn't hedge. She wasn't CP-trained. She wasn't CP-intimidated, -blackmailed, or even -overawed. She just answered any and all questions in her own freewheeling style, willing to talk to the HUAC, just as she would have been willing to talk to George Lincoln Rockwell or the Grand Wizard of the Klan. A woman with nothing to hide! A woman who disdained to conceal her views and openly declared them! Yes, she answered, she would accept Communists.

Yes, she answered, she would accept Nazis, if she could get 'em. In the cause of peace, one needed them all, one needed everybody.

It was the fall of HUAC's Bastille. Whether or no the Committee and its unfriendly witnesses hitherto had "deserved each other," they had come to need each other as playmates in a game with by now agreed rules. It was nice to ask a question knowing that the witness would refuse to answer, and that you'd get him for contempt. How disconcerting, then, if the witness spoiled everything by answering the question and reversing the roles, playing cop to their robber, hero to their villain! Of course, silence had been heroic—in intention. And Arthur Miller had tried to apotheosize this heroic refusal to speak in dramatic literature (*The Crucible*). In real life, unhappily, such refusal was rendered suspect and ambiguous by its whole background in the life and hates of the Communist Party. Liberation from the murk of this ambiguity was to be found in ending the silence—but singing quite a different tune from the one the HUAC wanted to hear.

> . . . once the keystone of [the Fifth Amendment] privilege was removed, the entire structure of investigative exposure so carefully erected through the years came tumbling down. The witness was at liberty to dispute and challenge all of the committee's most cherished assumptions, to parry and thrust, to insist upon counterstatements. Since there is nothing in the Federal contempt statute that forces the witness to confine his answer to a narrow formula or that bars him from objecting to questions ad nauseam, the witnesses at the hearing, liberated from the Fifth Amendment and its ancillary restraints, made the committee pay an exorbitant price for the answers it received. Overnight a new kind of witness was born: the witness who boils over with talk, who pleads no privilege and fills the record with his views and objections. He is exactly the old-style friendly witness with one important exception: his testimony attacks the committee, its premises and its claimed legislative subject matter—bitingly, humorously, solemnly and fearlessly.*

The hearing here described took place in August 1966. The view of Marx and Engels on concealment had finally come into its own, logically enough, by way of young members of the Marxist-Leninist Progressive Labor Party. They had prepared speeches presenting their views, and they delivered them as fully as they were allowed to, paying as much or as little attention to the questions the Committee asked, or tried to ask, as they wished. It was a matter therefore not only of open declaration but of a rather violent war of nerves—rebel sons of America against fuddy-duddy fathers. And no one could have been better cast for this father role than the Chairman of HUAC's Subcommittee, the late Joe R.

* "HUAC: From Pillory to Farce" by Frank J. Donner, *Nation*, September 5, 1966.

Pool of Texas. Jerry Rubin was on hand, dressed as a soldier of the Revolutionary War. Very much, at the time, a show in its own right, the 1966 hearing seems in retrospect more of a rehearsal for Judge Julius Hoffman's courtroom (1969–1970).

But this is to forget to credit HUAC with its own rehearsal procedures. They hauled in David Dellinger, Rennie Davis, and Tom Hayden in October 1968. These three didn't run wild like the Progressive Laborites, but they did exploit the committee room as a forum for their views, and, in effect, they imposed their own rules of procedure, since there was nothing the Committee could do to stop them from talking, let alone to ensure that their vocabulary, syntax, and tone should be what Congressmen regard as proper.

The HUAC road show, after running so merrily for thirty years, stopped right there. Yes, it was to continue under another name—the House Internal Security Committee—and might well remain a menace for a long time to come. But something more than a title had ended. The 1960s killed the Committee that all of us knew and some of us didn't love, that Committee whose spirit is perhaps best caught in the utterances of its most eloquent investigator, the late Richard Arens:

Do you remember the quotation from Lenin on that, that they will encircle the United States and it will fall in the hands of the Communists like an overripened fruit?

Within the framework of the Communist operation, is there room for concepts of God and spiritual values as we were taught them at our mother's knee?

Are you now thoroughly disgusted with the fact that you have been associated with the Communist ideology, which is atheistic, which is the very antithesis of Christian morality as we know it in this country?

Are you now, or have you ever been, a member of a godless conspiracy controlled by a foreign power?

Or, finally:

Kindly tell us, while you are under oath now, and in the aura of patriotism which you have surrounded yourself [with] in your opening statement, whether or not you betrayed your country by being executive secretary of this organization designed to subvert the security of this great nation?

A question which Arens reworded, when the witness objected to it, as follows:

For the moment, may we change to say, Were you executive secretary of this innocent little organization, this patriotic organization, this organization for the uplift of humanity, the Southern California Peace Crusade?

That is unmistakably the tone of the 1950s. But the mentality is much older, as old as persecution perhaps, and certainly as old as the thirties and forties, when the lady who had falsely denounced Hallie Flanagan to HUAC as virtually a Communist was rewarded for her pains by being hired as a Committee investigator and, after duly warning HUAC against Herman Shumlin and Woody Guthrie, reported on Helen Hayes as follows: "While Helen Hayes is one of our leading actresses, she was head of the milk fund for the North American Spanish Committee." The radicals of the sixties put the Committee—for the first time—on the defensive. Earlier, the witnesses were generally meek; now Committee members were generally meek. And in seizing the offensive, the new type of witnesses seized what was dearest to HUAC's patriotic heart: the headlines. On August 10, 1969, it was announced in the *New York Times* that, at long last, the courts had allowed a direct challenge to the Committee's constitutionality.

> The ruling, by a unanimous three-judge panel of the United States Court of Appeals for the Seventh Circuit, sitting in Chicago, will apparently have the effect of placing on trial the controversial 31-year history of the committee.

One Committee chairman was sent to jail years ago, but this was only for thievery. Now HUAC as a whole may be found to be unconstitutional, and, in that case, what would be the difference in status between its investigators and ordinary snoopers and spies? And who would have betrayed their country, the witnesses or the Committee members? Some of both perhaps; but only the HUAC members could claim to be traitors ex officio.

The Hollywood screen director Robert Rossen had come before HUAC in 1951 as an only partially repentant Communist. According to his own account, he then spent two years "thinking," only to return in 1953 with these conclusions: "I wouldn't like to see young people today believe what I believed in. I wouldn't like to have them feel there is no growth left in this country . . . that it's a dead society. . . . It's a young society, it's a growing society, it's a healthy society. It . . . can . . . realize its hope only in terms of the system of government that's been devised." "I don't feel that I'm being a stool pigeon," he said a little later in the day, "or an informer . . . that is rather romantic—that is like children playing at cops and robbers." For the Committee had got him to name names, as they had Granville Hicks, Daniel Boorstin, and Robert Gorham Davis. Of these three, it was Davis, probably, who was most concerned with this particular matter. Reviewing James Burnham's Web of Subversion *in 1954, he wrote: ". . . those most opposed to 'informers' are often intellectuals whose profession it is to inform and be informed, and who fight for freedom of inquiry in every direction but this." Now those, through the centuries, who have indeed fought for freedom of inquiry would be quite surprised to learn that, under that heading, could come inquiry into the beliefs and associations of former comrades. That is a kind of inquiry we associate with J. Edgar Hoover rather than Socrates, Galileo, or Voltaire. It is true that the Communists were equally disingenuous on the subject, since they would not allow anyone the right to turn against them in good conscience: it must always be a betrayal and have venal or other base motives. Two wrongs, however, don't make a right. The Communists and the anti-Communists, high- or low-browed, in vying with each other in disingenuousness, combined to evade the truth of every subject they touched. "I believe," said the once-Communist Hollywood director Frank Tuttle, "there is a traditional dislike among Americans for informers, and I am an informer. . . . The aggressors are ruthless, and I feel it is absolutely necessary for Americans to be equally ruthless." Neither side wanted to go into what actually underlies this traditional dislike, not merely American, of informers. The Communists were saying, "You know we are right, so any informing you do is in bad faith." The anti-Communists were saying, "You'd inform the police about arsonists, so you should inform Hoover about these political arsonists." Whereas someone who felt the traditional dislike without feeling that the Communist Party could command his loyalty might well have reasoned: "Tuttle exaggerates the threat in order to avoid complexity. In fact, there is not a clear and present danger of the kind he envisages, and it is quite dubious whether such utter ruthlessness is simply imposed upon us without any question. Since I owe the CP no loyalty, it is obvious that I don't think the Communists are right on all this. It is not obvious, though, that I should therefore give any information I may have about Communists to their enemies. I do not wish to protect the CP, but I may properly wish to protect past and even present members of it. And I dislike informers because they are phony avenging angels, 'phony' because their motives are seldom free of personal malice and perhaps suprapersonal vindictiveness. Tuttle says he is willing to be ruthless because it is absolutely necessary. That is phony: the testimony of these Hollywood people was in fact extremely unnecessary. The FBI had the information, such as it was, already. No, not an urgent political necessity, but fear and/or the American overconcern for public relations, was what made people like Frank Tuttle tick. In these circumstances, is not the traditional dislike of informing a better guide than the various 'rational' arguments? We all feel there is something slimy about informing. Because there is."*

(1971)

The Political Theatre of John Wayne

Mr. [Charles] Chaplin, who retained his British citizenship during 40 years residence in the United States, left this country in 1952. James P. McGranery, then Attorney General, announced that the comedian could not re-enter this country unless he could prove his "moral worth."
—*New York Times,* October 14, 1971

Showing up in Dallas to accept the Veterans of Foreign Wars Americanism Gold Medal, John Wayne said: "I have found that a peaceloving man fights if he has something to fight for. The V.F.W. represents many who died to give this country a second chance to make it what it is supposed to be—God's guest house on earth."
—*New York Times,* August 17, 1971

Of recent years I have repeatedly heard two things said of the black list in the theatrical profession. One is that it is now a thing of the past. The other is that the good guys got reinstated, whereas the bad guys, like Joe McCarthy himself, curled up and died. Happy ending. Triumph of the democratic process. And if not without tears, at least working itself out automatically and predictibly: God is good.

Well, there is no denying the disappearance of those particular bad guys. To the younger generation, Godfrey Schmidt and Vincent Hartnett would simply be Godfrey and Vincent who?, yet the first was president of Aware Incorporated, and the second was one of its directors as well as coauthor of *Red Channels*. In 1954 Aware called for a "full-fledged official investigation of the entertainment industry in New York" and got together with the House Committee on Un-American Activities to put it through. Where are the snows of yesteryear?

There is no denying the reinstatements and rehabilitations. Dalton Trumbo lives, and his screenplays are attributed to no one but himself. Vincent Hartnett and his collaborator, Laurence Johnson, a Syracuse supermarket owner, were sued by the black-listed actor John Henry Faulk, who won a three-and-a-half-million-dollar libel verdict (even if he didn't collect). Pete Seeger appears on TV (even if the script is censored to save face for Lyndon Johnson, the face unsavable). Millard Lampell and Lionel Stander report former privations in the *New York Times* and contrast them with present glory.

Yet one can only relax in satisfaction, or even sigh with relief, if one sees the conflict as a self-contained one between two small and rather peculiar groups: the theatrical profession on the one hand (including in the term "movie and TV people") and the radical right in business. This has been how the nonradical right has seen it, not to mention the center and the public at large, including many who consider themselves liberal. The moral drawn is that our system, if not always fast enough, of itself rejects such madness and returns the country to sanity—a thesis which has lost its cogency of late in that Vietnam has hardly been sanity. And Vietnam is not an isolated phenomenon but the result of a strict, if horrifying, logic, all things working together for bad.

In the perspective of the sixties, a perspective still deepening and darkening in the seventies, the fifties must be differently seen, not, alas, as some kind of social measles that we had and could not have again but as a spreading virus which we still have, and have much worse. Joe McCarthy was not really a failure, any more than other martyrs. Like these others, he only agreed to take the rap, and he complaisantly allowed himself to be a guinea pig in experiments not equally successful in all directions. But the battles he lost were stages in a war which his side still hopes, not without its reasons, to win. This was not a war against the theatrical profession, nor was it, really, a war against the tiny Communist Party of the U.S.A. It was a war against the Soviet Union, the People's Republic of China, and the Third World, against all Socialists who still believe in socialism and against all liberals neither enthralled nor intimidated by anticommunism. To prosecute this war it would be necessary for the United States to attack as well as defend and so, implicitly, to pass from nationalism to imperialism. Imperialism in turn implies racism, in which the United States was in any case uniquely schooled by its handling of the red, the black, and the brown.

The radical right at times let the cat out of the bag by admitting much of this, even boasting of it. Overfrank rightists tend to share the fate of McCarthy, and no one denounces them more shrilly than the main body of anti-Communists, but the latter really owe the former a debt of gratitude, though it would hardly be shrewd of them to admit it. Better to accept the services of such rightists and disown them. For the new imperialism must not call itself imperialistic, any more than a member of an all-white golf club calls himself racist. There are indeed differences between the new imperialism and the old. The old was less hypocritical. The problem of the new order is: how to be hypocritical successfully, a problem not economic or military but political and diplomatic, to be solved in the communications media. Which is how it becomes the problem of those of us who write or speak or act, particularly if we do any of these things for a powerful constituency.

The most important American of our time is John Wayne. Granted that all good things come from California, Richard Nixon and Ronald Reagan are only camp followers of Wayne, supporting players in the biggest Western of them all, wagons hitched to Wayne's star. In an age when the image is the principal thing, Wayne is the principal image, and if the soul of this image is *machismo* (a topic for another essay, a topic for a book, for *the* book of our time), its body is the body politic, and its name is Anti-Communism.

The 1947 Hollywood hearings of the Un-American Activities Committee have never been entirely forgotten. Forgotten, however, is that those hearings would probably not have happened but for California's own Fact-Finding Committee on Un-American Activities (1941–1949) under Jack B. Tenney and the Motion Picture Alliance for the Preservation of American Ideals, an organization founded in 1944 for the greater glory of free enterprise and what is now called Middle America, or, in its own words, to combat "the growing impression that this industry is made up of, and dominated by, Communists, radicals, and crackpots." It was made up of what a HUAC member called "old-time American producers, actors, and writers," and its president was John Wayne. "Let no one say that a Communist can be tolerated in American society and particularly in our industry," said Wayne on March 22, 1951. "We do not want to associate with traitors. . . . We hope those who have changed their view will cooperate to the fullest extent. By that I mean names and places, so that they can come back to the fellowship of loyal Americans. The bankers and stockholders must recognize that their investments [in the movie industry] are imperiled as long as we have these elements in our midst."

If, as Kierkegaard thought, purity of heart is to will one thing, Wayne's strength was always as the strength of ten, and his career described one consistent curve from that time forth until the day when Richard Nixon saw him on screen at the California White House and rushed out to say to the whole world that this was good old America, whereas bad new America was represented by gunmen of a different stamp like Charlie Manson, whom it seemed the President might have mixed up with Abbie Hoffman. In an age when God's son became a superstar, why shouldn't a superstar become God himself?

Patron saint anyway. England's patron saint had slain a dragon. America's —even if camouflaged as a paper tiger—would slay all dragons. All alike had red blood, and Wayne made some anti-Red movies, culminating, if that is the word, in *The Green Berets,* which was advertised with a picture showing Americans happily blowing up little, no doubt yellow villagers. But the movies labeled anticommunist were the least of it. Motion pictures, as Nixon intuitively recognized, are by nature anticommunist, if only they are good pictures, healthy-minded, and put together by old-time American producers, actors, and writers. That they are so is the meaning of John Wayne's whole career. It is amazing that students of art and politics have ignored this fact, and even more amazing that critics of a conservative turn of mind have remained skeptical of the power of propaganda, "conservative" propaganda at that. It is all too true that the concerted efforts of antiwar propagandists have failed to prevent, let alone stop, a single war. John Wayne on the other hand, an explicit champion of pugnacity and an implicit instigator of aggression, might claim to have got wars started. Along with the statesmen of the Pentagon Papers, he is one of "the people who brought you Vietnam."

Have I made it any clearer what the black list was all about? Out of the thirties came a sizable Red, or at least Pink, minority. This minority was generously represented in our profession. If even Helen Hayes (as cited on page 304) was a little bit pink, you can guess how flaming Red, in HUAC's eyes, were Tom, Dick, and Harry. Sociologists will find reasons for the radical enthusiasm of theatre folk, some flattering, some not—some, that is, having to do with our generosity of soul and some with our rootlessness and vagabondage.

World War II created a special situation. Soviet Russia was for the first time a political friend of the United States. It seemed all right, also for the first time, for Reds to be *openly* pro-Soviet, but when the war ended in 1945, the German menace had been removed, thus leaving (from the American viewpoint) the Russian menace all over again, in fact more so, or (from the Russian viewpoint) the American menace all over again, in fact more so. Which is how it has remained. And which is what put John Wayne ahead; and started the careers of his friends and colleagues, like Nixon and Reagan. Before 1945 life had several aims, which for the common man has advantages, since he can hope to get lost in the shuffle. After 1945 it had only one aim: to combat communism. I read in the *Times* just the other day a comment on the Pentagon Papers by a member of LBJ's cabinet who said that, in occasionally disagreeing with LBJ, he hadn't meant to rock the boat, he just meant that *Vietnam might not be ideal terrain.* Life still had only one aim. And if Wayne was the icon, Nixon has long been the iconographer. It has been said that Nixon played rough, or even dirty, in the kind of opposition he offered to Jerry Voorhis and Helen Gahagan Douglas, who obstructed his first steps to power. But why not? If liberalism in that era was tainted by communism, and even chained to it, then Voorhis and Douglas were, in effect, Communists, who, in turn, are Russian espionage agents. Only a few years later—and while Hiss was still in jail—J. Robert Oppenheimer was declared a Soviet spy in so many words by a United States official who never apologized and was never reprimanded. Indeed it is characteristic of this whole era in America that many were punished for words that did no provable harm to anyone whereas others were permitted to speak with maximum destructiveness and mendacity and were not punished at all.

Conceivably, Nixon bore no ill will to Voorhis or Mrs. Douglas, nor will it suffice to describe them as victims of his personal ambition alone. They were victims of something much more important, in which I would not doubt he believes with complete sincerity: anticommunism. I have never heard that Hartnett and Johnson hated Faulk. If they did, the case would be an exception. This was no war of individuals, and if it was a war of groups, it was not a war of these groups only: all were participating in the great religious war of our age, which differs from the religious wars of the past in that the religion is only superstition or, more accurately, melodrama. Hence, an actor who fell in this war was not the victim of personal venom, nor yet of a group feud between, say, sponsors and performers. No one bore him any grudge. It was just that as a Communist—well, a Pink, a liberal, what have you—he was a Russian agent, and Russian agents are always air-mailing atomic secrets to Moscow. The minute the Russians have stolen our atom bomb they will drop it on New York, you can be sure of that much.

Why did certain actors have to be black-listed? Because they were Russian agents, as I have just proved. And why is it bad to have Russian agents strutting our stages? Because, as I have suggested, they may be making a long-distance phone call in the intermission. There is another reason, just as important in the long run, if there is a long run. We gotta keep old-time America the way it always was, and those guys (Red, Pink, what have you) are in the way: they must go.

I would ask the actors not to get too discouraged at the thought. After all, we often hear the argument that actors are of no political importance anyway; probably they should stay out of politics altogether; when they go in, they don't do too good. Actors, says a friend of mine, are just *children*. To this I would answer, first, that we are all just children in many respects, and I don't see that actors can claim any kind of monopoly there. Second, it is not just "going into politics" that has political importance. More important is *what an actor seems to the public to stand for*. On this point we must hand it to John Wayne that he never keeps his public in the dark. Off screen, he does not, like many liberals, hesitate to join organizations or to sign declarations. He even seeks, which is fairly unusual in Hollywood, to put his art at the service of his beliefs, and, even in his less deliberately propagandist efforts, he succeeds. As his President has acknowledged, he is a definite part of the education—or should we say conditioning?—of most Americans. If John Wayne is the artist a President like Nixon deserves, Nixon is the President a nation of John Waynes would deserve.

While some people say it doesn't matter what actors think and stand for, the Establishment knows it does matter what actors think and stand for, because actors are in the public eye, are the royalty and aristocracy of a society that still craves these things after getting rid of them, are idols in a society that has lost its gods. For "actors" read "theatre people" generally. It was always said that investigators and black-listers were publicity hounds. They were, but not altogether wrongly. Publicity is a huge reality in our America, and our friends of the HUAC felt threatened by the publicity which attended radical activities in the theatre as elsewhere. I don't think they all believed their own mythology, which would have made Russian spies of all their enemies, yet their invention of such a mythology proves how lively their hallucinations were. Hallucinations are real. Rather than be crushed by the power of anti-Communist propaganda, shouldn't we take these people at their word and retort, "You think we are important? O.K., we'll be important. To borrow a phrase from Khrushchev: We will bury you."

Around 1950 a section of the Establishment decided that the world situation was so grave America had better move anyone suspected of communism out of any responsible public position. Theatre and film artists of left-wing persuasion resisted the trend at first but, in considerable part, surrendered to it later. Before Robert Rossen could work again in Hollywood he had to undergo, or pretend to undergo, or hope he'd undergone, a conversion. "I don't think," he reported, "that any one individual can indulge himself in the luxury of individual morality or pit it against what I feel today very strongly is the security and safety of this nation."

It is true that none of these people ever seems to have felt these things spontaneously, but only when threatened with the loss of contracts. At the same time one has to allow for the communism of some having been as insincere as their subsequent anticommunism: people are only people. And people are various. All degrees of sincerity were exhibited. Then again the definition of sincerity is an open one, and the value of certain types of sincerity is unproven.

I am not digging up this "ancient history" to score points off anyone, but I do think the preparation for the disasters of the sixties goes further back than the Pentagon Papers, and I do think the exposures should cover material of the fifties, and perhaps earlier. The aim should be to understand our plight now, which all agree to be grave. I don't think we of the entertainment world have played a very large part either for good or evil, but some part we have played, and we owe it to ourselves to assess it. If we are not that important, we are—and this is my real point—not that unimportant either, and if a John Wayne can labor so manfully (that's the word) to prolong a certain social order, others in his profession can labor, instead, to replace it. They did so in the past, I know, but latterly I have seen them get very discouraged. One actress told me she could never again do any "signing or joining," though she agreed in her heart with many of the current causes: her back had been broken by her experience of the McCarthy era. In such an instance we see the lasting strength of McCarthyism: it works. As much as we let it. It fails to work insofar as we stop it. If some members of our profession passively suffered under the black list and HUAC, or even surrendered to them and the forces behind them, others did not. At least one man recanted his communism at the behest of HUAC and the FBI and then later recanted his anticommunism at the behest of his conscience. This was Sterling Hayden, who wrote in his autobiography that he was "a stoolie for J. Edgar Hoover."

(1971)

"Your generation's frontier should have been Tanganyika," he [Wayne] contends, recalling the African country—independent Tanzania now—where he made *Hatari*. "It's a land with 8 million blacks and it could hold 60 million people. We could feed India with the food we produced in Tanganyika! It could have been a new frontier for any American or English or French kid with a little gumption! Another Israel! But the *do-gooders* had to give it back to the Indians! Meanwhile your son and my son are given numbers back here and live in apartment buildings on top of each other."

—*Life* magazine, January 28, 1972

The Mask of Unity

Woe to him that buildeth a town with blood, and stablisheth
a city by inquity!

—Habakkuk

The whole world is wet with mutual blood; and murder,
which in the case of an individual is admitted to be a crime,
is called a virtue when it is committed wholesale.

—Saint Cyprian, about 250 A.D.

Midnight, then one o'clock, then two
Sleep came to West End Avenue
Where at number 711
I had a dream, and not of Heaven

Fifth Avenue, I'm on a grandstand
A parade is approaching, band on band
And float on float—a gorgeous one
Shimmering scarlet in silver sun
Scarlet: But why is the paint not dry?
I shall see better when they pass by
Why are their clothes and faces red?

Why are their hands wet? No one said
But leaning forward as far as I could
I saw EACH PARADER WAS DRIPPING WITH BLOOD
Pressing forward against the rails
I saw it drip from their fingernails
It covered the floats, overflowed on the ground
While the bands kept up their cheerful sound
Up and down Fifth Avenue
It spread like a scarlet carpet of glue

On giant floats that filled the street
Came the cream of the power elite
High in the rigging, low on the decks
The men of the military-industrial complex
In the balmy brilliant weather
All the VIPs together
Missis Big and Mister Bigger
With every other famous figure
Big shot, bigwig, fat cat, fat ass
The whole American ruling class
Each general, chairman, president
That makes up THE ESTABLISHMENT

First, on a float like a tank and as weighty
Reserved for wisemen over eighty
Rode Harry S. Truman bearing this sign
THE CREDIT FOR HIROSHIMA WAS MINE
And up to his ankles and up to his knees
The blood of two hundred thousand Japanese
GIVE 'EM HELL, HARRY, shouted one,
And Harry answered THAT'S WHAT I'VE DONE

Lyndon B. Johnson was on the next float
And the sign he wore about his throat
Read: I AM SUPERHUMAN
I KILLED MORE MEN THAN HARRY S. TRUMAN
And since the blood had got up to his chin
He was getting set to drink it in
With the help of his eight bloodhounds strong
Who loyally had come along
McNamara, Humphrey, Rusk, Rostow: four
Two Bundys, Westmoreland, Abrams: that's four more

Said Rusk: IT'S ALL THE FAULT OF THE CHINESE
And returned his face to the deep freeze
Said Rostow: THAT THE RUSSIANS ARE OUR FOES
I CAN PROVE WITH DOMINOES
Hubert Humphrey, a happy boy
Proclaimed the politics of joy
A world away the farmhouse rafter
Shook at the rumble of Hubert's laughter
McNamara in his fashion
Stated the case for true compassion
Drinking warm blood he wept full well
His tears turned to napalm as they fell

A couple came riding tandem style
Not on a float but a crocodile
The first was Everett Dirksen who
Gurgled at Johnson: ME! ME TOO!
The second was Cardinal Spellman, he
Was telling his beads about victory
Chanting in ecumenical tone
MY FAVORITE CATHOLIC IS ROY COHN
The pair of them hurled themselves in the gore
And came up soaking and screaming for more
The crocodile's back was their diving raft
The crocodile threw back his head and laughed

The next VIPs
Were from overseas
Spain and Taiwan sent each a generalissimo
Singing GOD BLESS AMERICA double fortissimo
And behind the Greek generals and Syngman Rhee
A man from Nazi Germany
Kiesinger, Kurt
On Hitler he'd staked and lost his shirt
Which was brown, so what'd he do?
Got him a shirt of red white and blue
Beside Kiesinger rode through town
On a guided missile Wernher von Braun
I MADE IT FOR HITLER, he said, IT'S TRUE
BUT THAT'S O.K., I'M GIVIN' IT TO YOU
With a pair of jackals to ride upon
Came the quislings of Saigon

The bootlickers of Washington
Ky and Thieu, and Ky did say:
WHAT'S WRONG WITH HITLER ANYWAY?
I'VE HAD IT WITH THE USA
But Kiesinger whispered: DON'T KNOCK THE YANKS
THE FBI IS HERE WITH LISTENING TANKS
And Kiesinger shouted: THE REDS ARE FALLING DOWN
SCREWED BY AMERICA AND BROWNED BY BRAUN
To Wernher, Kurt murmured: THIS PARADE THOUGH JOLLY
DOES NOT TURN ME ON LIKE A NUREMBERG RALLY

And J. Edgar Hoover *was* listening
As he had to Mrs. Roosevelt and Martin Luther King
In one hand a flag, in the other a six-shooter
Hoover came next on a computer
With six pretty G-men bringing up his rear
Their equipment sticking out to here
OLD SOLDIERS, yelled Hoover, NEVER DIE
AND DIRECTORS OF THE FBI
WILL ONLY AGREE TO FADE AWAY
WHEN THEY CAN DO IT ON GOVERNMENT PAY

Behind J. Edgar's popular behind
Came the Voice if not the mind
Of America on a float of wire
Broad as a liberal, tall as a liar
Beaming to victims of creeping socialism
The holy scriptures of galloping Americanism

The next float to be seen
Was a traveling latrine
Which was no commonplace shit machine
For instead of dropping its load on the ground
It lifted it up, it spread it around
The air was pissy, the air was shitty
For this was the Un-American Activities Committee
And as the shit flowed from their every nude ass
They chanted in unison: WE LIKE JUDAS!
WE CHARGE YOU WITH HERESY, shrieked one wraith
BUT YOU CAN BE SAVED BY ACT OF FAITH
KISS RUSSIA AND TELL! SEND A FEW REDS TO HELL!
GIVE US SOME NAMES! ANOTHER! ANOTHER!

YOUR PASTOR, YOUR MASTER, YOUR TWIN BROTHER
WHICH OF YOUR PALS HAVE BIG RED DICKS?
TURN 'EM IN! THEY'RE HERETICS!
From a toilet seat in the shape of an eagle
The chairman declaimed in a voice of treacle:
ALL THROUGH HISTORY THE BEST OF PEOPLE
HAVE SENT US LISTS OF NAMES AS TALL AS A STEEPLE
THE IMMORTAL WHITTAKER CHAMBERS, THE INEFFABLE LOUIS
  BUDENZ
TURNED IN ALL THEIR MOST INTIMATE FRIENDS
—NOWHERE INCIDENTALLY DID WE HAVE IT SO GOOD
AS AMONG THE GREAT AMURRICANS OF HOLLYWOOD.

(And here in my dream, out of the shit machine, in living color, rose a giant
rosebud which suddenly burst open to reveal the Academy Award winners of
the past three decades, reciting in chorus:

> We are the movie makers
> And we are the dreamers of dreams
> And we are the movers and shakers
> Of the Western World, it seems
> Yes, we are the benders and breakers
> Of pink boys and scarlet dames
> We are the movie makers
> And we are the namers of names!

And there was joy in Hollywood over many a scarlet sinner who repented before the throne of the Almighty Dollar:

> Many a pink lady, many a scarlet man
> A Lee J. Cobb, an Elia Kazan
> And swimming with the big red sharks
> A little pink minnow named Larry Parks
> Trick trick trick trick
> Edward Dmytryk
> And oh with rue my heart is laden
> For Robert Rossen and Sterling Hayden!)

> And in my dream I saw that day
> Machos of Califor-ny-ay
> The barge they sat on like a burnished throne
> One of Warner Brothers' own
> Bled on the pavement, spouted blood
> Shed by Chicanos and flown in from Hollywood

Spraying the barrio but good
Symbol of Latin blood brotherhood
Saint George Murphy the Hollywood honky
Trotted in from Culver City on a dopey dapper donkey
Right on cue pronto
On a fucking bucking bronco
Simpering, pouting
Whimpering, shouting
Came at a gallop Sir Ronald the Reagan
A PLAGUE ON
CHAVEZ AND HIS GRAPES! ELDRIDGE CLEAVER?
THAT BLACK NAME PUTS WHITE-BLOODED MEN IN A FEVER
LOCK UP YOUR DAUGHTER
BEFORE CLEAVER HAS CLAWED 'ER
SAVE US, WHITE GOD, FROM THE SEX MANIAC
SAVE THY WHITE LAMBS FROM THE PANTHER BLACK!
Sir Ronald concluded, taking a bow
I WANT A BLOOD BATH AND I WANT IT NOW

Then a voice piped up: ISN'T RONNIE A GAS?
LEMME GET MY TONGUE STILL FARTHER UP HIS ASS
At which behind Reagan was seen to lower
A prick of a president, Hayakawa
And a prick has hair, and hair has crabs
Hayakawa had brought from classrooms and labs
Men in tweed jackets and silk striped ties
Each of whom had squinting eyes
One eye sought out a college
Overflowed with love of knowledge
The other looked cross-eyed at Washington
And winking whispered POWER IS FUN
These are the experts on government
Advisers to the President
From mock Gothic halls of academe
Smart as horsewhips, smooth as sour cream
From the prostitute institutes of technology
Wise as serpents and twice as slippery

HOW CALIFORNIANS SWEAR AND CURSE!
Quoth Grayson Kirk passing by in a hearse
A PRESIDENT'S JOB IS TO HOLD HIS PEACE
THEN AT THE RIGHT MOMENT CALL THE POLICE

POOH said Hayakawa THAT GETS YOU HARD?
I CALL IN THE NATIONAL GUARD
AND WE HAVE OUR VIETNAMS IN OUR OWN BACKYARD
AS FOR HIPPIES WITH LONG HAIR
AND THEIR CHICKS WITH THEIR BOSOMS BARE
THE DUPES AND THE KOOKS
AND THE STOOPS AND THE GOOKS
ALL THE SOCIALIST COMMUNIST ANARCHIST DISRUPTERS
I PICK 'EM OFF WITH HELICOPTERS!

WHICH IS WHAT I THINK AS WELL
Snarled the president of the A. F. of L.
He rode bareback on a jaguar
(The animal, not the British car)
And the two of them let out those jaguar cries
Which some call music and others call lies

Next in line (Hooray, HOORAY)
The top brass of the A.M.A.
In the white masks of the Ku Klux Klan
Each with a knife to stab or trepan
A sight to set the Hudson on fire
They rode in an ambulance with a flat tire
And a banner aloft, saying THIS PARADE
IS A PROTEST AGAINST MEDICAID
AND SOCIALISM AND ALL WE FEAR
WILL STOP US EARNING A HUNDRED GRAND A YEAR
On the ambulance's side
The following graffiti I espied:
MONDAY MORNING, DON'T DIE TOO SOON
WE'LL GET YOU TO HOSPITAL FRIDAY AFTERNOON
ALSO FOR YOUR INFORMATION
A.M.A. MEANS AMERICAN MURDER ASSOCIATION

Next, a dilapidated stage coach
Crawling with maggot, louse, roach
Sprawling inside it an emaciated hag
Draped in a stinking Confederate flag
And these words dripping from her ruined mouth
AH AM THE SOUL OF THE OLD SOUTH
AND ONCE AH MADE OUT WITH ROBERT E. LEE
TODAY 'NEATH A DEAD MAGNOLIA TREE

MADDOX AND THURMOND AND THEIR GANG
KNOCK ME OVER AN' IT'S BANG BANG BANG
BUT AH AIN'T GRUMBLIN', AH'M A MERRY OL' SOUL
AN' THE GUYS THAT RAPED ME GOT THINGS UNDER CONTROL
Behind the stage coach, robber bands
White gloves on their bloody hands
Gentlemen-gamblers all, of high degree
Riverboat captains of exquisite courtesy
Rednecks of white supremacy
At their head with nightstick and gun
Mississippi's favorite son
Gennleman Jim Eastland. With this dastard
George C. Wallace, Alabama's favorite bastard

All, all of our great ones played
In my bloody dream parade
And had played out the game without a hitch
But for voices raised to hysterical pitch
GET OUT OF VIETNAM! THOU SHALT NOT KILL!
Of a sudden the warm air was chill
Cops moved in at the shouters' calls
Plainclothesmen kicked them in the balls
But other voices took the cops on
POWER TO THE PEOPLE! BOMB THE PENTAGON!
The fire of the hecklers' rage
Sent a tremor through the cortege
And I saw from behind the rails
The Establishment bite its nails
DO SOMETHING FOR CHRIST'S SAKE, said one
Another reached for a submachine gun
HOLD IT cried a third with a hiccup and a groan
WE NEED A CHANGE OF TONE
A CHANGE OF PACE
A CHANGE OF FACE
Says a fourth, WAIT A MINUTE
GET A LOAD OF THAT FLOAT, JUST LOOK WHO'S IN IT

Along the affluent avenue
A plastic float hove into view
Billy Graham at the prow
Norman Vincent Peale in the bow
At all points in between

The cream of the cream
Pin-stripe grandfathers, D.A.R. aunts
Episcopalian debutantes
Diamond-pin diplomats and above all
Businessmen fat, executives tall
All of their faces in quite a short while
Blending into one toothpaste smile
By a mast that reached infinity
Stood a not so holy trinity
They too had their molars bared
They were Mitchell, Rogers, and Laird
Mitchell, leaning on a banister
Carried a tear-gas canister
At any hapless heckler to be hurled
That brought to his mind Ten Days That Shook the World
And Martha stood at Mitchell's side
And CRUCIFY FULBRIGHT Martha cried
BUT REHABILITATE BONNIE AND CLYDE
At the word "CRUCIFY"
Out of Mitchell's fly
Jumped J. Edgar Hoover who quietly said:
FRED HAMPTON'S DEAD
WE GOT HIM IN BED
THERE'S A JESUIT PLOT
TO ABDUCT A BIG SHOT
AND YOU BETTER LOOK OUT, MITCHELL JOHN,
OR THEY'LL HOLD YOU HOSTAGE IN DANBURY, CONN.
DAN BURY DAN
DAN BERRI GAN
FATHER DAN
SON OF MAN
MAN SON SHARON TATE
CHARLIE MANSON'S KIDNAPING THE SECRETARY OF STATE
DAN MAN AN AN AN ANGELA DAVIS
DAVE IS
DELLINGER
JOHN DILLINGER
WHO'S THAT COMIN' AT ME IN THE DARK?
BOBBY KENNEDY? RAMSEY CLARK?
ANGELA DAVIS IS A NIGGER
LEMME GIT MY HAND ON THE ATOMIC TRIGGER
Just above Hoover slicked and sleek

Stood an authentic synthetic Greek
His name is Christian and rhymes with Nero
But he's the last Homeric hero
In my dream he was naked like Apollo Belvedere
His body tattooed in Greek from here to here
On his ass I read:
CRONKITE, DROP DEAD
And just above:
MAKE WAR NOT LOVE
And higher yet: FUCK PEACE
UP THE JUNTA AND MY FASCIST FOLKS IN GREECE
Across his chest: LIBERALS ARE DYKEY OLD BAGS
MC GOVERN AND FULBRIGHT ARE FAGS
On his belly: REDS ARE FREAKS
PIPSQUEAKS
EFFETE SNOBS IN MOD APPAREL
ROTTEN APPLES OF THE BARREL
In pig Latin on his left ball:
WHEN YA SEEN ONE SLUM YA SEEN 'EM ALL
Agnew stands there like a rock
Caressing a Herculean cock
Agnew stands there and masturbates
While announcing: the president
PRESIDENT
PRESIDENT
OF THESE UNITED STATES!
I looked for Nixon but found
An escort of Greyhound
Busses and heard a rumor he
Was home watching football on TV
Then I saw pass by
Towering over the busses twenty feet high
A statue of plastic folderol
An Ersatz President, a Political Doll,
A Puppet, whiter than Agnew forsooth
Cleaner than Eisenhower's hound's tooth
Shinier than a new-made pin
Like a soul scoured pure from sin
What he'd done in former years
Washed away now in crocodile tears
And what was left just a big Plastic Thing
A Giant No-Thing, a Bit Player King!

(And suddenly in my dream, there was our President's voice making a speech, accompanied by our President's face, a TV face with only two dimensions. The voice said:

Let me make one thing quite clear. My heart is so full, I cannot put into mere words, even my speechwriters cannot put into mere words, how they, I, feel. When I was a little boy in California, or was it New York, no, Illinois, the biographies are so far from clear on such points, my father, just a plain, working American, that was all my father was, said to me, Dick, he called me Dick, thou shalt not kill, and quite literally I never did, great as the temptation was when I ran against Helen Gahagan Douglas. [A flashing smile from the face told me that this was humor but voice and facial muscles were out of sync.] Let me make another thing quite clear. Remember when I was in Thailand? Of course you do, if you stayed glued to your TV sets in the real old-fashioned American way, even if what they show these days doesn't always stay old-fashioned, eh, Spiro? The Thais came to me and said, Mr. President, how about those promises to defend us all to the death of the last GI? [Here the voice stopped, and the face chose a nicer expression.] When I was a little boy in New York, California, got it: Illinois, my old mother, a typical rugged fighting Quaker American, said to me, Richard, she said, Richard, George Washington was the fella who never told a lie, you can be the fella who never broke a promise, even someone else's promise, given in a moment of temporary insanity. [There had been Six Crises, our President's book had said. Now came the Seventh.] So, friends, naturally, we are gonna defend Thailand. All of Southeast Asia. All of Asia. Africa. Western Europe. South America, well, and naturally Mexico, even more naturally the Caribbean, Canada, Greenland . . . Oh yes, did I hear someone say just now, GET OUT OF VIETNAM? Well, my friend, where you been this past year? We ARE gettin' out of Vietnam. You ain't heard of Vietnam-iz-ation? Ts ts ts. They're gonna fight this thing on their own. Indefinitely. For centuries. Light years maybe. . . . Where was I? Yeah, I'm ending this war but also, so's not to disappoint a lot of good Amurricans down in Thurmond country, Agnew country, Mitchell country, actually it's all MY country right now, ha ha ha! I am keeping the war going—in a new way—new—what else is progress? I'm even EX-TENDING the damn thing. What's Vietnam? Not enough, that's what. I WANT CAMBODIA. I WANT LAOS. [At this the two-dimensional face looked straight at me.] You look surprised. [I might have answered, but he didn't let me.] Didn' expect Tricky Dick to come clean thisaway, didya? [Hey, that ain't Nixon's voice, I told myself, but it *was* coming from his face, maybe this was the real Nixon that I'd heard about once?] Tellin' the truth, did you say, "for a change"? Oh, come on now, Martin Luther King

had a dream. *You're* havin' a dream. [This straight at me.] Can't Richard
Milhous Nixon have a dream? He can, and this is my I-Have-a-Dream
Speech—made in your dream, you could say, but—it was me said it
first: THE COUNTRY NEEDS THE LIFT OF A DRIVIN' DREAM. My
own thing—well, my speechwriter's own thing. An' now I'm King. Nah,
not Martin Luther King. Prexy! Which it's the All-American Dream to be,
right? An' what else has always always always been the All-American
Dream? [Here at last I got my courage up and answered his question. I
said: Genocide. He said:] Wha? Whadda you say—genocide? [His face
changed color here, first very white, then quite ruddy—was it *color* TV?]
Yeah! That's the answer! We did it to the Indians and by God we'll do it
to you! [Here our President emitted a Texas rebel yell, but soon thereafter
got a grip on his PR.] Genocide, cried Huey P. Newton, and On to Hanoi!
cried li'l' ol' Lyndon, but something was wrong. Lyndon's genocide looked
like genocide, it even sounded like genocide, oh those speeches, ts ts, so my
staff went back to the old book or someplace and d'you know what they
found? This dictum: LOWER YOUR VOICE. Lower your voice, then genocide WON'T sound like genocide, no, for we will have made genocide genteel. [And our President again gave it to me right in the eye.] Like this parade in your dream, it's a parade of blood, so let me make just one more
thing quite clear. We have the Nixon Doctrine now, and this doctrine is:
NO VISIBLE BLOOD. No blood in the press, Spiro, no blood on TV, and a
little less blood all the time in the *New York Times.* Reverend Graham, go
slow on that blood-of-the-lamb stuff. Reverend Peale, give us some positive
thinking: the lamb has white wool, pale gray, anyway, how about the black
sheep? dip'em in white dye. . . . To make genocide genteel, we want no
black, no red, anywhere in this, after all is said and done, white man's land.
Now *this* is more than the Nixon *Doctrine,* it is that without which there
wouldn't be any Nixon. [Here the voice stopped again, and the face again
became that of your friendly neighborhood president.] Well, here's wishin'
all you kids a white white Christmas from my white White House, isn't that
white of me?)

> The power elite of power-mad nation
> Wore appropriate expressions of transfiguration
> And even the hecklers in the crowd
> No longer talked out loud
> The only remaining noise
> A PA system's bleary voice:
> BLOOD IS OKAY BUT ENOUGH IS ENOUGH
> HIDE THE DAMN STUFF
> AND CUNNINGLY

WHITEWASH THIS BLOOD-STAINED SOCIETY
WHAT GOES FOR RED GOES ALSO FOR BLACK
COVER WITH WHITE PAINT AND SHELLAC
The Establishment underwent conversion
Confirmed in baptism by total immersion
Covered from head to foot in paint
Each black flunky a white saint
Ere long there was no blood in sight
Fifth Avenue was a study in white and white

(Which was the end of my dream except for a sort of chant which everyone was intoning as I woke. By "everyone" I mean it seemed the whole Silent Majority was gathered there on Fifth Avenue, and had given up silence to intone these words:)

GIVE THANKS TO NIXON AND TO GOD
FOR KEEPING THE VIETNAMESE OFF CAPE COD
PRESERVING THE AFFLUENT WAY OF LIFE
FROM THE YELLOW DWARF WITH HIS POCKET KNIFE
GIVE THANKS TO US THE SILENT MAJORITY
FOR CREATING NIXONIAN NATIONAL UNITY
WHICH BLENDS THE FAR-OUT BLISS OF NIRVANA
WITH THE GOOD CLEAN FUN OF POLLYANNA.

(1970)

Men's Liberation

For *Martha Saxton*
I tried to get this "comment" published in various magazines, including some that would normally publish anything I sent in. It was rejected by male editors on Esquire, Modern Occasions, New American Review, New Republic, Partisan Review, *and* Playboy. *When Martha Saxton got word of this she accepted it for her* Works in Progress.

It is ridiculous that one has to be *for* homosexuality or *against* it. Such a thing should simply be accepted as part of the world, like the sea or the seasons, but, since it is not so accepted, and our society is against it, it is incumbent upon all who are not against it to be for it. As with negritude. That too should all along have simply been accepted as the handiwork of the gods. Since it wasn't, however, men who wish the gods' handiwork to be accepted one day must today do the work of defending it that precedes any acceptance—and leads to acceptance, though by a detour.

I am afraid the whole radical movement is committed to the defense of homosexuality, for radicals are against formalism, and hostility to homosexuality is nothing if not formalistic, being based on an overweening, if not exclusive, respect for stance and gesture. What matters is which protuberance is placed in which orifice on bodies of which sex. It is important not to have an unlicensed orgasm, since what counts is not the orgasm but the license. Licenses are issued by society—the current order of society, naturally, there being no other— the current order of society as it has flowed out of history, out of the nature of things. Whatever has been is right, and cops and judges are there to see that it stays that way.

This formalistic logic bypasses the content, and it could seem that the Faggot-Baiters thereby miss the opportunity to remark that the content of homosexual relationships is so often thin, bloodless, heartless, mindless, everything-less, almost a vacuum, but the fact is that they are smart not to use such an argument, as it could only lead to the further observation that the content of *hetero*sexual relationships is so often thin, bloodless, heartless, mindless, every-thingless, almost a vacuum, and, oh dear, if they made *this* observation they wouldn't be Faggot-Baiters any more, they would be . . . radicals. And not just in matters of sex. That there is something radically deficient in the personal relations of this society is a problem of the society as well as of the persons. Or, if you prefer, the society and the persons being identical, the problem must be seen as a total *Gestalt* made up of factors broken down for mere convenience as social and personal.

We live in a *society* with *persons* in it like Richard M. Nixon, and his spouse Pat Nixon, and many other Richards and Pats in all fifty states, and, if the Nixon name already makes some people shout for political revolution, what I am saying is that it might just as logically make them shout for sexual revolution. History is a nightmare from which we hope one day to awaken. The good society will be all that our present postindustrial society is not, politically, socially, and every other way. Yet when Pat Nixon tells you, as I'm sure she'd be glad to, that you shouldn't have sex without love, she isn't wrong. It is just that her husband perpetuates the kind of society which makes love more and more difficult, thereby making sex more and more empty and silly, as in *Oh! Calcutta!*

Besides, definitions of love vary, and not just according to love's inherent possibilities, but also according to historical trend and social context. La Rochefoucauld said none of us would fall in love if we hadn't read books about it. Certainly, love has always been what people expected it to be: the society, if not the individual, can take its pick. What is picked, being human, is imperfect and shot through with error, and it is usually easy to see the imperfection and error in definitions dead or dying. Such as the Victorian ones right now, which live tenuously on, at least in provincial places like the White House. These were over-moralistic definitions. Sex-with-love meant sex fogged over with high ideals. The ideals could even be antisexual and debilitating. That was most clearly evident in the classical image of woman during the eighteenth and nineteenth centuries—woman as decorative but useless, woman as virtuous but passive, woman as charming but weak: what Bernard Shaw ironically called the womanly woman, and what the Victorian poet Coventry Patmore, without irony, called the Angel in the House. No doubt we are unhistorical, and lacking in understanding, if we do not allow that such an image corresponded to a wider reality and could hardly be obliterated merely by rational recognition of its irrationality, but, by the same historical token, we are entitled to conclude that such an image belongs at best to an earlier condition of human culture and no longer provides, as ideals should, vital content for human relations.

If socialist humanism has a future—in practice, that is, as well as theory —we shall no doubt get sex-with-love but in a different definition of both. I don't know what definition. I can't know. To attempt one's own verbal formulations is to extend present-day theory while making a minimal contribution to tomorrow's practice. If the formulations of even a Herbert Marcuse or a Norman O. Brown affect the future it will chiefly be by breaking down some of the intellectual structures of the past. The new definitions will be hammered out not between typewriter keys and paper but between the penis and the vagina.

Or between the penis and the anus. Or the penis and the mouth. Or the vagina and the mouth. Erogenous zones were born equal and, if the whole body is holy, most holy are those parts of it on which human action and human imagination choose to confer most holiness. Or which human beings choose to employ to raise joy to ecstasy, to get as close as possible to another person, and to remind themselves of the sacredness of life itself. If I use enthusiastic language, it is because I feel the enthusiasm, not that I wish to sell anything to anyone, nor would I elevate the body above the mind, the nonverbal above the verbal. Even in love-making, it could be said, there are more words than actions. Except under demoralizing conditions, "sex" is preceded by torrents of words and accompanied by looks and caresses, by a behavior pattern which I would like to propose calling: fraternal.

If you wish to study the sexual inadequacy of our postindustrial society, you really needn't pore over Kinsey or peep through bedroom keyholes, you need only study the present state of the art of friendship. At a time when monogamy and the nuclear family are disintegrating, it is possible that homosexuals have a mission, not only to themselves, as is implied in the very idea of Gay Liberation, but also to everyone else; for they would seem to be in a better position than the others to affirm fraternity and the centrality of friendship in the humanistic—the human—scheme of things.

From Kinsey's first and most famous volume one gained the impression that orgasms are what matter, and it was important to have a lot of them, whatever their content in love, joy, or anything else. Such is sex when Middle America stops going to church and takes courses in sociology. Well, perhaps the position I'm taking is as simple as Kinsey's, but it's a little different. It is that the orgasms would be bigger and better if they came as the overflow of friendship. Today, in the wake of Kinsey, Middle America has taken up fucking strangers —"group sex" is the approved euphemism. There must be a fascination in this, or it wouldn't happen. Is it gratifying, though? Satisfying? An acceptable alternative to the marriage hearse? Or is it not, rather, an emanation from this hearse, an acting-out of the failure of love as Mom and Dad and Teacher handed it down to us? Woman couldn't be a friend to man, it was always said. That was because she was More. Angel in the House or, on nights out, Cleopatra, Isolde, or at least Mae West. But today, since that More is Less, friendship might be looked at afresh by all—and exhibited in some of its more positive possibilities by homosexuals.

At this point I hear the voice of one of my schoolteachers explaining to the class that what is a bit hard to understand about Shakespeare's *Julius Caesar* is that those fellows were all friends. Brutus is Caesar's *best* friend, and that is the main point, but he is also Cassius's best friend—these two have the greatest friends' quarrel in literature, and yet, and at the same time, this is a political play par excellence. A bit hard to understand, is it? Can this be for any other reason than that we don't have fraternity in our politics today, we just have public relations? Oh yes, everyone is called My Good Friend So-and-So, but Lyndon Johnson's good friend Walter Jenkins is out on his ass the moment public relations so dictate. The only milieu, perhaps, in which any of that Brutus-and-Cassius business is now permitted is that of gangsters; in which case one might say that fraternity does after all survive, if only in the Mafia.

But no, in fact, fraternity has been *revived*—in the radical movement. I'd say that was the secret of the movement's success, except that the movement hasn't been all that successful. Anyway, it is the source of the movement's appeal. Even our enemies, who think we don't understand Liberty and Equality —or that we are against them—know we mean business about Fraternity. All men are not brothers and sisters, not yet, but we in the movement are brothers and sisters, and call ourselves so: that's precisely what and who we are, that's "where it's at." This is why Women's Lib and Gay Lib are around, and are in the movement.

Everyone is putting down Kate Millett's *Sexual Politics* now. That's what she gets for having been overpraised at first. In my view, one of her ideas alone would make the book a landmark. This idea is that Women's Lib and Gay Lib are one: the enemy is the Man, the supermale, John Wayne or Spiro Agnew. There is no woman problem; there is only a man problem; yet the modern "unwomanly" woman has a natural ally in the modern "unmanly" man. When to be "manly" is all—is to take charge, and "achieve," run the world, and get the credit—to be "unmanly" is to be at best the helper and server, the half-man, at worst the weakling, the misbegotten, the pervert, the thing, the nonentity. A large section of straight society has now accepted homosexuals—as clowns. Limp wrist or lisp get an immediate yack out of any straight theatre or club audience, for Middle America views its way of life as the Aristotelian golden mean. Well it might. The world has *not* been run by females and faggots.

Their opportunity rests in the fact that Grandfather's world, already in ruins, is now threatened with total extinction. If another human world is to be built on the ruins, Women's Lib will have had something to do with it: this idea is already entering the general consciousness, though, as for Gay Lib, even those, among outsiders, who welcome it have not, I think, seen that much is at stake except perhaps reform of the sodomy laws. In liberal America today homosexuality is given at best a kind of diplomatic recognition: that it exists is admitted. Of course it must be tolerated, only that doesn't mean you gotta like it. Or that you could let your son "marry" one. More likely, if your son has "tendencies," you will send him to a Freudian psychoanalyst to be, in two senses, straightened out.

Perhaps our radical rage at Freud is excessive these days, but no wonder. His phase of history and ours live under opposite signs. He would have succeeded, if such things could be done singlehanded, in holding the patriarchal family together for another century. That was hardly an irrational goal while it could still seem an attainable one, but, now that the century following Freud's birth has shown itself one of disintegration, our goals are perforce different and, with them, our criteria. Under the old dispensation, it seemed so important to strengthen the system that homosexuals, like women, were gladly offered up as sacrificial lambs on its altar. Today they are crying, Hell no, we won't go. Which in turn means that at least some of "the others" are wondering if the sacrifice was "fair to homosexuals" in the first place. Ruthlessness is diminished, and is denounced by liberals, when it no longer pays off (as with Vietnam).

Insofar as the Freudians have collected well-observed facts about a number of homosexuals of a certain time and place, their surveys are as welcome as any others, and their facts, like other facts, will retain their status as part of the truth. At the time, the Freudian points were well taken. Surely an excess of Mother was very threatening, if what the culture must at all costs avoid was a threat to Father. But, by this time, Father is not only threatened, he is just about done for. That particular father image survives, if at all, only as an oppressor—*the* oppressor. In the long run, it is he—and not his projection in heaven—that will be found to be dead. Consequently, we of today do not wish—we wish it, anyhow, in smaller and smaller numbers—to become Father later on or to take those steps against Mother, and the Mother within us, which would make us cowboys, presidents of the board, Nixon, Agnew, General Abrams, or Lieutenant Calley.

That culture has gone, or is fast going. It is a loss—of Freuds as well as Calleys. But why shouldn't it be—and even more—a gain? Disintegration, yes, yet, if we are lucky the disintegration of shackles mainly. In short, liberation. Not total, of course. But liberation of a specific part of our human nature, a rather large part, that has been concealed, displaced, distorted, twisted for the greater glory of the Man.

What therefore is now demanded of society is not *tolerance* of a *perversion,* permissiveness toward behavior that is seen as bizarre, ludicrous, unsavory, or immoral, but *approval* of *liberation,* endorsement of a positive development in human history. Even this demand treats society in an overabstract way as a mere onlooker. Actually, no one is going to be an outsider in the mutation now under way. Women are doubly involved: first, as women, the oppressed sex, it-self moving rapidly toward liberation; second, as actual or potential homosexu-als. Men who see themselves as heterosexual are also involved, since the defini-tion of their heterosexuality is affected. That is the sense in which they are indeed threatened—in their innermost nature and to the quick of their sex-uality. They won't give in without a fight, and the fight will take the form of sexist ideology, propaganda, and persecution: that is "normal," isn't it? Still, the liberal wing of straight society will be a little different. It is (1) less violent and (2) undermined by guilt—two interrelated factors, which together, as conser-vatives often remind us, spell capitulation.

However all this may be, and whatever the later results of present changes will be, homosexuals are making a contribution even now, not only to them-selves but to society at large. They are the carriers—not the only ones, but quite special and signal ones—of fraternity in our time. "Love" has broken down. Neither married bliss nor the thrill of adultery is working out. Woman, who was so much more than a friend to man, has become distinctly less. Later no doubt she will become, at last, a friend to him, just that. Meanwhile, she must go out on her own. She may be lucky, in this period, to be homosexual: that way she too can experience fraternity (sorority?). In any case, I shall leave women to speak for themselves. What we males are aware of is a tradition of our own. It makes the history books in coy evasions with names like Platonic Love or the Cult of Friendship. It has shown its head, shyly or panic-stricken, in "crushes" of students on teachers, the dedication of apprentices to craftsmen, the emulation of athletes, the loyalty of younger to older warrior. Shakespeare made such a *blatant* display of such friendship in his sonnets that it has taken genera-tions of straight professors to re-establish law and order with the declaration that our greatest poet was no more than *latent*. Other scholars used the more fragile argument that the language of such friendship was conventional, and so not incriminating to Shakespeare in particular. Overlooked here is that conven-tions come out of people: homosexual conventions come out of homosexual people. What one must challenge, of course, is the assumption that Shakespeare should at all costs be relieved of a certain imputation.

Someone will suggest that surely there can be fraternity, and even friendship, without sex, homo- or hetero-? To which I would retort: Well, perhaps, but must there be? Do we need it? The suggestion would not be made were it not that middle-class culture has always regarded sexlessness as a virtue. Even mor-ally, that is more than dubious, and morality is only the half of it. The other half is vitality. Why speak of friendship as pure when all you mean is that it is asexual? Why shouldn't the sexual element in a friendship be the life of it—that which makes it more personal than an ideological alliance, more actual than a spiritual affinity? Wasn't it always the Platonic friendships that were un-healthy? As for fraternity, it has been at best a concept in abstract political theory, at worst the emptiest word in the politician's vocabulary of empty words. The life of actual fraternity is passion. Now if it is likely that any human passion will have an erotic element in it, it is surely unnecessary and perverse (a good word to use here) to try to exclude the erotic element from the passion of fraternity. Think. We have seen revolutions without fraternity, or from which fraternity disappeared soon after the revolutionary government took power. From Robespierre on, we have seen revolutionary leaders, preaching fraternity, who themselves, even when they were not dried-up old maids, lacked fraternal warmth. One way, after all, of stating what was wrong with Stalin is simpler and truer than the way the books state it. It is that he did not love the people—did not love people. This victor in the revolutionary battle lost touch, if he ever had it, with the original spirit of revolution, that without which revolution is just technology, if not abomination: the warm-blooded love of brothers and sisters.

Fidel Castro conspicuously had it. That was the edge he had over Kosygin and all the little Kosygins of the People's Democracies. It is the tragedy of Castro that he let ideology—and rotten old "bourgeois ideology" at that— prescribe limits to the very real fraternity in his movement. He denounced homosexuality, and has tried to exterminate it. Alas, this is not just an offense against a certain minority; and a protest asserting that minority's rights is a very inadequate response to it. The offense is to socialist humanism as a whole, to our humanity as a whole. This is the way to dry up such fraternity as did exist and give us, in a few more years, another gray, bureaucratic people's democracy. The fear of homosexuality in this socialist semihumanism is fear of love as such, love as it exists in human beings of flesh and blood.

What a contrast there is between the gray, bureaucratic brand of democracy and the vision of democracy of America's great democrat, Walt Whitman! But, hitherto, this vision has been a little more than anyone could take, and right now there is probably no stronger support for Whitmanic democracy in Washington than in Havana or Moscow. The homosexuality is the problem, of course. I read in a magazine just the other day that Whitman's disciple Pablo Neruda was more acceptable as a democratic poet because his love poetry is heterosexual. In the universities of the United States it is taught either that Whitman's homosexuality is an insuperable stumbling block or that it is irrelevant.

If Whitman is read afresh in the light of our own situation, his homoerotic emphasis is seen to have its reasons in something other than his separate and possibly eccentric existence. It is an *over*emphasis, certainly, in the way that black literature overemphasizes that black is beautiful; and, by the same token, it has been a *necessary* overemphasis and remains so, a correction of the balance. He is "unfair to women" in that he is unable to make the feeling of loving a woman as real as the feeling of loving a man. But it is always men who protest against this. Women never mind. For one thing, the feeling of loving a man is what they can share with Whitman, if they are heterosexual. The men protest because they feel threatened, even exposed. After all, it had been the traditional purpose of erotic poetry to encourage males to be more heterosexual than they were by giving heterosexuality more allure than it actually had.

Heterosexuality, as we have known it, has in no way favored its female component. On the contrary. Any enemy of this heterosexuality is, potentially at least, a friend to women; and, by paradox, the poet who did not understand women—or rather men's love for women—was a good friend to women, and had their interests at heart. For our liberation into Manhood is, like woman's liberation into womanhood, liberation from the Man.

(1972)

Living Theatre in a Dying World

Quantity and Quality

For Louis Kronenberger and Marshall Lee

It would be convenient if one could clearly and surely distinguish between quality in theatre and quality in the other arts. Certainly, most of us have our preferences as between one art and another. When D. H. Lawrence tells us that the novel is the one great book of life, he would seem to be implying that the novel is the greatest art. When Robert Frost says that everything written is as good as it is dramatic, he would seem to be saying that the drama is the greatest literary genre. How, though, can these claims be tested? Are they really anything more than heartfelt compliments, rhetorical expressions of enthusiasm, and applicable, with appropriate changes, to any art that takes one's fancy? It seems to me that preference of one art or genre to another might more sensibly be treated as a personal, temperamental, constitutional affair. Blind men, for example, seldom prefer painting, but one could not be surprised if a child who had shown a discriminating ear took easily to music—and perhaps ended up declaring music the highest, deepest, broadest—yes, the best—of the arts.

Furthermore, what blind men say about painting must be received with a certain amount of caution, for all their eloquence on the subject of music, and since no one is equally sensitive to all the arts and equally privy to their secrets, no one is really *in a position* to make those objective and definitive distinctions which alone could dispose of this matter. What one can learn at second hand —as, for example, by reading music history without having an ear for music —will not serve the purpose. The honest man, I fear, must admit that he can only take hold of those arts which take hold of him. Much of what he says about his favorite art may seem to others to apply just as much to their own favorites. This is natural, inevitable, and perhaps even valid. It is not clear that what people go to different arts for is always something different. Different arts, in some degree, perhaps a high degree, convey the same satisfactions, but to different people, people of different disposition.

Intensity, for example. But it is more than *an* example: it is *the* example. As surely as when they make love, when they expose themselves to an art human beings are seeking an intensification of their normal experience. That may be what they are mainly seeking; and it may be the principal and normal *raison d'être* for art. The quest may be seen in terms either of causes or results, antecedents or goals; and any such seeing yields an aesthetic. Nietzsche, for instance, stressed one result of such intensification: it invigorates, and thereby leads us to affirm existence, however irrationally. Which proposition implies a view of the causes and antecedents too. In advance of exposure to art, modern man tends to boredom, nausea, despair, nihilism. Nietzsche could see art as a cure, even, at times, as the sole cure and therefore our one hope of salvation.

And so the art which has the greatest intensity for you, though it will not have the greatest intensity for all and cannot claim to be, objectively, the intensest art, must for you represent a special opportunity and may well seem a special dispensation, a special revelation—God's way of getting through to you. As a theorist, you can grant that another art may be as intense to someone else, but as a man you will have great difficulty really believing this. I, for instance, like to think I have a fairly lively response to painting and architecture and yet for the life of me I cannot conceive how a painting or a building could take hold so hard, could move so deeply, as *Oedipus* or *Lear*. I am even tempted to marshal arguments why drama in general is more intense than fine art.

It is more sensible, though, to drop the competitive mode and deal with the intensities of the theatre in their own right. Where to begin? To begin with *Oedipus* and *Lear* would be beginning at the end—that is, with the noblest and most intricate intensities, those with the largest human and spiritual meaning. Where is the beginning? The point, surely, where there is a performer's body on stage and a spectator's eye out front. Whence the intensification of the spectator's experience? From whatever the performer's body communicates. Goethe said of the theatre: "It is corporeal man who plays the leading role there—a handsome man, a beautiful woman." The art of the theatre starts in the simple sensuousness of direct physical attraction (as against the indirectness of painting and sculpture where we do not encounter the actual human body).

The first reference the word "quality" would have in this context would be to the beautiful bodies of performers. The public's love of matinee idols, insofar as it is founded in the good looks of the stars, is basic and sound. The theatre, if it does nothing else, should exhibit fine male and female specimens, so that the spectacle may, at the very least, be a sort of human equivalent of a horse or dog show.

And of course the theatre can do *much* else. It can present the whole sensual lure of this world, and that through the world's darling allurement, the human body. So no wonder the theatre incurred the wrath of Saint Augustine and of all those for whom man's body, and the world's, represents mainly a threat. Saint Anthony, tempted, might just as well be depicted in an orchestra seat as in a garden, for what is theatrical spectacle but the literally shameless exhibition of all that which Saint Anthony is committed to fighting?

Yet only Saint Anthony's commitment can make pure sex appeal all that interesting and keep it so. For persons less committed, and less deprived, the mere exhibition of bare bodies palls sooner than they probably expect. In modern America there has to be tremendous ballyhoo about it, lest people lose interest altogether. Before American youth becomes preoccupied with breasts, millions of dollars are spent on establishing the prestige of breasts. Bare bodies also represent *the easy solution*. Their effect is overrated, and so is exploited to divert attention from poverty in other departments. And thus the physical appeal of other things than skin and the shape of mammary glands is forgotten about. Acrobatics is also purely physical; and yet need not have any sex appeal at all. What interests us in the acrobat's body is not how it looks but what it does: not bodily beauty but bodily prowess. Even the Folies-Bergères do not just "look": they find it necessary on stage to be going somewhere, doing something. Drama, as our teachers delight to mention, is action. And prowess is action, whereas handsomeness is not. The agile body is a truer archetype of theatre art than the beautiful one.

But, then again, beauty and prowess are not antagonists. On the contrary, they united at the very threshold of theatre art to produce admiration. I wonder if we realize how crucial a product that is. We tend to think of admiration as but a stamp of approval added at the end but, psychologically, it is a prerequisite at the outset and throughout. One cannot pay attention with any pleasure unless admiration is aroused; and that one should pay attention *without* pleasure, in art, is never intended and would indicate a fatal breakdown. Once again the naïvest, commonest responses are a reliable guide to the rudiments. When spectators whisper, "Isn't he marvelous?" as an actor goes to work, they are "with it," they are "into" theatre, "warmed up" to the theatre experience. Words like "competent" and "adequate," which in some fields would convey sufficient praise, are as damning in theatre as words like "dull" or "bad," because theatre is an engine which competence and adequacy will not drive. "Astonish me," Cocteau reports Diaghilev as saying to him. It was tantamount to saying, "Make me admire you inordinately"; and I am adding that this, functionally speaking, may not be saying much more than, "Hold my attention in the theatre." For, in the theatre, when there is nothing to marvel at, there is likely to be nothing, period. "Theatre of marvels" is a phrase to describe not only the special phenomenon of miraculous scenery and the like but any true theatre, any theatre that really "works." Every theatrical artist must be an acrobat in his own way, and the acrobat himself is the purest possible example of theatre, exhibiting, as he does, the most breathtaking feats that the human body is capable of. Nietzsche maintained that art embodies the will to power. If we apply the thought to acrobats, the operative word will be "embodies." Generally, the word "power" brings only politicians to mind, men in search of an abstraction, whom we can admire, if at all, only rather guiltily. The acrobat's power is concrete and corporeal. The wonder it arouses in us is lovely and innocent.

I once heard a man exclaiming upon the wonder of a trapeze artist's movements and being put down by his neighbor who said, "What's so wonderful? A bird would think nothing of it." Now one can wonder at the flight of birds too, but one would probably not wonder at a bird whose performance duplicated that of a trapeze artist. Why then do we wonder at the trapeze artist himself? That we do is the proof that movement is not found wonderful in itself but only as we hold a certain opinion about the mover's capacity for it.

> He floats through the air with the greatest of ease,
> The daring young man on the flying trapeze.

Ease. That is: nonease overcome. Our admiration for the daring young man has its root in the knowledge that, for a human body, such feats are not easy, as they are for birds. They require prowess, they require daring. And here we stumble upon a *difference* between acrobatics and regular theatre, namely, that the stage, unlike the circus ring, is not dangerous in the literal sense, only in the metaphorical. But the prowess circus artists and actors have in common. In order to understand our respect for it we should recognize that we do not make our minds a *tabula rasa* for artists to write upon but, on the contrary, bring to art all manner of attitudes and assumptions. In the present case, we bring our own estimates of what is difficult and of how difficult it is, and we respond to the acrobat's prowess insofar as we see it as a conquest of very considerable difficulties. In that sense, watching acrobats is an intellectual pursuit. More important: what the intellect addresses itself to is the will to power. It measures mastery. "All the world loves a winner." The Spanish proverb may bring to mind much that is dubious in ethics, but it embodies a truth of psychology that is not to be ignored by any student of the arts.

The stage is dangerous only in a metaphorical sense. "When you go out on stage," Sir John Gielgud once told a cast of actors whom he was directing, "think of it as a battlefield—because, by God, it is." In a metaphorical sense. And good theatrical work which comes across to us through our sense of difficulty overcome also comes across to us through our sense of danger survived, of risk successfully taken. Actors are heroes in the most primitive way: voyagers through perilous seas, climbers of crags, leapers of chasms, slayers of dragons. Those who are not are boring and, in effect, not actors.

What gives the actor his best chance of bringing to his audience that intensification of experience which is the aim of all art? It depends what is meant by "best." His simplest and most direct chance would be afforded by the simplest and most direct forms of dramatic art—such forms as melodrama and farce. Thrillers thrill. "Hilarious comedies" do induce hilarity. And indeed it is often assumed that nonthrillers thrill less, as also that less farcical comedies are less hilarious. It might even seem to stand to reason that the more *thought* you inject into a play the less *feeling* goes into it. But what would follow from this? That any successful melodrama or farce would be marked by greater emotional intensity than *Oedipus* or *Lear,* than *Volpone* or *The Misanthrope.* Which is not so: I need only appeal to the opinion of anyone who would claim to have experienced these works for an answer. Evidently the highest intensity is not reached by the most direct route.

Returning to our first postulate, which was that the theatre presents the beautiful body, the simplest and most direct procedure would be to take the actors' clothes off and send them out on stage; and since we live in a simplistic time, we find this procedure being adopted nowadays. What we do not find is any notably heightened intensity. Nor may we expect to find it even when—as is now being threatened—the actors make love on stage to the bitter or sweet orgasmic end. In doing this, the actors may indeed be experiencing intensity, but an actor's orgasm does not give me one. If I were brought to the point of orgasm by an enactment, it would presumably be through *non*orgasm on stage, through seductive cunning and device, erotic calculation and fantasy—in short, not through life but through art.

Sir Kenneth Clark has taught us that, in painting and sculpture, nudity is a kind of norm. But on stage it is not: it is a kind of exception. I affirm this, in the first instance, as a matter of history in all parts of the world of which I have any knowledge, but it could equally be affirmed as a matter of principle. Nothing seems more clearly written into the lawbook of dramatic art as it is known to us than that its first principle is concealment, its first implement (as well as symbol) the mask. True, this concealment can be regarded as a paradox. Just as one can *reculer pour mieux sauter,* so to conceal can be preparatory to revealing: dramatic plot might be cited as a leading example. But here again we are in the realm of metaphor. Nothing physical is uncovered at the end of a comedy, or, if it is, as for instance by the removal of a disguise, there are other clothes underneath. This last point is of importance to others than puritans and policemen. Pirandello called his plays "naked masks," not "naked faces," to express, among other things, his sense that the mask is itself an ultimate in the theatre. Nudity there, when it exists, will be a spiritual nudity; physically, the method of theatre is to cover, drape, and swathe. Hence the importance to naturalistic theatre of walls and ceilings, even of carpets, wallpaper, paint, light fixtures, everything that covers the nakedness of nature. But the great nonnaturalistic theatres go in for concealment every bit as much, and in some cases more. What is the baroque stage but this world decked out for carnival or upholstered to simulate a rather materialistic heaven? As for Shakespeare's stage, even if it was as bare of scenery as critics have liked to suppose (and it probably wasn't), it undoubtedly liked to flatter and distort the human form in all manner of rich raiment.

Seeing Edgar undressed, King Lear makes his famous speech about nakedness and himself starts to strip:

> Thou art the thing itself. Unaccommodated man is no more but such a poor, bare, forked animal as thou art. Off, off, you lendings, come, unbutton here!

He doesn't continue stripping, however, and the playwright twice tells us that Edgar's loins remain covered. Even if this latter point be regarded merely as a concession to a puritanic age, what is in question here is not what Sir Kenneth Clark calls nudity. The nudity of art, as Clark defines it, is an idealization of the human form, the human form transfigured by an idea of the *super*human. In other words, this idea itself becomes a kind of clothing. Quite different is your nakedness or mine, signalizing, as it does, the absence of an important part of our normal image, an impoverishment of our total ego, and it is this our nakedness—not Clark's nudity—which Shakespeare introduces into *Lear*, though even then not literally. Similarly, the taking off of clothes is shown in *Lear* not as an act of liberation but as an act of degradation, almost of mutilation. Lear may come to appreciate his common humanity in such a process, yet this is only to say he learns humility by being humiliated. Lear may speak of unclothed man as "the thing itself," as man in his essence, his animal essence, but there is no implication that the playwright agrees. The Shakespearean image of human dignity is an image of man as king, in other words, of man not only clothed but sumptuously arrayed, crown on head and scepter in hand. One might make the point that in this Shakespeare was a man of his time, but I am making the point that he was a man of the theatre—where Homo sapiens is not unaccommodated, poor, bare, and forked, but accommodated, rich, clothed, and raised above the animal by all the lendings and buttons that the dramatic poet can devise.

My larger point is that the theatre does not, cannot, go right at its intensities. If it could and did, showing copulation on stage would be a piece of theatre which no dramatic literature and no feats of what is normally called acting could possibly compete with. Even those modes, like melodrama and farce, which I have described as the *most* direct are still not *entirely* direct. They have their indirectness, and are dependent for their success on the operation of certain dualities. Farce depends upon a contrast between appearance and reality, lightness of heart and violence, gravity of manner, and zaniness of substance. Melodrama is as close to a direct, unmediated image of life as the art of the drama ever comes. It may often be a pretty literal mirror image of our fantasy life. But since it offers itself as art, not as raw fantasy, it is permeated by a sense of irony. We recognize this at those points in a melodrama where we laugh at it without ceasing to enjoy it. In pure melodrama the smile is never quite absent. If we received these heroisms, these disasters, these secrecies, without a smile we would be taking them seriously, taking them as more than melodrama, attributing to them a greater and higher complexity. But even melodrama which, since everything is relative, we can refer to as simple, is not as simple as all that.

At this stage in the argument we have to admit that intensity itself is not as simple a thing as is commonly assumed. The archetype of intensity, in common assumption, is sudden sharp sensation, such as a twinge of pain or a spasm of pleasure. Of late years, some advocates of drugs have offered to increase the intensity of such spasms for us as well as their frequency, and, logically enough, the suggestion has been made that the arts might prove unable to compete with the pleasures that drugs afford. I obviously cannot tackle here the whole topic of psychedelic experience, but it might be relevant to touch at least upon a claim for it that was put forward by its most widely known spokesman. In a lengthy exposition published by *Playboy,* Dr. Timothy Leary laid the stress on pleasure in the most directly physical sense: specifically, on many, many orgasms in place of the good old-fashioned single orgasm. It is not surprising that some of his colleagues immediately jumped on him. They wish to make a far more spiritual claim for psychedelic experience, and perhaps in the end, who knows? they will be able to make this stick. For the present, however, one may be justified in complaining that the talk of spiritual exploration is fairly vapid, like the talk of expanded consciousness, since one is given no clear account of *what* territory is explored or *what* the drug takers are aware of that they weren't aware of before. Even to say that drug experience improves one's experience of art itself— Beethoven sounds even greater when you're high—is to communicate very little if neither the previous experience of art nor the allegedly improved experience of it is adequately described. And at this stage, I find, most drug users fall back on the traditional copout of the mystics: their experience is by definition ineffable.

But while some things inaccessible to reason may be above reason, others may just be below it, and I would take my cue from Leary's confessions to *Playboy* for assuming that what he mainly looks to drugs for is *sensation.* The experience seems mostly subrational, and the experiencer's stance antirational. Art, including dramatic art, has to be considered, I'm afraid, in less animal and more human terms, much as one may resist the rhetoric that surrounds the word "human," and even though one may suspect that the human/animal dichotomy is unfair to animals. What I have in mind is not so much man's high claims for himself but rather what seems to be a fact of his make-up, namely, that with him, feeling does not exist separately, but is bound up with his thoughts. "Deep thinking," says Coleridge, "is attainable only by a man of deep feeling." And this is not all. There would seem to be some dynamic relation between a particular "deep thought" and the "deep feeling" of the man to whom the thought, as we say, "comes." Gabriel Marcel says, "Emotion is actually the discovery of the fact that 'this concerns me after all'"; which may not be a definition of all emotion but is certainly a very astute adumbration of the kind of feeling we find in dramatic art. Indeed we often find it twice over: in *Oedipus Rex* as in Ibsen's *Ghosts,* both characters on stage and spectators out front discover that "this concerns them after all," and are thereby deeply moved. Now to discover facts is the work of the intellect, and both Sophocles and Ibsen ask the intellect to perform its most characteristic chore: puzzle solving. Spectator and leading character must carefully and logically piece together a case history. It is in this sense that one theorist of the drama calls plot its most intellectual element: the most intellectual in order that the play may be most emotional.

But the intellectuality inherent in plot is by no means the same thing as "the thought" in a play. Does the latter as well as the former contribute to the emotional impact? There is plenty of thinking in plays which contributes to nothing, least of all to thought itself, and thoughts thrown in for whatever interest they may have in themselves are so much dead weight dramatically. One playwright has wittily said that characters in plays shouldn't have thoughts at all —thought should be something that emerges only from the play as a whole. The word "thought" is being used here in two quite different senses. In the first sense, a thought is an idea, often a general idea about life stated by an individual character with no special bearing on the plot and theme of the play. Oscar Wilde's characters get off such ideas all the time. The other kind of thought may have no general interest or reference. It is simply the intellectual part of the process of discovery and realization, either by a character or a spectator: "I see that that is so." Marcel is speaking exclusively of the latter kind of thought. First, one sees that that is so; then one recognizes that "it concerns me"; finally one is moved.

Possibly even this kind of thinking seems closer to crossword puzzles than to thought in the higher sense, but it need not be so. People who take *Oedipus Rex* as a crossword puzzle—and there have been some, even among classical scholars—regard the play as melodrama, which is to say that it has not brought them to any "this concerns me." Those who do derive this mes-

sage from the play will unanimously claim that there is more to it than in-
genious plotting. To say what this "more" is would be to offer a whole theory
of the drama, or at least of tragedy. What is pertinent here is that when the
thought is made a matter of personal concern it is deeply felt. Which is the ob-
verse of the fact that we are narcissistic: we feel very little except when we take
things personally.

The psychiatrist Victor Frankl has observed that while life and philosophy
can normally be regarded as separate, as per the adage, "First live and then philosophize," extreme situations can break down the separation and bring men to
believe, "First philosophize and then die." Knowing that they must die, prison-
ers in the Nazi camps were desperate to find the meaning of death, of life:
their extreme emotion drove them to an unwonted intellectuality. . . . In tragedy we watch the inmates of this prison the world (as one of Shakespeare's
tragic heroes calls it) in *their* desperate search for meaning, and, as has been
known at least since Aristotle, we do more than watch. We enter in. We say,
"This concerns me." It might seem a miracle that a single work can make all
men feel that it concerns them personally. Certainly, the tragic writer has to be
blessed with genius to practice successfully, and genius is a miracle. At the receiving end, however, neither miracles nor genius need be presupposed, but
only the humanistic postulate of Montaigne: "Each man carries within himself
the complete structure of the human condition."

Without breaking my promise not to claim that drama is a superior genre, I
might point to a unique feature of it which for many of us has great appeal and
which helps to explain the intensity of the genre. Although the playwright's
characters are imaginary, like the novelist's, and cannot walk on stage (though
Pirandello can imagine that they can), they are presented *to* human beings *by*
human beings, and this is a degree of actuality and humanity unique in the an-
nals of art. Its uniqueness is so striking and so attractive that I for one find it
hard to believe that the theatrical scheme of things could ever be replaced by cin-
ematography or any other mechanism. Its intensities are all its own, in that vibrations move from actor to spectator and back again, as they obviously cannot
in the movies and television. In this respect, theatre is closer to group therapy
than to "the media." J. L. Moreno's psychodramatic therapy is indeed based on
theatre and can be regarded (though by me it is not) as the ultimate form of
theatre.

What first strikes one about this scheme—human beings presenting other
human beings to yet other human beings—is that it makes of theatre the
most directly sensuous of the arts. That is why I mentioned physical beauty at
the outset. But I hurried on to state that prowess was more important than
looks; and perhaps by now my reasons for doing so are apparent. It would be
hard to overestimate the importance of the actor's physical presence, but easy to
overestimate the importance of his looks, because the dynamic of theatre is not

beauty but interaction as between human beings. A double interaction: first, between actor and actor, second, between actor and spectator. Thus the quintessential event in theatre is the human encounter. In one respect, this art is very simple. A child's impression, "All that happens is that a few people keep coming and going," is very proper, provided the child has also noticed that, before going, these people *meet*. Jean Racine remarked that his plays were quite easy to write once he had figured out the entrances and exits. This remark could be misunderstood only by someone who failed to realize what a Herculean labor the figuring out represents. Why, it is everything! For, as Nietzsche put it, "In every action of a human being the complete evolution of his psychic life is gone through again." The actions which playwrights show are encounters, and the great playwrights have known in their bones that each encounter is somehow crucial and comprehensive. That is the meaning of classical concentration in Racine and his Greek masters. But, equally, Shakespeare, whose methods were so different, evinces the fullest awareness of the possible bigness of the smallest encounter. The encounter of Cinna the Poet with the Roman mob is one of the shortest scenes in drama, and contains no character present in the rest of *Julius Caesar,* yet it both takes its place in the design of the play and remains indelibly stamped in the mind as a universal image.

"There seems to be no agent more effective than another person," writes Erving Goffman in his book *Encounters,* "for bringing the world alive for oneself." This is another of those principles of human life which are incorporated in the art of the theatre. Bringing things alive would, I think, be widely recognized today as the purpose of the arts in general, a purpose doubly worthy and urgent in a civilization like ours which is actually less a civilization than a massive assault on all forms of vitality, not to mention on life itself. Modern poets have stressed the need to give back to words their full emotional content. Dramatic poetry could be included in this proposition, and one might add that, the subject of drama being what is nowadays called "interpersonal relations," the art of the theatre, in which persons present persons to persons, is in a specially favorable position to set up live vibrations, to set the human engines revving again.

I would like to squeeze another idea out of Goffman's dictum: that one *needs* another person. A page or two back I was saying that one encounters oneself in the theatre. "This concerns me" means "this *is* me," and our identification with the tragic hero is perhaps the most celebrated fact in all theatrical psychology, finding its last squeaky echo in the newspaper reviewer's search for "human" characters whom he can "identify with." It is very well to begin with the hero as long as one proceeds to acknowledge the villain. But even a melodrama has a villain as well as a hero; tragedy, like serious modern drama, has many characters who may be neither heroes nor villains; and comedy can present a whole cast of characters whom one cannot identify oneself with, a world of "other" persons.

It is a recognized principle—Goethe, for one, states it—that one must find oneself, if at all, not by turning in on oneself but through human activity and relationship. This is something else that the dramatists intuitively know; it is implied already in Aristotle's insistence on character as doing rather than being. And so, in seeing a play, one can begin by feeling, "this concerns me, this is me"; one can go on to feeling, "this concerns others, this is the other fellow"; and one can end up feeling that the Me that "this" is has been redefined by the Non-Me, by the other fellow, or, more precisely, by interactions between the Me and the Non-Me—more precisely still, by interactions between aspects of the Me and aspects of the Non-Me. One realizes at this point why a playwright might need a big cast of characters. One realizes, too, that if he operated in abstract awareness of what he was doing (as most artists do not), he might well lay out the cast list in terms of various aspects of the Me and Non-Me, possibly with subdivisions according to which elements of the Me could be mixed with elements of the Other. Strindberg went some distance toward such a procedure in his dream plays, as did the German Expressionists who followed his lead.

I am assuming that Schopenhauer was right to believe that the stage offers the perfect mirror of life, but if it be asked, "How then is it to be distinguished from life itself?" one would have to admit that the image is misleading. On stage we see the "interpersonal conflicts" of real life in their full intensity; in life, however, we do not see them, or not in their full intensity. The effect of "full intensity" is, if you like, a trick, achieved above all by excluding from view all that is irrelevant to the conflict. Selectivity is the first principle of all art. But it is not a sufficient principle: another one enters in, more of an X ray than a mirror, in that underlying realities, normally unseen if not necessarily invisible, are exhibited in art, not least in dramatic art. Now the words "underlying" and "exhibited" are both metaphors. The stage cannot literally exhibit either of the two sets of realities involved—the inner facts of individual lives or the general facts of social and historical life—but what it does make visible—and audible—will make these realities real. Art is life even more than life is.

The intensities of theatre are very many. Thousands of pages could easily be filled illustrating their variety. Let me provide one illustration which I consider unusually important. Its character will best come clear if I permit myself a comparison, but not an invidious one, with fiction. Whereas a great, long novel can give an unmatched impression of the ramifications of experience, its extent, and many of its undulations and slow developments, and so may be regarded as having an enormous horizontal range, a supremely great drama can claim to pack in as much of life, but one will more easily see it as a vertical structure, layer on layer or floor on floor. *War and Peace* presents human lives with an incomparable richness of personal detail; it also places them within a particular span of history, and seeks to relate them to history in general. *King Lear,* on the other hand, forgoes much that a long novel has to offer in detail and process; willingly accepts instead what critics, with gratuitous sneers, call "melodrama" and "mere intrigue"; but all the same contrives to present the life of man "whole" and on the grandest scale, a life cosmic, social, and individual—all the time, all three.

As a schoolboy, I was puzzled by the description of Sophocles as seeing life steadily and seeing it *whole:* I could mention many things about life which Sophocles does not mention, so how could his account be "whole"? Well, it is the outline of a whole, without most of the details. This would be part of the answer, but, finally, a more important part, I think, is that, for Sophocles, life possessed a *wholeness,* and that his work communicates a sense of it. Unity of action, for example, flows from this sense: drama can have beginning, middle, and end when dramatists feel that life has beginnings, middles, and ends. Today, when, on the contrary, the consensus is that "things fall apart, the center cannot hold," it is harder to write drama, easier to write the kind of prose fiction which doesn't require unity of action.

Unity of action makes for the highest intensity in drama, as Aristotle knew, but the phrase "unity of action" goes only a short way toward describing the unified and unifying vision of such a work as *Lear,* or even of smaller masterpieces like those of Ibsen. I have been saying that the playwrights portray the essential conflicts of human beings. It should be added that they do not situate the conflicts outside time and space. On the contrary, the playwright who can manage it projects the very archetypes of his epoch. The characteristic intensity of Ibsen arises from the feeling we so irresistibly receive of being at the very nerve center of his civilization. Critics of an "aesthetic" bent shake their heads over Ibsen's choice of the middle-class drawing room as his "favorite" locale, but favoritism is not involved; rather, an unerring instinct for the significant. And the setting is just one example. Everything about an Ibsen play helps to provide a theatrical image, not of individuals, or even families alone, but of a culture.

In our own time, what would be the status of *Waiting for Godot,* if we did not believe it rendered a state of soul which is that of an epoch? No wonder that such a work arouses emotion, for in it I recognize not only *me* but *us.*

In setting up intensity as the criterion, one is attempting to speak in terms of quantity rather than quality. On the one hand, one asks how much emotion is generated in people, a purely quantitative query, and on the other one answers that the emotion is the greater the more the dramatist can pack into his play, a purely quantitative answer. It remains only to measure the quantities.

Only! Ay, there's the rub. One might believe in the eventual measurement of responses if indeed one simply wished to measure twinges and spasms, but if one believes that the total response of a human being is evoked by art, and that human beings—for worse as well as better—are what has been called spiritual as well as physical entities, then all prospect of measuring responses vanishes for the indefinite future. As for the amount of life that the playwright can pack into his play—life on the cosmic, social, or individual scale—this could definitely be measured so long as by *amount* is meant what a sociologist might mean and not what a dramatist has to mean. By the sociologist's standards more is recorded of human life in *The World Almanac* than in Dante's *Divine Comedy*. The Almanac's account of things is a lot "truer," too. When one says Shakespeare packs *everything* into *Lear*, one is using not only hyperbole but also irony. One means that Shakespeare makes certain things so important that everything else shrinks into insignificance. Yes, he packs a lot in, but an even greater achievement was to reduce to nothingness, in our minds, the larger lot that he left out. In short, our apparently rather "objective" comment on *Lear* depends on a whole cluster of value judgments, and these judgments have been made not by the eye of an all-seeing deity, but by me—or you, dear reader —in the somewhat murky depths (and shallows) of our limited and muddled being. God can think, no doubt, of greater or less intensity in a play much as we think of it in an electric bulb—a matter of pure quantity. You and I can see His point in principle, but when we try to measure these differences in watts, we begin to flounder. The straw to clutch when, in such circumstances, we find ourselves drowning is the word "quality."

(1968)

Theatre in Extremis

Since, finally, I reject the Living Theatre, I would like to begin by conceding what I concede can be conceded. The Living Theatre represents the most resolute attempt during the past twenty years to create a theatre which would be a radical alternative to Broadway and Off Broadway. In principle I favor such attempts. I also recognize certain achievements. I have long considered Julian Beck as just about the best stage designer around. He still is. Even in the current productions (which as a whole I consider disastrous) there are beautiful things. Many are visual effects devised by Mr. Beck, whose work in *Frankenstein* is the best pop art our theatre has seen. Some are directorial effects devised by Mrs. Beck (Judith Malina), particularly in the department of pantomine. Yoga exercises pay off choreographically, and also build bodies. Although most Living Theatre girls are still pretty unappetizing, several of the boys are edible in the extreme: an important thing for any theatre but especially for one in which the actors are prone at any moment to cry with King Lear, "Off, off, you lendings, come, unbutton here." And if the Living Theatre's efforts finally evaporate in sound and fury signifying nothing, the occasional moments of authentic, quiet feeling stand out the more by contrast. The Living Theatre's brilliant distortion of the most famous of Sophocles' choruses (on man as a wonder) was well worth the dirty subway trip to Brooklyn and the mostly meaningless sitting around in the Academy's theatre there. Taking a hint from Brecht, the Living

Theatre represents man, not as wonderful, but as monstrous; and a sense of the monstrousness of United States power was rendered in calmly intoned phrases which, helped by sober and spacious choreography, really sank in. I think it must have been harder afterward for any Humphrey supporters present to accept the Vietnamese enterprise for the "great adventure" that Mr. Humphrey has said it is.

If I am right, then for these moments the Living Theatre was effectively a political theatre, as it wishes to be. But for how many moments in the course of all these hours of performance (four shows, mostly very long) is this the case? I would say very few and that, even for those few, too many spectators will have been rendered unresponsive by what came before. They may even, and very justifiably, have gone home.

It has been said that sending "such people" home is an aim of this theatre. I would raise the question, though, whether that is a shrewd—let alone a generous—aim. It was certainly not shrewdly expressed when, at one performance I attended, an actor called out to the audience, "Which of you paid taxes this year? Get out of this theatre and make room for the people standing outside!" Now the people standing outside were just a mixed bag of humanity, some of whom presumably paid taxes, and others of whom were too young to have been asked to. What reason was there to pick on those who had shown sufficient interest to reserve their seats? Are all taxpayers worse men than all nontaxpayers? More relevant: mustn't future tax refusers be recruited from the ranks of present taxpayers? How then can any propagandist who has not taken leave of his senses ask the present taxpayers to get the hell out?

The Living Theatre *has* taken leave of its senses. I approve of that as a momentary thing. "The man who cannot lose his head has no head to lose." But as a permanent state of affairs? As a position publicly taken? In the *East Village Other*, Miss Malina says of Eugene McCarthy, "He's a murderer . . . a letter-writing murderer. . . . Just because he's more liberal, that's the worst kind of murderer." In the same interview, Mr. Beck states a case for astrology.

Can one accept *advice* from such people, off stage or on? Only, I should think, by an abdication of one's own intelligence, and this is precisely what the Living Theatre's performances ask of us: this is the point of its method and style. Hence the absurdity of considering these things in purely aesthetic terms, as I'm afraid Clive Barnes did in the *New York Times*. Mr. Barnes would add that, to a degree, the method and style are those of the *avant-garde* in general and may represent the future, but to that I retort: so what? Only a small sector of the future is involved in any such calculation, and maybe a particularly nasty sector. Mr. Barnes may fear being one of those critics who failed to recognize all the great new things of their time. Unhappily the opposite possibility also looms: that a critic may too easily accept claims to futurity at face value.

Why play guessing games about the future? A critic's tools are his intelligence and sensibility. Both are affronted by Living Theatre tactics. What the intelligence demands in the theatre (and I believe outside it too) is dialectics—a sense of the interplay of opposites. This is particularly evident in great political theatre from the *Oresteia* to *Henry IV,* from *Don Carlos* to *Galileo.* But where the Living Theatre offers opposites they are *so* opposite that their interaction is abstract and unreal. A prime instance would be their Creon and Antigone—presented as Ubu Roi versus Judith Malina. How remote this frankly monstrous Creon seems! An up-to-date American *Antigone* would require a Creon with a "splendid liberal record," since America's contribution to imperialistic war is precisely to cloak it in liberal ideology. The Living Theatre's conception is so lifeless it needs constant injections of theatrical Benzedrine—which, however, in turning on the actors, does not turn on the audience.

Dialectics means that a proposition elicits a counterproposition; and dramatists are people with a keen sense of this to and fro. The Becks are people with a weak sense of it. They are people who just state their convictions. Example: "If you go out and use violence against your enemies, you will return and use violence against your own people." Hearing this, any intelligent person will have many counterthoughts. Example: Do the Becks mean that Ho Chi Minh should refrain from violence against the Americans, lest he become a fascist and later go berserk against the Vietnamese? No one on the Becks' stage ever has such thoughts. Or any other thoughts. Only the original "convictions." Various actors *repeat* the original proposition, presumably on the Lewis Carroll principle that "what I say three times is true." Only, some people out front, unbeknown to the Living Theatre, are human beings, and possessed of the spirit of contradiction. If you keep drumming the same thing into my ears, what I think of is *Brave New World,* and my reaction is: Go brainwash someone else.

The Living Theatre does not present dialectics, but their failure to do so is dialectical: intellectual bankruptcy, in a natural, if shocking, process produces emotional hysteria. If this process had been worked out consciously, the thought would have been: "To fill the intellectual vacuum, emotional overexcitement"; but the Living Theatre does not think, so it is something that just happens. "Since we lack the means to persuade, we will overpower." Art is a seduction. The Living Theatre substitute is a rape. Only, as I think Confucius had it, you can't really be raped against your will. So it's only attempted rape; an attempt that fails.

Oh, but, someone will reply, the Living Theatre has a following: it does not fail with everyone—it fails only "with squares like you." (Definition of a square: anyone who rejects the Living Theatre.) Let us examine this following, who it is, and what it does. When the Living Theatre launches its various insults against the audience as a whole, a section of this audience detaches itself from the rest and joins the actors, sometimes literally, sometimes figuratively, on stage. Nice work if you can get it—from a certain point of view. But is this point of view that of political theatre? Or any theatre? When you abolish (or, which comes to the same thing, expel) the audience and merely enlarge the acting company, what do you have? Well, the nearest thing in American life would be a revivalist meeting. "Come up here in the pulpit and bear witness for Christ." I am not against conversion to Christianity, but I don't know that I'm for conversion to Living Theatre. In any case, no one asks my opinion on that. As a dramatic critic—no, let me just say as a member of an audience with a ticket and a seat—I am asked only to stop, look, and listen. True, there is all this stuff in the books about the origins of theatre in ritual and religion. What the books seem to have forgotten is that the theatre *parted company* with ritual and religion the first time that it had spectators instead of fellow worshipers, at the moment that the event lost all semblance of orgy and became, alas for the Living Theatre, a spectator sport.

I speak without prejudice to orgies. I speak with prejudice against the current pseudo-orgiastic theatre because of an ingrained prejudice in favor of orgies themselves. They just shouldn't take place in theatres, that's all. Theatres presuppose an audience; orgies presuppose total participation and total absence of mere onlooking. Otherwise we get bogged down in those two rather chilling perversions: exhibitionism and voyeurism. Which is what the theatre of Tom O'Horgan is about, insofar as it is about anything.

In New Haven the laugh was on the cops. Which is a good place for the laugh to be. The Living Theatre people said they weren't really naked when they were busted at Yale, and I believe them, because what one witnessed all evening was a display not of nudity but of underwear. Dare to undress! That was the challenge flung at us "squares" out front, but if any of us had taken the Living Theatre up on it, we'd have been doing what they didn't do: they only stripped to the traditional undress of the floorshow—a fancy G-string—and the only orgy that ensued was a petting party peered at by the clothed multitude. No house mother among them would have found anything to disapprove of. The voyeurs were catered to, but only with a kind of *coitus interruptus*.

If I have stressed the political errors of the Living Theatre, I should not overlook the aesthetic errors, since they include the prize blooper of the current *avant-garde*. This is the cult of intimacy, which is based on false psychological assumptions, both as to what is the normal relation of audience and actor and as to what can be done to upset it. Perhaps the root error is the notion that you can with impunity simply *ignore* the barrier between public and player and cross it like an abandoned frontier. How this fails to work out can be checked by any anthropologist who cares to thread his way through the jungles of Off and Off Off Broadway. Even an otherwise sound enterprise like *The Concept* —in which Daytop group therapy is exhibited on a Sheridan Square stage —is vitiated when, at the close, a performer asks a spectator if he can love her.

The spectator should answer, "I doubt it very much: I don't know you. Also: you are impertinent to ask. How d'you know I can love anyone? How d'you know whether I even prefer girls?" What actually happens? The spectator is nonplussed, embarrassed, overpowered. In which act of overpowering, the modest, otherwise very human little company of *The Concept* verges upon the totalitarianism of the Living Theatre. Some are born loving, some achieve love, but ticket buyers for our current *avant-garde* theatre have love thrust upon them.

Only that ain't love, and, as far as the Living Theatre is concerned, one must point to the contrast between verbal tributes to love and the nonverbal, indeed visceral, displays of hostility of which their productions mainly nowadays consist. This contradiction received unintentionally comic expression at Yale when the company spent a couple of hours working up an ugly, aggressive mood in the theatre and then had someone step forward and say, almost in so many words, "Now, please don't get violent, we are apostles of *non*violence." The comedy here is black, of course, and suggests just what is most hateful in the Living Theatre's archenemy, the Establishment: the habit of praising nonviolence while bringing more and more violence into being. Black comedy and sad irony. The Becks differ from most non-Broadway theatre people in that they are not motivated by a secret desire to be *on* Broadway, but this does not prevent the extremes from meeting in all-too-significant ways, as indeed they do in polarized America generally. The more intransigent and irrational student rebels at Columbia had many things in common with Grayson Kirk, and especially the ability to live inside a cocoon of defensive rhetoric. The Living Theatre likewise comes full circle, and reflects, in an odd distorting mirror, the faults of Establishment theatre. It is "against the star system," and yet the Becks themselves are more than stars, they are astrologers, they are gurus, they are the focus of a mystique of personality. How otherwise would it be possible to interrupt the telling of a story by Sophocles in order to make a reference to the "banishment" from the United States of Judith Malina? How otherwise could a company have existed for seventeen years and produced no directors and designers other than Julian and Judith who produced *it?* There are no actors here. Mrs. Beck was never a very good actress, and Mr. Beck was never really an actor at all, yet they hire (if the bourgeois concept is permitted) only devotees—potential yogis, yes, potential actors, no.

It may be said that in one particular the Living Theatre inverts the Broadway formula: Broadway flatters its audiences, the Living Theatre spits on its audiences. But this is truly no inversion. Flattery itself implies contempt, using, to lick boots, the same spittle which the Living Theatre aims at your eyes. An effective theatre of commitment, however dim a view it takes of the society at large, must perforce receive its own guests with courtesy. I am not talking public relations only, though the relation actor-spectator is a public relation par excellence. I am talking politics and therefore ethics. One could do without the testimonials to love, if only someone loved someone, if only one could sense the presence, in the theatre, of a little actual humor and goodwill. Of radicalism, Marx said the root was man. A radical theatre—before it arrives at the problems, before it tangles with obstacles—needs to testify, in a concrete manner, to its own humanity. Otherwise one must wonder if one would prefer an America in which the Becks won out to the America of the Nixons and the Humphreys.

(*1968*)

From Protest to Resistance

I applaud the statement recently issued by the Resist group in Cambridge, Massachusetts. It reads in part:

> During these past four years, we have realized that we cannot be honest and constructive by attempting to use the political mechanisms of a society which is dishonest and destructive. We believe that those mechanisms merely facilitate struggles between "conservatives" and "liberals" who fall within the supra-partisan consensus that has determined U.S. foreign and domestic policy for more than two decades. That consensus rests on the premise that those who run the American government know what is best for the non-white, the poor, and the uneducated people of America and the world. It does not believe in freedom or democracy for South Vietnam or the Dominican Republic, for Watts or Harlem. In perfect analogy to the reasoning which produced Soviet intervention in Hungary and Czechoslovakia, the American government uses all of the terrifying force and violence at its command to deny its subject peoples the right to effect solutions to their problems by means of their own choosing. Thus we see military and economic repression all over the world in the name of freedom, and at home in the name of law and order. . . . We therefore find ourselves engaged in an effort to reconstruct American society by deliberately going outside of the existing political system.

I think we are saying the same thing, if more naïvely, when at our * DMZ Cabaret in the Village Vanguard, to the tune of a Stefan Wolpe march, we sing:

We turn from protest to resistance
Since all our protests came to naught.
Since all our protests came to naught
We turn from protest to resistance.

We can't accept your law and order—
Your law and order are corrupt.
Your law and order are corrupt—
We can't accept your law and order.

We're not dissenters, we are rebels
Since disagreement's not enough.
Since disagreement's not enough
We're not dissenters, we are rebels.

Resistance first; then liberation:
We break your laws to break your power.
We break your laws to break your power:
Resistance first; then liberation.

What good does it do to sing this? By which question I mean: what contribution can be made by singers, by entertainers, by us theatre folk so rightly classed by our ancestors with vagabonds and beggars? My mind jumps here to another DMZ song, "Buddies in Bad Times" (Prévert-Kosma):

Box-office receipts have been so small. . . .
I sang the melancholy tale of a miserable abandoned dog
And people don't go to concerts to listen to a dog's despairing howls!
That other song about the dog pound
That number hurt us most of all. . . .

So the singer, like Chaplin at the end of a film, takes to the road. This of course is only dropping out, and falls short, not only of liberation but of resistance, and not only of resistance but of protest. And yet even this—which is my point here—does some good both negatively and positively. Negatively in detaching the singer from the system, positively in cheering him up. The idea that entertainment should entertain, which we usually fight because we usually encounter it only in its commercial context, is of course fundamentally right, and that section of the *avant-garde* that forgets it and falls into disorder and the merely

* "Our," strictly speaking, would mean mine and Isaiah Sheffer's, since the two of us were the producers of the Cabaret, but I am really including in the first-person plural all who contributed to it, especially the actors, the composers, and the writers.

nauseating is fundamentally wrong. What's wrong with Broadway is really that it is *not* amusing. And conversely the first thing we have to do—we, the army of the lost, the exiled, yes, the alienated—is cheer ourselves up. How shall we amuse (let alone instruct) others if, to begin with, we are not amused? What is wrong with much *"avant-garde* theatre" (this time I put it in quotes) is that the actors are so damned depressed. Probably Broadway actors are depressed too, but that's what's wrong with them, and partly they hide it. *Avant-garde* actors don't hide it, they boast of it—whereas what they are really called on to do is get over it. Yes, even in the circumstances. Laugh and mean it—even in the circumstances. There was music and laughter even in the concentration camps, so why not in the air-conditioned nightmare of America 1968? Even in the most political sector of *avant-garde* theatre one shouldn't be so overcome with thirties-ish altruism that one cannot begin by having a good time for oneself. When you conclude that this is not possible, you are concluding that the theatre art is impossible.

Which is always the real question. Those who become conscience-ridden at the smallness of their contribution through the arts should—must—abandon the arts altogether. There are certainly times when the sword is mightier than the pen, and it is generally a hell of a lot swifter. In any case, taking up the sword, and putting down the pen, is something a given person may simply have to do if only for subjective reasons—*good* subjective reasons. Whether you reduce these reasons to a neurosis or elevate them to a Calling, it is equally an individual matter. To think of society as a whole is to realize that not everyone is going to leave his job to devote all his time to some Cause. It follows that the planning of social change should not presuppose such a thing. Rather, it must make use of people *in* their jobs. Which means it must make use of us *in* the theatre. This, and not a lot of messianic talk, is the real justification of any theatre that calls itself political. Allied with it is the truth I glanced at a moment ago: that "theatre" persists, even in unlikely, unfavorable, and painful conditions. (In Germany, concentration camps got so bad with time that entertainment, finally, was out of the question, but in the years when it was allowed it had for the inmates an understandably quite enormous spiritual meaning and value.)

Granted that the theatre's contribution to social change is small—like most other contributions for that matter—how might that contribution best be made? I must prevent this question from bringing out the doctrinaire in me; and so must you, dear reader. The point is not for each of us to put down the other and put ourselves up but to live and let live, each doing his "own thing." Probably all the forms of political theatre that have been proposed have some validity: in any case this has to reveal itself in the praxis. The only advice to give is to be quick to drop what obviously has no efficacy. (The criteria are simpler than you think. Megan Terry would have cut the Hanoi Hanna bit out of

Viet Rock had she just asked herself which side she was on.) One battle that can be stopped where it has begun and forestalled where it has not is that between literary and nonliterary political theatre. I, for example, seem to have got caught on the literary side in these polemics; Richard Schechner on the nonliterary.* In other words, I championed *The Deputy;* Schechner has worked on guerrilla theatre. In either case, by their fruits ye shall know them. I can imagine circumstances in which *The Deputy* would be ineffective and should not have been chosen in the first place, and I think Schechner did find guerrilla methods unsuitable to some situations: it is a matter of that. At Columbia University, in our troubles of spring 1968, the Pageant Players—a guerrilla group—had a place, and the dramaturgy of Hochhuth hadn't. It's all a matter of the place and the moment. Another battle I'd like to frustrate, rather than have won for one side or the other, is that between free theatre and box-office theatre. Where free theatre is possible, good; but a lot of people have money and can pay, and this makes possible a lot of political theatre that would otherwise not be there at all. I am not thinking of Broadway or even Off Broadway. As far as both these are concerned it might be smart to forget about political theatre. By all means Jerome Robbins, Leonard Bernstein, and Stephen Sondheim can dress up Brecht's *The Exception and the Rule* for Broadway, but what will they do to it? More to the point, what difference does it make what they do to it: the announced price of an orchestra seat is fifteen dollars.** Where large chunks of capital are needed, you are dealing with the Establishment, and it would be a mistake, as Brecht liked to put it, to expect them to finance their own liquidation. That they enjoy co-opting a Shaw or a Brecht is another matter: one must only take careful note *on what terms* this is done. And of course the "critics" belong to the club and so will duly report that the politics of Shaw and Brecht are boring anyway and that it's only as "artists" that they remain of interest. . . . At the DMZ, on the other hand, we have never needed more than about five hundred dollars as capital, and this could be put together from the savings of my partner and myself. This is the only kind of box-office theatre I am justifying here. We couldn't have done our type of show if we didn't pay

* Schechner had written in the *New York Free Press:* "Where I split from Eric Bentley is that he still believes in 'drama' and I don't. . . . Revolutions are fought by disruption, dislocation, and finally, guns."
** This project was never completed, though not because anyone acknowledged its inherent absurdity. The following related facts are of interest to all students of theatre and life. While *The Exception* was under option for Broadway, its producers tried to stop the play's being performed in its original form by a street theatre which would have played in ghetto areas only for nonpaying audiences. Meanwhile Leonard Bernstein prepared a theatre piece called *Mass* for the multimillion-dollar Kennedy Cultural Center in Washington, D.C. On opening night the architects of the Vietnam war sat in the audience while Bernstein, in his *Mass,* told them their war was wrong and they ought to love their fellow men. By all accounts, they enjoyed this very much! It was the music and drama critics, appealing to purely aesthetic standards, who put the *Mass* down. What price the political theatre of Leonard Bernstein? [1972]

the actors and get our money back from the public, but since we never needed wealthy backers, we did enjoy freedom—relative freedom, if you insist, but what freedom is absolute? Unlike some theatres that aren't charging admission, we have not asked foundations for money. Perhaps this indicates a bizarre scruple since I as a person have never hesitated to ask foundations for money. But the DMZ is in effect part of the Resist movement: if any foundation official, reading this note, wishes to invest in the Resistance, he might take it up with us. . . .

If I have run on a bit about the little theatrical effort I happen to be up to the eyes in at the moment, it is because I'd like everyone to be pragmatic and down to earth about political theatre. Politics, Marx and Engels maintained, have an economic base. It is good to talk about money. The Living Theatre burns dollars on stage, but they also keep asking for dollars and, when you're solicited, you wonder if they're just collecting kindling. Burn *your* money by all means. But not mine. And if you burn money publicly, don't ask for more from the public. The *avant-garde* never had any sense! Political theatre must part company not only with the commercial theatre but also with the *avant-garde*. A political theatre needs a politics that makes sense, and no one will believe your politics makes sense if your theatre doesn't make sense. Good sense begins with good housekeeping, therefore (in our world) with money. Even to abolish money—perhaps supremely then—you need to have some sense about money.

In short, solve your economic problem without recourse to foundations, let alone to angels, but don't solve it by idiot attempts to liquidate it. Come to terms with money. Know how you're going to get the sums you need. Then do the kind of political theatre which most commends itself to you, whether it is based on a written script and performed indoors by professionals, or whether it is improvisatory material performed out of doors by amateurs; or whatever it is. *You need have no views at all on the aesthetics of this.* For whether the show is any good by artistic standards doesn't depend on your views, it depends on your talent. If *you're* good, the show will be good; so forget this subject. It's the politics your attention must be on: this is where your views do show. And since I have just been churlish about the Living Theatre, let me close by defending them against a criticism I consider unsound. Some hold it against them that their politics are simple. I see no possibility of representing the *complexities* of politics on the stage. Some few complexities of politics find their way no doubt into plays of Shakespeare or Shaw but not many, nor can we expect too many Shakespeares or Shaws to report for duty at Resist headquarters. Political theatre can be bad precisely by attempting complexity. It is bad when it is unclear. When it is good, it is often very simple. Walter Kerr may comment that he figured out how the show would end during the first five minutes, but this he could have done in the first five minutes of any Greek tragedy. Seldom would the political theatre try to give the sophisticated Mr. Kerr a new idea: he probably wouldn't admit any idea was new anyway. It might try to rob him of some old idea. More likely, it would try to shake him out of some old attitude. Impossible, I suppose. Yet one hopes other spectators are more tractable. Julian Beck says he works on the rigidities of the audience. He also says it would be satisfying to think that two members of any audience had become a little less rigid by eleven p.m. So Julian Beck does have *some* sense after all. In theory, if not in practice, he knows what a political theatre can hope to achieve and what it had better forget about.

(*1968*)

Oppenheimer, Mon Amour

In the program of *In the Matter of J. Robert Oppenheimer* at the Vivian Beaumont Theatre, the director writes, "The play answers no questions, rather it begs the question." I wouldn't have put it *that* strongly, but it is certainly true that the Heinar Kipphardt play seems to seal its subject off rather than open it up.

Both the author and the Lincoln Center management have stressed that this work is a play, a dramatization of Oppenheimer's "trial" by the Personnel Security Board in 1954. Our first question must be: What kind of drama results? And our first answer might be that there is always a little ginger in courtroom questions and answers, and that much of *Oppenheimer* is no better and no worse than many another courtroom drama based on a significant case and put together by a theatrical pro. You could drop in on this show at any time between eight-thirty and eleven and enjoy the parry and thrust of forensic cross-questioning, and probably this is the simple base of most of the pleasure the play has provided in the various countries where it has run successfully.

But it has a second claim to interest as art: that it dramatizes issues, and issues of the greatest urgency as well as magnitude. "Guilt by association." "Where does loyalty to a brother end, and where to the state?" "Loyalty to a government, loyalty to mankind." "What kind of people are physicists? " "Can a man be taken to pieces like the mechanism of a fuse?" And there is none of these themes that does not light up for a moment or two during the evening, ignited by some vehement bit of aggression or debate, the trouble being that the play as a whole is but a series of such flickerings: the conflagration which we as theatregoers cannot but hope for never happens. In other words, there *is* no play-as-a-whole, there are at best energetic dialogues laid end to end. Too many themes spoil the broth: needed is a single theme.

Needed also is a complete Action to carry the theme. In basing his play almost solely on the transcript of the 1954 hearings, Heinar Kipphardt gave himself no opportunity to find real antagonists for Oppenheimer. The result is that the source of all evil, in the script, too often seems to be Roger Robb, counsel to the Atomic Energy Commission. Which in turn makes the actor in the role force the pace, pretending to be an instigator, where in fact the gentleman was only the rather inept servant of Admiral Lewis Strauss, who cannot be brought into the play because he did not attend the hearings. In short, this play, for which it is claimed that it dramatizes issues, *cannot* dramatize issues, since too many essential factors are excluded *ex hypothesi,* and the excluded parts are the most dramatic, being the most human. The *in*cluded parts are the most abstract ("What is absolute loyalty?" etc.).

The nearest Kipphardt comes to providing Oppenheimer with a worthy and plausible antagonist is in his vignette of Edward Teller, strongly played at the Vivian Beaumont by Herbert Berghof. But the framework of the show requires that Teller be presented solely in formal answers to formal queries. Essentially, the episode is an exegesis of the Teller position, nothing more. As it ends, Teller and Oppenheimer confront each other. Shall we at long last get an actual encounter, a real scene? No. That wouldn't be part of a "hearing." There are no lines. After extracting as much from a glare as may be extracted from a glare, Berghof can only make his exit.

Leaving on the stage the protagonist. And does even he exist—in the theatre? On the contrary, it is not the smallest weakness in this play of many weaknesses that the title role is so passive, is brought so little in dynamic relation with other characters, a feature which is stressed in the physical production by having Oppenheimer sit on one side all the time. (At the Vivian Beaumont, when not speaking, he sits with his back to the audience.) Character, on stage, is a precipitate from action: an anvil is struck, the sparks that fly are characters. But Kipphardt wants us to accept Oppenheimer as a given quantity, like Jesus in Catholic movies, and with the same effect of pious torpor. The actor is expected to just sit there and be Oppenheimer. Obviously what he *will* do is the usual actor's job of tweedy-college-professor-with-pipe-and-prissy-voice. Not interesting; even when the patina of Joseph Wiseman's very great sophistication—body held just so, voice held one degree from plaintive quiver—is added.

I've spoken of *Oppenheimer* as, in the first instance, theatre, but I don't actually regard it as more important to write a good play than to tell the truth about J. Robert Oppenheimer. The life of Oppenheimer is far more interesting than most good plays, and I for one would gratefully accept a bad play, or a good nonplay, about him, provided it made a fascinating contribution to biography, to history. I have noted that Kipphardt's commitment to an historical document hampered him as artist: did it make him that much better an historian, and that much more reliable a student of the actual Oppenheimer? Unfortunately not. His play cannot even have the value of a movie like *Point of Order*, since it shuttles between fact and faction without letting the audience know which is which.

The claim implicit in Kipphardt's published notes is that, while small facts are shifted around a bit, no damage is done to the essential truth of history. It is, however, Kipphardt who decides what the essential truth is, and, as far as his audiences are concerned, he decides in secret: only the researcher who goes over the same ground will ever know what he discarded as inessential or what he added to the record by way of "truth" which was not actually documented as fact. Going over some of this ground myself, I find a number of the changes merely melodramatic. Kipphardt has Oppenheimer spending the night with a lady friend in a hotel where their presumably amorous conversation is recorded on tape by security officers. In fact, I believe, the "hotel" was the house of the lady's parents, who were present; and nothing was tape-recorded: security merely knew where Oppenheimer was. Again, it is strange, in a documentary style of play, to exaggerate what an archexaggerator like Joe McCarthy actually said, yet Kipphardt did just this in the one McCarthy excerpt in his original script. (At Lincoln Center, *echt* McCarthy has been reinstated.)

I would agree with Kipphardt that all such details fade into insignificance beside the question: What is the essential truth of the whole Oppenheimer story? The trouble, here, is that as we pass from fact to truth we also pass from knowledge to opinion: on the truth of the story there will be no agreement but only Kipphardt's opinion, my opinion, and yours, dear reader. A couple of comments may be in order.

For those who take a friendly view of Oppenheimer, the most thrilling and dramatic account to date is not the Kipphardt play but *Lawrence and Oppenheimer* by N. P. Davis.* Yet, like Kipphardt, Davis is so busy rescuing Oppenheimer from fools and knaves that he fails to draw a credible portrait of the man himself. For, quite apart from the notorious "Chevalier incident," which has never been fully clarified, Oppenheimer seems far more problematic—far less sweetly reasonable—than his liberal admirers think. This man of thought was overawed by power. In the thirties he felt the attraction of Soviet power.

* Later, there came along a rival to Davis in Philip M. Stern (*The Oppenheimer Case*), 1971.

Offered, however, a fantastic opportunity to add to the power of Russia's chief rival, the United States, he dropped his "left-wing ideas" overboard, freely denounced ex-comrades to the security police, and agreed to see modern life paranoid-style, as a struggle for a "Free World" against Russia. This quick footwork is explained away by Davis and blandly passed over by Kipphardt. The latter does not even notice that Oppenheimer's approach to the Security Board was one of extreme servility throughout. While considerably heightening the malevolence of Roger Robb, Kipphardt protects his audience from the knowledge that Oppenheimer presented to Robb nothing other than the classic Eichmann line of defense: "I was not in a policy-making position at Los Alamos. I would have done anything I was asked to do."

It is therefore quite possible that if other dramatists write about Oppenheimer they will completely reverse the liberal image presented by Kipphardt and Davis and follow in the wake of Haakon Chevalier's two books on the subject. In one of these Chevalier states that Oppenheimer was a sort of Greek tragic hero: tremendous but with a fatal moral flaw. The flaw he sees as pride which finally becomes megalomania. In both books Chevalier maintains that the older Oppenheimer was power-crazed, corrupt, ruthless, totally dehumanized.

But this isn't convincing either. The liberal interpretation and this illiberal one seem to me polar opposites and both equally incredible. Yet both parties have something. Both parties may have a great deal. Oppenheimer was not only a very gifted but a very big man—much room in him for good *and* evil. He was not the liberal that Kipphardt and Davis make him: he passed from the illiberalism of Stalin to that of the Congress of Cultural Freedom without a qualm. But he was not dehumanized, even at the end. He remained human-all-too-human, especially if we bear in mind that the human, though not always amiable, is always contradictory.

Oppenheimer's stature is not in question, but do we have a playwright big enough to depict him? While the German playwright Kipphardt may not have achieved a masterpiece here, he has at least produced a lively, thought-provoking drama. It is depressing to think that no American dramatist has tackled the subject at all, and it is even more depressing to think what some of them would do with it if they did.

A bizarre feature of the New York production is that some of the characters have their real names (Oppenheimer, Teller, *et al.*) whereas other have fictitious names. It seems that the real names were removed on the advice of lawyers, libel suits being feared. This raises several issues. One is whether the legal advice was well-grounded or overfussy. If it is well-grounded, then the laws obviously need changing to permit documentary drama to exist. As to the present, pragmatic solution it is thoroughly unsatisfactory. If Edward Teller can be presented under his own name as a heel, why should a very engaging version of my Columbia colleague Isidor Rabi be called "Jacob Lehmann of M.I.T."? (These are all lawyers' games anyway, as the whole transcript of the "trial" was published, and the published text of the play—Hill and Wang, 1969—uses all the real names save one.)

(1969)

The Theatre of Interpretations

There are no facts, there are only interpretations.
—Nietzsche

Clearly the outstanding fact about "the theatre of fact" is that it is vehemently suspected of propagating nonfact, even lies. Rolf Hochhuth is the *cause célèbre*. Both his plays were based on factual propositions which most people utterly reject: in the one case that Pius XII acquiesced in attempted genocide, in the other that Churchill brought about the death of Wladyslaw Sikorski. A recent play by Conor Cruise O'Brien deals with an alleged crime that stands midway between these other alleged crimes of Pius and Churchill: O'Brien believes that Dag Hammarskjöld and Andrew Cordier,* while they did not bring about the murder of Patrice Lumumba, were worse than acquiescent in it, since they could and should have prevented it but (according to *Murderous Angels*) deliberately and purposefully refrained from doing so.

Our most natural expectation of a documentary theatre is that it would either translate the history books into stage terms, or, dealing with very recent times, that it would remind us of what we know we lived through. Actually, the play-

* Reference is to the mimeographed script in which I first studied *Murderous Angels*. In the published version (Little, Brown, 1968) Cordier's name occurs only once, and only as "Andy" (p. 162). In the version produced on Broadway in 1971, it did not occur at all.

wrights, if dealing with earlier history, are revisionist and rebel historians of what the profession could only regard as an extreme sort. If dealing with recent years, they remind us of nothing but charge that we never knew the truth and regarded Pius, Churchill, Hammarskjöld, and Cordier as men who not only did not stand for murder but couldn't conceivably stand for it: not being that kind of person. The gist is, then, (a) that the history books are wrong and (b) that the men whom we idealists have most admired were not themselves idealists but at best ruthless realists, matching Hitler's crimes with their own (Churchill), at worst megalomaniacs (Hammarskjöld), schemers (Cordier), or organization men (Pius). Implicitly the plays call on us to (a) see history in terms quite other than those taught in the schools and (b) repudiate the idols of the Establishment: the unusually holy Pope, the gallant spokesman for anti-Nazi heroism, the religious poet who raised high the banner of the United Nations. And why not? That was exactly "where the action was" in the 1960s, and the force of any type of historical drama resides in its topicality: it must quiver with the life not of the era depicted but of the period of the performance.

The Deputy was successful. Which is not say it was universally acceptable. This type of play will be unacceptable to those who are its target, but it can be held unsuccessful only if it misses the target—that is to say, if it can be shown to be mendacious or otherwise unsound. Marginal errors or dubieties will not wreck them. Central ones are another matter, and here *Soldiers* was in trouble. Hochhuth was unable to make even his best-disposed readers and spectators share his belief that Churchill was guilty as charged. That Hochhuth tried to make the crime less incredible by arguing that it was tragically *defensible* only compounded his problem. For, with this, *Soldiers* just became confusing and confused. It is, indeed, one of those out-and-out failures which no ingenuity can redeem: for every device or idea to which the author has recourse only reveals itself *as* ingenuity—in the one lost cause. Seldom has so much intelligence produced such a stupid result. My only emotion upon seeing *Soldiers* was distress at the thought that the author of *The Deputy* could come to this. I suppose the case is instructive. The two plays are very obviously of the same authorship. *The Deputy* has some of the shortcomings of *Soldiers,* especially a Schillerian type of dialogue unrelieved, as in Schiller himself, by humor, but lacking Schiller's sheen and poetry. *Soldiers* has none of *The Deputy*'s merits. Hochhuth's talent is for shared outrage. The material of *The Deputy* offered him a foothold, the material of *Soldiers* did not.

O'Brien's play stands midway between the two Hochhuth plays in yet another respect: its main accusation is more firmly grounded than that of *Soldiers* but less firmly so than that of *The Deputy*. I speak here not for historians but for spectators. When we see *The Deputy,* whatever we may be unsure of, we are sure that Pius XII did stand idly by when he could at least have attempted to do something. When O'Brien urges the complicity of Hammarskjöld and

Cordier, we receive his presentation as an opinion, a sort of prosecutor's brief, and, however much we may be taken with its wit and thrust, which are considerable, we remain willing to listen to other reconstructions of the evidence.

The New Yorker has raised the question: What legal recourse have the villains of such plays? It seems that libel actions have been threatened in some cases. Faced with such threats, Lincoln Center changed the names of some characters in the Oppenheimer play (though not all of these were villains). People can hardly be pleased to find themselves badly thought of by a playwright, but it would be a gross infringement of freedom of speech to prevent playwrights from thinking badly of people. Yet replacing one name with another is a transparent trick, and I am surprised that most of the aggrieved have settled for it. Probably many in the future will not—a pilot involved in the crash that killed Sikorski is already suing Hochhuth in London.* What seems to be needed is a loosening of the libel laws as they apply to the stage. What the journalist can say in an editorial or article—possibly even what Drew Pearson can say in a column—the playwright too must be permitted to say.

I am assuming that the best corrective for untruth on stage will not be litigation but criticism: that of the dramatic critic and that of playgoers in general. If what a playwright says is truly scandalous, the proper retort is in the scandal itself, as it is talked about and as it finds its way into print. By all means, let the admirers of Pius XII present their case. If some argue that when mud is slung some of it always sticks, one has to reply that this consideration cannot justify a ban on mud-slinging. That argument is not a universal truth, anyway. Much mud was slung at Joan of Arc (by churchmen, as it happens), but none of it has stuck.

The documentary play is a little trickier than it looks. That a play is documentary at all means that it surprises and probably appalls its audience with material of which it can and indeed must be said, "Yes, and this actually happened." Hence it was nothing less than cheating when a fictitious episode was inserted into an otherwise "factual" Pittsburgh Playhouse presentation of HUAC proceedings. People left the theatre thinking certain things had really happened which hadn't. That is how the theatre becomes an *un*educational institution!

In this country, the producers of *In the Matter of J. Robert Oppenheimer* stressed that the dialogue was spiced with fiction. For their aim was to forestall libel suits. In Europe, everyone had thought that "it was all true," and one would have had to do a good deal of research to learn that Kipphardt gave a twist of his own to almost everything. Peter Weiss's *Investigation* kept pretty

* May 4, 1972: the *New York Times* announced that Edward Prchal, pilot of the plane that crashed on take-off from Gibraltar, killing Sikorski, has been awarded $130,000 in damages.

close to the printed records but was criticized for a certain kind of editing (the word "Jew" kept being replaced).

Would it be a solution to some of these problems if the dramatist did not add any words at all of his own? That he adopted such a course is stressed by Donald Freed in his recent play *The United States vs. Julius and Ethel Rosenberg*.* "Every word you will hear or see on this stage is a documented quotation," he tells his audience. They could well ask what difference it makes, since the principle of selectivity leaves Freed with so many options still open. He has a picture in mind, and he picks the quotations that support it. Theatre of fact in a world where the facts are so many and so various leaves elbowroom for some very large elbows, and selection is not all, there is also the little matter of ordering the material, both as to juxtaposition (montage) and cross-reference. Cross-reference is one form of repetition. There are others, the simplest of which—immediate simple repetition—can have a remarkable effect. Freed repeats anything that takes his fancy. *"Un bel dí."* "The Battle Hymn of the Republic." Strong stuff that, repeated at crucial points of the evening. Freed has noticed that Joe McCarthy used to say, "I have here in my hand a list of . . . ," giving various nouns and statistics at various times, so in the play he has McCarthy repeat the phrase half a dozen times *without interruption*. Now, a single beat of a drum is one thing; repeat it a single time, a little is added; repeat it a few times and the phenomenon is quite different; repeat it many times and all hell has broken loose. This is the principle involved in repetition of words too; and can easily nullify the principle implied in "Every word you will hear or see on this stage is a documented quotation."

What is the moral? That we can do without documentary drama altogether? That Freed should have presented his material with less manipulation? Or with more—introducing *un*documented material? Well, to begin with, it is a matter of indifference whether material is "documented" if one does not know the value of the documents concerned. Anything is documented that comes from a book, even a bad book. Next, the main question is not whether a speech is documented (in any sense) but whether the audience is on firm ground because it knows what it is getting. The fiction in *The Deputy* is acceptable because it is not taken for nonfiction: to get Hochhuth's message we don't have to believe that there was a Father Fontana who confronted the Pope. It follows that there is no special virtue in the plea that all such fictions have been eliminated, especially when we begin to realize how much artifice there can be in cutting, rearrangement, repetition, etc. But, in turn, a work in which every word is a quotation could be valid on the grounds on which we must judge all documentary drama, such as honesty and intelligibility. In the case of Freed, I have in effect argued that there is dishonesty (no doubt unconscious) in what is evidently claimed in the way of authenticity. Freed is also unintelligible in the sense that

* Later called *Inquest*.

he does not really tell the story but takes for granted that we know it, or even that, having our hearts in the right place, we can guess it: So-and-So *must* be innocent, or So-and-So *must* be guilty, these things follow from correct ideology. All of which is an evasion because this way the playwright shirks his obligation to tell the story and create the participants. Instead, we see marionettes dangling on the string of our present discontents.

To tell the story and create the participants. Am I right in assuming that these are things the playwright has to do? Peter Weiss has suggested, on the contrary, that it is permissible for the documentary playwright to "quote" characters rather than create them. He himself, presenting the Lyndon Johnson Cabinet in his *Vietnam Discourse,* does not ask the actors to do clever, lifelike impersonations, let alone caricatures à la *Macbird,* but merely "cites" these people. I have not seen *Vietnam Discourse* staged, but I hear from admirers of Peter Weiss that it is his least theatrical effort so far.

O'Brien is also in trouble—or at least in problems—in this department, as I have reason to know. Herbert Berghof wanted me to direct *Murderous Angels* with himself as Hammarskjöld. I asked O'Brien if it could be more a play, especially in certain parts. Could Hammarskjöld be given scenes in which O'Brien's tragicomic sense of him would be more fully realized on stage? For it seemed to me that, while the author's view of Hammarskjöld was clearly stated, little was done to enable Berghof to walk on and *be* such a person. O'Brien in effect asked me to accept his stage figures as Weissian "citations," and I, for my part, would have been glad to attempt a sort of political spectacle, influenced by the Living Newspaper and Piscator, in which character is subordinated to documentation. News clips. The UN on TV, etc. I could even have done a little boasting about my use of "multimedia" but even had the rights remained available,* Berghof really did not wish to play a citation, he wished to play a man. Was he wrong? In my book *The Theatre of Commitment* (1967), I myself argued the case for certain political and polemical simplifications. These included a two-dimensional form of character—political caricature, if you will, but not necessarily comic—in which the playwright forgoes psychology (*full* characterization) in order to channel outrage through an expressive stage figure. An example of such a figure is Hochhuth's Pius XII. It does not provide a rounded picture of the actual man. It does dramatize—or, if you prefer, theatricalize —what Hochhuth believes to be Pius's role in World War II, and I would have no complaint against Kipphardt's Oppenheimer or Freed's Rosenberg pair or O'Brien's Hammarskjöld if as much could be said of them. But, in all three instances, the theatregoer can only feel frustrated. The material exudes drama, and it should be remarked that none of the three plays could have any trouble holding an audience. (A hint for the young: in this genre you can hold your au-

* They went, first, to the National Theatre in London and, later, to the Mark Taper in Los Angeles and the Phoenix in New York (1972).

dience without being much of a playwright.) Yet in each play we long for scenes that never take place. Shouldn't Oppenheimer be confronted by Admiral Strauss, Hammarskjöld by Lumumba? If not, surely there should be *some* confrontation which brings action and character into dramatic focus? Of course, our authors have alibis. These are documentary plays, and such confrontations could not be documented. Even so, when told what the Rosenbergs did not do (commit espionage), couldn't we, this being drama, be shown what they did do? The point applies equally to the Oppenheimer play. Oppenheimer is also shown as "not a spy." But what is he? What was he actually up to in Los Alamos and earlier? Here the author will cite another alibi. His play is based on the "trial" record, and so *cannot* show Oppenheimer before 1954. The Rosenberg play cannot show what their "record" doesn't show: the life they did lead, the kind of people they actually were. But such alibis only raise the question whether the decision to be documentary in this way was a shrewd one. O'Brien, to do him credit, leans on no such alibis but argues in his preface for certain freedoms à la Hochhuth. (His whole play is a *Deputy* with a Protestant "Pope"—an interesting point, considering that he is of Catholic background, Hochhuth of Protestant background.) But *Murderous Angels* would be a better play—would be "more a play" if the author were freer, if he would let go, if he would let *his* Hammarskjöld come into being—by natural childbirth, as it were.* In the plays of Kipphardt and Freed, certainly, one feels the absence not only of full characterization but also of any effective two-dimensional protagonists. The final paradox of their theatre of fact is that their protagonists are balloons inflated with liberal legend and liberal sentimentality.

(*1969*)

---

* Seeing the play in the New York production of 1971, I was struck by the *un*natural birth of a certain sexism in it. We were to admire Lumumba the more because he was a womanizer. We were to think even less of Hammarskjöld because he was a homosexual. Sexism rears its head high in an assumption, clearly made by O'Brien, that warm, human feelings flow naturally in the veins of a heterosexual, whereas a homosexual is a cold fish. The second part of this proposition effectively prevents O'Brien from dramatizing the relationship between Hammarskjöld and his black lover. The over-all structure is, of course, mechanical as well as sexist: hetero hero with white mistress *versus* homo hero with black lover in a play subtitled "a political tragedy and comedy in black and white."

The Naked American

America in the sixties has been a paradoxical place. A member of Lyndon Johnson's staff was rumored to have threatened the Vietnamese in the following terms: "Behind the irresistible might of all this expensive hardware stands the indomitable will of a nation of free faggots." The President who wished to inaugurate a Great (that is, just and peaceful) Society succeeded only in escalating an unjust war. Meanwhile, on the American left, many who talked liberation and liberty helped only to forge new shackles or tighten up the old ones.

For "paradox" read "ambiguity" or even "equivocation." All the phenomena of the sixties which might claim to be positive are also negative. One can only hope that in some instances the opposite is also true: that there is a positive aspect to what is first seen as negative. For instance, that "sexual revolution" from which nudity in the theatre and other such things have stemmed. Here one must remark how much too easily the word "revolution" is used these days, and how it attaches itself to any notable changes whatsoever, however destructive, and unaccompanied as they may be by any hope of restructuring the social order as a whole. Thus it is a sexual revolution in Scarsdale if adultery is up by fifty per cent; and what used to be called the decadence of the Roman Empire would in current discourse be the Roman revolution.

What about public disrobing? How revolutionary is that? Let us be simple. Over the long span the primary phenomenon has been the strip-tease. Women took their clothes off in front of a crowd of horny men, who thereby got hornier. Strip-teasing was found more exciting than merely sending naked girls out on stage. That is how it *became* the primary phenomenon in this line of business. Let us continue to be simple. The topic *is* business, for what all our noble fighters against puritanism and censorship are doing is making a lot of money in the easiest way, there being no safer bet in the whole gambling den of capitalism than male horniness, and if some of the horny males also get orgasms from liberal ideology, so much the better for the bankbook of those who produce nude shows or publish "pornographic" pictures and texts. Students of the sixties will undoubtedly find it interesting that, at a time when an imperialistic war was being preached and fought by liberal politicians, the old trade in "dirty" literature and show biz was plied by liberal critics, publishers, and producers. War and "pornography" are not new to human history but, in the America of the sixties, they certainly made new friends. This is not to say that all these liberals sold out. Some of them had never sold in. Of others it could be said that, if they confused the issue of pornography, they were justified to this extent: that pornography itself represents a pretty confused situation.

Not to rehash this whole matter once again, let me point to a single historical factor: that autumn is also seedtime, that a period which can reasonably be seen as a decadence in relation to what is ending can often be seen quite differently in relation to what is just beginning. In any event, the commercial motive of the entrepreneurs does not completely cancel other motives in the "pornographers" and "nudists" themselves. The latter may share the commercial motive yet have other motives as well. It is pretty clear that the desire to strip in public, during the sixties, has passed all commercial bounds. Ultimately, it springs from some source even deeper, even less rational, than money.

What source is that? Before this question can be answered, one must concede that public stripping has a variety of meanings. A Jewish actor who stripped in *Fortune and Men's Eyes* in London told me he hated it because it made him think of Auschwitz. The meaning of such phenomena is largely a matter of emotional association, and here the association of stripping was with the most terrible powerlessness and humiliation. Usually, I think, girls are more apt than boys to respond in this direction; but any of us may feel powerless and (somewhat) humiliated even when stripped in a hospital. On the other hand, stripping in front of one person—your spouse—can lose all affect after a few months of matrimony.

If the stripper can be the attacked, he can also be the attacker. My colleague Richard Schechner reports that when he stripped at the very outset of a Living Theatre performance, he was trying to "show them." The first wish of the contemporary American male is to be thought to have balls! (Males of other nations assume that balls are what they do have.) Well, seeing is believing, and balls have been on display quite a lot lately. But it is the penis that people pay to see. The women's genitalia are not seen, or are not much to see, and their breasts, even with uncovered nipples, no longer provide the big, big surprise: Hugh Hefner has seen to this. No, the main reason for American theatregoing in the late sixties has been to see the penis. The penis has an enormous dual audience: women, who after centuries of restraint, have broken down and confessed that this is what they wish to see, and homosexuals, or rather men with a marked homosexual component, which is more men than one used to think. It is probably important that, alone among the erogenous zones, the penis is visually dynamic. Whether or not, on stage, its size actually varies, hope does spring eternal, and an audience is forever on the *qui vive* to see *if* a penis will do its thing. From strip-tease, then, to cock-tease: such is the history of America in the late sixties. In New York the district attorney's men were excited to the point of dementia. There they were at the nude show *Che,* as I gather, actually having hallucinations: they saw erections where there were none to see. Which proves either that there is something rather strong about the new theatre or that there is something rather upsetting about the DA's office.

If stripping can have a variety of meanings in life in general, it can also have a variety of effects upon theatre audiences. The old strip-teases either sent the horny men out to masturbate in the washroom or left them in a half-pleasant, half-frustrating state of turbulence. The same probably applies to much of the new nudity, even if there is now much less of deliberate teasing. Perhaps more typical of today is a certain humorous neutralization of emotion, a cool, half-laughing reaction. Even pornographic movies are received in this vein, not an erection in the house, whenever a bunch of young New Yorkers foregather to air their caustic wit before the bawdy screen. Watching my fellow spectators at the Off Broadway play *Geese,* I saw few of the tense temples and anxiety-drawn lips that I associate with audiences of veteran pornographers; equally few, incidentally, of the romantic celebrants of love (i.e., sex) whom the show's producers address themselves to; but many sophisticated worldings who found the show's daring distinctly groovy. Swingers out front were showing respect for swingers on stage; and that was the nature of the whole transaction. Like *Private Lives* back in the twenties.

In all the discussion of the proprieties, the actual effect of nudity and disrobing in a theatre has as yet been little studied, even by producers and directors. Some people who are very sophisticated, or wish to seem so, declare that stage nudity has already become as boring as conjugal nudity. This is not true for most people, however, and since it is not true for me either, I can report a quality of feeling in my own response which was a little different from the reactions which managements usually reckon with. It was not a state of high excitation. It did not seem to contain the promise, or even the hope, of orgasm, but, at what

I suppose must be called the sexier moments of *Geese* and of *Oh! Calcutta!*, I had the sensation of having gained entry to a special world with its own feeling tone and a certain shivery fascination.

I would advise producers and directors to explore that world further if they want to do something more with theatrical nudity. Meanwhile, alas, I can only concur with other critics who, in effect, have complained of the lack of this and any other kind of exploration in most of the nude shows. The devisers of *Oh! Calcutta!* seem to have been taken in by the biggest but by now best-known hoax of the century (not merely the sixties), namely, that the wife swapping and other high jinks in the suburbs can be taken at face value. Hadn't they heard the news—published widely enough in the twenties already—that all this hectic fun expresses mere misery? Though many of the listed authors of *Oh! Calcutta!* are American, one has the impression that it is all written by a British public-school boy, aged sixteen, preoccupied with gamy perversions, and believing that sex is a hayride. It is therefore all too vulnerable to the criticisms of anyone who has not been to a British public school and/or is at least eighteen. . . . At times I was able to enjoy just looking at the naked bodies, but not as much as at *Che* because, like most of the big audience, I was too far from the stage. Another lesson of the occasion is that this sort of thing requires a very small theatre. Uncovering objects only a few inches long or broad can have no interest except for eyes within a few feet of those objects.

From *Geese*, the lesson one learns is that stripping can easily destroy the world of a play. When, as in Brecht's *Arturo Ui*, an actor removes a mustache in front of the audience, he thereby dismantles the role he has been playing. How much more so when, as in *Geese*, he removes his entire costume and underwear! The skin underneath the Hamlet costume is not Hamlet's, it is John Barrymore's. So what have the actors in a play like *Geese* done for its author? Made him rich, perhaps, but by taking his play away from him. One need shed no tears—it isn't that good a play—but one wonders about the pattern. It belongs, of course, to a wider situation which has been much discussed. The drama (as usual, one could say) is felt to be dead, and the new theatre is looking elsewhere for its ideas: to action painting, to tape recordings, to light shows, to street happenings, to movies and TV, and then again to social events outside show biz altogether, and, most notably, *parties*. Now parties, you may say, are as dead as drama. Ah yes, but, unlike drama, they have been livened up lately. Some hostesses in Manhattan are holding group-therapy sessions instead of parties. Some therapists are letting their sessions *become* parties. Some group-therapy sessions have no therapist on hand: the members just "encounter" each other, and the gleam in each eye spells ORGY. Not that an orgy will necessarily be had. Just that the hope of it is signaled from eye to eye. As in the new theatre. Life is all one. Group therapy, parties, and theatre have merged, and their *promesse du bonheur* is the hope of an orgy.

Look through the advertising columns of the *East Village Other,* and, alongside the "encounter groups," you will find advertised *body-painting studios.* Follow up the ad, and you will find yourself naked in the presence of a naked model. For a stated sum paid by you, you paint each other. In some cases, the model is also a geisha girl or boy and will, as the expression now suitably is, "have sex" with you. Well, the transaction represents a distinct improvement over the American whorehouse which grandfather knew, and incidentally provides a clue to the character of the American theatre in this time of undoubted decadence and possible promise. To begin with, we shouldn't need Jean Genet to tell us that the whorehouse is itself a theatre. It is the legitimate theatre's illegitimate-sister institution. While the whorehouse is, on the one hand, a place where men settle for less than romance, it is, on the other, a place where they have consistently sought more than marriage and more than a respectable bourgeois love affair. On the one hand, as I was saying about the current literature and theatre of sex, it is all about money, but, on the other, human yearnings, fantasies, and hopes are involved of considerable scope and, in part, of real beauty.

What then, finally, to make of the naked American of the new theatre? For one thing, he or she is but old whore writ large. If stripping has many meanings, one of the first is undoubtedly the invitation to the sexual dance. To take off your clothes says: make love to me. In the theatre this is usually a little on the symbolic side, but the message is understood, even when the love is only made with the eyes. Above all, it is understood on the actor's side of the footlights. For the actor knows he is a whore and that violation by the eyes is humanly as thoroughgoing as any other. The wish to be naked on stage is the wish to offer oneself. I do not say "give oneself," as these are not amateurs, and admission is not free. The front rows at *Oh! Calcutta!* now go for twenty-five dollars a seat.

What's wrong with whores? Like other professions, they constitute a conspiracy against the public, but unlike some other professions they make no radically false claims for themselves, and in the course of a long history they have always imparted much pleasure, which is more than lawyers can say. But the naked American is not all whore. (Even a whore is not all whore.) In some degree, he is a rebel. Now rebels aren't necessarily better people than whores. It depends what they are rebelling against, and also what they are fighting *for.* I don't think the naked American knows. But he may be justified in his ignorance. For his rebellion is but a tiny part of the gigantic rebellion with which our land at present is all but convulsed. Against what? For what? Let history decide, we say. Which is all very well, provided we remember that Clio can be very mean. If the current revolt comes to nothing, or if it comes to some result which all acknowledge to be bad, then the many little revolts which it is made up of will also be adjudged nothing, and their cultural by-products will be condemned as decadent. If, on the other hand, there is someday a positive result to show for all the current effort, then even its minor manifestations will be seen positively. In this case, the naked American will be honored for defying a social order that needed to be defied, and a positive content will be found in his activity: at a time when our urban civilization was most unnatural and unnerving, he asserted the claims of natural man, the claims of the body. If you want evidence that the body has been betrayed in our time, it is there, and personally I don't think our soul is going to be saved until our body is joined to it again.

(1969)

Dear Grotowski

Dear Grotowski:

I won't say I know exactly what theatre is, but I know that it is a factor in the whole community's network of communications. What is *your* theatre? How does it relate to your environment, the Poland of 1969? There is little of Karl Marx in it, but then there isn't all that much Karl Marx in your Communist Party, is there? So does your theatre represent a retreat to old Catholic Poland? Your published disclaimer of belief in God doesn't prove it isn't. The Church exists for you, whether God does or not, and the Church has reality for you, whether God does or not: a disproportionate degree of reality, even. Your slogan as a director would seem to be: When in doubt, fall back on ritual, and even the Church never went so far as to believe that in ritual there was salvation.

I am saying that what comes through from your theatre to a radical spectator—and in America many of your spectators will be radicals—is a certain conservatism. And it will be our conservative press that will most readily call you *avant-garde*. Are you a reactionary, and, if not, does your work lend itself to reactionary interpretation and use? What attracted you to Calderón's play, *The Constant Prince?* The tacit assumption, throughout it, that Spain is entitled to a chunk of Africa because its princes are such devout Catholics? A nice retort to Peter Weiss's *Lusitanian Bogey!*

I'm kidding, but only just. Christianity without belief has a tradition, but an ugly one, one that, for my generation, recalls certain Frenchmen who supported Hitler. Even when not fascistic, that kind of Christianity was snobbish. T. S. Eliot, whom you draw upon, sometimes seemed to suppose that Christianity was beyond the reach of common folk, was a religion for cultivated, superior chaps only. For Pharisees, not for publicans, whores, and sinners, let alone fishermen. Such was the spirit breathed by *your* Constant Prince, I thought. Not by Calderón's, though judged in our unhistorical way he was an imperialist. Calderón believed in a Jesus, who, though divine, was no superior chap. Your Constant Prince might equally be called the Good Boy with a Slight Case of Masochism.

Conservatism in art, as is well known, often brings a certain formalism in its train. Your version of Auschwitz is overaesthetic and therefore distressingly abstract. Mythological analogies indeed! When the curtain goes up on Peter Weiss's *Investigation,* we see young Auschwitz guards dressed up, as by that time they were in real life, in senility and business suits. For dramatic truth and expressivity that moment (I thought) is worth any fifteen minutes of your *Acropolis,* and in it we forget Peter Weiss as we seldom if ever forget you in *Acropolis.* Which means that in that moment *The Investigation* is art and not cult of personality. Those who disliked Weiss's show complained that its subject was too unpleasant. Those who liked yours praised various technical devices. In New York City, thousands of whose families lost relatives in the extermination camps, you show us an Auschwitz that is of technical interest to theatre students! If that isn't an example of a deplorable formalism, what would be?

Am I too ideological? Very well, let's just speak of your tone, the tone of your book, *Towards a Poor Theatre,* the tone of your program notes, and the tone, apparently taken from you, of all other persons connected with your shows, right down (or up) to the ushers. Not that the ushers are all of one kind. They are of two kinds. Only one is hostile, snippety, peremptory, quasi-military. The other is a little unctuous, mealy-mouthed, reverential. Why the absence of humor? Why can no one relax? You have been a traumatic experience for New York and while this might do New York a lot of good, it would certainly seem that our city had a lot to put up with. Have you any idea how many people have suffered rebuff, if not insult, in their encounter with the Polish Laboratory Theatre? I seem to have spent the past two months visiting the wounded. Their cries still ring in my ears. Church doors have not suffered such blows since Martin Luther drove great nails into them. Rumor has it that Theodore Mann went on pounding on yours all through the night and never did get in. Other luminaries of our benighted American theatre (no irony) got in and roundly declared your theatre was no good anyway. They were so miffed.

And so on. And so forth. A book could be written, and probably will be, on the mess *around* your performances. May it be a better one than yours! Do you realize that the Anglo-American version of your book isn't even in good English? And this was what, for many of us, heralded your visit. Mind you, we could have penetrated bad prose, if that was the only problem, but this, surely, must be a bad book in any language. If there is a new theatre, it deserves a properly articulated description, if not a grandly conceived theory. You have made the mistake of publishing a bundle of scraps and *pretending* that it is a worthy manifesto. A book that oscillates between the trivial and the grandiose.

In short, for many of us, your work got the worst conceivable send-off. Don't reply that so many have swooned over you, fawned on you, etc., etc. We know that is true, and it only made the whole thing all the harder to take. It was not till the evening of your third show that I recovered from the trauma. During this show, *Apocalypse,* something happened to me. I put it this personally because it was something very personal that happened. About halfway through the play I had a specific illumination. A message came to me—from nowhere, as they say—about my private life and self. This message must stay private, to be true to itself, but the fact that it arrived has public relevance, I think, and I should publicly add that I don't recall this sort of thing happening to me in the theatre before or even in revivalist meetings, though maybe I haven't attended enough of the latter.

Do I digress? Say so at your peril. Your theatre is redeemed, it seems to me, by just this peculiar intimacy. Peculiar: not the "intimacy" of our own Off Off (off, off, off . . .) Broadway efforts, one part ineffectual goodwill, two parts clumsy aggression. A man shows you his penis, a woman clouts you over the ear, while the whole acting company shouts four-letter denunciations at you—that's our intimacy, our charming "audience involvement." When I see your theatre, and now that I've even got to the detraumatized point where I *can* see it, I note that your work, in this respect as in others, is a corrective to everything that happens here in your name. Any rudeness stops in the lobby. In your theatre a spectator is a person and is allowed to keep his dignity, his individual separateness. Sometimes your actors come within inches of us, but they never lay hands on us, nor whisper in an individual ear. In the space our body occupies, we are inviolate. Now if the closeness to the actor brings us something extra, the fact that it is not a merger like sexual intercourse seems to me equally important, embodying a dialectical law of art according to which, if there is closeness, it must be balanced and, as it were, canceled by distance.

Dignity is involved too. In your conservatism you aren't afraid of being considered bourgeois when what is bourgeois is rather nice. Chairs are rather nice. The floor is, well, rather uncomfortable and, in New York, extremely dirty. The bourgeoisie's case against discomfort and dirt is definitive. Besides, a third of the American people have bad backs: they need a chair to prop them up. I noticed that you had chairs for spectators right next to the ovens of Auschwitz. Actually, one could have wished they were less near, for it was too comical to see a mustachioed man in garish mod clothes leaning against a gas oven. That is where I am even more conservative than you, and want my spectators "off stage," but I'm glad you hold on to chairs. Make your American disciples buy some.

Apocalypse is a beautiful thing. It vindicates your idea of a theatre, and since only thirty-nine of my readers (or some small multiple of forty), will have seen it, I should perhaps tell what it is about: Jesus. Who else? He's your man, if not your Man, and this time you were, in his phrase, a fisher of men and caught him in your net. Him or someone else by the same name. Yes, there was a slight feeling of *déjà-vu,* and your program notes spelled out for us the word "Dostoevski." Who was it said you are antiliterary? You are too literary by half. You have read all European literature, and haven't forgotten nearly enough of it. But, literary though it is in inspiration, your image of Jesus becomes theatrical in its incarnation. That's how it becomes yours and, through the performance, ours.

Yours is a Jesus *sui generis,* a small young Pole, wearing an unbuttoned raincoat over just a pair of black shorts, and carrying a white stick. His eyes protrude. His mouth tends to hang open. He tends to run, to be "on the run." He has a strange, loping way of running, and when people stand in his way so he will collide with them, he is as much confused as frightened. . . . Now possibly, as far as this description goes, there is nothing that could not be projected, say, by Marcel Marceau from the stage of a very large theatre. You insist on a very small theatre. Correction. You insist on no theatre. What you insisted on in New York was the Washington Square Methodist Church, and when I saw *Apocalyse* I saw, too, *why* you had been so fussy. Fussiness is the name given to perfectionism by those who see no need of it. You needed it because, in addition to clear outline, you wished your image to have many delicate, shifting details which would get lost in a larger place. Your nontheatre is so small, it has many of the advantages of movie close-ups. One watches the play of wrinkle and muscle on your actors' bodies.

Here's an aspect of your conservatism that I'd call positive: you have created the conditions in which you can achieve a theatrical equivalent of modern poetry. I call this conservative because the kind of modern poetry your work evokes, and was suggested by, is that of the great, and now long past, generations, the poetry of the symbolists and (again the name!) T. S. Eliot. Perhaps one would have the right perspective if one were sweepingly to say that the theatre tends to be out of date and that at last, with you, it arrives where poetry was some fifty years ago.

There is a question in my mind whether your work is dramatic. It's certainly lyric. You're a poet. And, as I say, it's theatrical. So it's poetry of the theatre. Drama comes about as a culmination, a kind of grand synthesis, late in any historical sequence (Fifth-century Athens, Elizabethan England). You, it seems to me, are going back to the beginning, scraping back, as Stark Young once put it (he was a painter) to the design. Stark Young was speaking of Martha Graham, for in America this return to the beginning, the rock bottom, of theatre has chiefly been undertaken by dancers. But you, too, are a choreographer.

Apocalypse presents Jesus and his disciples *by the means of choreography,* and, looking back, I now see much more clearly than at the time how *The Constant Prince* and *Acropolis* were put together and how they present themselves to us. I would call your poor theatre "elemental theatre" to avoid those jokes about poor theatre at two hundred dollars a seat, which is what your tickets were selling for on the black market. Poor theatre is theatre reduced to its elements, and this not as an economy in the money sense, but as an attempt to discover the necessary by removing anything that might prove superfluous.

In your notes on *The Constant Prince* you congratulate yourself on catching the "inner meaning of the play." Cool it. The inner meaning of a three-act masterpiece cannot be translated into any one-act dance drama. Its meaning is tied indissolubly to its three-act structure: otherwise Calderón himself would have reduced it to one act—he was a master of the one-act. What you caught in *The Constant Prince* was the meaning—outer, inner, as you will—of another play, your own, which is vastly simpler and cruder than Calderón's and would probably bore his audience if it could return to life, but which for us is valid and therefore *not* boring. In retrospect, I very much admire the way in which each of your evenings was a *separate* exploration. I understand "environmental theatre" now, just as I now see what intimacy means. In *The Constant Prince* we were medical students looking down on an operating table or a bull-fight crowd looking down on the fight. In *Acropolis* we were inside the world of the play and the players within the electrified barbed wire of an extermination camp. In *Apocalypse* we were a small group of onlookers, small enough to feel ourselves disciples of the disciples. The decision to limit the number of "customers" to one hundred at the first two plays, and to forty at the last, may be arbitrary, but now that we know what you were after, we will grant that *some* arbitrary figure must inevitably be named. These events are planned as a whole: such-and-such actors to be seen by so-and-so many spectators from such-and-such an angle at such-and-such a distance.

If I have indicated my initial revulsion from some aspects of the first two shows, I should add that I now think of them with more satisfaction. Can an experience change after the fact? Clearly not, but one can realize after the fact that one had more fun than one has been admitting to. Irritation tends to make one forget, or disregard, nonirritating elements, and you came to us attended by more irritants than anyone in the whole history of the American theatre. The few of us who were lucky enough to see all of your work learned to be grateful for all three shows.

I do not withdraw the criticisms offered above. For one of my temperament and my views, those objections remain, but I can attest that the longer one stays with your work the more one finds to engage attention and even win admiration. Better than that: one perceives, finally, that the irritating things (other than those for which you bear no responsibility) are the defect of a quality, the negative aspect of a fanaticism which is your main source of energy. "Fanaticism" is perhaps too strong an expression; "enthusiasm" would be too weak a one. In hostile moments, one thinks of you as self-important. That is the note you sound in your published pronouncements, not least when you tell us you're not as important as all that: when you asked critics to pay attention to the rest of the company, it was as if you said you wouldn't settle for rave reviews for yourself, you demanded rave reviews for all your pals. But behind your self-importance is your importance.

If, on the one hand, you are conservative and at points even reactionary, you are, on the other, radical in the most radical sense of the word: you are digging for the roots, all the time for the roots of your art, and intermittently for the roots of the unprecedented sufferings of our time, man's unremitting inhumanity to man. Politically, your theatre would help, I should think, to undermine a bad regime or to bolster a good one. *Salud!*

Fraternally yours,
Eric Bentley

(*1969*)

Theatre and Therapy

For better or for worse, the principal event of the 1968–1969 theatre season was the visit to New York of the Living Theatre. Of their offering, they made a kind of take-it-or-leave-it proposition. I was one of those who "left it," but not in the sense that I left off thinking about it. What I propose to pursue here is the question: What has all the talk of the Living Theatre and kindred theatres really been about?

There is no one correct answer but a central topic has certainly been "audience involvement." The Living Theatre was trying to change the character of the theatrical event. They wanted to move the audience onto the stage. They wanted to exercise a therapeutic influence. On the audience, of course; but also, as they proclaimed, on themselves: the audience was to help cure *them*. I asked myself when had I heard something of the sort before. The whole conception seemed to be one of group therapy, rather than theatre as previously conceived, but had not one celebrated group therapist already effected a merger of these two, and, in his system, was the actor not indeed the patient, and did not the audience assist in treating him?

The therapist was Jacob Levy Moreno; his name was in the Manhattan phone book, and I had no difficulty getting myself invited to attend the group-therapy sessions of the Moreno Institute on West Seventy-eighth Street. Meanwhile I was seeing various shows around town that claimed to be doing something special with audience participation, and/or trying to give theatre a push toward therapy. I saw *The Concept, The Serpent, Dionysus in 69*. . . . Even the current nudism proved relevant. Insofar as it was more than a pursuit of a quick buck, it was an affirmation of the body, the health of the body, and was related to "nude therapy," sensitivity training, encounter groups, etc. I visited some of these groups and also saw *Hair, The Sound of a Different Drum, We'd Rather Switch, Geese, Che, Oh! Calcutta!*, and so on. Of the theatres, I think the Play-house of the Ridiculous and the Ridiculous Theatrical Company were probably the most cathartic, being founded on the deepest rejection of The American Way, and inspired with the cockiest faith that they can get along without imitating that form of life. But gradually I found myself seeing shows less and Moreno's "psychodramas" more. If one wanted theapy in the theatre, why not go the whole hog? At the Moreno Institute, therapy was the acknowledged and sole aim in view, yet the sessions there were emotionally affecting and intellectually interesting to a much greater degree than the New York theatres. What more did I want?

For the moment, nothing. And I concluded that, rather than attempt any sort of survey of the new trend in theatre,* I would simply try to explain what is at stake. Should drama be psychodrama? Is psychodramatic therapy the same as dramatic art? Are certain mergers called for? Or are certain separations—certain firm distinctions—in order? If we could attain to a degree of clarity on these matters, "current trends on and off Broadway" would be child's play.

Since it was psychodrama that prompted this approach and underpins the reasoning that follows, it will be as well to state in advance just what a psychodramatic session is. Perhaps a hundred people are placed on three sides of a platform. The platform itself has steps on all sides, is in this sense an "open stage." A patient, here called a protagonist, presents himself for a psychodramatic performance. A director-psychiatrist talks with him briefly, to find out what he sees as his problem, and what scenes from his life might be enacted. A scene being chosen, the roles of others taking part in it are played either by trained assistants or by anyone else present who might volunteer. What and how they are to play is briefly explained to them by the protagonist and director. If they then seem too far wide of the mark, the protagonist may reject them. But in each session, successful scenes do develop, "success" here being measured by the degree of spontaneity attained: if the protagonist does not "warm up" to his role, he cannot play it in its vital fullness.

Generalizations about the course of psychodramatic sessions are hazardous, since one session differs widely from another, but a typical line of development would be from relatively trivial scenes with friends in the recent past to serious and crucial scenes with parents in the more distant past. It will often happen

---

* As I had been invited to do by *Playboy*. When the present "comment" was submitted to them, they declined to print it.

that a protagonist will have an illumination, or at least a surprise, in one of these later scenes. He may suddenly realize that where he had seen only love there was also hate, or vice versa, in one of his main relationships. And here the stress should be on the word "realize," for it is likely to be a powerful emotional experience: a given insight is borne in upon a person in the midst of a very lively distress. The distress has opened the channels of communication. It may also have reached a kind of climax. The patient may, for the time being, feel cleaned out. The director now ends the play-acting and asks the audience to share common experience with the protagonist. The point is not to elicit interpretations but to discover what chords were touched in the onlookers, what degree of therapy was in it all for them.

I

Dramatic art and psychodramatic therapy have a common source in the fact that life itself is dramatic. In other words, life is not a shapeless stuff which is given form only by a dramatist or clinician. Human life, like the rest of nature, has been shaped, indeed so markedly that this shaping has always been the leading argument for the existence of God. As the beauty of leaves or seashells is attributed to God the Creator, so the shape of events, large or small, is attributed to God the Dramatist: life, as Dante classically stated it, is a divine comedy. The idea that "all the world's a stage/And all the men and women merely players," is not a clever improvisation casually tossed off by Shakespeare's cynic Jaques, it was written on the wall of Shakespeare's theatre, the Globe, in a language older than English: *Totus mundus facit histrionem*. To speak of life, as many modern psychiatrists do, as role-playing is only to make a new phrase, not to advance a new idea.

I shall return later to role-playing and would only at this point call attention to the positive side of the pattern. The negative side is all too familiar: it is that people are often hypocritical—use a role to pretend to be better than they are and deceive other people. It is curious how the phrase "play-acting" has come to be a slur: it implies insincerity. Yet the commonplaces I have cited imply that one has no alternative to play-acting. The choice is only between one role and another. And this is precisely the positive side of the idea: that we do have a choice, that life does offer us alternatives, that one's will is free within whatever limits, and the end is not yet determined. Life is not merely going through the motions, it is an adventure: which is often all that people mean by calling it dramatic.

What else might they mean? In the vernacular, these days, "dramatic" means little more than thrilling, and if it also means "spectacular" the sense of an actual theatrical spectacle is probably not intended. Dramatist and psychodramatist give the term "dramatic" a much more elaborate interpretation. Just as they see more roles to role-playing than Jaques' seven, they break down the "stage" which "all the world" is said to be into various departments. Given that there are roles to play, how are they played? A full answer to this question would be by way of a description of myriad different roles and relationships. A short answer, aiming at providing a basic scheme, might run somewhat as follows.

A role is properly and fully played by being brought into living contact with another role played by another actor. The "full" playing of the role implies that living contact is made, that if "I" am playing one role, "I" feel that the other role is a "Thou" and not an "It." (I am using terminology that most people will associate with Martin Buber, though J. L. Moreno has long thought along these lines too.) Buber's point has been that the modern person reacts to others as an It, and so forestalls communication. "I," too, become an It, if the other is an It. Neurosis walls us off from each other. That's modern life.

Now drama does not depict a utopia in which neurosis is absent, but, with an exception to be noted in a minute, it is utopian to the extent that it normally, not exceptionally, shows human beings in living contact with each other, shows couples who are "I" and "Thou" to each other. It may be living hatred that communicates, as in Strindberg's *Father,* or love, as in *Romeo and Juliet,* but that there *is* direct and lively communication is not only obvious, it is what interests us, it is what we want from theatre. Could it be said, then, that life is not dramatic in this respect, only theatre is? Perhaps. But the point is that this is a norm, not just for our theatregoing, but for our living. The "I" and "Thou" relationship is present enough in actual life for us to want to see more of it, and when we do see it in the theatre, our attitude need not be, "but that's because theatre is not life" but rather "this is what is trying to happen in life if only we would let it." For art need not be regarded as a more abundant life, but unreal. It can be regarded as an attempt by the life force (or what have you) to make our real life more abundant.

If life does afford real I/Thou relationships, and also, which is crucial, holds out the hope of ever more successful I/Thou relationships, drama can, for its part, portray the failure to achieve such relationships. But how could this possibly prove dramatic? Wouldn't the absence of live contact kill the stage action stone dead? It would—if nothing else is added. Drama characterized by a mere absence of emotion is dead. Suppose, however, the absence of emotion, of flow, is the very point? That, you say, is ridiculous. Then, I reply, the way to give it life is to give it ridiculous life. The dramatic form which regularly presents people who are out of contact with each other is the art of comedy, whose mode is ridicule. The role-playing in *The Importance of Being Earnest* is all a game of pretending to have living I/Thou relationships—friend to friend, parent to child, man to woman—when such relationships are not in the cards. Again, when we say comedy presents types, not individuals, we might just as well say it presents individuals who cannot make contact with other individuals because of a crust of nonindividual class characteristics. This is not a *man,* Molière or Shaw is forcing us to say, it is a *doctor.*

The question whether tragedy or comedy is closer to life becomes rather a snarled one. Tragedy presents us in our emotional fullness; it has, therefore, more of life in it. Comedy presents our customary failure to live that way and, in presenting less of life, gives a more characteristic version of it. As for I/Thou relationships, if they are per se dramatic, then we may say that life aspires to the condition of drama.

Does the I/Thou relationship, granted that it includes role-playing, amount to drama? If we would be inclined to say yes, that is because we have taken ourselves for granted. *We* are watching the "I" and the "Thou." We are their audience, and from their viewpoint a "They." Theatre is this completed circuit: an "I" and a "Thou" on stage and a "They" out front. Which is a very radical, if schematic, version of the rudiments of living: *I* relate to *you,* while *they* watch. I, Romeo, relate to you, Juliet, while the other Montagues and Capulets watch. This example, if extreme, serves to remind us how much those watchful eyes modify the I/Thou experience. We live out our lives in full view of other people. We do not live in a world of our own. We live in "their" world. How much tragedy, both of life and literature, lurks in that formula!

II

This, at any rate, is the image of life which psychodrama has appropriated: an "I," talking on stage to a "Thou," in front of a "They." By that token, psychodrama may be said to resemble life or even to be a slice (many slices) of it. Visitors are surprised how close it comes to the real thing. And its watchword is spontaneity. Nonetheless, psychodrama has to depart from life in a number of ways, notably:

(1) The "I" is not presented in a sheer, naked, literal state but buttressed, clothed, supplemented by another person. When the protagonist, at a psychodramatic session, is found to be reluctant, silent, overdefensive, another person is asked to play his double and to come forward with exactly those responses which the protagonist is holding back. Thus to take a crude instance, in the matter of ambivalence, if the protagonist keeps saying, "I *love* my mother," and clamming up, the double will say, "I hate her guts." This is as different from life as can be, since help is being given precisely where it was, perhaps disastrously, lacking. (The double can of course guess wrong, but this fact will probably emerge from what the protagonist then says and does. In any case, there is nothing definitive in a possibly false suggestion. The situation remains open.)

(2) The "Thou" is rendered in more or less the form not of life but of drama, namely: impersonation. Any partner the protagonist's story requires is enacted either by a trained assistant or by a member of the audience at the ses-

sion in question. Since this is a "stranger" to the protagonist, the difference, for him, from the real thing is very great indeed. Often it is necessary for the protagonist to reject outright what the player of such a role says. Sometimes he has to have him replaced. "My father just wouldn't react that way."

But—and this is what matters—some degree of I/Thou relationship is generally worked out before a session is over. Indeed what needs calling attention to is not the difficulty of reaching a degree of direct communication under the conditions of a psychodramatic session but the fact that life is outdone by psychodrama in this respect, somewhat as it is by dramatic art, though not by as much. It must be galling, for example, for a parent to learn how his child enters into rapport with a substitute parent far more readily than with the real one, but a moment's thought explains this: the "objection" is precisely to the real parent, and the "false" one is the real one minus the objection. Hence psychodrama is not "naturalistic," is not a duplication of actuality but, in the most relevant way, an improvement on it in exactly the same way as nonnaturalistic art is, for nonnaturalistic art is actuality not merely reproduced, but interpreted normatively, which means: to a certain extent transformed. Psychodrama and drama have in common a thrust toward human *liberation*.

To take up a single example. When a person fails to communicate with his nearest and dearest, he is apt to reach the extreme conclusion: "If I cannot reach them, I can reach no one." Actually, it is only they whom he cannot reach. The rest of the human race is more accessible. And psychodrama is not an argument to this effect but the living proof written in letters of emotion upon a person's whole nervous system: the kind of proof even philosophers don't easily reject when it's their own nervous system that is responding.

The form taken by scenes created in psychodramatic sessions stands, correspondingly, at a remove from actuality. The patient-protagonist is not encouraged to rack his brains for accuracy in reporting, as when someone tries to be very honest and self-disciplined in telling the police what occurred on a given occasion. What he does, after reminding himself as vividly as possible of the actual moment and location, is to let go and *throw* himself into the situation with a lack of reservation that at the time he hadn't actually achieved. Thus what is "brought back" from that actual happening is, in one sense, more than was there in the first place—more than was *known* to be there, more than actually emerged. Which is, of course, the reason for going to all the trouble. Mere rehash is a waste of energy for the rehasher, as well as being a great bore for those who have to listen. But I shall leave further comment on the psychology of recapitulation till later. The point here is that the "Thou" who is less, in that he may be a mere stranger, is also more, in that he is really a "Thou" where the nonstrangers were not.

(3) A third way in which psychodrama deviates from life is in making use of a director. There are few who feel, these days, that the drama of their lives is

directed by God. That was hard to believe with any constancy at any time; today, if there is a God at all, He is an absentee landlord, a director on perpetual sick leave abandoning the actors to their own resources. Jacob Moreno, though, always wanted to play God, and the modern age obviously placed no special obstacles in his path. He modestly called himself—or any of his standbys—directors; but they preside over the psychodramatic sessions in fairly godlike fashion.

In psychodramatic sessions, the director intervenes in several ways. In the beginning, he elicits the information on the basis of which a first scene is set up. He then *interrupts* whenever it seems to him the drama is (a) repeating itself, (b) wandering off, or (c) petering out. Since anyone could easily be wrong on any of these three matters, it is clear that considerable shrewdness is called for, not to mention knowledge. Interruption is, in any event, a very dynamic factor in itself, as some playwrights (e.g., Brecht) have known. It gives a jolt, which can be salutary or disastrous according to the moment when it occurs.

Interruption is the director's chief negative act. But he does something positive, too, and usually right after the interruption: he *suggests* an alternative path. Having stopped the patient-protagonist from pursuing one course, he propels him into another. Again, the possibility of error is considerable, but again much can be expected from knowledge and know-how. And again, errors need not be final. On the contrary, given the patient's set of mind, they will probably be exposed rather soon. A dead end is a dead end, and is seen to be so by patient and/or audience.

In one sense, then, the director is *not* called on to be God and always right, but only to be resourceful and always quick. The right moment to reach a stop or institute a change passes fast. The director must have instantaneous reactions that indicate immediate conclusions such as: "This is when a double is needed," "We must go straight to the scene just suggested in the dialogue," "Let's reverse roles here."

Reversal of roles, incidentally, is one of the chief devices of psychodrama, and perhaps one of the most efficacious. At a word from the director, the protagonist plays the "other fellow" in the scene. Thus "I" is forced to see and feel out the situation from the viewpoint of "Thou." Which is not only morally edifying but generally illuminating and specifically therapeutic. Our whole failure as human beings can be found in the failure to take in the reality of the other person. But merely knowing this doesn't help. Psychodrama can help by the *work* involved in "I"'s playing seriously at being "Thou."

In a sense, too, the director is not outside the psychodrama, but inside it. His is a voice that the patient sorely lacked the *first time around;* which was why seemingly fatal mistakes were made. *This time,* on stage, the voice speaks, like that of another double. *Next time,* if all goes well, the voice will be that of a double successfully internalized: it will be the patient's own voice. It is a "He" that becomes a "Thou" and that ends up as an "I."

Obviously the most important single instrument in psychodramatic therapy is the director, and this is not just saying that the director is the psychiatrist: it is saying that he has to possess the specific talents required by the situations that arise on the psychodramatic stage.

(4) If the "I" and "Thou" of life are modified in the psychodramatic theatre, so is the "They." The "They" of life is by definition general and amateur. The "They" of psychodrama is specialized and professional. At Dr. Moreno's public demonstrations the audience consists partly of those who see themselves as possible patients, partly of students of psychodrama. Any third element—such as the scoffers or the visitor who finds himself there by accident—is minor. So we are limited to people with a pre-established involvement, a curiosity that is really keen because it comes from need or greed.

It is perhaps seldom realized that in all theatrical situations there is a specific, understood relationship between actor and spectator, a kind of unwritten contract between the two. And it is probably just as seldom realized that the contract holds for only one type of theatre, while other types make other contracts. Thus what an expense-account executive at a Broadway show is buying from the actor is different from what, say, the Athenian people were buying from their festival players, which in turn was different from what Louis XIV had contracted for with Molière, and so on. A clear difference in aim, not to mention relationships outside the theatre, produces a clear difference in the actor/spectator relationship.

Such relationships, insofar as the facts are before us, can be examined in such terms as the degree of passivity (or its opposite) on the audience side. Lack of passivity can show itself in what I have just called need or greed: a felt need for what the spectacle intended to convey, an eagerness to know and in some sense possess it. At one extreme, audiences are both bored and bossy. "Entertain me," they say with a patronizing yawn. The actors are their slaves, their jesters, and will get whipped if they failed to be funny: what sharper whip than economic boycott? At the other end of the scale, the performer is looked up to: much is expected of him. The spectator is humble: it is he who hopes to profit by the exchange. The psychodramatic audience inclines to this other end of the scale, and its humility, combined as it is with neurotic involvement and intellectual curiosity, will show itself largely in the form of sympathy and human understanding.

It is not the audience's attitude in itself that is interesting but the way it functions in the reciprocal actor/spectator relationship. And it is necessary here to anticipate somewhat and say that one of the chief differences between drama and psychodrama is this: while drama is judged, fairly enough, by the effect the actor has on the audience, in psychodrama the highest priority goes to the effect the audience has on the actor. This effect, like that of the director's interventions, is by way of *propulsion*. The audience's sympathy oils the wheels; the audience's eager curiosity speeds things along. The whole occasion is a form of *public confession*. There is relief, and therefore pleasure, in such confession. The person who takes over much pleasure in it is called exhibitionistic. But if a degree of exhibitionism is normal, so is a degree of shyness. The presence of an audience makes it harder to be frank. Psychodrama addresses itself to this shyness and asks that it be tackled, not avoided, as it largely is by psychoanalysis.

(5) A psychodramatic session differs from another two hours of living in that it is *literally* theatre while life is theatre only metaphorically speaking. I mean, to begin with, that there is a stage and that otherwise there is only an auditorium. This organization of space is so ruthlessly selective that most of the detail of actuality is omitted. To say the world is a stage is one thing. To represent the doings of this world *on* and *by* a stage is another. The physique of the psychodramatic theatre bears no resemblance to the world-in-general and not too close a resemblance to the world-in-particular. A scene in a garden will be redone without the garden. A scene about a man as a child will be redone without a child—the physical presence of a child—on stage. Conversely, the physical characteristics of *theatre*—a floor of a certain type, steps, suggestive bits of furniture, the spectator's seats arranged in a certain pattern, the rows of faces above the seats—have a quality (reality, atmosphere) of their own which contributes to the character of psychodrama as a whole.

The sheer physical nature of a theatre does more to determine the nature of the whole theatrical event than has commonly been appreciated, except by recent writers on environmental theatre who have gone to the opposite extreme. Yet, if we turn now to the psychodramatic event as a whole, there is one feature more decisive than environment, and that is—it is so obvious, one could forget to notice—re-enactment itself. Such and such was done in life: it will now be acted. Or, to return to the premise of role-playing, such and such was enacted in life: it will now be re-enacted. The first thing the director does is to ask the patient to *show* (instead of narrating) what once happened. Psychodrama is not life but recapitulation of life, living life over a second time, having your cake and eating it.

And this, which is indeed the key idea of psychiatry as we know it, can properly be the cue for a comparison of psychoanalysis with psychodrama. It was Freud who encouraged us to believe that, if anything at all could be done about our mental illnesses, it would be by going back to the time of their origin and reliving it. *The first time around,* we retreated at a certain point or stood still. The hope which therapy holds out is that, returning to this exact spot, we can *this time* make the needed advance from it. It is a repetition with a difference: an innovation, a nonrepetition.

All life is repetitious. There is the salutary and needed repetition by which good habits are formed. There is the baleful repetition by which bad habits are formed. There is the endless repetition of therapy sessions before the point is reached when any positive result is attained. Then, in the midst of repetition itself, the breakthrough. A paradox, if you will, and yet one which seems built into the process of living. Even love-making is all repetition—of words, of caresses, of body movement—until the breakthrough of orgasm. Scientists report similarly of the breakthrough into discovery; artistic performers of the breakthrough from the repetition of the rehearsal into performance.

As for bad habits, by innumerable repetitions an undesired action has become a habit. The habit is to be broken by yet another repetition, the repetition of perhaps the earliest performance, the original act, which is then *not* repeated, even once. It now leads when it should have led in the first place. In order to be freed from the old captivity one re-enters it one last time.

Now psychoanalytic therapy is itself psychodramatic—up to a point. At one time, certainly, it specialized in the search for the early traumatic scene which was re-enacted, with the patient playing his childhood self and the analyst, for example, the hated father. Freud's first great discovery in the therapeutic sessions themselves was that the analyst did become father, mother, etc., in other words, that the patient assigned him roles—the main roles in his personal drama. Such *transference* was the key to the whole patient/doctor transaction, and therapy came about through the pain the patient endured in reliving the old troubles. If the patient fought back, he could hope to work through neurotic darkness into light.

It is unfortunately impossible to make any survey of the results of Freudian therapy and compare them with the results of any other therapy. One can only assert the a priori likelihood that one person might get more help from one form of therapy, another person from another. One can also point to what for many patients would be an unnecessary limitation in Freudian procedure. Freud in his day had to be much concerned with what one might term the sanctity of the confessional. His patients would never have "got it out" had anyone but the doctor been listening. Even at that they needed further encouragement by the device of the couch. You lie down and avoid looking the doctor in the eye. So in a way you are alone and can get into a reverie and say things you couldn't say into anyone's face. Freud preserves his patients both from the "Thou" and the "They." The patients' efforts to convert the analyst into a "Thou" are stoutly resisted. They are seen only as interference with the intention of making the latter a receptacle for roles not truly his, a ghost. "Look," the analyst must always be imagined as saying, "you have attributed to *me* all these characteristics of your father, but that's *your* problem."

Whatever help may be provided by such constantly re-enacted dramas of disenchantment, it may plausibly be maintained that there is often much to be gained by a contrary procedure: introducing the "Thou" by way of an actor and the "They" by way of an audience and letting the analyst emerge into daylight as a director. That the director can then be accused of pushing things too much is inevitable, but this risk may be worth taking, and there are self-corrective elements, as noted above. The "Thou" of the psychodramatic stage is neither the actual "Thou" nor a duplicate, but if he is a poor substitute in some ways, he is superior (as also noted) in others. The slow pain of free association, in conjunction with transference, produces certain realizations and has doubtless been curative on some occasions in some degree. But no patient is overly satisfied with the results, and that alone is justification for other methods than this Freudian one. And, as against transference, there is much to be said for engaging the other fellow, if not in his own person, at least in flesh-and-blood form. This encounter too inflicts a degree of salutary pain. And very painful indeed (as well as the opposite) is the presence of onlookers: something one has to face in life, something it may be needful to face in therapy. Many of us suffer specifically from fear of the others, and it may be doubted if psychoanalysis tackles this fear boldly enough. Many fear the flesh-and-blood actuality of the "Thou." It is often just this fear that makes a potential "Thou" into an actual "It." Here again, why not take the bull by the horns? There has been in the Freudian tradition itself a certain vestige of the Judaeo-Christian hatred of the body. In this respect Karl Kraus may have hit the mark when he said, "Psychoanalysis is the disease of which it purports to be the cure." And after all, Dr. Moreno is not the only one to ask if Freud hadn't overweighted things on the mental side in reaction against the physiological emphasis of nineteenth-century medicine. If today we talk in psychosomatic terms, by that token the somatic element is half of the whole. Is it not just as reasonable to get at the spirit through the body as vice versa? But these queries go beyond my topic, which is—to summarize this section—that, while there is drama as between couch and chair in the dimly lit office, there is an ampler drama when "I" meets "Thou" upon a stage in the presence of a director and an audience.

III

If psychodramatic therapy is at a remove from life, dramatic art is at two removes from it, for while the protagonist of psychodrama is "spontaneous" and presents himself, the protagonist in a play is held to a script on the basis of which he presents someone else.

If we see these two rearrangements of life—psychodrama and drama—as running in competition with each other, which one do we regard as the winner? It depends wholly on our own angle of vision. The psychodramatist inevitably looks with horror upon the written text. Dr. Moreno contemptuously terms it a "cultural conserve," and sees it exclusively as a hindrance to spontaneity, the highest value in his philosophy. From the viewpoint of therapy, I believe his point is well taken. Here there is nothing but advantage in improvisation.

The protagonist is a patient, and only his life matters. I have remarked that even the audience in psychodrama exists for the sake of the protagonist, not vice versa, as in drama. The dialogue, a fortiori is all his. Even the director is not an author but at best a sort of film-editor. Nor are there any prescribed forms of dialogue or character, as with the *commedia dell'arte,* which the psychodramatic "actor" must follow. Improvisation in any art—*commedia dell'arte* or a jazz combo—is free only within narrow limits. By comparison, psychodrama offers its protagonist freedom indeed!

It is obviously possible that "confinement" within the rules of an art may become a neurotic problem for a given individual. Dr. Moreno reports that this was the case with John Barrymore. This actor was sick (literally) of playing Shakespeare: he wanted, he needed, to play Barrymore. Of course, one thing one would need to know to make anything of this example would be whether psychodramatic therapy, if diligently pursued, would have cured Barrymore of alcoholism and of whatever else ailed him. That he wanted to play himself only proves him human: every infant wants the same. But I am prepared to grant that subjection to a written role may have compounded rather than solved this particular man's problems. No written role was ever intended to solve such problems anyway.

Spontaneity, as Dr. Moreno sees it, is a very useful, even an inspiring idea. I would define it as one of the forms of human freedom, a subjective form, in that it is a psychological, not a political, one. It is a matter of how one feels. A spontaneous man feels free. He feels disburdened of all the inhibitions and evasions and shynesses which normally hold him back from fully feeling what he could and would otherwise feel. If this is correct by way of definition, I would add that, like other forms of freedom, spontaneity operates within limits— within an iron ring of unfreedom, of unspontaneity. A completely free and spontaneous man would not only feel what he wants to feel but say what he wants to say—which would abolish politeness and saddle him with libel suits, to say the least. He would also do what he wants to—which would interfere grossly with the freedom of others. Life, then, has to set bounds to spontaneity. Indeed, some neurotic problems derive from such limits. Psychodrama moves the boundary posts out a little; but it doesn't throw them away.

What the psychodramatists have worked on, and worked for, is one particular kind of spontaneity which we may call solidification of the present moment. The neurotic's trouble is seen as the disintegration of the present: all is diffused into memories of the past and fantasies of the future. This entails great instability in the whole emotional system and, since joy is of the present, an incapacity for enjoyment: life is stale, flat and unprofitable. To re-create the present tense, to create spontaneity, is to bring a person back to life, it is to enable him to experience life in its fullness. For, as Blake put it,

He who catches the joy as it flies
Lives in eternity's sunrise.

If all this makes it sound as if the purpose of psychodrama were to stimulate to momentary pleasure I should go on to say, first, that this is no contemptible purpose but, second, that no one has claimed that a single achievement of that sort is a cure for any mental illness. Nor am I retracting the statement that psychodrama, like psychoanalysis, is painful: both therapies believe in possible progress through pain to pleasure. The difference between the two therapies, in regard to past and present, is that the Freudians keep constantly in mind the persistence of ancient hurts into the present and until recently have tried to refer the patient back just as constantly to the trauma of long ago, whereas the psychodramatist has always worked gradually back from the present. This labor, and not the discovery of trauma, is what "works through" the trouble: its pain, and not the vestigial pain of the trauma itself, is what the psychoanalyst assumes to be therapeutic. He begins "spontaneously" (i.e., as spontaneously as possible) in the present; works back to the obstacles, the rigidities, the nonspontaneities; only to help the patient back to the present; if he is lucky, with a true spontaneity.

Such a conception of spontaneity has in its favor that it is unpretentious. Its normal field of vision is a restricted one. Envisaged (initially at least) is not a whole life, a whole civilization, remade. In the clinical situation faced by the individual, doctor and patient can concentrate upon moment-to-moment experience. (If an invalid is still breathing, his breath will becloud a mirror.) Much psychiatry goes astray by overextending the field of vision: asking so many questions that there can be no coherent, compact answers. In psychodrama the question can usually be limited to: Is the patient's soul still breathing? Can this man warm up to an encounter with another man? Can he feel? Will his limbs go along with his feelings? Can he blush? Shout? Whisper? Kiss? Embrace? It is useful not to have to ask if a man is this or that type of neurotic, but instead: Is he in shape to survive as a human being among other human beings? Can he face the suffering? Can he experience the joy?

Limits are placed on spontaneity in life; in psychodrama; and in dramatic art. To the psychodramatic therapist the limits placed on spontaneity by art seem particularly threatening because, indeed, to impose a script and a role on someone would be to nip their psychodrama in the bud. This and the fact that psychodrama itself throws up scenes with considerable strength as dramatic *art* have encouraged Dr. Moreno to view the two activities as competitive and to feel that, in this competition, psychodrama wins. Actually, there is no competition. The problem, if it is a problem, is only that this therapy and this art overlap, and if chunks of a psychodramatic session are art, pure theatre could in some ways be therapeutic. More useful than taking sides, it seems to me, would be an attempt to sort things out a little.

To maintain flatly that theatre itself is or should be therapeutic will only lead us to the conclusion that it has less to offer than other therapies. If one had a serious mental illness, no amount of theatregoing in even the greatest of theatres could be expected to help very much. Dr. Sophocles and Dr. Shakespeare would find themselves hopelessly unable to compete with Drs. Smith and Jones on Central Park West, neither of whom has ever laid claim to genius.

This is not to say that the notion of a *connection* between drama and therapy, between all the arts and therapy, is ill founded, only that it has been exaggerated, often by a kind of literal-mindedness. Take the most famous notion in the whole field: catharsis. There is a certain agreement, now, among scholars that the word should be taken as a medical term, that it signifies a purge, and not a moral purification as scholars used to think. Even so, there remains much to say, and chiefly that the word was pounced upon by psychiatrists of the 1890s and applied to a much lengthier and deeper process than any that a visit to a theatre could elicit. The word now described what happened in five years of psychoanalysis. Which, I would say, effectively takes it out of dramatic criticism altogether.

Was Aristotle wrong? Did he exaggerate? Did he mean something else? I doubt that a great pother is called for. After all, Aristotle said very little about catharsis, but the accepted modern interpretation of the word does apply to many works of art, provided we can forget psychiatry for a moment and remember art for quite a few moments. Is it the case that a psychiatric session provides a thoroughgoing catharsis, whereas a play provides an inadequate one? To be sure, patients have often been known to vomit after a session; the theatre could seldom achieve such a result even if it tried.

What is needed, perhaps, is not that we judge art as therapy but that we distinguish one kind of therapy from another. Society needs therapy on two different scales. In the case of individual breakdowns, something more drastic than art—any art—is needed: that's why we have psychiatrists. But these complete breakdowns do not exhaust the list of psychic ill that flesh is heir to. At present, it is true, the others are just let go, if not actually encouraged, because they serve this or that sinister interest. Mother Nature does what she can. Many mental illnesses arise, take their course, and are gone, like physical illnesses. As Freud noted, there are even happy therapeutic accidents. But by and large, mental illness is left to flourish, is *encouraged* to flourish, as physical illness was in the Middle Ages. Which means both that individual special therapy is needed by more and more people and that whole societies can be described as sick in something more than a metaphorical sense.

Now the arts are helpless in the face of such serious maladies. They can only help counteract such tendencies when other forces are doing so on a much larger scale than art itself: in other words when the situation is not as bad as all that. The Greeks viewed the arts as just a part of the good life, and the arts do need a good life to be part of, even if it's a good life that is beset by bad life. In such a context it makes sense to speak of a poet's "healing power" and even of the "corrective effect" of comedy. Poetry could not heal, and comedy could not correct, if things had gone more than just so far, *and not even then on their own.* But if there exists a real civilization, then, just as there are cures effected by nature, and others by lucky circumstances, so one could speak of the arts, too, as therapeutic, alongside other therapeutic agencies of a nonclinical sort. If it is a mistake to see art as standing alone, when it is in fact part of a common effort, a common culture, so it is a mistake to see art as therapy alone, when in fact, as we are all aware, it is other things as well.

What is the total function of art? That might seem too large a question to pose here, especially as there has never been any agreement on the answer. Yet there is no getting any further till the question *is* posed, and it is possible that the disagreements are not relevant. Suppose we just forge ahead.*

The function of art, say some, is to please. The function of art, say others, is to instruct. But what if being pleased is itself instructive? What if being instructed is itself a pleasure? The artistic impulse is the impulse to make something for fun. Why is it fun to make something?

The human creature has destructive urges. Little children wish to kill their parents. But destructive wishes trouble the conscience. We would like to atone for the sin of "thought crime." We would make restitution. We would repair the crockery we have broken, and restore it to its owner. The toy that a child willfully breaks but then guiltily repairs—or better still, replaces—and returns to its owner is perhaps the prototype of artwork. What arouses that "pity and terror" of which Aristotle spoke? Destruction and the resultant disorder. The tragic artwork is the poet's restoration of order and restitution for wrong. And his audience receives it as such. I offer these sentences only as thoughts that might help us understand the actual effect of tragedy, which is in part a healing effect, not indeed in the outright sense that tragedy would cure a case of epilepsy or schizophrenia, but in the sense that it springs from a need to feel that one can make good one's destructions. Without such feelings, I suggest, one would go mad. I am not saying nothing but tragedy, or nothing but art, can provide them. I *am* saying that art, that tragedy, can provide them.

If the therapeutic element is only part of a whole, what is the whole? I'd suggest that the best name for the whole is *education,* though you may prefer, at one pole, *child-rearing* or, at the other, *culture.* I mean that art is the pabulum

---

* Not, of course, alone. In the following paragraphs I am drawing upon Shaw's Preface to *Misalliance* and two articles by the Scottish psychoanalyst, W. R. D. Fairbairn, "Prolegomena to a Psychology of Art" and "The Ultimate Basis of Aesthetic Experience," which appeared in volumes 28 and 29, respectively, of the *British Journal of Psychology.*

of the people, and that they should be nourished by it from childhood on: this (along with other contributions) makes a culture, makes up the spiritual life of a civilized community. The function of art is to educate, but to say so is not to plump for a didactic type of art: rather, for the idea that art per se is didactic, whereas what is called didactic art tends to fail to be didactic, fails actually to teach because it is boring and therefore soporific. It is because art is *fun* that it can succeed in being didactic, for there is no true teaching except in eagerness, amusement, delight, inspiration.

On the one side, then, all the deadly hate and destructiveness; on the other, the desire to make restitution by creating something for fun. Such restitution is therapeutic, among other things, not to the extent that it alone can clear up the acute sicknesses of either individuals or societies, but on a smaller scale which is nevertheless not all that small and which, in any case, is without time limit. Once there is a good society, even a society good enough to earn the name of civilization not chronically sick, art will join with Mother Nature and with Happy Accident, as also with other branches of culture, to attend to the psychopathology of everyday life, neutralizing many minor toxins, killing many small germs. Which is but a modern and clinical way of restating the ancient belief that art is part of the good life.

Returning to the idea of spontaneity: if all spontaneity is a little unspontaneous too, as I believe, one can certainly find in art—and specifically in theatre—a kind of spontaneity. And indeed a true theatre person is one who craves this type of spontaneity. John Barrymore's problem, as I see it, was that he didn't want to be a theatre person, even though he had the talent for it: which is like being allergic to your own hormones.

Let me try to describe the spontaneity of an actor in a play. On the face of it he has surrendered it to the playwright: Barrymore mustn't be Barrymore, he must be Hamlet. But consider what really happens—from the first rehearsal on. At the first rehearsal, the actor hasn't yet built his characterization, so presumably what he brings along is himself and nothing but himself, and no script ever made an actor feel inhibited about this. As rehearsals progress a little, he comes into contact with his colleagues on stage. Maybe a little electricity is generated. He's attracted by the leading lady. He hates his male partner. Or vice versa. The electricity, in any case, is not between characters, it is between actors. Now the fondest hope of any professional actor (as of his director) is that the electricity generated in rehearsals will be preserved in the performance. That, to a large extent, is what rehearsals are for. Is such electricity a form of byplay, an additional stage effect like background noise? Just the opposite. Properly handled, it does not damage or distort the characterization itself, but is combined with it. Quite a trick! The characterization is to be what the author wanted: that, to be sure, is a principle of drama that there is no getting around. But the actor still meets the eye of another actor, not of a character, which is to say that both actors are still present: their own bodies and all that two human beings have that is not body. And they continue to use all of this, in live contact, as "I" and "Thou."

Should they fail to maintain the contact, could we say, "The actor having now withdrawn his own personality, what is left must be the character"? By no means: when the actors seem dead, as now they would, the characters would never be born. In other words, the life of the stage is a dual life, and through one of these two lives the principle of spontaneity enters, and is indeed essential: that the character may *seem* to have a spontaneous existence, the actor must *actually* have a spontaneous existence. The pulling-off of this "trick"—it is of course much more—is perhaps the main task to which the actor addresses himself. Other things are important. There has to be a characterization to animate. But unless the actor animates it, a characterization has no theatrical value whatever. Conversely, if an actor comes on stage as his spontaneous self, and throws characterization to the winds, we may possibly get something of *psycho*dramatic interest—but even this not really, because the other actors won't relate to it properly, nor will we ourselves relate to it properly: it isn't what we "paid our money for." Whether we know it or not, we have different criteria for dramatic art, different expectations. Barrymore was finally ruined precisely by playing himself instead of the stage character. Life is life. Therapy is therapy. Drama is drama. All afford some freedoms, some opportunities for spontaneity, but, in all, freedom and spontaneity are very strictly circumscribed, so that the acceptance of the circumscription is as necessary an attitude to human beings as love of freedom. Freedom, says Engels, is the recognition of necessity. Goethe says, *"In der Beschraenking zeigt sich erst der Meister"*— "only in his confrontation of limits does a master show his mettle." This is another way of saying: we marvel that spontaneity exists at all; and we marvel how much spontaneity can be created by masters of living; of therapy; or of art.

(*1969*)

White Plague and Black Terror

For Phillip

I

I can't think of any theatre I would rather sit down in than the New Lafayette in New York City, at Seventh Avenue and 137th Street, just around the corner from Mother Zion Church. It is an auditorium that combines the best of both worlds—the hospitable informality of Off Off Broadway buildings which are obviously theatres only by conversion and transfiguration and the comfortable formality of conventional theatres with seats fixed to the floor and arranged in neat rows. The New Lafayette is nice to sit in also because they don't have the house lights full on before the show. "A dim religious light" burns, as does incense which, however, has an odor agreeably unsuggestive of either the Pope or the Maharishi: a hedonistic, irreligious incense.

It's a good place to see a show, too. There are three banks of seats, two of them raised high, stadium-fashion. The audience sits on three sides of the spectacle, which is on the floor, not on a stage. For the show I saw there, *The Psychic Pretenders,* this floor was covered with carpets of different colors, and these colors became different again and again in the constant play of a color wheel. A charming effect, and, in the course of the evening, I found it to be typical of the whole show in its subtle combination of energy and regularity, turbulence and repose.

The subtitle is "Pageant of the Black Passion in Three Motions." The "motions" are through three gates, the gate of the searchers, the gate of love, and the gate of intuitive knowledge. In other words, the whole thing is a quest, a story of trial-by-ordeal, of education and growing up, of a type familiar to many of us from Bunyan's *Pilgrim's Progress* and Mozart's *Magic Flute*. The special twist here is that the pilgrim is black. This brings about an inversion of the familiar color scheme. Whereas in *The Magic Flute* the villain is a queen of blackest night, and the black man in the opera, Monostatos, is a blend of barbarian and devil, while both the young hero and his ancient mentor are pillars of white civilization, in *The Psychic Pretenders* the mentor is a black mother-figure, while the pilgrim is a black youth whose problem is that he wears a white mask and white pants—that is, he is pretending to be white, he has gone over to the enemy. He will be making headway in the degree that he is reclaimed by blackness. Regress to the black maternal womb will be this pilgrim's progress—this prodigal's return, not to Heavenly Father, but to Earthly Mother.

The Psychic Pretenders is not an opera, but neither is it what most people would consider a straight play. On a high platform at the back of the floor-space are several musicians who play almost uninterruptedly from beginning to end: a good score, redolent of Africa and New Orleans, mostly drum used with delicacy. Even the trombone is delicate in this combo, not the same instrument you've heard in a brass band. There is spoken dialogue, but not much, and it is rather less distinguished than the nonverbal elements. You watch the actors a great deal more intently than you listen to them. Call it a dance drama: there is plenty of outright dance, all movements are large and ceremonious. It is a spectacle choreographed throughout.

A work of art, but what kind of art, exactly? And what is art? I ask this last question advisedly because it is categorically answered in the program, an amazing fact when you consider that this program does not even give the name of the author or the composer, nor tell which actor plays which role, nor yet explain the quite obscure title of the show. "The raising of consciousness," says this otherwise reticent document, ". . . is the purpose of art." Having always wondered what the purpose of art was myself, I can't but admire the glorious self-confidence. In the afterglow of reading this, I'll even overlook, for the moment, all the art that has *not* been dedicated to raising of consciousness (at least in the sense here intended). In any case, I am among those who welcome all art that does make a respectable stab at raising consciousness, and obviously this is the task to which all black literature, all black art, addresses itself today.

> A Community Art Institution takes on responsibility for the creation and presentation of images which are vivid enough to activate the minds of the community audience to considerations of their everyday existence from points of view consistent with that community's place in history and its efforts toward the future.

That's our program again. To activate people's minds. Get them to see what's happening to them. By means of images. So that what is *called* a community —Harlem, in this case—might *become* a community. So that a bunch of paupers and semislaves might become a family of fully human beings. Through solidarity to power and fulfillment. A beautiful conception.

What success black theatre is having in raising consciousness I am not equipped to say, and in the nature of things it is hard to measure. What a non-black observer can observe is the very considerable variety of approaches among black theatre people, and *The Psychic Pretenders* strikes me as far more successful than the naturalistic efforts I've seen, such as the current *Black Terror* at the Public Theatre, written, as it happens, by one of the Playwrights in Residence at the New Lafayette, Richard Wesley. *The Black Terror* comes across as a conventional—in that sense, white—play which, by the appropriate conventional standards, does not make the grade. Even if it were a better piece of writing and of playmaking—even more so then—one would have to ask what messages come through, and not what messages the playwright may have intended to send. At the Public Theatre this "black" work simply confirms for the largely white audience what White America brought them up to believe about Terrorism in general and Terrorism by "Nigras" in particular, namely that all terrorists are nuts and black terrorists are savages into the bargain. Any comparisons between this play and *The Battle of Algiers,* or even with *La Chinoise,* are entirely unearned. Its effect, as opposed to its intention, is reactionary and racist.

If Richard Wesley ends up making use of the white man's stereotype of the black (the native, the savage, the cannibal, the Hottentot), what shall we say of equally "far-out" cartoon images of the villainous White Man? The strongest piece of theatre I have seen in the past few years is *Slave Ship* by LeRoi Jones, as produced in 1969 at the Chelsea Theatre Center. Where Wesley merely falls backward into racism, Jones leaps delightedly into it, face-forward. What is the white theatregoer to do? Stay away from Jones's plays? Play at being black? That surely is an effort at identification with the victim which soon becomes ludicrous. Enjoy being put down by such a fanatic down-putter? That surely is an exercise in white masochism that only black sadists can contemplate with satisfaction. White middle-class liberals can be counted on for a goodly amount of breast beating, it is true, but not for this much. As for myself, though I'm as guilt-ridden as the next man, I didn't really feel guiltier for seeing Jones's play, for, rightly or wrongly, I just didn't identify myself with the whites in it. How could one? They were monsters. Then I identified myself—sentimentally—with the blacks? Not that, either. Not that *exactly.* Feeling detached from both groups, I found myself instinctively taking the play as an image of all such struggles. Finally, I did identify myself with the blacks but for me they weren't necessarily black. They were yellow, and from Vietnam. They were red, and from Manhattan. They were white-skinned and black with coal dust like the miners of Lancashire, where I come from. As a Socialist, I read LeRoi Jones's play as a series of extremely vivid images of capitalist exploitation, and this is not something I thought of later, it is only my later formulation of what I was actually feeling during the performance. So, as a Socialist, I got my consciousness raised by a writer who (I must assume) wants me liquidated as a carrier of the white plague; and whom I disapprove of as a racist.

A few years ago most white people would have said that antiwhite literature was by definition racist. It is not necessarily so. In *The Psychic Pretenders* two blacks produce a tiny white baby doll with the stars and stripes painted on it. They light matches, as if to burn it. Symbolically speaking, it *is* burnt. Such an incident is typical of *The Psychic Pretenders* but, as I see things, did not have the force of racism because, in this work, though certainly white culture is seen as the enemy, the extermination of white men is not seen as the remedy. Rather, the drawing apart of black men from the white culture. Here's an analogy. In Vietnam, the American is the enemy, and is fair game for the satirist as well as for the antiaircraft gunner. This is not to say the Vietnamese represent any threat to the American people, let alone that they encourage racist doctrines that would include themselves "in" and most of us "out."

When I call *The Psychic Pretenders* more successful than *The Black Terror,* I am ignoring economics: *The Black Terror* may well be earning more money. Can black theatres ignore economics? Hardly: the dependence of many of them on white foundations is notorious. The issues are complex, but come down to Lenin's: who whom? Are the foundations buying off the revolutionaries, or are the revolutionaries taking advantage of the foundations? Again, some people see a theatre in the ghetto as principally a way of bringing culture to the uneducated. This process carries the reactionary implication of opium for the people. Should black theatres refuse money from white foundations? Or would this be a display of unrealistic idealism, futile pride? Why doesn't the ghetto itself support ghetto theatres? Because they are too radical? Because they are too arty, and the ghetto prefers Channel 2?

The problems are those of the theatre of commitment generally. There are probably no pure solutions or, if there are, they may not be better than some of the impure ones. Or purer. The contradictions will be there willy-nilly. If anything is certain, it is that results will be achieved not by living in dread of contradictions or contemptuously rejecting them but by taking for granted that they are going to be there. Working against them, we can hope in time to work through them. Meanwhile, we are working *with* them.

When Blacks talk racism they invariably become rhetorical, as if to indicate they aren't serious, they just want to let off steam. There is another *ism* in the Black radical community that, to the contrary, is always serious and is therefore going to be more of a problem, and that is sexism, the sexism of LeRoi Jones and Eldridge Cleaver, the sexism of Stokely Carmichael's famous intimation of the proper position of women: prone.

My piece "White Plague and Black Terror (I)" was reprinted by the New Lafayette management and distributed by them as publicity. I myself received two unsolicited packets of publicity material from the New Lafayette, one of which contained my piece. Although I had not given permission for this use of my work, I had, in fact, no objection, and was flattered that it had been thought of interest.

At first. But when I read on I discovered, with a shock, that this was not the kind of literature I would want to be associated with. Even more clearly I saw that its writers would not want to be associated with me if they knew me. Speaking less personally, and more to the political point, I found positions taken in this literature that run counter to socialist humanism—to *any* humanism, really—counter to common sense, counter to the truth.

I found rampant sexism. As evidence let me quote the full text of one of the six panels of a brochure:—

IF THEY CAN KEEP YOU BUYING WHAT THEY WANT YOU TO BUY THEY CONTROL YOUR LIFE. Diahann Carroll wears a wig. Sidney Poitier goes with a white girl. [A black male celebrity] is a white girl. Niggers who could sing, dance, and act the fool have always been a dime a dozen whether they had a T.V. Special or not. And everybody knows that some people will do and say anything for money. A suit of clothes and a pair of shoes better than the man standing next to him. That's what it's all about isn't it?

One of the packets I was sent contained a copy of *Black Theatre,* No. 5, 1971, edited by Ed Bullins (managing editor, Richard Wesley, associate editors, Roscoe Orman and Marvin X). I quote, uncut, an editorial footnote that appears on page 3:—

The editors of Black Theatre magazine do not think that *any* Black people should see The Blacks. Jean Genet is a white, self-confessed homosexual with dead, white Western ideas—faggoty ideas about Black Art, Revolution, and people. His empty masochistic activities and platitudes on behalf of the Black Panthers should not con Black people. Genet, in his writings, has admitted to seeing himself as a so-called "nigger." Black people cannot allow white perversion to enter their communities and consciousness, even if it rides in on the black [sic—E.B.] of a Panther. Beware of whites who plead the Black cause to their brothers and fathers who oppress us; beware of Athol Fugard of South Africa and Jean Genet, a French pervert; disguised white missionaries representing Western cultural imperialism. Black people, in this stage of the struggle, have no use for self-elected "niggers."

Now how can one handle all this? It is not presented as an argument—as reason—and one would therefore be falling into a trap if one argued back, if one even presented the *reasons* why all this is dangerous and false. So I will limit myself to saying:

Beware of blacks who seek to oppress their brothers and fathers (and sisters and mothers) with sexism! Beware of Ed Bullins, Richard Wesley, Roscoe Orman, and Marvin X, who, wearing a cloak of black nationalism, spread around the white plague of sexist machismo! I'll take Diahann Carroll, Sidney Poitier, and Jean Genet,* and they can keep their John Wayne.

(1972)

---

* The name of the person referred to in brackets on page 406 is here omitted at the request of The Viking Press.

Theatre and the Movement

If there is one thing we are agreed on today it is that we are agreed on nothing: the nation is united only in the belief that the nation is disunited. The words "Establishment" and "anti-Establishment" may not sum it all up, but they come as near to doing so as any such dualities of former times ever did—Red and White in Russia, Northerner and Southerner in this country, Roundhead and Cavalier in Britain. And it is time to see the problems of theatre art not merely in the terms of Broadway and Off, or even Off Off, Broadway, terms which tend to triviliality, but in the larger and more dynamic context of a general social conflict which is the total national destiny.

"Our struggle today is for the right to wear our hair long." Declarations like this sounded eccentric if not preposterous a year or two ago, but time has shown that; comic as they are, they are not without truth. Taken as symbolic, they are even legitimate. "We are fighting for a life style." If hair-dos and clothing are hardly, in themselves, worth a fight to the death, in the 1960s they did become symbols of more than just a life *style:* they became symbols of another *life,* and this the essential life of human beings, the life of their deep affections and their cherished thoughts.

The middle classes, and even the highly paid working class, had "pursued happiness," according to the prescription of the Declaration of Independence, but it was more and more evident that this pursuit only led to a brave new world of consumer goods. As in Aldous Huxley's great archetype, this world took over, not just the body, but the spirit of man. The new Homo sapiens not only bought material junk at the supermarket, he bought spiritual junk from the movies and TV, those supermarkets of the soul. Man was now "happy" by definition. Whether this was the happiness which the rebels of 1776 had in mind is another question. It was not happiness for the rebels of the 1960s. They saw it, rather, as a form of consciousness too narrow to be dignified with the word "human." The antidote, quite logically, was consciousness-expanding drugs. Is it not remarkable how inventions and discoveries are timed? The invention or discovery of drug culture in the sixties was hardly something that merely happened to happen. It was the answer to more than a prayer. I am not one of those who believe it solved the problem to which it was addressed, but it was certainly one of history's cleverer bits of footwork.

So was rock music and (more literally) so were the dances that went with it. The subculture of America in the sixties was the quickest way out of Westchester. I need hardly say it had its real achievements. Never have achievements been either so widely or so instantly applauded. It is safe to say that, if I were to criticize the Beatles or the Stones *in the Establishment press itself*,* the editors would be bombarded with outraged letters.

Yet criticism is called for. The fact that rock music was produced by a good revolt does not make all rock music good, and indeed anyone who really "digs" the more enterprising and adventurous things would be the first to admit that most rock, *like most art of all kinds*, is mediocre, and that quite a lot of it is atrocious. The subculture is not a utopia of supermen. Like all subcultures before it, it consists of a few people who are too good for the main culture, many who are just good enough for the main culture, and some who are not good enough for it. The notion that a subculture is a new and separate culture is an illusion. However rebellious, it remains part of the main culture: it may want to break but it has not broken. Sometimes the wish to break is more apparent than real. It has been remarked that rock music and kindred phenomena are quickly co-opted by the System. This is incorrect. Though they represent revolt against the System, they were never outside it; revolt, by definition, is always from within; anything else would be invasion and conquest. Hence, if we are to talk not of the impulse that created the rock beat but of those who manage the rock "scene," we are talking of people who are exactly as revolutionary, or even dissident, as the directors of General Motors. Though, like other mortals, they make mistakes (as when Atlantic Records undertook to make an Off Broadway hit of Brecht's *Mahagonny*), they can, over the longer span, be trusted to run their own show, so long as the big show of which theirs is but a part—capitalism itself—is still running. It is not even true that they de-revolution-

* This "comment" was written for the *New York Times*.

ize every revolutionary work. As yet they haven't needed to. The System is an ocean that can absorb these tiny countercurrents quite comfortably. Picasso is a revolutionary painter in more senses than one, but how much revolutionary effect does one of his paintings have when it is placed on Nelson Rockefeller's wall? Yet we may be sure that the Governor hasn't scraped off any red paint. Even a Picasso painting disappears quite easily into the wallpaper of plutocracy.

Just as anti-Establishment politics duplicates the faults of Establishment politics, so anti-Establishment culture duplicates the faults of Establishment culture. Now the worst fault of capitalist culture has always been that it is capitalist—that is, money-based. Anticapitalist culture, before the advent of socialism, is also money-based, being based on the same money, the same money system, the universal cash nexus. Money swallows all, and the most important thing it can swallow, in respect to culture, is aesthetic standards. The Establishment offers two alternatives: box-office standards and snob standards. Snob standards apply in cases where the Establishment decides that a given institution should be supported even though it loses money. The most obvious instance would be symphony orchestras, which are supported because they have "class" (a great word in the circumstances) and help hold the present social order in position with ropes binding it to the dignified past. I don't think they should, as threatened, drop the custom of wearing white tie and tails.

Anti-Establishment culture has its own ties with big money and its own snobberies—generally forms of inverted snobbery, pseudo-proletarian or traditionally bohemian. More important, it inherits a sheer lack of aesthetic standards. In lamenting this, one is not lamenting an inability to pass judgment in the manner of the critic and expert, one is lamenting something far more disastrous: lack of interest in what any art really is, lack of contact with what each art is actually doing. In the brave new world of consumer culture, all music aspires to the condition of Muzak, "dinner music," a background to other activity that is much more important, like buying Wheaties or quarreling with the wife. *But this is true of the subculture as well.* I have even heard some of our young "rebels" declare that Marshall McLuhan says this is all right; which would *make* it all right. Music has other purposes besides being listened to. Again, there is listening and listening, and especially: listening when you're high. Though some reporters on this experience tell of hearing everything *better,* others boast that, in their "expanded" state, they deleted most of the sounds in a performance and just listened to the bass. I have a feeling Beethoven wouldn't have relished this prospect, and that he would have a point, to wit, that a work of art, while it may in a sense be more than the sum of its parts, can never be less.

After drugs and rock, in countercultural esteem, come the movies. The reasons are in part a credit both to this medium and to those who appreciate it but partly the movies flourish among the rebels for exactly the same reason they have long flourished among the population generally: because, like peanuts, they are so undemanding. Indeed, like Muzak, they scarcely even demand what in former times one would have thought *had* to be demanded: attention. Can this be true of *avant-garde* films? Yes. The discontinuity in Jean-Luc Godard's films may, on the one hand, be an artistic alienation effect helping to structure a film and our experience of it but, alas, it can just as easily be yet another invitation to that half-attention (not even half, more likely one-tenth) which is the bane of spiritual life in this epoch.

Is this attaching too much importance to too little? Not if that little is duplicated a million times in a million different activities. And it is. While a degree of distraction is legitimate, and perhaps even necessary, in human life, and is implicit in the whole idea of entertainment in all media, a spiritual life that is all distraction is by that token sheer evasion, inauthentic, and vicious. All the more so if the distractions are manipulated for evil political ends. I note that when the present Administration couldn't come up with any poets or orators to sing its exploits in Vietnam, it fell back—Honor America Day, July 4, 1970—on professional entertainers.

We live under a regime that needs nothing more than to deflect our attention from what it is doing. In that respect, Bob Hope and Red Skelton, who honored America on the Fourth, deserve medals for services above and beyond the call of theatrical duty. In these circumstances our need is for the strength to resist such distractions, against the time when the circumstances themselves may be changed.

Instead of distraction, concentration: this is the principle that applies inside (yoga) and out (radical action). It applies on a large scale and on a small. My own field—theatre—is small, compared not only to, say, warfare and politics but also to other fields of communication, like TV. Nonetheless, it has a mission that the giant and more modern media cannot carry out. A sense of this fact underlies all that has happened in radical theatre in the sixties, from Grotowski to the Becks, and from the playwriting of Hochhuth to the nonliterary guerrilla and street theatres. What all these very different men, women, and children of the theatre shared was a conviction that they could recall people from their distracting daydreams and make them concentrate on some brute (i.e., human!) reality. The theatre has much in common with other media. What is peculiar to it is the flesh-and-blood encounter of flesh-and-blood human beings. The work of radical theatre in our time has been nothing more nor less than an attempt to put across three propositions: (1) This happened to flesh-and-blood human beings; (2) We who show it are also flesh-and-blood human beings; (3) You, our audience, are flesh-and-blood human beings. The propositions are simple, it is the putting across that is hard, and yet is the special contribution of theatre. The forces that are peculiar to the flesh-and-blood encounter of human beings are mobilized to penetrate that elephant-hide of resistances ("hangups") with which the Establishment has equipped us. Cerebral persuasion is beside the point or at best grossly insufficient. So is pathos: what is usually implied in the words "touching" or "moving" is but a passing sensation or mood, as soon forgotten as last week's orgasm. If there is truly a touching, it must touch to the quick. If there is movement, it must be visceral or, better, must penetrate the whole psychophysical system.

Well, no abstract formulation is going to prove satisfactory, but anyone who has seen either Grotowski's troupe or the Living Theatre will have seen an attempt at such communication and may even have got the message. If I may revert to my own critique of the Becks, I'd want to admit that my vehemence testified to their success, since their aim was less to command my assent than to rouse me to spontaneous feeling. I think they were seduced into violent excesses by exasperation, much in the way that the Weatherman faction of SDS has subsequently been: in both cases, the new, secret weapon proved to be only the same old, all-too-efficient boomerang. The Becks certainly put across the second of the above three propositions; they were far less successful with one and three. Grotowski also is in difficulties with number three: we, the people, are a little ghostly and insubstantial to this aristocrat. But he gives a poignancy to both one and two that, in the experience of most of us, is unparalleled.

That *The Deputy* was wordy and long-winded should not blind us to the fact that its main achievement, like that of other radical theatre, was to expose a raw nerve. If the play is overliterary, it is because Hochhuth has made our insensitivity into a *subject* which, in the context created, has to be dealt with in words. As a result, we may conclude that this is to preach in favor of feeling rather than to make us feel. On the other hand, Hochhuth is a good enough dramatist to arouse authentic feeling precisely in his portrait of the man who cannot feel, Pope Piux XII. When his hero, Father Fontana, bleeds, we may just sit back and listen, but when his villain, the Pope, fails to bleed, then *we* bleed.

If *The Deputy*—written less than ten years ago—already seems remote, that is less because of its content than of its habitat: it belonged to the professional theatre, which in turn belongs to producers, backers, and landlords. It is in habitat, and not in playwriting, that radical theatre changed most during the sixties. Up to and including Hochhuth, a radical playwright was a radical who persuaded a producer to do his play on Broadway. His highest hope had to be that his work would be found entertaining, though radical. More often he would have to hear a critical chorus chanting that, though radical, it was a terrible play. Now, heaven knows, many radical plays are terrible, like many nonradical plays, but it can still be a mistake to put the radicalism and the merit or demerit in separate compartments. *Viet Rock,* for example, had an aesthetic flaw—uncertainty of point of view—which was also a political flaw. I hope, after what I've said above, no one will suspect I have no artistic standards, but at the same time I must champion the need for each type of theatre to be judged in accordance with its own nature and aim. It is no prime aim of a political, propagandist theatre to convince Establishment journalists that it is purveying good Establishment entertainment, yet, if you think back, you will realize that perhaps the only compliments Shaw and Brecht ever got in New York were for doing just that. *My Fair Lady* is Shaw reduced to the stereotypes of Establishment entertainment. The Blitzstein *Threepenny Opera* was Brecht similarly reduced.

It seems to me that, in the sixties, something else was worked out. Often, now, the radical playwright did not place his script in the hands of a Broadway producer but got together with a group and put it on himself. In a number of instances, an Off Broadway producer, with an eye to the main chance, then picked up the "property"; but even this is quite a bit different from the earlier procedure, and in any case did not happen every time. Nor was it just a matter of getting a script accepted and produced. It was a matter of ending up with a show which would be a radical act. Now nothing is a less radical act than placing a radical script on a Broadway stage for ratification by Broadway critics. That's like going to the czar in the hope he'll say Bolshevism is really quite amusing. And even if he says it's high-minded but boring, that hardly seems to be the response a rebel should desire to elicit from his enemy.

If the duty of the revolutionary is to make revolution, the duty of a theatre of radical action is to perform radical acts of theatre. Not only is this not a matter of getting a radical script accepted by a nonradical theatre. It may not be a matter of a radical script at all. Unless we broaden the usual definitions quite a lot, *Terminal,* the recent Open Theatre show, was not really a radical script. It was an indeterminate script which would reach definition, no, not in performance alone, but in performance before particular audiences. That it passed muster as conventional entertainment (and therefore pleased conventional critics) isn't necessarily bad, but how good is it? Would it justify the effort? I hear from people who saw performances of *Terminal* which were dedicated to the Black Panthers that the show received a powerful electric charge from this little ritual and was transformed thereby into theatre of commitment.

Would Neil Simon's plays become radical if and when performances were dedicated to the Panthers? Maybe; to some slight extent. Conceivably the dedication would "alienate" the action in some degree, making it seem that Mr. Simon is critical of that whole world of which he is so successfully uncritical. But I wouldn't count on it, particularly if there weren't many Panthers out front. When the Open Theatre decides to dedicate a performance to a cause, the decision is a solemn one, taken by the group as a whole, and modifying, transfiguring the whole occasion, actor and spectator alike.

Even the fact that such an event does not take place in a "Broadway" building can have its importance, just as it is important that a Catholic Mass not be celebrated in a whorehouse. The milieu of the radical theatre today is the church, the schoolroom, the loft, the cellar, the meeting hall, the store front, and of course the street. The 1960s have seen a kind of transfer of ownership, or at least allegiance, from the actual theatres, with their real-estate men, producers, agents, etc., to the Movement, and indeed one may expect radical theatre to succeed or fail in the seventies as the Movement itself succeeds or fails.

(1970)

INDEX

Index

This index lists all names of persons (though not of fictitious characters) and all titles of books, plays, periodicals, songs, and the like. It indicates personal names and titles as they occur in the text. However, where a Comment or succession of Comments is devoted to a single writer, either by name or by title of his work, entries for the author and work are given with the first and last page numbers hyphenated. Titles of shorter works are given in quotation marks.

Index by David Beams.

Y

Yeats, W. B., 108, 135, 205
Yevtushenko, Yevgeny, 234
You Never Can Tell, 3
Young, Stark, 383
Yvette, 18

Z

Zhdanov, A. A., 116
"Zinc Box, The," 99
Zinoviev, Grigori, 160, 161
Zola, Émile, 187